ROGER LEROY MILLER   UNIVERSITY OF MIAMI

ECONOMIC ISSUES FOR CONSUMERS

WEST PUBLISHING COMPANY
ST. PAUL • NEW YORK • BOSTON • LOS ANGELES • SAN FRANCISCO

CREDITS Photography by Marge Agin except for the following: Page 16 the Bettmann Archive, Inc.; page 193 photo by Dave Bellak, Jeroboam, Inc.; page 211 photo by Frank Siteman, Stock, Boston; page 271 photo by J. Berndt, Stock, Boston; page 350 photo by Ken Graves, Jeroboam, Inc.; page 436 photo by Peter Vilms, Jeroboam, Inc.

Other credits are as follows: Page 127 disclosure statement reprinted courtesy of Sears Roebuck Co. Page 172 editorial cartoon by Pat Oliphant. Copyright, *The Denver Post.* Reprinted with permission Los Angeles Times Syndicate. Page 301 cartoon from *Best Cartoons of the Year, 1967,* edited by Lawrence Lariar. Copyright 1967 by Lawrence Lariar. Reprinted by permission. Page 363 advertisement reprinted by permission of Source Securities Corporation. Page 405 cartoon reprinted from *The Wall Street Journal* by permission of Cartoon Features Syndicate.

COPYRIGHT © 1975 By ROGER LEROY MILLER INC.

All rights reserved

Printed in the United States of America

Library of Congress Cataloging in Publication Data

Miller, Roger LeRoy.
    Economic Issues for Consumers.
    Includes index.
    1. Finance, Personal. 2. Consumer education. 1. Title.

HG179.M48   332'.024   75–6957

ISBN 0–8299–0039–X

CONTENTS IN BRIEF

Preface   xxi

1   **THE AGE OF THE CONSUMER**   1

2   **MAKING UP YOUR MIND**   11

3   **THE INFORMATION GLUT**   31

4   **THE ECONOMICS OF LOVE AND PAIN**   53
CONSUMER ISSUE I
Making a Decision about Children   63

5   **THE CONSUMER AS WAGE EARNER**   69

6   **YOU HAVE TO LIVE WITH WHAT YOU HAVE**   79
CONSUMER ISSUE II
How to Budget Your Limited Income   99

7   **THE OVEREXTENDED AMERICAN**   111
CONSUMER ISSUE III
Coping with the Credit Maze   135

8   **THE $BILLION STOMACH**   149
CONSUMER ISSUE IV
How to Get the Most for Your Food Dollar   171

9   **MORE THAN JUST KEEPING WARM**   185
CONSUMER ISSUE V
Getting the Most for Your Clothes Shopping
Dollar   199

10   **PUTTING A ROOF OVER YOUR HEAD**   205
CONSUMER ISSUE VI
How to Buy or Rent a Place to Live   227

11   **GETTING THERE BY CAR IS HALF THE
WORRY**   251
CONSUMER ISSUE VII
Buying Transportation   264

12   **THE HEALTH CARE DILEMMA**   279
CONSUMER ISSUE VIII
How to Keep Your Medical Costs Down   294

1st Reprint

13 OTHER FORMS OF PROTECTION: LIFE INSURANCE AND SOCIAL SECURITY   **307**

CONSUMER ISSUE IX
How to Meet your Insurance Needs 329

14 WHAT TO DO WITH YOUR PIGGY BANK   **339**

CONSUMER ISSUE X
How to Be a Rational Investor 360

15 THE HIGH COST OF LIVING   **371**

CONSUMER ISSUE XI
Protecting Yourself against Inflation 384

16 PAYING FOR GOVERNMENT   **393**

CONSUMER ISSUE XII
Easing Your Tax Burden 409

17 THE CONSUMER GETS A VOICE   **415**

CONSUMER ISSUE XIII
How to Get Help from the Government 430

CONSUMER ISSUE XIV
How to Use a Small Claims Court 443

CONSUMER ISSUE XV
Do Consumers Have Responsibilities, Too? 449

18 ECOLOGY AND THE MARKETPLACE 453

19 YOUR FUTURE AS A CONSUMER   **463**

APPENDIX A
Estate Planning: Wills, Trusts, and Taxes 471

APPENDIX B
All You Need to Know about Metric (for your everyday life) 477

Glossary Index 479
Index 481

CONTENTS

Preface xxi

1 THE AGE OF THE CONSUMER   1

WE ARE NOT JUST CONSUMERS   1

  A growing nation   1

  Income differences   2

THE COMPLEXITIES OF CONSUMPTION   2

  Fraud   3

  Producers everywhere   3

SOME PAST AND FUTURE SOLUTIONS   5

THE AGE OF CONSUMERISM   6

THE INFORMATION EXPLOSION   6

QUALITY OF LIFE   8

INFLATION, INFLATION, INFLATION   8

WHAT IS TO COME   8

  Summary   9

  Questions for thought and discussion   9

  Things to do   9

  Selected readings   9

2 MAKING UP YOUR MIND   11

EXCHANGE AND RATIONAL DECISION–MAKING   11

WHAT DETERMINES YOUR CHOICES?   13

  Goals   13

  Customs   14

CONSPICUOUS CONSUMPTION   15

BUYING HABITS   15

  Impulse buying   15

  Planned buying   16

MOTIVATIONAL RESEARCH   16

CONSUMER SOVEREIGNTY VERSUS
  PRODUCER SOVEREIGNTY   17

BUYING AND SEARCHING   18

YOU'RE THE BOSS   19

ALTERNATIVE LIFE STYLES   20

FORESIGHT AND HINDSIGHT   23

TIME, TIME, TIME   24

CLARIFYING OUR VALUES   25

PARKINSON'S LAW   26

  Breaking the law   26

  Summary   27

  Questions for thought and discussion   28

  Things to do   28

  Selected readings   29

3 **THE INFORMATION GLUT**   **31**

HOW MUCH INFORMATION SHOULD
  WE ACQUIRE?   31
THE ADVERTISING EXPLOSION   32
  Who pays?   33
  The value of brand names   33
  Brand name loyalty   35
TYPES OF ADVERTISING   35
  Informative advertising   35
  Competitive advertising   36
  Comparative advertising   36
FALSE ADVERTISING   37
  Bait and switch—the case of beef   37
DOOR TO DOOR SALESPERSONS   39
  Cooling off periods   39
THE FEDERAL TRADE COMMISSION   39
CORRECTIVE ADVERTISING   41
THE FTC AND RALPH NADER   42
OTHER AGENCIES HELPING YOU OUT   43
THE WHY AND WHERE OF RADIO AND TV ADVERTISING   43
  Way back when   43
  There is no such thing as free TV   44
COMPARISON OF TV, RADIO, AND OTHER MEDIA   45
BUYING PRIVATELY PRODUCED INFORMATION   45
  Consumers' Research Magazine   47
  Other information sources   47
  Information produced and distributed by government agencies   47

  Summary   48
  Questions for thought and discussion   49
  Things to do   49
  Selected readings   50

4 **THE ECONOMICS OF LOVE AND PAIN**   **53**

STATE SANCTIONED LOVING   53
  Estimating economic values   55
  Marriage costs and benefits   55
CRYPTO–SERVANTS   56
MEASURING THE VALUE OF HOUSEWIVES' SERVICES   57
VOLUNTARY MARRIAGE DISSOLUTIONS   57
THE LIBERATION OF WOMEN   58
SPECIALIZATION AND LIBERATION   60
NONMARRIAGE AND THE OUTSIDE WORLD   60
A NEW BENEFIT OF STAYING SINGLE   61

  Summary   62
  Questions for thought and discussion   62
  Things to do   62
  Selected readings   62

CONSUMER ISSUE I   **Making a Decision about Children**   **63**

The cost of consuming   63

A grave decision   64

When is the best time to have children?   65

Family planning information   65

Social pressures to become a parent   65

The joys of parenthood   66

Summary   66

Questions for thought and discussion   66

Things to do   67

Selected readings   67

5   **THE CONSUMER AS WAGE EARNER**   **69**

INVESTING IN YOURSELF   69

Wages and productivity   70

THE RATE OF RETURN TO EDUCATION   71

Costs, too   72

THE CHANGING WORLD OF FEMALE ENDEAVORS   72

OCCUPATIONAL WAGE DIFFERENTIALS   74

WAGES AND AGES   75

OCCUPATIONAL CHOICE   75

Summary   76

Questions for thought and discussion   77

Things to do   77

Selected readings   77

6   **YOU HAVE TO LIVE WITH WHAT YOU HAVE**   **79**

WHY FIGURE OUT A BUDGET OR SPENDING PLAN?   79

DEMOCRATIC DECISION–MAKING   81

The family council   82

Coping with the teenage consumer   83

HOW DOES THE TYPICAL HOUSEHOLD ALLOCATE ITS INCOME?   84

Different level budgets   87

CITY VERSUS COUNTRY   87

BUDGET–MAKING GOALS AND VALUE CLARIFICATION   89

TRADE–OFFS   91

WHAT HAPPENS WHEN INCOME SUDDENLY CHANGES   92

FITTING IT ALL INTO A LIFETIME PLAN   93

Day to day tasks   93

Summary   96

Questions for thought and discussion   96

Things to do   97

Selected readings   98

CONSUMER ISSUE II   **How to Budget Your Limited Income**   **99**
Steps in budget-making   99
College student budgets   101
Budgeting for the nonstudent spending unit   103
Keeping records   103

Summary   109
Questions for thought and discussion   109
Things to do   109
Selected readings   109

7   **THE OVEREXTENDED AMERICAN**   **111**
THE AMERICAN IN DEBT   111
   Bankruptcies   112
THE INDEBTED SOCIETY   112
SOURCES OF CREDIT   113
   Commercial banks   113
   Finance companies   114
   Consumer finance companies   114
   Credit unions   114
   Credit cards   114
NONCREDIT CARDS—PAY CASH AND PAY LESS   114
LOANS ON YOUR LIFE INSURANCE   115
WHY BORROW?   115
DON'T BE FOOLED   116
WHAT IT COSTS TO BORROW   118
   Origins of interest   118
INFLATION AND INTEREST RATES   118
THE WHY AND WHERE OF USURY LAWS   119
   Washington state usury laws—an example   120
   Looking at Arkansas   122
TRUTH–IN–LENDING   122
ENFORCEMENT   124
REVOLVING CREDIT   125
REGULATING BANKS   126
   Now is the time for NOW   129
TOTAL BANKING SERVICE FOR ONE FEE   129
THE CASHLESS SOCIETY   130

Summary   131
Questions for thought and discussion   132
Things to do   132
Selected readings   134

CONSUMER ISSUE III   **Coping with the Credit Maze**   **135**
When should you borrow?   135
What is the maximum you can borrow?   137
What to do when you are refused credit   140
Shopping for credit   142
Nothing is free   144
Debt counseling   144

Summary   145
Questions for thought and discussion   145
Things to do   146
Selected readings   146

APPENDIX: If you have to declare personal bankruptcy   146
Danger signals   146
How to keep from going under   146
If that fails   147
Going into personal bankruptcy   147

8   THE $BILLION STOMACH   149
FOOD AND INCOME   149
GOVERNMENT INSPECTION AND LABELING REQUIREMENTS   150
    Fair packaging   151
    Net weight sometimes spells nonsense   153
    USDA grades—another labeling confusion   154
WHAT IS GOOD NUTRITION?   155
    Recommended dietary allowance   157
ON NOT BUYING OLD STUFF   158
THE GOVERNMENT'S HELPING HAND IN AGRICULTURE   160
    The depression and the AAA   160
    The results   161
    And milk, too   162
TRENDS IN FOOD RETAILING   163
    Buying food by TV   163
    The growing trend toward frozen convenience food   165
    Discount stores   166

    Summary   166
    Questions for thought and discussion   168
    Things to do   169
    Selected readings   170

CONSUMER ISSUE IV   How to Get the Most for Your Food Dollar   171
    To buy or not to buy that TV dinner   173
    Nutrition   174
    Americans on the move   174
    Making sure the bacteria is down   177
    Ways that you can be cheated by food stores and what to do about it   179
    Actually doing it   180

    Summary   181
    Questions for thought and discussion   182
    Things to do   182
    Selected readings   183

9 MORE THAN JUST KEEPING WARM   **185**
WHERE WE BUY OUR CLOTHES   185
WHY SO MANY CLOTHES?   185
  Customs   186
  Mental attitude   186
  Social class identification   187
CLOTHES, FAMILY HAPPINESS, AND BUDGET FORMATION   188
  Individuality and conformity   189
  The budget again   189
THE FASHION INDUSTRY AND WHO DECIDES   189
  Who dictates fashion?   189
CHANGING ATTITUDES TOWARD CLOTHING   190
DURABILITY VERSUS PRICE   191
  Why purchase clothes that wear out so fast?   191
  Durability not free   192
THE TREND TOWARD LESS FLAMMABLE PRODUCTS   192
  The costs involved   194
THE TREND TOWARD BETTER LABELING   194

  Summary   196
  Questions for thought and discussion   197
  Things to do   197
  Selected readings   198

CONSUMER ISSUE V **Getting the Most for Your Clothes Shopping Dollar**   **199**
  Where to buy and how much to look around   199
  Should you shop around for values?   199
  Using the mails   200
  Cash or charge?   200
  Buying principles   201

  Summary   202
  Questions for thought and discussion   203
  Things to do   203
  Selected readings   203

10 PUTTING A ROOF OVER YOUR HEAD   **205**
THE HOUSING INDUSTRY   205
  Different types of roofs   207
  Tax advantages   209
RENTING A PLACE TO LIVE IN   209
COPING WITH THE HOUSING PROBLEM   210
  Urban renewal   211
  Are there any solutions?   212
CRIME   213
  The private security industry   213
WHY DOES IT COST SO MUCH TO BUY A HOUSE?   214
DETERMINING THE VALUE OF LAND   214
  Pollution effects   214

BUILDING COSTS, BUILDING CODES, AND YOU   215
   Unions and building suppliers   216
INVESTING IN A HOUSE   216
   Mobile homes   217
THE TAX GAME   218
HOUSING AND EDUCATING YOUR CHILDREN   219
HOUSES DO NOT LAST FOREVER   221
MAKING THE MOVE   221

   Summary   222
   Questions for thought and discussion   224
   Things to do   225
   Selected readings   226

CONSUMER ISSUE VI   **How to Buy or Rent a Place to Live   227**
Renting versus buying as investments   227
How much can you afford?   228
Selecting where you want to live   231
When to use a real estate broker   233
How to bargain   234
Before you sign anything   234
What happens when you decide to buy?   237
Closing costs   237
Title insurance   237
Getting a mortgage and what it is all about   238
The kinds of mortgages   239
More flexible payment arrangements   241
Prepaying insurance and taxes   242
Coping with repairs   243
If you want to rent   244
Making the move   245

Summary   246
Questions for thought and discussion   248
Things to do   248
Selected readings   249

11   GETTING THERE BY CAR IS HALF THE WORRY   **251**
WE SPEND A LOT ON CARS   251
FOUR-WHEELED COFFINS   251
   The cost of safety   253
   Alternatives available   253
THE PRIVATE COST OF DRIVING   254
   The repair industry   255
   The automobile insurance industry   255
NO FAULT INSURANCE, PROS AND CONS   256
SHOULD YOU BUY AND HOLD   257
THE SOCIAL COSTS OF DRIVING   258

MASS TRANSIT   259
    Subsidizing the automobile   260
    Summary   261
    Questions for thought and discussion   262
    Things to do   262
    Selected readings   263

CONSUMER ISSUE VII   **Buying Transportation   264**
    Should you buy a new or a used car?   264
    If you decide to buy a new car   265
    Trading in your wheels   269
    If you buy a used car   269
    When those repairs go wrong   270
    Financing that purchase   272
    Getting an adequate amount of insurance   272

    Summary   275
    Questions for thought and discussion   276
    Things to do   276
    Selected readings   277

12   THE HEALTH CARE DILEMMA   279
MEDICAL CARE EXPENDITURES   279
WHY DOES MEDICAL CARE COST SO MUCH   279
    When Medicare started   280
    Insurance schemes   280
THE SHORT SUPPLY OF MEDICAL CARE   281
    The production of medical doctors   281
    Restrictions   281
    The past   281
WHY DID THE AMA SEEK CONTROL?   283
AMA'S MOTIVES NOT SATISFIED   283
    Self-treatment   284
    The future supply   285
DRUGS, DRUGS, DRUGS   285
    What the FDA does   286
    The benefits and costs of FDA requirements   286
    Restrictions in pharmaceutical sales   287
    Boston an anomaly   287
ALTERNATIVE HEALTH CARE DELIVERY SYSTEMS   288
    Group health   288
    HMOs   289
NATIONAL HEALTH INSURANCE   289
DIET AND HEALTH   290
    Health and organic foods   290
    Dieting   291

    Summary   291
    Questions for thought and discussion   292
    Things to do   293
    Selected readings   293

CONSUMER ISSUE VIII   **How to Keep Your Medical Costs Down**   **294**

How to keep your medical costs down   294
Keeping healthy   294
Voluntary prepaid medical care insurance   295
Types of medical insurance   295
Where should you go for health insurance?   297
Blue Cross and Blue Shield   297
Group health   298
When you get older   299
What about mail-order health insurance?   301
Providing for the ultimate expense   302

Summary   303
Questions for thought and discussion   304
Things to do   304
Selected readings   305

13   **OTHER FORMS OF PROTECTION:**
LIFE INSURANCE AND SOCIAL SECURITY   **307**

SECURITY   307
PREMATURE DEATHS   307
SELLING LIFE INSURANCE   308
PRINCIPLES BEHIND LIFE INSURANCE   308
THE DIFFERENT TYPES OF LIFE INSURANCE   309
THE TWO BASIC TYPES OF INSURANCE   309
WHOLE, STRAIGHT, OR ORDINARY LIFE INSURANCE   309
   Premiums   309
   Living benefits   310
   Borrowing on your cash value   310
   When you reach retirement age   311
   Death benefits   312
LIMITED–PAYMENT WHOLE LIFE   312
TERM INSURANCE   314
   Convertibility   315
   Other types of life insurance policies   315
ANNUITIES   317
   Variable annuities   317
   Fixed annuities   317
INVOLUNTARY BENEFIT PROGRAMS—THE CASE OF SOCIAL SECURITY   320
   The provisions of the Social Security Act   321
BASIC BENEFITS OF SOCIAL SECURITY   321
PROBLEMS WITH SOCIAL SECURITY   322
HOW SOCIAL SECURITY IS PAID   322
IF YOU WORK, YOU DO NOT GET PAID   322
OTHER FACTS ABOUT SOCIAL SECURITY   324

   Summary   326
   Questions for thought and discussion   327
   Things to do   328
   Selected readings   328

CONSUMER ISSUE IX   **How to Meet Your Insurance Needs**   329

Some insurance buying rules   329
Are you underinsured?   329
Getting your Social Security figured out   330
Figuring out how much insurance you should buy   330
Now that you have figured out how much, what should you buy?   332
Some additional considerations   334
Take advantage of group plans   334
Shopping around for insurance   334
Should you get a participating or nonparticipating policy?   334

Summary   336
Questions for thought and discussion   336
Things to do   336
Selected readings   337

14   **WHAT TO DO WITH YOUR PIGGY BANK**   339

THE TENDENCY TO SAVE   339
WHY SAVE AT ALL?   339
  Saving among the poor   340
WHAT DETERMINES HOW MUCH YOU SAVE?   341
THE NATURE OF COMPOUND INTEREST   343
  The power of compounding   343
TYPES OF SAVINGS INSTITUTIONS   344
THE SIMPLE FACTS ABOUT INVESTING   346
RISK AND RATE OF RETURN   347
  Some facts on the stock market   347
  Preferred stocks and bonds   348
  Capital gains and losses   348
  What affects the price of a stock?   349
MAKING MONEY IN THE STOCK MARKET   350
  Getting advice on the market   350
  Public information   351
  Capitalization   351
  Hot tips   352
  The random walk   352
  What about investment plans?   353
  The two types of mutual funds   354
  Is there no way to get rich quick?   354
OTHER SUREFIRE SCHEMES   355
  Real estate   355
PENSION AND RETIREMENT PLANS   356

  Summary   356
  Questions for thought and discussion   358
  Things to do   359
  Selected readings   359

CONSUMER ISSUE X   **How to be a Rational Investor   360**
Inflation and the interest rate   360
Evidence on the stock market   361
Real estate deals   366
Variety is the spice of investment   366

Summary   368
Questions for thought and discussion   368
Things to do   369
Selected readings   369

15   THE HIGH COST OF LIVING   371
HISTORY OF PRICES   371
INFLATION IN OTHER COUNTRIES   372
WHO IS HURT BY INFLATION?   372
Pocket money   373
Others who suffer from inflation   373
Contracts negotiated in real terms   375
RISING PRICES AND YOU   375
AND INCOME, TOO   377
ANTICIPATING INFLATION   377
INTEREST RATES AGAIN   377
HOW TO TELL WHERE YOU STAND   379
What is a cost of living clause?   379
IF YOU KNOW THE PRICES ARE GOING UP, SHOULD YOU BUY NOW?   379
INFLATION AND INCOME TAXES   380
What has happened?   380
ARE YOU BETTER OFF OWNING A HOUSE DURING INFLATION?   380

Summary 382
Questions for thought and discussion   383
Things to do   383
Selected readings   383

CONSUMER ISSUE XI   **Protecting Yourself Against Inflation   384**
Minimizing the costs of cash   384
Investments   384
Funds for investing in short-term securities   385
Adjust your life insurance   388
Taking out loans   388
Retirement plans   388
Your wages   389
Taxes   389
Minimizing cash holdings   389
In conclusion   390

Summary   390
Questions for thought and discussion   390
Things to do   391
Selected readings   391

16   PAYING FOR GOVERNMENT   393

THE WHYS AND WHERES OF TAXATION   393
FIRST, A LITTLE THEORY   393
THE ABILITY TO PAY DOCTRINE   396
   The sacrifice doctrine   396
THE PERSONAL FEDERAL INCOME TAX   397
HOW OUR PROGRESSIVE SYSTEM CAME INTO BEING   398
LOOPHOLES   399
   Capital gains   399
   Income redistribution   401
HOW YOU SHOULD EXPECT GOVERNMENT TO SPEND YOUR TAX DOLLAR   401
CAN WE IMPROVE OUR TAX SYSTEM?   404

   Summary   406
   Questions for thought and discussion   407
   Things to do   407
   Selected readings   408

CONSUMER ISSUE XII   Easing Your Tax Burden   409

The minimum   409
Keeping down your taxes   411
Americans are honest   411

Summary   411
Questions for thought and discussion   412
Things to do   412
Selected readings   412

17   THE CONSUMER GETS A VOICE   415

A HISTORY OF CONSUMER PROTECTION   415
   Business wanted them, too   416
ANTIMONOPOLY POLICIES   416
   Food and Drug Act   416
   Why the renewed interest in the consumer?   418
PROTECTION AFTER THE FACT   418
THE PRESIDENTS SPEAK UP   419
STATE AND LOCAL GOVERNMENT AND PRIVATE CONSUMER PROTECTION   420
   The private sector   421
   Product standards   422
RECOVERY OF DAMAGES   423
PRIVATE AGENCIES   424
ACTIVE CONSUMER GROUPS   425
   Cost vs. benefits   426

   Summary   427
   Questions for thought and discussion   428
   Things to do   429
   Selected readings   429

CONSUMER ISSUE XIII   How to Get Help from the Government   430
Where to go?   430
A strategy   431
Getting your money back   431
What happened to me shouldn't happen to anybody   433
The Federal government   434
The old guard   434
Consumer protection by the CPSC   437
Powers of the CPSC   438
How to get in touch with the CPSC   438
Do you want to do it yourself?   439

Summary   441
Questions for thought and discussion   442
Things to do   442
Selected readings   442

CONSUMER ISSUE XIV   How to Use a Small Claims Court   443
Why were they founded?   443
Criticism of the courts   443
But you have to watch out   446
How they work   446
Preparing for trial   446
What happens in court   447
Where, what, and how much?   447

Summary   447
Questions for thought and discussion   448
Things to do   448
Selected readings   448

CONSUMER ISSUE XV   Do Consumers Have Responsibilities, Too?   449
Reverse rip-offs: consumers who cheat business people   449
Selected readings   451

18   ECOLOGY AND THE MARKETPLACE   453
IS THE PROBLEM AS NEW AS IT SEEMS?   453
AIR POLLUTION   454
The unpaid social costs   454
New regulations   455
No-lead gas   456
The future of the auto   457
Electricity generation   457
WATER POLLUTION   457
The harm from water pollution   458
WILL THERE EVER BE AN END TO AIR AND WATER POLLUTION?   459

Summary   460
Questions for thought and discussion   461
Things to do   461
Selected readings   461

19 YOUR FUTURE AS A CONSUMER   463

A MORE COMPLEX LIFE   463
THE NOT SO GOOD OLD DAYS   463
   Income uncertainty   464
AND LIFE ITSELF   464
OUR COMPLEX SOCIETY   464
   What can you do as a consumer?   466
RECREATION AND CALLING IT QUITS SOONER   466
ALTERNATIVES TO EARLY RETIREMENT   468
WRAPPING IT UP   469

   Summary   469
   Questions for thought and discussion   470
   Things to do   470
   Selected readings   470

APPENDIX A   Estate Planning: Wills, Trusts, and Taxes   471
Estate planning is not just for the rich   471
The basics   471
Basic wills   472
What to do with your will   472
Letter of last instruction   472
Trusts   473
Minimizing estate taxes   474
Gift taxes   474

APPENDIX B   All You Need to Know About Metric (for your everyday life)   477
Metric is based on decimal system   477
Basic units   477
Other commonly used units   478

Glossary Index   479
Index   481

PREFACE

The 1970s have been called the "age of the consumer." If we were to use as evidence the growth in interest in consumer economics courses, we would certainly have to agree; consumer economics is now being offered not only in home economics departments, but in departments of economics and in business schools as well. More and more students want to find out how they can be rational consumers. They also want to know what economic issues face consumers both as individuals and as a group. It is with this growing interest in mind that I have written this text.

You will notice a somewhat unusual format throughout the following pages. I have attempted to present the major areas of consumer economics in chapter form. At the end of many of these chapters, a consumer issue has been presented. For example, after an explanation of what inflation is and how it affects the consumer, an issue follows that outlines how the individual can best protect himself or herself against the ravages of inflation. As another example, after the chapter on food, a consumer issue outlines the steps that the individual can take to become a better food-shopper. To a large extent, the consumer issues offer more practical advice than do the chapters.

Students will find a number of pedagogical aids in both the chapters and the consumer issues. Each chapter starts off with a Chapter Preview that indicates to the reader what will be covered. Then, to "ease the blow" of new terminology, a Glossary of terms that might not be known to the reader is presented before the actual text begins. At the end of each chapter, there is a point-by-point Summary that can be used for review. Then Questions for Thought and Discussion that follow the Summary may be used as the basis for class discussion or as the basis for individual thought or even discussion in groups of students without the aid of an instructor. Things to Do gives some projects that a class can do as a group or that individuals can do at the request of the professor or on their own. Lastly, Selected References are presented. This list is not merely a rundown of academic articles that students can never hope to understand. Rather, it presents some alternative sources of reading for those students who wish further explanations of certain sections of the chapter.

The consumer issues have basically the same pedagogical devices, except that there is no preview and the issue summary gives more practical hints on certain consumer decision-making problems.

You will notice a wide use of illustrative materials—photographs, charts, and cartoons. In my experience, visualization of certain ideas not only aids the student in understanding the material but also makes the task of reading the text more enjoyable.

Professors certainly need not use this book in the order in which the chapters and issues are presented, nor need they feel that they must use every single chapter in the book. This may be particularly true in situations where professors wish to use extensive audiovisual supplementary materials.

Since it was important to consider a new consumer economics text as a project and not just as another book, from the very beginning, I have had the pleasure of working with Dr. Phillis Basile, who has prepared one of the most pedagogically helpful student workbooks that I have ever seen. This workbook, which brings the student along and makes any difficult area of study comprehensible and usable, will be found by most students, I believe, a valuable supplement to the text itself. Dr. Basile also was kind enough to offer detailed review of my original drafts.

Additional supplements complete this project. Nancy Spillman, of Los Angeles Trade-Technical College, has developed a lively and interesting Reader that can be used with this text as well as others. She also reviewed the manuscript intensively. And, for the instructor, there is a complete Instructor's Manual which was developed, in conjunction with me, by Dr. Phillis Basile. In the Instructor's Manual you will find other topics for class discussion, exam questions, selected references, and other helpful teaching devices.

A number of other individuals were instrumental in this project. Major reviewers who offered detailed, incisive, and certainly very constructive criticism were:

Professor Howard Alsey, Department of Economics, Arkansas State University

Professor Jean S. Bowers, Department of Home Economics, Ohio State University

Professor Judy Farris, Department of Home Economics, South Dakota State University

Professor Barbara Follosco, Department of Home Economics, Los Angeles Valley College

Professor Ron Hartje, School of Business, SOUK Valley College

Professor James O. Hill, Department of Economics, Vincennes University

Professor Eugene Silberberg, Department of Economics, University of Washington

Professor Faye Taylor, Department of Home Economics, University of Utah

Professor Margil Vanderhoff, Department of Home Economics, Indiana University

Professor Joseph Wurmli, School of Business, Hillsborough Community College

I have found through the years that the best way I can improve on what I write is by soliciting the comments of those who use my texts. I therefore stand ready to answer any and all comments, criticisms, or questions relating to what follows in this book. It is with the help of those who want the best for their students that I can find out what is best for the ultimate reader of *Economic Issues for Consumers.*

RLM
Coral Gables, 1975

ECONOMIC ISSUES FOR CONSUMERS

CHAPTER PREVIEW

☐ What are the characteristics of our consumer-oriented society?

☐ What are some of the suggested solutions to many of the problems facing American consumers?

☐ What is the information explosion all about?

GLOSSARY OF NEW TERMS

Consumption or Consuming: The process of acquiring products and services, using these products and services, maintaining the products (if applicable), and disposing of remnants, residue, etc.

Consumers: Individuals who act in the capacity of purchasing, using, maintaining, and disposing of products and services.

Capitalist: An individual who owns all or part of an income-producing asset.

Real Level of Living: The level at which individuals are able to enjoy the fruits of their wages and/or profits and rent. Generally, the average real level of living per person in the United States has been defined as total amount of income per year divided by the number of people in the country, then corrected for any changes in overall prices.

Purchasing Power: The implicit amount of goods and services that can be bought with a given amount of money.

Service Sector: That area of economic activity involved in such things as repairing and cleaning products, and serving people in general.

Inflation: A sustained rise in prices.

THE AGE OF THE CONSUMER

You consume. I consume. Your friends consume. We all consume in one way or another. As **consumers**, we number at least 215 million in the United States alone. And the dollar value of what we consume is staggering —in 1975 an estimated $910 billion. That comes out to over $13,000 for every household in the United States.

What do we buy as consumers? A grab bag of goods as varied as 18 carat gold toothpicks, toothpaste, five-bedroom houses, movie cameras, TVs, hamburgers, hot dogs, and terrariums. Table 1-1, on the next page, lists some of the broad categories of goods and services that we spend billions of dollars on.

WE ARE NOT JUST CONSUMERS

The world is a cruel one: we do not usually get something for nothing. Hence, most of us are more than consumers. At one time or another we have to work; we have to act as employees or producers. In fact, there are about 95 million of us in the measured labor force, earning incomes as professors, truck drivers, typists, engineers, artists, construction workers, businessmen, or any of the other ways for making a living. Additionally, many, such as housewives, work to provide services for family members, but are not given monetary payment. Those of us who are paid to work for a living receive wages or salaries that account for about three-fourths of all of the income generated in any one year in the American economy. The other 25 percent of that income goes to those of us who are owners of things like land, stocks, bonds, oil wells, and apartment buildings.

Most of us are, therefore, at one and the same time consumers, employees, and/or **capitalists**, for we consume in order to survive and be happy; we work for others in order to receive the income necessary to buy what we want; and often we obtain income from our savings, whether they be in the form of stocks or houses. In fact, more than 35 million Americans have purchased shares in American companies.

A GROWING NATION

We are a growing nation: While the population is rising at a slower rate than in the past, it is still in fact

TABLE 1-1 PERSONAL CONSUMPTION EXPENDITURES BY MAJOR TYPE, 1974 (in billions of dollars)

This table shows an actual tabulation of the billions of dollars that are spent by American consumers on various categories of goods and services. (The last category, "All others," includes everything that was not listed specifically.) You can check the latest issue of the *Survey of Current Business* to find out how much personal consumption expenditures have grown since 1974. Source: *Survey of Current Business*, October, 1975.

TOTAL	$869.1
SUBCATEGORIES:	
Automobiles and parts	50.6
Furniture and household equipment	59.5
Food and beverages	183.5
Clothing and shoes	74.4
Gasoline and oil	36.8
Housing services	124.9
Household operation services	51.7
Transportation	25.6
All others	262.1

rising, as can be seen in Figure 1–1. And we have a dynamic economy. As a nation, our **real level of living** is almost continually rising, as can be seen in Figure 1–2, which shows the amount of **purchasing power** available (after taxes) per person in the United States over the last several decades. But this growth in real living levels has not been obtained without cost. Nor can we categorically state that all Americans have shared equally in the economic cornucopia.

INCOME DIFFERENCES

Soon after World War II, in 1947, the bottom 20 percent of income earners in this country received about 5 percent of total income. A quarter of a century later, the bottom 20 percent is still getting only about 5 percent of the total pie. Clearly, income inequality exists now. In principle, the government (particularly the federal government) has been empowered to alleviate this imbalance in incomes. Voters have presumably elected officials who would institute programs aimed at helping the relatively poor in society through income redistribution. Unfortunately, the evidence indicates that many attempts at helping out poor people have in fact not helped them, and in some cases have actually hurt them. The poor, of course, face special problems induced by their poverty. But they also face many of the challenges that virtually all consumers face (although the errors of poor consumers can often be more costly to them than such errors to others).

THE COMPLEXITIES OF CONSUMPTION

In a growing, dynamic economy such as ours, the task of being a rational and informed consumer may have become more and more complex. For example, in 1974 alone, almost 32,000 trademarks were issued. With so many new things being offered, it is not surprising that many consumers feel overwhelmed. In addition, they are bombarded with continually increasing amounts of advertising as producers compete for consumer dollars. Figure 1–3 shows the per capita advertising expenditures over the last several decades. Whereas in 1935 only $13.28 was spent on advertising per capita in the U.S., in 1975 it is estimated that almost $130.00 will have been lavished on each man, woman, and child.

FRAUD

Not surprisingly, problems of false advertising and fraud continue to plague the sometimes bewildered American buyer. What percentage of these complaints are real is unknown, but the sheer number of them gives some idea of the problems facing many unwary consumers (and even the wary ones, too!).

PRODUCERS
EVERYWHERE

In spite of many allegations that the country is becoming monopolized, there are about twelve million firms in the United States. To be sure, in certain manufacturing industries, a very few firms do dominate. But in the ever-increasingly important service sector (repairing, cleaning, etc.) of the economy, there are literally hundreds of thousands of firms. The service sector in our society is projected to grow in importance until by

FIGURE 1-1
POPULATION IN THE UNITED STATES
We see that from 1920 onward population has been growing quite steadily, and is projected to reach about 225 million Americans by 1980. (Before 1940, the data did not include Alaska and Hawaii.) Source: Bureau of the Census, Current Population reports.

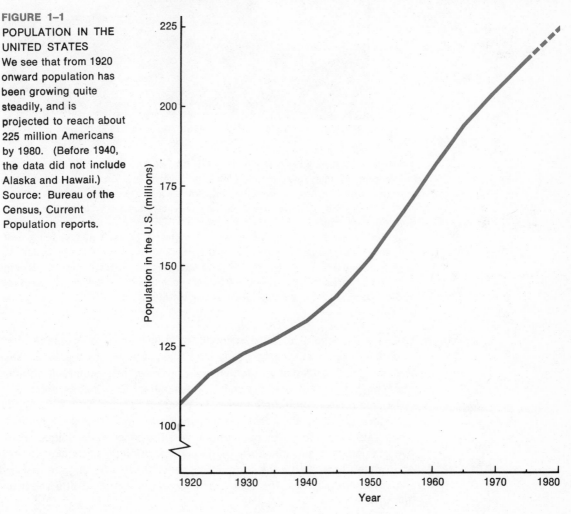

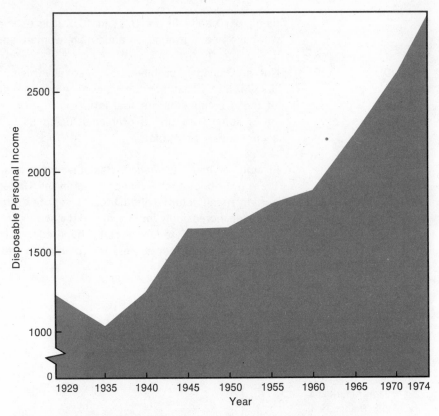

FIGURE 1–2 REAL PER CAPITA INCOME IN THE UNITED STATES
In the United States the amount of income available for spending per person, after taxes, has been growing quite steadily from just before the Great Depression in 1929 until today. Of course, there was a severe downturn during the Depression, but that can be considered an unusual occurrence in this nation's history. Note that the dollars here are expressed in terms of 1958 purchasing power. If they were expressed in terms of 1975 purchasing power, the figures would be quite a bit higher. The data before 1960 excludes Alaska and Hawaii. Source: U.S. Bureau of Economic Analysis, *National Income and Product Accounts of the United States, 1929–65,* and the *Survey of Current Business.*

1980 it will account for 30 percent of all money spent on personal consumption; hence we can be pretty sure that there will always be at least one area of the economy in which the consumer has numerous choices when buying a particular service. These numerous choices are at the same time a blessing and a curse. The blessing is obvious: the consumer has more choices, and, presumably, the larger the number of choices, the greater the degree of competition for the consumer's dollar. However, the curse is still there: the huge number of producers makes it harder to detect and distribute information about those who engage in fraud and who generally give the customer a low-quality product at a relatively high price.

**SOME PAST AND
FUTURE SOLUTIONS**

Concerned citizens and government officials have attempted to eliminate many of the problems facing a consumer in this age of complexity. Many of us are aware of some of the solutions, such as truth in labeling, truth in lending, standardization, fair weights and measures, occupational licensing, and so on. Unfortunately, the results of such attempts have not always been to the advantage of the consumer. Occupational licensing is a good example. As we shall see, in some cases occupational licensing is used to protect those in a particular occupation from competition by potential entrants into that occupation. Hence, in those cases, the consumer generally loses out.[1]

Numerous devices to regulate specific industries have also sometimes had mixed results. Consumers, we must remember, are a diverse group of people with diverse interests, while producers have very specific interests. An agency operating with the intent of regulating an industry in the interests of consumers will face pressure from producer groups that would be directly hurt by the agency's actions. However, there is generally no consumer group which will put pressure on the agency to act in the interests of consumers, since consumers represent such diverse interests. It is not surprising that regulatory agencies have often passed

[1] Thomas G. Moore, "The Purpose of Licensing," *Journal of Law and Economics,* Vol. IV, 1961, pp. 93 ff.

FIGURE 1–3 PER CAPITA ADVERTISING EXPENDITURES IN THE UNITED STATES (estimated total in millions of current dollars)
Expressed in purchasing power of dollars that actually existed in each year, per capita advertising expenditures have been rising quite rapidly in the United States. The estimate for 1974 is almost $13,000 per every American. Source: McCann-Erikson Advertising Agency, Inc., for *Printer's Ink* Publications, New York, 1935–66. *Market Communications,* 1966–69. After 1970, *Advertising Age* (Crain Communications).

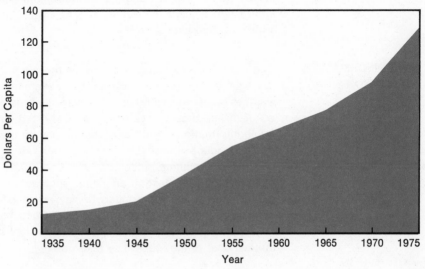

rules and regulations at the behest of those that they regulate. The Interstate Commerce Commission and the Civil Aeronautics Board are good examples. In both cases, the producer groups in question—carriers and airlines, respectively—have benefited from the restrictive rules and pricing methods allowed by the commissions, for the regulating agencies have forbidden price cutting and other forms of competition. As a result, the consumer has generally lost out and has been paying dearly in the form of higher shipping and transportation costs on trains, buses, trucks, and airplanes.

That does not mean, of course, that there is no way to regulate business practices that are fraudulent or otherwise detrimental to the consumer. We are indeed no longer in the era of *caveat emptor*—"let the buyer beware." Rather, we are in the era of a more balanced view where *caveat venditor*—"let the seller beware"—also applies.

THE AGE OF CONSUMERISM

In this most recent age of the consumerist movement, legislation has produced agencies and rules designed to protect and help the consumer in his or her quest for getting the best products at the best prices. Of course, the consumerist movement has not always benefited consumers. And more particularly, certain groups of consumers have often been hurt by legislation designed to help everybody. What is certain, though, is that the consumerist movement is here to stay. More than 10 years ago, the late President John F. Kennedy sent a message to Congress outlining a declaration of rights for consumers in a modern society, which included the rights to information, safety, and choice.

All of these rights have since been greatly expanded. However, the consumer also has a set of responsibilities which we will look at later on. We will have occasion to discuss many of the consumer-oriented acts which have passed Congress and state legislatures. Many of these acts involve, among other things, the requirement that producers provide more information to consumers. And indeed we find ourselves in the midst of an information explosion.

THE INFORMATION EXPLOSION

One of the tenets of the consumerist movement is that the consumer has the right to be informed. Before the movement got started, the consumer was not totally uninformed. However much he or she may have mistrusted or disliked most advertising, part of it did, and still does, provide valuable information. Such information may be merely a statement that certain products are available and at certain prices. Or the information may be detailed technical accounts, provided either by producers themselves or by independent testing agencies, such as the Consumers Union (an organization we will have much to say about later on). Information may also be found on the product labels. Consumers can now obtain such information as the unit price of the food they buy, or the actual annual interest cost of the loans they take out.

The provision of more information does not, however, guarantee that consumers will use that information wisely. Therefore, one of the aims of this book is to help you, the consumer, choose among the many sources of information in the most beneficial manner. It will certainly not be worth your while to spend all of your time checking out every product you ever buy. But then again it may be worthwhile for you to investigate carefully when purchasing certain products. When and where to look for information and how much of it to consume is no less a difficult decision than deciding what products to buy and when, how to use them, etc.

Once you treat information as a scarce resource with a cost—which it is indeed [2]—then you can more rationally acquire information and become a better consumer. When we talk about your being a better consumer, we mean that you will be more satisfied. We will not restrict our discussion merely to your purchases of material goods; we will also talk about what you do with your leisure time and how much of that you have, what you select as your lifetime goals, and how you form some of your values. How all of these problems are solved partly determines what the quality of your life is. Numerous other things do, too, and sometimes they are out of your control.

[2] Just estimate how much time you have to spend getting yourself set up when you move —what bank you should use, where you should establish credit, where you should do your grocery shopping, and so on.

QUALITY
OF LIFE

The quality of your life depends in part on your occupation, your income and how you spend it, how carefully you use your time, and so on. But it also depends on your surroundings, your environment. Today more than ever before, we are aware that the quality of our life is deteriorating, and is doing so in good part because the quality of our environment is deteriorating.

Some of our present ecological problems are a function of our market system—of the way you and I have decided to spend our consumer dollars. Of course, as *individuals* we are not to blame for foul, smog-filled air in the cities or polluted rivers and ocean beaches. But we are part of the problem, and we cannot deny it. The other part of the problem, however, lies in how certain resources are allowed to be used. Generally, the areas of environmental decay that bother us most are areas in which resources, such as air and water, are not owned by anyone, so many abuse them. We will look at ecology and the marketplace in the last chapter of this book.

INFLATION,
INFLATION,
INFLATION

By now Americans have come to expect **inflation** -a sustained rise in overall prices. There are many theories about who causes inflation: some say businessmen, some say workers, others say neither, but rather government policies. Although this is not the book in which to discuss the causes of inflation, we will discuss the effects of inflation, and the personal economic policies that one can follow to at least partially avoid these effects. The prices of most goods have been rising on average over 5 percent a year for more than five years now. Sometimes prices rise faster than in previous years, sometimes slower. So, without due care, you may, for example, put your savings in investments that fail to guard against these unanticipated swings in the rates of inflation, or you may sign contracts in which you lose out to that same unanticipated inflation. There are ways in which you can protect yourself against what has come to be this perpetual demon. These are treated in Chapter 15 and Consumer Issue XII.

WHAT IS TO COME

Besides covering all of the topics just mentioned, many areas will be explored in which consumer decision-making is important—medical care; buying on credit; purchasing food, housing, and transportation; saving for the future; insuring yourself; reducing taxes; and other concerns. The basis, though, of the rest of this book is much simpler—how to achieve your full potential as a consumer, worker, parent, taxpayer, and simply as a person. There will not be a simple decree of strict rules of the road. There will be numerous suggestions, and many general principles of which you may want to be aware. Even then, you may often throw the principles to the wind, for your tastes may be different than mine, and mine are different than those of anyone else. Ultimately, the values that you have discovered are appropriate for you will be paramount in all of the decisions you must make throughout your life. No book on consumer economics can ever attempt to account for these values, for they are many and ever-changing. That, of course, is what makes life interesting.

And now onward to the next chapter for some thoughts on consumer decision-making.

SUMMARY

After every chapter and every issue, there will be a point-by-point chapter summary stressing the key ideas, concepts, and aids to being a better consumer. Since this is an introductory chapter, there is no chapter summary.

QUESTIONS FOR THOUGHT AND DISCUSSION

1. Do you think that the standard of living in the United States will continue to rise throughout your lifetime?

2. Does the fact that 35 million Americans own shares in American companies mean that the ownership of American business is widely dispersed throughout the nation and throughout all income levels?

3. Do you think that it is more difficult to be a rational consumer today than it was when your parents were your age?

4. Is the information that you receive about products ever free?

THINGS TO DO

1. Find out what personal consumption expenditures were in the United States during the last three months. You can do this by looking at the latest issue of the *Survey of Current Business,* which you will find in the reference section of your library.

2. Go back to some very old issues of the *Survey of Current Business* and compare the numbers then with the numbers you found in a very current issue. Can you notice a difference in percentages? That is, are we spending a larger or smaller percentage of total expenditures on automobiles today than we were, say, 20 years ago? You probably will not find a heading for mobile homes in the government data for 20 years ago. Why is that?

3. See if your parents own any stocks in American companies. If they do, ask them how they can influence the management of those companies.

4. Find out what the Bureau of Census thinks the U. S. population will do in the next 50 years.

SELECTED READINGS

After each chapter and issue, there will be selected readings that you may wish to consult to get a broader idea of the concepts presented in each chapter and issue.

CHAPTER PREVIEW

☐ What is involved in rational decision-making?
☐ How do goals affect your consumer choices?
☐ What else determines how you act?
☐ What determines your buying habits?
☐ How much information should you seek before you make a purchase?
☐ What are some of the aspects of alternative life styles?
☐ Why is value clarification important?

GLOSSARY OF NEW TERMS

Barter: The exchange of goods and/or services without the use of money. If I give you two pencils for one eraser, you and I have exchanged by way of barter.

Credit: A loan that someone offers to you in exchange for a payment, usually called interest.

Conspicuous Consumption: Consumption of goods more for their ability to impress others than for the inherent satisfaction they yield; buying and using consumer goods in a flashy or noticeable manner.

Motivational Research: Research done by a psychologist into the reasons why consumers buy what they buy. Motivational researchers attempt to find out the hidden reasons that you buy one brand of something rather than another.

Monopoly: A firm which controls to a large extent the sale of a good or service. A monopoly usually involves the prevention of others from competing for customers.

Rational Consumer Decision-Making: Deciding how to buy, where to buy, and what to buy in such a manner that the highest satisfaction is obtained from the consumer's total income including the time the consumer has.

Sunk Costs: Costs that have been incurred already and that cannot be changed. An example of sunk costs is the initial cost of buying, say, a television set. That cost never changes after purchase, but the cost of running it can change—the longer it is kept on, the higher will be your electricity bill.

Parkinson's Law: Work will expand to fit the time allowed.

Even if you were absolutely the wealthiest person on this earth, you still would have to make decisions. Say even that all your material wants could be satisfied at the touch of a button; one valuable resource still would be scarce for you, and that resource is your time. You have only so much time in a day and so many days in a life. Even in that nirvana of total abundance, you would still be faced with making a choice about the use of your time: you would have to learn the *art* of decision-making.

We know that in the real world, in which we are all more or less distant from being the richest person on earth, the art of decision-making applies to the use not only of our time, but of our other resources as well. Intelligent, rational consumer decision-making thus becomes all the more important. We are all faced with a budget problem. We cannot have everything we want, so we must make choices. And once we make them, we must also carry them out in a rational manner. We cannot simply decide to buy a new car. We must also decide what kind of new car—foreign or domestic, small or large, luxury or economy, sedan or station wagon, and so on. We must then decide where to look for the car of our choice, and then whether to pay cash or buy it on credit. If we use credit, we must decide where to obtain that credit. Decision-making never seems to stop.

MAKING UP YOUR MIND

EXCHANGE AND RATIONAL DECISION–MAKING

All consumer decision-making ultimately results in a choice that is carried through by exchange. When we decide to enter a certain occupation and take a job with a particular firm, we exchange our labor services for that firm's payment of wages. When we decide to buy a TV, for the set itself we exchange the purchasing power implicit in the money paid for it. When we decide to put our savings into a savings and loan association, we exchange the purchasing power implicit in those savings for shares in the savings and loan association. Actually, we expect to receive at a later date what we put into the savings and loan plus a reward, that is the interest on our savings.

Rational consumer decision-making generally involves seeking out those exchanges that are most beneficial

Should I buy a new car?

Yes

What size should I buy?

Compact

What body style should I buy?

Station wagon

Automatic or manual transmission?

Manual

FIGURE 2–1   A TYPICAL DECISION–MAKING PROCESS

to you, the consumer (or that are most beneficial for another person or group if you happen to be the decision-maker with that responsibility). But determining the most beneficial choice for yourself presupposes the ability to analyze the benefits (and costs) of alternative choices. This is sometimes impossible, or at best extremely difficult. Whenever your personal values or feelings enter into your decision-making, you may have a difficult time in quantifying them sufficiently to make what we deem a rational choice. Or you may even have a difficult time putting priorities on the different values you have.

We can generalize the decision-making process into several steps:
1. Define the problem in light of goals and values.
2. Select and explore possible alternatives.
3. From these, select one alternative.
4. Then proceed to accept and evaluate your responsibilities after having selected this one alternative.

This last step is important because many persons have a tendency to blame others when things fail to work out.

There are many ways in which exchange can be facilitated. In a market economy such as ours, these ways include, among others, the use of money instead of trading goods for goods **(barter)**, the use of **credit**, the branding of particular products to give certain types of information, the use of media to transmit product information, and so on. As rational consumers, we may attempt to facilitate our transactions in the market-place as much as is economically worthwhile: we may sometimes attempt to acquire information that is not provided to us by, say, the seller of the product. Or we may sometimes want private or government agencies to facilitate the exchanges we like to make. A national job-market bank might be one means of getting such information; a rental agency listing the available apartments in an entire city might be another means. A magazine that presents test results is yet another. The list could go on and on.

WHAT DETERMINES YOUR CHOICES?

There are many determinants of the choices we make in our day-to-day living. If this were a book dealing exclusively with the principles of economics, we could talk about how our choices are governed by our income and the prices of various goods and services. For example, we would find out that, in general, as the price of one product goes up relative to all others, a smaller quantity of the product will be demanded. We would find that as people's income goes up, so, too, does their demand for most goods and services.

But more generally, the choices we make can be looked at as also depending on the goals we set for ourselves and our family, and the customs already laid out before us in our society.

GOALS

Everybody has goals, whether or not they are well defined. To start off, we know that except for pathological cases, the main goal of most individuals is to be happy, however each of us defines it. But to attain that goal, we make numerous subgoals. Yours may be to finish college or to get a good job or to play the guitar well; you may have goals set for your children, if and when you have them; you may have a goal set in your job or your business. These goals will often determine your consumption behavior. If one of your goals is to be relatively well off by the time you are 50, you may then decide to work hard, spend little, and save a lot. That means you will not be tempted to take long vacations or buy higher-priced housing, at least not in the earlier stages of your career. On the other hand, if your goal is different, you may take those longer vacations. You know that you will pay for them later on in the sense that your savings will be smaller.

Individuals change their goals all the time. In fact, experts who specialize in helping persons plan for the future often advise that goals should be made for the immediate run, intermediate run, and long run, and be revised often. You might have a goal for the next two months of finishing a particular project, doing well in certain classes, increasing your sales, or what have you. Obviously, at the end of the stipulated period, you will see if you attained those goals and you will make new ones for the next immediate time period. In the *intermediate* run, your goals may involve improving your tennis game, painting the house, or getting a new car. And then there are the long-run goals, five-year, 10-year plans, even 20-year projections into the future. As most people find out, these are often revised according to new information on where you are going in your job, on the size and circumstances of your family, and on your own thinking. Just look back at what you thought five years ago you were going to do. Did you actually end up doing it? Some of you have, but many others have not. Does that mean you planned wrong? It certainly does not. When you make decisions for the future, you use the information presently available. But information is not perfect, or complete. If you used the information rationally and economically, then the goals you set would be rational also; but they will not be unchangeable, because you will continuously acquire new information about yourself and the world around you.

Goals and planning go hand in hand. Consumer decision-making is sometimes based on plans that are themselves based on goals. Planning is sometimes a painful procedure, particularly when a family is involved and numerous diverse interests within it must be considered. Compromises must be reached. Compromises must also be reached within one's own mind. Men and women often have a tendency to "want the stars," but since scarcity still hangs heavy, they can't have it all.

Consumers who plan in a rational manner may be accused of lacking spontaneity. Certainly that is one of the costs of planning, but one of the benefits is that goals can often be met through proper planning and adherence to those plans. To be sure, you must decide. If indeed you do decide to become a consumer who plans, then you may be able to satisfy many of your desires and needs. If your values are such, however, that spontaneity is important in your life, then a set of plans will not be your only way to happiness.

CUSTOMS

Primitive societies are usually ruled by custom. But even modern societies have customs that determine people's choices. Although it is impossible to avoid custom, we might say that in the United States custom plays less of a role in our decision-making than it does in many other nations. Nonetheless, if you examine your own behavior as a consumer, you may be surprised at how much you do depend on customs already established. Here are just a few of the things we do that are controlled more or less by custom:

1. the types and combinations of food we eat.
2. our exchanging Christmas cards.
3. the style of clothes we wear.
4. how we dispose of the dead.
5. the type of marriage ceremony we use.

Take, for example, clothes. The two or three buttons on the sleeve of a man's suit jacket are there by custom; they are totally nonfunctional otherwise. You can probably think of numerous other features of clothing that have no function other than to fit the dictates of custom. The fact that men in our society do not wear skirts is also dictated by custom, for we partly identify sex role by established dress.

Many of our food-buying habits certainly are affected by our culture. What we consider acceptable for eating may not be considered acceptable in other cultures, and vice versa.

Customs do serve a useful purpose: without them, we could not predict behavior; the result would be considerably more confusion than now exists in our society.

Your consumption patterns may also be determined by your desire to influence others' opinions of you. Many years ago, a famous American economist, Thorstein Veblen, gave a name to this pattern.

CONSPICUOUS CONSUMPTION

Professor Veblen pointed out, in his *Theory of the Leisure Class*, that many people desire to consume in a conspicuous manner. **Conspicuous consumption** is the use of the goods and services we can afford to show what our social worth is, on the implicit assumption that the more we can afford, the worthier we are. Such consumption is based on conformity—the conformity that one wishes to have, at least in appearance, to the consumption practices of one's neighbors and friends. This type of behavior, also known as "keeping up with the Joneses," is familiar to all of us, and is considered by many to be undesirable behavior because it shows a lack of individuality. But although individuality carries high praise in American society, it is not an overriding characteristic of *any* society. Even if individuality is more preached than practiced in our society, the theory of conspicuous consumption still fails to adequately explain people's consumption activities; for as the old adage has it, "one man's meat may be another man's poison." Tastes do indeed differ, as do people's values. Today, motivational psychologists no longer place overriding emphasis on Veblen's theory to explain consumption patterns in our economy.

BUYING HABITS

In one respect, there are as many varied buying habits as there are consumers. But in other respects, for the purposes of analysis and to better understand our own buying habits, we can categorize them into several broad groups, the two most obvious being impulse buying and planned buying.

IMPULSE BUYING

Impulse buying is just that—buying on a whim, walking into a store, seeing something we like, and purchasing it. Obviously, impulse buying cannot explain all of our buying habits because we have certain needs that must be met if we are to survive, the most obvious being minimum amounts of food and shelter. Thus, at least part of what we consume has to be in some way planned. The rest, however, could conceivably be based on pure spur-of-the-moment impulses. Nonetheless, there is a limit to impulse buying. That limit is our income, plus our available credit. Scarcity exists everywhere and it starts right at home. Once we run out of income, plus our credit line, we can no longer buy on impulse. Most consumer economists tend to argue against impulse buying because it often wrecks a well-thought-through budget and may lead to financial difficulties.

PLANNED BUYING

Planned buying is also sometimes called rational consumer decision-making. While it may lack spontaneity, planned buying does have the virtue of safety if it is consistent with available resources. Consumers will generally not overstep their income if they plan carefully to keep in line with available or anticipated income. But even the best-laid plans can go awry. And, to top it all off, some motivational psychologists believe that businesspersons can affect our plans, and certainly our impulsive buying sprees, by using a tool now well known in the marketing trade.

MOTIVATIONAL
RESEARCH

Many Americans first learned of motivational research when Vance Packard's exposé, *The Hidden Persuaders*, became a best seller. In this book, he revealed the techniques that marketing researchers use to find out the best ways to manipulate consumer wants. Motivational research is just that—seeking out the motivations behind consumer buying habits, and using this information to direct advertising and product development. You are probably aware of some motivational research results. When cigarettes used to be advertised on television, it was not just coincidental that every ad had an attractive female in it. The same was true of car ads. Sellers, who knew that many purchases were made by men, discovered that they responded well to the "appropriate" he-man image in ads.

"A man works from Sun to Sun. But a woman's work was never done" Until Ferriff's Perfect Washer came to her ken, And now she's through before the men.

It must be remembered, however, that motivational research is not a perfect science. Researchers can be wrong. And the resultant marketing and product development efforts can therefore also be wrong. To make matters worse for producers, thousands upon thousands of them are bidding for our attention, telling us to buy this or that or another thing. Since we have only a limited income, we have to make decisions. Competition for our limited dollars by all of these different advertisers may in fact have the result that no one of them is more successful than any other. In other words, competition for the consumer's dollar may make motivational research totally ineffective on what we consume.

There are also marketing campaigns designed to make us *not* spend. How many times do we see ads for savings and loan associations wanting our dollars in a savings account? Since the average amount saved in the United States, as a percentage of total income, has changed little over the last hundred years, we know that advertisers trying to get us to save more are at a standstill with advertisers trying to get us to spend more. This, of course, leads us to an area of contention in the field of consumer economics: Does the consumer determine what is produced and sold, or does the producer?

CONSUMER SOVEREIGNTY VERSUS PRODUCER SOVEREIGNTY

Every day in every way we are bombarded with advertisements, as producers attempt to manipulate us into buying their products. How successful are they? Some say very successful; others say not so much. The saving rate in the United States does at least give some evidence that producers have not made us spend any more now than we had in the past, measured as a percent of our total income.

But from there it does not necessarily follow that producers have not encouraged us to buy a bundle of goods we would not have bought without their sometimes hard-sell techniques. For example, John Kenneth Galbraith, the noted Harvard economist and author, has often maintained that American consumers have been persuaded to consume too many private goods and not enough public goods, such as schools and parks. His conclusion is that the government should step in to wrest away part of consumers' incomes and direct it to public enterprises such as those just mentioned.

In the ideal world where the consumer is sovereign, we consumers, through our dollars, vote for the products or services we want most. Those products that get the most votes yield the highest profits and therefore attract the businesspersons' money from other areas in the economy where dollar votes are smaller. In this manner, the profit system directs resources to areas in the economy where they yield the highest value to the population.

However, even in this ideal world, income may be so maldistributed that very few people are commanding large amounts of resources; hence, the dollar voting system does not distribute goods and services in the way that society deems best. But, setting aside for the moment the problem about distribution of income, the consumer sovereignty issue also rests on an assumption about the economy itself.

That assumption has to do with the degree of competition within the system. If there are many monopolistic practices and restrictions of entry into various industries, a high price may not in fact cause resources to flow into those industries because outside resources are not *allowed* to enter. This is the age-old problem of monopoly. To be sure, if you believe that the United States is made up of monopolies, then you may have some serious doubts about the validity of the consumer sovereignty principle.

One thing we have to remember about this entire unsettled issue is that even if producers as a whole want to influence our buying habits, they must somehow get together to decide how to influence our habits in unison. Otherwise, competition among them (except in the case of monopolies) will not necessarily lead to any predictable conclusion. Even with motivational research, sophisticated marketing techniques, and heavy doses of advertising, consumers, at least on occasion, have demonstrated their desire to be sovereign. Witness the failure of the Edsel in the 1950s, which cost the Ford Motor Company a quarter of a billion dollars because consumers refused to buy it. Witness also the reluctance of the American woman to accept the midi-length skirts, even though the fashion industry pushed them hard. It has been estimated that nine out of every ten new products fail within one year.

BUYING AND SEARCHING

All consumer decision-making generally rests on information, which must be acquired through some searching procedure. What is the best search procedure? Of course, for each person it will be different, but a general rule for rational consumer decision-making can be made:

The larger the expected payoff from searching for better information in the marketplace, the greater the cost that should be incurred to acquire the information.

What does that mean? In plain language, we probably will spend considerably less time trying to get the best deal on a tube of toothpaste than we will spend trying to get the best deal on a new car. The expected gains from getting a "good" deal on toothpaste may be at most a few cents; but on a car the gains may be a few hundred dollars. What separates rational from so-called irrational buying habits is that in the former, expected costs and benefits of seeking out the best deal are looked at.

Some people, such as doctors, lawyers, and top executives, consider their time so valuable that they seek out very little information. They may, for example, find a very expensive store in their neighborhood where they buy many products. They may be willing to pay the higher price because they have found that the store carries relatively higher-quality brand names, and they make no attempt to gain more information about other sources of the products because they consider the time involved in doing that better spent on their careers.

But for any one of us, it is not *always* beneficial to spend more time trying to get a lower price or higher quality in a product. At some point, we have to stop our search. We will not search *every* store in our city for the lowest toothpaste price, even though we know that the next store might be the one with the lower price. The point at which we stop searching is determined by the information we already have, and a comparison of what it will cost to acquire new information against what we expect the benefits to be from that new information. A study done in Chicago revealed that when buying a car most people sampled no more than two car dealers. We also have to realize that searching for the best deal may not mean searching everywhere in a large geographical area. Would you buy a new car at a dealer 30 miles away because it is a hundred dollars cheaper than the dealer two blocks away? If you happened to have warranty or service problems and must take the car back to the dealer who is 30 miles away, you will incur time costs, additional gas costs, and probably car rental costs that you would have been spared had you purchased from your local dealer.

Expected potential benefits must be weighed against actual and expected costs. That is the rule by which you can become a rational consumer decision-maker.

YOU'RE THE BOSS

Remember in all of this discussion that you're the boss: you determine your values and make decisions based on those values. Think about that when you analyze the behavior of others, too. If you think somebody is stupid because he or she purchased a product for a price that you thought was too high, you may be trying to impose a low time value on that person just because *you* have a low time value. But that person may not like to spend the time looking for deals, while you may like to. Also, you are generally imposing your values on other people if you consider what they bought to be in poor taste. Their taste is merely a reflection of a value system of theirs that is different from yours. Thus, while the tenets of rational consumer decision-making as outlined above are universal, one person's decision-making may be rational for him or her but not for someone else. Do not fall into the trap of trying to apply the rules of others to your behavior, or your rules to the behavior of others.

**ALTERNATIVE
LIFE STYLES**

Whenever you compare yourself with others, you will find contrasts. You may often ask yourself, why does so-and-so seem to have so much free time? How does your best friend manage to work on that TV course you always wanted to take? Or you may find instead that *you* seem to go on vacation all the time and your friends stay around in the city fixing up the house on all their days off. You may come home exhausted at the end of every workday. Or you may be able to take your work in stride and fit in many gratifying extra-household activities. Or you may be the type who constantly complains that "my work is never done."

What we have said in a roundabout manner is that all of us have different life styles. In fact, we can, and often do, choose among alternative life styles. You may be making that choice right now. And you may want to reconsider it later. You make the choice whether or not you want to, and whether or not you are aware that you are making it. What may be important for you, however, is to be aware of all the decisions you are actually making. Look at a few alternative life styles to see what they have in common and how they differ.

THE FRUSTRATED INSURANCE SALESMAN: Joe Smith went to college and majored in business administration. He was not a particularly conscientious student, and consequently when placement time came around before his graduation, not too many firms were interested in him. He did like to talk, though, and an insurance company recognized this ability and offered him the best job at that time. He took it, all the while thinking he would eventually find something better.

Marriage came and somewhat altered his outlook about changing jobs, at least for the time being. He felt obliged to make sure he provided for his wife and coming child. A job change would come later. That was 15 years ago. He never did get around to looking for another job. He makes good money now, but keeps telling himself he should have done something else after a few years. He keeps telling himself that he actually could be doing something more exciting with higher pay. But Joe Smith will be a disgruntled insurance salesman until he retires. (He nonetheless might be a good one, as reflected in his high income.)

THE SATISFIED EDITORIAL ASSOCIATE: Sue Jennings majored in English when she went to college. She was always excited about books and writing and thought someday she could be a writer. In the meantime, when she got out of college she took a low-paying job in a New York publishing firm as a copy editor. Eventually she worked her way up— with much overtime and many frustrating moments in the highly competitive publishing world—to an editorial associate working directly under the executive editor of the whole company. She still thinks that she will someday write a book. In the meantime, she's happy. In fact, she's ecstatic. She has a job with much responsibility; her husband doesn't try to dictate her career plans; and she feels that she is indeed independ-

ent and is in the right job, even though her life appears to be hectic with little time for long vacations and leisurely three-day weekends.

AN OVERWORKED COUPLE: Sharon and John Halsing did not finish college. They got married when they were both sophomores and decided they wanted to see the world. So together they "bummed" around Europe for a couple of years taking odd jobs. Finally, when they came back to the States, they both realized, after three or four years of changing jobs, that they could not be happy working for somebody else. So they had a plan. They were going to go into business for themselves. They were both art "freaks," spending many leisure hours in museums. So what was more natural than to start an art supply store which could eventually become a place selling lithographs and paintings? John borrowed some money from his life insurance policy. Sharon took out all of her savings from the bank, and they also got a loan from the Small Business Administration. They started a small store selling art supplies near a local university. The hours they worked were tremendous, but they kept telling themselves that they at least were not working for somebody else. Raising a family was going to have to wait; it just would not fit in right now.

Eventually, the store caught on and students from other universities were even coming there to buy their art supplies. The lithograph section grew by leaps and bounds, and so, too, did the small medium-priced painting gallery. And they were still working long hours six days a week, and had not yet taken more than three or four days off at a time in all the years they had had the store. Were they happy? They could not quite tell. When they were working, they were happy, but when they thought about all those missed vacations, they sometimes got morose. They finally decided that it was too late to raise a family and Sharon often regretted that decision. But they certainly weren't unhappy, as all their customers could tell you, for they were served with a smile and good cheer. Did Sharon and John make the right decision? Sometimes they think they did; sometimes they think they didn't.

THE IDENTITY-CRISIS HOUSEWIFE: Lana Stellen got married even before she finished high school. The kids came fast and furiously: there were four at the end of seven years. Her husband, backed by his father, slowly built up an extremely profitable dry cleaning company with franchises throughout the city. He provided well for her. She was even able to hire help to come in and clean the house once in a while. She thought she was happy, and in fact motherhood suited her well, at least for the time being. Her kids sometimes gave her problems; she spent many a sleepless night with them, and she often had to arbitrate the fights among them. But they did give her a constant source of joy. As they started to grow older, Lana and her husband were able to take three-day weekends, leaving the children with babysitters. Soon they were able to take longer vacations, and often the family went camping weeks on end. Lana had not stopped learning just because she did not go to college. She watched a lot of talk shows on TV, read nonfiction best sellers, and discussed politics with her husband and friends.

At some point in her life, however, she started getting a vague feeling of uneasiness; a feeling of incompleteness sometimes overcame her, especially when she saw newscasts about prominent women in the United States and the rest of the world. Every once in a while she would get a letter from her former best high school friend who had not gotten married until much later in life. This friend had developed a promising career in interior design. Lana started going through periods of moroseness and depression. Finally it hit her. She had to get a job. She had to get out of the house and do something on her own. It turned out after she figured the costs of babysitting, transportation, and taxes she would have to pay that no matter what she did, she would not end up adding much money to the family income. Nonetheless, she had to do it and she did. Many adjustments had to be made in the family at that time, but after the initial shock and disappointment, her husband made a sufficient number of compromises so that it all worked out. Lana had become aware of her frustration and acted on it. She still was not perfectly happy, but of course no one ever is. She did think, however, that she was a better person, and of course that is what counts.

The alternative life styles above should enable you to quickly realize that what is appropriate for one person may not be appropriate for someone else; and the criterion for appropriateness is simply that which makes you happy. Even before experimenting, though, you can figure out some of the boundaries within which you have to work. For example, Joe the insurance salesman had a steady income, but he felt that there was not much excitement or much challenge after a while. But that feeling is common. The more risky and challenging a job, the greater the chance of not having any income at all in certain years. Whenever we decide on a life style that has security, we are generally choosing, at least in our work, a life style which has less excitement, perhaps, than some other life style. If we want to be sure that the pay check will always come in, we can get a government job that has tenure after twelve months' work. We may never make a fortune, but neither will we ever starve. If we want to take a chance on hitting it rich, we may pass a good part of our lives never knowing how we will feed ourselves from one day to the next. Such a decision we have to make ahead of time. After the fact, we might say we made a mistake, but we cannot change what has already happened. Ultimately, any decision on life style is intimately tied up with a decision about a career or a field of occupation.

FORESIGHT AND HINDSIGHT

When you decide on your life style, even if it is one in which you risk not only your money but your time, you have to make a decision with incomplete information. You will never have perfect information; you can never know how you will feel in the future, what your values will be and what your job situation will be. But you nonetheless have to make a decision. Little did you know that you were going to get tired so fast of sitting at a desk, or that your business was going to go bankrupt, or that what you really needed was an extra year of bumming around the country before you started to work. Had you known it, you would not have done things the way you did.

When you look back five years later, if you want to kick yourself, remember that hindsight is always more reliable than foresight. The best thing you can do with hindsight is perhaps to use it in making a decision about what to do in the future. Since there is no way to reverse your *past* life, you will only cause yourself untold grief if you bemoan the decisions you made then. As trite as it may sound, the saying "let bygones be bygones" is appropriate. To express this fact about the past, we can use the economists' term, **sunk costs:** sunk costs are forever sunk. Assume they have sunk to the bottom of the ocean. Stop worrying about them and look to the future. If you can extract some information from mistakes you made in the past, it is all the better. But do not think you were stupid simply because you disapprove of what has happened to your life through a decision you made five years ago. You likely based it on the best information available at the time.

TIME, TIME, TIME

In every possible alternative life style, one element remains constant: the amount of time you have available. The question you must answer is how you want to use that time. One life style you choose may involve being always busy, with no time to be with your family or friends, and no time for vacations. Most likely you see this all around you; your husband or wife or brother or sister or father or mother or friends may fit into this category. Successful businessmen are often like this. They use every second of their time to maximize their prestige, income, or fame. These people may work so much that they have little time to spend their large incomes. Compare such persons with men and women who decide to work on a factory assembly line. Their jobs last seven hours a day and may seem boring. But when those seven hours are over, they need not use their remaining hours thinking about the job. After 4:30, the time is their own, as are their weekends and vacations. Their lives are quite a bit different from those of executives who never leave their jobs no matter where they are because they are always thinking about problems. Assembly line workers certainly will never make as much money as the busy executive, but they will have a freedom from worry that makes free time truly free.

It is important to look at time as a commodity that you purchase. But it is also important to judge the quality of that time. Say, for example, you are a busy executive; if when you go home, no matter what anybody says to you, you are still thinking about your work, that time may be of low quality to you as leisure. It is not of the same quality as the time you might have at home were you to devote yourself to your own interests or those of your friends or family. Once in a while you might find it a good idea to take stock of how much time is actually your own in your own life style. You might decide that you need a change in life styles. It need not be of the abrupt kind you read about every once in a while when a company president chucks it all at age 42, buys a house in Mexico, and lives on $100 a month for the rest of his life, which he spends fishing in the harbor. It might instead simply involve going to another firm or working for another person and starting out with the expressed understanding that the amount of time you will spend on that new job will be limited to 35 hours a week instead of 60 as in your old job.

The same is true for those who decide to devote much of their time to the household. Specialization of tasks may be fine for some, but perhaps not for you.   Maybe you want to have a part-time job and let others in the family share with you responsibility for the household chores while you share with them responsibility for earning the family income.   Such possibilities all involve a decision about how you, and the others affected, want to use your time.   You can wisely make this kind of decision, though, only if you have some general notion about what your values are.

**CLARIFYING
OUR VALUES**

From the time you were around five years old, people probably started asking you what you wanted to be in life.   You might have said a musician, a mother, an artist, a scientist, a doctor, a lawyer, a stewardess, a fireman, or any one of the numerous occupations you might have been aware of at that time.   Later on, however, you had to start making some hard-nosed decisions.

It starts for many of us in high school: Should we drop out or stay in? Should we be a vocational education major?   Should we be a precollege major?   Should we take more math or less?   Once we have decided to stay in high school, we face another choice: Should we go on to college after high school, or get a job?   In either case, we have to start deciding what we really want to do.   Once in college, we have to decide what we want to specialize in.   When we get out (if ever), we again have to decide where we want to work and how, the amount of free time we want to have, what kind of risks we want to take, what kind of people we want to be with, and so on.

Often, however, many of us let ourselves be drawn along by whatever happens to come our way—the "path of least resistance," we might call it.   And just as often, when this happens we look back and think we made a mistake.   We realize we did not *clarify our values* about life and how to live it.   For this reason, career guidance counselors, psychologists, and sociologists increasingly stress the need for individuals to engage in their own soul-searching, their own value clarification.

Clarifying our values is an ongoing process.   All of us change throughout our lives (or at least we think we do).   You are probably not the same person you were five years ago in your values and your view of the world. Sometimes just a roundtable discussion with your family or friends or even a career guidance counselor is useful to point out in which directions you have actually moved in the last few years.

What we are all striving for is easy to say—happiness.   The way we get there is another matter.   Continued value clarification is possible, but how each of us does it might of course be difficult for someone else to dictate.   What is important, though, is that you do not wait until you have a nervous breakdown to decide that your values have changed and are no longer in line with your life style.   Gradual change is generally less painful and less costly than abrupt change.   For example, if you have spent the last six years as a homemaker and you had not given a thought to what your values are and what you are doing, but now suddenly realize that you are tired of washing dishes, you might become so disapproving of your current situation that the decisions you make will mean abrupt and painful change in your life. But if, on the other hand, all along you had every once in a while clarified your own values and related them to your actual living conditions, you could have gradually changed your life style to suit your changing values. The mental and emotional costs to yourself and to other members of your family would probably be lower.

PARKINSON'S LAW

Whatever our values may be and whatever our life style becomes, most all of us share a certain psychological trait, commonly known as **Parkinson's Law.** Parkinson made an observation that unfortunately seems to have universal validity: work expands to fit the time allowed. If you are aware of Parkinson's Law, you can fight it. If you are not, it sometimes will overtake you. Say you have allotted yourself four hours to write a report. You had better believe that the report will take you *at least* four hours. However, had you allotted yourself, say, three hours, it would have taken only three hours and probably would not have been neither worse nor better. In fact, it might have been better because you would have started in earnest right off the bat instead of twiddling your thumbs, sharpening pencils, and looking at additional reference materials for the first two hours. If you have spent much of your time taking care of your children and cleaning house, you know what Parkinson's Law is. If you do not believe it, just see what happens when you take a part-time job and find half of your day is taken away from household tasks. You probably end up doing exactly the same amount in half the time. But when you have the full day, you can be extremely inefficient and essentially make the job full-time, yet still feel an awful lot is left to do.

**BREAKING
THE LAW**

Personal time plan. One way that some people get around Parkinson's Law is to plan and draw up lists of things they have to do. The more specialized and specific the lists are, the more efficient they become. Of course, this can be carried too far and we can become fanatical about it. But for many people this is the only way to do enough things so that they feel satisfied with how they spend their lives, that is, with their particular life styles. Instead of telling yourself that you really ought to read more books, one way to make sure you do it is to chart out book time every day. It does not have to be five hours at a sitting, because you know that is impossible. It might be 15 minutes at a time, four different times during the day.* You will be surprised how many books you will have read that way. If you really would like to keep up correspondence with old friends, stop putting it off: set up a specific time and do it. Another way of making sure you get things done and use your time efficiently is to reward yourself. A famous writer once had a plan: because he was an avid smoker and craved nicotine, when he had a contract to fulfill he would re-

_____
* See p. 94 for an example.

ward himself with one cigarette after he finished each page. That way he never missed his deadlines. Probably you may not make the same use of cigarettes, but you might find another self-reward that is appropriate to you.

Such a technique can be extended to lifetime planning, by which you have goals for each day, each week, each month, each year, each five-year period, and you keep redefining these goals. Some extremely efficient people always put down more goals each day than they know they can possibly do. But sometimes they do more than they thought they could because they had set such standards for themselves.

SUMMARY

1. Since we live in a world of scarcity, we are forced to make choices and therefore must involve ourselves in decision-making.

2. Rational consumer decision-making involves seeking out exchanges that are most beneficial to you.

3. Decision-making involves: (1) defining the problem in view of goals and values; (2) selecting and exploring possible alternatives; (3) selecting of one alternative; and (4) accepting and evaluating consumer responsibilities after selection has been made.

4. Your goals generally determine the choices you make, and these goals change from time to time.

5. Goals and planning occur together through feedback during decision-making by the consumer.

6. Many of our actions and habits are determined by custom, such as the style of the clothes we wear.

7. Consumers generally engage in either impulse buying or planned buying.

8. Information must be acquired before purchases can be made. However, it is only useful to acquire information up to the point where the expected payoff from searching for more information is not as great as the expected costs of that additional search: the larger the purchase contemplated, the more one should spend seeking out information on the best product and the best financial deal. Hindsight is always 20/20, but what has happened in the past cannot be reversed. However, it is useful to analyze past decisions and actions to make better decisions in the future.

9. Even if you have decided to accomplish certain goals because they fit in with your values, you may not be successful if you fall prey to Parkinson's Law (work will expand to fit the time allowed). That is where your personal time plan comes into play.

**QUESTIONS FOR
THOUGHT AND
DISCUSSION**

1. Can you think of any product, service, or resource that is actually free? Is your time valuable?

2. Why does scarcity force you to make decisions?

3. We mentioned several things in our economy that facilitate exchange, such as the use of money and credit. Can you list any others?

4. How do your goals determine your choices?

5. Do you think that as an American you allow custom to be more important in determining your consumer decisions than you would as a citizen of a European country? Why or why not?

6. Look around you. Do you think most people engage in some forms of conspicuous consumption? Why?

7. Are there any psychological benefits that individuals might obtain from allowing themselves to "impulse buy" once in awhile?

8. The debate is still raging about whether or not you, the consumer, determine what you buy. Do you feel you have any effect on what producers are willing to produce and offer you for sale?

9. What determines the life styles that different people choose? What determined your life style?

10. What does the statement "sunk costs are forever sunk" have to do with consumer decision-making?

11. Why do you think Parkinson's Law seems to work all the time?

12. What have been some of the influences helping you to clarify your own values? What are those values? Are they the same as your parents', your friends', your neighbors'? If they are different, why do you think they are different?

THINGS TO DO

1. Go back to a recent consumer decision that you made—say in the purchase of an article of clothing, a book, a record, a TV, a radio, or whatever. Outline the steps you undertook to reach your final decision. How did you decide when to buy it, what to buy, where to buy, how much to pay, what brand, what quality, and so on? See if you can draw a chart showing the step-by-step progression of your consumer decision-making. Now see if there is anyplace within that process where you should have (looking now after the fact) obtained more information? Why did you neglect or fail to obtain more information? After reviewing your decision-making process, do you think it can be improved? In what ways? Do you see a general behavioral pattern that you want to change?

2. Check Vance Packard's *The Invisible Persuaders* out of the library and read it through. Do you think that book, written a number of years ago, is still valid today? If not, why? Has the world changed so much, or have we become smarter consumers? Has legislation affected anything in advertising that Packard talked about?

3. Write down a set of long-term, intermediate, and short-term goals. Are these the same goals that you had last year; the year before; or the year before that? Do you think you will have the same goals five years from now? If not, why do your goals change? Is there any way you can predict how they will change?

4. Draw up a list of consumer actions that you engage in which are at least in part determined by customs in the United States. We mentioned five within the text itself.

5. Draw up a list of those things that you purchase on an impulse and those that you plan to purchase very carefully. If the impulse list is very long, does that bother you? How could you change your buying behavior?

6. Try to determine the way you decide how many places to shop for any particular item. Does it depend on the price of the item? Does it depend on your knowledge or lack of knowledge of alternative sources of that item? Is there any way you could make a rule that would tell you when to stop looking for a better deal?

7. List the times when you are most likely to suffer from Parkinson's Law.

SELECTED READINGS

Feldman, Saul D., *Life Styles—Diversity in American Society* (Boston: Little, Brown & Co.), 1972.

J. C. Penney Co., "Value Clarification," *Forum*, Spring/Summer 1972.

Packard, Vance. *The Hidden Persuaders* (New York: David McKay Co.), 1957.

Packard, Vance, *The Status Seekers* (New York: Pocketbooks, Inc.), 1959.

"Values and Decision Making," Home Economics Research Abstract, No. 6 (1968), Washington, D. C.: American Home Economics Association.

Ward, Scott. *Effects of Television Advertising on Children and Adolescents.* Cambridge, Mass.: (Marketing Science Institute) July 1971.

Veblen, Thorstein, *The Theory of the Leisure Class* (New York: The Macmillan Company), 1899.

CHAPTER PREVIEW

☐ Has there been an advertising explosion?
☐ Who pays for advertising?
☐ What are the characteristics of informative versus competitive advertising?
☐ What are some of the forms of false advertising and how is it being regulated?
☐ How can door-to-door salespersons be handled?
☐ How does the Federal Trade Commission operate?
☐ Why are radio and TV advertising the way they are?
☐ How do you go about obtaining privately produced information?

GLOSSARY OF NEW TERMS

Comparison Shopping: A shopping technique that involves comparing values of different products both from the same retailer and from different retailers. Comparison shopping involves using time to acquire information about different sellers and different products.

Informative Advertising: Advertising that gives information about the suitability and quality of the product you are considering buying. To be contrasted with competitive advertising.

Competitive Advertising: Advertising that contains basically little information and is used only to allow a producer to maintain a share of the market for that product. An example is cigarette advertising.

Comparative Advertising: A type of advertising that specifically compares the brand in question with other brands of the same product.

Corrective Advertising: Advertising required by the Federal Trade Commission that is supposed to correct previous misinformation supplied by previous ads.

Bait and Switch: A selling technique that involves advertising a product at a very attractive price, but then informing the consumer once he or she is in the door that the advertised product is either not available, is of poor quality, or is not what the consumer really "wants." A more expensive item is then substituted by the salesperson.

Whether you like it or not, you are subjected to about $29 billion of advertising every year: whether you like it or not, every time you turn on a commercial TV channel, you are treated to some sort of ad at least every 10 minutes; when you turn on a commercial radio station, the melodious sounds of advertising strike your ears at least every five minutes; every time you open your local newspaper, advertisements cross your field of vision. And if for some of you that is still not enough, you can purchase more information about every good or service you might conceivably want to buy: you can buy books on how to invest money in the stock market; how to buy a house, real estate, a car; how to keep fit and trim; how to avoid being defrauded. You name it, and there is some bit of information that you can buy or get free. Information is all around us. In fact, we are bombarded with it constantly every second of every waking hour—or so it seems.

Now, obviously some of this information is useful to us, but some of it is not. And just as obviously, more information might sometimes be useful for us if we could get it at a "reasonable" cost. Information, however, happens to be a valuable commodity. It generally requires resources to provide and to obtain. That is why you and I never have *perfect* information about any of the products we buy. Of course, we never really expect to get perfect information because it would be too costly for anybody to provide it to us.

THE INFORMATION GLUT

HOW MUCH INFORMATION SHOULD WE ACQUIRE?

What we want is good information at the "right" price. In our own daily lives we *acquire information up to the point where the cost of acquiring any more would outweigh the benefits of that additional information.* When we decide to go shopping for food, we may look at advertisements for only a few supermarkets instead of trying to find out the price of specials at all 46 in our city. Why do we look at only a few? Because we have found that it just does not pay to look at any more than those few pieces of information. When we go shopping for a new car, we may go to only a few dealers within our immediate area. Why go to only a few and not all? Because, again, we have found that it does not pay to go to all of them.

FIGURE 3–1
ADVERTISING
EXPENDITURES IN
THE UNITED STATES
Source: McCann-
Erikson Advertising
Agency, Inc. Not
deflated.

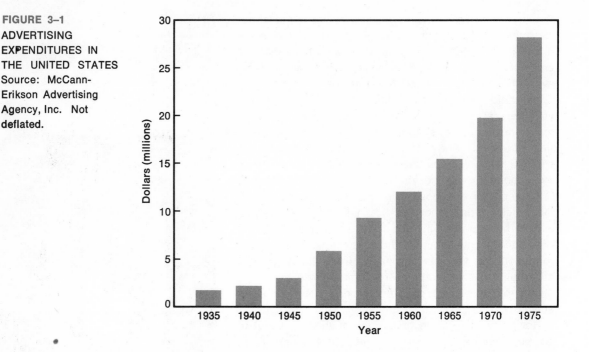

Some of us may not do any comparison shopping at all. We may not even bother to read advertisements or to seek out additional information about the products and goods we wish to purchase. Instead, we may decide to shop at a very expensive store where only the most expensive brands are carried. Why? Perhaps we are "status-seeking," or perhaps because we consider our time too valuable to spend in comparative shopping, in acquiring additional pieces of information. We may believe that high price means high quality, which is possible but not necessarily true. If we shop in this manner, we are not necessarily poor shoppers; we may simply have determined that it is not worth our while to acquire quantities of information. We are then essentially nonshoppers.

Information, in the form of advertisements, relating to products in our economy has been on the upswing, as can plainly be seen in Figure 3–1, which shows the expansion of U. S. advertising. A detailed look into advertising will show why it pays sellers to advertise, who pays for it, and the problems of false advertising.

**THE ADVERTISING
EXPLOSION**

There must be a fairly good reason why you and I are subjected to so much advertising, and why the amount of it is increasing each year. Look at it from the advertiser's point of view. Most businessmen are in business for one reason and one reason only—to make money. Obviously they would not advertise if they did not think advertising could make them more money, or at least maintain their current sales and level of profits.

Thus, by common sense alone, we can assume that they believe the additional sales they will make through advertising will at least cover the costs of advertising. In this sense, advertising can be treated like any other expenditure. If it fails to pay for itself, it will be reduced. If it more than pays for itself, it will be expanded. So the advertising explosion can be attributed to the realization by businessmen that more advertising yields them more than enough additional sales to justify the expenditure. Of course, when you look at it this way, you also come to a startling realization about who ultimately pays for advertising.

WHO PAYS?

Since businessmen are out to make money for themselves and are not necessarily altruistic, you can be pretty well certain that if they can help it they are not ultimately going to lose money by advertising. Only when they make a mistake about the profitability of a particular advertising campaign do they pay for it themselves, by taking a loss on that particular expenditure. In general, however, the cost of advertising is built into the price of the products you and I buy. This should not surprise you, should it? After all, the costs of labor expenses are built into the price of the products we buy. So are the costs of buildings and machines. So why should the cost of advertising not be built into the price of advertised products? Well, it is, and there is very little you can do about it, except, of course, to purchase nonadvertised items that are similar in quality to advertised ones and are lower in price. This can be done in supermarkets with nonnational brands of food products, and with a number of other products that you certainly must come across elsewhere in your shopping forays. But here we reach a dilemma; for if it is possible to purchase nonadvertised products at lower prices than advertised products and get the same product indeed, why would any of us be so stupid as to buy nationally advertised brands, to fall for the "brand name game" (if it is one)?

THE VALUE OF BRAND NAMES

Obviously, many of us have decided that brand names have value in and of themselves. There must be a few reasons why at least many of us purchase brand names.

1. **Brand names may mean less variance in quality:** If we generally have learned that brand name products vary less in quality than do other products, then obviously the brand name has a value, for it tells us to anticipate fewer problems. This may be true, for example, with electronic equipment: you may decide to purchase, say, Sony stereo components because you have found out, or have heard from your friends, that the brand name "Sony" gives you a lower probability of having to take the equipment in for repairs. Therefore, if you go to a stereo shop and see two amplifiers next to each other, one by an unknown company and the other by Sony, you may be willing to pay a higher price for the brand item.

The same is true for food or services, or anything else. People some-times prefer to pay slightly more for nationally advertised tree doctors because they have more confidence in them. Whether or not national brand names and quality are always related is a moot point. Advertisers have been selling brand name reliability for years. Only now is some questioning being done, and from most of it has come a denial that brand name and reliability are associated. We do know, however, that many consumers are willing to pay more for national-brand products.

2. **Brand products may offer better guarantees:** When something goes wrong with the national-brand product you bought, if it has a superior guarantee then the service you can get on it may be quicker and less of a hassle than for a nonnational brand. Hence, you may decide to pay more for the national brand.

3. **National-brand products may have a larger number of repair facilities:** It may be difficult to get nonnational-branded products repaired as easily as those of a national brand. This fact is quite obvious with automobiles, especially with an exotic foreign job. How many gas stations can help out when a Maserati refuses to start? And even if they knew how, how quickly would they be able to get the parts?

BRAND NAME
LOYALTY

The discussion above illustrates the reasoning behind brand name loyalty, which is fostered by national advertising. Brand name loyalty is rational for some people and not rational for others. It is up to you to decide whether you wish to pay the higher price for nationally advertised items. If none of the above considerations seems important, then perhaps you should not. This might be particularly true with nonnational-brand foodstuffs, like canned peas and carrots and such products. At least it is obvious why much advertising is done merely to establish brand name loyalty.

The question remains, of course, whether such loyalty actually helps the consumer. Many critics of advertising contend that such advertising does nothing for the consumer, and in fact ultimately does nothing for the producer. To understand this argument, we have to look at the various kinds of advertising.

TYPES OF
ADVERTISING

Basically, its critics and students place all advertising into either of two categories, which, however, sometimes overlap. The first category is informative advertising, which is presumably always good, and the second is competitive (persuasive) advertising, which presumably is always bad. (Of course, there is also false advertising, which we treat in the following section.)

INFORMATIVE
ADVERTISING

Informative advertising is just what the term says: it informs and nothing else. You can think of a tremendous amount of informative advertising you see all the time: supermarkets advertise their prices; stereo shops advertise the brands they sell and their prices; producers advertise new products that were not previously available. In other words, you the consumer are being informed about prices, products, and availability. You can take that information for what it is worth and use it in any way you want. You are not asked to believe that a product is better or worse than another one, or that a company does a good or a bad job. Rather, you are simply given the relevant information about the key aspects of a good or service, and those key aspects are price and availability.

Believe it or not, in the United States there is a tremendous amount of informative advertising, advertising that even the critics of advertising would not suggest we get rid of. There are some very weird products you would never think would be advertised because the market is so specialized. But did you know, for example, that the producers of multimillion-dollar steam electricity generators send salesmen around to various electric utilities to inform them about the availability and the costs of different types of steam generators? Did you know there are literally hundreds of specialized trade magazines that treat very narrow fields of interest, and that companies in those fields subscribe to them just to find out what is happening and what products are available? There are journals for printing, publishing, electric utilities, leatherworks, paper producers, flour millers, and so on. In fact, any industry worth its salt has a trade magazine or two in which very specialized informative ads can be found.

COMPETITIVE
ADVERTISING

The other kind of advertising is called competitive and, again, it is just what the name implies. It comes about through brand name competition. Cigarettes are a good example. The big cigarette companies advertise a tremendous amount. Up until recent legislation, they advertised on television to the tune of millions and millions of dollars a year. The question is: What good is this type of advertising? If you look at it from the consumer's point of view, none at all, according to many critics. For ultimately each of the large tobacco companies puts out a tremendous amount of advertising, and no single one of them gets the edge on all the others through this advertising. In other words, they reach a stalemate. Although if any one of them stopped advertising it would lose sales, it gains no more by advertising than it would if *none* of them advertised at all. This is what competitive advertising is all about.

Any time we try to regulate competitive advertising, we run into a problem: the risk of eliminating informative advertising. Who is going to be wise enough to decide what is competitive and what is informative? Where does the cut-off point lie? How would advertising actually be regulated? For example, if you were in charge of deciding about car ads, what would you let manufacturers say? Could they list only the obvious, such as horsepower and the size of tires? Or would you let them say that their new model "handled better" because of an improved suspension system? You would have a hard choice to make, indeed. The Federal Trade Commission has begun to specify what is and what is not informative advertising, but its rulemaking procedures are not yet settled.

Recent years have seen the growth of a kind of competitive advertising that approaches informative advertising in certain respects—at least if it is done honestly.

COMPARATIVE
ADVERTISING

Until the last few years, there was very little of what we call **comparative advertising**—that is, advertising that actually names competitor brands when making comparisons between them and the advertised brand. This is a change from the standard comparison between something and "Brand X." Today, for example, Volvo has started comparing itself with other brands of cars, like Saab and Mercedes. Numerous other examples of comparative advertising should readily come to mind. Although many people had thought that such advertising is illegal, it never actually was; but in the past radio and television stations were either reluctant to take it or refused it altogether. When properly and honestly done, comparative advertising is obviously a benefit to us consumers, for it saves us the time of doing the comparisons ourselves.

One type of advertising that everyone agrees about concerns that which is false, for fraudulent information dissemination is certainly not in the public interest, particularly if it can be stopped without spending too many resources.

FALSE ADVERTISING

Certainly no one needs to be told what false advertising is, but an example of it should give you the flavor of what you have to watch out for.

BAIT AND SWITCH— THE CASE OF BEEF

Perhaps you have had the joy of reading some of the great beef baiting ads, such as "government inspected, tender, delicious beef sides, only 90¢ a pound, including all the cuts of beef steak, roasts, etc." Well, what may await you if in fact you are dealing with a false advertising claim is diagrammed in Figure 3–2.

**FIGURE 3–2
BAIT AND SWITCH**

Advertised meat at 90¢/pound

Actual edible meat available at $1.60/pound

Trimmed meat at $2.00/pound
Additional trimming if dishonest dealer

True cost $3.10/pound

As soon as you walk in the door of the meat store that advertised the beef side, you are met by the friendly but persuasive salesman. You ask to see the 90¢ a pound beef advertised in the local paper. You are shown it, and obviously you would not feed it to your dog, let alone your family. He agrees, stating that this "is the type of meat they use in institutions." Next, you are shown an extremely good-looking side of beef. It has little fat and is exactly what you had in mind. In fact, it looks a lot like the picture in the ad you saw in your local newspaper. But, of course, the salesman informs you that this beef is going to cost you $1.60 a pound. If you agree to buy, you sign a contract.

But $1.60 per pound isn't actually what you end up paying for the beef, because the butcher is going to have to trim away about one-fifth of the beef side's hanging weight in fat and bone; a more dishonest beef baiter may trim away as much as one-half. However, the price you pay is for the *gross* weight, the weight *before* trimming. And if you do not stay around to look at the cutting and packaging of your meat, a dishonest dealer may give you a side that you did not select, one of a lower quality. But even if you do make sure that he gives you the side of beef that you chose, if you have no freezer of your own and use his "freezer plan," you may ultimately get lower quality cuts, anyway, as he replaces the beef you left with him.

Beef baiters practice a classical variety of a standard fraudulent practice called **bait and switch.** When you, the buyer, take the bait from an advertisement and go to buy the advertised item, the advertiser gets you to switch to a higher-priced quality or brand. The key to never being tricked by one of these schemes is to learn how to recognize the pattern of a bait and switch scheme and to walk out when you think you're being had. No one forces you to take the bait and then accept the switch. The Federal Trade Commission puts bait and switch at the top of its list of common fraudulent practices or deceptions on the part of businesses. Other deceptions include, to name a few:

1. **Contest winner:** You are told you have won a contest, but it turns out you must buy something in order to receive your prize.
2. **Free goods:** You presumably will get something free if you buy something else. But you may be paying a higher price for that "something else" than you would have otherwise.
3. **Merchandise substitution:** In place of what you thought you were buying the seller substitutes a different variety, make, or model, or quality of a good.

Again, you do have ways to avoid deceptive practices by sellers, or at least reduce their probability. One way is to establish yourself as a steady customer of reputable sellers in your area. Once sellers know you are a steady customer, even if they are tempted to cheat you, they would realize its unprofitability, since they rely heavily on your repeat purchases for their business.

DOOR TO DOOR SALESPERSONS

There are probably more fraudulent practices used in door-to-door sales than in many other aspects of product selling. You would probably be appalled if you looked at the methods used by salespersons for encyclopedias, vacuum cleaners, land, and even Bibles. Their sales pitches range from quoting phony list prices of their products in order to make their own price look like a bargain, to getting people to sign a questionnaire that is really an installment credit contract. So notorious are their techniques that it is not worth our while to go into detail about how door-to-door salespersons ply their trade. Suffice it to say that again you have the option of escaping their grasp. One way you can make sure you never get taken by someone peddling at your door is by never letting them *in* the door. You have that choice. If this fails, you can always call the police to get rid of an unwanted salesperson at your door.

It should not be forgotten, though, that sometimes door-to-door salespersons may provide you with a product or service that is useful and is a good deal. In fact, certain products are sold only door to door, and cannot be gotten anywhere else—for example, special types of household cleaning aids; and certain cosmetics and toiletries, like Avon products. If you happen to like these special products, you have no choice but to accept a door-to-door salesperson. But, then, in these cases you are not dealing with someone trying to sign you to a 36 month installment contract on a set of 58 books at a total price of $650. Rather, you deal with smaller sale prices and, hence, less risk of really getting taken.

COOLING OFF PERIODS

Many states now have a "cooling off" law that must be applied to many if not all installment contracts. For example, Ohio has a three-day cooling off period. Say a door-to-door salesperson gets you to sign a contract, for example, to purchase a set of encyclopedias and pay for it over 36 months; during a three-day period, you can renege on that contract. Essentially, you are given three days in which to think over what you have committed yourself to, and also to acquire information about alternative means of purchasing the product you contracted for. That is, you have time to investigate to make sure that you did not in fact get "taken" by a high pressure door-to-door salesperson.

This cooling off provision in the law in Ohio and other states was adopted as a rule in 1972 and 1973 by the Federal Trade Commission. The exhibit on page 40 is a typical "Notice of Cancellation" that should be available from any door-to-door salesperson.

THE FEDERAL TRADE COMMISSION

There are government agencies, both state and federal, that are making an attempt to control advertising. More than half of all advertising is national in its coverage. Since it therefore involves interstate commerce, the Federal Trade Commission (FTC), created by Congress in 1914, has control over that advertising. Currently the FTC is organized into two principal operating bureaus—the Bureau of Consumer Protection and the

EXHIBIT

NOTICE OF CANCELLATION

(enter date of transaction)

_____

(date)

You may cancel this transaction, without any penalty or obligation, within 3 business days from the above date.

If you cancel, any property traded in, any payments made by you under the contract or sale, and any negotiable instrument executed by you will be returned within 10 business days following receipt by the seller of your cancellation notice, and any security interest arising out of the transaction will be canceled.

If you cancel, you must make available to the seller at your residence, in substantially as good condition as when received, any goods delivered to you under this contract or sale; or you may, if you wish, comply with the instructions of the seller regarding the return shipment of the goods at the seller's expense and risk.

If you do make the goods available to the seller and the seller does not pick them up within 20 days of the date of your notice of cancellation, you may retain or dispose of the goods without any further obligation. If you fail to make the goods available to the seller, or if you agree to return the goods to the seller and fail to do so, then you remain liable for performance of all obligations under the contract.

To cancel this transaction, mail or deliver a signed and dated copy of this cancellation notice or any other written notice, or send a telegram, to

_____

(name of seller)

at _____ not later than midnight of _____
(address of seller's place of business)   (date)

I hereby cancel this transaction.

_____   _____

(date)   (buyer's signature)

Bureau of Competition. The former has chief responsibility for "monitoring advertising, labeling and deceptive practices, reviewing applications for complaints, drafting proposed complaints concerning . . . practices and, of course, prosecuting cases after the commissioner issues a formal complaint." The FTC has 12 regional offices in various parts of the country. At each regional office, a staff of attorneys and specialists in consumer protection has the responsibility of monitoring advertising and competitive practice in an area of several states. The staffs also conduct investigations of complaints and suspected violations, and will try cases concerning alleged unfair practices in that particular geographical area.

The FTC receives letters or other communications complaining of violations from many sources, including competitors of alleged violators, consumers, consumer organizations, trade associations, better business bureaus, other government organizations, and state and local officials. In addition, the commission staff has a large program for monitoring radio and TV commercials, national advertising media, and, through field offices, local advertising media. In the last few years, the FTC has created in major cities consumer-protection coordinating committees that attempt to bring local, state, and federal consumer protection officials in a particular geographical area together in an attempt to provide a coordinated "one-stop" consumer complaint service.

The statutes administered by the FTC are many. Those that more specifically involve advertising are the Wool, Fur and Textile Fiber Products Acts of 1939, 1951, and 1958, respectively. (We treat these in detail on page 194.) In addition, a 1938 amendment to the original FTC Act of 1914 specifically prohibits false advertising of food, drugs, cosmetics, and devices. The Truth-in-Labeling Act of 1968, administered by the FTC, requires full disclosure in advertising that makes representations about credit terms.

CORRECTIVE ADVERTISING

Lately, the FTC has stepped up its rulings against what it considers to be false advertising. A famous case involved requiring Profile bread to eliminate its advertising claim concerning the weight-reducing qualities of its product. It turned out that the reason Profile bread has fewer calories per slice than other breads is because it is sliced thinner. The FTC has also stepped in to stop a number of companies from advertising claims which it considers fallacious or misleading. The most controversial aspect of this campaign is the requirement by the FTC that certain companies spend a specific amount of money advertising the fact that they did indeed present false information.

Sometimes the FTC's attempt at "corrective advertising" has seemed a shock to much of the industry in question. For example, the FTC claimed that Wonder Bread was wrong in advertising its nutritive value because the implication was that Wonder Bread is unique. The FTC reasoned that it was not unique because other enriched loaves had the same nutritive value. Notice that the FTC did not claim the ads were *false,* nor that they misrepresented the product. It simply said that what was claimed was not unique to that product.

It is also possible for information about the falsity of advertising itself to be misleading. This is, of course, true for individuals as well as for government agencies—sometimes you are wrong about the charges you make against somebody else. The FTC found itself in this position. It happens that a product named Zerex was advertised as an effective stopper of radiator leaks. The TV ad showed a puncture in a can of Zerex being sealed over from within by coagulating action of the contents of the can. The FTC charged that Zerex's advertising was false and publicly maligned the company for using deceptive illustrations, threatening, in addition, to remove the product from the market altogether. However, a few months later, the FTC withdrew its charges; it admitted that the ads in question were not actually deceptive. The FTC unfortunately was not financially accountable for the sales lost by the Zerex company. We can hope that no federal, state, or local agency charged with protecting you, the consumer, will be so hasty in its judgment of deceptive advertising. On the other side of the coin, even when the FTC does apparently prove its case against deceptive advertising, some companies still are allowed to continue that advertising. An example is the case that the FTC initially won against Preparation H; because of the time-consuming judicial appeal procedure, the company has been able to continue its ads for years despite rulings against them.

**THE FTC AND
RALPH NADER**

Ralph Nader and his associates issued a report in 1969 [1] recommending a complete overhaul of the FTC's staff, practices, and policies. His findings and recommendations included, among others:

1. There has been too much secrecy about what the FTC is doing.
2. The FTC has been preoccupied with the trivial while ignoring large-scale deceptions.
3. The FTC "fails woefully to enforce its laws properly. It relies too heavily, nearly exclusively, on voluntary non-binding enforcement tools. These cannot be expected to work at all unless backed up by stricter coercive measures, which are almost completely lacking now."
4. The FTC essentially "proceeds in purely random fashion" in seeking out improper or illegal business behavior.

The chairman of the FTC at the time, Mr. P. R. Dickson, was accused by Nader and his associates of having "institutionalized mediocrity, rationalized a theory of . . . inaction, delay and secrecy, and transformed the agency into the government's Better Business Bureau."

[1] Edward F. Cox, Robert C. Fellmeth, and John E. Schulz, *"The Nader Report" on the Federal Trade Commission* (New York: Richard W. Baron, 1969).

Basically, the Nader report indicated that the federal government organization with the most responsibility for protecting consumers from deceptive and unfair selling practices was wasting too much effort on trivial matters which merely gave the impression that it was vigorously policing the American economy. The American Bar Association panel that studied the FTC, at the request of President Nixon, came up with many of the same criticisms that Ralph Nader's associates did. In the last half decade, the FTC has taken account of both Nader's and the American Bar Association's criticisms. However, despite its "new look," it still does not move very fast and still suffers from many of the criticisms outlined above.

OTHER AGENCIES HELPING YOU OUT

The FTC is not the only agency charged with control over advertising. There is also the Food and Drug Administration, the U.S. Postal Service, the Federal Communications Commission, and the Securities and Exchange Commission. Their basic laws result in some overlapping jurisdiction. Consequently, for example, the FDA and the FTC operate under a voluntary agreement giving specific areas of authority to each agency.

THE WHY AND WHERE OF RADIO AND TV ADVERTISING

At the beginning of this chapter we asked a question: Why are you subjected to so much advertising on radio and TV? Well, now we can answer it. There is no basic reason why you should not be able to purchase the services of radio and TV signals without paying the cost of watching sometimes deceptive, sometimes disturbing, but also sometimes entertaining advertisements. I personally find it annoying (and this is, of course, a value judgment) that in order to watch a full-length movie on commercial (nonpublic) television, I must be subjected to an advertisement every time the plot gets good and thick. That may not bother you. But I do not have a choice—at least not in most states in the Union. Neither do you. Why? Because TV and radio are regulated by the Federal Communications Commission (FCC). TV and radio waves are emitted within a publicly controlled monopoly franchise. If you do not have a license from the FCC, you do not have the right to transmit TV or radio signals.

WAY BACK WHEN

This was not always so. When radio first came into being, anybody who could set up a transmitter could in fact transmit. But soon the government decided to regulate what was occurring. Rather than become the policeman of the airwaves, and to insure that whoever owned a particular airwave frequency was not bothered by someone else's pirate transmission, the FCC was set up to allocate a certain number of radio frequencies to the various and sundry people who wanted to transmit. However, the rights to transmit radio waves were not sold to the highest bidder. Rather, they were allocated in some "fair" manner to a more-than-willing set of demanders. Since the FCC can rescind valuable licenses, it eventually got control over the content of radio and TV transmissions. That is why the FCC can now set rules for how much and what kind of sex or violence can be exhibited on TV and radio.

More important for us, however, in relation to the amount of advertising we see, is the fact that the FCC has refused for many, many years to issue licenses to pay-television stations. Although a long while ago pay-TV was technologically impossible, it is now technologically a reality. But this presents a problem to the owners of commercial television stations. As you can imagine, they would prefer not to have competition; and, in fact, the FCC has been more than willing to help them fight the competition of pay-TV.

**THERE IS
NO SUCH THING
AS FREE TV**

Of course, the fact is that you do not get free TV even on commercial channels. You pay for the TV both in the time you spend watching advertising and by purchasing advertised products. Any products you purchase that are advertised on TV include in their price the cost of that TV advertising. If, however, you buy products that are not advertised on TV but you do watch television, you are getting a subsidy from those who buy the TV-advertised products. Now, when you purchase *pay*-TV—that is, in the six or seven states that now have it—you buy a program by paying $2 or $3 each time you want to watch it. You have chosen to see no commercials, but you certainly pay a higher dollar price for the program. In future years, pay-TV may arrive in most states in the Union. You will find much more diversity in the program material you can purchase than you now subsidize on commercial TV.

You may be wondering why television has been so "mediocre" in the past, why it has catered to the lowest common denominator. To begin with, the number of television channels, particularly in the earlier years

**FIGURE 3–3
ALPHABET SOUP**

of television, was severely limited by the FCC's caution in granting TV licenses. Now those monopoly holders of TV licenses made their money by advertising, purely and simply; and advertisers were, and are, willing to pay more for a minute of advertising the larger the TV viewing audience is. How do you expect the commercial television program to get the largest audience? Easily: by catering to the average viewer with average tastes.

It should be pretty easy to figure out why television was once called a "wasteland." The average viewer's desires (when considered by academics, government officials, intellectuals, and so on) are pretty "common." What would you expect? Not everybody can like opera, sophisticated drama, symphonies, and foreign films. The cards were stacked against the TV station owners (who respond to advertisers that want their products seen by the largest possible audience) when the FCC started looking into the content of television. For TV was a "wasteland" because the Federal Communications Commission had in fact taken upon itself the duty of restricting the number of TV stations in any particular city. In addition, the FCC had itself helped cause this problem by helping the existing commercial television station owners fight pay-TV. Although the FCC may contend that it regulates the air waves in the public's interest, it would be hard for us, using any form of dispassionate analysis of the FCC's actions, to reach a similar conclusion. Recently, for example, the FCC stalled the growth of *cable* TV basically because it was supporting the self-interest of existing TV stations and networks. The actions of the FCC, however, are not unusual for a regulatory agency. If one thing has become clear from the numerous studies by Ralph Nader and his "raiders," it is that regulatory agencies end up serving the interests of the regulated instead of the interests of you and me, the consumers.

COMPARISON OF TV, RADIO, AND OTHER MEDIA

When you think about it, there is little difference in principle between radio and television and all the other information/entertainment media. Newspapers and magazines can influence the American public as much as radio and TV can. Nonetheless, print is very little censored, while radio and TV are very much censored. Perhaps it is true that spoken and visual media face a problem with children's education. However, some might say that such a problem is for parents to handle and not for a federal agency.

BUYING PRIVATELY PRODUCED INFORMATION

If you want to buy a product but are not quite sure which brand to purchase, you need not rely only on the advertisements by the various manufacturers. You can purchase product brand information; you can, for example, purchase *Consumer Reports or Consumer's Research Magazine.*

Consumer Reports

Consumer Reports is the publication of Consumers Union, chartered in 1936 as a nonprofit organization under the laws of the State of New York. The object of Consumers Union has been to bring more useful information into the seller/buyer relationship so that consumers could buy rationally. The first issue of *Consumer Reports,* in May 1936, went to 3000 charter subscribers. They were told about the relative costs and the nutritional values of breakfast cereals, the fanciful claims made for Alka Seltzer, the hazards of lead toys, and also good buys in women's stockings, toilet soaps, and toothbrushes. Consumers Union's policy has always been to buy goods in the open market and bring them to the lab for testing.

Now approximately two and a half million subscribers and newsstand buyers read *Consumer Reports* every month. Consumers Union accepts no advertising in its magazine, and tries to objectively test various types of consumer products. In addition, it gives advice on purchasing credit, insurance, drugs, and so on. One of the major aspects of Consumers Union's testing involves automobiles: which are the best buys, which are safe, which have good brakes, which have safety defects, and so on. Recently, Consumers Union has put in its reports articles on ecological topics such as pesticides, phosphates in detergents, and lead in gasolines. It also strongly criticizes government agencies when they act against the consumer's interests.

If you decide to take the recommendations of *Consumer Reports* to heart, you have to realize that it is difficult for even highly objective researchers to present you with purely objective results. That is not to say that you will get misinformation, but you may sometimes get emphasis on certain aspects of products that are consistent with the tastes of the researchers but not with your own. For example, recommendations about cars may give more weight to safety, gas mileage, or comfort than you personally want to give. You may opt for a different car because you prefer styling or low cost as opposed to safety. Even though the occupants of VWs face a higher probability of serious injury in an accident than do occupants of bigger cars, people continue to buy VWs, presumably because they are cheaper. But you will face this problem of acceptance with any information you obtain either free or at a price. In the last analysis, only you can make a decision, and it has to be based in part upon your personal value judgments. If you are a lazy shopper, you can probably get away with looking at *Consumer Reports* for whatever you want to buy, picking either the "best buy" or the top of the line, calling up your local dealer, and having it delivered. You may get some products you dislike, but on average, if your tastes correspond with those of the persons running Consumers Union, you will have saved much time searching, and will have probably avoided getting burned by basically defective products.

*Consumers' Research
Magazine*

Consumers' Research, Inc., founded in 1929, puts out a monthly *Consumers' Research Magazine,* similar to *Consumer Reports,* with a readership of several hundred thousand. It gives product ratings, as well as ratings of motion pictures and phonograph records, and gives short editorials, just like *Consumer Reports.* No advertising income is permitted. The product testing policy of Consumers' Research often involves its borrowing test samples of large, expensive items from manufacturers who sign affidavits that the goods are typical and were selected at random. Sometimes the goods are rented—for example, typewriters—for testing. Consumers' Research often restricts its tests to brands or goods that are nationally distributed, while *Consumer Reports,* on the other hand, sometimes tests brands that are distributed in various high-density localities.

Again, it cannot be stressed too much that ultimately you, the consumer, must decide whether you want to accept the information given in *Consumers' Research Magazine* or *Consumer Reports.* You may not agree with the tastes of the people presenting the objective information. You should consider that information as simply one contribution to your consumer decision-making process.

OTHER
INFORMATION
SOURCES

There is an increasingly large number of privately produced information sources in addition to the two mentioned above. For example, a monthly magazine by Time-Life, called *Money,* is aimed at families of middle income and above. Nonetheless, even for lower-income families, it often has valuable information about making better consumer choices, such as articles about deceptive selling practices, better nutrition for your family, and so on. A less well-researched, but perhaps still useful, alternative private source of information is the magazine *Your Moneysworth.* However, *Changing Times,* the magazine published monthly by the Kiplinger Service for Families, is perhaps a better source of consumer information. Any given issue may give you information on "gimmick" reducing machines, how to buy insurance like an expert, new tax rulings that might affect you, how to get interest on your checking account, and why extra long auto loans are bad deals.

Better Homes and Gardens, Good Housekeeping, Sunset, as well as other magazines, give helpful consumer information on such things as money-saving recipes, furniture maintenance ideas, do-it-yourself projects, and the like.

INFORMATION
PRODUCED AND
DISTRIBUTED BY
GOVERNMENT
AGENCIES

Persons who are willing to take a few minutes to send away for free or nominal-cost booklets will find a wealth of valuable information available from various consumer agencies. Your local Extension Service of the Department of Agriculture is a good source. In addition, you can get free every three months an index of selected federal publications of consumer interest by writing Consumer Information, Public Documents Distribution

Center, Pueblo, Colorado 81009, and asking to be put on the mailing list for their publication, "Consumer Information." You may also wish to get on the mailing list for the U.S. Government Printing Office's publications list. Merely write the Superintendent of Documents, U.S. Government Printing Office, Washington, D.C. 20402, and ask to have your name put on the list for "Selected U.S. Government Publications."

SUMMARY

1. Comparative shopping involves acquiring information about alternative sources for a particular product. The acquisition of information, however, requires the use of your time and perhaps other resources, such as gas for your automobile. Therefore, there is a limit to how much comparative shopping you want to engage in.

2. There has been an advertising explosion in the United States. Expenditures have increased to an estimated $28 billion in 1975.

3. Ultimately, the consumer pays for advertising in the form of a higher-priced product. This is true for products advertised on television and radio also.

4. Individuals often associate brand names with (1) less variance in quality, (2) better guarantees, and (3) a larger number of repair facilities.

5. The way to avoid the undesirable consequences of deceptive selling practices, such as bait and switch, contest winner, free goods, and merchandise substitution, is to know before you shop what you are looking for. When a salesperson attempts to sell you something you do not want, leave or be insistent. Generally, you do not get anything free, and if one retailer is selling an item at a drastically reduced price, you should be suspicious unless you know why.

6. Make sure that if you ever decide to buy something from a door-to-door salesperson you sign a "Notice of Cancellation," which gives you without any penalty or obligation three business days from the date of the transaction to decide whether you want to cancel the contract.

7. The Federal Trade Commission is empowered to monitor advertising and deceptive practices of businesses. If you think that you have been the victim of deceptive advertising, you might want to contact the local bureau of the FTC. The field office can be located in your telephone directory.

8. Ralph Nader recommended that the Federal Trade Commission undergo a complete overhaul. Among other things, his group of researchers pointed out that the FTC "proceeds in purely random fashion" when it seeks out improper or illegal business behavior.

9. You end up paying for "free" radio and TV when you buy the products advertised in those media, for those products are relatively higher priced in order to pay for radio and TV commercials.

10.   There are numerous places where you can obtain privately produced information about products and services that you might want to buy. You can, for example, subscribe to *Consumer Reports, Consumers Research Magazine, Money, Changing Times, Moneysworth, Better Homes and Gardens, Good Housekeeping, Sunset, Media and the Consumer.*

11.   Publicly produced information can be obtained from the U.S. Government Printing Office.

QUESTIONS FOR THOUGHT AND DISCUSSION

1.   Who do you think should bear the responsibility for honest advertising? The manufacturer? The advertising agency? The government? The consumer?

2.   Do you think that all corrective advertising is necessary?

3.   Can advertisers regulate themselves? Is there any evidence that mass advertising has become a less effective marketing device?

4.   Do you think there is any end in sight to the advertising explosion?

5.   Why do consumers still prefer brand names?

6.   Can you distinguish between informative and competitive advertising?

7.   Listed in the text are several deceptive advertising techniques. Can you think of any others?

8.   Why would a manufacturer want to have its product sold door-to-door rather than in a retail outlet?

9.   Do you think that there should be an increased amount of noncommercial, that is, public, television? Who should pay for it?

10.   Why are there more privately produced sources of information, such as magazines of the *Consumer Reports* type, on the market today than there were, say, 50 years ago?

THINGS TO DO

1.   Read the Nader Report on the Federal Trade Commission. Find out from your local FTC field office whether any of the recommendations in the Nader report have been taken to heart.

2.   Examine some marketing journals, such as the *Journal of Marketing* and the *Journal of Advertising Research.* See what some of the authors writing in those magazines believe is necessary for successful advertising.

3.   When you see what you believe to be a false or misleading ad, write the manufacturer of the product being advertised asking an explanation. If you are not satisfied with the explanation, ask your local FTC office if in fact the advertising is deceptive.

4. Experiment with some potential bait-and-switch ads. These are especially prevalent for appliances and locker meat. For example, if you see an appliance ad in your local newspaper, cut it out and go down to the store offering that product at that specified price. See if the salesperson in fact attempts to get you to buy a higher-priced product. If that happens, ask that salesperson if he or she is aware of the FTC's rulings on bait-and-switch cases.

5. Write a list of products that you buy mainly because of the brand name. Then decide which of those products can be bought at a lower price by going to a nonbrand name. Why have you been choosing a brand name for so long?

6. Make a list of products for which competitive advertising is the norm. You can start the list with cigarettes and go on to toothpaste, and then add all the others you believe fall into this category.

7. Take note of the corrective advertising you see on television. Analyze it from the point of view of the consumer. Does the corrective advertising give you information that will change your buying behavior with respect to the product in question?

8. Do research on the argument by commercial television companies against pay-television. Do you think you would be better off if pay-television were allowed throughout the United States? Why or why not?

9. Compare the various information consumer magazines, such as *Consumer Reports and Consumers Research Magazine,* as well as *Money* and *Changing Times.* If you had a limited amount of time, which one or ones would you read most often? Why?

10. Send away for the index of selected federal publications from Consumer Information, Public Documents Distribution Center, Pueblo, Colorado 81009. Order those government-provided information booklets that might be of help to you in making your consumer decisions.

**SELECTED
READINGS**

Advertising Age, various issues.

Buxton, Edward, *Promise Them Anything.* (New York: Stein & Day), 1972.

Cox, Edward F., Robert C. Fellmeth, and John E. Schulz, *"The Nader Report"* on *the Federal Trade Commission* (New York: Richard W. Baron), 1969.

Hearings before the Senate Committee on Commerce on Truth and Advertising Act, .1971, October 4, 1971, (Washington, D. C.: U.S. Government Printing Office).

Levitt, Theodore, "The Morality (?) of Advertising," *Harvard Business Review,* July/August 1970.

Nader, Ralph. *The Consumer and Corporate Accountability* (New York: Harcourt Brace Jovanovich), 1973.

Packard, Vance. *The Hidden Persuaders* (New York: David McKay Company), 1957.

Telser, Lester G., "Advertising and Cigarettes," *Journal of Political Economy,* No. 70 (1962), 471–499.

Ward, Scott, *Effects of Television Advertising on Children and Adolescents* (Cambridge, Mass.: Marketing Science Institute), July 1971.

CHAPTER PREVIEW

☐ What is the history of marriage in the Western world?
☐ What are the economic costs and benefits of marriage?
☐ Are women "crypto-servants" in our society?
☐ What is the women's liberation movement all about?

GLOSSARY OF NEW TERMS

Patriarch: The male head of a family or clan in which he takes on an authoritarian role, generally, which extends not only to his own immediate family but also to the families of his sons.

Pair Bonds: Generally, male-female relationships in which the two persons involved share in significant mutual activities and life planning.

Specialization: The dividing up of various tasks so that one individual concentrates only on certain tasks while leaving the other individual or individuals time to concentrate on the remaining tasks. Also called the DIVISION OF LABOR.

Crypto-servant: John Kenneth Galbraith's name for the woman's role in America. They are, he says, secret or not-seeming servants, but servants nevertheless to the males in the society.

Let us look at the life cycle of the average person in American society. Having, obviously, been conceived, then born, for about the first three years you are totally dependent on adults for your care and feeding. If left alone, you could not survive. After a while, however, you become increasingly self-sufficient: you can feed yourself, dress yourself, and make your wishes known in other ways than crying or laughing. All the while, you are being formed by your environment—friends, family, surroundings. When school starts for you, the family takes on less importance. Environmental stimuli outside of the family become more important in formulating the values you will have throughout the rest of your life. If you are the typical American, you will finish high school and go on to some form of higher education. Today, more than 60 percent of high school graduates go on in their schooling. Also, if you are typical you will eventually get married. For women, the average age of first marriage is 20; for men, 23.

The life cycle starts over again for your offspring when you begin to raise a family. What does this mean? Simply that a tremendous part of the average person's lifetime is involved in family activities. It is not surprising, then, that the family occupies a key role in the study of economic and consumption decision-making in general. However, the family is not the unique spending unit in this country. Today there are twelve million one-person households. Of college-age students, the vast majority live with roommates or in dormitories, fraternities, sororities, rooming houses, communes, etc. No matter what your present or contemplated future living arrangement might be, the principles and rules outlined in this text for your personal economics are still going to be valid. Nonetheless, it might be useful to look into the economic aspects of marriage, and its counterpart, the dissolution of marriage.

THE ECONOMICS OF LOVE AND PAIN

STATE SANCTIONED LOVING

Marriage, as we know it, is an old institution. The form that it takes in our modern Western civilization is the product of a long development in which Greek, Roman, Hebrew, and Christian traditions were combined. Before the rise of Christian notions of marriage, the Germanic peoples and the Jews had a type of marriage similar, it seems, to that of the Greeks and the Romans. It fitted well into a society composed of kinship groups headed by patriarchal chiefs, fathers with great authority over their grown sons and unmarried daughters, and over their sons' families. Every person, male or female, belonged of necessity to a clan dominated by a patriarch. When a woman married, she was allowed to leave the clan of her birth and enter her husband's clan. However, marriage was not a transaction between the two partners involved but, rather, between the chiefs of the two clans, as was also the dissolution of a marriage. By the time of Jesus, custom and law allowed a marriage to be terminated arbitrarily by the husband, but the wife had no such power.

Some contemporary observers maintain that the institution of marriage is dying out. Divorce statistics indeed indicate a slight downward trend in the percentage of young adults remaining married. In addition, the average age at which people first get married has been increasing throughout the history of the United States. But marriage is not a dying institution, at least not yet. Since it is not, we might investigate why the mar-

riage contract is such a popular arrangement. Perhaps we might better observe that the "traditional" marriage contract is undergoing a transition; it is being modified by changing motives and roles.

ESTIMATING
ECONOMIC VALUES

It is of course easiest for us to look at marriage as an institution in which love plays a primary role. This view reflects our modern culture, for in the marriage institutions of past societies, particularly in the East, love had little if anything to do with getting married. But today, at least for most people in this country, love plays a role. In fact, we might consider the major benefit of marriage to be a reduction in the search costs for love and companionship. Once a mate is found and a marriage made, love and companionship (sexual and otherwise) can be obtained with much less effort than must be expended by, say, single individuals in search of the same goals. Of course, long-term pair bonds need not always be legalized by the state in order for people to obtain the mutual benefits. Whatever be the reason, however, most persons seek legal bonds. Perhaps the state sanctioning of the marriage contract and the difficulty of reneging on that contract give a sense of security to the partners involved. More importantly, perhaps, there are definite materialistic reasons for legalizing marriage: to establish clear lines of inheritance of material property; and also to establish legal responsibility for the care of any children resulting from the marriage (although marriage is not necessary, only legally admitted paternity).

MARRIAGE:
COSTS AND
BENEFITS

If we are willing to make some fairly general assumptions, we can estimate the economic value of marriage to both men and women. Marriage is often viewed as beneficial only to the male partner. As long before today's feminist and liberation movements as 1884, Friedrich Engels maintained that monogamous marriage as it had developed in the West was little more than a contractual system by which men exploited women.[1] This argument, of course, ignores some of the important features of marriage today. For one thing, the marriage contract is usually voluntary; hence, both parties can be presumed to be better off married than unmarried (at least for a while). Marriage also involves specialization; members of the family specialize in individual endeavors in order to increase the general welfare of the family unit. Moreover, the female member of the family unit, *particularly if she does not work for wages or salary*, receives at least part of the income remaining after the male makes his own consumption expenditures. In other words, for example, the nonworking wife obtains services from jointly consumed goods, such as houses, cars, and stereo systems, in addition to making her own personal consumption expenditures, such as on food and clothing. Of course, she does not obtain these goods and services free of charge, because the specialization aspect of the marriage may require that she do certain tasks.

[1] Friedrich Engels, *The Origin of the Family, Private Property and the State* (New York: International Publishers, 1942).

Although people certainly would not marry if the benefits were not at least equal to the costs, the benefits of marriage most often mentioned are such nonmonetary ones as love, companionship, and children. But there are also economic benefits; most obviously, to a woman the economic benefit of marriage is total family income minus the personal expenses of other family members, for this represents the income available for her benefit.

From Bureau of the Census data for lifetime incomes, adjusted for taxes paid and personal consumption expenditures of other members of the family unit, we get an average lifetime figure for a two-person family of $314,262 usable by the wife. Thus, marriage is a valuable economic alternative for many women.

CRYPTO-SERVANTS

This number may be large, but certainly does not tell the true story. In fact, the women's liberation movement today is attempting to make known the true costs of marriage to the female partner and, even more, the benefits of marriage to the male. One of America's best-known economists, John Kenneth Galbraith, believes that a tremendous amount of social anxiety has arisen from the conversion of women to the role of "crypto-servant" (*crypto* meaning "secret, not seeming"). That is, women are consigned to the function of managing and executing for their families the high level of consumption the modern economy permits. Galbraith considers this to be a degrading exploitation:

The conversion of women into a crypto-servant class was an economic accomplishment of the first importance. Menially employed servants were available only to a majority of the preindustrial population; the servant-wife is available, democratically, to almost the entire present male population. Were the workers so employed subject to pecuniary compensation, they would be by far the largest single category in the labor force. The value of the services of housewives has been calculated somewhat impressionistically at roughly one-fourth of total Gross National Product.[2]

Dr. Galbraith has a strong point, but at least some facts contradict the notion that there is an *increasing* amount of female exploitation within the family unit. For example, from 1950 to 1972, the proportion of married women working or seeking work outside the home rose from 24 to 42 percent. (Of course, this does not mean that women are not exploited outside of the family; but we will say more on that later.)

In much the same way that we earlier estimated the value of marriage to the woman, we can numerically show the value of marriage to the man.

[2] John Kenneth Galbraith, *Economics and the Public Purpose* (Boston: Houghton Mifflin, 1973).

**MEASURING
THE VALUE OF
HOUSEWIVES'
SERVICES**

In numerous tragic accidents every year, women who are both wives and mothers are taken away from their families, most commonly in automobile accidents. When a negligent party is at fault, the husband and family often sue to recover the lost economic value of the woman. Added up, the numbers are indeed startling. To replace a wife and mother requires housekeepers, tutors for the children, extra repair services around the house, extra gardening services, and, of course, some sort of compensation for the "loss of consortium" (affection, companionship, etc.) suffered by the husband. In a sample calculation, it was found that to compensate the family for lost housekeeping services alone (with no allowance for tutoring, love and affection, etc.) would cost over $100,000 for a 37-year-old wife and mother until age 65.

It is certainly not clear who is getting the better deal in marriage, because at least economically, the man and the woman both benefit.

**VOLUNTARY
MARRIAGE
DISSOLUTIONS**

In some cities in the United States, there are more divorces than marriages on any given day. Just look at the vital statistics page in the Los Angeles *Times,* for example. The trend is obvious: divorces are increasing, not only in the United States but also in the rest of the world. Figure 4–1 shows the per capita number of divorces in this country over the past half century.

FIGURE 4–1 U.S. DIVORCES PER 1000 FEMALES 15 YEARS OR OLDER
Before World War II, averaged fewer than 9 divorces per 1000 females. The half decade right after the war saw a rise in divorce rates which settled down to an average figure of fewer than 10 per 1000 females from 1950 on to about 1963. (Beginning in 1960, figures include Alaska and Hawaii.) Then the rate started rising again, reaching over 15 per 1000 in the 1970s. Source: *Current Population Reports, Series P–120.*

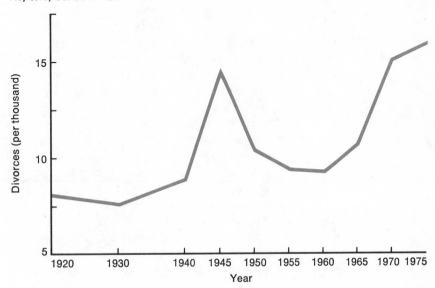

The dissolution of a marriage is, of course, an economic as well as a noneconomic act. Divorce may occur for any number of reasons. And those reasons may not correspond very well with the legal reasons given in court: couples wishing for more than just a friendship may decide to divorce after they "fall out of love"; marriages often dissolve because of money problems or the simple incompatibility of two human beings. When children are involved, they too partake in any of the costs and benefits of the decision. Child psychologists have recently discovered that children are often better off living with a single parent than living with both parents in an uncomfortable, disruptive family situation.

The upsurge in divorces may be accounted for by two key changes in American society, one economic, the other social. In the first place, the cost of divorce has fallen as the legal fees have dropped and the courts have become more lenient on the grounds for divorce. Of course, many states still recognize only such things as provable adultery as grounds for divorce; but others, such as California, Ohio, and Washington, have essentially eliminated the need for seeking any grounds at all when both parties involved are mutually agreeable to the divorce settlement and there are no children. In other words, "no fault" divorce is in the process of being legalized in some states. Divorce "by mail" is becoming increasingly popular throughout the United States.

The act of divorce has become more acceptable and the treatment of divorcees by friends, in general, more favorable and, hence, less costly. Divorcees may not be treated in exactly the same way as they were when they were married by all of their friends, but the social stigma once attached to divorces is slowly but surely dying out.

Another reason for relatively high divorce rates in recent years has often been placed at the feet of the women's liberation movement, an important subject to which we now turn.

THE LIBERATION OF WOMEN

The women's liberation movement is not new. The first women's rights convention was held in 1848 in Seneca Falls, New York, with Elizabeth Cady Stanton and Lucretia Mott its promoters. The purposes of that convention included expanding women's employment and educational opportunities.

Today's women's movement is referred to by its members as the Second Wave, coming after a 50-year pause following the passage of the Nineteenth Amendment and the achievement of suffrage for women in 1920. The current movement can be said to have begun with Betty Freidan's book, *The Feminine Mystique,* which detailed "sexism," or the "disease which has no name" in the suburbia of the 1950s.

Though often identified as a middle-class movement, the women's liberation movement seeks to define and eradicate sexism from all spheres of life for all women. Although the movement seems to be centered in the United States, demands of women in many other countries for such

"Henry, I've gone as far as I can in this field. I'm leaving you."

things as safe and legal abortions are rising. In this country, such organizations as The National Organization for Women (NOW) seek to promote equal opportunities for women in employment, education, obtaining credit, and so on. They seek such equality largely through the courts and by lobbying legislatures. In addition, local organizations focus on such issues as eliminating sexism from grade school textbooks (in which Dick runs and Sally watches him), and challenging sexist advertisements. Apart from such attempts to alter the institutional framework of American society, including a national campaign to ratify the Equal Rights Amendment to the U.S. Constitution, there is widespread use of "consciousness raising" groups to foster communication among women who sometimes feel isolated in their homes, and to develop an alternative to the sex role conditioning that the women's movement sees as the root of sex bias in society.

Today's women's liberation movement has succeeded in creating an awareness of discrimination in the labor market based on sex, as indicated in Table 4–1. Recently, through the efforts of the federal Equal Employment Opportunity Commission, the movement obtained a $50 million settlement against AT&T for alleged sexist practices. Though it presents many diverse demands and speaks with no single voice, the effects of the women's movement are being felt in every household in America.

TABLE 4–1:
MEDIAN WAGE OR SALARY
INCOME OF FULL–TIME
YEAR–ROUND WORKERS, BY
SEX AND SELECTED MAJOR
OCCUPATION GROUP, 1968
Here we present the median wage or salary income of men and women in various occupational groups. Women's median wage or salary income expressed as a percent of men's reaches a high of 65.9 percent for professional and technical workers down to a low of 40.5 percent for sales workers. Source: U. S. Department of Commerce, Bureau of the Census: *Current Population Reports, P–60, No. 66.*

MAJOR OCCUPATION GROUP	Median wage or salary income		Women's median wage or salary income as per- cent of men's
	Women	Men	
Professional and technical work- ers	$6,691	$10,151	65.9
Nonfarm managers, officials, and proprietors	5,635	10,340	54.5
Clerical workers	4,789	7,351	65.1
Sales workers	3,461	8,549	40.5
Operatives	3,991	6,738	59.2
Service workers (except private household)	3,332	6,058	55.0

SPECIALIZATION AND LIBERATION

We should note that if in fact women wish to have complete equality within marriage, then one of the reasons for marriage as it exists in our culture is eliminated. That reason is *specialization*. For those who wish to specialize in specific activities such as earning income or raising children, *complete* equality of work load within the family unit may not allow for this specialization. The general economic welfare of the family unit may fall. Of course, despecialization within the family unit is not necessarily bad, for if in fact it brings more emotional harmony to the household, then even though the household may be worse off in economic welfare, it may be better off overall. Of course, specialization does not imply that it is necessarily the female who should specialize in housework.

NONMARRIAGE AND THE OUTSIDE WORLD

For those women who decide not to marry, or are widowed or divorced, important social and economic pressures await them. Of course, we are talking about discrimination. Even though the Civil Rights Act of 1964 specifies that it is illegal to discriminate by sex (as well as by race or national origin), not all groups will necessarily be treated equally in the job market or the marketplace in general; nor will they be treated equally by their peers or society in general. Until recently, single women generally had an extremely difficult time obtaining credit—purchasing houses, cars, etc., on time, and so on. In many places, divorced women who have children have had, and still have, difficulty renting houses or apartments. Because the single, widowed, or divorced woman has been considered less "stable," entrepreneurs in their role as profit-makers have sought to treat these groups of potential buyers differently from other groups.

In the job market, a single woman often faces tremendous barriers, not the least of which are created by the past behavior of single women taken as a whole. In the past, the life cycle of a woman generally involved getting married and having children, for whom she was expected to care full-time. Employers have often been reluctant to hire a young single woman at the same wage rate at which they would hire a man for fear that the woman would eventually quit to get married and raise a family, thus taking with her all of the specific training that the employer had invested in her. This reason for giving less pay for equal work to women is, of course, slowly changing as more and more women continue to work throughout their married and child-rearing years. At most, such women are gone from the job market only during the pregnancy and nursing period, but then re-enter the market, giving the child or children to babysitters or child care centers during working hours. Men are gone from the job during temporary physical disabilities, also. (Recently it has been suggested that *both* men and women be given pregnancy leaves!)

A NEW BENEFIT OF STAYING SINGLE

Of course, all of the facts and figures above should not be your ultimate guides for your decision about marriage. We have simply attempted to point out both the costs and the benefits of marriage and divorce. One fairly new hidden cost of marriage is worth mentioning to conclude this chapter. Getting married used to lower your tax burden because Uncle Sam treated married people differently from how he treated single people. But single people got together and lobbied to have the taxes changed. Now the law has gone the other way. Table 4–2 shows the tax savings that can be had today if you decide to live "in sin" and not get married. If your income is relatively high, the savings can be quite considerable. You might question what Congress is up to, for, usually, when the benefits of doing something increase, more people want to do it. Should we conclude that Congress is trying to break up the institution of marriage and promote legally unsanctified cohabitation?

TABLE 4–2:
PERSONAL INCOME TAX REFORM,
1973

Family Income	TAX * ON BASIS OF		
	Joint Return	Two Unmarried Persons	Saving from Living "in Sin"
$10,000	$ 1,257	$ 1,114	$ 143
15,000	2,298	2,136	162
20,000	3,582	3,192	390
25,000	5,068	4,356	710
30,000	6,794	5,738	1,056
40,000	10,858	8,902	1,956
50,000	15,635	12,640	2,995

* Assumes standard deduction throughout.

SUMMARY

1. Our Western view of marriage should be contrasted with the view of past Eastern Societies, for example, in which love had little to do with the act of getting married. Rather, marriage was a type of economic arrangement negotiated by a family patriarch.

2. Friedrich Engels once said that marriage developed in the West as a contractual system whereby men exploited women.

3. Specialization within a household may allow for both the wife and the husband to have a higher standard of living.

4. If we measure the value of housewives' services to their husbands and families, the number becomes very large very quickly. For example, some economists believe that the typical housewife's services would cost her husband at least $5000 to $10,000 a year to replace.

QUESTIONS FOR THOUGHT AND DISCUSSION

1. Do you think it is appropriate to study consumer economics within the framework of the family unit? Or would it be better to discuss it for a one-person household?

2. Do you think that costs outweigh the benefits of any marriage? Why?

3. Does specialization necessarily imply that women should do housework and men should work outside the home for money income?

4. Do you think Professor Galbraith's contention that women are crypto-servants in the United States is a valid one? Why?

THINGS TO DO

1. Look at the vital statistics page of your local newspaper and see what the ratio is of marriages to divorces in your community. Go to the library and look at that same page, say, 30 years ago. Has there been any change?

2. Try to figure out how you would measure the implicit—that is, unstated—value of the services of a housewife. What would you add to the normal things, such as housecleaning and preparing meals? Would companionship be included? Would gardening activities? Would your computations change if the person in question enjoyed doing those things?

SELECTED READINGS

Cotton, Dorothy W. *The Case for the Working Mother* (New York: Stein and Day), 1965.

Engels, Friedrich, *The Origins of the Family, Private Property and the State* (New York: International Publishers), 1942.

Galbraith, John Kenneth, *Economics and the Public Purpose* (Boston: Houghton Mifflin), 1973.

Horner, Matina. *Femininity and Successful Achievement: A Basic Inconsistency* (Lansing, Mich.: University of Michigan Research Study), 1972.

Roszak, Betty, and Theodore Roszak, eds., *Masculine/Feminine: Readings in Sexual Mythology and the Liberation of Women* (New York: Harper & Row), 1969.

Making a Decision about Children

Once a new family unit is formed, its members initially are the husband and wife. The decision whether to enlarge the family unit must be faced from the very beginning. Long ago, when there was little knowledge about conception and the possibility of its prevention, this decision usually was not even considered: the children came when they did and there seemed little way to stop them. Of course, men and women always had the choice of forestalling marriage to a later date, and abstinence has always been, and continues to be, an effective means of preventing conception. However, things have changed, at least for most people in the United States.

Decisions about when to have children and how many to have can now be considered by both parties in the pair bond. This is a particularly relevant decision to be made in an era in which children are not the **productive asset** they used to be. On the farm in the old days, raising children was a means of obtaining needed manpower. But today, with less than 5 percent of the population working on farms anyway, children are raised mainly as a **consumption good;** that is, not as an investment which will yield income for the parents later on.

THE COST OF CONSUMING

To figure out rationally the size of family desired, a couple might be interested in knowing the expected costs of raising children. Are you ready? The estimates of these costs range from about $30,000 to $150,000 per

Productive Asset: Anything that you own which produces income or satisfaction for you. A productive asset might be, for example, a tractor that you would use on a farm.

Consumption Good: A product or service that you use up in a very short period of time, as opposed to a PRODUCTIVE ASSET. A movie, for example, is a consumption good. So are food and similar products.

Opportunity Costs: The true cost of any action you take. For example, the opportunity cost of your reading this book could be measured possibly by the wages you would receive if you were working during the same time instead of reading the book. The opportunity cost of your education could be measured by what you might have been able to make at a full time job.

child! The costs, of course, are dependent on the income level of the parents: an upper-class family spends more on clothing and on education than a lower-class family. If, however, you expect to be a middle-class family in which all of your children go to college, be prepared to come up with the upper end figure for each child. Many families start providing for college education as soon as their children are born, by way of trust funds and insurance programs.

More Costs Involved

None of the cost estimates of raising children take account of the *time cost* for the parents. When the wife or husband is prevented from working or from doing other things she or he would rather do because the child or children must be cared for, a cost is incurred. Generally, this cost is called the **opportunity cost** of raising children. If the mother or father must give up the opportunity to pursue a career, to get more education, to learn ceramics or photography or whatever, then these foregone alternatives are obviously a real cost.

Often forgotten in discussions of whether or not children are advisable in a marriage are the problems that children bring into the family unit. A recent survey by the University of Michigan Institute for Social Research discovered that most women seem to identify as the happiest times of their marriage those before the arrival of their first child and after the departure of the last grown child. Some sociologists and marriage counselors maintain that childless couples have happier marriages than do parents.

At the very least, the married couple can expect the birth of the first child to create difficulties in their relationship with one another. In this period the sexual life of the couple is disrupted; and in this period there is potential for jealousy, since the new mother spends a large amount of time either being

with or thinking about her child that she probably once spent with her mate. Not every husband adjusts gracefully to such a change.

It must be anticipated, also, that with the arrival of a new child or more children, considerably more housework has to be done. This is particularly true during the first six or so years of each child's life, when it is difficult to get the child to clean up after himself or herself, or to assume responsibility for his or her own personal care. Couples who are used to immaculate households often have difficulties readjusting to the disorder brought by children's playthings scattered at random throughout the home.

A GRAVE DECISION

The decision to become a parent is the decision to bring into the world other human beings who must be cared for and for whom the parents will feel a responsibility to raise in a suitable manner. To become parents is to take on the responsibility of fostering a suitable environment for their children, that is, of creating an economic, social, and moral foundation for each new member of the family. This task is generally not taken lightly and, hence, is a subject of numerous soul-searching sessions between the parents and later among the parents and children. It is particularly true when children get to be teenagers and reach the stage at which they rebel against their parents. In any event, in the United States decisions about having children are certainly changing. In 1970, the birth rate was 88 per 1000 women age 15 through 44. By 1973, it had dropped to 69 per 1000, and is estimated to be about 60 per 1000 in 1975. A recent survey conducted by the U.S. Department of Commerce indicates that young married women between 18 and 24 plan to have an average of fewer than 2.3 children. Contrast this with the 1965 planned average of 3.1.

WHEN IS THE BEST TIME TO HAVE CHILDREN?

If you ask a random sample of people when the best time to have children is, you will usually get three answers: (1) never; (2) right away; (3) later. (We will discuss below the people who answer "never.") Let us look at the other two answers, in which it has been decided to have children. If pregnancy and childbearing occur at the very beginning of a marriage, the benefits are that the parents are younger while their children are growing and can perhaps relate to them easier than if they waited. Moreover, by the time the children leave home, parents are still relatively young and can enjoy an active child-free marriage for a good number of remaining years.

On the other hand, the costs of early pregnancy and childbearing are just as important. The sooner children come into the family unit, the less time the couple has to be alone with each other. One thing that new parents are amazed at is their lack of privacy and spontaneity in their life once they have children. Unless you find yourself in a pretty unusual situation, you cannot do everything you want to do once you have children, particularly when they are small. Also, because most couples are financially less well off when they are young and just married, the financial burden of children is heavier then. Older couples may have larger and more stable incomes to support children.

At the other extreme, waiting until the family is financially secure to have children presents problems of its own. The costs of waiting are, of course, the benefits of not waiting: the parents are older while the children are growing up and therefore (although no generalization is certain) may be less able to relate to their children; by the time the children leave home, the parents think they are too old to enjoy an active child-free life themselves. An important medical consideration is that the higher the age of the mother at conception, the

higher is the probability of mental retardation. New mothers over 40, for example, run an 18,000 percent greater risk of having a mongoloid infant than do new mothers under, say, 25.

Obviously discussions about deciding when to have children imply the ability of the parents to control conception. It may be useful, then, to outline the available information centers where prospective parents—or even non-parents—may seek information.

FAMILY PLANNING INFORMATION

Of course, a couple seeking family planning information can look first to their private doctor. If the private doctor is a general practitioner or internist, he or she will usually recommend that the woman see an obstetrician who specializes in these matters. The "OB" will usually require a complete physical examination of her and will learn about her medical history in order to choose the most suitable birth control technique, whether it be pills, intrauterine device, diaphragm, or some other method. Or instead the man can have a vasectomy; but this method is advisable only if the couple wants to remain permanently childless, for the rate of successful reversal of vasectomies is extremely low. (Of course, if an unwanted conception has occurred, abortion is an alternative.)

A couple who feel that they cannot afford the services of a private medical practitioner have an alternative in most states. The woman can go to Planned Parenthood centers where, after she has attended a class on birth control, volunteer doctors provide the contraceptive of her choice at a nominal fee, often no more than the supply cost.

SOCIAL PRESSURES TO BECOME A PARENT

Besides the tax deduction that every child gives to parents, there seems to be in much of American life a bias in favor of having children. It can be expected that about after two years of marriage, outsiders to the family unit will start to wonder—discreetly, of course —when the children are coming. According to Ellen Peck, author of *The Baby Trap* (Bernard Geis Publishers, 1971, New York), people "exert ingenious pressures on you to have children. People say you're selfish, that you're missing the greatest things in life or that you're denying your maternal instinct. And the smuggest threat: 'You'll be sorry when you're old.' " To fight against this bias in America, a group has been founded called the National Organization for Nonparents (NON). It has linked itself with Planned Parenthood and Zero Population Growth (ZPG). But whereas Planned Parenthood and ZPG recommend that all couples limit themselves to one or two children, NON is asking whether it would not be preferable if some couples had no children at all and others had six or seven. Margaret Mead, the well-known anthropologist, contends that "childbearing will become a vocation to be pursued by a diminishing group of people who really want to become parents."

Whether NON and Margaret Mead are right remains to be seen, but the pro-child bias in America today is obvious, at least to any married couple that has put off having children for a while.

THE JOYS OF PARENTHOOD

When all the cards are counted, however, and even after looking at all the costs we outlined above, couples become parents because of the expected joy of raising a child, of watching him or her grow and develop into a young adult. But while it is difficult to put in monetary terms the benefits of having children, nonetheless the *costs* remain and must be reckoned with, and the distribution of those costs within the family unit must also be understood. That is why the decision to have children generally works out for the best when both the man and the woman can agree as to the advisability, the number, and the timing. The decision to get married, as well as the decision to have children, must rank highest among the lifetime decisions that most of us must face. It can be hoped that the information contained in the previous chapter and in this consumer issue will help you make the right decision for you. (If you are already married and/or have children, they may have given you some retrospective insight into your decisions and their consequences.)

SUMMARY

1. Children are no longer the productive asset they used to be when we had a predominantly agricultural society and they could work on the farm.

2. The costs of raising children include not only all the actual money spent, but also the time involved in their upbringing. This time is called the opportunity cost of child raising.

3. The birth rate in the United States has been falling dramatically in the last couple of decades. Its present level will probably give us zero population growth in the not-too-distant future.

4. Family planning information can be obtained from (1) a general practitioner or internist, (2) specialists such as obstetricians and urologists, (3) Planned Parenthood centers.

QUESTIONS FOR THOUGHT AND DISCUSSION

1. What would happen to birth rates if families were taxed on the number of children they had?

2. Would it be possible for our society to die out because of an insufficient birth rate?

3. Is there any way you could ever determine whether child-free couples have happier marriages than other couples?

4. When do you think is the best time to have children?

5. Do you think that the social pressures to become a parent are increasing or decreasing?

THINGS TO DO

1. Try to figure out the costs that your parents incurred in raising you to age 18.

2. Is there any way you could figure out the time cost that your parents incurred in your upbringing? If you have children, what are your time costs?

3. Find out the latest U.S. Department of Commerce, Bureau of Census statistics on birth rates. Have our rates actually dropped below those that produce zero population growth? What are the Bureau's projections for the future?

SELECTED READINGS

Bettelheim, B., "Look into Your Future: Child Raising," *Today's Health*, April 1973, pp. 56–57.

Cutright, P., "Timing the First Birth: Does it Matter?" *Journal of Marriage and Family*, November 1973, pp. 585–595.

Hoover, Mary, and Charles Modsen, Jr., *The Responsive Parent: Meeting the Realities of Parenthood Today* (New York: Parents Magazine Press), 1972.

Maddsen, Clifford K., *Parents/Children/Discipline: A Positive Approach* (Boston: Allyn & Bacon), 1972.

Peck, Ellen. *The Baby Trap* (New York: Bernard Geis Associates), 1971.

Piotrow, Phyllis Tilson, *World Population Crises: The United States Response* (New York: Frederick Praeger), 1973.

"Planned Parenthood; Education for Parenthood Program," *Saturday Review of Education*, March 1973, pp. 61ff.

Shannon, W. V. "Right On! To Responsibility," *Parents Magazine*, May 1973, pp. 35–38.

CHAPTER PREVIEW

□ What does investing in yourself mean?
□ What determines how productive you are and, therefore, how much you earn?
□ What is the pay-off to going to school?
□ What are the differences between wages made in the various occupations?

GLOSSARY OF NEW TERMS

On-the-job Training: Training which you receive while you are working on a particular job. On-the-job training will raise your productivity and therefore your value to your employer.

Investment in Human Capital: Any activity that makes you more productive. You as an individual can produce just like a machine, which is physical capital. You are, on the other hand, human capital, and when you go to school, you make an investment in yourself because you make yourself better able to perform on the job.

Age-earnings Profile: The profile of how earnings change with your age. When you are young and just starting out working, your earnings are low; as you get older, your earnings go up as you become more productive and work longer hours, and then they start to fall.

Participation Rate: The percentage of any given group who participate in the labor force. If, for example, there are 75 million females between the ages of 16 and 65, and of those 75 million, 50 million are working or looking for a job, then the female labor force participation rate would be two-thirds, or 66.67 percent.

How much you are able to spend as a consumer depends to a large part on decisions you made about your education and training, and about which occupation you chose. To be sure, there are many different causes of differences in our incomes. Some persons are more clever than others, and so in a similar situation might make more income than others. Some persons have more artistic ability than others, and this, too, can cause a difference in income. Some persons prefer riskier jobs at higher rates of pay than others do: if you are willing to work as a welder on the tops of high-rise buildings, you will certainly make more money than you would as a welder in a very safe ground-floor welding shop. If you decide that you want to have lots of savings when you are older, your income will be higher today because you work more than other people.

But more important, at least for those of you who are now making the investment (right: I said you are making an investment), is your decision to go to school; that will permanently affect the level of your command over goods and services in your role as a consumer. Now, what could this possibly mean? You may think you have never made an investment in your life, but you will soon see that you did, and for most of you, not a bad one, either.

THE CONSUMER AS WAGE EARNER

INVESTING IN YOURSELF

Few persons think it strange or unfair that somebody with an M.A. gets paid more than somebody with a grade school diploma. In the first place, the M.A. has spent a long time acquiring his or her specialized knowledge; in the second place, the grade school graduate probably could do little of the work the M.A. does (and vice versa). And a basic fact of life is that individuals are generally paid only what they are worth to employers. Education can be looked at, then, as a process of making workers more productive. That is why we could say, above, that you were making an investment in yourself: going to school is an **investment in human capital**, as it is called, an investment in human beings. Usually, the longer you go to school, the more new skills you learn. You may become a better thinker; you generally become a more responsive person, at least in working situations. Why otherwise would businessmen pay more for college grads than for high school grads when they could get the less-educated people to work for them for less money?

Do not get the mistaken impression, however, that going to school will automatically guarantee you a higher income. If you specialize in an activity or a field that no one cares about, the *demand* for your services is going to be quite small. No amount of services you could supply would induce others to hire you at high wages, because what ultimately determines the individual's wages or income is the supply and demand for different types of labor.

WAGES AND PRODUCTIVITY

For any given specialty, the more trained you are, the more productive you will be and, therefore, the higher will be the demand for your services. One way to predict your future income is to analyze how productive you can be in doing something. Employers have a tendency to end up paying workers their exact worth, no more, no less. (Of course, like any general rule, this one has a few exceptions.) Thus, anything you can do to make yourself more productive will result in a higher wage rate for you, and a higher total lifetime earnings.

Now, formalized schooling is not the only way to invest in yourself; you can learn on your own by reading and practicing skills, or you can learn on the job. In fact, **on-the-job training** is one of the chief means by which individuals increase their productivity, by which individuals invest in themselves. (Persons engaged in on-the-job training—for example, as apprentices—are usually paid less than after that training is over.) However, productivity cannot occur in a vacuum. You could be very productive at something that nobody values highly. That means that

**FIGURE 5–1
AGE–EARNINGS
PROFILE FOR
SELECTED DEGREE
HOLDERS**
Source: U.S. Department of Commerce,
Consumer Income,
Series p60, No. 74.

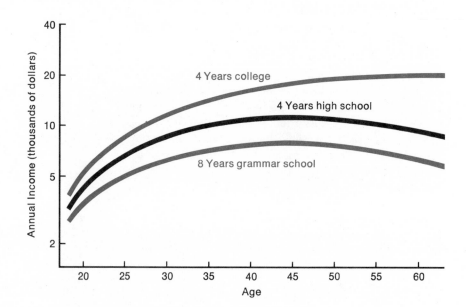

TABLE 5–1:

AVERAGE LIFETIME EARNINGS OF
SELECTED DEGREE HOLDERS

The average lifetime earnings of selected degree-holders are given in this table. The difference between eight years of grammar school and four years of college is over $500,000. These figures are averages only, and are not corrected for the timing of the income received. (Strictly speaking, these figures should be corrected [discounted] for timing, and all made comparable on a present value basis.) Source: U.S. Department of Commerce.

LEVEL OF EDUCATION	AVERAGE LIFETIME EARNINGS
8 years of grammar school	$1,134,264
4 years of high school	1,406,160
4 years of college	1,691,343

unless you choose wisely, your area of specialization may be something that society does not value highly and, hence, for which you will be relatively poorly paid. No one would now think of specializing in learning how to make horseshoes. But of course some people were doing just that right at the time when horseshoes were no longer worth very much because of the introduction of mass-produced automobiles. Those people who spent time learning how to make horseshoes, after the fact, had made a mistake.

Ultimately, then, investing in yourself requires careful planning. That is to say, you must invest in yourself in a way that increases your productive capacities in areas that are demanded by the economy. If it looks like computer keypunch operators will be unneeded in the future because of optical scanning techniques, then you certainly do not want to specialize in computer keypunching. Choosing an occupation that benefits you most may require an investment in acquiring information about future demands for different types of jobs.

**THE RATE OF
RETURN TO
EDUCATION**

While the evidence is overwhelming that an education is valuable, the old saying, "get all the education you can get," does not apply equally to everybody, and it certainly is not meaningful without qualification, because you could be acquiring formal education for the rest of your life (as some perennial students do). We can give a general rule, though, and one that will be familiar to you: acquire more education as long as the expected benefits at least cover the costs. As to some of the expected benefits, Figure 5–1 shows the **age-earnings profile** for three levels of degree holders—grade school, high school, and college. Note that the more education you get, the higher the curve is. For example, the average high school graduate at 40 years of age may be earning 40 percent more than the average grade school graduate at 40 years of age. In dollars and cents, the figures are even more impressive. Table 5–1 shows the average lifetime earnings of various degree holders: college degree holders obviously make more than grade school degree holders.

What is often ignored in the discussion of college, or of higher education in general, is the noneconomic aspects of the whole process. Individuals change in some ways when they go to college: their tastes change; they are exposed to a broader array of possible life styles; and so on. How does one measure the value of these noneconomic goods? It isn't easy. Ultimately, only you, the individual, can make that measure for yourself.

COSTS, TOO

Of course, our general rule has its limits, because it might be more expensive to acquire the higher amount of education; and in fact it is. The main cost of going to college is *not* tuition and books; this cost ranks second. The main component is the cost of foregone income—that is, the *opportunity cost* of not working. In other words, had you not gone to college, you could be working full time at, say, some average salary for the four years you are in college and out of the job market. But even with the costs of foregone earnings, tuition, and books, the rate of return to investing in education is at least as good as the rate of return to investing in something like the stock market, and certainly higher than putting your savings into a savings and loan association account.[1]

Now, it may be true that in certain years some college graduates cannot get jobs. But rather than meaning that going to college is a bad deal, it means only that during up-and-down movements in business activity, the demands for different types of college degree holders shift. Although you may be caught unaware and out of a job in your area of specialization during college, you still may have made the right choice.

Some of you, however, definitely will have made the wrong choice. In fact, according to the Carnegie Commission, 300,000 to 900,000 students should not be in college. Apparently, this large number of students is attending college mainly because of social and parental pressures, rather than from personal choice.[2]

THE CHANGING
WORLD OF FEMALE
ENDEAVORS

Numerous data have been collected to show that women earn less than men. In fact, we commonly hear that women on average earn 60 percent of what men make. While this figure does not in itself prove that discrimination and sexism operate in the labor market, it does indicate the prospects facing women in the labor market. What we want to look at is the changing characteristics of female labor-market participation. In the first place, the **participation rate** of females has been rising steadily from 18.2 percent in 1890 to around 45 percent by 1975. That is, by 1975 45 percent of females over the age of 14 were in the labor force.

[1] This is obviously true for some people only; the statistics reflect only those who were successful at college. For computation, see Gary Becker, *Human Capital: A Theoretical and Empirical Analysis, with Special Reference to Education* (New York: Columbia University Press, 1964).

[2] *More Effective Uses of Resources: An Imperative for Higher Education* (The Carnegie Commission on Higher Education, June 1972).

With the new women's awareness in the air, it is not surprising that labor-force participation has increased for women as a whole. Civil rights legislation and changing views on the role of women in society have opened to women an increasing number of occupations once restricted to men. Merely a partial listing of women workers in New York alone now yields women carpenters ("Women's Woodwork"), movers ("Mother Truckers," "Tinkerbell Memorial Trucking Company"), restauranteurs ("Mother Courage," "Food Liberation Inc."), bar owners ("Bonnie and Clyde"), acting companies ("New York Tea Party"), housepainters ("Women Can Do"), and paperhangers ("Paper Hanging Lady"), as well as electricians, landscape artists, structural draftswomen, stock brokers, sound engineers, and recreational consultants. Elsewhere, the advertising of large firms is beginning to feature women in atypical occupations, such as Bell Telephone's female linepersons.

Sexism has worked two ways, though, and males have been discriminated against in certain occupations; there have been few if any male telephone operators, airline stewardesses, or nurses. We are finally hearing male voices when we call the operator, and being served by male stewards on airplanes—although women are not yet in evidence as pilots, air-traffic controllers, etc. In spite of the complaints that many males have lodged against the women's liberation movement, at least some of them have benefited, because the Civil Rights Act of 1964 has been used to eliminate discrimination against males in many occupations.

**OCCUPATIONAL
WAGE
DIFFERENTIALS**

Among the incomes of different occupations, at the top of the ladder, as we see in Table 5–2, are the so-called professions—medicine, dentistry, and law. Does that mean you should automatically go out and start studying medicine, dentistry, or law? Obviously not. For one reason, you may be wasting your time. For example, unless you are able to get into an accredited medical school (and, of course, graduate from it), you cannot legally practice medicine in the United States. The ratio of applicants to acceptances in most medical schools is astounding. Therefore, unless your father is a doctor or you are an extremely good student in an extremely good school, the odds are against your admission to medical training.

The same is not true of law, however. There are numerous law schools that you can attend; you can even learn law at home by mail. Of course, you should not look only at the high salaries in law. To obtain a law degree you must take three additional years of training after college, three more years of not earning any income. This additional cost of becoming a lawyer means that the rate of return to becoming a lawyer may be no higher than your doing something else.

Moreover, you may "starve" for a number of years before you become a junior partner in a law firm, for at the start of your age-earnings profile, you will be getting relatively low salaries. Even doctors start their practices at low wages. So, even though the average salary for the occupation is very high, you should not anticipate that your impressive amount of schooling will start making you a nice sum of money right away. To see why this is not necessarily "unfair" or "unjust," we must look at the reasons behind the shape of the typical age-earnings profile as represented in Figure 5–2.

TABLE 5–2:
MEDIAN EARNINGS BY
OCCUPATION FROM
THE 1970 CENSUS
Source: U. S. Department of Commerce, *Statistical Abstract of the United States, 1973.*

Occupation	Male	Female
Physicians, medical and osteopathic	$15,000	$ n.a.
Dentists	15,000	n.a.
Lawyers and judges	15,000	n.a.
Civil engineers	12,675	n.a.
School administrators	11,612	7,600
Accountants	10,627	5,818
Insurance agents, brokers and underwriters	10,024	4,835
Secondary school teachers	9,002	6,723
Bank tellers and cashiers	7,265	4,190
Plumbers and pipe fitters	7,123	n.a.
Carpenters	7,001	n.a.
Bakers	6,422	n.a.
Sales clerks, retail trade	5,532	2,226
Construction laborers	4,617	n.a.
Farm laborers and farm foremen	2,619	1,112

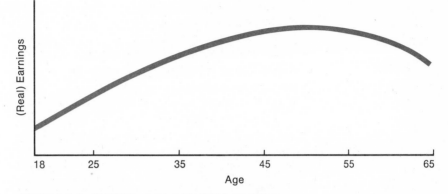

FIGURE 5–2 TYPICAL AGE–EARNINGS PROFILE
Within every class of incomes earned, there is usually a typical age-earnings profile. Earnings are lowest when starting out to work at age 18 and reach their peak at around 45 to 55, then taper off until retirement at around 65 when they become zero for most people. The rise in earnings up to age 45 to 55 is usually due to more experience, working longer hours, and better training and schooling (abstracting from general increases in national productivity).

WAGES AND AGES

Look at it this way: when you first start a job, you are inexperienced (you might even need on-the-job training). Your employer will not be inclined to pay you as much as a more experienced worker who can be more productive. Gradually, as you become more productive and better-trained, and also as the number of hours you work increases, so, too, does your wage rate (even corrected for inflation). Your employer gets more and more information on your productivity and your reliability from all of your previous employers.

You may peak out at age 45 to 55, and then slowly come down until retirement when you cease work altogether. The slow downturn in the age-earnings profile has several causes, one being that older people generally work fewer hours and also are generally less productive than middle-age people.

OCCUPATIONAL CHOICE

Not only are there vast differences among the wages for different occupations, as shown in Table 5–2, there are also vast differences in the qualifications, the amount of training, and the type of work required in each occupation. In an occupation that has highly variable periods of employment, the average wage rate is relatively higher than similar work with steadier employment; all this means is that the wage rate is higher to compensate for the periods of unemployment. You must also remember that wages alone are not going to determine whether you made the right choice. If you have a spirit of independence, you will certainly not be satisfied in a large insurance office doing paperwork; if you have a spirit of adventure, you will not be happy as a sales clerk. Therefore, you may finally choose an occupation that promises you a lower wage rate than some others but a more acceptable work situation. After all, most of us work most of our lives, and if we hate our work, we will not be very happy, even if we make quite a bit of income.

You also have to decide whether or not you want to live in one area for a long period of time. If you become a junior executive in a company that has a history of switching its executives around the country every 18 months, you will be very unhappy if you dislike moving. On the other hand, you might be very happy if indeed you want to see the country while you are young.

Your choice of occupation in some ways depends on your values and your desired life style. It also will determine how much leisure you will have. These matters were treated in Chapter 2. As you have already seen, very few things come free of charge. If you want a job with more leisure, you will generally have less income to spend than from a job with less leisure. If you want a job that is highly stable and risk-free, you will pay for it in the form of a lower income than is earned in the opposite kind of employment.

SUMMARY

1. Many income differences are caused by inherent differences in human beings, but they are also caused by the amount of training and education an individual has obtained, the amount of on-the-job training, the riskiness of the occupation, and so on.

2. Going to school is an investment in human capital because it makes you, the human, more productive in the future. Generally your investment in human capital should pay off in the form of a higher wage later on.

3. However, you must specialize in an activity that is in demand and for which there is not a surplus of supply. Hence, choosing your occupation requires predicting both the demand and the supply for that particular occupation in the future.

4. Generally, individuals are paid according to their productivity. Therefore, anything that raises an individual's productivity may ultimately lead to a higher income.

5. The rate of return to education is as high as the rate of return to investing in other things. A college degree holder may make as much as a half a million dollars more on average than a grade school degree holder.

6. The greatest cost of going to college is the opportunity cost of not being able to work and make an income during those years.

7. The female labor market role has been changing and there is some evidence that male/female wage differentials are narrowing.

8. An individual's wages (corrected for inflation) are usually lowest when the individual first enters the labor force. That's because the individual is least productive then.

**QUESTIONS FOR
THOUGHT AND
DISCUSSION**

1. What are some of the most important factors that contribute to differences in income?

2. Have you ever considered going to school as an investment in your own human capital?

3. Is the act of going to college pure investment, or not?

4. Does it seem fair that some students specialize in areas in which they cannot get a job once they get a degree? What would you do about that situation?

5. Why does the government subsidize much of higher education?

6. Do you think college is a good investment?

7. What is the highest cost of going to college?

THINGS TO DO

1. Go to the career guidance center of your college or university. Look at the books on occupations that you could enter. Make a list of the highest-paid occupations. Then ask someone in the center whether or not you would be eligible for those occupations. Try to determine why you would or would not.

2. Get the latest data from the Department of Commerce on lifetime earnings of various degree holders. Is it still worthwhile for individuals to complete college?

**SELECTED
READINGS**

Abelson, P. H., "Career Choices," *Science*, July 28, 1972, pp. 293ff.

Becker, Gary, *Human Capital: A Theoretical and Empirical Analysis with Special Reference to Education* (New York: Columbia University Press), 1964.

Berg, Ivar E., *Education and Jobs; The Great Training Robbery* (New York: Center for Urban Education, Praeger Publishers), 1970.

Cochran, S., and D. P. Eldridge, "Employment and Personal Consumption Expenditures," *Monthly Labor Review*, March 1972, pp. 39–47.

Deutermann, W. V., "Educational Attainment of Workers, March, 1971," *Monthly Labor Review*, November 1971, pp. 30–35.

Erlick, A. C., "Youth, Education and Jobs," *Intellect*, October 1972, pp. 10ff.

Gordon, Margaret S., *Higher Education and the Labor Market* (New York: McGraw-Hill), 1974.

Iris, B., and G. V. Barrett, "Some Relations between Job and Life Satisfaction and Job Importance," *Journal of Applied Psychology*, August 1972, pp. 301–304.

Johnson, L., and R. H. Johnson, "High School Preparation, Occupation and Job Satisfaction," *Vocational Guidance Quarterly*, June 1972, pp. 287–290.

Michael, Robert T., *The Effect of Education on Efficiency in Consumption* (New York: Columbia University Press), 1972.

CHAPTER PREVIEW

☐ Why do we have to follow a budget?
☐ How can a budget work into democratic decision-making for the family spending unit?
☐ How important is teenage spending in our economy?
☐ What do typical family budgets look like?
☐ How can one fit a budget into a lifetime plan?

GLOSSARY OF NEW TERMS

Scarcity: The limit that exists in our world where we can not have everything we want. Nature creates this limit. Most goods that we want are scarce. That is, there is not an unlimited quantity available at a zero price. Scarcity causes us to make choices.

Trade-off: The realistic choice that one must make between alternatives. For example, if you buy a couple of new books, by necessity you must trade off that purchase with something else—say, a night out on the town. All choices involve trade-offs between alternatives.

Transfer Payments: Payments made by the government to individuals for which no services are rendered. A transfer payment might be a Social Security check, or an unemployment check.

Luxury Good: A good, the purchase of which increases more than in proportion to increases in income. Jewelry, gourmet foods, sports cars, etc., usually fall into this category.

We American consumers are rich. That is, we are rich by comparison with the British consumer, the Indian consumer, the African consumer, the Spanish consumer, or the Venezuelan consumer. Table 6–1 shows that the average per capita income in the United States is considerably higher than in most other countries of the world.

But per capita income does not tell the story we want to tell. Table 6–2 shows the different percentages of U. S. families that make particular amounts of income, ranging all the way from poverty to extreme opulence. Most of us, as you can well imagine, find ourselves somewhere in the middle of income earners: we are not absolutely broke, because we do have some form of income, but on the other hand we are not Rockefeller, Howard Hughes or Hugh Hefner.

However, all of us, whether we be rich or poor, have something in common. You may not want to believe it, but no matter how rich you are, you still have a problem: you can not buy everything you would like to buy. The problem is universal—a problem we call **scarcity** All of us are faced with a limited budget, even Howard Hughes: for if he wanted to buy every single jet in the world, he would not have enough money to do it. (I have no idea what he would do with all those jets.) Since we all face this universal problem of scarce resources, we can better understand why personal money management is important for all of us, no matter what our income level.

YOU HAVE TO LIVE WITH WHAT YOU HAVE

WHY FIGURE OUT A BUDGET
OR SPENDING PLAN?

If you find yourself at either end of the income spectrum, you may think it a waste of time to formulate a budget. Obviously, if you have no income, a budget is not what you should be looking for. If you have a seemingly infinite amount of income, you need not formulate a budget with respect to your usual purchases. Most of us, however, lie somewhere in between, right? (I dare you to deny that.) Since we have limited incomes, every action of ours that involves spending part of that income means we sacrifice something else. Economists term this the opportunity cost of spending.

TABLE 6–1:

PER CAPITA GNP, 1973, U.S. DOLLARS. If we accept the amount of total income divided by the population, or per capita GNP, as an indication of living standards, the United States is still at the head of the list, though followed closely by Canada and Sweden. Down at the bottom are the less developed countries such as Turkey, Korea, the United Arab Republic, and India. Sources: Agency for International Development; Center for International Studies, M.I.T.

COUNTRY	PER CAPITA GNP
United States	$5,980
Canada	4,920
Sweden	4,910
Denmark	3,860
West Germany	3,830
France	3,750
Norway	3,720
United Kingdom	2,670
Japan	2,610
Italy	2,110
Israel	2,080
Czechoslovakia	1,920
Soviet Union	1,800
Portugal	830
Brazil	530
China (Taiwan)	520
Turkey	370
Korea (South)	310
U.A.R. (Egypt)	230
India	110

If you decide to spend more on entertainment, you have less left over for all the other things in your budget. Or if you decide to spend more on transportation, you have less for all other things. In other words, every spending decision that you make involves an opportunity cost: you are giving up the opportunity of spending that income on something else. Why? Simply because you have a limited budget; simply because you face a problem of scarcity.

Planning a budget and attempting to stick to it forces the issue of scarcity and opportunity cost out into the open. You cannot deny the fact that you are giving something up when you decide, for example, to take that trip to Mexico. For if you plan it in your budget, you will realize that somewhere else along the line something has to be cut out of the budget. A budget, then, is a way of managing your money in a more or less systematic and rational manner. It is also, however, a control mechanism that causes you to be aware of decisions you are actually making—decisions that are there even if you do not wish to make them an obvious part of your decision-making process. Now, some of you may be gifted with the ability to determine instantaneously the **trade-offs** involved every time you make a purchase. But we mortals who cannot always do such quick mental computations may be helped out by a budget. With it, we may be able to hold in check undirected spending activities that can ultimately lead to unhappiness and, occasionally, financial disaster when the household must declare bankruptcy.

A budget also works as well as part of long-range lifetime planning, a topic we discuss in the final part of this chapter. Budgets are generally meant to last for a short period of time, perhaps a month and sometimes as short a time as a week, although they then become too complicated and too time-consuming for most people to bother with. Understanding the "why" behind budget formulation is also linked to value clarification, which we discussed in Chapter 2. A budget can be a basic part of putting into play values that have been clarified as part of lifetime goals in a consumer's lifetime planning process.

A budget is also useful for bringing harmony into a household in which money may be a sore point among the family members.

DEMOCRATIC DECISION-MAKING

If you live alone, of course, you need not be concerned about or consider democratic decision-making, unless of course you find yourself being rather schizophrenic about purchases you make—in which case, you might want to consult both sides of your mind for two different opinions on everything.

If, on the other hand, in your situation more than one person is affected by the way each month's income is spent, then you have to make a choice about how decisions are to be arrived at. Will decision-making be unilateral or dictatorial? Will decision-making be democratic, in which case everybody participates? This problem comes up not only in traditional family situations, but also in communal and group-living situations, too. The principles are the same: if you decide that one person is going to make unilateral decisions, then those whose lives are affected may at one time or another feel cheated, left out, or trod upon.

The formulation of a spending plan can (if you wish) become an integral part of increasing harmony within any living situation by bringing into light everyone's desires, needs, preferences, and complaints. Each time a major economic decision has to be made, a democratic decision-making unit will involve everybody in the process. On the other hand, situations

TABLE 6–2:
MONEY INCOME OF FAMILIES BY INCOME LEVEL, 1971. The largest percentage of families earn between $7000 and $25,000. Only 5.3 percent earn above $25,000 (in 1971) and less than 10 percent earned under $3000. Source: Bureau of Census, Current Population Reports, Series P–60.

Income	Percent
Under $1000	1.5
1000–1999	2.6
2000–2999	4.2
3000–3999	4.8
4000–4999	5.4
5000–5999	5.7
6000–6999	5.5
7000–9999	18.5
10,000–14,999	26.9
15,000–24,999	19.5
25,000 +	5.3

more akin to tyranny will involve only one person in the decision. In most families today, the so-called male breadwinner is no longer freely allowed all the decision-making powers simply because he brings home the "bread." After all, everybody, including John Kenneth Galbraith whom we talked about in Chapter 4, realizes that the housewife also contributes to the total implicit income of the family, to the tune of at least $4000 a year in a family of four. If she is contributing income, even though it is not in the form of dollars brought home in a paycheck she too will want to take part in the formulation of the budget, and therefore in the formation of the lifetime goals and plans of the family unit. In some states, such as Washington, the wife has the legal right to share in controlling family finances. That is, either partner is empowered to act independently on behalf of the "community," except for a few specified instances in which the signatures of both spouses are required, such as the signing of a mortgage when a house is purchased.

Our discussion above also applies to such nontraditional spending units as groups and communes.

THE FAMILY
COUNCIL

Often, in truly democratic households, there is a meeting of a family council when budget-making time comes around. At this time, everybody airs his or her desires; and everyone, especially children, faces the problem of scarcity and the trade-offs that have to be made with a fixed income. Everybody must realize at the onset that no one person's every desire will be satisfied. This is so because many decisions are mutually exclusive; if, for example, a new TV is purchased, it may be impossible to buy a new 10-speed bike. If the family unit decides to trade in the old clunker for a brand new sedan, there may be no vacation in the mountains this year. The beauty of the democratic family-council budget-making process is that everybody's cards can be laid on the table—and the biggest card of them all, of course, is the fixed amount of income that the family has to spend. Even the parents may have much clearer notions of the opportunity costs of their actions and the effects of these trade-offs on other members of the family.

Viewed in this light, the budget-making process has another, separate goal: not only can it hold in check undirected spending and prevent financial crises, it can also help to solidify family relationships. Love of money (often considered the root of all evil) is the basic cause of so many marital squabbles that democratization of the spending process would seem a natural desire of all families who wish to have unity, tranquility, and harmony within the household.

No matter how democratic the process may be, however, there will always be problems with children, particularly when they get to be teenagers and want to assert their own independence (and with adults, too, who wish to assert *their* independence).

COPING WITH
THE TEENAGE
CONSUMER

As a group, teenagers form a powerful consumer bloc. Did you know that in 1974 there were over 28 million teenagers in the United States, and they spent an estimated $23 billion? That means that every one of them spent on average $800 a year on records, tapes, cosmetics, etc. It is not surprising that advertising agencies have increasingly focused their attention on the teenage market. Teenagers, of course, get much of their money from their parents in the form of an allowance or payment for household chores. Many of them also do work on their own—paper routes, part-time sales jobs, and so on. In one survey, over half of the high school students questioned reported at least two sources of income. Quite a large percentage of teenagers have their own savings accounts, have their own sets of U. S. Savings Bonds stashed away, and belong to Christmas or vacation clubs; some of them have even already obtained insurance.

To a large extent, teenagers pick up the spending habits of their parents. Hence, if the parents are always complaining about never having enough money to finish the month out, if the parents always are fighting about money worries among themselves, then the teenage children cannot very well be expected to act differently in their own spending. Hence, it may be useful to look at the teenage years as a time when parents can engage in what we might call money training. The best teaching method is setting a good example. But more than that, parents can engage in a subtle form of money training that will prepare their children for adulthood.

Of course, most important in money training is to make the teenager realize that everything in life involves a trade-off, spending money being no exception. This realization can be encouraged in a variety of ways. If the teenager is made part of the democratic family council in which budget formulations are made every month or so, then he or she is given first-hand knowledge of how painful trade-off decisions might sometimes be and what the trade-offs actually involve. If the parents then want to spend a little more time with their teenager, they can try to get him or her to formulate a personal budget. In this way, the teenager sees in black and white the trade-offs that he or she faces with this very limited income. It is a wise parent who informs a teenage child that even though the teenager's income will be larger later on in life, he or she will still be faced with the same basic problem of scarcity. Many teenagers believe that it is irrelevant to learn good spending and budgeting habits during the teen years because they are convinced that later on they will have "so much money" they will have no worries about how they spend it. We all know, painfully so, that this is wrong; our wants and desires seem to always be one step ahead of our incomes. Hence, we are always faced with the problem of figuring out how to allocate our limited budget to a large number of competing desires and needs. The transition from childhood to adulthood certainly will be less painful if the teenager understands that the budget problems he or she faces as a teenager are no different in principle and in practice from those he or she will face as an adult member of a family or living unit, even if this living unit consists of one person— himself or herself. For some thoughts on allowances, see Exhibit 6–1.

HOW DOES THE TYPICAL HOUSEHOLD ALLOCATE ITS INCOME?

Averages can sometimes be deceiving. But it may be instructive for you to see how typical households in the United States allocate their fixed incomes to the many competing demands. The U. S. Department of Labor, Bureau of Labor Statistics, has for some time obtained survey data on the spending patterns of households of various income levels. Figure 6–1, a pie graph, shows how an average American family spends its income. The largest chunk usually goes for housing services (which include utilities and maintenance). Equal to that expenditure, and sometimes even larger, is the chunk of income that goes for food. Food and housing often account for over 50 percent of the average American family's expenditures in any one year.

This may seem to be a frighteningly large percentage, but it is not when compared with those of other countries. Table 6–3 shows the percentage of total income going to food in different countries of the world. Notice that there seems to be a relationship between the percentage of income spent on food and the level of development of the country. In fact, for an accurate measure of how well off a country is, all you would have to look at is what percentage of each family's budget went for food. The larger the percentage, the less developed the country. (Of course, there will be exceptions to this.)

FIGURE 6–1
AVERAGE AMERICAN FAMILY BUDGET (based on annual budgets for a four-person urban family, intermediate level of living)
The average American family spends at least one-fourth of its income on housing, and almost one-fourth on food. The rest is divided among transportation, clothing, medical care, personal care, taxes, and other. Source: U.S. Department of Labor, Bureau of Labor Statistics.

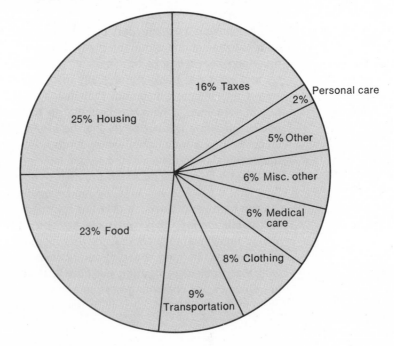

16% Taxes
Personal care
2%
5% Other
6% Misc. other
6% Medical care
8% Clothing
9% Transportation
23% Food
25% Housing

EXHIBIT 6–1
A child's allowance shouldn't be hit-or-miss

Some families are free and loose about children's allowances. Others play it tight and hold the kids accountable for every dime. Both ways work.

Psychologists and educators point out that there are no hard-and-fast rules. Any sensible approach is good if it is in line with the family's income and mode of living and is followed consistently. "Trouble comes when the allowance is hit-or-miss," says a top New York child psychologist. He adds: "What's really important to understand is that *your* attitude toward money rubs off on the kids. They'll tend to do with pennies or a dollar what you do on a bigger scale."

A Connecticut educator and psychologist who specializes in teen-age problems notes that "a parent's feeling of confidence about money is soaked up by the kids very early—or the parent's feeling of fear and doubt."

A small child should be given a dime or so once or twice a week but never more money than can be managed easily. By 10 the child should be getting a regular weekly amount of pocket money—maybe $1 or a bit more—to provide some spending options. The habit of saving requires some excess cash that makes it possible.

Pre-teenagers, say psychologists, develop confidence by having more money in hand, but it should still be on a weekly basis. Starting at 13 or 14, a monthly allowance should teach the youngster something about budgeting. But here the advice comes full circle: The parents' spending habits are what the kids really look at.

By 15 or 16, the child should have at least some idea of family finances, though too much information may be worse than too little. "Give them a clear, honest understanding if they question you," says a Harvard University psychologist. "But don't make a big thing of it. Don't impart anxiety by forcing the issue."

An obvious blunder at any age is to give a youngster more than friends get. "He should be in line with his peers," says a specialist. "If he gets too much, he may waste it and feel guilty about it in the bargain." Giving too little in the hopes of instilling a sense of frugality is equally bad.

TABLE 6–3:

PERCENTAGE OF TOTAL INCOME GOING TO FOOD IN SELECTED COUNTRIES. The U. S. spends the smallest percentage of total income on food of any nation in the world. As much as 60 or 70 percent, or more, of total income is spent on food by some less-developed nations, such as Uganda, which spends 79 percent of total income on food. Sources: FAO Review of Food Consumption Surveys, 1970, and *Fortune* Magazine, February 1974.

COUNTRY	PERCENT Total Food Exp./Total Income
Argentina	40
Brazil	37
Chile	64
France	36
Honduras	41
Hungary	42
Indonesia *	60
Japan	27
Kenya	38
Korea	49
Malawi *	40
Netherlands *	29
Pakistan	51
Philippines	63
Poland	45
Saudi Arabia	74
Somalia *	60
Spain *	49
Sudan *	70
Switzerland *	21
Thailand	55
Tunisia *	50
Uganda	79
United Kingdom	28
United States	15
Venezuela	25
Yugoslavia	35

* Percent of total expenditures.

Clothing, personal care, and medical care take up another large chunk of each family's budget in the United States. Medical care itself has been taking up an increasingly large percentage of total U. S. consumption spending. The reasons why, and what to expect in the future, will be treated when we study medical care in detail, in Chapter 12. Taxes, unfortunately for many of us, take up an ever-increasing amount of our income.[1] For the average American, fully 40 percent of every dollar earned goes to federal, state, and local taxes. Some of those tax monies are returned in the form of transfer payments, such as Social Security benefits and unemployment compensation, but the remainder, which is almost 25 percent, is still a large fraction of our total income in the United States. Again, this percentage is not as large as in most other countries of the world, where taxes are higher and total government expenditures as a percentage of total income are also higher.

[1] See Chapter 16.

DIFFERENT
LEVEL BUDGETS

The make-up of the various budget categories change as we go from lower income to higher income spenders. Table 6–4 shows the U. S. Department of Labor's estimates of the expenditures for typical low-, medium-, and high-income families. Notice, for example, that as percentages of total income, food spending falls and housing expenditures rise as income goes up. That means that as our incomes go up, we buy proportionally more housing and proportionally less food. Housing, then, is often considered after a certain point to be a type of luxury good, for people buy a disproportionate amount of it as they get wealthier, as they earn more income. Food, on the other hand, has the opposite characteristic and is often called a necessity.

We have to be careful of such labels as luxury and necessity, however, because they have some subjective connotations. Remember that one person's meat is often another person's poison, so it is not really just to talk about luxuries and necessities. One person's luxury may be another person's necessity, and vice versa. Most of us have a hard time deciding our own values and goals, let alone deciding for other people. But that is exactly what we do when we consider somebody else's spending to be wasted on so-called luxury items, or frivolous consumption.

CITY VERSUS
COUNTRY

Not only are there differences in budget allocations among low-, medium-, and high-income families, there is also a difference in typical income levels between urban and rural areas. The costs of living in cities differ from those of living in the country. And the costs of living in a large city differ from those of living in a small city. The U. S. Department of Labor has come up with annual family budgets according to the areas where people live. In Table 6–5 we show high, intermediate, and low budgets, their values for the year 1973, and where they apply. A low family budget

TABLE 6–4:
SUMMARY OF ANNUAL
BUDGETS FOR A
4–PERSON FAMILY
AT 3 LEVELS OF LIVING,
URBAN UNITED STATES,
AUTUMN 1973

Source: U.S. Department of Labor, Bureau of Labor Statistics

	LOWER BUDGET	INTERMEDIATE BUDGET	HIGHER BUDGET
TOTAL BUDGET	$8,181	$12,626	$18,201
Total family consumption	6,580	9,761	13,450
Food	2,440	3,183	4,020
Housing	1,627	2,908	4,386
Transportation	563	1,014	1,315
Clothing	696	995	1,456
Personal care	205	275	390
Medical care	660	664	692
Other family consumption	389	722	1,191
Other items	385	611	1,024
Taxes	1,216	2,254	3,727
Social security and disability	492	647	647
Personal income taxes	724	1,607	3,080

TABLE 6–5:
SUMMARY OF ANNUAL
FAMILY BUDGETS AT
3 LEVELS OF LIVING IN
THE UNITED STATES,
ACCORDING TO AREAS,
AUTUMN 1973
Source: U.S. Department of Labor, Bureau
of Labor Statistics.

AREA	Low TOTAL BUDGET	Intermediate TOTAL BUDGET	High TOTAL BUDGET
Urban United States	$ 8,181	$12,626	$18,201
Metropolitan areas	8,305	12,909	18,760
Nonmetroplitan areas	7,626	11,363	15,708
Northeast:			
Boston, Mass.	8,988	14,893	21,986
Buffalo, N. Y.	8,201	13,223	18,920
Hartford, Conn.	8,909	13,721	19,127
Lancaster, Pa.	8,101	12,385	17,470
New York-Northeastern N. J.	8,661	14,448	21,999
Philadelphia, Pa.-N. J.	8,415	13,022	18,851
Pittsburgh, Pa.	8,002	12,299	17,703
Portland, Maine	8,283	12,694	17,578
Nonmetropolitan areas	7,960	12,334	16,913
North Central:			
Cedar Rapids, Iowa	7,933	12,603	18,183
Champaign-Urbana, Ill.	8,582	12,943	18,723
Chicago, Ill.-Northwestern Ind.	8,635	13,213	18,919
Cincinnati, Ohio-Ky.-Ind.	7,733	12,137	16,896
Cleveland, Ohio	8,105	12,806	18,172
Dayton, Ohio	7,785	11,715	16,912
Detroit, Mich.	8,246	12,810	18,591
Green Bay, Wis.	7,922	12,557	18,701
Indianapolis, Ind.	8,171	12,738	18,074
Kansas City, Mo.-Kans.	8,098	12,481	18,126
Milwaukee, Wis.	8,220	13,211	19,186
Minneapolis-St. Paul, Minn.	8,269	13,020	18,970
St. Louis, Mo.-Ill.	8,056	12,390	17,691
Wichita, Kans.	7,796	11,876	16,919
Nonmetropolitan areas	7,921	11,760	16,471
South:			
Atlanta, Ga.	7,716	11,684	16,683
Austin, Tex.	7,233	10,959	15,743
Baltimore, Md.	8,425	12,519	18,192
Baton Rouge, La.	7,333	11,368	16,582
Dallas, Tex.	7,494	11,408	16,473
Durham, N. C.	7,923	12,111	17,206
Houston, Tex.	7,532	11,343	16,188
Nashville, Tenn.	7,583	11,667	16,633
Orlando, Fla.	7,827	11,358	16,210
Washington, D. C.-Md.-Va.	8,547	13,043	18,869
Nonmetropolitan areas	7,253	10,766	14,830

TABLE 6–5:
SUMMARY OF ANNUAL
FAMILY BUDGETS AT
3 LEVELS OF LIVING IN
THE UNITED STATES,
ACCORDING TO AREAS,
AUTUMN 1973
(Continued)

AREA	Low TOTAL BUDGET	Intermediate TOTAL BUDGET	High TOTAL BUDGET
West:			
Bakersfield, Calif.	$ 7,827	$11,761	$16,531
Denver, Colo.	7,976	12,107	17,422
Los Angeles-Long Beach, Calif.	8,525	12,520	18,489
San Diego, Calif.	8,229	12,216	17,763
San Francisco-Oakland, Calif.	8,939	13,378	19,316
Seattle-Everett, Wash.	8,407	12,667	17,924
Honolulu, Hawaii	9,924	14,937	21,901
Nonmetropolitan areas	7,898	11,338	15,730
Anchorage, Alaska	12,010	16,520	23,011

in New York City may be the equivalent of a high family budget in Podunk, Somewhere. But of course, people are generally paid more if they work in big, expensive cities. In fact, you would not expect that moving to a city would necessarily make you better off just because you were offered a higher salary.

Of course, such a comparison is only part of the information you need to decide whether or not to move from one city to another, or from the country to the city or vice versa. A move to the city involves a move to an area where a tremendous amount of cultural activity can be found that is unavailable in less-populated areas. "Specialization is a function of the size of the market," said Adam Smith, the father of modern economics. That means that the larger the size of the city, the more specialized services you'll be able to buy. Just think of how many movies, restaurants, theaters, operas, and concerts you can go to in cities of 5000 as compared to cities of 5 million. Many people are willing to pay a relatively high cost in such things as increased congestion, increased living expenses, and increased crime in order to have available the numerous recreational activities found in large metropolitan areas and not found in small rural areas. All of us would certainly like to be able to have the benefits of big cities without paying the costs, but so far nobody has figured out how that can happen. Again, we live in a world of scarcity where, generally, every benefit has a cost. You have to decide whether the benefit is worth the cost. And, of course, in deciding that, you have to bring into play your goals and values.

BUDGET-MAKING GOALS AND VALUE CLARIFICATION

Remember that in Chapter 2 we talked about value clarification, about how you decided what your goals were, what your values were, and what they meant in respect to how you should spend your time. Ultimately, this all related to what kind of life you want to lead. Now you can put this more-or-less abstract problem into perspective by applying it to an actual dollars-and-cents decision-making process—budget formulation. When you sit down alone or with the other members of your spending unit, you have to bring to the forefront the values that you place on the various things you want to do with the income available.   To be able to have a clear idea of your values, you first have to have formulated your goals and those of the spending unit as a whole.   Then you must set *priorities* among your goals.   These priorities will be linked to the three types of goals that you probably will set for yourself or your household, which might be set under the headings:

1.   short-term
2.   intermediate
3.   long-term

If, for example, one of your main long-term goals is to have a super-athletic family in which all members are as physically fit as possible, this will have strong implications for how you spend your income.   The decision may be made that the family will go to a tennis camp or join a tennis club, or that jogging uniforms for wet-weather running will be purchased for the family.

On the other hand, if part of your goals for your family or yourself happen to involve the appreciation of the arts, a large part of your budget may be allocated to the purchase of books, records and tapes, and theater, opera and concert tickets.

More basically, you may have the goal of a well-nourished and adequately housed family, or one that is medically protected or has adequate transportation. Here, however, your goals may involve choices. To have a well-nourished family, you may have to stint on housing; to have medical protection, you may have to stint on transportation needs.

Everybody's main goal, of course, can be subsumed under one heading —to be happy. The problem is clarifying your values enough so that you can establish goals that taken all together will spell happiness for you and those around you. When you formulate a budget, you can see exactly what these goals cost. You force yourself to rethink and to reformulate your values when you realize that either they are unattainable or extremely costly in the sense that you must give up the opportunity to do numerous other desired or necessary things.

TRADE-OFFS

Any seeming overemphasis here on the problem of trade-offs should not upset you, for they are the key to understanding why families and other spending units often run into so many problems. Frequently, it is not realized that trade-offs must be made, and hence when they come up unexpectedly, they seem to be either one person's fault or another's when in fact no one is at fault. Rather, nature is at fault, because nature is so stingy and does not give us everything we want. That is, nature makes things scarce for us, and ultimately the scarcity reflects itself in the income of the spending unit—an income that is insufficient to satisfy everyone's desires and wants and needs.

For example, assume that you and the other members of the spending unit have decided that physical fitness is an important value you wish to maintain so that your goal for the next several years is good health, stamina, and athletic prowess for the children and the adults in the family. There are many ways you can accomplish this goal. Jogging is probably the cheapest way of building stamina; after the initial outlay for warm, waterproof suits for the winter and sturdy running shoes, there is nothing else to buy. But not everybody can be satisfied with jogging; and even if they are, they may want to engage in more competitive sports. While the children may be able to engage in competitive sports that require no additional outlays in the family's budget plan, the parents might be less fortunate. If they wish to engage in sports such as, for example, tennis or golf, equipment might have to be purchased, fees might have to be paid for the use of courts or greens, and so on.

The benefit of laying budget-making out on the table, so to speak, is that it becomes difficult to escape knowing the actual cost of attaining the goal that came from clarification of the family's values. Those members of the spending unit who will feel cheated if, say, the parents decide to play tennis indoors during the winter, can express their feelings, and perhaps a compromise can be reached. But in this method of formulating a budget, individual values can come into conflict and must be compromised. If compromise is accomplished in a democratic way through, for example, the formulation of monthly budgets, then those in conflict may be willing to compromise because they know that in future months they will gain.

Goal definition and value clarification are integral parts of budget formation and may be considered the only way to arrive at a good budget. A good budget, of course, is one that works and a budget itself has many tasks to accomplish besides keeping a family's spending in line. No one should try to overwork that poor budget, however. It will not miraculously bring family happiness to the unhappy family. It will also not work if it lacks an equal chance of being an underestimate as well as an overestimate of the family's spending. In fact, if the budget is made always to be broken in the upward direction, then for many families it is just as bad as having no budget at all. The accusations start coming fast and furiously; fingers are pointed at the person who may have overdone the spending in a particular budget category. Such a spending unit is right back where it started from without any budget at all.

A budget also cannot be considered a cure-all in times when there are big changes in income.

WHAT HAPPENS WHEN INCOME SUDDENLY CHANGES

Often families experience windfall gains and losses in their incomes. You are all aware of the plight of families whose breadwinner is suddenly out of work. Spending must be drastically reduced, if the spending unit is to escape financial ruin. Here a budget is necessary. If a family finds itself in financial straits, a well-constructed budget that has been followed over many months or many years can in fact present the family with categories where they know they can cut back. And when the cutback has to come, again it probably is best to involve the entire family. Unilateral decisions will not be any more appreciated in this situation than in any other.

Every year, many U. S. families suffer a generally unanticipated decrease in income. When this happens, there is a high probability of family discontent. Fights will break out among members more frequently when income has dropped below normal without warning than when such a drop was expected. Unanticipated income drops may also require otherwise nonworking members of the spending unit to seek employment if the income level is to be kept high enough to satisfy the basic wants of the family. In such a situation it is helpful to be psychologically prepared for the increased discord that will come about from a big drop in income. Also, the budget itself, as mentioned above, can help pinpoint the areas of least need where expenditures can be cut back.

Also, during any one year many families find themselves with more income than they anticipated. Would that all of us found ourselves in that situation often! Unfortunately, not too many of us do. But when it happens, a budget can again be useful, for without it, unilateral decisions on how to spend the extra income may be made to the detriment of some members of the spending unit; discord may again occur because some people will think they are being cheated. Moreover, without budgets, families that discover they will have a higher income in the next twelve months may end up in financial distress by overcommitting themselves. Each member of the spending unit individually starts making plans on how he or she will spend the extra money, but when all those individual increments are added up, the sum is greater than the increment in income. The result is disaster—financial hardship through overspending when income is rising. The way to avoid this is to expand the budget process in the democratic spending unit council to take account of anticipating the problems inherent in a sudden, unpredicted rise in income.

FITTING IT ALL INTO A LIFETIME PLAN

Today there is much talk about early retirement and the decisions that must be made if it is to be a happy period, and also much talk about more leisure time to be spent and the need to purchase more leisure-related products. These matters should be considered as part of a lifetime plan, one that is revised periodically to take account of changing values, income, and consumption situations. To some extent, lifetime planning can involve taking the spontaneity out of life. But spontaneity need not be lost. Nobody said lifetime plans could not be altered. Their purpose is to rationalize your behavior as a consumer in the most fundamental meaning of the word. If you have certain values and goals and you set them out clearly for yourself and your family, then you can work towards them and have ways of measuring your progress. This can give you a sense of satisfaction that enables you to feel tranquil about life itself. If, however, you are maniacal about your plans, any failure to meet them may cause grief. The suggestion might be then that if you can use plans to mold your decisions so that no important elements of your values or goals are omitted, then by all means sit down right now and figure out where you are and where you want eventually to be. As we mentioned before, such a method is a very effective way to give you motivation, if motivation is what you want, and is also a very effective way to get things done instead of having them hang over your head and make you miserable. Below are a few hints about how you can make lifetime planning work for you. Of course, there are no cut and dried rules, and you may not even want to bother with such methods. It is for you to decide.

DAY TO DAY TASKS

For many people, the best way to handle day to day tasks is to make a list. Lists are not enough, however; all the items on your list must be weighted every day to make sure you get done what is most important to get done. Most people who start making lists of tasks to be done tend to do the simplest one first simply to be able to cross something off the list.

EXHIBIT 6–2   **PERSONAL TIME PLAN**

FIXED APPOINTMENTS   ITEMS TO DO

8:30   Class   A–1.   Read 2 chapters in consumer
                                   econ book
9:30   Class   A–2.   Study 2 hours for math quiz
                            O–3.   Wash clothes
10:30   B–4.   Write parents
                            O–5.   Swim at gym
11:30   O–6.   Call about part-time job
                            O–7.   Read some more of novel
12:30 Lunch with friends

1:30   Class

2:30

3:30   Dentist's Appt.

4:30

5:30   KEY: A = do first
                                   B = do after A's
Evening   O = fit in odd times

ORGANIZATION IS THE WATCHWORD

You should avoid this tendency unless at first you need a psychological boost to get you doing the things you really should be doing. One way to escape such a tendency is to use a system whereby you give the highest weight, A, to those tasks that are most important (and usually the hardest to get around to doing), B to those that are of secondary importance, and O to those that are really quite unimportant (and usually the easiest to do). Now, obviously you will not finish your list every day; in fact, most people find it best to make the list too long so that they always run a little short of their desired goals. As long as this does not frustrate you, it can be a useful aid in getting your life running as smoothly as you would like it to.

Next comes a weekly list of things to do. This can be more general and can also guide you in figuring out what to do each day. You might jot down the days you think you should do the different things and therefore include those tasks on your list for given days.

Much more important to you as a consumer are monthly and yearly lists of goals, tasks, and ideas. The monthly list, for example, would tell you when to have scheduled maintenance on your car, when to have services performed on household appliances, what days sales are coming up at various stores, and so on. The yearly list, of course, can do the same thing but with an even greater scope. This list will tell you what goals you want to have attained by the end of the year, what purchases you would like to make, and other such items. This way you can decide well in advance the kind of savings program you have to undertake and also the composition of your spending program so that you spend in such a way as to maximize your happiness from your income. If you keep telling yourself, "I really wish I could get around to affording a new camera or a new stereo," you can stop complaining about never getting the things you want by being realistic, making these part of your yearly goals, and saving towards them so that in fact you buy them by a specific date. When you are working toward a goal, it is easier to make the appropriate decisions and take the appropriate actions.

Your goals can be stretched to five years, 10 years, and even 15 years, but of course they will be much broader and will be revised every year. Your five-year goal may be to acquire a bachelor's degree, to learn how to ski better or to play tennis better, to become fluent in Spanish, to become an active participant in a minority affairs program, and so on. You have to work out a program to attain those goals, and here your yearly plans come in; next you go to your monthly plan, weekly plan, and daily plan. Every once in a while you have to take stock of where you are and of your progress towards all of these different goals for the different time-period plans. You will probably want to do this with those around you who would be most affected by these different plans. In fact, it would not be a bad idea to have a family planning period whereby the family council gathers to decide where the family stands and where it wants to be a year from now, five years from now, and so on. If a new house with a view of the ocean is really strongly desired by everyone in the family, then a program to attain that goal can be worked out. That program might require sacrificing many consumption expenditures over the next few years in order to save up the down payment on that house.

Long-range planning is quite simple in concept but sometimes difficult to put into operation, mainly because people do not always like to face up to the difficulties of attaining certain goals. For example, the only way to attain a higher level of consumption activities is to make more income, and the only way you can generally make more income is to become more productive in your job or to change jobs, moving to one where you are in fact more productive. That may involve going to night school, taking additional training, working on weekends, and so on. If you are aware of such requirements, then you know the cost of getting to your goal for yourself and/or your family.

SUMMARY

1.   Even the richest among us do not have an unlimited budget and must therefore make choices.

2.   Budgeting or making a spending plan forces you to realize that you do face the constraint of a limited income and you must make trade-offs among those things you desire to purchase.

3.   Democratic decision-making within a spending unit can involve a family council in which the budget is decided upon.

4.   Teenagers represent an important spending group in our society. Teenage spending habits are usually acquired from parents' spending habits. Therefore, the way to have a teenager become a rational consumer is to set a good example and to perhaps get him or her to formulate a personal budget.

5.   A typical household in the United States spends about one-fourth of its budget on housing and about one-fourth on food. As a family's income goes up, the percentage spent on food goes down and the percentage spent on housing goes up.

6.   Before deciding to live in different cities or areas in the United States, it is worthwhile to check with U.S. Department of Labor statistics on the cost of living in these areas, for they vary widely. An income of, say, $200 a week means a different standard of living in New York City from what it means in Ames, Iowa, because the cost of living is higher in New York City.

7.   When setting your goal structure, it is important to put in priorities. These can be worked into short-term, intermediate, and long-term goals. These goals must be made consistent with reality, and that is where trade-offs come in.

8.   Your goals and values relate to your day-to-day behavior, which can best be handled by establishing a personal time plan and then reviewing what you have done at different points in the year from those personal time plans.

**QUESTIONS FOR
THOUGHT AND
DISCUSSION**

1.   Do you know anybody who does not face a budget constraint?

2.   Do you think citizens of the United States have different problems in meeting their budget constraints than do, say, citizens of India or Turkey?

3.   It is sometimes argued that budget making, personal time plans, etc., cut down on one's spontaneity. Do you agree or disagree? Is there any way the two can be reconciled?

4.   Democratic decision-making by way of a family council sounds old-fashioned to many individuals. What might be a more modern alternative if this is indeed the case?

5.   How much say-so do you think a teenager should have in family budget making?

6.   Why would Americans end up spending more on housing as their incomes went up than on, say, food?

7.   Can you explain why the cost of living is higher in the city than in the country?

8.   Why must trade-offs be made?

9.   "If I only had 50 percent more income, I could buy everything I wanted." Evaluate this statement. Have you ever made it? Has it proven to be true?

10.   Very few people do serious lifetime planning. However, do not many individuals implicitly have a "plan"?

THINGS TO DO

1.   Check with the latest edition of the United Nations book about income around the world. Does the United States still lead? Will it continue to lead the rest of the world in per capita GNP?

2.   Make a list of the typical items that a teenager might buy. Do the consumer choices that have to be made by a teenager differ from those that have to be made by an adult?

3.   With the help of your reference librarian, go back to the earliest publication you can find from the Department of Labor, Bureau of Labor Statistics, and see what the average American family budget looked like then. How has it changed over the years? Are we spending more or less on food? On housing? What about taxes?

4.   Go to your reference library and look at the United States Department of Labor cost of living indexes for various cities. Does the city you live in appear to be more expensive than the average? Can you figure out why or why not?

5.   Make a detailed list of your short-term, intermediate, and long-term goals. How do these goals fit in with your overall values?

6.   Work up a personal time plan for the next five days. Use as an example the one given in this chapter. After the five days are up, go back

to see how effectively you used your time. Did that time plan allow you to make more rational use of your time? If it did not, why not? Try to figure out how a time plan can work into a lifetime plan.

**SELECTED
READINGS**

A Guide to Budgeting for the Family, HG–108 (Washington, D. C.: U. S. Department of Agriculture, Office of Information).

Bailard, Thomas E., David L. Biehl, and Ronald W. Kaiser, *Personal Money Management* (Chicago: Science Research Associates, Inc.), 1973.

Helping Families Manage Their Finances, HERR #21, U. S. Government Printing Office.

How to Buy Your Dreams with Cash Left Over (Deerfield, Illinois: Jackson Hinch, Inc.).

Make Your Money Count, HXT–34 (Berkeley: Agricultural Extension Service, University of California), 1963.

Margolius, Sidney, *How to Make the Most of Your Money* (New York: Appleton-Century-Crofts), 1969.

Morse, Richard L. D., *Money Management Process* (Manhattan, Kansas: Department of Family Economics, Kansas State University), 1966.

Mumey, Glen A., *Personal Economic Planning* (New York: Holt, Rinehart and Winston), 1972.

Ryan, Mary E., and E. Scott Maynes, "The Excessively Indebted: Who and Why," *Journal of Consumer Affairs,* Winter 1969.

Smith, Carlton, and Richard P. Pratt, *The Time-Life Book of Family Finance* (Boston: Little, Brown), 1970.

"Who's Going Bankrupt and Why," *U. S. News and World Report,* July 19, 1971.

CONSUMER ISSUE II
How to Budget Your Limited Income

Once you decide to do some positive money management, you have to get practical: you have to figure out a budget, and then you have to stick to it. The budget, remember, is a planning tool to help you hold in check undirected spending. In this consumer issue we will look at two different types of budget for two different situations; one is for college students, and the other is for persons not in a college living situation.

STEPS IN BUDGET-MAKING

Very briefly, after your goals are determined, the following basic steps can be followed in creating a spending plan. Goals are implicit in the budget sheet of Table II–1.

1. Keep records.

2. Determine **fixed expenses,** such as rent and any other contractual payments that must be made even if they come infrequently, such as insurance and taxes.

3. Determine **flexible expenses,** such as for food and for clothing.

4. Balance your fixed plus flexible expenditures with your available income. If a surplus exists, you can apply it to your goals. If there is a deficit, then you must re-examine your flexible expenditures.

Now let's go on to some specific budgets that you might wish to work out.

Fixed Expenses: Expenses that occur at specified times and cannot be altered after the fact. A house payment would be considered a fixed expense once the house is purchased or rented. A car payment would be thought of similarly.

Flexible or Variable Expenses: Expenses that can be changed in the short run. The amount of money you spend on food can be considered a flexible expense, for you can buy higher- or lower-quality food than you are now doing.

TABLE II–1 A GENERAL WAY TO BUDGET

CASH FORECAST, MONTH OF _____

cash on hand and in checking account, end of previous period

	ESTIMATED	ACTUAL
Receipts		
net pay		
borrowed		
other		
TOTAL CASH AVAILABLE DURING PERIOD		
Fixed Payments		
mortgage or rent		
life insurance		
fire insurance		
auto insurance		
savings		
local taxes		
loan or other debt		
other		
TOTAL FIXED PAYMENTS		
Variable Payments		
water		
light		
fuel		
telephone		
medical		
car		
food		
clothing		
nonrecurring large payments		
contributions, recreation, etc.		
other		
TOTAL VARIABLE PAYMENTS		
TOTAL ALL PAYMENTS		
Recapitulation		
total cash available		
total payments		
cash balance, end of period		

COLLEGE STUDENT BUDGETS

There are approximately 8½ million men and women in American universities and colleges. While many students live at home, many others live in dormitories, fraternity and sorority houses, rooming houses, and apartments. Students who live away from home can rely only on themselves to make decisions about what to spend their limited incomes on, whether those incomes be obtained from parents, scholarships, or part-time jobs.

Table II–2 presents a suggested budget form for college students. Expenses are anticipated both for the college year and for each month. College students have many expenses that other people do not, such as tuition, fees, books and supplies, and dues to fraternities,

sororities, and honorary societies. But students can also anticipate income that most others do not: gifts from parents and others, and scholarships and prizes. All of these have to be taken into account, or else the budget content will prove to be fairly inaccurate and of less value than it could be.

You can alter the budget form to fit your particular situation. But the key to making it work for you is to go over it every month and see how close to your budget specifications you actually came in your spending. If you really are out of touch with reality, this is how you can find out, and the sooner the better. How many of you in college have friends who continuously come around to you at the end of each month for a "light touch" so they can

TABLE II–2 SUGGESTED BUDGET FORM FOR COLLEGE STUDENTS

						MONTH					
	YEAR	9	10	11	12	1	2	3	4	5	6
EXPENSES											
College											
Tuition											
Fees											
Board											
Room											
Books, supplies											
Fraternity or sorority											
Honorary societies, clubs											
Transportation to and fro											
Other											
SUBTOTAL											
Personal											
Clothing											
Cleaning, pressing											
Laundry											

TABLE II–2—Continued

| | YEAR | MONTH | | | | | | | | | |
		9	10	11	12	1	2	3	4	5	6
Personal—Continued											
Dental care											
Medical											
Barber or beauty shop											
Toilet articles											
Telephone, telegraph											
Postage											
Newspapers, magazines											
Donations											
Gifts											
Recreation											
Beverages											
Snacks											
Tobacco											
Insurance											
Automobile											
Local transportation											
Taxes											
Bank charges											
Other											
TOTAL											
INCOME											
Gifts from parents											
Gifts from others											
Drawn from savings											
Current earnings											
Scholarship											
Prizes											
Other											
TOTAL											

buy food until their next check comes at the first of the following month? Such spending behavior is generally due to an inability to realize that a limited budget means you just can not buy everything you want when you want it. A more-or-less permanent budget program that is reviewed every month is one solution to such a problem.

Of course, a budget is not for everybody. You may decide that budgeting your limited income is not worthwhile. You can buy so few things that it really does not matter. You know you have to eat and pay for a room, but in addition to that you do not spend enough money to bother figuring out what you can and cannot buy. Thus, for many of you it may be quite rational to get by without drawing up a budget because the time spent in budgeting would be in excess of the potential benefits. However, you might want to consider a budget and planning program as an investment in money-management skills for later years when in fact you will have a lot more money than you need to just cover basic necessities. Often the rate of return to such an investment can be high indeed.

BUDGETING FOR THE NONSTUDENT SPENDING UNIT

Those of you in nonstudent family units face a slightly different problem from the college student's. Your income is generally more predictable and is less a function of the generosity of others. But your expenses are also generally much higher, and involve payments on life insurance policies, mortgages, and so on. Naturally, you would have to expect a slightly different set of classifications for your budget than does the college student. Tables II–3 through II–7 are examples of possible budget sheets you might want to use every month. These budget sheets, remember, would be worked into a yearly expenditure tally. And this expenditure tally for the year fits in with a lifetime plan, which you of course

have decided on with the other members of the spending unit, and which you of course change as your values change, your goals change, and your economic situation changes.

Notice that in the budget sheets there are entries for savings. We cover savings in more detail in Chapter 14. Suffice it to say here that you save in order to optimize your level of consumption throughout your lifetime. In other words, you save to provide for those periods when your income is very low so that your consumption—that is, your expenditures for things you like to buy—does not have to fall drastically. Saving allows you to smooth out your consumption expenditures even though your income may be variable. We all realize that we have to save for the day when, as older persons, we no longer can work. But what we do not realize is that we also save for the day when something happens to us as younger persons that temporarily keeps us from working. Saving for a rainy day is a trite but true analysis of the act of saving. The savings umbrella allows you to keep dry during the storm. After the storm is over, then you start again to repair that umbrella for the next time you need it. But more on that in Chapter 14.

KEEPING RECORDS

Your budget-making, whether you be a college student, a single person living alone, or the head of a family, will be useless if you do not keep records. The only way to make sure that you are carrying out the plans implicit in your budget is by having records to show what you are actually spending. The best way to have records is to write everything down, but that becomes time consuming and time is costly. Another way to keep records is to write checks for everything. That way at the end of different months you can put the checks into different categories. (Many banks offer no-cost checking accounts if you keep a certain minimum balance of, say, $200.)

TABLE II–3 MONTHLY LIVING EXPENSES. Does not include fixed monthly obligations, important future expenses, or savings and investments.

Market purchases: food, beverages, sundries $_____

Automobile: operation, servicing, minor repairs   _____

Utility bills: electricity, gas, water, garbage, telephone, cable TV   _____

Laundry and cleaning   _____

Clothing   _____

Incidental expenses   _____

Medical and dental expenses, prescription drugs (not covered by insurance)   _____

Adult allowances   _____

Children's allowances   _____

Family recreation: eating out, hobbies, movies, home entertainment   _____

Miscellaneous labor: babysitter, housecleaning, etc.   _____

Subscriptions: newspapers, magazines   _____

Dues: union, lodge, club (other than deducted from paycheck)   _____

Education: evening courses, school charges and fees, special lessons   _____

Religious contributions   _____

Charity contributions (other than deducted from paycheck)   _____

Unexpected expenses   _____

Other expenses   _____

TOTAL MONTHLY LIVING EXPENSES (Average Month) $_____

TABLE Ii–4 FIXED MONTHLY PAYMENTS. Fixed by lease, mortgage, contract, court order or conscience

Rent or mortgage payment on home $ _____

Auto loan payment—car no. 1   _____

Auto loan payment—car no. 2   _____

Appliance, TV, furniture loans   _____

Personal loans   _____

Other loans   _____

Credit card payments   _____

Major store contracts   _____

Other contract debts or payments   _____

Taxes due   _____

Regular contributions to others—parents, etc.   _____

Alimony or child support   _____

TOTAL FIXED MONTHLY PAYMENTS $

TABLE II—5 IMPORTANT FUTURE EXPENSES. Divide total of yearly expenses by twelve for average amount to be saved each month for big payments to come.

MONTH	TAXES—FEES	INSURANCE	SHOPPING	VACATION	OTHER	TOTAL EXPENSES
JANUARY						
FEBRUARY						
MARCH						
APRIL						
MAY						
JUNE						
JULY						
AUGUST						
SEPTEMBER						
OCTOBER						
NOVEMBER						
DECEMBER						
TOTALS						

TABLE II–6 MONTHLY MONEY PLANNER.

INCOME

Salary and wages—(take-home pay) husband $_____

Salary and wages—(take-home pay) wife   _____

Interest (average month)   _____

Income from securities (average month)   _____

Received from income property (average month)   _____

Other monthly income   _____

                    TOTAL CASH INCOME FOR AVERAGE MONTH $_____

EXPENSES

Total monthly living expenses $_____

Total fixed monthly payments   _____

Total future expenses—monthly average   _____

                              TOTAL AVERAGE MONTHLY EXPENSES $_____

                INCOME AVAILABLE FOR SAVINGS AND INVESTMENTS $_____
                     (Total expenses subtracted from total income)

TABLE II–7 YEARLY MONEY PLANNER.

MONTH	INCOME	LIVING EXPENSES	FIXED PAYMENTS	FUTURE EXPENSES	SAVINGS AND INVESTMENTS	TOTAL ALLOCATIONS
JANUARY						
FEBRUARY						
MARCH						
APRIL						
MAY						
JUNE						
JULY						
AUGUST						
SEPTEMBER						
OCTOBER						
NOVEMBER						
DECEMBER						
TOTALS						

SAVINGS	NOW	END OF YEAR	INVESTMENTS	NOW	END OF YEAR
Emergency fund			Savings bonds		
Education fund			Mutual funds— securities		
Special purposes			Real estate		
Other			Other		
TOTAL			TOTAL		

SUMMARY

1. Budget making requires (1) keeping records; (2) determining fixed and flexible expenses; (3) balancing fixed plus flexible expenses with available income; and finally (4) reorganizing and redetermining priorities if there is a budget surplus or deficit.

2. A cash forecast for each month can be estimated and then compared with what actually happened after the fact. Any difference must be made up and can be a signal as to excessive spending.

3. A college student's budget is slightly different from a general budget because of regular college expenses that come in and also because of gifts from parents and others that may occur irregularly.

4. Record-keeping is essential to effective budgeting. Perhaps the easiest way to keep records is to use a checking account and save the canceled checks.

QUESTIONS FOR THOUGHT
AND DISCUSSION

1. Do you feel that a budget is worthwhile for young people? When would it not be worthwhile?

2. Does making a cash forecast seem too time-consuming for you?

3. What individuals would be most likely to benefit from making detailed budgets?

4. Is it possible to live through a life without ever having to worry about meeting your budget?

THINGS TO DO

1. By all means, start making out your own budget.

SELECTED READINGS

"Family Budgets in Forty Big Cities," *U.S. News & World Report,* July 2, 1973, pp. 80ff.

"Five-Year Plan for Managing Your Money," *Changing Times,* October 1973, pp. 43–46.

Holland, B., "How to Stop Scrubbing and Start Living," *McCall's,* June 1974.

Pellegrino, V., "Teaching Your Child About Dollars and Sense," *Today's Health,* October 1973, pp. 50–55.

"To Save or Invest Successfully, Make a Money Plan," *Changing Times,* May 1974, pp. 15–18.

☐ How much are Americans in debt, and what are the characteristics of that debt?
☐ What are the various sources of credit?
☐ Why do individuals borrow?
☐ What are interest rates all about, and what is their relationship to inflation?
☐ Can interest rate ceilings help consumers?
☐ How does the Truth-in-Lending Act affect you?
☐ How are banks regulated?

GLOSSARY OF NEW TERMS

Bankruptcy: The state of having come under the provisions of the law which entitle a person's creditors to have his or her estate administered for their benefit.

Consumer Durables: Goods that consumers buy which last more than a short period of time. Examples of consumer durables are stereos, television sets, cars, and houses.

Service Flow: The flow of benefits that are received from an item that has been purchased or made. Consumer durables generally give a service flow that lasts over a period of time. For example, the service flow from a stereo may be a certain amount of satisfaction received from it every year for five years.

Collateral: The backing that in many cases an individual puts up to obtain a loan. Whatever is placed as collateral for a loan can be sold off in order to repay that loan if the debtor cannot pay it off as specified in the loan agreement. For example, the collateral for a new car loan is generally the new car itself. If the finance company does not get paid for its car loan, it then can repossess the car, sell it, and thereby attempt to pay itself off.

Inflationary Premium: An amount added to the cost of obtaining a loan to take account of the effects of inflation. If, for example, prices are rising at 5 percent a year, a dollar loaned out today will have a value of only 95¢ when it is received a year from now. The person who loaned that dollar will require an inflationary premium of 5 percent to take account of the decreased value of the dollar to be paid back.

Transactions Costs: The costs associated with any economic activity. For example, the transactions costs of obtaining a loan might involve searching for the best deal, reading a lengthy contract, and so on.

Right of Rescission: The right to back down, or "bow out," on a contract or an agreement that has been signed. For example, before you sign an agreement to buy a set of encyclopedias, you might want to obtain the right of rescission during a three-day period.

In 1786 in the city of Concord, Massachusetts, the scene of one of the first battles of the Revolution, there were three times as many people in debtors prison as there were in prison for all other crimes combined. In Worcester County the ratio was even higher—20 to one. Most of the prisoners were small farmers who could not pay their debts. In August of 1786 mobs of musket-bearing farmers seized county courthouses to halt the trials of debtors. Led by Daniel Shays, a captain from the Continental Army, the rebels launched an attack on the Federal Arsenal at Springfield; although they were repulsed, their rebellion continued to grow into the winter. Finally, George Washington wrote to a friend:

> For God's sake, tell me what is the cause of these commotions. Do they proceed from licentiousness, British influence disseminated by the Tories, or real grievances which admit to redress? If the latter, why were they delayed until the public mind had become so agitated? If the former, why are not the powers of government tried at once?

THE AMERICAN IN DEBT

Debt, as you can see, has been a problem in the United States from its colonial beginnings. In fact, The Society for the Amelioration of the Condition of Debtors was formed shortly before the American Revolution by a group of New York businessmen. Today, the overextended American is still with us. He or she is not the type of person you might think. Instead of a poor ghetto dweller in a disadvantaged situation (who has a hard time getting credit anyway), the overextended American is more accurately portrayed as a reasonably well-off blue-collar worker who makes $900 a month, typically with a wife and two or more children. But his indebtedness (excluding the mortgage on his house) is in the neighborhood of $4000 to $5000. While he might be what people call "credit drunk," a compulsive buyer, he is more realistically described as simply an average American who bit by bit got into debt deep over his head. When he starts to drown, he declares personal bankruptcy.

THE OVEREXTENDED AMERICAN

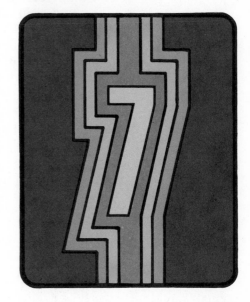

BANKRUPTCIES

Bankruptcies are on the rise. Every year almost a quarter of a million Americans seek refuge in personal bankruptcy proceedings from what they consider to be excessive debts. The Constitution, you will remember, allows Congress "to establish an uniform Rule of Naturalization, and uniform Laws on the subject of Bankruptcies throughout the United States." So we have Chapter XIII of the Federal Bankruptcy Act to help us out. In 1960, there were not even a hundred thousand personal nonbusiness bankruptcies. By 1970, there were almost 180,000, and by 1975 the estimate is 300,000. Just because a person has filed for bankruptcy does not mean his or her life is ruined. In fact, many of those who have gone through bankruptcy proceedings eventually start using credit again; one estimate is that 80 percent of those who file for bankruptcy use credit and are in debt trouble again within five years.

In spite of people who continue to go into debt over their heads, and in spite of all the cries of the overextended American, the amount of debt outstanding in the United States keeps on going up.

**THE INDEBTED
SOCIETY**

At least 50 percent of all Americans have outstanding installment debt at any given time. In 1971, the median debt for families with debt was almost $1000. For families of adults under 45 years of age and no children, fully 25 percent had $2000 or more of outstanding debt. Figure 7–1

FIGURE 7–1
AGGREGATE DEBT IN
THE UNITED STATES
Aggregate indebtedness
of Americans has been
on the rise for the last
two and a half decades,
reaching over $2 trillion
in 1974. We also
indicate the per capita
amount of debt in the
United States, corrected
for increases in the price
level. By 1975, it
reached a figure of
$14,000 expressed in
terms of 1967 pur-
chasing power. Source:
*Survey of Current
Business,* May and June
issues.

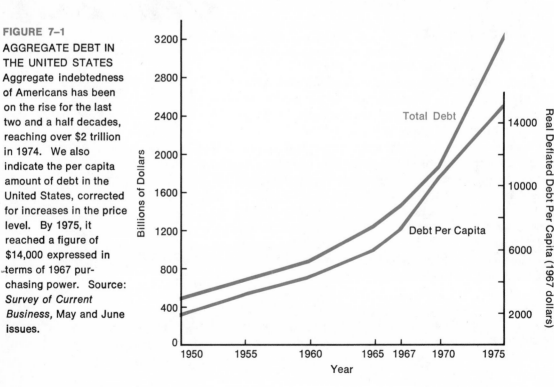

TABLE 7–1:
CREDIT BREAKDOWNS
Source: *Survey of
Current Business,*
October 1974.

	DOLLARS (billions)
Total credit outstanding	187.4
Installment	154.5
Automobile paper	52.8
Other consumer goods paper	49.3
Repair and modernization loans	8.2
Personal loans	44.2
Noninstallment	
Single payment loans	13.2
Charge accounts	9.3
Service credit	10.4
Installment credit	
Extended	15.2
Repaid	12.9
Consumer installment credit by holder	
Total	
Financial institutions	136.9
Commercial banks	73.3
Finance companies	38.9
Credit unions	21.4
Miscellaneous lenders	3.3
Retail outlets	17.6

shows the total amount of aggregate debt in the United States over the past few decades. It has risen to a monumental $2¼ trillion and is expected to rise even more. Of course, part of this is due to inflation and another part is due to a rising population. For a better perspective, the bottom line in Figure 7–1 gives the inflation-corrected per capita debt in the United States.

We break down the total credit into categories in Table 7–1. Today, installment debt repayment now takes almost 15 percent of disposable personal income. People get credit from a variety of formal sources which we now look at.

**SOURCES OF
CREDIT**

There are numerous places where you can go to get credit when you want to buy something on time. While not exhaustive, the list below indicates the range of possibilities.

COMMERCIAL
BANKS

The most obvious place to go for credit is a commercial bank. Today, the personal loan departments of commercial banks make perhaps almost 60 percent of loans for automobile purchases as well as almost a third of all loans for other consumer goods.

FINANCE
COMPANIES

Finance companies buy installment credit from retail merchants; in this way, retailers sell the risk involved in loaning money. For example, a finance company may take over title to the car you bought. It collects a monthly or weekly payment from you and hands over the title to the car when you have finished the payments. Finance companies supply almost 30 percent of automobile credit and account for about 35 percent of all personal loans.

CONSUMER FINANCE
COMPANIES

Consumer finance companies are small loan companies generally making small loans to consumers at relatively high rates of interest. These are the loan companies you hear advertised on radio and on TV, and are the largest suppliers of installment cash loans—that is, loans that consumers obtain for buying other things than such durable consumer goods as cars, TVs, and stereos. There are perhaps 25,000 licensed consumer finance offices in America today.

CREDIT UNIONS

Credit unions are special consumer cooperative agencies that are usually chartered by various states and the federal government. You have to be a member of a credit union in order to use it. Teachers generally have their own credit unions, as do workers in large unions or companies. Credit unions account for about 13 percent of all consumer installment credit.

CREDIT CARDS

Today, more than 50 percent of all families have at least one nongasoline credit card, and fully 25 percent have three or more. You are probably familiar with the most widely known of these—Mastercharge, BankAmericard, and Chargex. There are about 6000 banks today that offer Mastercharge, and 4000 that offer BankAmericard.

**NONCREDIT
CARDS—PAY CASH
AND PAY LESS**

When you use a credit card, the merchant accepting it generally has to pay the credit card company a fee of up to 8 percent. Moreover, he doesn't get his money until he turns in the credit slips and they are processed. Hence, if you pay him cash, you save him some money. There is a way in which you can sometimes get some of the saving passed on to you.

Today there are at least three plans at work which will sell you a "cash" card that you can show to member merchants and obtain a discount on the products or services you buy. By the beginning of 1975, it was estimated that almost 400,000 members are using their cash cards at the 3000 or so outlets accepting them. By comparison, however, BankAmericard alone is held by almost 27,000,000 people and is accepted by about 1,000,000 outlets in the United States. In any event, we list below the three plans in effect at the beginning of 1975.

1. Equity Club International
   Jenkintown, Pennsylvania   19046

   Discounts available at about 3000 outlets with New York City area best represented.

2. Savers Clubs of America
   Shaker Heights, Ohio   44122

   Available through about 25 savings and loan associations and banks in 11 states.

3. United International Club, Inc. (UNIC)
   Beverly Hills, California   90212

   The UNIC card is accepted at about 800 outlets, mostly in Los Angeles.

**LOANS ON YOUR
LIFE INSURANCE**

If you have a life insurance policy with a cash value (whole or straight life, usually),[1] then you may indeed be able to obtain a relatively low-cost loan on your life insurance policy. We discuss various life insurance policies in Chapter 13. Suffice it to say here that you usually pay something less than 10 percent for a loan on the value of your policy. You cannot be turned down for a loan from your insurance company, and no questions are asked about what the money will be used for. Your credit rating has nothing to do with whether or not you get the "loan." You can take as long or as short a period as you wish to repay. In fact, you need not repay at all if you choose. However, whenever the policy becomes payable, either because it matures or the owner of it dies, any outstanding loan is deducted from the amount of the insurance claim that the company must pay. Hence, any loan you take out reduces your insurance protection.

Since there are so many ways to borrow and so much debt around, there must be a reason why all this is happening.

WHY BORROW?

Why should you ever borrow money? Some of you may be puritanical about it and answer, "There is no reason that you should ever borrow money. Pay cash for everything and never have debt hanging over your head." This is the attitude throughout much of traditional Europe today; there is a moral dislike of borrowing as a way to purchase goods and services.

The reason most of us borrow, however, is very simple. For example, you have decided that you want to buy an automobile. Now, you are not buying an automobile per se. What you are really buying is the *services* from that automobile for each day, week, month, and year that you will have it. In fact, what is really important to you is the cost per service flow per period. In other words, what does it cost you per month to op-

[1] See p. 310 for an explanation of these policies.

erate that Ford, as compared to that VW or that Toyota? What will it cost you per month or per year to buy a new car instead of keeping your old one? Cars are sometimes called consumer durables, just as are houses, TVs, stereos, and other things that last a relatively long time. You do not consume them immediately; rather, you consume the services from them over a period of time: they are durable.

Now, when you go to the movies, you consume that movie during the hour and a half or two you are there, and you also pay for that movie when you consume it. When you go out to dinner, you eat the meal and that is the end of it. You pay for it on the spot, usually. What are you doing when you consume things and pay for them at the same time? You are synchronizing the payment for the good or service with the rate at which you are consuming it. Why not think of this as the reason for borrowing? You want to synchronize the payments for the services you are consuming from a consumer durable, such as an automobile, with the services themselves. Therefore, you do not feel obliged to pay for the car with cash because you are going to be using it over a certain number of years. What you decide to do usually is to purchase the automobile on time. You decide to borrow. *When you borrow, then, you are merely synchronizing your cash outlay to correspond more or less with the* service flow *from the good you purchased.* That is why you may wish to borrow.

DON'T BE FOOLED

A very astute savings and loan association once ran an ad in some national magazines. The ad pointed out that if you were to save for 36 months and buy a car with the savings, the car would cost you, say, $5000 and you would have had to put in the bank only $4600, the rest being made up by the interest you received over the three years. On the other hand, pointed out the ad, if you bought the car immediately and paid for it over 36 months, not only would you not receive interest on your savings, but you would have to pay a finance charge on the installment debt. The total price of the car might be $5800. There is obviously a big difference between the two: $4,600 and $5,800. The conclusion, according to the savings and loan association: it is better to save now and buy later than to buy now and go into debt.

Is anything wrong with the reasoning in that ad? A crucial point was left out: during the three years in which you saved, you would not be enjoying the services of the car, or of the other things you could buy. You would be putting off your purchase for three years. Most people do not want to wait that long; they would prefer to have the services of the car immediately and pay the finance charge in order to do that. After all, the finance charge is merely a payment for using somebody else's money so that you can consume and that other person can not, the other person being the saver who decided not to consume. You have decided that the implicit utility you get per service flow of whatever you buy is greater than the interest payments you have to pay your creditor in order to get the total amount of money to buy the goods right away. No moral judgment need be passed here: it is simply a question of comparing costs and benefits. The benefit of borrowing is having purchasing power today; the cost is whatever you have to pay in finance charges. Obviously, if the cost were zero, you would borrow as much as you could because you could buy everything you wanted today and pay back whatever you owed at some later date without any penalty. In fact, the ultimate consumer probably would like to die with an infinite debt. That way, he or she could consume all he or she wanted at everybody else's expense. You must remember, though, that creditors take a dim view of this type of behavior because it means financial losses for them. When you buy something on credit without the intention of paying back that loan, there is little difference between that action and stealing. You are taking something from somebody else without intention of paying for it.

The benefits of borrowing are something that only you can decide. But the costs of borrowing are something that all of us can be made aware of.

WHAT IT COSTS TO BORROW

You are all well aware that borrowing costs. This should not surprise you: nothing is free. Why do you have to pay to borrow? Because somebody else is giving something up. What are they giving up? Purchasing power, or command over goods and services today. For other people to give up command over goods and services today, they have to be compensated, and they are usually compensated with what we call interest. Ask yourself if you would be willing to loan, say, $100 to your friend with the loan to be paid back in 10 years, with *no* interest, just the $100 to be returned. Would you do it, even if you were sure of getting the money back? Probably not. You would have to sacrifice what the $100 would have bought, while your friend enjoyed it. Most people will not make this sacrifice for no reward.

ORIGINS OF INTEREST

The concept of interest dates back to the time of the Romans when the law stated that the defaulting party to a contract had to pay his creditors some sort of compensation. During medieval times lawyers used this legal tactic of *damna et interesse* to extract such compensation. Thus, *interesse* became a charge for the use of money under the guise of compensation for failure to perform a contract.

It is best to think of the interest rate you pay on a loan as the price you pay the lender for the use of his money. What determines that price is no different from what determines the price of anything else in our economy. The various demands and supplies for credit ultimately result in some sort of interest rate being charged for the various forms of credit.

But we cannot really talk about a single interest rate or a single charge for credit. Interest rates vary according to the length of a loan, the risk involved, whether or not the debtor has put up something as **collateral** for the loan (i. e., secured it), and so on. One rule is fairly certain: the higher the risk involved, the more the creditor will demand in interest payments from the debtor. Do not be surprised, then, that interest rates in the economy range all the way from relatively low to relatively high. Much of that difference in interest rates has to do with the riskiness of the loan involved.

Let us see why today interest rates are just about the highest they have been in the history of the United States.

INFLATION AND INTEREST RATES

You and I are well aware of what has become more or less expected of the economy—rising prices, or inflation. There is a very definite relationship between rising prices and high interest rates. But the relationship is not the simple one of causation that you may have been taught to expect. Contrary to popular belief, high interest rates do not, and cannot, *cause* inflation. While inflation is a sufficiently important subject to merit a chapter later in the book, here we can point out that when prices are rising, interest rates will have an **inflationary premium** tacked onto them. A simple example will show you why.

Suppose that you are a banker who has been loaning out money at 5 percent a year for the last 20 years. Suppose also that for the last 20 years there has been no inflation. That 5 percent interest you have been charging is the *real* rate of interest you are receiving. It just covers your costs and gives you a normal profit for your lending activities.

Now prices start rising at 5 percent a year, and you expect that they will rise at that rate forever. If someone comes in to borrow money, how much do you think you would want to give him at the 5 percent rate of interest just like you have always charged?

Well, think about it. Say a person comes in to borrow $1000 for a year. At the end of the year, with an inflation rate of 5 percent, the actual purchasing power of that $1000 paid back to you will only be $950. If you only ask for 5 percent, or $50 in interest payments, you will just be compensated for the erosive effect of inflation on the value of the money you lent out. What will you do? You will want to tack on an inflationary premium to the real interest rate that you had been charging when there was no inflation and none was anticipated. Hence, in periods of inflation, we find the inflationary premium tacked on everywhere. It is not surprising, then, that during an inflationary period when prices are rising at 5 percent a year, that interest rates would be 10 percent.

You, the demander of credit or the potential debtor, should not be put off at this higher interest rate. After all, you are going to be repaying the loan in cheapened dollars—that is, dollars that have lost part of their purchasing power through inflation. In fact, some interest rates did not react very rapidly to rising inflation in the early 1970s. Credit unions, for example, were giving out automobile loans at an effective interest rate of 8 percent per annum. If the rate of inflation is 6 or 7 percent, those loans cost people only a 1 or 2 percent real rate of interest. For example, I took out a National Defense Education Act student loan while I was in college in the 1960s. The rate of interest on those loans was 3 percent. Now that I have to pay them back, I am actually making money! That is right, I am making money on a loan, because the real rate of interest on a 3 percent loan with, say, a 5 percent rate of inflation is *minus* 2 percent. That is, there is a profit of 2 percent in holding off paying those loans back. This is not the kind of deal that most people get, because potential creditors generally tack on inflationary premiums whenever they think inflation is going to occur.

One thing that inflationary premiums have brought to a head is the problem with usury laws, to which we now turn.

THE WHY AND WHERE OF USURY LAWS

There have always been restrictions on interest rates, both for the lender and for the borrower. Everybody seems to think that moneylenders have some unique monopolistic power over others in the economy. Indeed, money men have been so long condemned that dominant ethnic groups have historically shunned the profession, leaving it to minority groups.

EXHIBIT 7–1

THE "REAL" RATE OF INTEREST

The rate of interest you are paying on a $100 loan for one year	10%
The rate of inflation (loss in value of money) this year	5%
The difference between the rate of interest you are paying and the loss in the value of dollars you will pay back	5%

So 5 percent is the real rate of interest you pay when you are charged 10 percent on a loan and the rate of inflation is 5 percent.

In the Western world the Catholic Church, in the Middle Ages, made laws against usury, the lending of money at "unreasonable" rates.

Today many states have laws against charging borrowers interest rates that exceed a specified limit. The persistence of legislation affecting the lending of money makes it clear that a widespread suspicion still lingers that the moneylender possesses some unique shady influence. Many individuals are in favor of limiting the amount of interest that can be charged on a consumer loan. However, since no action is cost-free, you should be aware of both the benefits and the costs of usury laws.

Remember, the selling of credit is no different from the selling of anything else. If usury laws are valid, then so, too, are government controls on every single price in the economy. While we really cannot go into the issue in this book, we can note some of the unpredicted effects of usury laws that went into effect in the state of Washington and of usury laws that are in effect in the state of Arkansas. Let us first take the case of Washington.

WASHINGTON STATE
USURY LAWS—
AN EXAMPLE

Prior to 1968, interest on consumer loans from the credit card companies—BankAmericard, Mastercharge, and so on—as well as on revolving credit loans from the big stores—Sears and others—were generally 18 percent per annum, or 1.5 percent per month in the state of Washington. Many consumer advocates and concerned citizens felt that this rate of interest was much too high, that poor people were not able to afford credit. At that time, for example, commercial bank loans to some customers were going for as low as 9 percent. Poor people who obviously could not get bank loans at that low interest rate were supposedly being discriminated against and they had to forego the benefits of being able to buy on time.

A movement was begun to pass legislation against such usurious interest rates. In 1968, a motion was put on the ballot to set the maximum legal interest on consumer loans at 12 percent instead of 18 percent. It was felt that lowering the interest rate would benefit those who could not afford the higher rate. The measure passed quite successfully and all the credit card companies and stores in the state were forced to lower their rates to 1 percent per month, or 12 percent per year.

What results would you predict? Obviously, lower-cost credit. That is indeed true, but it turned out that the lower-cost credit was not necessarily given to people whom the formulators of this new law had in mind. Two academics, John J. Weatley and Guy G. Gordon,[2] did a study of the effects of the law one year after it took force. Their conclusions were startling:

> Low income people who are marginal credit risks seem to have suffered the most from the enactment of the law because of the general tightening of credit.

What in fact did creditors do? They raised some prices, adjusted their credit practices and merchandise assortment, and raised charges or instituted new charges on other services, all in an effort to make up the lost revenues from their credit accounts. You have to realize that both before and after the legal maximum limit was put on interest rates, there was a tremendous amount of competition for consumers' credit dollars. According to a study made of the profits of credit institutions, the price being charged did not lead to above-normal profits. That is, the price being charged reflected only the costs of providing credit plus some normal rate of return or profit to the companies. (The results of the study by Weatley and Gordon confirm this supposition.) Creditors had to make up the lost revenues in one way or another. One way of doing it was by raising prices. Another way, of course, was by eliminating risky debtors.

In fact, a further study by Sauter and Walker [3] shows that "the largest proportion of retailers expect to react to interest ceilings by becoming more selective in granting credit." This reaction would be in keeping with the retailers' desire to reduce costs and increase profits. Who is burdened by this reaction? Obviously, low-income and other "marginal" customers are forced to forego credit purchases and turn to more costly sources of funds, such as small loan companies, loan sharks, and pawnbrokers.

Another striking credit situation is found in the State of Arkansas.

[2] "Regulating the Price of Consumer Credit," *Journal of Marketing*, Volume 35 October 1971, pp. 21–28.

[3] R. F. Sauter and O. C. Walker, Jr., "Retailers' Reactions to Interest Limitation Laws— Additional Evidence," *Journal of Marketing*, Volume 36, April 1972, pp. 58–61.

LOOKING AT
ARKANSAS

For many years now, the State of Arkansas has had a maximum interest limit of 10 percent. In the face of inflationary premiums that reflect expected inflation of 4, 5, 6, and sometimes 7 percent, a 10 percent rate of interest is insufficient to induce many retailers and credit companies to provide credit in the state of Arkansas. The results are predictable, as evidenced by the city of Texarkana, on the border between Texas and Arkansas.

Interest rates in Texas are not looked at so carefully—that is, they are not really regulated. On the main street in this city, one side is Arkansas, the other side is Texas. On the Texas side, there are numerous finance companies, used car dealers, and TV and appliance stores. On the Arkansas side, there are many fewer, and in places none. The number of credit purchases in Arkansas is small, small indeed, per capita, compared to the credit purchases in Texas, the neighboring state. Why is this so? Simply because the usury law is so restrictive in Arkansas that no suppliers of credit want to do business there. But there are suppliers of credit in Texas.

Are the people of Arkansas better off because of the 10 percent limitation in interest rates? To be sure, some of them are. But many of them are not. They must go to other states or forego credit purchases altogether. Or they may in fact end up working with loan sharks outside of the law in order to borrow money when they think they need it desperately. Almost all economists agree that usury laws are usually detrimental to the general welfare of the people who are supposed to be helped.

In any event, given the variety of types of lending institutions, all in competition, the truth-in-lending legislation, passed by Congress in 1968, is a step in the right direction, and is an alternative to interest-ceiling regulation.

TRUTH-IN-LENDING

The Truth-in-Lending Act, which is Title I of the Consumer Credit Protection Act of 1968, is essentially a disclosure law. Most kinds of installment debt now have to be properly labeled so that the consumer knows exactly what he or she is paying. The bill finally passed in the Congress in 1968 had a long history. Former Senator Paul Douglas had introduced similar bills in the 86th, 87th, and 88th Congresses. He titled his bill "A Bill to Assist in the Promotion of Economic Stabilization by Requiring the Disclosure of Finance Charges in Connection with the Extension of Credit." The testimony and exhibits presented at the hearings before the Senate Committee on Banking and Currency, in 1960, '61, and '63, filled nearly 4000 pages. Hearings in 1967 added another 1200 pages. Lending institutions, retailers, and their trade associations put up strong opposition to these bills; that is presumably why they were blocked for so many years. When President Johnson signed the act, he stated succinctly, "As a matter of fair play to the consumer, the cost of credit should be disclosed fully, simply and clearly."

How does a 5¾ percent discount rate compare to a 6 percent add-on rate? Is one percent per month on the unpaid balance a better deal than either of the two above? And what are finder's fees, points, and service charges? These kinds of questions, couched in terms which were typically used to describe credit plans prior to the enactment of Truth-in-Lending, provide an obvious reason for the legislation. Prior to 1969, the majority of consumers were unable to understand the variety of credit terminology or the many methods used for rate calculations. Consumers therefore found themselves poorly equipped to make intelligent comparison among types of credit plans or among competitors.

The Congressional purpose of the Act is "to insure a meaningful disclosure of credit terms so that the consumer will be able to compare more readily the various credit terms available to him and avoid the uninformed use of credit." The Act attempts to accomplish this purpose in several ways. It requires that all the various terms used to describe the dollar cost of credit, such as interest, points, etc., be described and disclosed under one common label, *finance charge.* Likewise, it abolishes all the various terms used to describe the cost of credit in percentage terms, such as discount rates, add-ons, and the like, and prescribes a uniform method of computation of a single rate known as the *annual percentage rate.* (We see below, however, that there are still problems with how this rate is computed.)

The Truth-in-Lending Act does not cover credit extended to corporations, trusts, governments, and partnerships; it does not apply to private loans among friends and families, or to loans for business purposes; and the extension of credit must be for $25,000 or less, unless it is secured by real property such as in a typical home mortgage in which no limit applies.

The Truth-in-Lending Act also grants the consumer-borrower a right of rescission (cancellation) for certain credit contracts. Section 125 of the Act gives the consumer three business days to rescind a credit transaction that results or may result in a lien on his or her home, or on any real property that is used or expected to be used as his or her principal residence. The right of rescission is designed to allow the person additional time to reconsider using his or her residence as security for credit. However, this right of rescission does not apply to first mortgages on homes.

The Truth-in-Lending Act also regulated the advertising of consumer credit. One of the primary purposes of the Act's advertising requirements is to eliminate "come-on" credit ads. For example, if any one important credit term is mentioned in advertisement—down payment or monthly payment—all other important terms must also be defined.

A 1970 amendment to the Act provides federal regulations on the use of credit cards. This amendment prohibits the unsolicited distribution of new credit cards, and also establishes a maximum $50 limit on liability for the unauthorized use of such cards—that is, the owner of a lost or stolen card that has been used illegally by another person cannot be made liable to pay more than $50 on its illegal purchases.

ENFORCEMENT

A relatively novel scheme of administrative enforcement has been created whereby the Federal Reserve Board is given broad authority to write and administer regulations implementing the Truth-in-Lending Act. The Board's regulations are spread among nine federal agencies. Generally, those federal agencies with preexisting supervisory authority over a particular group of creditors were also given Truth-in-Lending enforcement responsibility over them. For example, the National Credit Union Administration is responsible for federally chartered credit unions, and the Federal Home Loan Bank Board is responsible for federally chartered savings and loan institutions. Other enforcers include the Comptroller of the Currency, the Federal Deposit Insurance Corporation, the Department of Agriculture, the Civil Aeronautics Board, and the Interstate Commerce Commission. Enforcement of all remaining creditors not covered by the above agencies falls to the Federal Trade Commission. The FTC in essence puts out the bulk of federal enforcement effort. In fact, it estimates that its responsibility extends to nearly one million creditors, including all retail creditors and finance companies.

Obviously, the FTC would have great difficulty in attempting to enforce the Act against *all* local retailers throughout the nation. Hence, the Truth-in-Lending Act allows the provision that any state which enacts legislation similar to Truth-in-Lending and provides for "adequate" enforcement may apply to the Federal Reserve Board for an exemption from the federal act and thereby obtain authority to enforce its own statutes instead. By 1973, Massachusetts, Maine, Connecticut, Oklahoma, and Wyoming had been granted such exemptions.

REVOLVING CREDIT

When the Truth-in-Lending Act was applied to revolving credit contracts, a battle was waged in Congress. Revolving credit, or open-ended credit, as it is sometimes called, is a growing part of total consumer credit. Many department stores allow you to have revolving credit accounts. An open-ended credit account has three main characteristics:

1. The customer may pay the balance in full or in installments.
2. The creditor permits the customer to make purchases (or loans) at irregular intervals, usually by means of a credit card.
3. The creditor usually computes the finance charge on the *outstanding* unpaid balance.

It is the last aspect of an open-ended credit account that has bothered consumers the most and for which the Truth-in-Lending Act ran into the most trouble. The fact is that many creditors used different techniques to compute finance charges on revolving credit accounts. The techniques are the following:

1. **previous balance method:** Here the creditor computes a finance charge on the previous month's balance, even if it has been paid.
2. **average daily balance:** The finance charge is applied to the sum of the actual amounts outstanding each day during the billing period divided by the number of days in that period. Payments are credited on the exact date of payment.
3. **adjusted balance method:** Finance charges are assessed on the balance after deducting payments and credits.
4. **past due balance:** No finance charge is assessed so long as full payment is received within a certain period, such as 25 days after the closing date of the last statement.

It is obviously important to know which method is used in assessing the finance charge that you are being made to pay, for the different methods can result in finance charges that vary by a huge factor: Table 7–2 shows the difference between the use of the previous balance method and of the adjusted balance method.

TABLE 7–2:
DIFFERING RESULTANT
FINANCE CHARGES

METHOD	OPENING BALANCE	PAYMENTS	MONTHLY FINANCE CHARGE	ACTUAL FINANCE CHARGE	ACTUAL MONTHLY RATE	ANNUAL RATE
PREVIOUS BALANCE METHOD	$300	$100	1%	.01 x $300 = $3	1½%	18%
ADJUSTED BALANCE METHOD	$300	$100	1%	.01 x $200 = $2	1%	12%

You see that the same monthly finance charge of 1 percent results in two different actual annual rates of finance charged, depending on which computational method is used by the creditor. The Truth-in-Lending Act requires that all revolving credit contracts and monthly bills must state the "nominal annual percentage rate." The nominal rate will equal twelve times the monthly rate. However, the nominal rate does not tell you the effective, or actual, annual rate. Retailers were given a further concession in one provision in the Truth-in-Lending Act whereby they are allowed to exclude from the disclosure of finance charges a certain minimum monthly charge on small unpaid revolving account balances.

The Truth-in-Lending Act does not actually give protection, only information. But information can be valuable; it can be the best protection around. It allows you, the consumer, who are looking for credit to shop around, to see exactly what you are paying, and to know exactly what you are getting into. Figure 7–2 displays a typical disclosure statement. What the Truth-in-Lending Act requires is that an accurate assessment of the annual percentage rate be given; that is circled for you, and that is what you should look at when you compare the various prices of credit from various dealers and companies. In addition, you may want to look at the finance charge, which is the total number of dollars you pay to borrow the money, whether directly or in the form of deferred payments on a purchase. These total finance charges include all of the so-called carrying charges that are sometimes tacked on to a retail installment contract, plus such things as "setup" charges and credit life insurance. These all contribute to your cost of having purchasing power today instead of waiting, of having command over goods and services right now, and of taking that command away from somebody else. Expressed as a percentage of the total price, it gives your annual percentage interest rate. In some cases, it may be very, very high indeed.

REGULATING BANKS

When you want to have a checking account so that you do not have to carry currency all the time, and so that you can have a record of many important purchases, you go to a commercial bank. In the United States, commercial banks are not unregulated; in fact, they are extremely regu-

FIGURE 7–2:   A TYPICAL DISCLOSURE STATEMENT

ACCOUNT NUMBER				

SEARS, ROEBUCK AND CO.
DISCLOSURE STATEMENT

Sales Check No._____   Date _____19____

☐ Easy Payment Plan

☐ Modernizing Credit Plan

DESCRIPTION OF MERCHANDISE

OFFICE USE ONLY (Code 4 Sales)	
NO. OF MONTHS	MONTHLY PAYMENT

CASH PRICE				
CASH DOWN PAYMENT				
UNPAID BALANCE OF CASH PRICE – AMOUNT FINANCED				
FINANCE CHARGE				
DEFERRED PAYMENT PRICE				
TOTAL OF PAYMENTS – THIS SALE				

This purchase is payable in installments pursuant to my Sears Easy Payment Plan—Modernizing Credit Plan Retail Installment Contract and Security Agreement.

Beginning _____ , I will pay $ _____ per month for _____ months and a final monthly payment of $ _____ until the amount financed and the finance charge for this purchase are fully paid.

If the **FINANCE CHARGE** exceeds **$5.00,** the **ANNUAL PERCENTAGE RATE** is [%]

In accordance with my Sears Easy Payment Plan-Modernizing Credit Plan Retail Installment Contract and Security Agreement, a subsequent purchase may change the number and amount of my monthly payments, the amount of the Finance Charge and the Annual Percentage Rate of this purchase. Any such change will appear on my next monthly billing statement.

A copy of my sales check is attached hereto and incorporated by reference. Ownership of the merchandise described in such attached sales check remains in Sears until paid for in full.

If I pay in full in advance, any unearned finance charge will be rebated under the Rule of 78, after deducting a charge of $5.00.

11078-202 (F11363 WW) Rev. 12/72

lated. Much of the regulation is to prevent practices in which you, the consumer, would be hurt. But some of the regulation seems out of date.

Today there are about 14,000 commercial banks in the United States. Together they have total deposits of $225 billion. The average per capita amount of checking account plus currency is over $1000. That is one large amount of money, right? When you go to a bank today and open a checking account, you have to make some decisions: what color folder to use for your checks, how personalized you want the checks to be (some banks even offer you pictures of sailing ships, or pictures of yourself embossed on every check you buy). A lot of banks give you an option. If you keep a minimum balance, there is no charge for any check you write. You can write as many as you want. Other banks periodically offer you small appliances if you open an account with them for a specified amount. Sometimes you see banks opening offices that are only blocks apart from each other and you cannot understand why.

The reason why is pretty easy to see. The explicit interest rate that banks can pay you on your checking account balances is fixed at a maximum of 0 percent per year—not very much, is it? But the deposits that you leave in the bank on average can be used by the bank to purchase interest-earning assets, like bonds or stocks or promissory notes in the form of loans to individuals and firms. Therefore, your unused checking account balances are used by the banks as an input in the sale of other services such as loans.

They certainly would like to have all those inputs free of charge—that is, at a zero interest rate. But there is competition in the banking system. Banks find that it is beneficial—that is, profitable—to try to induce you and me to put our checking accounts in their particular one instead of another. How do they try to induce this? Well, the first thing they can do is offer us free checking services or pretty pictures on our checks, or, where legal, they can offer us convenience in the form of multitudinous branch offices. They can sometimes offer us small appliances to get us to put money in their particular bank. These are all ways of getting around the regulation that prevents banks from offering interest on checking account balances.

It is strange that the government is still regulating banks in a manner that seems not to be in the consumer's best interest. After all, we consumers would like to have the option of being paid a small interest rate on our checking account balances instead of having to receive a more or less hidden interest rate in the form of free services and many convenient bank locations. But the Federal Reserve instituted Regulation Q fixing the maximum interest rate on checking accounts as zero in order to prevent what it called cutthroat competition. That argument seems a little thin these days, does it not? Even pro-regulation Consumers Union came out against this restriction on interest rates in its June 1973 issue of *Consumer Reports* (pp. 420, 421).

Actually, in some cities you now have an option. A few savings and loan associations have gotten around Regulation Q and are offering a new type of account.

NOW IS THE TIME
FOR *NOW*

Several state savings banks have started what are called Negotiable Orders of Withdrawal, or NOWs. When you open a NOW account you get a checkbook. It is not called that—it is called instead a negotiable order of withdrawal book. But it is a checkbook nonetheless, and in most cases merchants are not going to turn it down. The difference is that your balance in your NOW account earns the same interest as a regular savings account, 5 to 6 percent. For each withdrawal, however, the customer is charged something like 10 or 15¢. Obviously, if you write a lot of checks you would not find a NOW account very convenient as a substitute for a checking account, for the service charges would be more than the interest you would earn. But if you have normally high checking account balances and do not write very many checks, this is an obvious way to earn a little extra money.

As you can imagine, the commercial banks are fighting NOW accounts tooth and nail. The American Bankers Association is backing legislation, which may already have gone into effect, to prevent the spread of NOW accounts throughout the United States. However, it is inevitable that sooner or later, competition in the banking system will allow you the consumer to earn money on those unused checking account balances. Just recently, in one major West Coast city, a "trans fund account" became available. You keep what you think is an adequate balance in your checking account to cover your expenses, and the rest in a trans fund account, where you get the normal interest rate on your savings. Whenever you need money you call the bank. It immediately transfers the amount of your request to your checking account and mails you a transaction memo in verification. That way, as long as you do not need the money in your checking account, you earn interest in your trans fund account.

TOTAL BANKING
SERVICES FOR
ONE FEE

A number of banks around the country have instituted a banking package for which they charge you a single monthly fee, generally only $3. For that $3 fee you get something called a Blue Chip Account or a Gold Account or an Executive Account. Included in the fee are the following services:

1. unlimited check writing.
2. personalized checks, sometimes with your picture embossed on them or with a reproduction of a famous painting or landscape in your area.
3. overdraft protection, whereby if you write checks for more money than you have in your account, you will automatically have funds transferred from either a credit card account or a personalized line of credit.
4. a safe deposit box.

5. unlimited travelers checks, cashiers checks, and money orders.
6. (sometimes) preferred interest rates on personal loans.

And, in some cities, banking services have become so sophisticated that you no longer have to write checks.

THE CASHLESS SOCIETY

Some cities, like Lincoln, Nebraska, and Macon and Atlanta, Georgia, are trying a system of cashless, checkless spending, and it seems to be working. What is it all about? And does it mean that money will be useless? No, it does not. It means only that money will take another form. Money in the form of cash, which consists of currency and checking account balances, we use as a means of storing purchasing power. Since our receipts do not always match our expenditures, we generally keep some money in a checking account balance or in our wallets in order to make expenditures later on each month. In the cashless, checkless society, you still would need a checking account balance on which to draw even though you did not write a check and even though the transmission mechanism was semiautomatic at the beginning of each month. You would have to deposit your income checks into your account at the beginning of each month, just as you do now, although that, too, can be done automatically.

In those cities that allow cashless, checkless transactions, although you still keep part of your wealth in the form of a checking account balance, you are using it in a semiautomatic manner. When you make a purchase in a store you merely give the merchant or salesperson a credit card which automatically transfers money from your checking account balance to the store's balance.

The cashless, checkless society is merely a means of reducing **transactions costs** Instead of your having to write out checks every month for your mortgage, your phone, your milk, and your electricity, a computer does it automatically. It saves you time and it saves the banks and companies money, also. After all, it is estimated that the banking system spend over $3\frac{1}{2}$ billion annually just to process checks. If somehow this processing can be reduced, you the consumer will benefit. Now, this might cause some problems, but not serious ones. Since most of your fixed expenses for car payments, house payments, and the like are anticipated, anyway, their being paid automatically is not going to change your behavior. In the cashless, checkless society, you will get a statement at the end of every month just as you do now, in fact you will probably always be able to phone in to find out where your finances stand. Since we are all faced with a budget constraint (we know that we cannot spend for long more than we make), checks and balances against overspending will have to be built in. And of course, that all goes back to formulating a budget and sticking to it.

You still may want to borrow money, even in this forthcoming society, so in the consumer issue that follows we find out when and where and how you should go about getting credit.

SUMMARY

1. The largest debt item in America for consumers is our home loans or mortgages. The second largest is automobile loans. At least 50 percent of all Americans have outstanding installment debt at any given time.

2. The sources of credit are many, including commercial banks, finance companies, consumer finance companies, credit unions, and credit card companies.

3. Individuals borrow in order to obtain the services of large consumer items without paying for them at one time. The installment payments can be thought of as matching the service flow from whatever was purchased, such as a house or a car.

4. Interest is the payment for using somebody else's money today. As such, it is like any other price. During inflation, interest rates must rise to take account of the rate of inflation. Hence, interest rates are relatively high when the rate of inflation is high.

5. The real rate of interest you pay on a loan is the stated rate of interest minus the rate of inflation.

6. Usury laws set a legal maximum on the rate of interest that can be charged a consumer. Some studies of usury laws have shown that they hurt some consumers while helping others.

7. The Truth-in-Lending Act requires that the total finance charge be clearly stated on a loan agreement as well as the annual percentage rate.

8. You must be careful when computing the actual percentage interest rate you will pay on an open-ended credit account. Ask specifically whether one of the following four methods is used: previous balance, average daily balance, adjusted balance, or past due balance. As you can see in Table 7–2, the resultant finance charge can be much higher if, for example, the previous balance method is used instead of the adjusted balance method.

9. Banks in the United States are regulated so that they cannot pay interest to you on your checking account balances. Therefore, you should find a bank that gives you the most free services in exchange for your checking account. For example, some banks offer six to nine services for $3.00 a month.

10. Eventually, the United States may not use currency. Everything will be done electronically. This, however, will not change your budget-making plans or processes: you still cannot spend more than you earn.

1. Why do you think the aggregate amount of debt in the United States has been growing so much? Does it have anything to do with increased incomes? increased population? increased price level?

2. What is the difference between credit and debt?

3. The interest rate charged by different lenders varies tremendously. Does this mean that some of them have a monopoly? If not, how can you account for the differences?

4. Does it seem fair that those who pay cash pay the same price as those who use a credit card?

5. Can you think of some very specific reasons why you would ever want to borrow money? or ever have?

6. Is it better to save and buy? or to buy and go into debt?

7. Do you think it is appropriate that interest rates be regulated? If your answer is yes, how does the regulation of interest rates differ from the regulation of other prices in our economy?

8. During a number of years in this decade, the rate of inflation exceeded the rate of interest that some borrowers had to pay on their loans. What does that mean about the real rate of interest those borrowers were paying?

9. Do you think the Truth-in-Lending Act has been effective? Why?

10. Can consumers figure out how they are actually being charged for their credit? What information would be helpful in addition to what now exists?

11. If you are charged a setup fee in addition to some annual percentage rate to borrow money from a credit card company, should that setup charge be included as part of the total finance charge? Would this raise or lower the annual percentage rate of interest?

12. Do you think banks should continue to be regulated so that they cannot offer interest on checking accounts? Is there a problem about possible cutthroat competition? What would be the result?

13. If you were the owner of a savings and loan association, how would you feel about the ability of commercial banks to offer interest on checking accounts?

14. Why have a number of banks started total banking services for a flat fee every month?

THINGS TO DO

1. See if you can find a grown, self-supporting person who has *never* gone into debt. (If you find one, ask how and/or why.)

2.   Make a survey in your area of the various sources of credit.   Find out what the various characteristics of those sources are and what the various charges on their loans might be.

3.   Pick a consumer durable good, such as an automobile or an expensive stereo.   Start calling around to find out where you could get the best loan.   If there are big differences in annual interest rates charged for the loan, try to determine why.

4.   Ask your neighborhood retailers who accept credit cards whether they give a discount for cash.   If they do not, find out why not.

5.   Ask someone who works in a savings and loan association what their feelings are about going into debt.   See if that person thinks it is better to save and then buy, rather than to go into debt and have today.

6.   Go to your reference library and find out from the *Monthly Labor Review,* or the *Federal Reserve Bulletin,* or the *Survey of Current Business,* or *Business Conditions Digest,* what the rate of inflation has been for the past five years.   Then compare that rate of inflation with the interest rate you would have had to pay to borrow for the purchase of, say, a new car.   Now calculate the real rate of interest that you would have been charged.   Does that real rate of interest seem high or low?   If it seems relatively low, can you figure out why it would have been so low?

7.   Find out if there is a usury law in your state.   Compare it to the so-called prime rate, or the rate of interest charged by banks to the lowest-risk borrowers, that is, best borrowers.   The prime rate can be found in the *Federal Reserve Bulletin* or in the local newspaper every once in a while.   Or you can call up any local banker and ask him or her what the prime rate is.   If your state usury law is close to the prime rate, ask the local banker whether that has caused any problems.

8.   Obtain the disclosure statements from a number of local department stores and appliance stores that offer credit.   Make a comparison of the annual percentage rates listed on the forms.   Then call the credit departments and find out whether they use the previous balance, average daily balance, adjusted balance, or past-due balance method of computing the finance charge.   Now see if that will make a difference in the annual percentage rate.   If it does, find out from your local field office of the Federal Trade Commission why there are such discrepancies.

9.   Make a survey of commercial banks in your area.   Ask to speak with the assistant manager.   Ask his or her opinion on the regulation from the Federal Reserve, called Regulation Q, which prohibits the payment of interest on checking accounts.   Make the same survey again, but now call the assistant managers of savings and loan associations.   Why do you think there will be a difference in your results?

**SELECTED
READINGS**

Annual Report to Congress on Truth in Lending, Board of Governors of the Federal Reserve System (latest edition).

"Before You Borrow or Say 'Charge It' . . .," *Changing Times,* January 1972.

"Charge Account Bankers: The New Merchants," *Consumer Reports,* January 1971, p. 53.

"Consumer Knowledge and Understanding of Consumer Credit," *Journal of Consumer Affairs,* Summer 1973.

"Credit Insurance: How You Can Get Soaked," *Changing Times,* August 1972.

Kaplan, Lawrence J., and Salvatore Malteis, "The Economics of Loansharking," *American Journal of Economics and Sociology,* vol. 27 (1968).

"The Credit Card Trap," *Consumer Reports,* November 1971.

"Use of Bank Credit Cards Grows," *Family Economic Review,* September 1970.

"Using Credit: Key Words You Need to Know," *Changing Times,* November 1971.

"Who's Going Bankrupt and Why," *U. S. News and World Report,* 71 (1971), 83.

"Workshop on Consumer Credit," *Journal of Home Economics,* January 1968.

CONSUMER ISSUE III
Coping with the Credit Maze

WHEN SHOULD YOU BORROW?

Some personal finance books give you cut and dried formulas to tell you when you should borrow. It is not unusual to find a financial adviser telling consumers that they should borrow only for major purchases, such as automobiles. Just about everyone who buys a house automatically assumes that it is respectable to borrow, for very, very few of us are in a position to chunk out $20,000, $30,000, $40,000, or $50,000 to pay the full cost of a house. Since we know that the housing services we consume per month represent a very small part of the total price (since houses last so long), it seems meaningless to spend all that cash; instead, we take out a mortgage. The same holds for cars, especially new ones. A car is such a large expense that very few of us consider that we should pay for it in cash; fully 71 percent of all new automobiles are purchased on time. After houses and automobiles, though, the reasoning gets pretty fuzzy. Is it all right to buy a stereo on time? Some financial advisers say yes, and some say no. Is it all right to buy furniture on time? Some advisers say yes, some say no. Of course, for clothes and food, most financial advisers are adamant about the desirability of paying cash.

A Dollar Is a Dollar Is a Dollar

When you think about it, the reasoning behind such cut and dried rules is pretty shaky. Gertrude Stein once wrote that a rose is a rose

Liabilities: Something for which one is liable or responsible according to law or equity, especially pecuniary debts or obligations.

Assets: The entire property of a person, association, corporation, or estate that is applicable or subject to the payment of his or her or its debts; or the items on a balance sheet showing the book value of property owned.

Net Worth: The difference between your assets and your liabilities, or what you are actually worth. If your liabilities exceed your assets, your net worth is negative.

Acceleration Clause: A clause contained in numerous credit agreements whereby if one payment is missed, the entire unpaid balance becomes due, or the due date is accelerated to the immediate future.

**EXHIBIT
Determining a safe
debt load**

ITEM	AMOUNT
Car payment	_____
Installment debt (department stores, etc.)	_____
1. _____	_____
2. _____	_____
3. _____	_____
4. _____	_____
Loan payments due	
1. _____	_____
2. _____	_____
3. _____	_____
4. _____	_____
Others	
1. _____	_____
2. _____	_____
Overdue accounts (e. g. phone, electricity, etc.)	_____
TOTAL OUTSTANDING	_____

Having thereby determined your short-term debt load, you are in a position to determine whether you want to extend it. Below are two methods by which you might decide:

A

10% of monthly income (after taxes) _____

multiply by 18 _____

SAFE DEBT LOAD RESULTS
(principal *plus* interest)

_____

B

Indicate your annual income after taxes _____

Subtract your annual expenditures on housing, food, and clothing

_____

Divide by 3

SAFE DEBT LOAD RESULTS

_____

is a rose, and so, too, a dollar is a dollar is a dollar. What does it matter what you say your dollar is going to buy? You cannot earmark it. If you make $100 a week and you spend $10 for clothes, $50 for food and lodging, and the rest on entertainment, how do you know which dollar you used for "essentials"—that is, food and lodging and clothes—and which dollar you used for "nonessentials"—entertainment? You do not, because you can not tell one dollar from another. What does it matter if you say you are going to buy your clothes on time and pay for your entertainment cash and carry? It does not matter. What is important for you is to decide what percentage of your anticipated income you are willing to set aside for fixed payments to repay loans. You should care about the total commitment you have made to creditors. You want to make sure you have not overcommitted yourself. In the accompanying exhibit, you get an example of what may be "safe" for you.

Values Enter In, Too

Value judgments enter in, too. Some will say that certain types of consumption activities are frivolous and therefore you should never borrow money to engage in them. Be careful here, however. It is hard to determine which activities are frivolous and which are not, particularly somebody else's activities and not your own. You may deem it absolutely essential that you spend a large part of your income on entertainment to keep your sanity. I may say that you are wasting your money; that it is frivolous consumption and therefore you can never justify borrowing for entertainment. Likewise, some people find it essential to get away from it all on their vacations, and therefore, if they run out of money before their vacation, they may be willing to go into debt in order to fly away to Hawaii or Mexico or Florida. This is how they keep sane for the rest of the year's work. Hence, this activity

may not be frivolous to them, although to an outsider it may look so.

Thus, when we judge each other's behavior, we can never tell whether the other's purchases are superfluous or not. Nor can we tell whether the other is borrowing for the "right" kinds of things or not. Again, what is important is that the total amount of indebtedness relative to a person's income not be excessive. In any event, you will be faced by a maximum amount of indebtedness that creditors will allow you to have. And they have some fairly simple rules for determining what your borrowing capacity is. Remember, however, that reliance on lending agencies to limit your borrowing is a mistake: you, the lendee, should be responsible for your own needs. Creditors check your credit worthiness to protect themselves, not you.

WHAT IS THE MAXIMUM YOU CAN BORROW?

If you go to a bank or a credit company and ask for a loan, the loan officer will more than likely require you to fill out a form. On this form you list your **liabilities** and your **assets** so that the credit officer can come up with an estimate of your **net worth.** Figure III–1 shows a typical net worth statement. You have to put down all of your assets—whatever you own—and all of your liabilities—whatever you owe. The difference is your net worth. Obviously, if your net worth is negative, you will have a hard time getting a loan from anybody unless you can show that your expected income in the immediate future is extremely large.

You still do not know what your maximum credit limit is. That, of course, depends on the loan officer's assessment of your financial position. This will be a function of your net worth, your income, your relative indebtedness, and how regular your situation is. What does regularity mean? It can mean different things

**EXHIBIT
Determining your
net worth**

Estimated amounts, end of this year

ASSETS

House (including furniture)—market value   _____

Car(s)—resale value   _____

Life insurance cash value   _____

Bonds, securities—market value   _____

Cash on hand   _____

Other (for example, stereo, cameras,
           savings accounts, land, etc.)   _____

TOTAL ASSETS   _____

LIABILITIES

Mortgage   _____

Loans   _____

Other   _____

TOTAL LIABILITIES   _____

NET WORTH   December 31, 197__   _____

An annual net worth statement may help you and/or your family to keep track of financial progress from year to year. Essentially, your net worth is an indication of how much wealth you actually own. We generally find that young people have low net worths—or even negative net worths: that is, they owe more than they own—because they are anticipating having higher income in the future. As individuals and families get further down the road, their net worth increases steadily only to start falling again, usually, when retirement age approaches and the income flow slows down or stops completely, thereby forcing the retired person or couple to draw on past accumulated savings. The above very simplified statement of family net worth can be easily filled out. Just make sure that you include all of your assets and all of your liabilities. Assets are anything that you own, and liabilities are anything that you owe. It is all very simple.

FIGURE III–1 TYPICAL NET WORTH STATEMENT

(Personal Financial Statement) .... **OFFICE**

Name .... Address ....

Business .... City .... Zip ....

Social Security Numbers:

Borrower: .... Spouse: .... Statement as of: ....

ASSETS				LIABILITIES			
Cash on hand and in banks....................				Notes payable banks:			
U. S. Government Securities—Schedule 1...........				Secured			
Stocks and Bonds—Schedule 1...............				Unsecured			
Accounts receivable				Notes payable other.........			
Notes receivable				Accounts and bills payable.........			
Cash surrender value life insurance............				Accrued taxes and interest.........			
Face Value $...............				Mortgages payable on real estate—Schedule 2.....			
Real estate—Schedule 2............							
Automobiles				Security Agreements			
Other assets—itemize				Other debts—itemize			
....				....			
....				....			
....				....			
....				Total liabilities			
....				Net worth			
TOTAL ASSETS				TOTAL LIABILITIES AND NET WORTH...........			

SOURCE OF INCOME				GENERAL INFORMATION
Salary				Married (name of spouse) ....
Bonus and commissions........				Single ....
Dividends				Number of children........
Real estate income........				Other dependents ....
Other income				Are any assets pledged?........
....				Defendant in any suits or legal actions?........
....				Personal bank accounts carried at........
....				Life Insurance - face amount, company, beneficiaries........
....				....
TOTAL				....

DO YOU HAVE A WILL? YES____ NO____

CONTINGENT LIABILITIES

Endorser or comaker..

Legal claims ....

Federal Income Taxes:

   1. Do you owe any Federal Tax for years prior to the current year? Yes ☐ No ☐ Amount $................

   2. Are there any unpaid Federal Tax Assessments outstanding against you? Yes ☐ No ☐ Amount $................

Other ....

(see over)

to different people, but in general it means the following:

1. You have been working regularly for a long period and therefore have been receiving regular income.

2. Your family situation is stable.

3. You have regularly paid off your debts on time.

Or your credit worthiness can be measured by the three C's that loan officers use as a guide to lending:

1. Capacity to pay back.

2. Character.

3. Capital or collateral that you own.

The behavior of loan officers may appear to some of you to discriminate against people with unstable living situations—that is, those who have unstable jobs, unstable family situations, and the like. That may or may not be true, depending on your definition of discrimination. But you can be sure that a loan officer is supposed to make decisions that maximize the profits for his company. At the going interest rate, he may decide to eliminate people who are high risks: loans will be refused to people who come in with records that indicate they will not pay off their debts as easily or as regularly as those people who seem more stable. If you are a credit buyer with an unstable living situation, one way that you can persuade loan officers not to refuse you is to candidly discuss your problems with him or her and produce a past record of loan repayments that was stable in spite of your unstable situation. Or, alternatively, you could offer to pay a higher interest rate.

You may sometimes nevertheless be refused credit because of a bad credit rating. Once, there was little you could do about this, but now under a new federal law you have some recourse.

WHAT TO DO WHEN YOU ARE REFUSED CREDIT

The Fair Credit Reporting Act (Title VI of the 1968 Consumer Credit Protection Act) was passed in 1970 and went into effect in 1971. Under this new law, when a credit investigating agency gives you a bad rating, you have recourse. Now, when you are turned down for credit because of a bad credit rating, the company that turned you down must give you the name and address of the credit investigating agency that was used. The same holds true for an insurance company.

The 1971 Act was meant to regulate the consumer credit reporting industry to insure that credit reporting agencies supply information that is equitable and fair to the consumer. The problems that led to passage of the Act seem to have been the reporting of incorrect, misleading, or incomplete information, as well as one-sided versions of disputed claims. In addition, many people were concerned about the invasion of privacy involved in the distribution of such reports to those who did not really have a legitimate business need for them. These reports often contained material about a person's general reputation, personal characteristics or mode of living, and character.

The Act applies not only to the usual credit bureaus and investigating concerns, but also to finance companies and banks that routinely give out credit information other than that which is developed from their own transactions.

When you go to a credit bureau, under the rules of the new law it must disclose to you the "nature and substance of all information" that is included under your name in its files. You also have the right to be told the sources of just about all that information. Now, if you discover that the credit bureau has incomplete, misleading, or false information, the Fair Credit Reporting Act requires that the bureau reinvestigate any disputed information

EXHIBIT
What you can do to
protect yourself
against unfair reports

If you are trying to get insurance, credit or a job, you may be subjected to a personal investigation. Under the Fair Credit Reporting Act of 1971—

☐ The company asking for the investigations is supposed to let you know you are being investigated.

☐ You can demand the name and address of the firm hired to do the investigating.

☐ You can demand that the investigating company tell you what its report contains—except for medical information used to determine your eligibility for life insurance.

☐ You cannot require the investigators to reveal the names of neighbors or friends who supplied information.

If the investigation turns up derogatory or inaccurate material, you can—

☐ Demand a recheck.

☐ Require the investigators to take out of your file anything that is inaccurate.

☐ Require them to insert your version of the facts, if the facts remain in dispute.

☐ Sue the investigating firm for damages if negligence on its part resulted in violation of the law which caused you some economic loss—failure to get a job, loss of credit or insurance, or even great personal embarrassment.

☐ Require the company to cease reporting adverse information after it is 7 years old—with the exception of a bankruptcy, which can remain in the file for 14 years.

"within a reasonable period of time." Of course, the credit bureau is not necessarily going to do it, but you do have the law on your side and you can go to court over the issue. In addition, at your request, the credit bureau must send to those companies that received a credit report in the last six months a notice of the elimination of any false information from your credit record.

Even if you have not been rejected for credit, you still have the right to go to a credit bureau and find out what your file contains. You also have the right to ask the credit bureau to delete, correct, or investigate items which you believe to be fallacious and inaccurate. The credit bureau then has the legal right to charge you for the time it spends correcting any mistakes. Also, the Fair Credit Reporting Act specifically forbids credit bureaus from sending out any adverse information that is more than seven years old. But there are important exceptions. Bankruptcy information can be sent out to your prospective creditors for a full 14 years. And there is no time limit on any information for loans or life insurance policies of $50,000 or more, or for a job application with an annual salary of $20,000 or more. That means that adverse information may be kept in your file and used indefinitely for these purposes.

Problems with the Act

Critics of the 1971 Act have been numerous, and various proposals have been before Congress to amend the statute to increase its effectiveness. One of the main criticisms is that consumers cannot obtain a copy of the credit reports, or have actual physical access to the files. Moreover, many critics contend that consumers who have asked for information from these agencies have been subjected to evasion, delaying tactics, or exorbitant charges. Many other consumers believe they are not receiving all of the information that is in their files. Of course, the credit reporting agencies have opposed any legislation that would give consumers direct access to the agency files. Their argument is that they would no longer have any sources of confidential information. And, moreover, there would be a substantial increase in the costs of providing accurate credit reports.

SHOPPING FOR CREDIT

Once you have decided that you want to buy some credit—that is, you want to get some goods now and pay for them later—then you should shop around. The Truth-in-Lending

Act, which requires a full statement of the annual interest rate charged, makes shopping much easier these days. This is certainly true if you are comparing, say, revolving credit accounts: if the actual annual interest charge for one is 22½ percent, you know this is not as good a deal as another one at 18 percent.

But when looking at loan agreements, you have to be careful, because all have various contingency clauses written into them that may or may not affect you. For example, if you sign a credit agreement that has an **acceleration clause**—meaning that all of the debt becomes immediately due if you, the borrower, fail to meet any single payment on the debt—you could not likely pay that large a sum. Obviously, if you could not meet a payment on the debt because you lacked the money, you certainly would be unable to pay the whole loan off at once. The addition of an acceleration clause in a credit agreement increases the probability that whatever you bought on credit will be repossessed.[4]

It is also possible for a court order to allow a creditor to attach part of your property. Your bank account may be attached and used to discharge any debts. Or your wages may be garnished (attached)—that is, if a judgment has been made against you, your employer is required to withhold wages to pay a creditor. (If this happens often, you may find it hard to keep or get another job.)

Interest Rate and Taxes

Note that to calculate the actual interest you will pay, you have to take account not only of inflation, but also of the taxes that you save by borrowing. All interest payments and finance charges are usually tax deductible. Every dollar of interest payments you make is

---

[4] Since loans with an acceleration clause usually can be obtained at relatively lower interest rates, they may still be a good deal for people who rarely or never default on loan payments.

**EXHIBIT
Actual interest paid
after tax deduction**

1. Assume your tax rate is 20 percent, that is, you must pay Uncle Sam 20¢ of the (last) dollars you earn.

2. Interest payments are tax deductible.

3. You borrow $100 at 10 percent, that is, you pay $10 in interest.

4. But when calculating your taxes you get to deduct that $10 from your income *before* you compute your taxes owed.

5. Hence, what you do not have to pay Uncle Sam is
.20 × $10.00 = $2.00

6. Your actual interest payment for that $100 loan is therefore $10 − $2 (in tax savings) = $8.00, or only 8 percent (instead of 10 percent).

one dollar less of income you pay taxes on. That means that your tax savings would be 20 cents on each dollar if you are in the 20 percent tax bracket; if you are paying an interest rate of 10 percent and your taxable income bracket is 20 percent, the after-tax interest payment you are actually paying is only 8 percent. Obviously, the higher your tax bracket, the less it really costs you to borrow.

Where Should You Go for a Loan?

Some kinds of asset purchases tell you immediately where you should go for a loan. If you are buying a house, you obviously do not go to your local small loan company for a loan. Where do you go? You go to a savings and loan association, a commercial bank, or a mortgage trust company or you sign a contract with the seller of the house. The real estate agent usually helps the buyer of a house to secure a loan. If you want to shop around, the easiest thing to do is to call various savings and loan associations to see what

interest rates they are charging. In Consumer Issue VI we discuss in more detail what you should look out for when you are borrowing money on a house.

To borrow for a car, again you probably will not go to a small loan company around the corner. Rather, you want to go to a credit union or a commercial bank, where the loan for a car will cost less. Note that the interest rate for new cars is usually lower than for a used car. Why? Because the car is used as collateral, and the new car is generally easier to sell than a used car (although this may not be true in the age of pollution control equipment on new cars). You should note also that if you buy a car which is technically "brand new"—that is, you would be the first owner—but you purchase it after next year's models have entered the showroom, the lending agency may consider that to be a used car and charge you the higher rate of interest.

If you want to borrow money for purchases of smaller items, a credit union loan might be cheapest, and the next best deal would be credit card companies, of which Mastercharge and BankAmericard are the best known.

The key to purchasing the best credit deal is to treat credit as a good or service just like anything else; use the same shopping techniques for purchasing credit that you would use to purchase anything else. Your having spent time to find the best deal for a car does not mean that your shopping should stop there. You may not be getting the best deal possible, if you buy the credit for the car from the dealership or its affiliate. You may do better going to your local commercial bank. But you cannot predict: you have to compare and contrast.

NOTHING IS FREE

You often hear ads for companies that want to help you help yourself. They propose to consolidate all of your debts into one fixed monthly payment that will be lower than the total of what you are paying now to all of your creditors. But do not be taken in. It is impossible for the claim to be true; you cannot actually end up paying a smaller interest rate by consolidating your debts than by paying for them separately. Remember, you have already incurred any setup charges involved in taking out the various earlier lines of credit that you want consolidated. Credit companies do nothing for free. Like any other company, they will not render you any service unless they make a profit on it. So if you let a credit company pay off all your existing debts and then lend you the total amount that they paid, you will have to incur the setup charge for that.[5]

---

[5] Sometimes debt consolidation *may* actually save you some money. If, for example, you consolidate all of your revolving credit accounts which charge you 18% into one 12% credit union loan, you will be better off (assuming that there are no early payment penalty charges on the revolving credit accounts).

Now, it may be more *convenient* for you to have all your loans consolidated into one big one. Then you have to write only one check a month instead of many. But this service will not be handed to you without charge. You may in fact have a smaller monthly charge, but it will be for many more months, and you will ultimately end up paying higher finance charges for the whole consolidation package, and thus a higher total payment. If you detest keeping records and writing out lots of checks, you may want to incur this additional cost (and additional debt) by taking a loan consolidation. As long as you realize that nobody gives you anything for free, you can make a rational choice, knowing that there are always costs for any benefits you receive. Loan consolidation is certainly not going to pull you out of financial trouble if you really are in trouble. The only way out of such trouble is either by making a higher income or by cutting back on your current consumption so that you can pay off your debts more easily. (You could, of course, sell some of your assets to pay off your debts, too.)

DEBT COUNSELING

If you have gotten into financial trouble by overextending yourself, you may wish to consult some of the good nonprofit organizations working with people in debt troubles. Such work is generally called debt counseling. For example, there is a Financial Crisis Clinic run at Long Beach State University, in California, as a part of the program in financial counseling under the auspices of the Home Economics Department. You may wish to consult the home economics department of your local college or university to find out if a similar program is available in your area.

Basically, many credit problems you run into result from the lack of a financial plan. While such influences as credit advertising, credit selling, and other credit-oriented selling techniques tend to push families into the overuse of credit, you, the consumer, ultimately are the one who signs on the dotted line. If you have a sound financial plan, perhaps along the lines outlined in Chapter 6, no amount of advertising or fast talk will get you to over-extend yourself financially.

SUMMARY

1. There is no definite way to decide which purchases should be bought on time and which should be bought with cash. Rather, one's total outstanding debt should not exceed what can be handled.

2. You determine your safe debt load by adding up all of your outstanding debt, which includes loan payments, department store pay-ments, credit card payments, overdue ac-counts on telephone and electricity, and so on. One way of determining whether this is a safe debt load is by taking 10 percent of your monthly take-home pay (that is, after taxes), and multiplying it by 18. If your monthly debt is greater than what is safe, you must take steps to reduce it. These are outlined in the appendix to this issue.

3. You should estimate your net worth regu-larly, perhaps once a year.

4. You determine your net worth by adding up all of your assets, which include the market value of your house, your car(s), your bonds, stocks, and other things. Subtract what you owe, such as your house mortgage and other loans. This gives you your net worth.

5. Keeping track of your net worth year by year gives you an idea of the financial prog-ress you are making. If your net worth stays constant or goes down, you are spending an-nually more than you receive.

6. When applying for a loan, you must realize that the loan officer will look at your capacity to pay back, your character, and what col-lateral you can put up to back the loan.

7. When applying for a loan, put your best foot forward—fill out the form either with a typewriter or print clearly. And when meeting the loan officer, dress appropriately: first im-pressions are important.

8. If you are refused credit, the Fair Credit Reporting Act allows you to demand that the firm hired to do the credit check tell you what its report contains; that it do a re-check; and that it insert your version of any facts in dispute.

9. When you shop for credit, shop as if you were buying any other good or service. Look for the best deal by (a) calling around to get the various offers of interest rates and monthly payments; (b) checking to see whether an ac-celeration clause is in your contract; (c) mak-ing sure all finance and setup charges are specifically stated in any contract; (d) recom-puting the finance charge yourself—do not take the loan company's word for it.

10. Be wary of debt consolidation schemes. They generally are expensive.

11. If you are in trouble, debt counseling may be required. Financial crisis clinics are run in many major cities in the United States. Check with your local college or university home economics department.

QUESTIONS FOR THOUGHT
AND DISCUSSION

1. Is it important for you to determine why you are borrowing money before you borrow? Would you feel safer borrowing money to buy a durable consumer good such as a refrigera-tor, TV, or stereo, rather than borrowing mon-ey for a vacation?

2. Do you think it is unfair for loan officers to delve into your character before they de-cide whether you are a good credit risk? Why or why not?

THINGS TO DO

1. Go to the Exhibit on page 136 and use either method A or method B to determine your safe debt load or the debt load of your parents. How much are you overextended or underextended? (Is it possible to be underextended in debt?)

2. Call several banks or credit departments of various stores in your area and ask them to send you a loan application. Fill out the net worth statement to see what your net worth is. Familiarize yourself with all of the various terms. If you do not know what they mean, ask your instructor or go to a dictionary. If it is appropriate, attempt to determine your net worth for the past five years. Has it gone up or down?

3. Call your local field office of the Federal Trade Commission. Ask to speak to someone about what activities the FTC performs in enforcing the Truth-in-Lending Act. See if they have changed over the last few years.

4. Calculate the actual interest paid after your tax deduction for a typical consumer loan. Try to calculate the actual interest paid by someone like Howard Hughes, who is probably in the 70 percent tax bracket. Is there a big difference between the two corrected interest rates?

SELECTED READINGS

Before You Sign a Contract, HXT–95 (Berkeley: Agricultural Extension Service, University of California).

Be Wise: Consumers' Quick Credit Guide (Washington, D.C.: U. S. Department of Agriculture, Government Printing Office), September 1972.

Buying on Time, HXT–93 (Berkeley Agricultural Extension Service, University of California).

"How Much Can You Borrow?" *Money*, October 1972.

"The How and Why of Credit Buying," *Forecast*, November 1972.

APPENDIX: If you have to declare personal bankruptcy

Certain danger signals will tell to you that you are not financially sound. If some of the following appear in your financial picture, you may have to take fast action to keep from "going under."

DANGER SIGNALS

1. You consistently postpone paying your bills.

2. You begin to hear from your creditors.

3. You have no savings, or not enough to tide you over a financial upset.

4. You have no idea what your living expenses are.

5. You use a lot of credit, having charge accounts all over town and several credit cards in your wallet, paying only the minimum on each account every month.

6. You do not know how much your debts come to.

HOW TO KEEP FROM GOING UNDER

You can do certain things to prevent yourself and your family from getting into deeper financial trouble. Some of the following common-sense actions will be of special help.

1. Itemize your debts in detail, making sure you note current balance, monthly payment, and when payments are due.

2. List the family's total monthly net income that can be counted on every month.

3. Subtract your monthly living expenses from your net income. Do not include the payments on debt you already have. The result will be the income you would be able to spend if you had no debts. Now subtract the monthly payments you are committed to making on all of your debts. If you come out with a minus figure, you are obviously living beyond your means. If you come out with a very small positive figure, you still may be living beyond your means.

4. If you think you are in fact living beyond your means, what you have to do is clear: Notify everyone in your family that the money situation is tight. Tell them things are going to have to be cut back. You and every other spender in the family unit will have to start shaving expenses, such as those on recreation, food, and transportation.

IF THAT FAILS

If you are still in deep trouble and cannot pull out of it yourself, then you may have to devise a plan of action by yourself or with a debt counselor, as we discussed in the preceding consumer issue: Once you have made up that plan of action, go to your separate creditors and discuss it with them to see if you can work things out without going into personal bankruptcy.

GOING INTO PERSONAL BANKRUPTCY

You have the alternative of getting out of debt by going to court. But you may spend a great amount of money in doing so, and lose some of your property besides.

The basic law that allows you to declare bankruptcy is Chapter XIII of the National Bankruptcy Act, the Wage Earner Plan. It is a court-supervised plan for paying off your debt; it is not true bankruptcy. With the help of a lawyer, you draw up a budget and a plan for repayment, usually over 36 months. You file your plan and your petition with the bankruptcy court in your area. Upon filing the plan

and petition, you are immediately given relief from creditor harrassment and collection pressures.

The plan must be approved by both the court and creditors. Once it is approved, the court will appoint a trustee who receives your payments and distributes the money to the creditors. You must pay the trustee 5 percent of the amount he distributes; here is where the cost comes in. Court costs and lawyers fees will add another several hundred dollars to filing a Chapter XIII.

Note that Chapter XIII is successful in only half the number of cases in which it is used.

True bankruptcy is the only legal way you can cancel your debts without paying them. For you to file bankruptcy in a U. S. District Court, your debts do not have to exceed your assets by any particular amount, but you do have to be in deep financial trouble.

After filing, in effect you give up all that you own. That is, the court has control over all your assets. A trustee is named to check on those assets available for distribution to creditors. The court will return to you tools and other items necessary for you to earn your living, as well as food, clothing, basic furniture, and perhaps, but not always, your home. Exactly what you can keep varies from state to state and should be looked into before you even consider declaring personal bankruptcy.

The benefit of declaring bankruptcy is that all your debts are wiped out except for taxes, alimony and support payments, and the debts that others have cosigned for you (which now become their debts).

The disadvantage has already been mentioned: you no longer have control over your property. But in addition, bankruptcy puts a black mark on your credit record. What is more, you can get back into debt right away. After all, you have court and lawyers' costs, which together might run to $500. And remember, you can not file for bankruptcy again for another six years.

☐ What are the characteristics of food consumption in the United States?
☐ How do government inspection and labeling requirements affect the consumer?
☐ Specifically, what does the Fair Packaging and Labeling Act do?
☐ What are some of the attributes of good nutrition?
☐ How do government agricultural programs affect consumer food prices?
☐ What are the trends in food retailing and what is the future of convenience foods?

GLOSSARY OF NEW TERMS

Engel's Law A proposition, first made by Ernst Engel, that states that as families' income rises, the proportion spent on food falls.

Marginal Buyers: Buyers who are just on the borderline between buying and not buying a product at the particular offering price. Marginal buyers for specific products are very concerned with price and quality of those products.

RDAs Recommended Dietary Allowances, usually specified in terms of a daily intake of a particular vitamin or nutrient.

Support Prices: A minimum price set by the government for a particular agricultural raw commodity. For example, the support price of wheat may be set at, say, $2.00 per bushel. That means that the farmer never has to sell his or her wheat below that support price.

Nonrecourse Loans: Loans made to farmers by a government organization in exchange for a particular agricultural commodity—say, wheat or corn. They are called nonrecourse because the government can never demand payment for the loan.

Target Prices: Prices set by the government for particular agricultural commodities, such as wheat and corn. If the actual market price falls below the target price, farmers get a kickback or subsidy from the government for the difference.

In one year, the average American consumes 170 pounds of red meat, 50 pounds of poultry, 14 pounds of fish, 41 pounds of eggs, 352 pounds of dairy products, 50 pounds of fats and oils, 80 pounds of fresh fruits, 140 pounds of fresh vegetables, 260 pounds of canned goods, 142 pounds of flour and cereal products, 120 pounds of sugar and other sweeteners, 15 pounds of coffee, tea, and cocoa, etc. The total amount of money spent on food products is just as staggering: $200 billion estimated in 1975 alone. Americans consume more than 30 percent of the world's total agricultural output. We are feeding a very large and hungry stomach. We buy our food products at 300,000 retail stores which carry an average of 2600 different products on their shelves at any one time. The number of brands of different types of foods—canned peas, carrots, soups, cereals—is probably many thousand when you include all of the regional specialties you can buy.

And since food bills take up between 20 and 35 percent of just about every American's budget, there is deep concern over rising food prices. Figure 8–1 shows the price index for foods over the last 50 years. When we talk about inflation in Chapter 15, we will discuss some of the significance of this rise in food prices, and below in this chapter we will discover that at least one reason why food prices are so high is that certain government programs are designed to keep them high.

FOOD AND INCOME

Even though we spend a total of $150 billion a year on food, that represents only 15 percent of total income in the United States. Figure 8–2 shows that the percentage of total U. S. income spent on food consumption has actually been falling. Is this surprising? Well, it should not be. Ask yourself how much more food could you buy if you had a doubling of income. You could certainly buy better quality, and perhaps you could eat out in restaurants more often. But there is a limit, at least for most of you; and that limit is a physical one. Your stomach can hold only so much at any one sitting and your body will maintain its weight only if you do not put more calories into it than you use up.

If people's expenditures for food had kept in line with their incomes over the past 150 years in the United

THE $ BILLION STOMACH

FIGURE 8–1
PRICE INDEX, FOOD
(1967 = 100)
An index of average
food prices shows
dramatic increases in
the last half decade.
In particular, since the
so-called food crisis of
1973 up to the present,
it has risen faster than
almost every other
component of the
overall price index in
the economy. Sources:
*Monthly Labor Review;
Federal Reserve
Bulletin.*

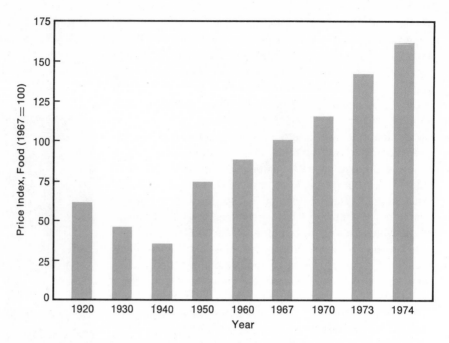

States, we would be a nation of balloons, each running into each other
and having trouble sitting in chairs, driving cars, and getting on buses.
While there may be some tendency for the average American to be slightly
overweight, we certainly are not a nation of corpulent slobs.

A long time ago, in 1856, a German statistician, Ernst Engel, made some
budgetary studies of family expenditures and found that as family incomes
increased, the *percentage* spent on food decreased—not the total amount
spent on food, of course, but the percentage. A family making $25,000
a year certainly spends more on food than a family making $10,000 a
year. However, even though the richer family has an income two and a
half times larger than the other family's, the richer family does not spend
on food two and a half times the amount that the other family spends.
It might spend, say, only twice or one and a half times as much.

Engel's Law has a fairly universal applicability, not only through time
but across nations at any given moment. Remember our discussion of
this in Chapter 6 in reference to the budgets of different families. Richer
nations spend a smaller fraction of their total national income on food
than do poorer nations. And we can predict that in the United States, if
we become richer, our expenditures on food will become a smaller percentage of total expenditures.

**GOVERNMENT
INSPECTION AND
LABELING
REQUIREMENTS**

Since food is an essential part of every consumer's budget, the government has through the years established a system of inspection and labeling designed in principle to aid us consumers in making wiser choices
about the food products we buy. You may not be aware of it, but the

government is busy inspecting meatpacking houses and various food processing establishments in order to insure that our food is processed in a clean, bacteria-free environment so that we will not suffer the harmful effects that sometimes result from improper food processing. The FDA goes so far as to periodically determine the quantities of rodent hair and insect residue in your peanut butter! The government is also attempting to force fair packaging and labeling, particularly in the form of the Fair Packaging and Labeling Act of 1966.

FAIR PACKAGING

The law came about through numerous criticisms directed at packagers. The quantity of contents were often inadequately or confusingly disclosed; there was no uniform designation of quantity by weight or fluid volume. For example, one producer would measure by ounces, while a competitor would measure by the quart or would measure by quarts and ounces combined. In addition, there was criticism of the use of presumably meaningless adjectives of exaggeration, such as "giant" or "jumbo," and the use of designations of servings, such as small, medium, and large, without any standard of reference.

The Act applies to such consumer commodities as foods and drugs, devices, or cosmetics that are subject to the Federal Food, Drug and Cosmetic Act, and to any other article customarily purchased for sale through retailers for consumption by individuals or for "use by individuals for pur-

FIGURE 8–2
PERCENTAGE OF TOTAL INCOME IN THE UNITED STATES GOING FOR FOOD
At the beginning of the Great Depression and for the following 20 or so years, the percentage of disposable personal income going for food remained at around 23 to 24 percent, but in 1950 it started dropping until it reached about 15 percent in the 1970s. It will probably continue to drop as our real income goes up.
Source: USDA Agricultural Economic Report No. 138; supplement for 1971.

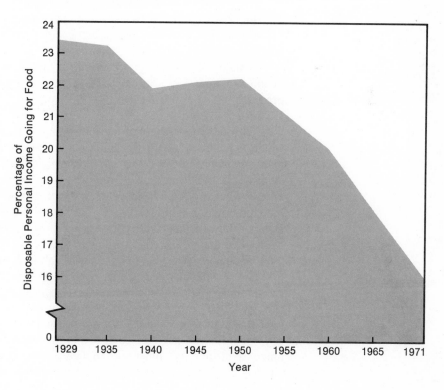

poses of personal care or in the performance of services ordinarily rendered within the household." The FTC at first proposed regulations that enlarged upon the term "consumer commodity" to include virtually everything. But when producers threatened substantial litigation if these enlarged regulations went through, the FTC instead listed 52 classes of products that it does not consider to be "consumer commodities" and therefore are not included under the Fair Packaging and Labeling Act of 1966.

The Act also authorized the Secretary of Commerce to attempt to limit "undue" proliferation of product package sizes. If the Secretary determines that there is such an undue proliferation that consumers suffer an "unreasonably" impaired ability to make product comparison, then the Secretary may request that manufacturers, packers, and distributors participate in the development of a *voluntary* product standard for that commodity. If no standard has been adopted within one year after such a request, or if the voluntary standard adopted is not observed, the Secretary of Commerce is supposed to report such determination to Congress.

The Act, which became effective in 1967, does not apply to tobacco, meat, poultry, and any other products covered by other federal laws. It requires, among other things, that the label of every consumer product that is covered by it must:

1. Give the net quantity per serving.
2. Not have "too much" air space or packaging material.
3. Identify the commodity and make clear the name and place of the business of the manufacturer, distributor, or packer.
4. Contain a statement in a standard location on the main display panel of the package of the net contents in units that seem appropriate for the product.

All of the federal efforts at fair packaging and labeling are aimed at providing consumers with a maximum amount of information so that we may make rational choices. And all such efforts may be gathered under the label "truth in packaging," or truth, plain and simple. But we have to be careful when we analyze the effects of truth in packaging acts passed by federal, state, or local governments. Take the case of air space in packages. If all consumers could be duped forever, the ultimate result of, say, cereal manufacturers putting their products in big boxes with quantities of air space would be that people would end up buying boxes of air. Since that has not happened (at least not yet), we know that *some* consumers are informed.

Many of the informed consumers who keep producers in line are so-called institutional buyers—that is, governments, hospitals, day camps, day care centers, summer camps, and places like that—which buy great amounts of food and have nutritionists who make sure that the best food value is obtained. Those large institutional buyers who take so much care in their food shopping are what we call marginal buyers, because if they find out that a particular product they have purchased turns out to be a gyp, they switch immediately: they are right on the margin between buying it and buying the second-best choice. Fortunately, there are always a number of these buyers around. In fact, one study showed that fully one-third of all shoppers are marginal shoppers; they are very price conscious and also take time and effort to establish the validity of the claims made by all ads, labels, and so on.

NET WEIGHT
SOMETIMES SPELLS
NONSENSE

Even though the Fair Packaging and Labeling Act requires that the net weight of canned foods be given, it is sometimes pretty hard to figure out what you are really buying. You have to find out, for example, what is the actual weight of the fruit in a can of pears because some brands will have more syrup than others. If you do not want the syrup, then you do not care how much *it* weighs. Table 8–1 reproduces a portion of the results—those for peach halves and peach slices—of a Consumer Union survey done in New York. Notice that the average drained weight

TABLE 8–1:
DRAINED WEIGHT VS.
LABELED WEIGHT
A study done by Con-
sumers Union produced
these results. The
labeled weight of
peaches and pears
showed a considerable
difference from the
average drained weight.
In general, the drained
weight was about 40
percent less than the
labeled weight. Source:
Consumer Reports,
October 1972, p. 666.

	LABELED WEIGHT	AVERAGE DRAINED WEIGHT		AVERAGE PRICE
PEACH HALVES, YELLOW CLING, IN HEAVY SYRUP				
A & P	16 oz.	9.8 oz.	61.3%	$.27
	29	17.0	58.6	.37
Del Monte	16	9.8	61.3	.28
	29	18.9	65.2	.37
Grand Union	16	10.0	62.5	.25
	29	18.6	64.1	.28
Waldbaum's	16	10.5	65.6	.25
	29	18.8	64.8	.33
PEACH SLICES, YELLOW CLING, IN HEAVY SYRUP				
A & P	16	10.6	66.3	.29
Del Monte	16	11.0	68.8	.31
Grand Union	16	9.6	60.0	.25
Waldbaum's	16	10.7	66.9	.27
PEAR HALVES, BARTLETT, IN HEAVY SYRUP				
A & P	29	16.2	55.9	.45
Del Monte	16	9.4	58.8	.35
	29	16.2	55.9	.57
Grand Union	16	9.2	57.5	.33
	29	18.4	63.5	.49
Waldbaum's	16	8.6	53.8	.29
	29	17.2	59.3	.37

of the peaches was about 60 percent of the labeled net weight, and that the degree to which the labeling was false was almost the same for just about all brands. That would mean that once consumers figured this out, they could still use the labeled weight as a guide and therefore figure out the best deal. Notice also that in the peach halves selection, the larger can always gave a lower cost per pound of drained weight, so that buying in larger quantities always led to a lower per unit price even if the can was mislabeled as to its net weight.

The Food and Drug Administration has numerous requirements for the canning industry. The usual rule of thumb is that a container must be at least 90 percent full. However, since packing liquid, such as syrup for peach halves, can be legally added, the FDA requirement is obviously not very useful. The National Canners Association takes the position that part of the nutrients of the canned food end up in the liquids used for canning and so the liquid is part of the food product. Therefore, the NCA is against disclosing the drained weights on the outside of cans. But since it appears that the drained weight averages about the same percentage of labeled weight for all brands of a given product, it probably would not matter. We consumers would know that we are actually paying a higher price per average drained weight, but we would still have the same selection at about the same prices we have always been paying. In this example, it seems that the additional information is not going to make us much better off.

USDA GRADES —
ANOTHER LABELING
CONFUSION

In addition to FDA labeling requirements for canned or processed foods, and meat inspection, the U. S. Department of Agriculture provides for grade marks on various meats and fresh produce. These grades are meant to guide the consumer as to the level of quality, but the labels are often misleading.

Meat. All fresh meats, with the exception of pork, are labeled as to grade. Until several years ago, the top grade available in supermarkets was "prime," followed by "choice," and so on. However, the prime classification had generally been eliminated, and "choice" had become the top grade available. This led to a degree of confusion in shopping for meats, fostered in part by the reluctance of both supermarkets and shoppers to give up the old labels. "Prime" is still associated with top quality, and meats are often still advertised as "prime." It was apparently difficult to accept "choice," which used to be viewed as adequate, but not the best, as now representing the most tender cuts available. And every city has a Prime Rib restaurant, also reinforcing the identity of that term with the top quality available. In any event, the current grading marks on fresh meats, which appear usually as a purple stamp on the product, have been undergoing significant changes. You will have to verify for yourself what current standards are.

Poultry. Poultry was not under federal inspection standards until the Wholesome Poultry Products Act of 1968. But it has for some time also been subject to USDA grading. And this leads to even greater confusion, for poultry is graded solely on physically observable characteristics, such as presence or absence of freezer burns, of wing tips or other missing parts, or breaks in the skin. In other words, a grade of A on a turkey may mean that you get a tough old bird that just happens to have all its parts and suffers from no *observable* flaws. Similarly, a B bird, though technically a lesser grade, may be delicious but have a wing tip broken. Poultry grading does not guarantee quality; but you can be sure that a C rating means that the product is likely to physically appear nearly un-marketable.

Other Food Products. The USDA also provides for the grading of other food products, such as eggs and milk, and also for fresh fruits and vegetables, usually those that come prepackaged. In this area particularly, the grading is often misleading. In Table 8–2 are listed some of the grades applying to produce. As you can see, "U. S. No. 1" is not a sufficient guide to quality; in some cases it represents the third grade. Similarly, "U. S. No. 1 Bright" represents the second grade of oranges, but the third grade of apples.

Obviously, the best way to shop for groceries is to obtain the most palatable, most nutritious foods for the least amount of money. Some guidelines for doing this are presented in the following consumer issue. But in order to understand some of the recent legislation involving labeling requirements, we had best look at the question of nutrition here.

**WHAT IS
GOOD NUTRITION?**

Even the experts are at odds. Many grade school students are taught about food in terms of the basic four: meat (or other protein sources); grains; vegetables and fruits; and dairy products. Sometimes the basic four are expanded to seven to include fruits, oils, and other food items. In its Family Food Plans, the USDA defines nutrition needs in terms of 15 food categories measured in weekly amounts; this is one of the few programs to specify other than daily intake suggestions.

Interestingly, most nutrition advice has stressed the importance of eating a balanced diet *daily*. Now a considerable group—for example, several cereal companies—talk about eating a nutritionally balanced breakfast, or lunch, or dinner. Several studies have shown, however, that daily balancing of nutritional intake (such as bread versus meat versus dairy products, or protein versus vitamins versus carbohydrates) is unnecessary. In fact, in a study of the eating habits of children who were offered a variety of foods representing all food groups, it was found that children did indeed balance their diets, but *over days or weeks*. Apparently, the "natural" eating pattern of human beings dictates a certain nutritional variety in a certain proportion over a longer period than a day.

TABLE 8–2: PRODUCE GRADING

The U.S. Department of Agriculture has instituted a rather complex system of grading of products. For example, in grapefruit, U.S. No. 1 is *not* the top grade, but in onions, U.S. No. 1 *is* the top grade. In fact for oranges from Florida, U.S. No. 1 is the third grade, the top grade being U.S. Fancy and the second grade being U.S. No. 1 Bright. Source: U.S. Department of Agriculture.

COMMODITY	TOP GRADE	SECOND GRADE	THIRD GRADE	FOURTH GRADE
Apples (all states but Washington)	U.S. Extra Fancy	U.S. Fancy	U.S. No. 1	U.S. Utility
Apples (Washington)	Washington Extra Fancy	Washington Fancy		
Grapefruit (all states but Arizona, California and Florida)	U.S. Fancy	U.S. No. 1	U.S. No. 1 Bright	U.S. No. 1 Bronze
Grapefruit (Arizona and California)	U.S. Fancy	U.S. No. 1	U.S. No. 1	U.S. Combination
Grapefruit (Florida)	U.S. Fancy	U.S. No. 1	U.S. No. 1 Bright	U.S. No. 1 Golden
Onions	U.S. No. 1	U.S. Combination or U.S. Commercial	U.S. No. 2	
Oranges (all states but Arizona, California and Florida)	U.S. Fancy	U.S. No. 1	U.S. No. 1 Bright	U.S. No. 1 Bronze
Oranges (Arizona and California)	U.S. Fancy	U.S. No. 1	U.S. Combination	U.S. No. 2
Oranges (Florida)	U.S. Fancy	U.S. No. 1 Bright	U.S. No. 1	U.S. No. 1 Golden
Pears (Summer and Fall)	U.S. No. 1	U.S. Combination	U.S. No. 2	
Pears (Winter)	U.S. Extra No. 1	U.S. No. 1	U.S. Combination	U.S. No. 2
Potatoes	U.S. Extra No. 1	U.S. No. 1	U.S. Commercial	U.S. No. 2

Note: Potatoes are also sold "unclassified" meaning ungraded.

COMMODITY	TOP GRADE	SECOND GRADE	THIRD GRADE	FOURTH GRADE
Tomatoes (Fresh)	U.S. No. 1	U.S. Combination	U.S. No. 2	U.S. No. 3

The study on children's eating habits also indicated that children were at least sensitive to their own nutritional requirements, that their bodies seemed to "crave" the proper foods, even though sugars and other sweets, often viewed as nutritionally empty calories, were also available.[1]

There is, however, some sense to the frequent admonition to balance food intake daily. In the first place, such attention to nutrition often avoids establishing eating habits that at a later date might confuse the body's own sense of what it needs, as excessive sugar intake can do.

[1] Obstetricians who often advise pregnant women to give in to their cravings thereby acknowledge that such cravings may represent real nutritional needs.

Second, new FDA guidelines on the nutrition labeling of processed foods are in RDA's—Recommended Dietary Allowances—and these are usually measured in daily intake. These new regulations specify that all processed foods state their nutritional content in terms of RDAs on the label.

RECOMMENDED
DIETARY ALLOWANCE

The RDA allowances for nutrition, established by the National Academy of Sciences, state nutritional requirements for some nutrients in metric measurements. Especially in regards to vitamins and minerals, the content of processed foods is increasingly specified on labels as percentages of daily RDAs contained: a breakfast drink label might state the contents as 30 mg. of Vitamin C, or 50 percent of the RDA. In Table 8–3 are given the recommended daily dietary allowances for men and women of those vitamins and minerals usually viewed as contributing to good

TABLE 8-3:
RECOMMENDED DAILY
DIETARY ALLOWANCES
FOR REFERENCE
WOMAN AND MAN [1]

NUTRIENT	UNIT	ALLOWANCE		ALLOWANCE PER 1000 CALORIES	
		Woman	Man	Woman	Man
Food energy	cal	2,000	2,800	1	1
Protein	g	55	65	28	23
Fat-soluble vitamins: [2]					
Vitamin A	IU	5,000	5,000	2,500	1,800
Vitamin E	IU	25	30	12	11
Water-soluble vitamins:					
Ascorbic acid	mg	55	60	28	21
Folacin	mg	.4	.4	.2	.1
Niacin	mg equiv	13	18	6	6
Riboflavin	mg	1.5	1.7	.8	.6
Thiamin	mg	1.0	1.4	.5	.5
Vitamin B_6	mg	2.0	2.0	1.0	.7
Vitamin B_{12}	mg	5	5	2	2
Minerals:					
Calcium	mg	800	800	400	290
Phosphorus	mg	800	800	400	290
Iodine	mg	100	140	50	50
Iron	mg	18	10	9	4
Magnesium	mg	300	350	15	12

[1] National Academy of Science-National Research Council, Pub. No. 1694, 1968. RDA were established for food energy and 15 nutrients; for other vitamins and minerals, RDA have not yet been established. Reference woman: age=22 years; height=64 inches; weight=128 lb. Reference man: age=22 years; height=69 inches; weight=154 lb.

[2] Needs of reference adults for vitamin D are assumed to be met by foods in a mixed diet and usual amounts of exposure to sunlight, so no allowance is specified.

Source: Judy P. Chassy, "Nutrient Needs and Food Costs of Women," *Family Economics Review*, Fall 1973, p. 21.

nutrition. While protein content is often indicated as a percentage of daily RDA, more frequently, however, protein, carbohydrates (starches and sugars), and ash, or nonnutritive materials are measured as percentages of the total contents of the package. As a guide to menu planning in terms of these categories, Table 8–4 presents the U. S. Department of Agriculture's recommended weekly food plan.

The next Consumer Issue goes into more detail on how to consider nutrition in buying food. But it is important that we first understand some more about the effects of government legislation on the food products we buy.

ON NOT BUYING OLD STUFF

We all like to buy fresh food. When we buy fruits and vegetables, we can see at a glance how old they are and whether or not they are worth the price. But when we buy canned items or processed meats and other such goods, we cannot really tell unless we open up the package or can. Few of us ever do that when we buy something wrapped in clear plastic. (It would be embarrassing if we were caught.) Since we do not know how old the processed food is that we buy, government truth in food labeling activities has centered to some extent on food dating.

Food dating is not new; there is already food dating on the cans and many of the cartons you buy. But most of the time, you have no knowledge of what the code numbers mean. In many states you are now able to figure out how fresh is the can, or salami, or cottage cheese, or whatever, through the open dating systems. In other words, the shelf life of the product in question is printed on the container in numbers which conventionally represent the date. This not only helps you pick processed food that is not too old, it also gives you information to use in your own day-to-day food planning. You make sure you use up your purchased foods in the order of their shelf life dates. For example, at the top of the carton of milk you bought you see a date. This is usually the date by which the food should be sold to insure its subsequent freshness for home use.

Photographers know about this already. Film has been dated for many years without government regulation, the date telling us would-be photographers when we should use the film by. Outdated film often sells at a lower price than in-date film because the film is less likely to be good once out of date. The same is true, of course, with pastry items and bread. You know you can buy day-old bread and such things at certain bakeries at a lower price than fresh items. Why? Because generally the day-old stuff is not as good or as desired.

Eventually, this is what will probably happen with many items that are now being dated for freshness in supermarkets, as required by law in some states. After the freshness date expires, the supermarket, to get rid of the products, will have to lower the price.

TABLE 8–4:
RECOMMENDED
WEEKLY FOOD PLAN

KINDS OF FOOD	CHILDREN AGE 7 TO 12	WOMEN ALL AGES *	MEN ALL AGES *
Leafy, green yellow vegetables	½ to ¾ lbs.	¾ lb.	¾ lb.
Citrus fruits, tomatoes	2½ lbs.	2½ lbs.	2½ to 3 lbs.
Potatoes	1½ to 2 lbs.	1 to 1½ lbs.	2 to 3 lbs.
Other vegetables and fruits	6½ to 7½ lbs.	5 to 7½ lbs.	7 to 9 lbs.
Milk, cheese, ice cream	6 to 6½ qts.	3½ quarts	3½ quarts
Meat, poultry, fish	3 to 4 lbs.	4 to 4½ lbs.	5 to 5½ lbs.
Eggs	4	4	4
Dry beans, peas, nuts	2 ounces	2 to 4 oz.	4 ounces
Cereals, flour, and baked goods (whole grain or enriched)	2 to 3 lbs.	2 to 2½ lbs.	3 to 4 lbs.
Fats, oils	¾ lb.	½ lb.	¾ to 1 lb.
Sugar, syrups, preserves	¾ lb.	½ to 1 lb.	1 to 1½ lbs.

* The smaller quantity for the age group over 55 years.

Source: *Family Fare* (Washington, D. C.: Human Nutrition Research Branch, Agricultural Research Service, United States Department of Agriculture, Home and Garden Bulletin No. 1), pp. 14–15.

Of course, many aware consumers of food products know that, even in the past when there was no dating on processed foods, one way you could be sure of not getting old food was by shopping at a store with a reputation for always having fresh items. Generally, that store probably charged a higher price for some of its products than other stores in which you could be less confident of freshness. But of course, you were getting a service for that higher price, the service being certainty about the freshness of the food you were buying. The dating information that is now being provided for various food items will help all of us, however, know at a glance whether we are getting fresh processed food or food that should have been used yesterday.

Many consumers are quite thankful for government help in requiring truth-in-labeling, truth-in-packaging, proper processing facilities, and the like. But consumers in general are increasingly dissatisfied with the government's consistent intervention in the food markets in order to keep the price of food high. You the consumer have been hurt by our various agricultural programs designed not to help you, but to help the farmer.

THE GOVERNMENT'S HELPING HAND IN AGRICULTURE

Farmers have always been considered an underprivileged group because, before government intervention, the price of their products suffered large swings from year to year. That meant that the variability in income for farmers was quite high. Some years it was feast; other years it was famine. To help out the farmer, the government entered into numerous arrangements of which you probably are not aware.

THE DEPRESSION AND THE AAA

During "the First Hundred Days" of the Franklin D. Roosevelt Administration, when the nation was suffering the greatest depression in its history, a variety of legislative acts were passed to bring the economy back to its feet again. Whether or not these acts were effective in that respect is not our concern here. Our concern is the Agricultural Adjustment Act of 1933 (and its later version of 1938), which was the legal foundation of the AAA, the Agricultural Adjustment Administration. As well as establishing a system of conservation of agricultural lands, acreage

restrictions, and so on, the act established support prices for a number of agricultural products.

What is a support price? Well, it is just what the term suggests. When the government supports the price of a product—say, wheat— at a certain fixed amount per bushel, any farmer who cannot sell his wheat on the open market at the stated support price can always sell it to the government. That means, in effect, that the price will not go below that fixed supported price. For many years, the support price was below the market price, so the government was not called upon to buy many agricultural products. However, after World War II, the situation changed.

The government found itself with larger and larger "surpluses" of agricultural products, because the unrestricted price was lower than the support price, and farmers were therefore selling much of their wheat and corn and other produce to the government.[2] To cut back on these surpluses, the government instituted more and more acreage restrictions. That is, farmers who wanted to take part in the price support efforts of the government had to agree not to cultivate a certain amount of their lands. But farmers are not stupid; they put into fallow (disuse) their worst lands and added more fertilizer, seed, and men to the lands that they could cultivate. As a result, over a seven-year period total acreage cultivated fell by 30 percent but total output increased by 17 percent!

THE RESULTS

What did these programs mean to consumers over all of these years? Obviously, one thing and one thing only—higher food prices. Had the government not attempted to keep the price of agricultural products high so as to help farmers, we would have been paying lower food prices all along, at least during the period from about 1948 to 1972. In 1973, the government scrapped some major aspects of its agricultural program. All of the acreage restrictions were to be lifted for 1974 and target prices were substituted for support prices. But because the world price of agricultural products was quite high in 1973, target prices were set at a relatively high level in comparison with past supported prices or past unrestricted market prices. Therefore, while in the future we may not be subjected to the higher food prices that once came from government supports, we *will* be subsidizing farmers whenever the market price falls below the target price.

During quite a few years in the 1960s and 1970s, we food consumers paid a total cost of $5 billion a year in higher food prices because of government programs. In addition to that, we made $5 billion a year in direct payments to farmers to bring their incomes up.[3] Many of us would prob-

[2] The transaction was not *called a sale.* The farmers got a *nonrecourse loan* from the Commodity Credit Corporation. But the effect is the same as a sale, because in a non-recourse loan the farmer can one day choose to buy back the produce on which the loan was issued, but no farmer has to do this.

[3] Charles L. Schultze, *The Distribution of Farm Subsidies: Who Gets the Benefits* (Washington, D. C.: The Brookings Institution, 1971).

ably not be so upset about that transfer to farmers if it were indeed the poor farmers who were getting the money. But that was not the case. In 1973, for example, 45 percent of all payments to farmers went to the top 7 percent of the income-earning farmers. That does not sound like a redistribution of income to the poor.

AND MILK, TOO

The Agricultural Adjustment Act of 1933 and of 1938 (the first one was declared unconstitutional by the Supreme Court) established another government program that makes the milk that you drink higher-priced than it would be otherwise. It is perhaps instructive to see why the government had to step in.

Earlier in the century, before government participation in the market for agricultural products, farmers, through their cooperatives, attempted to bargain with dealers for a two-price system in which milk that was to be resold for fresh milk would fetch a higher price for the farmer than milk which would be resold for manufacturing cheese, butter, yogurt, and cottage cheese. However, in the absence of monopoly power, it is extremely difficult, if not impossible, to maintain price differentials that do not reflect production cost differences. Milk dealers who are going to resell what they buy as fresh milk could inevitably find milk producers who would sell their milk at about the same price as the cost to those manufacturing milk products. There was occasional violence and there were milk strikes in order to maintain the two-price system that farmers wanted for their own benefit. But in the absence of any government support, such two-price systems are unstable and led to instability in milk prices both for producers and for dairies and bottlers (usually called handlers).

Since farmers could not maintain a monopoly pricing situation, they decried the market for milk as being extremely "unorderly." Milk price instability, caused by the efforts of farmers to maintain discriminatory pricing for their output, was deemed socially undesirable and therefore the competition which caused this was to be eliminated. Since such a large number of producers were involved, it was impossible for competition to be eliminated without government support.

Because milk producers therefore increased their efforts to obtain support for their monopoly pricing efforts, the AAA has a provision for federal control over the marketing of fluid milk. The AAA still allows producers of milk sold to the public as fresh milk to force marketing controls upon dairies and handlers. The federal government controls over 60 percent of today's milk markets and the states control the majority of the rest. It is quite obvious to any disinterested bystander, and particularly to you and me as consumers of fresh milk, that federal marketing milk controls have been established for the benefit of milk producers, not for the public at large.

The effect of federal tinkering in the milk market has been to help out fluid milk market producers and hurt manufactured milk market producers. If you happen to like cottage cheese, yogurt, butter, and the other products made from milk, you are perhaps better off, because the supply of those products is larger now than it would have been without federal controls. But if you happen to like fresh milk, you are worse off, because you are paying a higher price than you would have paid in the absence of controls. A few years ago the Justice Department brought suit against 13 milk associations because they were violating antitrust statutes. They had banded together to keep the price of fresh milk artificially high.

In general, the types of government programs designed to help special-interest groups must be looked at with a cautious, skeptical eye. Businessmen are at the bottom of them, and hence you can well imagine that the consumer will not benefit. Many advocates of regulation and government programs realize that in the past producer or business interests have been served much more than consumer interest or public interest. However, that does not necessarily mean that such government regulation and programs should be scrapped. Rather, according to some, all interests should be involved in making many of the decisions that are now made by government regulators. That is, producer interests, labor interests, *and* consumer interests would be represented on the boards of many of these regulatory agencies. Then perhaps the public interest, which may be a compromise of producer, labor and consumer interest, would be best served. This interesting idea is receiving growing support in Congress.

TRENDS IN FOOD RETAILING

If you wanted to buy something to eat for dinner in a small village in Africa or India or some other less-developed country, you would not drive down to your local supermarket and pick out meat in clean plastic-wrapped packages and vegetables in cans or freezer packages. Rather, you would go to small stalls in an open-air market and buy what you wanted from a local merchant, who might even be the person who had raised the steers or the corn, peas, or carrots. In fact, that is how much food shopping used to be done even in the United States; and we still see some remnants of it like roadside fruit stands on well-traveled highways in agricultural areas. But in general, as consumers of food products, you and I do not go to open air markets; we go to a supermarket or, at the very least, to a small mom-and-pop store on the corner. Today, as we mentioned in the opening paragraph of this chapter, there are 300,000 retail markets in the United States. In some areas, the trend is towards closed-circuit TV shopping.

BUYING FOOD BY TV

In Stockholm, Sweden, the Home Shop is one to which you never have to go to buy your food. You merely dial in whatever you want to buy from the store's bi-weekly catalog. Ordering is done quickly and is filled by a conveyor belt system, and your order is delivered to your door. Stockholm food customers give this store almost 3½ percent of the city's total food business.

Certain self-contained living units around our country also have closed-circuit television food shopping. In some apartments, there is a closed circuit TV. You dial the grocer in your building. If he or she is not busy, your call is accepted and through your TV you get to watch your choices being picked for you. You specify what size piece of meat you want to buy and what size head of lettuce, and so on. We have come a long way from the one-to-one food buying experienced by our ancestors in open-air markets.

Some of us may get a tinge of nostalgia when we think about how exciting and pleasurable buying food in those big markets must have been. In fact, some of us still can do it in the few open-air markets that still exist in the U. S. Remember, though, the reason why we now have impersonal supermarkets and may someday have closed-circuit TV or telephone food shopping is that many of us do not like to spend, or cannot afford to spend, much time getting food to eat. (This may also explain some of the "food jag" fad diets, like those in which you eat nothing but grapefruit for two weeks—it certainly simplifies and cuts the time needed for grocery shopping!) It may be fun to shop for food every day in small towns in France. But French food shoppers spend many hours every week getting that great food that they eat. Americans appear unwilling to pay that time price, and so we see trends toward faster and faster retailing methods which save us more and more time. Many observers feel that our entire life style emphasizes speed, "efficiency," and machine effort, and that our social values, perhaps reinforced by marketing techniques, push us to these choices.

"For dessert, we have Twinkies, Hostess cupcakes, or Devil Dogs."

Basically, then, the so-called work ethic has come to mean work for money income only, while time spent on other activities is considered wasted. Hence, it is not surprising that we see such a big trend not only towards faster shopping techniques, but also towards the use of more and more convenience foods.

THE GROWING TREND
TOWARD CONVENIENCE
FOOD

The food industry is now providing us with buttered peas, frozen corn on the cob, stuffed baked potatoes, cheese in a spray can, complete frozen dinners, frozen tacos—you name it and you can buy it already prepared. Just pop it into the oven and wait.

Why convenience foods. Why are Americans buying so many convenience foods? The answer is quite easy: because our high incomes lead us to place a high value on our time. Americans are no lazier than other people. We are merely willing to pay more than others in both money and lower food quality to save time. We prefer to use our time otherwise.

One of the reasons people like to buy convenience food is that it equals built-in maid service. You need none of the pots and pans and cutting utensils of old for something that is already prepared and frozen, buttered and made ready to eat after only heating. This eliminates a good part of kitchen chores. Now, certain convenience foods give you less nutrient value than if you spent the time making the dish yourself. Again, that is just part of the price you pay for convenience and you should be aware of it. People who are more concerned about nutritional value and dislike consuming large quantities of food additives shy away from convenience food, but they pay a price for that: the people who always cook fresh vegetables spend more time in the kitchen than the people who always cook frozen vegetables.

We can make no ultimate judgment about whether convenience foods are good or bad for the American consumer. As long as you know exactly what you are getting, then you can make the choice. We will point out in the following consumer issue on food buying that, looked at realistically, the cost of convenience is sometimes astronomical. If you decide that the cost is sometimes too high, you will choose foods that are not so convenient.

Not all convenience foods the same. But perhaps it is incorrect to lump all convenience foods together. While some increase sugar in the diet, such as Tang in place of frozen orange juice, and others provide non-food, such as frozen cream pies, others provide real convenience, such as frozen fresh-cut string beans. The latter gives you a reasonably fresh vegetable out of season with the time-consuming preparation job (i. e., cutting and cleaning) already done.

The trend towards packaged foods is definitely on the upswing, though, because restaurants, even some of the best ones, now have prefrozen convenience foods on their menus without your knowledge. It might surprise you to find that some parts of a $35.00 meal in an expensive French restaurant in Chicago are actually frozen foods. Well, you should not be surprised, because the cost of food-preparing labor in restaurants has risen so much that to stay in business, even the best restaurants have to cut corners. And one way of cutting corners is to buy convenience foods.

DISCOUNT STORES

The nation's discount stores are growing at a rate of at least 15 percent a year. In 1974 they accounted for 20.4 percent of the nation's nonfood retail stores. In 1960, there was one discount store for every 39,600 households; by 1980 it is estimated that there will be one store for every 8000 households. Numerous discount stores are now selling food at prices that are sometimes distinctly lower than their nondiscount cousins. Back in the 1960's, the National Commission on Food Marketing saw that food discounting in general merchandise discount houses had increased from practically nothing to upwards of 10 percent of all food business by the end of the 1960's. Also, increasing numbers of supermarkets are becoming discounters.

How does a discount store operate? Easily. It cuts its costs in servicing you, the food consumer, and hence is able to cut its prices to induce more of you to buy from the discount store instead of from a regular market or department store. How does it cut costs? An important technique is to reduce the variety and number of brands it sells, and in some cases to entirely eliminate nationally advertised brands in favor of local, usually cheaper, versions. Thus, the store has lower inventory costs, lower ordering costs, and lower stocking costs. These costs can be significant, and may account for a large part of the price reduction in discount establishments. A discount store can also cut costs by having less check-out help, no box boys to take your groceries to your car, and so on. You pay for discount prices by getting less service.

Fortunately, there is a wide range of choice for the food consumer. Those of you who want to pay high prices and have many services can go to high-priced food stores, and those of you who do not want to pay the price can go to discount stores. How much choice you actually have is, of course, dependent on the size of the city you live in—the larger the city, the larger the choice.

The following consumer issue should enable you to stretch your food dollars further and to get the best deal for your monthly food budget.

SUMMARY

1. The percentage of total United States income spent on food has been declining steadily since the beginning of this nation. This is characteristic of goods that are necessities as opposed to luxury items. As income rises, the percentage spent on necessities falls.

2. A German statistician named Ernst Engel made this statistical discovery back in 1856 and it is now called Engel's Law.

3. The Fair Packaging and Labeling Act became effective in 1967; it requires that the labels of most consumer products give the net quantity per serving, identify the commodity, and make clear who manufactured, distributed, or packed it and where. The Act also authorizes the Secretary of Commerce to limit undue proliferation of product package sizes.

4. There are a number of so-called marginal buyers who shop carefully for many food items. They have an important effect on the price and quality of what we buy. The most obvious marginal buyers are large institutions that must feed a large number of individuals.

5. The U. S. Department of Agriculture provides grades for meats, fresh produce, poultry, and other items. However, these grades can be confusing. For example, prime grade meats no longer existed in most areas; the best you could get was choice. Nonetheless, there are many prime rib restaurants throughout the United States serving choice grade meat.

6. Produce grading is even more confusing. The top grade of grapefruit is U. S. Fancy, but the top grade of pears is U. S. No. 1. In order for you to understand which the top grades are, you must learn Table 8–2.

7. The National Academy of Sciences has established Recommended Dietary Allowances for a variety of foods. These can be found in Table 8–3 and should be consulted when making up balanced diets, which is gone into in the following Consumer Issue.

8. Open dating of food products can be helpful not only in determining whether the product is out of date, but also in determining which product should be used first.

9. Since the Great Depression, an agricultural program has been in effect in the United States. For many years, the government set minimum prices for various products such as wheat and corn, guaranteeing that consumers would end up paying higher prices for food products in order to benefit the incomes of farmers. The current agricultural program now has three sets of prices: the market price is what is paid for, say, wheat and corn on the market. The target price is the price that the government thinks the farmers should receive; if they receive less, the government makes up the difference. The support price is the minimum price that farmers can receive on the open market for their goods.

10. In most instances, milk prices are "stabilized" by government regulation or government-supported private regulation.

11. There is a growing trend toward frozen convenience foods because as Americans become richer, they are willing to pay more to save time. That is, their higher incomes lead Americans to place a higher value on

their time, and they therefore prefer the built-in maid service of a convenience food even though it costs them considerably more than putting the food together themselves.

QUESTIONS FOR THOUGHT AND DISCUSSION

1. Why would you expect the citizens of less-developed countries to spend a larger percentage of their income on food than the citizens of the United States?

2. Is it useful to look at the price index of food to figure out whether food is a "good" or "bad" deal? (Hint: How many hours does it take today to obtain enough income to buy a week's food compared to the number of hours it took 50 years ago?)

3. Is there a limit to the reduction in the percentage of disposable personal income going for food? Could it ever reach zero?

4. When you go to the supermarket to buy meat, do you look for a particular grade of meat? Does USDA grade labeling help you make wiser consumer choices?

5. Is it possible to get two identically graded cuts of meat from two different markets and have one be much better than the other?

6. Food manufacturers are adamant in their distaste for fair packaging laws. Why should they care?

7. Do you think it would ever be possible to get food manufacturers to voluntarily reverse the proliferation of product package sizes?

8. Do you think that the net weight of canned items should exclude any liquids?

9. Why do you think food grading came into being?

10. Do you engage in food planning to make sure that you get the proper amounts of different types of nutrients? Why or why not? If you do so, how much time does it involve?

11. How closely do you follow the USDA weekly food plan?

12. Open dating for film has been around for many, many years, yet it has only recently been used in food packaging. Why do you think it has taken so long to be used for food?

13. What are the pros and cons of government agricultural price support programs? Is there any way that these programs could reduce the price to consumers of critical food products?

14. Do you prefer to have a constant price for milk throughout the year or a fluctuating price whose average is lower than the constant price?

15. Are there government controls that can benefit both producers and consumers simultaneously? Or is it merely a trade-off?

16. How much of your diet consists of convenience foods? Is that good or bad?

THINGS TO DO

1. Add up how much food you eat every week. Now add that up for the entire year. Do you eat more or less than the average for the nation?

2. Look at the latest issue of the *Monthly Labor Review* or the *Federal Reserve Bulletin*. See what the index of food prices has done in the last few years. Is there a continued upward trend?

3. At your local meat market, try to determine the differences among the various grades of meat. Ask the butcher if there is a distinct difference between the top two grades of meat, and if the top grade is worth the extra money.

4. Run an experiment with fruit cocktail similar to what *Consumer Reports* did. Find out whether the average drained weight, expressed as a percentage of labeled weight, differs significantly among brands.

5. Go to the produce section of your local market. Try to figure out the U. S. Department of Agriculture labeling on the various types of apples, grapefruit, onions, oranges, and pears. Can you tell the difference between U. S. No. 1, U. S. Fancy, and U. S. Extra No. 1? Ask the grocer what he or she thinks the differences are between the various grades.

6. Write down what you have eaten in the last seven days. Now attempt to add up the daily dietary allowances as presented in Table 8–3. Do you meet the minimum recommended? Do the same thing, but in terms of Table 8–4.

7. The next time you go grocery shopping, find out which products use open dating. If some of the cans you purchase have numbers on them, ask the grocer what those code numbers mean. Often they refer to canning dates and other dates that might be important in your purchase decision (although they might merely identify the packing plant).

8. Call up your local dairy. Find out the difference between the price of fluid milk—that is, milk that will be resold only as a fluid—and the price of manufacturing milk—that is, milk that will be used for ice cream, butter, yogurt, cottage cheese, etc. Ask the dairyperson to explain why there is such a big difference.

9. Look at some of the convenience foods you buy. Try to estimate the price you are paying for convenience. Then try to figure out whether that price is relatively high or low in terms of the time you save by buying and eating the convenience food.

**SELECTED
READINGS**

Boyd, Jacque, "Food Labeling and the Marketing of Nutrition," *Journal of Home Economics,* May 1973.

Cost of Food at Home Estimated for Food Plans at Three Cost Levels (Hyattsville, Md.: U. S. Department of Agriculture).

Fleck, Henrietta, *Introduction to Nutrition* (New York: The Macmillan Company), 1971.

Key Nutrients, Second Edition (Washington, D.C.: U. S. Government Printing Office), 1971.

Manno, Anne, "The Importance of Protein in the Meatless Meal," *Forecast,* January 1973.

Martin, Ethel Austin, *Nutrition in Action* (New York: Holt, Rinehart and Winston), 1971.

Nutritive Value of Foods (Washington, D.C.: U. S. Government Printing Office), 1971.

Starr, J., "The Psychology and Physiology of Eating," *Today's Health*, February 1973.

CONSUMER ISSUE IV
How to Get the Most for Your Food Dollar

The high cost of food should make you want to economize in food shopping. In this issue are given some general ideas on how to get the best dollar value in relation to some very specific food attributes, the most important being nutrition. But you will want still more food information, because no one shops for nutritional value alone, no matter on how limited a budget. You can probably satisfy all your nutritional requirements for a mere fraction of your present food spending by living on soybeans and raisins, or some such stuff. But you are not likely to take that kind of a nutritional diet to heart. If you want to see why, read on.

Unit Pricing

In several U. S. cities, **unit pricing** of all food items is now required by law. What is unit pricing? Well, instead of a label on the shelf under the product indicating only the price, there must now be a label also specifying the price per convenient unit of measurement (i. e., weight or liquid measure). Whereas before you needed a calculator to determine if 7½ ounces of tuna fish at 65¢ is cheaper than 6½ ounces at 59¢, the store has now calculated this for you and posted the results for you to see. This makes it much easier to determine the "best buy" of any particular item. In effect, for canned goods and other prepackaged foods, you are now being told what you have always been told for meats and produce—that is, that pork chops are $1.19

Unit Pricing: Pricing of food products expressed in a well-known unit, such as ounces or pounds.

Complementary Resources: Resources that are used when purchasing or using other resources. For example, the complementary resources used in shopping are your time, and often your automobile.

per pound, but pork blade steaks (which look nearly the same, but are slightly tougher and fatter) are $1.09. Of course, unit pricing does not account for differences in quality or personal preferences. It merely translates into comparable figures the price differences you observe in the market. In so doing, it usually makes it possible for you to capitalize on what "specials" are available. Formerly, when certain brands of, say, canned goods were on special, they still might cost more than the usual price of other brands not being featured. While some price differences reflect differences in quality, other differences might be due to advertising. In some cases, neither may matter to you—you may feel that canned tomatoes are canned tomatoes, and whether one brand is firmer than another does not matter since you are just going to mash them into spaghetti sauce, anyway. It is especially when you do not prefer one particular brand over another that unit pricing is valuable. And in all cases, it allows you to see just what you are paying for your favorites.

Shopping for Specials

Many shoppers know that one way to save money on food is to shop for specials, and that the way to find specials is to look in the local newspaper. Some consumers attempting to get the best possible deals will spend time combing through supermarket ads. They will cut out the ads and go to the various supermarkets to get whatever they need that is on special. While this method is fine for some individuals, you have to realize that the time you spend looking for specials is valuable, both the time spent looking in the ads and that spent shopping. Also valuable is the money you spend shopping for specials, the money spent as wear and tear on your car and on the gasoline that you have to consume when you go to several stores instead of one.

Unfortunately, there can be no hard and fast rules about how long you should spend looking through newspaper ads and how many stores you should go to. Against the potential savings from buying specials at various supermarkets, you must compare the antici-

4/24/72

Between the Producer and the Consumer stands the Grabber.

pated costs of driving your car to those supermarkets, plus the value you place on the time that would be involved. Hence, you know it would not be worthwhile to drive five miles to a more distant supermarket merely for its special on mustard and black peppercorns. However, if that same market had a special on meat that you could purchase for the rest of the week's meals, then it might be worth your while to go to it.

Substituting One Thing for Another

From our discussion about shopping for specials, you should realize that you can substitute various resources to do a particular task. If you decide that you want to spend fewer dollars for food, you can spend more time looking for specials. In other words, you substitute your time for the food dollars that you would have spent had you not looked for specials. When you take a car to shop at several different markets, you use a complementary resource in your attempt to reduce your food budget. Whenever you use a **complementary resource**, you have to realize that you incur a cost, even if you did not pay for it directly or immediately.

Once you understand substitution and complementarity in resource use, then you are well on your way to being a rational, and indeed thrifty, shopper. Some consumers become fanatical about buying food on specials only. They have lost track of means and ends. The original end in mind, of course, is getting the most value for your food dollar, taking into account all of the combined resource costs that go into food shopping. While fanaticism for specials can lead to an uneconomical overuse of time, only you can decide whether that has happened to you, because only you know the value you place on your own time.

The optional use of time leads us to a discussion of when it is rational for you to purchase convenience foods that you know will cost more at the supermarket.

TO BUY OR NOT TO BUY THAT TV DINNER

Convenience foods are just that—foods made for convenience to save you time and energy. Whether or not you like their taste is, of course, up to you, but you should be aware of the cost of convenience. For example, perhaps you have seen breaded veal steaks on the shelves these days. A close look shows that there is an average of about 30 percent breading, and 20 percent beef (which may be more nutritious than veal in amount of usable protein, but nonetheless usually costs less) added to the veal, for this is the limit permitted by the U. S. Department of Agriculture's regulations. So, all in all, those breaded veal steaks are only about 50 percent veal. If the price per pound package is, say, $1.65, then you are paying $3.30 per pound for ground veal steaks with some hamburger and bread thrown in. However, if you can find the same ground veal in the market, you will find that it costs, say, $1.98 a pound; ground beef is, say, $.98 a pound, and readymade bread crumbs are, say, $.40 a pound. That means that homemade veal steaks made just the same way as you buy them in the package would cost you $1.35 per pound.

In addition, for example, you will find that the sugar in presweetened breakfast cereals is costing you $1.50 a pound. You will find also that you pay about twice as much per ounce for peas that are frozen in butter sauce as for peas for which you have to add your own butter during cooking. (And the frozen butter sauce includes not only butter, but water, too.)

What are you paying for convenience? In some cases, you are paying as much as 100 percent or more (as above) for convenience. Is it worth the price? That, of course, depends on how highly you value your time, and on how highly you value the taste differences between what you prepare and what the producer does.

American families seem to be placing more value on their time: the percentage of total food budgets spent on frozen convenience foods is rising from about 27 percent in 1955 to 35 percent in 1965 to an estimated 45 percent in 1975.

What's in Convenience Foods?

In deciding about convenience foods, you ought to keep in mind several other considerations. If we have no real reason for staying out of the kitchen, why pay the price of convenience? And further, it sometimes seems that the only way to make any sense out of the labeling and fancy packaging of some convenience foods is by trusting to providence that what you are buying is wholesome. In other words, if you want to figure out just what nutritive value many convenience foods actually have, you must spend at least part of the time that such foods are meant to save. Further, they often come "gift-wrapped" in layers and layers of packaging designed to preserve freshness. This creates additional problems for the environment, some of which we shall discuss in Chapter 18.

NUTRITION

According to some nutritionists, many convenience foods do not give a high amount of nutrition for their cost. We buy food for two reasons: the pleasures of eating, and nutrition to keep our bodies healthy. The nutritional aspect of food is often ignored by on-the-go, busy consumers who have "better" things to worry about. But after a little time deciphering the nutritional value of different types of food, the wise food consumer can purchase more nutrients per food dollar.

Protein

One of the basic nutrients needed to maintain a healthy body is protein, and there are various inexpensive ways of obtaining it. Further, protein exists in many forms. Seven basic amino acids in various configurations make up the proteins that are usable by the human body. The only food which approximates the ideal relationship among those amino acids is eggs. Other protein sources come more or less close, and often need to be supplemented. For example, the protein in most dried beans and peas is made more usable within our bodies by the addition of a small amount of meat protein, hence the custom of adding salt pork to baked beans. (In fact, many so-called "soul foods" merely reflect the necessity of using complementary proteins to render them usable to the body).

Thus, while bacon may taste good with those eggs in the morning, it is among the costliest ways of obtaining protein. Table IV–1 shows the cost of protein in various of its sources. A 1972 Consumers Union study of frankfurters, for example, showed that the average price per pound of protein in hot dogs ranged from a low of about $5 to a high of $11.70.

Surprisingly enough, a major source of quite inexpensive protein is peanut butter. The average protein content in most peanut butter brands is about 25 to 30 percent, and the total protein supplied by two peanut butter sandwiches and an 8 ounce glass of milk would be almost 85 percent of the daily protein allowance recommended for a ten year old by the National Academy of Sciences-National Research Council. Peanut butter is also a great source of niacin, phosphorus, and magnesium. At the same time, this above-mentioned meal would provide fully one-third the daily calorie need of a 10 year old.

Knowing the nutrient values of different foods is important for obtaining a good diet.

AMERICANS ON THE MOVE

Most Americans do not always consume a good proportion of the different types of foods that a good diet requires. In fact, the percentage of Americans who have poor diets—that is, who have less than two-thirds of the allowances indicated by the RDAs—appears to be increasing. According to the U. S. Department of Agriculture surveys, 15 percent of the American population had poor diets in 1955, 21 percent in 1965, and 24 percent is estimated for 1975. (Using a broader definition of nutrition, a 1974 Agricultural Department study indicated that more than half the people of the United States do not eat nutritionally correct meals.)

Since real incomes are rising in the United States, the same U. S. Department of Agriculture surveys show that the percentage of poor diets decreases as the income level of the family unit increases. No one has yet explained this anomaly. It may in part be due to the increasing availability of "empty calories," that is, calories with little or no nutritive content. It is often easiest, particularly if you value your time highly, to eat a huge amount of sugars and starches; they are readily available, and are often the easiest things to grab "on the run." But there are other reasons as well why an estimated 24 percent of families have poor diets in 1975. First and foremost, of course, is ignorance of what good nutrition means. But many of us who should, and often do, know better simply do not take time to have a good diet. Either we are in too much of a hurry or are on miracle diets to become slim and attractive, or our lives are simply too disrupted.

To counter this growing trend towards poor diets, the government and representatives of the food industry have cooperated to produce an informative 32-page booklet on nutrition. The booklet, "Food is More than Just Something to Eat," explains how diet at any age can affect the length and quality of your life. For example, experts say what a young girl eats now is likely to affect the kind of pregnancy she will have years later. The booklet tells what foods are the best sources of various nutrients and how to combine them into a helpful diet. (To get a free copy, write Nutrition, Pueblo, Colorado 81009.)

In addition, the commonly held idea that a good diet is economically costly turns out to be a myth. A study done by George Stigler in 1945 [1] used a technique called linear programming to figure out what a good diet would actually cost. Can you guess the figure he came up with in that year for a good diet? He came up with the grand total of $59.88. In today's dollars, that would still be less than $250. How did he do it? Well, you would have to eat quantities of soybeans and cabbage to remain on Stigler's diet, but you would get all the nutrients your body requires.

That means, of course, that all Americans except the very, very poor could have a nu-

[1] "The Cost of Subsistence," *Journal of Farm Economics,* 1945.

TABLE IV–1:   COSTS OF PROTEIN. Source: *Diet for a Small Planet,* by Frances Moore Lappe, New York: A Friends of the Earth/Ballantine Book, 1971, pp. 272–274, Appendix C.   It lists the prices at which the foods were calculated.

PROTEIN SOURCES LISTED IN INCREASING ORDER OF COST	COST PER 43.1 g USABLE PROTEIN *	PROTEIN SOURCES LISTED IN INCREASING ORDER OF COST	COST PER 43.1 g USABLE PROTEIN *
1. DAIRY PRODUCTS		Oatmeal (@ 28¢/lb)	28¢
Dried nonfat milk solids (@ 39¢/lb)	10¢	Spaghetti (@ 23¢/lb)	34¢
Cottage cheese from skim milk (@ 31¢/lb)	19¢	"Protein Plus" (@ 45¢/lb)	35¢
Buttermilk (@ 19¢/qt)	29¢	Bulgar, red (@ 27¢/lb)	35¢
Whole egg (@ 63¢/doz)	33¢	Barley, pot or Scotch (@ 22¢/lb)	37¢
Whole milk, nonfat milk (@ 26¢/qt)	44¢	Macaroni (@ 25¢/lb)	37¢
Dried egg whites (@ $3.66/lb)	51¢	Brown rice (@ 21¢/lb)	38¢
Swiss cheese (@ $1.05/lb)	53¢	Gluten flour (@ 68¢/lb)	41¢
Cheddar cheese (@ $1.13/lb)	62¢	Wheat bran (@ 42¢/lb)	46¢
Ricotta cheese (@ 53¢/lb)	62¢	Barley flour (@ 28¢/lb)	46¢
Blue mold cheese (@ $1.16/lb)	75¢	Buckwheat flour, dark (@ 37¢/lb)	46¢
Parmesan cheese (@ $2.14/lb)	82¢	Egg noodles (@ 37¢/lb)	47¢
Yogurt from skim milk (@ 44¢/lb)	$1.52	Millet (@ 35¢/lb)	60¢
Camembert cheese (@ $1.98/lb)	$1.56	Cornmeal, whole ground (@ 32¢/lb)	63¢
		Whole wheat bread (@ 38¢/lb)	66¢
2. LEGUMES (DRY SEED)		Rye bread (@ 39¢/lb)	69¢
Soybeans, soygrits, and flour (@ 33¢/lb)	15¢	"Super-cereal" [2] (@ 59¢/8 oz)	$1.06
Cowpeas (Blackeyed peas) (@ 16¢/lb)	16¢		
Split peas (@ 19¢/lb)	19¢	**4. SEAFOOD**	
Lima beans (@ 23¢/lb)	20¢	Turbot (@ 49¢/lb)	28¢
Common white beans (@ 23¢/lb)	26¢	Squid (@ 39¢/lb)	28¢
Chickpeas (garbanzos) (@ 25¢/lb)	27¢	Herring (@ 45¢/lb)	31¢
Lentils (@ 23¢/lb)	31¢	Cod (@ 75¢/lb)	33¢
Kidney beans (@ 28¢/lb)	31¢	Swordfish (@ 79¢/lb)	34¢
Mung beans (@ 43¢/lb)	31¢	Perch (@ 59¢/lb)	37¢
Black beans (@ 39¢/lb)	40¢	Tuna, canned in oil (@ 96¢/lb)	48¢
		Catfish (@ 79¢/lb)	54¢
3. GRAINS, CEREALS, PRODUCTS		Sardines, Atlantic, canned in oil (@ 85¢/lb)	56¢
Whole wheat flour (@ 19¢/lb)	21¢	Salmon (@ 89¢/lb)	62¢
Rye flour, dark [1] (@ 22¢/lb)	22¢	Oysters (@ 69¢/lb)	76¢
"Roman Meal" (@ 25¢/lb)	27¢	Crab, in shell (@ 59¢/lb)	84¢
Whole grain wheat, hard red spring (@ 27¢/lb)	27¢		

* 43.1 g of usable protein is the daily allowance for the "average" American male weighing 154 pounds.   "Usable" protein means that the protein has been reduced

$$\frac{price}{\% \text{ protein x number of oz x NPU (as a \%)}} \times 1.54 = \text{cost per 43.1 g usable protein}$$

[1] Note: other types with less protein would be relatively more expensive per gram of protein.

by the NPU score to the level that the body can actually use.   Formula for calculating price per 43.1 g of usable protein:

[2] Included to show that brand-name high-protein cereals may not necessarily be good "protein buys."

TABLE IV–1: COSTS OF PROTEIN (Continued).

PROTEIN SOURCES LISTED IN INCREASING ORDER OF COST	COST PER 43.1 g USABLE PROTEIN *	PROTEIN SOURCES LISTED IN INCREASING ORDER OF COST	COST PEF 43.1 g USABLE PROTEIN *
Clams, soft, in shell (@ 59¢/lb)	$1.41	Raw cashews (@ $1.31/lb)	$1.30
Shrimp, canned wet pack (@ $3.79/lb)	$3.03	Brazil nuts (@ $1.00/lb)	$1.33
		Black walnuts (@ $1.96/lb)	$1.82
5. NUTRITIONAL ADDITIVES		Cashews (@ $2.41/lb)	$2.19
Wheat germ (@ 47¢/lb)	27¢	Pignolia nuts (@ $3.56/lb)	$2.23
"Tiger's Milk" (@ $1.98/lb)	46¢	Pistachio nuts, in shell	
Brewer's yeast (nutritional yeast) (@ $1.20/lb)	54¢	(@ $2.61/lb)	$5.20
Baker's yeast (@ $1.60/lb)	87¢		
		7. MEATS AND POULTRY	
6. NUTS AND SEEDS		Hamburger, reg. grd. (@ 63¢/lb)	51¢
Peanut butter (@ 61¢/lb)	54¢	Chicken breast w/bone (@ 69¢/lb)	62¢
Raw peanuts (@ 66¢/lb)	47¢	Pork loin chop med.	
Sunflower seeds or meal (@ 90¢/lb)	62¢	fat, w/bone (@ $1.09/lb)	$1.15
Sesame seeds or meal (@ 71¢/lb)	69¢	Porterhouse steak choice	
Peanuts (@ 92¢/lb)	76¢	grade, w/bone (@ $1.58/lb)	$1.67
Pumpkin and squash kernels (@ $1.80/lb)	$1.00	Lamb rib chop, choice grade, w/bone (@ $1.49/lb)	$1.81

tritional diet if they were willing to sacrifice variety in their food intake, but most of us are not willing to make such a sacrifice. And in fact we pay quite a bit for variety. We do not merely eat to live, some of us live to eat (at least a little bit). We enjoy eating and we like it to be an occasion to look forward to. How many of us would look forward to two meals a day of soybeans?

Of course, there are many alternatives between the low-cost, high-nutrient soybean and cabbage subsistence diet and the high-cost, low-nutrient diet of junk foods and empty calories. Nutritionists have insisted for years that a healthy, balanced food intake need not be unpleasant or dull. Why do Americans shun the healthy diets they can afford better than anyone else in the world? The ultimate answers are beyond the scope of this book. But while too much of our food has too little of what our bodies need, much of our food also has something else, besides empty calories, that we do *not* need.

MAKING SURE THE BACTERIA IS DOWN

You would be surprised at how many of the foods you buy have high bacteria counts. One food that most of us are enamored with is hamburger. Several studies done by Consumers Union and news reporters in several cities [2] showed that the per capita consump-

[2] See the accompanying Exhibit, and *Media & Consumer*, Vol. 1, No. 12 (November 1973), pp. 6–7.

EXHIBIT

Coliform count in the hamburger you buy

A survey done by a number of news organizations throughout the country showed that the average coliform count per gram of hamburger bought in supermarkets was quite high, ranging from 400,000 coliforms per gram down to less than 500. The average bacteria count per gram in the seven cities sampled was 1,351,972. Source: *Media and Consumer*, Vol. 1, No. 12 (November 1973), p. 6.

CITY	NEWS ORGANIZATION	NUMBER OF SAMPLES	AVERAGE COLIFORM COUNT/GRAM	NUMBER EXCEEDING 100 COLIFORMS /GRAM	WORST COLIFORM SAMPLE	PRESENCE OF E.-COLI	NUMBER EXCEEDING 50 E. COLI /GRAM	AVERAGE BACTERIA COUNT/GRAM	WORST TOTAL COUNT SAMPLE
Chicago	*WTTW-TV*	20	14,372	18	240,000	4 of 20	1 of 20	2,352,625	10,000,000
Dayton	*Daily News*	20	24,877	16	400,000	14 of 20	5 of 20	159,156	1,700,000
Louisville	*Courier-Journal*	10	34,786	10	220,000	10 of 10	10 of 10	2,229,800	7,800,000
Boston	*WBZ-TV*	9	29,978	8	120,000	Not Tested	Not Tested	1,970,533	7,200,000
St. Petersburg	*Times*	20	540	16	1,500	20 of 20	12 of 20	1,008,900	3,260,000
Philadelphia	*Bulletin*	20	10,480	20	29,600	20 of 20	6 of 20	1,304,900	1,980,000
San Francisco	*Bay Guardian*	30	3,430	28	10,800	4 of 30	Not Tested	437,983	2,600,000
Total or Average		129	16,923	116 of 128		72 of 120	34 of 90	1,351,972	

tion of hamburger was almost 60 pounds a year! Consumers Union contended that "the heavy consumption of hamburger looks like a great, but often unwarranted, act of faith." Why? Because by their findings, in shockingly large percentages, the hamburger purchased is well on its way to putrefaction (rottenness). In addition, a good number of the samples contained more fat than unadulterated hamburger would normally contain. (In some areas, fat content of hamburger must now be specified on the labels.) Some samples contained more fat than the law allows, and the test results hint that at least some ground beef labeled as chuck or ground round may have been something else.

Of course, your first worry is whether you will actually become sick from eating the hamburger you buy. One way of making sure you do not get highly putrefied meat is to buy your own meat grinder, buy your own unground meat, and make your own hamburger—something that an increasingly large number of consumers are doing these days, just to be sure. The other alternative is to shop in a highly reputable supermarket or meat market where you have learned from experience that you never get sick from eating their hamburger. But you will pay more for the certainty of unputrefied meat, in money and/or time.

A discovery from the Consumers Union study that may surprise you was that the hamburgers purchased in the New York area from such "fast-food" stands as Burger King, Burger and Shake, Hagers, McDonald's, Wetson's, and White Castle were of meat in many respects better than the average supermarket product—lower in fat and often in coliform count. However, the actual price you pay for a quick burger is quite a bit more than if you made the burger yourself. But now we are back again to the value of your time and whether or not you should buy convenience foods. The fact that McDonald's has already sold 12 billion hamburgers must mean something.

WAYS THAT YOU CAN BE CHEATED BY FOOD STORES AND WHAT TO DO ABOUT IT

Probably, the bulk of food stores attempt in no way to cheat you. But since some do, you should be aware of the methods that they can use, and of how you can guard against these unsavory practices. A few of the better-known techniques for robbing you of value for your food dollar are:

1. Water may be added to the cereals used in making processed meats, thereby adding the weight of the water. You end up paying meat prices for H_2O.

2. Turkeys, oysters, chickens, and hams can be soaked in water or juice overnight, thus adding several ounces to their weight.

3. Poultry dealers can place rolled up chicken-neck skins in the breast cavities of the birds. Hence, you pay chicken prices for neck skins.

What you can do: Call your local weights and measures inspectors, who can be found in your telephone directory yellow pages, and tell them you think you may have been cheated. Save your purchase so that it can be used as evidence. After your accusation has been confirmed by an inspector's purchase in the same store, the offending merchant will be warned, or will be prosecuted if he or she is a repeat violator.

4. Sellers may bore holes in counterpoised weights, reducing them by anywhere from 10 to 20 percent. This short-weighing technique has been found in several states.

5. A lead sinker may be hooked to the underside of the weighing pan.

6. A one-ounce magnet or several, can be attached under the scale pan.

Edict of Louis XI, King of France
A.D. 1481

"Anyone who sells butter containing stones or other things

(to add to the weight) will be put into our pillory, then

said butter will be placed on his head until entirely melted

by the sun. Dogs may lick him and people offend him

with whatever defamatory epithets they please without

offense to God or King. If the sun is not warm enough,

the accused will be exposed in the great hall of the gaol in

front of a roaring fire, where everyone will see him."

What you can do: The easiest thing to do is to purchase a good household scale and use it to check-weigh all purchases that you suspect have been short-weighed. If you find the items short-weighed, you may try taking them back to the store manager. In this way, the manager is given a chance to correct an honest error, if it is one, or a warning signal that you are a smart shopper who cannot be easily cheated.

7. There are probably an infinite number of other ways in which you can be short-weighed. It is up to you to figure out if in fact this trick is being played on you. If you think this is consistently happening, you have the choice of either shopping at a different store or reporting the dishonest operator to the proper agency, such as the weights and measures inspectors in your area.

ACTUALLY DOING IT

Before we leave this topic, we should consider your actual trip to the supermarket. There are several things to consider.

First of all, what kind of preparation for the trip have you made? Many shoppers prefer planning menus for the week (at least the suppers), often taking into account the meat specials that week. Generally, once the meats are decided upon, the rest of the supper menus follow rather naturally. Usually, such advance meal planning would encompass a week at a time, although some shoppers prefer to do it just once every 10 days.

If you have decided not to pay much attention to advertised specials, and therefore not to reading the supermarket ads in your newspapers, meal planning can often take place in the store itself in much the same way. You go first to the meat counter and decide what your meals will center on by looking at the specials (or even just the prices). Some times, especially with relatively high meat prices, you may also wish to check the prices of canned or fresh fish, or eggs, or cheese, and feature these or other meat substitutes in your meals.

Other consumers prefer to engage in a kind of "reasoned" impulse buying. In other words, they know roughly what they consume in any given week, and vary only a few items on any given trip to the supermarket.

In any case, whether you do your food planning at home beforehand or in the supermarket, two things should be kept in mind:

1. Does your time schedule for the week indicate that one or several days are going to allow very little time for preparing meals? If so, either you might purchase convenience foods (although some of them take more time to heat than would be required, say, to fix a mushroom omlet, and are also relatively more expensive), or you might choose to plan and cook at one mealtime enough food for two meals, using the leftovers for the more hurried day.

2. Remember to keep a shopping list of at least those incidental items that you seldom have to replenish. These include most spices and baking ingredients—or whatever else is not used up too rapidly. It can be quite disconcerting to decide to make your favorite

salad dressing, for example, and discover you are all out of white vinegar.

Apart from meal planning, there are two other "rules" to follow in the trip to the supermarket:

1. Never go hungry! If you do, you might purchase either too much food, or too many of whatever your favorite snack items are.
2. Don't take the kids (or spouse, or whatever indulgent eaters you might have in your household). First, their demands for food items will make it nearly impossible for you to concentrate on shopping sensibly and doing comparative pricing; and, second, you then have additional sets of whims and fancies to contend with (apart from your own) that could greatly detract from making sound, nutritionally based decisions.

Bon apetit!

SUMMARY

1. Unit pricing is generally required by law in many states. When you go shopping for food, you should compare unit prices instead of trying to determine whether a 7½ ounce can of tuna fish is cheaper than a 6½ ounce can when the former sells for 72¢ and the latters sells for 64¢.

2. Shopping for specials is one way to save consumer dollars for food. Specials are generally listed in throwaway newspapers or ads in regular newspapers, as well as in the markets you shop at. Be careful, though: do not drive 15 miles just to go to a market that has salt on special. The savings you will realize on the salt will be less than the cost in extra gas (unless, of course, you are buying a ton).

3. Generally you should compare the potential gains from shopping for specials with the potential costs, particularly in terms of your time and other complementary resources.

4. You end up paying about twice as much per ounce for peas, string beans, and carrots that are frozen in butter sauce. Ask yourself if this price is too high for the extra convenience.

5. The only food that gives you just about all of the seven basic amino acids are eggs. All other protein sources are incomplete and must be supplemented. One major source of inexpensive protein is peanut butter, which has a protein content approaching 25 to 30 percent.

6. Even though American incomes are growing, the percentage of families estimated to have poor diets is rising.

7. Many of the ground meats that you purchase in a supermarket have high bacteria and coliform content. One way to avoid this is to grind your own meat. Simple hand-operated meat grinders are very inexpensive.

8. One way to avoid being cheated by food retailers is to measure what you buy with your own scales. Once you find a store that does not cheat you, you can continue to shop there with some assurance of honesty on the part of the retailer. In fact, repeat buying will usually yield high returns because the retailer's income is mostly from customers who continually come back.

9. Advanced meal planning can be helpful as a guide to careful shopping in the supermarket.

10. Two cardinal rules should be followed to avoid overspending in the supermarket: (a) never go shopping when you are hungry, and (b) never take children or a spouse with you.

QUESTIONS FOR THOUGHT AND DISCUSSION

1. Why did it take so long for unit pricing to become more or less common in retail food markets?

2. Is it ever advisable to comb through all supermarket ads? If so, when?

3. Some nutritionists contend that TV dinners lack many basic nutrients. Others contend that they taste awful. Nonetheless, TV dinners sell very well. Why?

4. Do you think the basic amount of nutrients should be clearly labeled on the front of every item sold in a market?

5. Why do you think meat is such an expensive food item?

6. How can you explain the fact that Americans have increasingly poor diets even though they are getting richer as a nation?

7. What is the most important aspect of your diet? Nutrition? Variety? Cost? Convenience?

8. How can you explain the fact that McDonalds hamburgers, for example, have a lower coliform count than hamburger purchased in your local supermarket?

THINGS TO DO

1. Check the markets in your area to see which ones engage in unit pricing if it is not required by law in your state. If some do not, ask the manager why. Do you think unit pricing adds to the cost of selling food products?

2. Look at all of the local newspapers one day and compare specials on national-brand food items. What is the percentage difference from the normal price and the special price? Can you compute the extra time it would require to obtain the specials? If so, what would have to be the value of your time to make it worthwhile for you to go especially to the one store with the special?

3. What other resources are complementary to food shopping besides your automobile or other form of transportation? List them and

estimate their yearly cost just for food shopping.

4. Sit down and write a list of all of the foods you eat that could be labeled as convenience foods.

5. Query your local restaurateur's food buying habits. Ask him or her how many of the items sold on the menu are prefrozen. When you go into a seafood restaurant, ask which items are fresh, fresh frozen, or just frozen. Try to get an honest answer. Can you tell the difference between fresh and fresh-frozen seafood?

6. Update Table IV–1 to determine the cost per 43.1 grams of usable protein for the products mentioned. Use the prices of the products in your area as they are today.

7. As an experiment, find out how much you spend on food without any advanced planning, and then compare it with what you will spend on food if you carefully plan your meals ahead of time for a week period. Is the difference worth the effort? (Usually it is.)

SELECTED READINGS

Anderson, W. Thomas, Jr., *The Convenience-Oriented Consumer* (Austin: University of Texas, Graduate School of Business, Bureau of Business Research), 1971.

"Combating Nutrition Misinformation," *Forecast,* May–June 1972.

Cross, Jennifer, *The Supermarket Trap* (Bloomington: Indiana University Press), 1970.

Erhard, D., "Nutritive Education for the Now Generation," *Journal of Nutrition Education,* Spring 1971.

Kramer, Mary, and Margaret Spader, *Contemporary Meal Management* (New York: John Wiley & Sons), 1972.

"Labels that Tell You Something," *Journal of Home Economics,* April 1972.

Lauda, Frani, "Playing the Supermarket," *Sphere,* April–May 1972.

Moolman, Valerie, *How to Buy Food* (New York: Cornerstone Library), 1970.

"Name Brands vs. House Brands," *Changing Times,* August 1973.

Nutritive Value of Foods (Washington, D.C.: U.S. Government Printing Office), 1971.

Taylor, E. T., "Unit Pricing and Open Dating," *Family Economics Review* (Agricultural Research Service, U.S. Department of Agriculture), June 1972.

Trager, James, *The Food Book* (New York: Grossman Publishers), 1972.

Your Money's Worth in Foods, G–183 (Washington, D.C.: U.S. Department of Agriculture, Government Printing Office).

CHAPTER PREVIEW

☐ What are the characteristics of the clothing industry?
☐ What determines the types of clothes we buy?
☐ Why do different socioeconomic classes usually dress differently?
☐ How do clothes fit into family budget formation?
☐ How does durability affect the price of clothing?
☐ How has the Flammable Fabrics Act affected the production and sale of clothes?
☐ What are the federal statutes relating to the labeling of clothing products?

GLOSSARY OF NEW TERMS

Cease and Desist Orders: Legal orders from a federal agency or a judge requiring that a certain activity stop immediately. For example, the Federal Trade Commission can issue a cease and desist order against a fur manufacturer's deceptive labeling practice.

Generic Name: The general or nontrade-mark name of a product. For example, the trade names of a particular type of fiber may be Antron, Cantrece, or Qiang, but the generic name of that fiber is nylon.

It is estimated that American families have spent $70 million on clothing in 1975. Together, all of us purchased $70 billion worth of shoes, pants, hats, jockey shorts, brassieres, panties, hose, suits, ties, shirts, skirts, and socks. Clothing expenditures account for between 9 and 13 percent of the typical American's total budget.[1] Clothing is a major industry, now employing over a million workers in any one year. The fashion business, of course, occupies large amounts of advertising space and media space, and probably, for many people, a significant amount of mental space.

WHERE WE BUY OUR CLOTHES

There are approximately 7000 wholesale clothing outlets, more than 90,000 retail clothing outlets, and 25,000 or more manufacturers. It is hard to tell how many manufacturers of clothing there are because so many small ones go into and out of business in any one year (or month, for that matter). In addition to all these market outlets for clothing, countless women make at least some of their own or their family's clothes, accounting for approximately $2 billion of sales in fabrics, notions, and other sewing needs.

Recent years have seen the upsurge of discount clothing stores, stores in which there are usually fewer salespersons, and in which you are charged for services, such as alterations and hemming, that are "free" in nondiscount stores. In general, discount stores that offer true bargains have a smaller variety of sizes, styles, colors, and qualities, and perhaps also fewer brand names. This is how they reduce their costs so that they can in fact sell you clothes at a lower price than nondiscount stores.

Shopping for clothing can be time-consuming. By one estimate, the typical housewife spends 100 hours a year shopping for clothes for herself and her children, and even sometimes for her husband. We are indeed a clothes-conscious society; that cannot be denied.

WHY SO MANY CLOTHES?

Everybody must be aware that the typical American has more clothes than he or she actually "needs" in order to provide himself or herself the physical protec-

MORE THAN JUST KEEPING WARM

[1] *The 1973 Yearbook of Agriculture*, Washington, D. C.: U. S. Government Printing Office; p. 8.

tion from cold, sun, wind, and rain. Obviously, then, most clothing is no longer within the realm of so-called necessity. Rather, it is a consumer good that gives pleasure and serves more than the basic necessities. In the last consumer issue, you were shown that a food budget, if wisely spent, of only $250 a year would allow you to have all the nutritional and caloric values you needed to stay healthy. Unfortunately, that food budget required you to eat soybeans for every other meal, or almost.

The same analysis can be made with respect to clothing. You could purchase very durable, sturdy, and even fairly good-looking clothing that would last you far longer than you may want to keep it. In this manner, you could reduce your clothing budget considerably. You could also buy second-hand clothes from Goodwill Industries and other second-hand establishments. These clothes would protect you from the elements, but they would not serve another purpose—variety. Variety, as has often been said, is the spice of life. Variety in clothing is no different.

CUSTOMS

The types of clothes we buy are often determined by customs in the community, although in the United States this is less true than it was. It was certainly only by custom that men wear trousers and women wear skirts. After all, in Scotland men wear skirts also, and in the United States, more and more women are wearing pants or pants suits whenever and wherever they wish without being exposed to ridicule or discrimination. Why do men wear ties and collars while women usually do not? Again, the only explanation is custom. These customs change slowly. It took many years before fancy restaurants admitted men without ties, but rather in turtleneck sweaters.

Have you ever asked yourself why men's clothing has buttons on the opposite side from women's clothing? Custom must be the answer. But customs are not created in a vacuum; most are created to appease or satisfy a large segment of the population. Once customs are well established, they are hard to break, simply because the majority of the society accepts them or even enjoys them. Only when a significant and aggressive minority find the customs disturbing, are they changed. Later in this chapter, we will talk about the changing attitudes toward dress in the United States.

MENTAL ATTITUDE

Clothing that pleases us as wearers, and that we think pleases those who see us, often contributes greatly to our attitude towards our fellow humans. One of the strongest motivations of dress is preservation of the self-concept or self-image of the wearer through the enhancement of the body. This is an aesthetic consideration, that is, one having to do solely with beauty. Even among primitive tribes, self-adornment is a stronger motivation than protection from the elements, or thrift, or durability. And this motivation in clothing selection has nothing to do with snobbery. It merely indicates a positive self-concept, which is healthy and beneficial.

Some of you may balk at such a value system because it places high importance on a material good. Nonetheless, it cannot be denied that many, many people feel better when they are dressed in a manner they think is attractive. In addition, many people feel better when they think they are dressing in a manner that identifies them to the rest of society as belonging to a particular socioeconomic class. This is an important problem in self-awareness and self-identification well known to psychologists. It also has another, more economic explanation that might be of interest to you.

SOCIAL CLASS
IDENTIFICATION

Generally, people in the same socioeconomic class feel most comfortable with "their own." If, for example, you are a blue collar worker, you probably would not feel comfortable (at least not at first) with someone like the executive of a multibillion-dollar corporation. The opposite is also true. If you are an intellectual who hates physical activity, you probably do not anticipate getting along too well, at least for any period of time, with someone who loves the outdoors and lives for physical activity. This fact is part of human nature and we all accept it even if we do not think it is "right."

Now ask yourself this: What is the easiest way for you to identify members of a similar socioeconomic class, or of similar visible preferences? Of course, you can sometimes identify them by where they work or where they live. But how can you tell if you meet them on the street, in a store, at a party, or somewhere else that gives you no immediate clues? One way you can identify their socioeconomic class is by their choice of dress. This generalization is sometimes risky, but we have to make generalizations in our own day-to-day behavior in order to reach economically meaningful decisions, because we do not have the time to acquire perfect information.

Herein lies the crux of differential dressing habits for different members of society: in effect, members of different socioeconomic classes minimize the cost of others' acquiring information about them by dressing in a manner that identifies them with their status in the community. This identification or dissemination of information, as it were, avoids many problems. What kind? The kind of problems that arise when two people are incompatible and cannot really be friends. Since the majority of us have limited amounts of time and therefore have only a select number of friendships that we can cultivate and keep, we welcome any aids in helping ourselves decide which friendships we should attempt to make. This is one way to explain so-called "hippie" dressing habits. Those who dress in a wild, flashy, or unconventional manner are essentially giving signals to the rest of the community that they are different and should be treated as such. They are indicating that their attitudes about life are, let us say, less conformist, less formal, and more open; hence, you are forewarned when you first meet the "hip" person. If open, unpretentious attitudes toward life do not sit well with you, then you know to stay away.

Thus, we can say that dressing habits are sometimes used to indicate not only socioeconomic classes, but also individual life styles and attitudes, and, often, aesthetic values. Sometimes people attempt to pass off "false" information about themselves by buying and wearing clothes that are expensive beyond their means. There is nothing wrong with such overspending if we remember the true cost of this "information" or "advertising" expenditure.

CLOTHES, FAMILY HAPPINESS, AND BUDGET FORMATION

How a family dresses can sometimes be important for adding to family satisfaction. Again, some of you may find this idea reprehensible because it puts too much weight on a material aspect of life instead of a spiritual aspect. But just as variety in diet contributes to more than physical well-being, so, too, can clothing be one of the material aspects of life that contribute to self-image and self-esteem. The fact remains, for example, that parents who approve of how their children dress are often more satisfied and proud to be the heads of the family. Similarly, children as well as their parents may take great pleasure in being part of the family unit which "dresses up" to go to church on Sunday or to visit friends. But each member of the family has his or her own idea about what fashions are appropriate for himself or herself and for the others in the family. This may cause conflicts within the family or spending unit for two reasons: (1) the family's budget will, by necessity, curtail some of the clothing spending desired by each member, and (2) members of the family who have clothing habits significantly different than those of other members may feel pressure to conform.

INDIVIDUALITY
AND CONFORMITY

To avoid the problem of family conflicts about individual dressing styles, it is important that each member's individuality or "living space" not be violated. This is something that can be discussed during family councils or between individual members of the spending unit. Since clothing habits reflect each person's values and aesthetics, no set rules about dressing can be made absolute for any person at any time. If one member of the spending unit wishes to rebel and buy clothes that are indeed different from everyone else's, this attempt at individuality must not only be understood but also accepted (at least in part). As with everything else, compromises will have to be made about dressing habits within a spending unit, as well as about the size of each member's clothing expenditures.

THE BUDGET
AGAIN

Clothing enters into the budget-making decisions of every spending unit. Such decisions cannot be avoided because clothes are so important. One way to decrease the friction within the family or spending unit is to discuss each individual's desires or needs for clothes at some sort of family council when the budget is being formed. The problems of democratic money management, and the agreed-upon rules of democratic decision-making, within any spending unit will apply to clothing decisions also. It is best that the head or heads of the spending unit not attempt to impose his, her, or their value judgments on the other members by dictating clothing tastes and rules of fashion.

THE FASHION
INDUSTRY AND
WHO DECIDES

The fashion industry is fascinating enough to merit an entire study in its own right. In the United States alone, it is the fourth largest industry in annual sales. How fashions are decided and how they affect you, the consumer, is important information for your clothing decision-making. We are all aware of "high" fashion, but most of us are not direct consumers of it. However, whatever happens in the salons of Christian Dior, St. Laurent, Chanel, or whatever is designed by Bill Blass, Geoffrey Beene, Sonja Rykel, and so on eventually filters down to less expensive ready-to-wear clothes. Indeed, the respected designers in France, the United States, and elsewhere have themselves entered the ready-to-wear market in the past decade.

WHO DICTATES
FASHION?

The immense size of the fashion industry and its supposed modes of deciding our fashions leads us back to the eternal question of consumer versus producer sovereignty. Are fashions dictated by you, the consumer, or are they dictated by the whims of producers? Nobody will ever know who truly dictates fashion, but we can consider a few salient facts. Not all fashions dictated by designers actually take hold. We mentioned in

Chapter 1 that the midiskirt failed through the resistance of women. Fashions in cars can also fail to take hold, as we also mentioned in Chapter 1: the Edsel cost the Ford Motor Company a quarter of a billion dollars in losses.

Although changes in fashions cause earlier "obsolescence" than some consumers would prefer, we do have the choice of either wearing classic fashions which seldom change, or of wearing old-fashioned clothes. We do not have to give in to the whims of the fashion industry. But if so many companies are able to make at least a normal profit by continually coming out with new fashions, there must be quite a few consumers who do want variety in their clothing styles, and who do want fashions to change so that they can buy different styles of clothes every year. You and I might find such changes a disagreeable waste of scarce resources. But who is to say what is important for making people happy? On the other hand, even if you have decided that your clothing needs consist of replacing your one pair of jeans every six months or so, you might find that in order to get the same style that you wore last year would mean a lot of hunting. So the success of the fashion industry might merely reflect changing availabilities of replacement articles: the fact that you now buy your jeans with flared pants legs may have nothing to do with your eagerness to adopt changing styles.

If, however, people are made happy by the availability of new fashions, then it would be a value judgment to say their happiness is false. As long as we consumers are aware of the cost of purchasing fashion happiness, we certainly must have the right to decide whether we want to give up other things in order to buy fashionable clothes at a higher price than merely utilitarian clothes cost. We consumers may not be king, particularly with respect to fashions; but since nothing is being forced on us either, the consumer always has the choice of not being drawn into the passing fashion parade.

CHANGING ATTITUDES TOWARD CLOTHING

The attitudes of people, particularly young people, toward clothing are changing. Although whether we are witnessing a trend or merely a random cycle is not clear, nevertheless a large number of young people prefer to dress in what might be termed a less than impeccable manner. Styles of the day, not only in the United States but also in such countries as France, often dictate blue jeans, T-shirts, sweat shirts, army fatigues, coveralls, boots, and the like. Adults sometimes cringe at this particular fad or trend, but nonetheless we must recognize one important aspect: casual dress is often less expensive than more formal dress, and less impeccability costs less than more impeccability; it is at least likely that it costs less in time and maintenance. The changing trends among young people's dressing habits might also reflect their lower valuation of material things as compared to intellectual and spiritual ones.

Many changes in clothing styles, even among adults, have come about apparently because of the increase in recreational and in particular, sporting activities.[2] The influence of recreational clothing styles on everyday dressing habits has been quite noticeable in the last few years. Fashions that have become popular for hiking, backpacking, skiing, sailing, and tennis have crept into day-to-day wearing apparel. In its share of total clothing expenditures, recreational clothing has itself been growing by leaps and bounds.

Are we going to ultimately end up in casual dress all the time? No one really knows, but in the last few years it has become quite obvious that many Americans are no longer happy in more formal attire even when they go to what are usually considered formal occasions.

No matter how informal you decide to become, you are still going to be faced with choices, and you still have to decide how to spend your clothing dollar. In the next consumer issue, then, we will see how your dollars can best be spent, and how to tell what you are actually buying.

DURABILITY VERSUS PRICE

Many people accuse the clothing industry of creating obsolescence. That may or may not be true. But it is certain that to have more durable goods we generally have to pay more; to buy a dress or a suit that should last five years, you must pay more than for a similar item of less durable material and workmanship that should last only three years.

All of us must decide how much durability we want to pay for. Some manufacturers, such as Monsanto, are now "wear dating" their clothing items: a tag is attached to the garment indicating the guaranteed wear period, usually a year. Thus, the consumer can sometimes determine how much durability is being purchased.

In some cases, we have tried to come full circle by producing paper underwear, paper dresses, and other items made out of paper products that are thrown away after they are used several times. This would be the ultimate in planned obsolescence. But at least in this case, the obsolescence is planned by the consumer, because those of us who buy such articles do so knowing that they will soon be thrown away. Nobody is being fooled for the manufacturers tell you explicitly how many times you can plan on wearing such a piece of clothing. Information is not a problem.

WHY PURCHASE CLOTHES THAT WEAR OUT SO FAST?

Now, why would any of us in our right minds purchase such a highly nondurable piece of clothing? The answer is pretty obvious: (1) you need not worry about upkeep or cleaning when you know the item will be thrown away; and (2) you can change fashions often this way, even as frequently as every three days. For you fashion-conscious consumers, this may seem ideal, if you are willing to pay the very high implicit price.

[2] The increased percentage of women who work outside the home, as well as higher valuation of time, may also be factors.

DURABILITY NOT FREE

If durability were a free good, we could be fairly certain that producers were creating obsolescence. But durability is not a free good. You usually have to pay more for materials that last longer; and that price may be more than you wish to pay. Depending on your tastes and your budget, you may be better off buying less durable clothes and replacing them more often—especially if the cost of cleaning rises relative to other costs. Whenever the maintenance costs of an item go up relative to other costs, you have more incentive to replace the item rather than to maintain it and repair it.

Once you know that durability is *itself* a good, you can make more rational choices when buying clothing items. You are purchasing a suit or a dress, for example, because of the service flow it yields per unit time period. Thus, if you buy, say, a jacket that you think will last five years, you should figure out what the cost per year is; if it costs $100, but another jacket that will last only one year costs $75, the first jacket is obviously not more expensive in cost per service flow per year. You should know, also, that many durable clothes are actually cheaper than the same type retailed as a "fad." For example, there is little durability difference between a $5.99 men's Dacron and cotton shirt and one for $10.99. However, the fit, stitching, and finishing may be far superior in the $10.99 shirt. That may be the only difference, but one that you may be willing to pay the extra $5 for.

In your own shopping forays, remember that you should figure out the cost per year of owning a piece of clothing. It would also be important for you to understand the maintenance costs of particular materials. A clothing label that says "dry clean only" may indicate that the item will cost you more to maintain than another item in the same line labeled "may be machine washed." This kind of information is important in your figuring out the relative costs of different pieces of clothing (and also a good reason for labeling requirements).

THE TREND TOWARD LESS FLAMMABLE PRODUCTS

The U. S. government has increasingly required that children's clothing be nonflammable. In 1953, Congress passed the Flammable Fabrics Act. It was passed in response to public indignation at the deaths and injuries caused by highly flammable wearing apparel. Congress enacted this particular piece of protective consumer legislation in order to create a federal regulatory scheme that would uniformly prohibit "the introduction or movement in interstate commerce of articles of wearing apparel and fabrics which are so highly flammable as to be dangerous when worn by individuals. . . . " In its original form, the Act was applicable only to the manufacturing and sale of a narrow range of articles susceptible to flammability—wearing apparel and fabrics to be incorporated into wearing apparel. Also, the Act explicitly excluded from its control certain items of wearing apparel, such as hats, gloves, and footwear. The original

version of the Act, although helpful, seemed to fall short of the protection it was expected to give the consuming public. Congress had failed to include many articles that created significant hazards, and had failed to permit establishment of more stringent standards of flammability.

The 1967 amendment specifically prohibits the manufacture and sale of any product, fabric, or related material that fails to conform to an applicable standard or regulation. More specifically, manufacture or sale of such a flammable product was to be considered an unfair method of competition under the Federal Trade Commission Act. In addition, the 1967 amendment repeals the specific wearing apparel exclusions of the 1953 Act. While the original Act gave the Department of Commerce power only to recommend new standards, but left Congress itself with the power to change the standard, the amendment gave the Department the authority to determine the need for new enforceable standards of flammability. The Department of Health, Education, and Welfare was made responsible for providing statistical data on test injuries and analyses.

As can be imagined, this divergent responsibility for administering the Act created substantial problems of coordination. In 1972, the entire responsibility for administration and enforcement of the Flammable Fabrics

Act, was taken from the three agencies—FTC, Department of Commerce, and HEW—and given to the newly created Consumer Product Safety Commission.[3]

THE COSTS INVOLVED   We all agree that we would like our products to be totally nonflammable, because whenever they catch fire, there is a potential high cost to the person wearing them. But consumers are not necessarily always willing to pay the higher price necessary to make fabrics nonflammable. And this is not always callous or irrational, because the probability that you or even your children will catch on fire with a flammable piece of clothing is still very, very small. The Act was originally aimed at children's clothing that "burst into flames" when near, say, a lighted match, causing serious injuries to many children. Such accidents as a result of the properties of some of the newer synthetic fibers, have been greatly reduced. But the trend seems to be toward even greater flame-retardant capabilities. Many of the families who are unwilling to spend part of their budgets to reduce this probability even more think it is low enough to start with. But they will have less and less of a choice because products, especially children's pajamas, will be sold only if they are extremely flame-retardant (the criterion often being that they never burst into flame, and ideally will smolder and self-extinguish).

Parental unwillingness to purchase flame-retardent clothing may be due to a lack of awareness of how flammable some items and many new synthetics have been or still are. But new synthetic fabrics appear on the market all the time and seldom are labeled as to flammability. Parents, whether motivated by reasoned concern for costs or by partial or total ignorance of product hazards, will still have the option of making their own children's clothes and using cheaper and more flammable materials. Even if the government requires that all children's clothing be totally flame-retardant to be sold in the marketplace, it will be impossible to entirely prevent such behavior. Some interesting repercussions of the current concern about flammability are already developing. For example, some of the sleepwear marketed by Sears in its nationally distributed catalog are marked "Not available in Washington State," because they fail to meet that state's more stringent flammability requirements.

THE TREND TOWARD   The government has been active in improving the labeling standards for
BETTER LABELING   furs, wool, and textiles. The Federal Trade Commission has, since its beginning, been responsible for enforcing federal statutes relating to wool, fur products, and household textile articles. For example, the Wool Products Labeling Act of 1939 protects producers, manufacturers, distributors, and consumers by requiring that manufactured wool products be uniformly labeled to indicate the percentages of wool and any other fibers in them. The FTC is authorized to issue rules and reg-

3 See pages 438–439.

ulations, to make inspections, and to issue **cease and desist orders**. The Fur Products Labeling Act was designed to protect consumers and competitors by making it unlawful to misbrand, falsely advertise and falsely invoice fur products. The statute was originally passed in part because of the widespread use of exotic-sounding euphemisms, such as "Baltic Lion," and "Isabella Fox," for such unexotic furs as rabbit, dogskin, skunk or alley cat. As the Wool Act does for wool, the Fur Act makes it unlawful to distribute or advertise and sell a fur product that is misbranded or falsely invoiced. The Fur Act goes one significant step beyond the Wool Act in that it requires *informative advertising* as well as labeling of fur products.

In 1958 the Textile Labeling Act was passed. Basically it requires that all wearing apparel, floor coverings, draperies, beddings, and other textile goods used in the household be informatively and truthfully labeled and advertised. A product is considered misbranded if it is not correctly labeled with the percentage of each fiber present that makes up 5 percent or more of the product's weight. Additional information must be stated, such as identification of the **generic (nontrademark) name** of the fiber, the country of origin, and the manufacturer.

Critics of the Textile Labeling Act point out that the information provided is only helpful to those consumers who understand the qualities of various clothing materials used. However, the type of fiber alone is often not sufficient indication of the wearing qualities of the garment in question. For example, yarn size in nylon products can yield one of the strongest of fabrics (such as "rip-stop" nylon used in tents and sleeping bags) and one of the most fragile, such as in hosiery, with many variations in between. Finishes can also cancel out fiber characteristics, or provide beneficial characteristics not available in the fiber. For example, cotton is one of the most absorbent fibers, but it can be made water-resistant, as is polished cotton. In sum, most labels containing fiber content (as provided for by the Textile Fiber Products Identification Act) are useful on clothes only to the extent that consumers have knowledge of fibers, fabrication methods, and finishes. As a guide to the maze of synthetic fibers and their various properties, you might want to order one or both of the following booklets:

1. A current fiber chart from:

   Man-made Fiber Producers Association, Inc.
   1150 17th St., N.W.,
   Washington, D.C. 20036
2. Fibers and Fabrics, NBS Consumer Information, Series 1. from:

   The National Bureau of Standards
   U.S. Dept. of Commerce
   Washington, D.C. 20230

More informative for your clothes buying excursions are the care instructions required as of July 1973 by the FTC trade rule of 1971. This ruling specifies that all fabrics be labeled as to the laundering or dry cleaning that will be required to maintain the garment's original character. In other words, now when you go to a store, you can assess how much time or money will be entailed in maintaining the garment you purchase. For instance, labels vary from "Dry Clean Only" to "Leather Clean Only" to "Machine Wash, Warm, Tumble Dry"—nine different classifications in all. Some manufacturers have even added further care categories.

As confusing as this might sound, it is an acknowledgement by the FTC and textile manufacturers that fabric content is not sufficient to tell you anything about what you are buying. Although durability information is still not explicitly available, permanent labeling as to care instructions is certainly a great aid in purchasing clothing. No longer will you find that that skirt or pants you just threw in the machine was supposed to be dry cleaned, or that another item should not have been put in the dryer. What these labels represent is a more sophisticated version of the "drip-dry" or "wash and wear" categories we previously had. It is now possible to determine just what you are getting yourself into when purchasing clothing—that is, you will have to iron this stuff, or wait for it to hang dry, or incur the sometimes higher expense of dry cleaning, or whatever. And the regulation does not apply solely to prefabricated garments; persons who choose to sew for their families are also being given care labels to sew into the garments with each piece of fabric they buy.

Now that you know what to look for on the labels, and have presumably decided what kind of styling, durability, and so on, you are in the market for, let us see how to economize on your clothing purchases.

SUMMARY

1. Clothes are purchased for other than mere physical protection. They are purchased because of custom and also because of the improvement in mental attitude that appropriate clothes give the wearer.

2. Different socioeconomic classes typically dress differently as a matter of class identification to impart information to other members of society.

3. Family conflicts about individual dressing styles and clothing budgets can be resolved through democratic family decision-making. Generally it is important to compromise in terms of the individual's desire to either conform or not conform with family dressing habits.

4. It has been said that fashions are dictated by the fashion industry. However, the flop of the midiskirt a few years ago is at least one instance of the consumer's rebellion.

5. Generally, more durable clothes are higher priced. When you are deciding which clothes to buy, it is important to take account of how long they will last. Then you can compare clothes on the basis of the price per year rather than on the basis of the total purchase price.

6. In 1953 Congress passed the Flammable Fabrics Act, which was amended in 1967. The Act requires that the manufacture and sale of fabric or fabric products conform to an applicable standard or regulation. This is particularly important for children's bedtime clothing.

7. Numerous acts apply to correct labeling of fabrics and fur. The Fur Act, for example, requires informative advertising as to the actual content of the products in question.

8. Current information on fibers can be obtained from the National Bureau of Standards or from the Man-Made Fiber Products Producer Association.

QUESTIONS FOR THOUGHT AND DISCUSSION

1. What determines how many clothes you buy each year? How much extra do you spend on clothing for variety and style?

2. How many of your decisions about clothing are based on custom?

3. Do you agree that clothing imparts information to the onlooker? Or do you think "you cannot judge a book by its cover"?

4. Do you think that every member of a spending unit should be allowed to dress in his or her own way without regard to the general ideas held by the spending unit?

5. Do you think that fashion designers dictate what fashions will be or that they cater to what the public wants? What evidence do you have?

6. Have you noticed a changing attitude toward clothing in your lifetime?

7. Do you think it is fair that more durable clothes cost more than less durable clothes? Do you care about durability in your own clothing purchases?

8. Why do you think it has taken so long for Congress to act on flammable fabrics?

9. Why are some parents unwilling to buy flame-retardant clothing for their children? Do you think that they should be required to do so by law?

THINGS TO DO

1. Write a list of all of the clothes you have bought in the last year. Also list all of the clothes that you no longer wear. From the first list,

decide what were actual necessities and what were "frills." From the second list, decide which clothes were still serviceable. Now ask yourself how much you have spent for clothing in excess of what was actually necessary.

2. Make as long a list as you can of all of our clothing habits that are based purely on custom. Why are customs different in different parts of the United States and in different countries?

3. Contact a fashion designer or a fashion designer's assistant. Try to find out how decisions are made on which fashions will be selected for any particular year or season. Why do you think spring fashions are shown long before spring occurs?

4. Examine the labels on all of the clothes you have. How helpful are they in telling you what the fabric is made of, how durable it is, how it should be washed, and so on? Can you think of better labeling that would be more helpful to you the consumer?

**SELECTED
READINGS**

Buck, George S., *Flammability Report,* Textile Industries, November 1971.

"Care Labeling of Wearing Apparel," *Family Economics Review,* March 1972.

"Fabrics and Fire: What You Don't Know *Can* Hurt You," *What's New in Home Economics,* April 1971.

"How Much Other People Spend on Clothes," *Changing Times,* August 1972.

Look for That Label, FTC Buyers Guide No. 6 (Washington, D.C.: Federal Trade Commission).

CONSUMER ISSUE V
Getting the Most for Your Clothes Shopping Dollar

WHERE TO BUY AND HOW MUCH TO LOOK AROUND

Where you buy clothing will be dictated by your preferences in styles. Some stores differentiate themselves by catering to different tastes, or by offering different qualities of goods, or by presenting a store atmosphere—in the kinds of salespersons and the help they offer—different from that of other stores. Also involved, of course (as we indicated in the previous chapter, is a certain amount of status: shopping at Saks Fifth Avenue implies a different self-image than does shopping at J. C. Penney.

In some stores you will find very modish, young looking clothes, and in other stores traditional styles or even old-fashioned, older looking clothes. (With the revival of 1930s fashions, it is sometimes difficult to tell the difference.) In any case, the style you prefer is the first consideration. The next consideration is whether or not you should go to a discount store (if there is one in your area). Whether or not you do depends on how much you value the variety and the services that may be offered by nondiscount stores (and, of course, whether or not you feel your self-image is consistent with discount shopping). One of the services that is often foregone in discount stores is the continuous help that may sometimes be received from a salesperson. Many consumers do not prefer to have assistance from salespersonnel, while others require constant attention. If you find a store where a salesperson is extremely knowledgeable about the durability and other character-

istics of the clothes that are sold in that store, you might be willing to pay a slightly higher price than you would in a discount establishment. The difference in price, you predict, will more than be made up for by the information that you are given by the salesperson. Again, this is a choice that cannot be made for you, and it is one that you cannot figure out perfectly. You may make a mistake; but this is one method by which you become an informed shopper. You acquire information ("experience") as you make mistakes so that the next time you will make the right decision about the purchase.

SHOULD YOU SHOP AROUND FOR VALUES?

Whether to shop around for values is another matter of personal choice. Obviously, if you can buy the identical piece of clothing for a lower price in one store than in another, and both stores give the same amount of service in hemming, alterations, allowing returns, and so on, you should buy the cheaper item. But finding the best deal involves using your time, and you must decide how valuable your time is. Also, you must decide whether you actually enjoy shopping. Some consumers detest going to store after store in search of the best deal on a particular piece of clothing. In such a situation, you might even end up ordering clothes through the mail. You are less likely to get exactly what you had in mind, but you are spared the time of walking, taking the bus or subway, or driving your car around to different stores. Many clothing

outlets, particularly those for shoes and recreational equipment, offer service by mail with take-back provisions. You can also order through catalogs from Wards, Sears, Penneys, Spiegels, or other stores, and again take-back provisions are usually very liberal. Here you save your time, but you do not get to see the article in question until it is delivered to your door. (Remember, however, that service to your door means that you pay a higher price for the product; in many cases, you can arrange to pick up the items at a catalog desk in the store nearest you.)

Characteristics of Stores

There are certain characteristics of each retail clothing store you may want to check into before you choose the one to shop in. How good a reputation does a store have? Can you be certain about the quality of its products? One way to find this out is to ask your neighbors or

your friends. Another way is to see what percentage of its sales is to repeat customers. If you find people going back often to the same store, it may give good service and sell a fairly reputable product. If you have your own predetermined evaluations of particular brands, then you pick the store according to the brands it carries. How you then decide which store to go to depends on:

1. What kind of service do you get?
2. How do you get along with the salespeople?
3. What are the take-back or exchange provisions?
4. What kind of sales does it have, etc.?

Most of your common-sense notions about shopping will apply here as they will whenever you spend money.

USING THE MAILS

As we mentioned earlier, if you want to save shopping time, you can use the services of some mail-order firm—that is, one which sends you catalogs from which you can choose those products you intend to buy. Most catalogs also provide you with useful information, such specifications as type of fabric, the warranties applying, and so on. This often allows for less hurried comparative shopping in the home. Moreover, if you decide to shop on credit, credit terms are usually spelled out. Note also that you may want to read the catalog first and then go to your usual clothing store to compare with what the catalog firm has to offer. This is comparison shopping the easy way. The key, of course, is to find a reliable mail-order house; there are literally hundreds of them.

CASH OR CHARGE?

Most consumer consultants generally recommend that all clothing be purchased with cash because, it has been stated, buying on credit costs more money. That is true for the reasons we discussed in Chapter 7. If you buy on time, you will have to pay a service charge (interest) for borrowing that money. But remember our earlier discussion on the flow of services from any item. If you buy, say, a nightgown and charge it, you can expect that it will last at least as long as the time period you might take to pay off the balance. In a sense, you are then spreading out the payments for the item so that they correspond with the use of that item.

Your considering the purchase of clothing does not give you any built-in reason to pay cash or to charge. Your decision will be based on how much overall debt you want to carry, and this depends on what income you expect to make in the future, how much you value present consumption over future consumption, and what the charges will be for purchasing things on time.

Remember, though, you are better off financially if you are allowed to charge goods for 30, 60, or 90 days without paying any interest. This way, you get the use of that money for that particular period and you also get the use of the clothes you buy, with no charge for that simultaneous use. But be careful to make sure that in fact there are no hidden charges for paying 30 or 60 days later. Also, see if there is a discount for paying cash. In this case, you may decide that you would rather get the cash discount because you were going to pay the bill fairly soon anyway.

BUYING PRINCIPLES

Many buying principles can be applied to shopping for clothes to guarantee that you get the best deal for your money. They are so obvious that we can treat them briefly.

Comparative Shopping

We know that you should compare values—that you should look at the price of a product in one store and compare it with a similar product in another. You have to be careful about similarities, though.

EXHIBIT
Figuring out your clothing needs

1. What do you have already?

2. What clothes are required by:
   a. your job or school?
   b. your social life?
   c. your recreational activities?

3. How many changes of clothes do you require to meet your minimum standards of:
   a. cleanliness?
   b. variety?
   c. social status?

4. How do your answers to questions one through three square with the income that you can spend?

Durability: Remember the discussion about durability in the previous chapter. That two pieces of clothing look the same does not necessarily mean they are the same: one may last longer than the other. You would not be truly comparing values if you automatically bought the cheaper item. You should find the most favorable relative cost per unit of service offered by each clothing item. And this service includes the ability to exchange easily with the store, to get a refund if the clothing is defective, and so on.

Styles: Quite obviously, if you choose basic or classic styles, you will have less of an incentive to change those styles and, hence, your desired clothing budget may be smaller. But of course you give some things up— the joy of wearing highly fashionable clothes, and of wearing new clothes more often.

Needs: You should be careful to buy clothes that, as some consumer economists say, "fit your needs." Only you come close to knowing what your *true* needs are. And you should avoid one pitfall in shopping for clothes: do not become a bargain fanatic. That is, do not buy everything on sale just because it is on sale. Instead, take an inventory of the items you have and decide where you really have a deficiency in your clothing stock.

In general, you should remember that you can save up to 25 percent on many clothing items if you buy store brands instead of national brands. If you are not enamored with brand names per se, you can make quite a few savings (depending, of course, on the quality of the house brand).

SUMMARY

1. Clothing shopping begins with a decision about what type of clothes to buy and in what price range. These two attributes will considerably narrow down the range of possible retail stores to go to.

2. Shopping for clothes you should take into account the time and use of complementary resources involved.

3. When making a decision about where to shop, check into the reputation of a store. You can find this out from friends who have shopped there before, as well as by seeing which brand names are carried in that store (if in fact you know which brand names are reliable).

4. Check out the kind of service you will get after you have made a purchase. What are the take-back guarantees and exchange provisions?

5. You can use the mails to save shopping time. Get catalogs from Sears, Wards, Spiegels, and other companies to find out the exact attributes of some of the clothes you wish to buy. Then you can use that information as a comparison when you go shopping in the retail stores in your area.

6. Whether to pay cash or to charge your clothing purchases should be decided by the total amount of debt you are already handling, not on the particular purchase made. Go back to Consumer Issue 111, Exhibit on page 136, to find out if in fact you have a safe debt load. Make sure you do not exceed it just because you are enamored of a particular article of clothing.

7. Durability is an important quality of any piece of clothing you purchase. Try to compare clothing articles by their cost per year. That means you have to know the durability and also the cost of maintaining the particular piece of clothing.

8. If you buy highly stylish clothes, remember that styles will change more often for you than if you buy more classical styles. You pay for stylishness.

9. Purchasing store names instead of national brand names may save you up to 25 percent. Consider it as a possibility.

QUESTIONS FOR THOUGHT
AND DISCUSSION

1. How often do you shop for durability?

2. Do you find that salespersons offer you help in clothing stores? Or would you rather pay a lower price and shop at a discount store?

3. How much time do you spend shopping for clothes? Do you spend more or less time trying to find good buys than you do for food? If you do, is this rational? Why?

4. Is it just being lazy to actually order articles of clothing through the mail? For whom would this be the most appropriate consumer behavior?

5. What determines your clothing needs? Do you think about them often?

6. Do you think that males looking for clothes spend more or less time than do females, or equal time?

THINGS TO DO

1. Make a list of your clothing inventory. Write down how often each item has to be replaced. Try to determine whether you replace the item more often than is absolutely necessary and, if so, why you do that.

2. Order some of the major mail order catalogs. After you've gotten several of them, compare the clothing in each with the prices in each. If there are significant differences, can you determine why? Now try to establish whether your local retailers sell the same items at the same price. If there is a significant difference, ask your local retailers why.

3. Order the two guides to fibers mentioned in the last chapter. Compare them with our partial guide to synthetic fibers. See how up-to-date this guide is compared to what you received in the mail. Why do you think that the characteristics of certain fabrics may change over time?

SELECTED READINGS

Buying Clothes for Your Family, HXT–N (Berkeley: Agricultural Extension Service, University of California) 1970.

Shopping Care to Fabric Care, HXT–55, Agric. Extension Service, Univ. of California, October 1970.

"Textiles of the 70's: Maze or Miracle?" *What's New in Home Economics*, September 1970.

Removing Stains from Fabrics, HG–62 (Washington, D.C.: U.S. Department of Agriculture, Superintendent of Documents) 1972.

"Ways to Make Clothes Last Longer," *Changing Times*, October 1970.

Your Clothing Dollar, Money Management Institute, Household Finance Corporation, Prudential Plaza, Chicago, Ill. 60601, 1972.

CHAPTER PREVIEW

☐ What is the nature of the housing industry?
☐ What are the different types of dwellings we live in?
☐ What are the advantages of renting over buying?
☐ What has the federal government done to cope with the housing problem?
☐ What is the nature of crimes against property, and what is being done about them?
☐ Why is housing so expensive?
☐ What are some of the problems with the moving industry?

GLOSSARY OF NEW TERMS

Pro Rata: Proportionately according to some exactly calculable factor.

Lease: A contract by which one conveys real estate for a term of years or at will, usually for a specified rent, and the act of such conveyance or the term for which it is made.

Housing Voucher: An alternative method of providing those in need with housing services. A housing voucher would be for a specified amount of money that could be used only in the purchase of housing services. It would be used as an alternative to providing public housing.

Site Value: The value of the land on which a house or other building sits. The site value is determined by many characteristics of the site, such as the view, the shrubbery, the proximity to a city, and so on.

Marginal Tax Bracket: The last tax bracket that a taxpayer finds himself or herself in after figuring out how much is owed the government. In our progressive tax system, tax rates go up as income goes up, but only on the last or marginal amount of income. Your marginal tax bracket could range anywhere from 0 to 70 percent.

Capital Gain: An increase in the value of something you own. Generally you experience a capital gain at the time you sell something you own, such as a house or a stock. You compute your capital gain by subtracting the price you paid for whatever you are selling from the price you receive when you sell it.

PUTTING A ROOF OVER YOUR HEAD

If you happen to be an Eskimo living in the Yukon Territory, putting a roof over your head is complicated, but not impossible: you make an igloo. If you happen to live in the bush country of Tanzania, putting a roof over your head takes some time, but eventually your thatch hut will be just what you need. If you were a pioneer settling down on some cleared land in the Old West, putting a roof over your head would have meant making a log cabin.

Today, by way of contrast, if you are Mr. and Mrs. Superwealthy, deciding on a new roof over your head may involve $30,000 in architect's fees, $100,000 for a plot of land (not too small, of course), and perhaps another $100,000 for quite a nice house. And then again, if you are the average American, you have a three-bedroom house with 1300 square feet of floor space, which, with its land, has a market value of $34,000.

Housing is a necessity, even for the poorest of humans, but we know that the various types of housing services that people seem to "need" vary drastically from region to region, from suburb to suburb, and from person to person. The variety of houses that one can purchase seems almost infinite. And the price range that one has to look at is also large. Housing is just like clothes or food: once we pass a certain minimum level, the rest depends on our tastes and preferences. And our tastes and preferences must be put into line with reality—our limited budgets.

Early Americans must have had just as many fanciful ideas about how they would like to live as we have. But today, some of us—in fact, most of us—live like kings compared to earlier Americans. Why is that? Simply because we are all richer. Each year for the last 150 years, our real incomes have gone up at about 1½ percent per capita. And we have spent an increasing proportion of our budgets on housing services, mainly because most of us really do like to cater to our fancies. We like the good life, and that includes a spacious house with many special features that make it seem like our own.

THE HOUSING INDUSTRY

There are now more than 47 million single-family dwelling units in the United States. There are at least 18

FIGURE 10–1
GROWTH IN HOUSING
IN THE UNITED STATES
The number of housing
units has risen from a
little more than 8 million
in 1890 to almost 75
million in 1975. Source:
Department of Com-
merce.

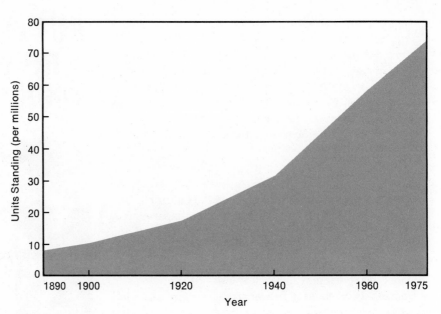

million apartments and another 3 million mobile homes. In almost any
one year, more than one million new houses are being built. Americans
also like to add on to existing houses, as evidenced by the $17 billion
we spend every year for add-ons, improvements, maintenance, and the
like. The number of the U.S. houses, as depicted in Figure 10–1, has been
rising at the rate of about 2½ percent a year for the last 25 years.

However, these figures can sometimes be deceiving. A truer picture of
our circumstances might emerge from measuring how much additional
services we are getting from the rising housing stock. It is one thing for
another one million one-bedroom apartments to be built, and it is another
to have one million four-bedroom houses instead. After all, why do we
buy houses or mobile homes, or buy or rent apartments? We buy or
rent them for the services they yield, just as we do clothes or cars or
anything else that lasts. When we buy a house, we expect to reap an
implicit rate of return in the form of housing services over a number of
years; thus, it is important not to get confused between the existing stock
of housing and the *flow* of services from that stock.

What we are buying is not the house itself, but how much pleasure
we get out of living in it month in and month out. And that pleasure is a
function of its size, the conveniences it has, how pretty the view is, what
the neighborhood is like, and everything else that can contribute to our
happiness when we are home. Generally, the reason there is "no place
like home" is because all of us try to make our homes as special as
possible so that we get the greatest amount of utility or services from
them. That is why, also, it is important to realize that when we buy a
$50,000 house, we are getting a larger flow of services per month than if
we had bought a $20,000 house.

People who have their own houses built incur tremendous money and time costs, worry, and stress. Why do they do it? Many of them incur all those costs so that they can specify the exact house that will maximize the utility and pleasure from the roof over their heads.

DIFFERENT TYPES OF ROOFS

We mentioned before that it is important to distinguish between the different levels of housing services that are being added to our housing stock. Everybody is familiar with single-family dwellings, but fewer people are as familiar with multiple-family dwellings, such as duplexes, high-rise apartments, and so-called tenements. Additionally, in the United States we have seen a rise in condominiums, cooperatives, and mobile homes.

Further below we will talk about why so many mobile homes are being built. Basically, the cost per service flow from mobile homes is considerably lower than from regular dwellings. One reason why is that mobile homes can be built by different rules and construction techniques than are required for regular houses. Many consumers know what a mobile home is, but few are totally clear about what a co-op or condominium is. So let us look at these two new types of ownership arrangements.

Co-ops: In a building of cooperative apartments, each dweller owns a **pro rata** (proportionate) share of a nonprofit corporation which holds the legal right to that building. Each individual dweller has a long-term proprietary lease on his or her individual apartment. All costs, such as real estate taxes and maintenance, are prorated (distributed proportion-

ately to) among all the owners. Much cooperative housing has been produced for middle-income families, although recently it has become more
popular with higher-income families in such places as New York City.
In 1975 it is estimated that there is well over $2 billion worth of coopera-
tive housing in the United States, serving more than 200,000 families.

Cooperative housing grew only slowly until 1950, when legislation was
passed that allowed the Federal Housing Administration (FHA) to insure
the mortgages of cooperative housing units. Today, numerous business
organizations design, finance, contract for construction, and then sell
cooperative housing projects to prospective member-residents. In many
cases, after the cooperative unit is sold, another profit-making organization can be hired to manage the entire unit. In New York, one of the
largest is the United Housing Foundation.

Since the new ruling in 1950, the FHA has insured over $2½ billion
in cooperative housing mortgages for 1¼ million middle-income families.
In certain states, there are state mortgage plans, which have worked out
quite well. For example, the United Housing Foundation, in New York,
built Co-op City in the Bronx. That "city" accommodates 15,000 families
of moderate to middle income.

Co-ops themselves are nonprofit organizations and are therefore owned
and operated solely for the benefit of the members. The FHA estimates
that the costs of living in cooperative apartments are about 20 percent
less than renting comparable apartments from a private landlord. It is
interesting to speculate how this 20 percent differential could continue to
exist. Perhaps it does because, for one thing, maintenance costs would
be lower in the co-op since the owner-members take better care of their
apartments than renters would. Also, fuller occupancy and lower turn-
over would contribute to lower operating costs. And, as we mention
below, owner-members can claim income tax deductions that are not
available to renters.

Members in cooperative units have a right to sell their particular unit
when they decide to move. They recoup any difference between what
they owe on their mortgage and what the resale price of their unit is. In
general, the co-op itself has the first option to buy the apartment that is
put up for sale. In most cases, if the apartment is to be sold to someone
else, the members of the cooperative must approve the sale.

Condominiums: In condominiums, which are a newer type of ownership
than the cooperative, the apartment dweller has the legal title to the apartment which he or she owns and to nothing else in the building except a
proportionate interest in the common areas in the underlying ground, such
as swimming pools, and so on. In other words, a condominium owner
owns the air space in which he or she is living. The ownership rights
are about the same as those of a single-family house. All maintenance
expenditures must be voted on by members. Condominiums have become especially popular in resort areas where the owners do not live

year-round. In 1972, 25 percent of all new housing units constructed were condominiums, and that percentage by 1975 was estimated to be up to 30 percent.

Some housing experts contend that condominiums have certain advantages over cooperative units, and therefore we should see a continued growth in condominiums relative to co-ops. In many situations, owners who want to sell their condominium apartments are under fewer restrictions than are the owners of a co-op unit. The condominium can be sold without the approval of a board of directors. With a condominium, if the owner of a unit defaults on a payment, it only affects the mortgage. In the case of a cooperative unit, any owner who defaults causes the other co-op members to chip in an amount to cover what has been defaulted. Condominium owners are free to rent or lease their units to anyone, and, lastly, condominium owners can own up to three units but are not required to live in more than one of them.

TAX ADVANTAGES

We will see below the various tax advantages of owning a home. All of them apply to condominiums and cooperatives. Basically, all local taxes and interest on the mortgage for the prorated share in the cooperative and the entire share for the condominium unit are deductible from income before taxes are paid. Because this benefit is not directly available to renters, it is one of the reasons why a number of people prefer to own condominiums or join a cooperative instead of renting an apartment, even though an apartment in a cooperative or condominium looks the same and gives the same types of housing services.

RENTING A PLACE
TO LIVE IN

Until fairly recently, it was not uncommon for renters to be looked down upon as people who were unable to manage their money correctly. The proof, of course, was a lack of home ownership. But this attitude has been changing, and today many people rent apartments or houses from choice even though they could easily buy their own home.

There are several reasons why individuals wish to rent instead of buy:

1. Renters have greater mobility than those who own homes.
2. No down payment is involved, or credit checks as in securing a mortgage.
3. Renters are freed from the maintenance tasks that home owners must face.
4. The exact cost of purchasing housing services can be easily figured.

Most apartments are rented on a month-to-month basis with the rent paid in advance. The renter or tenant automatically gets the right to live in the apartment for the next month. In this type of tenant/landlord relationship, the contract may be terminated on 30 days' written notice.

Given the proper 30-day notice, the rent can be raised at any time, or the tenant can be asked to leave. There are advantages and disadvantages to this short-term contract. On one hand, renters can move when they wish without giving a long advance notice. But on the other hand, there is the uncertainty of possibly being asked to leave on short notice, or of finding the rent raised sooner than had been anticipated.

Alternatively, renters may obtain a **lease**. This is simply a long-term contract that binds both landlord and tenant to specified terms. The lease, which is usually for one year, will require generally one month's rent in advance, and perhaps one month's rent as a cleaning deposit.

COPING WITH THE HOUSING PROBLEM

The federal government has been concerned with the problems of slum housing since the initiation of public housing programs in the 1930s. The goal of the Housing Act of 1949 was "realization as soon as feasible . . . of a decent home and suitable living environment for every American family." Twenty years later, the problem was still with us, and in passing the Housing and Urban Development (HUD) Act of 1968, Congress reaffirmed the 1949 goal and specified the construction or rehabilitation over the next 10 years of 26 million housing units, at least six million of which were to be for low- and moderate-income families.

After four decades of government attention, the problem still persists, and federal policies have been at best a mixed blessing. Between 1950

and 1960, for example, the fraction of U.S. dwellings deemed "substandard" fell from 36.9 percent to 18.2 percent.   However, a substantial contribution to this reduction during this decade was made by the private housing market, which upgraded more than two million substandard dwelling units to standard quality.   In the next decade, the National Commission on Urban Problems found that one million dwellings, most of them inhabited by lower-income families, had been demolished under one government program or another.   Through 1967, only 700,000 public housing units had been constructed in their place.

URBAN RENEWAL   Of the various government efforts, the urban renewal program alone was responsible for the plowing under of 400,000 dwelling units. This program, which was the federal government's major attack on the decay of the central city, has failed to eradicate slums, as we are all painfully aware. Urban renewal is a cooperative program between the federal government and local authorities. Local authorities develop a comprehensive, detailed plan for urban renewal—including the area to be rehabilitated, and that to be leveled, and the complex of housing and other facilities to be erected in place of the existing buildings. The new facilities typically include low-income public housing to replace that destroyed and in addition, usually middle- and high-income apartments, hotels, and commercial enterprises that will be financed by private capital.

Once approved by the federal government, the program gets underway with the leveling of the area to be reconstructed. Thereafter, typically, a long period, five to ten years, follows before construction begins. During this period, the area remains a wasteland. The delay has been the result not only of bureaucratic red tape, but also of the reluctance of private capital to construct enterprises of doubtful profitability in such circumstances. The consequences—according to many impartial observers and even those in government itself—have been quite simply that the poor have become worse off; for during the five to ten year interval, the supply of low-income housing has been reduced. Forced out of the areas to be leveled, the poor have had to find other homes, thereby increasing the demand for existing low-income housing and raising the price of those dwellings further.[1] As the price of low-quality housing rises, the owners of better-quality housing on the fringes of slum areas have had an incentive to break up their dwellings into smaller ones and to allow them to deteriorate to be consistent with the quantity or quality demanded by the poor potential residents. Hence, urban renewal has not eliminated slums but—according to some—has actually caused them to spread to other parts of the city. Demolition of slums serves mainly to relocate them, not to eliminate them.

ARE THERE ANY
SOLUTIONS?

Obviously, the past solutions to the lack of "adequate" low- and middle-income housing have not been overwhelmingly successful, although a number of people have benefited from the government programs. One solution has been suggested by a number of home economists, consumer advocates, and government economists. Since we have had such bad luck in the past with trying to have the government build housing units or subsidize them, why not merely give poor people **housing vouchers** (or more income, for that matter)? In this way, they themselves could choose whether they wanted to spend more for housing or buy a minimum amount with the housing vouchers. The problems, outlined above, that arise when the government itself gets into the housing market would occur no more. Instead, as the demand for certain types of housing increased because people with the housing vouchers desired it, private industry would start to provide it. In the long run, the supply of housing would grow—which is, in fact, what we really want. Not only do we want the supply of housing to grow as fast as the population, but we want the quality of housing to improve for less-wealthy Americans. While housing or rent vouchers would be no cure-all, it is clear to most observers that our past efforts to solve our housing problems have not worked out perfectly either.

[1] Some observers contend that there currently is plenty of low-income housing in places like San Francisco, but that the middle-class won't move out of it!

FIGURE 10–2
BURGLARIES OF
HOMES AND
APARTMENTS
Burglaries of homes and
apartments have been
on the rise for many
years now, as can be
seen in this chart.
Source: FBI, *Crime in
the United States*
(Uniform Crime Reports).

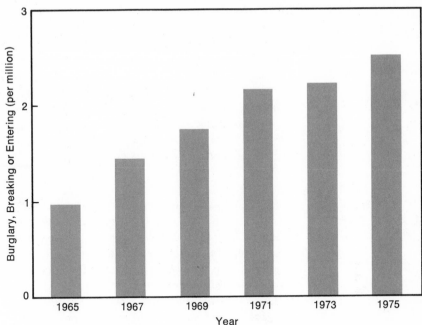

Another problem that is facing all homeowners and all apartment or
housing renters is one of crime.

CRIME

The 1960s saw a 147 percent increase in crimes against property, and
that rate has not fallen very much since then. We see in Figure 10–2
that burglaries in homes and apartments have increased over the past
10 years. More than two million homes are burglarized each year.

Burglaries in dwelling units are something that all of us have to worry
about. While this is not the place to go into the sociological reasons for
such crimes, its magnitude and current seriousness merit comment. The
crime business is big, of that there is no doubt. In fact, the economic
costs of all crime in the United States probably exceed $30 billion a year,
of which almost $8 billion is for police, prosecution, courts, jails, and
certain private methods of preventing crime. That is where you, the
home owner or apartment dweller, come in. You can privately protect
yourself from crimes against your property with a number of various and
sundry devices.

THE PRIVATE
SECURITY INDUSTRY

Very wealthy individuals now are hiring more and more personal guards
to make sure that their property is not invaded by would-be burglars. In
certain areas in the United States where there is already police protection
from the government, citizens have hired additional guards to patrol the
area. The amount of employment for private security has increased from
282,000 to 505,000 persons in the last 15 years.

Even more important, the security hardware business has grown as people become more frightened about the problem of theft. There are increasing numbers of companies that sell security devices ranging from better locks to intricate electronic surveillance equipment that can only be rivaled by the fertile imagination of a science fiction writer. You can buy such things as 3M Ultrasonic Intruder Alarms disguised as dictionaries, pick-resistant Medeco cylinder locks, VigilPane (an impenetrable lamenated glass), or Ademco photoelectric unit, plus pressure-sensitive floor mats, vibration sensors, and wired magnets. Home-protection expenditures are supposed to reach $500 million by 1980.

WHY DOES IT COST SO MUCH TO BUY A HOUSE?

In 1955, the average single-family house cost $14,500. In 1975, the estimate is over $30,000. Not only have the costs of houses themselves gone up, but so, too, have property insurance rates, the costs of maintenance repairs, mortgage interest, and property taxes. Why do houses cost so much today? And what determines their costs in different areas of a city—or, for that matter, of the world?

One reason that the price of housing units has been going up so much is because the value of their sites, the land they are on, has also been going up. Let us find out what determines site values.

DETERMINING THE VALUE OF LAND

Land is generally thought of as being in fixed supply. Of course, we can fill in areas of a bay and do other such things, but not much of an increase in the total supply of land results. The value of a piece of land is determined by the same things that determine the value of anything else: the forces of supply and demand interact. Why does a piece of land with a view over a bay cost more than the same piece with no view? Obviously because the demanders—that is, you the consumers—place a value on having a view and you are willing to pay for it. Demanders like you will bid up the price of the view lot so that it reflects the utility received from having the view.

But many other things besides the view determine the **site value** of land. One of the most important determinants is property taxes. If you own an acre in one section of town and you have to pay $5000 a year in taxes, that same acre in another section of town where you would only have to pay $2000 in taxes will be worth a lot more. Why? Simply because the cost of owning it would be smaller and therefore people like you and me might bid up the price of the lower-taxed land to reflect the tax savings.

POLLUTION EFFECTS

The amount of pollution in an area also affects the price of the land, because pollution is a source of disutility. The same piece of land with the same house on it will have a lower value in a highly polluted area than in a less-polluted area. Why? Simply because consumers like you and me bid up the price of the land where there is less pollution. You have an indication of what might happen if suddenly all of the smog was eliminated from the Los Angeles Basin: property values in the hitherto smoggy areas would immediately rise, and the relative value of land in the outlying, less smoggy areas would fall, because those pieces of land would now be less special. If you are a property owner in a polluted area of a city, you obviously will benefit from any unanticipated reduction in pollution in your area. Your benefit is in the form of an increase in the value of your property, which means that when you sell it, you can get more for it.

There are a host of other aspects of land that determine its value. If a freeway that takes you downtown in 10 minutes is near your land but out of ear shot, the value of your land is going to be higher than if the freeway did not exist. Land close to stores, shopping centers, schools, and other such facilities will also be more valuable.

In other words, all the amenities of living are somehow figured into the site value of land. Whenever any of them changes, the site value changes also. If you live in a pollution-free area but suddenly a factory moves in, the value of your land will fall. If a bridge is built across a lake, thus shortening the trip between your land and the city from one hour to 20 minutes, your land will increase in value. If the crime rate increases in your area, the value of your land will fall; if the crime rate decreases, it will rise.

BUILDING COSTS, BUILDING CODES, AND YOU

To build a house, you cannot just buy the lumber, bricks, pipes, and so on, and put it up. Why not? Because many, many elements of that house must be checked out by a city building inspector. For unless you live in an otherwise uninhabited area, there are city, state, or federal building codes to be met.

What are building codes? They are codes by which builders must abide if they are to get certification for their work. Building codes are generally thought of as a means by which consumers are protected from unscrupulous methods of putting together a dwelling. A building code which gives a certain thickness of wire for electricity presumably protects you against short circuits and fires from them. A building code which gives a certain thickness plasterboard protects you from having a poorly insulated house, or one that will crack easily.

However, not everybody who has studied housing codes thinks they are all for the good of the consumer. Considering how unbelievably rigid local building codes can be, many observers are amazed that we have as much housing as we actually do. If you look at an identical house in different cities, you will find that the price of building it varies greatly because of variations in the codes. Some codes require, for example, that roof trusses be spaced 24 inches apart; others say that 16 is the necessary minimum. There are at least 13,000 code authorities in the

United States; and in each city or state there may be hundreds and hundreds of inspectors making sure the codes are carried out. Now, a house need not be safer in Sacramento, California, than in Mesa, New Mexico, but the codes, when looked at in this way, certainly will tell you differently. Why is there all this variation? Much of it is due to custom and habit, but much else is due to the lobbying of very powerful special interest groups when the codes were drawn up.

UNIONS AND
BUILDING SUPPLIERS

If you are a member of a plumbers union and someone invents inexpensive plastic pipe that does not require a sophisticated plumber, you would realize that in the future there will be less demand for your services if houses could be built with this plastic pipe. It would be in your best interests to make sure that the housing code was not changed to allow the less expensive plastic pipe to be used. This is exactly what happens, as the hearings for plastic pipe in Seattle, Washington, exemplify. The people against plastic pipe contended it was unsafe. How did they demonstrate it was unsafe? They took a brick and dropped it from 10 feet over the pipe and showed that the pipe would break. They poured gasoline on the pipe, lit it, and showed that it would melt, therefore "proving" that it was unsafe. What was actually being done? People— that is, plumbing union members—were fighting against a new innovation that would bring the cost of housing down, and also the income of plumbers.

But not only the building tradesmen have a special interest in making sure building codes favor them; so, too, do local suppliers. Local suppliers may persuade the drafters of building codes to require very specific materials, sometimes even by brand names. In this way, the supplier will benefit from the building code, and you, the consumer, will often lose out.

Basically, building codes are materials-oriented instead of function-oriented. They specify, for example, the number of studs instead of the strength of the wall. They specify the thickness of the wallboard instead of its insulation properties. Consumers would be much better off if in fact building codes were altered to specify functional characteristics that were deemed adequate to protect the consumer, rather than specifying the types of materials used and the ways houses must be built.

**INVESTING
IN A HOUSE**

Figure 10–3 shows the increase in mobile home construction since 1963. Mobile homes are one of the most popular forms of low-income housing in the United States today. Why? One reason is favorable tax treatment in those states that tax them as vehicles instead of as homes. Another reason is that with mobile homes you may get more housing services per dollar spent, since mobile homes are often built on an assembly line with nonunion labor, and without very restrictive building codes. That means that alternative, less-costly building techniques can be utilized. Evidently, since so many Americans are buying mobile homes, those circumstances detract little or nothing from the quality or safety of the dwelling unit. However, we should note that not all has been perfect in the mobile home industry: California, for one, has felt the need to regulate the way mobile homes could be built.

Quite obviously, whether a union or nonunion tradesman works on a housing unit does not necessarily determine its quality. And if you were aware of how much more expensive union workers are than nonunion workers, you would understand the trend towards using assembly line methods which do not require anybody from the plumbers union, the construction workers' union, or the electricians' union. Figure 10–4 shows the average wages of building union members over the last 25 years. They have risen faster than just about any other wages in the economy. It is not surprising that, for example, most of the time a large percentage of union construction workers do not have union work, because their wages in 1975 averaged over $7 an hour. Many of them prefer to take nonunion wages on the side (and presumably against union rules) rather than remain unemployed for so many months out of the year.

MOBILE HOMES

It is fairly certain that the population will continue to grow for some time to come, and, hence, there will be pressures on land prices in spite of everything else. Does this mean that you should invest in a house with land around it because you are certain that it will go up in value?

If you consider your housing purchase an investment, you are not *guaranteed* of making any more than if you had invested in something else. The reason is fairly simple. Because it is well known that the value of land

FIGURE 10–3

MOBILE HOMES BUILT EACH YEAR
The growth in mobile homes over the last decade and a half has indeed been startling. The reason behind such a rapid growth rate is obviously because home buyers are finding mobile homes a better buy than conventional housing. Sources: Federal Reserve Board of Governors, and Mobile Home Manufacturers Association.

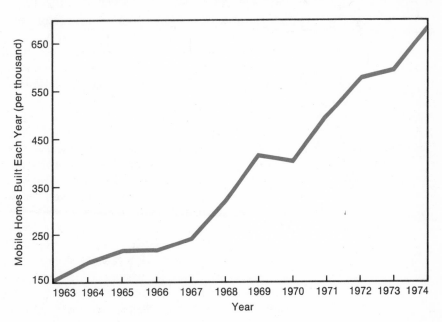

FIGURE 10–4

GROWTH IN WAGES OF
UNION CONSTRUCTION
WORKERS
Average hourly earnings
of union construction
workers has been on
the rise for many years
now. In 1975 it is
somewhere in excess of
$7 to $8 an hour.
Source: Department of
Labor, Bureau of Labor
Statistics, *Handbook of
Labor Statistics;* and
*Survey of Current
Business.*

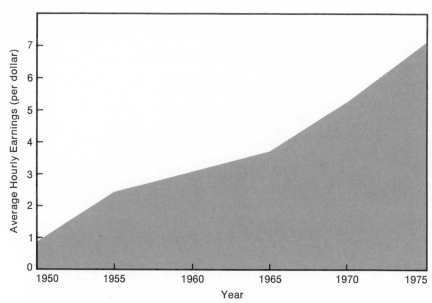

has risen over time as population increased, many people take that into account when they try to purchase land or houses, and the price of land is consequently bid up. If something is so obvious that you and I know about it, how can we expect to make a killing on the obvious? If we think we can, we are fooling ourselves. Buying a house may or may not be a good investment, but do not expect to get rich simply because you bought a big house with plenty of land. The price you paid for that house probably reflected everybody else's anticipation of rising land values. What you will usually get is a normal rate of return on your investment, which will be equivalent, in essense, to the rate of return you could have gotten had you invested the money elsewhere and rented a house. Many people nevertheless want to buy instead of rent, and many of their compelling reasons have to do with the special tax advantages that we briefly mentioned earlier.

THE TAX GAME

Did you know that if you buy a house and borrow the money to pay for it, all of the interest payments that you pay to the bank can be deducted from your income before you pay taxes? This may not mean much to you if you are not in a very high tax bracket, but when you get up into a higher one, it will make a big difference.

For example, suppose you buy a $30,000 house and were somehow able to borrow the entire $30,000. Let's say that the interest you paid every year on that $30,000 came to $3000. You would be able to deduct that $3000 from your income before you paid taxes on it. If you were in the 20 percent tax bracket, you would get a tax savings of $600. But if you were in the 70 percent bracket, you would get a tax savings of $2100; the interest on your loan would in effect only be costing you $900, which is pretty inexpensive. Now you know why, as people get into higher income tax brackets, it generally pays them to buy a house instead of renting.

This tax policy is an implicit subsidy to the housing industry and to all of you who own houses and have any taxable income. The Joint Economic Committee figured out that the implicit subsidy was costing the U.S. Treasury $2.6 billion a year.[2] Unfortunately, the benefit from this implicit subsidy is directly proportional to your **marginal tax bracket** which, of course, is directly proportional to how much you make. Since poor people are poor because they make little money, they are not in a high marginal tax bracket. Thus, even if they deduct all of their interest payments for their house, the implicit tax savings will be little, or sometimes zero. This interest rate subsidy to homeowners has not been very useful in helping out lower-income people.

Taxes and housing are related in another way that you may want to know about. If you buy a house for $20,000 and sell it ten years later for $30,000, you have made $10,000. And generally, you would be taxed on that sum, for it is a **capital gain**.[3] However, if you buy another house of equal or higher price within a year (or have a new one built within 18 months), you pay no capital gains taxes at all.

HOUSING AND EDUCATING YOUR CHILDREN

Most education from kindergarten through twelfth grade is provided by public school systems. Because these public school systems are at least in part financed by property taxes, it is not unusual to find more agreeable school systems in areas where property values are high and the total property taxes collected are usually large. Of course, between property tax revenues and quality of education there need not be this relationship, but it is sufficiently common to consider it when buying a house (or even when deciding where to rent). In other words, when you buy a house, you are buying a complementary good that goes with it—education for any younger children you happen to have. In areas that have better elementary (or "primary"), junior, and senior high schools than other areas, the housing prices may be correspondingly higher.

Education through twelfth grade is mandatory in most states, and in all states it is provided by tax-financed institutions. Usually there's not much choice: you must pay the taxes, whether or not you have children in school or whether or not you want to send them to a public institution. Wealthier parents obviously have more choices, but they are limited. While there are private grade schools, junior highs, and high schools, there are not very many. And the reason is easy to see. Since all of us have to pay for education through property taxes no matter where we

[2] Joint Economic Committee, "The Economics of Federal Subsidy Programs" (Washington, D. C.: U.S. Government Printing Office, 1972).

[3] Capital gains tax rates are generally lower than normal personal income tax rates.

live, many of us do not feel we can afford, or that we want to pay, the extra amount for whatever additional value we would receive from sending our children to private school instead of public school. Those of us who send our children to private school pay twice, first in the form of property taxes and second as tuition to the private institution.

As parents we have some choice in the quality of our children's schooling even without sending them to private schools, but only if we are willing to move to where we feel the better schools are. The quality of schools is obviously a strong selling point for some suburban areas. One need only drive around with a real estate agent in Scarsdale, New York, or in Beverly Hills or Palo Alto, California, where the public schools are considered above average. The real estate agent will certainly let you know.

"And just think, in another thirty years you'll be a gray-haired old couple, and you'll be sitting here burning the mortgage in this very fireplace!"

**HOUSES DO NOT
LAST FOREVER**

Remember that when you buy a house, you are not buying the house for itself but for the services that it yields. And the way you get a constant level of services from a given house is by maintaining it. Houses have a tendency to fall apart just like anything else you own. And repairing them can sometimes be expensive. We mentioned already that the average increases in craftsmen's wages are among the highest in the nation. The same is true for the wages of persons who come to fix your sprinkler system, your clogged drain, your leaking roof, your broken furnace, or whatever. Since the maintenance expenses on a house can be extremely important, when you consider purchasing a house you should figure out how much it will cost to keep up. If you have one with a large front and/or back lawn and much shrubbery, you know that you will have high maintenance expenses for the grounds. You or someone else in your family must do the work, alone or together, or you must hire a gardener. In either case, you pay more for your housing services—but, of course, you get more in aesthetic pleasure. When you own anything (except a brick house), you have to plan to repaint it every few years. If it has carpets, they have to be cleaned professionally every once in a while.

All maintenance costs should be included in the costs per year of having any particular house. After all, you are buying a service flow for, let us say, a year at a time, and you should not be fooled into ignoring some of the very important costs of obtaining those services.

MAKING THE MOVE

Ours is a mobile society. One in five U.S. families moves once every year; among people 25 to 34 years old who have gone to college, almost 38 percent move every year. The decision to move often comes from a desire to change location, to go to a place with a better school system, to be in a different climate. Sometimes a move is forced on a family by a job commitment. Whatever the reason, when moving comes around (unless you are lucky) you have too many personal possessions to be moved in your Chevy or Volkswagen. Either you rent a U-Haul truck or you must call in a mover, a professional one to be sure. Even in the best of circumstances and with the best movers to help you, you are not in for a picnic. Moving at its worst can be a total disaster causing an incredible amount of stress. In the next consumer issue some pointers are given about how to choose a moving company, what to prepare for, and how to make things generally easier for yourself. Do not expect too much, however. Moving is never easy.

There are many problems in the moving industry, some of which can never be worked out. Many of them, however, are the result of government-business relationships that do not seem to benefit the consumer at all. Moving is an industry regulated by the Interstate Commerce Commission, an agency set up in 1887 to regulate some of the abusive practices of railroads. Since then, the ICC has increasingly taken over regulation of all forms of transportation, including, as we mentioned, moving. As a result, at one and the same time you have a friend and a foe. You have a friend because many ICC regulations are designed to benefit you; in addition, if something goes wrong and you think you have been cheated, you can complain to the ICC and often you will get a redress of your grievances. On the other hand, you have a very definite foe, because the ICC frequently does things at the behest of the industry to help the industry and not the consumer.

For example, the stifling of competition, with the help of the regulatory agencies involved, is not unknown in this industry. For example, say a large moving company wants to service a state in which it does not yet have a license to service. Hearings are held to find out whether the company should be allowed to service that state. Now you and I know that there are generally no reasons to prevent such competition because we, the consumers, will benefit from it ultimately through better service and/or lower prices. However, since the movers already servicing that state will lose some of their business to the new competition, they fight tooth and nail to prevent the competition.

How they do it is rather interesting. A hearing is held in which the competitors find people who have been moved by the company wishing to gain entrance into the state. These people have to be special: they have to have had problems in their moves. The competitors pay the travel expenses for them to come to the hearings to complain. But the company that wants to move into the new state fights back. It pays the travel expenses for individuals who it has moved and who are content to come testify in its favor. What a comedy! The battle of sob stories versus glowing reports! Somehow it seems no better than a hearing at which gasoline is poured over a plastic pipe and set on fire to demonstrate the unsafeness of the pipe. But consumers should expect such behavior, because special producer interest groups always look out for their own special interests and not for general interests. If it happens otherwise we are lucky. Here perhaps is where organized consumer groups could help out.

When you decide to buy a house and to move, you should have some idea of the best way to buy a house, and that is explored in the following consumer issue.

SUMMARY

1. Americans purchase many different types of housing services—those from residential houses, those from apartments, those from condominiums or cooperatives, and those from mobile homes.

2. Individuals purchase or rent a house or apartment, or whatever in order to obtain the flow of services from that particular asset. The flow of services from an expensive house is obviously more than from a less expensive house.

3. Cooperatives and condominiums are becoming increasingly popular types of ownership arrangements. In a cooperative situation, the co-op is a nonprofit corporation that is owned and operated solely for the benefit of its members—that is, the individuals who own residences in the building. Members of a co-op can sell their particular unit when they decide to move, but the members of the co-op must approve the sale.

4. Condominiums provide legal ownership to the airspace in which the individual is living. The condominium owner has fewer restrictions than the co-op owner. For example, the condominium owner can rent or lease the unit to anyone, and can own up to three units although living in only one of them.

5. Renting is an attractive alternative to buying because (a) there is greater freedom of mobility, (b) there is no downpayment, (c) there are no maintenance tasks, (d) the exact cost can be easily figured out.

6. Urban renewal involves destruction of dilapidated housing and construction of better housing in its place. However, urban renewal has been judged less than a total success because during the time that leveling and construction of new units are underway, the supply of low-cost housing to the poor is greatly reduced.

7. An alternative to urban renewal and public housing is the institution of housing vouchers: needy families would be given certificates with a specified amount of money on them that could be used only to purchase housing services.

8. Crimes against property are increasing dramatically in the United States. What you can do as an individual to counter this increase is purchase various devices that will prevent or will signal the attempted entrance of a robber.

9. Housing is so expensive for two reasons—the cost of construction, and the cost of the land or site on which the house is put.

10. The more attractive the site, the more expensive it will be. A site can be attractive for any number of reasons, such as the absence of air pollution and noise pollution, a beautiful view, closeness to shopping, nice neighborhood, etc. Construction costs are high because of restrictive building codes that require expensive construction materials and techniques, and because of relatively high construction industry wages.

11. An alternative to the normal house is a mobile home, which is less expensive because it is not generally constructed by union laborers, nor is it as well regulated by construction codes.

12. Do not get the mistaken impression that an investment in a house guarantees you a higher than normal rate of return on your investment. In fact, in our system, any investment that is well known cannot guarantee you ahead of time a higher than normal rate of return.

13. Remember that all interest payments on mortgages for houses are deductible from your taxes. Therefore, if you are in the 20 percent tax bracket and you pay interest of $1000 on your house mortgage, you will get a reduction of 20 percent times $1000, or $200, in the taxes you owe the government. Hence, the actual cost to you of that interest will be reduced by $200.

14. Your choice of housing may determine the education for your children, since public school systems are financed in part by property taxes which depend on the value of the property in the area around the school.

15. The moving industry is regulated by the Interstate Commerce Commision. That regulatory agency is both a friend and a foe, for it has allowed the elimination of much competition in the moving industry, but will often set regulations that do benefit you when you make a move.

QUESTIONS FOR THOUGHT AND DISCUSSION

1. Why do you think housing is such a special commodity?

2. When somebody tells you that they are going to buy a $30,000 house, does that sound like a lot of money? (What is the average price of a new house today?)

3. Is it better to buy or rent a house?

4. If you had to live in either a co-op or a condominium, which would you choose? Why?

5. Do the tax advantages of owning a home benefit everyone equally? (Hint: What about our progressive tax system?)

6. Why has there been a change in the attitude towards renting versus home owning?

7. Why do you think urban renewal has often been deemed a failure?

8. If you were in charge of solving the housing problem, what would your solution be?

9. Do you think housing vouchers would be a good alternative to current government attempts at helping poor people have adequate housing? Why or why not?

10. Can you make a list of other determinants of the value of land than those given in the text?

11. If you buy a house for $20,000 in 1975 and sell it for $30,000 in 1980, are you better off? (Be careful: What about inflation?)

12. What are the costs of having building codes? What are the benefits?

13. Why has there been such a rapid growth in the construction of mobile homes in the last 10 years?

14. "Since the amount of land available is fixed and the population is growing, land has to be a good investment." Evaluate.

THINGS TO DO

1. If you are living in a house, or you know someone who is, try to determine the exact cost per month of living in it. Make sure you include the maintenance costs, the opportunity cost of the difference between the value of the house and the mortgage (sometimes called the equity in the house), the interest on the mortgage, and so on. When you have come up with a monthly figure, search around your neighborhood to find out what sort of apartment or house you could rent for that amount. Is buying obviously a better deal than renting?

2. Send away for literature on the numerous condominiums that are advertised in the travel section of newspapers and also in the housing section of the Sunday editions. See what advantages there are to buying a condominium rather than a co-op or other dwelling unit. Do you find advantages that were not listed in the text? What are they?

3. See if there is a local office of HUD (Housing and Urban Development). Ask them to send you all of their literature on what they are doing to help out the housing problem. Evaluate it for its impact on the poor, the middle class, and the upper class. Find out if there have been any objective standards set by which to judge the success or failure of various housing programs.

4. Discuss the concept of housing vouchers with anybody who is convinced there is a housing problem. Find out what the pros and cons are from other individuals' points of view. Could the concept of vouchers be applied to other specific necessities, such as education, food, entertainment, and so on?

5. Check out a copy of the FBI Uniform Crime Reports. See what has been happening to crime in your area of the United States. Are the trends down or up? If crimes against property were given in dollar terms, what should you do to find out what is really happening? (Hint: What about correcting for inflation?)

6. Call up a real estate agent and ask where the best housing investments should be. If the agent tells you that land on the water or land with a view always is a good investment, ask why.

7. Call up City Hall. Try to get a copy of the building codes for your area, or at least find out how you can read parts of them. Find a specific feature, such as wiring or plumbing, and ask when those codes were set up. Find out if there have been any technological advances since then, and try to determine whether the building code should be changed.

8. Make a comparison between the cost per square foot of buying a new mobile home and the cost per square foot of buying a regular home.

9. Get a copy of the pamphlet issued by the Congress of the United States, Joint Economic Committee, entitled "The Economics of Federal Subsidy Programs" (Washington, D.C.: Government Printing Office, 1972). Read the section on housing and draw your own conclusions.

10. Can you see how decisions about what kind of car to buy resemble decisions about what kind of house to buy when you consider maintenance problems?

SELECTED
READINGS

"Age of Automation Arrives for Housing Industry," *What's New in Home Economics*, April 1972.

"A Man's Home Is His Capital," *Money*, December 1972.

"A Mobile Home vs. a House—How the Costs Compare," *Changing Times*, January 1971.

"Dollars and Sense Condominiums," *American Home*, January 1970.

"Landlords vs. Tenants: Rules of the Game Are Changing," *Changing Times*, May 1972.

"Modular and Mobile Homes, Recreational Vehicles," *Consumer Bulletin Annual*, 1973.

"Moving? These Families Tell What It's Really Like," *Changing Times*, August 1972.

"New Patterns in Housing," *Forbes*, April 1970.

Perl, Lila, *The House You Want* (New York: David McKay Co.), 1965.

"What's Happening to the Cost of Building a House?," *Changing Times*, June 1973.

CONSUMER ISSUE VI

How to Buy or Rent a Place to Live

When you want to obtain housing, your first decision must be whether to buy or rent. If you have already decided to rent, you can go directly to the last section of this issue. But before you decide either way, perhaps you should know what you are getting into in either case. There is a perennial argument among family spending experts as to whether it is better to buy or to rent. Surveys done with home owners show that at least a fourth of them own homes because they think it is cheaper than renting, and at least a fifth of them own homes because they think they are a good investment. Others own homes because they like the idea of being a home owner and being their own landlord, so to speak.

RENTING VERSUS BUYING AS INVESTMENTS

Consider the argument that rent money is wasted by the tenant, whereas payments on a home are not wasted because you are building up equity. This is clearly ridiculous. In either case, you are paying for a housing service. For example, even if you buy a $25,000 house and pay for it with cash, you still have costs, even though you have no house payments. You have the costs of maintenance and taxes. But more important, there is an implicit opportunity cost, because you have $25,000 tied up in that house. After all, that $25,000 could earn a return if you invested it in the stock market or got interest in a savings and loan association. Realistically speaking, the implicit opportunity cost

Earnest Money: Sometimes called a deposit on a contract or an offer to purchase a house. It is the amount of money that you put up to show that you are serious about the offer you are making on a house for sale. Generally you sign an earnest agreement or a contract which specifies the purchase price you are willing to pay for the house in question. If the owner selling the house signs, then generally you are committed to purchase the house and if you back down, you can lose the entire earnest money or deposit.

Title: The physical representation of your legal ownership to a house. The title is sometimes called the deed.

Title Insurance: Insurance that you pay for when you buy a house so that you can be assured that the title or legal ownership to the house is free and clear when you buy the house. If, for example, you purchase a house and pay for title insurance and six months later the builder who put on a new bathroom sues you because the former owners did not pay for the work, the title insurance company may be forced to come up with the money.

Discount Points: Additional charges added to a mortgage that effectively raise the rate of interest you pay.

of the $25,000 you paid for the house might be as high as 10 percent, or $2500: you are paying $2500 a year, plus taxes—say, of $500 plus maintenance and depreciation, which might add another $1000. That means that even if you pay cash, the implicit cost of owning a $25,000 house will be around $4000 a year.

Against this cost you must weigh the value of the services you receive plus any appreciation in the land value. Say the land itself is worth $10,000. It might appreciate at, say, 7 percent a year. That would mean you would deduct $700 from the total cost to get a net cost per year of a little over $3000. Do you still think that to buy is cheaper than to rent? What equivalent value in services could you get in a rented house or apartment for, say, $250 a month? There is no other cut and dried way to make the decision.

Buying a house rather than renting one presupposes that you have made a fundamental value judgment. Owning your own home involves many hidden costs. You are the one who must worry about upkeep, maintenance, changes in zoning laws, and so on. If you rent, you have no such worries. The question is: can you get what you want in a rented apartment or house? If your tastes are similar to the average, perhaps that is possible. If you have special unusual preferences, you will have a difficult time renting exactly what you want. When you rent you are usually not allowed (or do not necessarily want) to make changes in the dwelling, at least not permanent changes. In a home that you own, you are free to make such changes.

The American dream seems to be that each of us will own our own homes. Let us assume that you share that dream. When you buy a house, you should figure out how much you can safely spend.

HOW MUCH CAN YOU AFFORD?

It is very easy to get carried away with buying housing services. A nice house is something that makes you and your family feel good, and

probably also proud. But a nice house may also mean many unanticipated financial headaches. To make a sound decision, you should first calculate the level of your *dependable* monthly income for, say, the first third of all the mortgage payments due on a house. In other words, if you happen to be making a quantity of extra money this year, to count that as permanent may get you into trouble. Be conservative.

Next, you must figure out prospective monthly housing expenses. This includes your payments on a mortgage, insurance premium, taxes, costs of maintenance repair, heating, air conditioning, electricity, telephone, water, sewage, and things like that. Your mortgage payments may be higher than you think. Table VI–1 shows the size of mortgage payments for various mortgages for 15, 20, 25, and 30 year loans at various interest rates.

Remember, rarely can you finance 100 percent of the cost of the house. Usually, you must pay one-fourth of the purchase price as a downpayment. In addition, there are closing costs, which we discuss below. Table VI–2 gives rules for estimating how much housing you can afford. It tells you, for example, that the purchase price divided by your annual income should come to 2.5 or less. Another helpful rule of thumb is that you should not spend more than one-fourth of your take-home pay for housing payments. These are only rough rules, but they do serve as a guide: if you buy a $40,000 house on a yearly income of $8,000, you are asking for trouble. After housing expenses, food, and transportation, you will have no money left over for desired recreation and other such things.

New versus Used

As with the purchase of almost any goods that last a long time, you can choose between an older house and a new house. The new ones you find advertised in the home section of your Sunday newspaper every week. In some years, as many as two million new housing units are built in the United States. On

TABLE VI–1: MONTHLY PAYMENTS AND TOTAL INTEREST COST TO BUY A $20,000 HOME.

You can see what your monthly payments will be at various interest rates on 15, 20, 25, and 30 year mortgages. You can also see how much you pay in total interest. If you want to consider borrowing an amount greater than $20,000, use the accompanying table, VI–1A, and multiply the amount borrowed times the number in the appropriate column and row. For example, if you had to borrow $30,000 at 10 percent for a 20 year mortgage, your monthly payment would be $289.86, plus whatever you had to pay toward insurance and property taxes. Source: *Family Economics Review, 1969,* U.S. Department of Agriculture, p. 15.

Down Payment	Amount Borrowed	MONTHLY PAYMENTS				TOTAL INTEREST			
		15 yrs.	20 yrs.	25 yrs.	30 yrs.	15 yrs.	20 yrs.	25 yrs.	30 yrs.
Dol.	Dol.	Dol.	Dol.	Dol.	Dol.	Dol.	Dol.	Dol.	Dol.
					7½ Percent Interest				
0	20,000	186	161	148	140	13,340	18,650	24,330	30,190
500	19,500	181	157	144	136	13,010	18,180	23,720	29,430
1,000	19,000	176	153	140	133	12,670	17,710	23,120	28,680
2,000	18,000	167	145	133	126	12,010	16,780	21,900	27,170
3,000	17,000	158	137	126	119	11,340	15,850	20,680	25,660
4,000	16,000	148	129	118	112	10,670	14,920	19,470	24,150
5,000	15,000	139	121	111	105	10,000	13,980	18,250	22,640
6,000	14,000	130	113	103	98	9,340	13,050	17,030	21,130
8,000	12,000	111	97	89	84	8,000	11,190	14,600	18,110
10,000	10,000	93	81	74	70	6,670	9,320	12,170	15,090
					8 Percent Interest				
0	20,000	191	167	154	147	14,390	20,110	26,280	32,780
500	19,500	186	163	151	143	14,030	19,610	25,630	31,960
1,000	19,000	182	159	147	139	13,670	19,110	24,970	31,140
2,000	18,000	172	151	139	132	12,950	18,100	23,650	29,500
3,000	17,000	163	142	131	125	12,230	17,090	22,340	27,860
4,000	16,000	153	134	124	117	11,520	16,090	21,030	26,220
5,000	15,000	143	126	116	110	10,800	15,080	19,710	24,580
6,000	14,000	134	117	108	103	10,080	14,080	18,400	22,940
8,000	12,000	115	100	93	88	8,640	12,070	15,770	19,670
10,000	10,000	96	84	77	73	7,200	10,060	13,140	16,390
					8½ Percent Interest				
0	20,000	197	174	161	154	15,440	21,640	28,200	35,340
500	19,500	192	169	157	150	15,050	21,100	27,500	34,460
1,000	19,000	187	165	153	146	14,670	20,560	26,790	33,570
2,000	18,000	177	156	145	138	13,900	19,480	25,380	31,810
3,000	17,000	167	148	137	131	13,120	18,400	23,970	30,040
4,000	16,000	158	139	129	123	12,350	17,310	22,560	28,270
5,000	15,000	148	130	121	115	11,580	16,230	21,150	26,500
6,000	14,000	138	122	113	108	10,810	15,150	19,740	24,740
8,000	12,000	118	104	97	92	9,260	12,990	16,920	21,200
10,000	10,000	98	87	81	77	7,720	10,820	14,100	17,670

TABLE VI–1:—Continued

MONTHLY PAYMENTS AND TOTAL INTEREST COST TO BUY A $20,000 HOME.

Down Payment	Amount Borrowed	MONTHLY PAYMENTS				TOTAL INTEREST			
		15 yrs.	20 yrs.	25 yrs.	30 yrs.	15 yrs.	20 yrs.	25 yrs.	30 yrs.
Dol.	Dol.	Dol.	Dol.	Dol.	Dol.	Dol.	Dol.	Dol.	Dol.
					9 Percent Interest				
0	20,000	203	180	168	161	16,490	23,160	30,220	37,820
500	19,500	198	176	164	157	16,070	22,580	29,460	36,880
1,000	19,000	193	171	160	153	15,660	22,000	28,710	35,930
2,000	18,000	183	162	151	145	14,840	20,850	27,200	34,040
3,000	17,000	173	153	143	137	14,010	19,690	25,690	32,150
4,000	16,000	162	144	134	129	13,190	18,530	24,180	30,260
5,000	15,000	152	135	126	121	12,360	17,370	22,670	28,370
6,000	14,000	142	126	118	113	11,540	16,210	21,150	26,480
8,000	12,000	122	108	101	97	9,890	13,900	18,130	22,690
10,000	10,000	102	90	84	80	8,240	11,580	15,110	18,910
					9½ Percent Interest				
0	20,000	209	187	175	168	17,560	24,660	32,370	40,490
500	19,500	204	182	170	164	17,120	24,040	31,560	39,480
1,000	19,000	199	177	166	160	16,680	23,430	30,750	38,470
2,000	18,000	188	168	157	151	15,800	22,190	29,130	36,440
3,000	17,000	178	159	149	143	14,920	20,960	27,510	34,420
4,000	16,000	167	149	140	135	14,050	19,730	25,890	32,390
5,000	15,000	157	140	131	126	13,170	18,500	24,270	30,370
6,000	14,000	146	131	122	118	12,290	17,260	22,660	28,340
8,000	12,000	125	112	105	101	10,540	14,800	19,420	24,300
10,000	10,000	104	93	87	84	8,780	12,330	16,180	20,250

TABLE VI–1A:

MONTHLY PAYMENTS PER $1000 BORROWED ON MORTGAGE

Source: *Selecting and Financing a Home,* Home and Garden Bulletin No. 182, Agriculture Research Service, December 1970, p. 15.

INTEREST RATE (percent)	PAYMENT PERIOD			
	15 yrs.	20 yrs.	25 yrs.	30 yrs.
7	$8.99	$7.76	$7.07	$6.66
7½	9.28	8.06	7.39	7.00
8	9.56	8.37	7.72	7.34
8½	9.85	8.68	8.06	7.69
9	10.15	9.00	8.40	8.05
9½	10.45	9.33	8.74	8.41
10	10.75	9.66	9.09	8.78

TABLE VI–2:

HOW MUCH HOUSING CAN YOU AFFORD?

Most savings and loan association loan officers will use the rules alongside to determine how much housing you can afford. Rule 1 states that the purchase price of the house should not exceed 2½ times your yearly gross income. Rule 2 states that your monthly mortgage payment should be no more than 25 percent of your monthly income. Rule 3 states that all of your debt payments combined, including your mortgage payment, should not exceed one-third of your monthly income. And Rule 4 indicates that most savings and loan associations will not loan you more than 95 percent of the purchase price of your house. And generally, the maximum is closer to 80 percent, and in some cases, even as low as 65 percent. Source: The United States Saving and Loan League.

1. $$\frac{\text{PRICE}}{\text{INCOME}} \leq 2.5$$

2. $$\frac{\text{MORTGAGE PAYMENT}}{\text{MONTHLY INCOME}} < 25\%$$

3. $$\frac{\text{ALL DEBT SERVICE}}{\text{MONTHLY INCOME}} < 33\%$$

4. $$\frac{\text{LOAN AMOUNT}}{\text{VALUE}} < 95\% \text{ (usually around 70–80\%)}$$

the other hand, an "older" or second-hand house might make as much sense or more for you than a new one. Of course, you must be more careful about future maintenance problems with an older home, but using an inspection service ahead of time can avoid that problem, as we will discuss below.

SELECTING WHERE YOU WANT TO LIVE

Even before you start looking for the kind of house you want to buy, you must first decide where you want to live. Below is a list of the most important kinds of variables you have to take into account.

1. Relationship to work: Is the area you are looking at near your work or distant from it? If distant, is there good transportation, by bus, train, or a freeway that is not congested at the time you have to go to work? If you happen to work in an area where most people in your city do work, you will find that the farther away from the work center, the cheaper land will be, all other things remaining constant.

But you make up the difference in this price of land by having to spend more time, which has a value, and more money for transportation to and from work.

2. Property taxes: Find out what the average assessment is in the area you are thinking of living in. This is an important out-of-pocket cost that you have to take account of in calculating your housing needs relative to your means. Property taxes, you are now aware, have a direct relationship to the school system. For an indication of by how much property taxes can vary from city to city, see Table VI–3.

3. Schools for your children: Make sure you check out the schools in the area you are considering. If you think they are not going to be suitable, then you will probably come to feel unhappy about your children's education and you may wind up spending money for private education. Go to the schools that you think you might have to send your children to. Talk with the teachers, the principal. See what kind of philosophy is behind the teaching

TABLE VI–3: HOW YOUR STATE AND LOCAL TAX TABS CAN VARY

State and local taxes can vary widely among cities in the United States. In the table below, we indicate income, real estate, sales, and automobile taxes assessed at the state and local level for a sample of 30 major cities in the United States. In the right-hand column is given the total tax burden measured as a percent of taxable income. In other words, in Boston you would pay on average 16.4 percent of your income to state and local governments in the form of taxes, whereas in Houston, you would pay only 3.1 percent. Source: *Business Week*, November 3, 1973.

| Cities | STATE AND LOCAL TAXES | | | | Total burden | |
	Income	Real estate	Sales	Automobile	Amount	Percent
Boston	$1,037	$2,688	$ 64	$319	$4,108	16.4%
Milwaukee	1,748	1,837	233	115	3,933	15.7
New York	1,586	1,503	417	204	3,710	14.8
Buffalo	1,241	1,619	417	152	3,429	13.7
Los Angeles	732	1,925	243	168	3,068	12.3
San Francisco	732	1,895	267	168	3,062	12.2
San Diego	732	1,549	243	168	2,692	10.8
Baltimore	1,264	1,014	202	151	2,631	10.5
Chicago	525	1,286	330	281	2,422	9.7
Washington	1,163	743	308	171	2,385	9.5
Pittsburgh	1,085	987	179	118	2,369	9.5
Philadelphia	1,403	665	179	118	2,365	9.5
Phoenix	713	1,079	317	226	2,335	9.3
Detroit	1,152	739	288	118	2,297	9.2
Cincinnati	815	929	185	99	2,028	8.1
St. Louis	875	713	293	130	2,011	8.0
Kansas City	875	761	252	113	2,001	8.0
Indianapolis	418	1,209	151	186	1,964	7.9
Denver	800	812	378	189	1,930	7.7
Atlanta	751	592	272	227	1,842	7.4
Cleveland	640	885	185	99	1,809	7.2
Columbus	765	714	185	99	1,763	7.1
New Orleans	309	649	396	96	1,450	5.8
Nashville	—	865	369	115	1,349	5.4
Seattle	—	729	408	188	1,325	5.3
Memphis	—	837	369	115	1,321	5.3
San Antonio	—	625	244	208	1,077	4.3
Dallas	—	408	244	208	860	3.4
Jacksonville	—	451	206	138	795	3.2
Houston	—	326	244	208	778	3.1
City average	**712**	**1,034**	**269**	**163**	**2,170**	**8.7**

experience there. If it differs from yours, be careful: you may not want to live in that area.

4. Shopping: How close will your house be to the kind of stores that have free parking? Or will you have to pay for parking every time? Generally, the farther away a house is from shopping, the lower will be the value of the land, all other things held constant. But you will make up the difference in extra time and expense transporting yourself to the shopping centers.

5. Air quality: Is the area polluted or clean? Is it close to factories or is it close to the mountains? The site value of the land will take account of the different levels of pollution, but you may place a much higher value on clean air than do the rest of the consumers in the housing market. If you have special respiratory problems, you definitely will be willing to pay for an unpolluted air environment in the form of higher housing costs.

6. Crime: If you are worried about crime rates in your prospective area, you can check with real estate agents in different sections of town, the police department, neighbors, and statistics from the Police Department Annual Reports. Usually, the police are obligated by law to give you those statistics. You can also check the deductible clause in homeowners insurance for an indication of theft in the area.

7. The neighborhood: What kind of neighbors will be around you? Are they people who have the same life style as yours? Will you feel uncomfortable at home? If you have children, do other people in the area have any the same age? If not, that can present problems.

8. Zoning and development: Are nearby undeveloped areas zoned for industry, housing, apartments? Is there going to be further development in the area? All these things should be checked out, either with a responsible real estate agent or by doing it yourself.

WHEN TO USE A REAL ESTATE BROKER

You can start a housing search by first looking in the classified section of a newspaper. This will require much time and many telephone calls, and actually going out to see houses that might interest you. If you are casually looking for a house, this may be the best way to do it because generally you will save a real estate broker's commission if the people advertising are selling the house themselves. However, perhaps the majority of ads are placed by real estate companies themselves, so you end up paying the brokerage fee even if you find the house through the newspaper. If you decide to use a broker, it is wise not to take the first one who comes along. To check out brokers, call several of them, tell them what you want, and have them show you a few houses. You will find out very soon how serious each broker is about servicing you. You will also find out whether he or she understands your tastes and preferences and can therefore act as you would act in searching for a house. If you know individuals in the area who have used brokers, find out which of the brokers have given satisfactory service. Information is hard to come by, but it may be close at hand.

What Does a Broker Do?

Essentially, brokers provide you with information, and also provide sellers of houses with information. Information, remember, is a costly resource. This is particularly true with such a nonstandard product as a house. Every single house is different from every other, and it is difficult to get buyers and sellers together for such nonstandard products. Generally, for standard products, or even for nonstandard products that do not cost very much, there are no brokers. But in the housing market, the reverse is true: a house is the largest purchase for any family, and it involves something that is, so far, completely nonstandardized. The broker, then, saves you information costs by engaging in the search procedure for you and for the seller. He or she becomes a specialist in matching up the wants of buyers with the supplies of sellers.

How Much Will You Pay?

For selling a house, most brokers in any state or area charge a fixed fee which is paid, at least nominally, by the seller. But do not be fooled about how fixed this fee is. In times of bad housing markets, you can bargain with a broker over a house you think you want to buy. You can stipulate, for example, that you will buy the house if a refrigerator, a stove, or some such thing is supplied. Or in a good market, the seller can do the same thing; the seller will agree to pay the fixed commission, but over a seven year period, which means that, in effect, the commission will be worth less to the broker and cost less to the seller of the house. Such arrangements are against the rules of brokerage societies, but that should not worry you. The very fact that brokers have fixed commissions is against present antitrust laws. If brokers can break the Sherman Antitrust Act, then, in your own best interests, you can try to persuade them to break their own rules governing fixed commission rates.

Brokers can do many things besides helping you find the house you want. They can also help you arrange for the financing, make sure that the papers are in order, and even do the bargaining for you.

HOW TO BARGAIN

Most Americans are unaccustomed to bargaining. Goods and services are sold in a marketplace at set prices that you can rarely get lowered. But people in many other countries, such as in Latin America and Asia, are used to bargaining. The asking price is generally not the final sale price. If you are unaccustomed to bargaining for a house, or you feel uncomfortable doing it, you can let a real estate broker do it for you.

Many times, sellers do not expect to get the price they are asking on their houses. They set a price that they think may be, say, 5 or 10 percent more than the price they will finally receive. It is up to you to find out how far they will go in discounting that list price. You can start out by asking the real estate broker whether he or she thinks the price is "firm." Since the broker's commission is a percentage of the sale price, the higher that price, the more the broker benefits, but not if it means waiting months or years for a sale. The broker's desire to get that commission as soon as possible is an incentive to arrange a mutually agreeable price so that a deal will be made. You may want to bargain, for example, on a $35,000 list price for, say, $32,000 plus the refrigerator, freezer, washer, and dryer that are already in the house. This sort of bargaining happens all the time. You should not accept the list price just because you think you want the house. While that price may be the lowest you can get it for, then again it may not be. You only know if you bargain, and if you are unwilling to do it yourself, ask your broker to do it. The broker may ultimately decide to take a lower (implicit) commission rate in order to seal the deal. The first stage of sealing the deal is signing a written earnest agreement, but before this is done, certain basic, common-sense precautions must be taken.

BEFORE YOU SIGN ANYTHING

Before you sign anything, make sure you are getting a house that is structurally sound. Pay an expert to go over everything in the house that could cause problems—wiring, frame, signs of termites, plumbing, sewage, and so on. Often, you can get this done for $25 or $50, but for more expensive houses you will have to pay $100 to $200. It is money well invested unless you yourself are an ex-

EXHIBIT
Homebuyer's (or Renter's) Guide, or how to decipher what the ads say

CONVENIENT TO SHOPPING	Bathroom window overlooks the local A&P parking lot
FAMILY ROOM:	unfinished basement with a 60 watt bulb
$200 to HEAT:	$640 to heat
DESIRABLE CORNER:	corner
ENTRANCE FOYER:	door
ONLY 10 MINUTES FROM . . .	only 45 minutes from . . .
MANY EXTRAS:	recent owners have left behind half-used bar of soap, numerous rags and coat hangers, and three switches that are connected to nothing
IMMACULATE:	the walls in the kitchen are not quite as greasy as the grease rack at Sam's Standard Station
PIAZZA:	porch
GLEAMING BATHROOM:	bathroom
COMFORTABLE:	very small
COZY:	even smaller
CUTE:	itsy bitsy
VICTORIAN:	many drafts
COLONIAL:	built prior to the first Eisenhower Administration
GRACIOUS COLONIAL:	forget it—too expensive
LEISURE HOME:	enter only during July and August
MAKE AN OFFER:	say something funny

EXHIBIT
An estimate of cost and cash requirements for purchasing a house

Loan Amount $_____   Purchase Price $_____

ESTIMATED COSTS

Service Charge $_____

Title Insurance   _____

Recording Fee   _____

Due Seller for _____ Taxes   _____

Fire Insurance Premium   _____

Interest from _____ to _____   _____

Tax Registration   _____

Allowed Toward _____ Taxes   _____

Assessments   _____

Credit Report   _____

Escrow Fee   _____

Appraisal Fee   _____

TOTAL $_____ *
                                                        _____

ESTIMATED CASH REQUIREMENTS

Down Payment $_____

Estimated Costs $_____

Subtotal $_____

Less Earnest Money $_____

TOTAL $_____
                                          _____

ESTIMATED MONTHLY PAYMENT AT ___% FOR ___ YEARS

Principal & Interest $_____

Taxes   _____

Insurance   _____

Mortgage Life Insurance   _____

Mortgage Disability Insurance   _____

TOTAL $_____
                                                    _____

* Plus Reimbursement to Seller for Unused Fuel Oil

pert at figuring out what can go wrong with the house just by looking at it. If there is no one listed under "building inspection service" or "home inspection service" in your telephone directory yellow pages, then you can call, without charge, the Nationwide Real Estate Inspectors Service, Inc., at 800–221–2165. They advertise 24-hour service for major cities nationwide. Again, they are selling the same thing that a broker is selling—information. Such information can save you hundreds, if not thousands, of dollars in repairs you would later discover had to be made. Often, if structural faults in a house can be shown up by a building inspector, you can have the seller of the house agree to pay for the repairs even after you take over the house itself. Or this can be a point in bargaining: the price that you agreed on can be reduced by the amount of the repair costs.

WHAT HAPPENS WHEN YOU DECIDE TO BUY?

Generally, when you have decided to buy a house, you make an offer and put it in writing, and you must put up what is usually called **earnest money** or deposit. The earnest agreement, which is usually good for 24 hours, states in some detail your exact offering price for the house, and lists any other things that are not normally included with a house but are to be included in this deal, such as washers and dryers. Within 24 hours the seller of the house either accepts or rejects the earnest agreement. If the seller accepts and you try to back down, the earnest money you put up, which may be several thousand dollars, is legally no longer yours. But sometimes you can get it back even when you decide against the house after signing the agreement. In any earnest agreement, it is often wise to add an escape clause if you are unsure about getting financing. Put in a statement like, "This earnest agreement is contingent upon the buyer's obtaining financing from a bank for

X thousand dollars." Remember, the earnest agreement (called an "offer" in California) is *your* proposal. Put in what *you* want. Let the seller change it—then you review it.

CLOSING COSTS

Table VI–4 indicates the typical closing costs on a $30,000 house. Quite a bit of money, isn't it? You didn't realize that it would cost so much. Generally, closing costs end up being 3 to 4 percent of the total purchase price, and that is money that you have to come up with in front, in addition to your down payment. That means that you've got to have cash for closing costs. (The accompanying Exhibit shows a form that you can use to figure costs when you plan to buy a house.)

Something mentioned in Table VI–4 that you should know about is title insurance.

TITLE INSURANCE

When you purchase something as large as a house, you must be sure that you really own it, that no one with a prior claim can dispute your **title** to the land and structure. Any one of the following four methods can insure that you do in fact have title, free and clear, to the property:

1. An abstract: Usually a lawyer or title guarantee company will trace the history of the ownership of the property. The resulting document is called an abstract, and it will indicate whether any claims are still outstanding. Note, however, that the abstract, no matter how lengthy it might be, does not guarantee that you have the title. Nonetheless, if the search has been careful, it provides reassurance.

2. Certificate of title: In some areas of the country, this is used in place of an abstract. An attorney merely certifies that all the records affecting the property have been looked at and, in the opinion of the attorney, there are no claims on it. Note, however, that the attorney is not guaranteeing his or her opinion, and cannot be liable if some obscure claim does arise in the future.

3. Torrens certificate: This is a certificate issued by a government unit giving evidence of title to real property. It is used mainly in large cities. You can get it faster and it is usually safer than an abstract or certificate of title. An official recorder or registrar issues a certificate stating ownership and allowing anyone who has prior claim on the real property to sue. If no suit develops, then a court will order the registrar to record the title in your name; a certificate to this effect will be issued.

4. Title insurance: A title guarantee company will search extensively through the records

pertaining to the property you wish to buy. When it is satisfied that there are no prior claims to that property, it will write an insurance policy for you, the new owner. The insurance policy guarantees that if any defects arise in the title, the title company itself will defend for the owner and pay all legal expenses involved.

GETTING A MORTGAGE AND WHAT IT IS ALL ABOUT

Unless you are really cash rich, you will have to pay for a good part of your house by a mortgage. What is a mortgage? A mortgage is merely a loan that a bank or trust company makes on a house. Usually, you do not hold title to the house; the mortgagor does (although in some states, such as California, you do hold the deed). As the mortgagee, you

TABLE VI–4: TYPICAL CLOSING COSTS ON A $30,000 HOME
The service or setup charge on a mortgage usually varies from 1½ to 2½ percent, the lower figure being applied to a loan that is 75 to 80 percent of the purchase price of a house. If, for example, on a $30,000 house, you put a down payment of 20 percent, or $6,000, you would have to pay a setup or service charge of 1½ percent of $24,000, or $360. Title insurance would range from $13 to $90. A recording fee would be another $6, and various other things added in would make the total closing costs 3 to 4 percent of the value of the house, or, for a $30,000 house, about $900 to $1200.

Service Charge:	on 75 or 80% loan = 1½%
	on 90 or 95% loan = 2 to 2½%
Title Insurance:	on 75 or 80% = $13.15
	on 90 or 95% = $60 to $90
Recording Fee:	about $6
Fire Insurance:	about ¼% of sale price
The bank also collects the taxes on the house	
Credit Report:	$10 to 15
Appraisal Fee:	$20
TOTAL CLOSING COSTS:	3 to 4% of house value

make payments on the mortgage until it is paid off. More than 90 per cent of all people who buy homes do so with a mortgage loan. Savings and loan associations, which make home loans exclusively, finance well over 40 percent of all the homes in the United States. Sometimes you can arrange to take over the mortgage that already exists on a house.

When you go shopping for a mortgage, you should know the language of the mortgage trade:

1. Prepayment privilege: You can prepay the mortgage before the maturity date without penalty. This is something you might do later on if interest rates in the economy fell below what you were actually paying. You would pay the mortgage off by refinancing it at a lower interest charge.

2. Package mortgage: This mortgage covers the cost of all household equipment as well as the house itself. This is something you might try to get if you do not have the cash to buy furniture and you think you can get a lower interest charge through a mortgage company than through other credit sources. (Some finance experts advise against this because you pay interest on the money for the furniture long after you have used up the furniture.)

3. Open end mortgage: This mortgage allows you to borrow more money in the future without rewriting the mortgage. With an open end mortgage you can add on to the house or repair it and have the mortgage company pay these new bills. The mortgage company then charges you a larger monthly payment or increases the life span of your loan.

THE KINDS OF MORTGAGES

There are basically three kinds of mortgages. Although you may not be eligible for two of them, all three are available from the same

sources: commercial banks, savings banks, mortgage bankers, savings and loan associations, and insurance companies.

1. Conventional mortgages: Most conventional mortgages run for 20 to 30 years. However, in recent years, savings and loan associations have been reluctant to write mortgages for 30 years and, in fact, some of them are charging higher interest rates for mortgages that last so long. Naturally, the rate of inerest charged is determined by conditions in the money market (but also subject to state usury laws, which we discussed in Chapter 7). Interest rates in the past few years have been at record highs. This should not, however, be a surprise when you consider the high inflation rates of recent years. The mortgagor's interest rate has to take account of any expected loss in the purchasing power of the dollars that will be paid back to it in the future.

With a conventional mortgage loan, the money that the lender risks is secured only by the value of the mortgaged property and the financial integrity of the borrower. To protect the investment from the start, the conventional lender, such as a savings and loan association, ordinarily requires the down payment of anywhere from 5 to 35 percent of the value of the property. As a general rule, you can plan on having to put up 20 percent. Some private insurers will protect lenders against loss on at least a certain portion of the loan. When such extra security is provided, the lender may go to a higher loan figure. The borrower, of course pays the cost of the insurance.

If you make a very large down payment, lowering the risk of lending, the lender may be willing to grant you a slightly lower interest rate, perhaps a fraction of a percent below the prevailing local rate.

Conventional loans can be arranged on just about any terms satisfactory to both parties. Different lenders favor different arrangements, which means it will pay you to shop around. And since most borrowers pay off their mortgages well before maturity, it is wise to look around for liberal conditions on prepayment; you will not want to pay a penalty if you wish to prepay.

2. Veterans Administration mortgages: These loans can be obtained only by qualified veterans or their widows. The interest rate charged is administered rather than determined strictly by the forces of supply and demand in the money market. The VA loan is guaranteed rather than insured. That is, the government simply promises that on an approved loan it will repay up to a certain amount, like $12,500, or a certain percent, say 60 percent. The borrower has no insurance premium to pay.

Nothing-down loans are possible under the VA program, often for amounts of $25,000 or more, and for up to 30 years. However, you cannot get a loan on a VA-financed house for more than the VA appraisal of its current market value, nor mortgage it for longer than the VA estimate of its remaining economic life. All VA loans can be prepaid without penalty.

Although the Veterans Administration makes some mortgage loans directly to veterans, usually in rural areas where lenders are not making guaranteed loans, in all other circumstances a would-be borrower should go to the usual funds of mortgage money, such as a savings and loan association, a mutual savings bank in states where they exist, commercial banks and mortgage companies. It is particularly useful to check with the bank, savings and loan, or mutual savings bank where you happen to be a saver or depositor. If they have a history of your past records, they probably will be more accommodating to you.

3. FHA mortgages: The Federal Housing Administration issues insurance covering the entire amount of an FHA loan. This added security enables qualified borrowers to obtain a

much more generous loan in relation to the value of the property than they could obtain with an uninsured loan. Of course, to the borrower, a bigger loan means a smaller down payment.

Generally, it is possible to borrow 97 percent of the first $15,000 of the appraised value of an approved house that you intend to live in yourself, plus 90 percent of the next $10,000, and 80 percent of the rest up to $33,000. The maximum interest rate that can be charged has usually been below market interest rates. But, you also have to pay a ½ percent premium for the insurance, and a 1 percent origination fee (a fee for the work of drawing up the papers) is also permitted. The loan can be for as long as 35 years, not to exceed three-fourths of what the FHA estimates is the remaining economic life of the dwelling. You may prepay up to 15 percent of the loan in any one year without penalty, but if you pay off the entire loan within the first 10 years, you may run into an "adjusted premium charge" of up to one percent.

You can apply for an FHA insured mortgage loan just as you would apply for any other loan. The lender, be it a savings and loan association, mortgage company, or commercial bank, will supply you with the necessary forms and help you complete them. If that lender is willing to make the loan, the application to the FHA insuring office will be submitted for you. When your application reaches the FHA office, the staff will process it, and this may be a time-consuming endeavor. The FHA staff will analyze the transaction, including your qualifications as a mortgagee, the estimated value of the property, and so on.

While the FHA has no arbitrary rules with respect to age or income, these factors are considered for their possible effect on your ability to repay the loan over the period of the mortgage.

The FHA also sponsors a subsidy program for low- and moderate-income families. In this program, down payments can be as low as several hundred dollars, and interest as low as a couple of percentage points.

The big difference between FHA loans and so-called conventional loans is that the FHA interest is not determined strictly by market conditions, but is set at an arbitrary rate by the Secretary of Housing and Urban Development. Usually, the Secretary tries to fix a rate well below the lowest prevailing market rate. However, this practice has been associated with a curious "point" system.

What About Points?

Sometimes you may be asked to pay **discount points.** This is merely a device to raise the effective interest rate you pay on a mortgage. This will occur whenever there are restrictions on the legal interest rate that can be charged you for your mortgage loan. You may think this unfair, but if you are faced with the possibility of either paying the discount points or not getting the loan at all, you may decide to pay the implicitly higher interest rate.

A point is a charge of one percent of a loan. This charge may be assessed against the buyer, or the seller, or both. To see how a discount point system works, say you have to pay four discount points on a $25,000 loan: that means that you get a loan of $25,000 minus 4 percent of $25,000, or only $24,000. However, you pay interest on the full $25,000. Obviously, the interest rate you pay on $25,-000 understates the actual interest you pay because you get only $24,000. Some states have laws against discount points, and FHA and VA have restrictions on buyers paying points (so they are charged to the seller, but ultimately passed on to the borrower in the form of a higher price).

MORE FLEXIBLE PAYMENT ARRANGEMENTS

Many young people who have been saving for a home may be able to buy one sooner than anticipated because of government rules that became effective in 1974. The aim of the new rules is to permit savings and loan associations to arrange schedules of flexible mortgage payments with borrowers.

In effect, young people may now be able to tailor their monthly mortgage payments to both their present budget and to any anticipated increases in income later on. The rules permit home buyers to contract to make lower monthly payments during the first few years of their mortgage, and increase the payments later on when presumably their income would be greater. However, the lower payments must at least cover the current interest on the mortgage and can continue for no more than five years.

As an example of how this new system works, below is a 30 year mortgage of $30,000 at 8 percent interest (an interest rate that is relatively high by historical standards but probably lower than the one prevailing when you read this book). Monthly payments are given for both a conventional and a flexible plan.

Notice that the interest charges under a flexible plan are somewhat higher than under a conventional plan. That is because you do not begin to pay back the principle until six years after you take out the mortgage loan. Essentially, then, you have the loan for a longer period.

Limitations on Flexible Payment Schedules

Flexible payments are limited to mortgages on single-family, owner-occupied homes. The down payment for any home subject to flexible payments may be as low as 5 percent of its price. Older people, perhaps those nearing retirement, can also take advantage of flexible mortgages given through savings and loan associations. A flexible mortgage here, however, would be the reverse of the example above—higher monthly payments during the first few years decreasing with time when the home buyer might be living on a fixed retirement income that is lower than his or her actual income when the mortgage was taken out.

Years	MONTHLY PAYMENTS	
	Standard Plan	Flexible Plan
First through the fifth	$ 220	$ 200
Sixth through the 30th	$ 220	$ 230
Payment on principal	$30,000	$30,000
Payments on interest	$49,200	$51,000
Total cost	$79,200	$81,000

PREPAYING INSURANCE AND TAXES

Most mortgage sellers require the mortgagee—that is, you the homeowner—to prepay taxes and insurance as part of your monthly payments. Say a savings and loan association is the mortgagor: a special reserve account is set up within the savings and loan association, the money from which home insurance and taxes are paid every year. This way the mortgagor does not have to worry about foreclosure on the house because of unpaid taxes or problems if the house burns down and is not insured.[4]

We will talk more about insurance in Chapter 13. Suffice it to say here that you should have 80 percent of the total value of the house insured—that is, 80 percent of its replacement value—for if you have at least that much coverage, you collect the full replacement cost, not the depreciated value, of any damaged property. For example, say your 10-year-old roof is damaged in a fire. It costs you $2500 to replace it. If you have at least 80 percent coverage on your house, your insurance company must pay you the full amount of the roof damage, whereas if your house is covered for less than 80 percent of replacement, the agent will decrease the value of your roof by 10 years and give you, say, only $1200.

You need not insure your house for the full market value for two reasons: (1) the land has a value that would not be destroyed in a fire or flood, and (2) even if the house is totally burned down, the foundation, sidewalks, driveway, and such things are still standing. Be careful, though: if you are living in a house you bought many years ago, the cost of replacement may be much more than you think. Remember that in the last chapter we discussed the phenomenal increase in construction costs. Take that into account now and make sure that your insurance keeps pace with it. You may want to have an arrangement with your insurance company whereby the value of your insurance is increased 10 percent every year or two, to keep pace with construction cost increases. Avoid being left in the cold if your house burns down.

Although lenders usually do not require that you have anything other than fire (and perhaps flood) insurance for the structure of your house, most home owners' insurance packag-

---

[4] The special reserve account that you must pay into monthly does not usually earn interest for you. Rather, the holder of that account uses it in a way that will earn interest for the mortgaging institution.

EXHIBIT
Nailing down house insurance rates

This sampling of rates for virtually identical homeowners policies gives an inkling of the big savings available to those who shop around. All policies are for $30,000, ordinarily enough to cover houses with a replacement value of $37,500 excluding land. INA's rates come down 10% after two years without a claim. Reprinted from the February 1974 issue of MONEY Magazine by special permission; © 1974, Time Inc.

	Marietta, Georgia	Mill Valley, Calif.	New Rochelle, New York	St. Cloud, Minnesota	Webster Groves, Missouri
AETNA	$127	$105	$125	$131	$140
FIREMAN'S FUND	114	138	129	124	143
GEICO	95	106	105	121	95
INA	122	121	124	112	150
NATIONWIDE	95	116	130	*	*
STATE FARM	99	114	113	98	92

*Not sold there.

es include provisions for insuring personal property. Usually unsecured personal property within the house is often insured up to one-half of the total face value of your insurance policy. If you have a $40,000 insurance policy on your house, you can insure up to $20,000 worth of furniture and personal belongings at the same time. Your insurance policy may also provide for living expenses while your house is being rebuilt if it has burned down, medical expenses, and in most cases liability in case somebody gets hurt on your property and sues you for negligence. A fairly large liability coverage for your house is not a bad idea, because it is relatively inexpensive and guarantees no financial disasters from some future law suit.

COPING WITH REPAIRS

One way to avoid having to make many repairs is to keep things well maintained, but this of course takes your time and money. It is often useful to keep a list of repairmen you know to have been honest and to have given you high quality service. Also, if you continuously use the same repair people, they establish a working relationship with you. There may be organizations in your city that, once you have joined one, can simplify your repair problems by reducing information costs. The American Homeowners Association, for one, which was organized in Milwaukee, Wisconsin, in 1969, has spread to at least six other states. If you become a member, you pay between $10 and $20 a year to cover emergency calls for which the first half-hour is given without charge. Everything else is paid for at straight time rates—that is, with no overtime pay. The AHA locates what they think would be competent workmen in your area. But in some areas problems have occurred with similar services, so you may wish to investigate the services you are thinking of subscribing to. Information on the American Home Owners Association can be obtained from 5301 West Burleigh Street, Milwaukee, Wisconsin 53210.

Also available is a prepaid repair and maintenance program called Palace Guard, which is a service of American Home Owners Association. It is similar to a life or casualty protection policy, except that instead of covering you it covers major equipment in your house, such as central heating and cooling systems, sheet metal duct work, electrical and plumbing systems, plumbing fixtures, hot water heaters, water softeners, and built-in appliances, including oven, range, dishwasher, and garbage disposal. Local divisions of the American Home Owners Association administer the Palace Guard program and can give you full details. Basically, you pay a set fee once a year for this service.

IF YOU WANT TO RENT

Renting an apartment or house, although not as complicated as buying a home, involves some of the same principles. First, you should know some of the rights that you have as a tenant as well as some of the responsibilities. Of course, your landlord also has responsibilities and rights. You are responsible, for example, for paying the rent on time and as

specified, and you must keep the apartment or house in reasonable order. Generally, you are not responsible for normal wear and tear, but rather only for major damage that you cause. You have the right to freedom from harassment by the landlord; in other words, the landlord cannot come into your apartment whenever he or she desires. Such a visit must be arranged in advance with you.

What to Look out for in a Lease

If you decide to sign a long-term lease, you should be careful about the following two provisions which seem to cause the greatest source of tenant abuse:

1. Confession of judgment. If your lease has this provision, your landlord's lawyer has the legal right to go to court and plead guilty for you in the event that the landlord thinks his rights have been violated—that is, that the property has been damaged or the terms of the lease have not been lived up to. If you sign a lease that has a confession of judgment provision, you are admitting guilt before committing any act.

2. Waiver of tort liability: If this provision is in your lease, you have given up in advance the right to sue the landlord if in fact you suffer injury or damage because of your landlord's negligence.

Many disagreements between renters and landlords are over the cleaning deposit. Have it made clear from the very beginning whether the cleaning deposit is in fact a cleaning *fee*: a nonrefundable charge. If it is a fee, and you know it from the start, then you will not be disappointed when you leave the apartment or house and that money is not returned to you. Moreover, you will not have to spend an undue amount of time cleaning up the premises before vacating them. When you rent an apartment or house, make sure that you go through it with the landlord to note all damages to furniture or structure that exist before you move in. Remember that since you have the right to normal wear and tear, the landlord cannot keep your cleaning deposit (if in fact it is a deposit), because of normal wear and tear during the time of the lease.

Also, note at this time any comments the landlord has about the condition in which the previous tenants have left the premises. Such comments often indicate what the landlord will expect from you at the time you vacate, and often include remarks on the state of the lawn (if you have rented a house) or how clean the stove has been kept, whether washing wall to wall carpeting is to be your responsibility, and so on. Such a discussion will give you clues about what you will have to do to get your deposit back, and also about areas of tension that might develop with your landlord. You also might want to determine whether your landlord feels you have the right to sublet in order to, say, take an extended vacation, without forfeiting your lease. Such provisions are often not specified in a lease. In sum, try to anticipate in your initial tour with the landlord all the contingencies that might arise during the period of your tenancy.

MAKING THE MOVE

If you are moving from one part of the country to another, you can employ the services of moving consultants. But this generally will be useful only if you are in an upper-income bracket. Otherwise, your time may be worth less than a moving consultant's time.

Although the goverment regulates movers, you can not necessarily be certain of a guaranteed move. Some new regulations apply to the moving industry, and you should be aware of the most important of them to take advantage of any benefits they might bestow on you:

1. The moving van must come on the promised day. The company can be fined up to $500 if it fails to do so.

2. The price estimates must be based on the moving company's actual physical inspection of whatever you ask it to move.

3. Well in advance of the actual moving day, a mover must give you, the customer, an *Order for Service*, which states the estimated price of the move and the mutually agreed-upon pick up and delivery dates.

4. The shipment must be delivered and all services performed on payment of the estimated amount plus no more than 10 percent additional in the case of an underestimate. Anything you owe them above 110 percent of what they estimated in writing you have 15 working days to pay.

How to Pick a Mover

Picking a mover is a very tricky problem because surveys of people's reactions to different movers show that even within one moving company there is extreme variability in quality of service. The level of complaints seems to be about the same for each of the largest firms: North American Van, United, Bekins, Allied, and Arrow Mayflower. If you get two or three estimates made of your moving task, do not be fooled into giving the job to the lowest estimate, because the ICC has made sure that the industry charges about the same price for weight and mileage.

Don't Cut Time Corners

Do not try to postpone your move to the very last minute. Make sure that you have the movers come a few days before you have to vacate your house. Sometimes movers do not come on time, and that may spell disaster if you are supposed to leave the day the mover has been scheduled to come. You can get by without your furniture for a day or two, but what will you do if you have to stay around after you were supposed to vacate the premises?

Appliances

You must pay extra to have appliances prepared for moving. It's probably better to call your regular repair services and have them do it. Also have them explain what must be done to put things back into service later on.

Watch Out!

When the movers are loading your stuff, make sure you see a copy of the inventory form and look at what they mark to describe the condition of your furniture. A series of code letters indicate scratched, marred, gouged, cracked, soiled, and so on. If you think the movers' description is exaggerated, make sure it is changed or threaten to call the whole thing off. For if the description of damage to your furniture is exaggerated before it leaves, then you will have no recourse for a damage payment if your furniture is damaged in transit. Since a full 25 percent of all moves end in some dispute over damages, you had better believe this is an important point.

When your furniture is finally delivered, be there. Do not sign an inventory sheet, no matter what the driver says, until you've had the time to notice all damage and all loss.

Making a Claim

There's a good chance you will want to make a claim for lost, broken, or damaged items. There's generally a claims bureau in your town and somebody will be sent out to estimate damage or to take things to be repaired. Note that, under a 1972 ICC rule, the van line on an interstate move is "absolutely responsible for all acts or omissions" of its agents. If you fail to get satisfaction, call the nearest Interstate Commerce Commission office. If that fails also, write to the Director of the Bureau of Operations, Interstate Commerce Commission, Washington, D. C. 20423. If you think you have been badly abused, you may want to go to small claims court, which we describe in Consumer Issue XIV.

An Alternative

If you have some extra time and some friends to help, and you want to save some money and avoid fights with movers, you can always rent a truck from U–Haul, EZ Move, U–Drive, or various other companies. The one-way rate across the U. S. is quite reasonable. Remember, though, you must count the time and fatigue costs of this particular moving method. Since the cost of moving yourself is directly related to the income you forego, or the implicit value you put on the leisure time lost in doing the moving, you may find moving yourself the most economical way. People who are students during the school year and do not have summer jobs, for example, have a very low opportunity cost and, therefore, may wish to take advantage of this low opportunity cost by renting a U-Haul. On the other hand, if you were a high-income executive, it would not make sense for you to spend two weeks driving a truck across the United States in order to save moving expenses, for you would give up much more in lost income.

SUMMARY

1. In trying to decide whether to buy or rent, be sure that in calculating the cost of buying, you include the opportunity cost on whatever the down payment is. A general rule of thumb in determining how much housing you can afford is no more than two and a half times your annual income. Recently, however, financial experts counsel consumers to be more conservative and to not pay for a house more than two times the consumer's annual income.

2. In deciding where you want to live, you must look at: (a) the relationship to work, (b) property taxes, (c) schools in the neighborhood, (d) proximity and completeness of shopping, (e) air quality, (f) crime, (g) the general neighborhood, and (h) how the area is zoned.

3. If you are buying or selling a house, you will probably find the services of a real estate broker helpful. However, remember that those services will cost you.

4. A real estate broker essentially brings together buyers and sellers. He or she is therefore a provider of information.

5. If you are selling a house, try to bargain with potential brokers on the commission they will charge you. You can bargain about when you will pay the commission (because a commission paid over a five-year period is less costly to you than a commission paid immediately upon the sale of the house) and certain other details of the sale. Shop around for a broker, just as you would shop around for anything else.

6. When you are buying a house, shop around for a broker, also. Find one that understands your needs and does not attempt to get you into a house that you do not want or will not be happy with. You can also bargain with brokers when you are buying a house. If, for example, you are ready to make a purchase, you may ask the broker to do such things as buy you a refrigerator and stove if he or she wants you to purchase the house, actually split the commission with you (where that is legal), put a new carpet in, or have the house painted at the expense of the broker.

7. You can let the broker do the bargaining for you if you are unused to that activity.

8. When bargaining on a house, never let the seller know that you are excited about the purchase. In fact, the seller should not learn anything about you at all. That is why it is best to have a broker do your bargaining so that your emotions cannot get involved in the activity, and so that you do not "show your hand."

9. It is usually advisable for you to have a building inspection service come out to the home you wish to buy before you make any offer whatsoever. Look in your Yellow Pages for such services. If you are really concerned, have more than one inspection service look at the house.

10. When figuring out the cost of a house, remember that you must take into account the closing costs, which can run as high as 3 or 4 percent of the purchase price of the house. This money must be in cash, as must the down payment on that house. Generally, you must purchase some form of title insurance in order to obtain a mortgage. However, if you are in doubt, hire your own lawyer to do the title search.

11. Shop for a mortgage just as you shop for anything else. Seek out the best deal in terms of the downpayment required, the annual percentage interest rate charged, whether or not there is a penalty for early prepayment in case you decide to sell the house after a few years.

12. If at all possible, you may wish to obtain a Veterans Administration mortgage or a Federal Housing Administration (FHA) insured mortgage. Ask your real estate agent or the banks you have contacted about these possibilities.

13. You may also wish to take part in a flexible mortgage payment plan whereby you pay a lower amount during the first five years and a higher amount from then on. You may have to pay a higher interest rate on a flexible payment schedule, however.

14. Make sure that you obtain sufficient insurance on your house so that at least 80 percent of its value is covered. Shop around for housing insurance, making sure you check out each company's policies with respect to how much they will pay you for personal furnishings lost in a fire, what they will pay you for alternative housing if you are forced to leave your home because of a fire, and so on.

15. When renting a place to live, make sure that before you sign a lease, you are not signing away a confession of judgment or a waiver of tort liability. Also, make it clear from the beginning whether the cleaning deposit is actually a deposit or a fee. If it is a fee, then you need not bother to clean up the apartment or house when you leave.

16. Personal household and liability insurance is important when you rent.

17. Moving can be a traumatic experience. You can avoid some of the traumas by taking several steps: plan well in advance; work all of the details out with the potential mover; set your actual moving day for several days before you must leave your house or apartment; take a complete inventory of what you are shipping; check the mover's log to make sure that more defects in your furniture are not recorded than actually exist; and do not expect perfection. You may wish to try some of the smaller movers. Many consumers indicate that they receive better service from other than the top five large moving firms.

QUESTIONS FOR THOUGHT AND DISCUSSION

1. Do you think that a mortgage rate of 8½ percent is high? Why?

2. Why would you want to borrow on a mortgage for 30 years instead of, say, 15 years?

3. Would you prefer to buy a new or a used house? Why?

4. Can you think of any other features of a house you should look at in addition to the eight listed in the text?

5. Do you think real estate brokers charge too much?

6. Would you ever pay more than the asking price for a house?

7. Which type of title insurance do you think is best?

8. Which is the best kind of mortgage: conventional, VA, or FHA?

9. Do discount points seem "unfair"?

10. Why do you think mortgage companies require you to prepay insurance and taxes?

11. Is it always best to repair everything that goes wrong in a house?

12. If you are certain that a cleaning deposit for a rented apartment or a house will actually end up being a cleaning fee, has your effective rent been raised or lowered?

THINGS TO DO

1. Call a number of savings and loan associations and find out what their interest rate is on a 20-year $30,000 mortgage on a $50,000 house. If you find significant differences, ask why.

2. Call up the local office of HUD or FHA. Ask what special government help can be provided you if you decide to buy a house. Find out what the income limitations are. In other words, does the special help apply only to poor people, or to middle-income people also?

3. Drive around your town into different residential areas. Try to figure out why one area is more expensive than another.

4. Look in the Yellow Pages under Real Estate Brokers and see what some of the large ads say. Try to figure out whether it is possible for one broker to do a better job than another.

5. Obtain a typical contract or earnest agreement from a broker in your area. Go over the details with the broker. Find out whether the agreement is more beneficial to the buyer or to the seller. (Actually, it should be most beneficial to the broker.)

6. Get a copy of a typical mortgage agreement from a savings and loan association. Try to read the small print.

SELECTED READINGS

Financing for Home Purchases and Home Improvements: A Guide to Financing Costs and Home Buying Ability (Washington, D. C.: Federal Housing Administration).

"For House Hunters: Sizing Up the Neighborhood," *Changing Times*, July 1970.

"Homeowners vs. Lenders: A Question of Interest," *Consumer Reports*, March 1973.

"House Buying: The Cost of Closing the Deal," *Changing Times*, November 1971.

"How Much House Can You Afford?," *American Home*, January 1969.

"How Much Should You Put Down on a House," *Better Homes and Gardens*, August 1973.

"How to Avoid the Ten Biggest Home-buying Traps," *Consumer Bulletin*, August 1969.

"How to Pick an Apartment," *Changing Times*, April 1971.

"Learn to Spot What's Wrong with a House," *Changing Times*, February 1970.

Mager, Bryon J., *How to Buy a House* (New York: Lyle Stuart), 1965.

Questions and Answers on Guaranteed and Direct Loans for Veterans (Washington, D. C.: Veterans Administration).

Selecting and Financing a Home, G–182, revised (Washington, D. C.: U. S. Department of Agriculture, Government Printing Office), 1972.

"The How and Why of Taking Over a Mortgage," *Changing Times*, January 1970.

"The Legal Side of Owning a House," *Changing Times*, July 1973.

"What Can You Afford to Pay for a House?," *Changing Times*, June 1968.

CHAPTER PREVIEW

☐ How much do we spend on transportation?
☐ What are the safety aspects of automobiles?
☐ How do safety standards affect the cost of a car?
☐ What are the characteristics of the automobile repair industry?
☐ What are the characteristics of the automobile insurance industry?
☐ Is no-fault a good deal?
☐ Why is there no more mass transit in the United States than there is?

GLOSSARY OF NEW TERMS

Private Costs: The costs that are incurred by an individual and no one else. The private costs of driving a car, for example, include depreciation, gas, insurance, and so on.

Social Costs: The costs of an action that society bears. Social costs include private costs, but to them must also be added costs that the individual does not bear. For example, the social cost of driving a car includes the private costs plus any pollution or congestion caused by that automobile.

No-fault Auto Insurance: A system of auto insurance whereby, no matter who is at fault, the individual is paid by his or her insurance company for a certain amount of medical costs and the material damage to the car.

Someone who wanted to name the twentieth century would not be wrong to call it the Age of the Automobile. From a modest beginning at the turn of the century, when a few courageous souls drove around in Stutz Bearcats, Hupmobiles, and Model T's, but especially from the moment Henry Ford developed low-cost mass-production techniques to put out a $870 "Tin Lizzie", until the mid-1970s, when fully 85 percent of all American families own cars, we have seen the automobile become a pervasive part of American life. There is no way to escape it, or at least it seems so. The trend towards multiple-car families is also continuing, as Figure 11–1 shows. Today, fully one-third of American families have two four-wheeled vehicles in their driveways.

WE SPEND A LOT ON CARS

In the United States today there are probably close to 110 million cars. The number of new cars turned out of the factories every year sometimes exceeds 11 million. Money spent on purchasing automobiles, on automobile repairs, and on other related expenses accounts for 11½ percent of total income in the United States. The automobile industry itself is also huge. One out of every six people in the United States is in some way concerned with automobiles, whether it be as a factory worker in Detroit or as an employee of a company making spare parts or servicing cars. The notion behind the famous statement, "Whatever is good for General Motors is good for America," could derive from the sheer numbers involved in automobile-related employment.

However, the total amount of money spent in the private transportation industry does not give true indication of the total cost to society. We will talk later about the *social* cost of driving, but first we will discuss that painful aspect of driving your car—accidents.

FOUR-WHEELED COFFINS

Some have depicted the automobile as a four-wheeled rolling coffin. Why? Because approximately 50,000 Americans are killed every year in vehicle accidents, and two million others are injured. The economic costs of the injuries and deaths, and property damage exceeds $20 billion annually. Then there is the cost of pain and suffering, both for those involved in the accidents and for their loved ones. We can put no dollar figure on this tragic aspect of private transportation.

Many highway deaths could have been avoided had the drivers been more careful. But, according to many observers, many others could have been avoided if additional safety features were required on automobiles. In 1958, the Ford Motor Company tried to sell additional safety to the American car-buying public, but nobody bought and Ford lost money. Finally, after the exposés of Ralph Nader in his book *Unsafe at Any Speed,* Congress started moving, and the result was the Motor Vehicle Safety Act of 1966, the basis of most current safety requirements on automobiles.

Some of the requirements imposed on car manufacturers by the National Highway Traffic Safety Administration are:

1. dual braking systems
2. nonprotruding interior appliances
3. over-the-shoulder safety belts in the front seat
4. head restraints on all front seats

FIGURE 11–1   TREND IN MULTIPLE CAR OWNERSHIP
The trend in multiple car ownership is continuing upward. In 1957, only 13 percent of families in the U.S. had two or more cars, whereas in 1971, the figure reached almost 30 percent. Source: *1971–72 Survey of Consumers,* Lewis Mandell, George Katona, James N. Morgan, Jay Schmiedeskamp, Contributions to Behavioral Economics (Institute for Social Research, The University of Michigan: Ann Arbor) 1973.

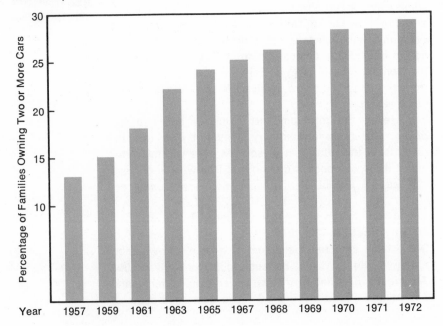

5. seat belt warning system and ignition interlock
6. collapsible, impact-absorbing arm rests
7. impact-absorbing instrument panel

THE COST OF SAFETY

All of the safety devices that must be put on cars these days constitute additions to the supply of safety for automobile transportation. Unfortunately, as we have continuously pointed out in this book, nothing is free. Automobile safety devices raise the costs of automobiles. You the consumer pay for that safety directly out of your pocket. But of course, you get a benefit—a safer mode of transportation.

It is not known, however, whether the total amount of automobile safety on the highway has dramatically risen because of the safety standards. After all, some people react to the higher relative cost of automobiles by not buying new cars as frequently as before. And the older the car, the higher is the probability of a mechanical failure that could cause an accident. The average age of cars being driven on the highway today has risen as the costs of new cars has increased because of the required safety devices.

ALTERNATIVES AVAILABLE

Alternatives are available that might reduce the numbers of accidents and injuries on the highway. Although their availability does not necessarily make these alternatives *preferable*, they are still worth thinking about.

At least half of all U.S. highway deaths are in one way or another related to drinking. Perhaps 50 percent of the 10,000 or so pedestrians killed every year are drunk, and 50 percent of the drivers involved in fatal highway accidents are legally drunk. To be legally drunk, a driver must have had the equivalent of three martinis on an empty stomach. Thus, many instances of poor driver judgment may be related to alcohol-induced slowness of mind and reflexes, which is not actually legal drunkenness, however.

If so many accidents are caused by drunk drivers, one alternative to the solutions already tried for increasing highway safety involves reducing the number of drunks on the road. This would mean, for example, much higher fines and stiffer jail sentences. In Sweden, for example, where there is an alcoholism problem, accidents caused by drunk driving are relatively few. Why? Simply because the costs of being caught driving drunk are tremendous—jail and huge fines. Any time people get loaded in Sweden, they either stay where they are or they let somebody else drive, or they call a taxi or take a bus. With stiff enough fines in the United States, the same thing could be true here. Generally, though, we are extremely lenient with drunk drivers no matter what they do on the road. You can find people with four and five drunk-driving arrests on their records still driving. Generally, only when they kill or maim somebody do they realize their mistake. And even then they may eventually be drunk on the road again.

Another way of preventing fatalities and injuries resulting from accidents is to cut down on the number of road hazards and increase the ease with which people can drive safely. This would require break-away signs, energy absorbing materials at off ramps and around bridge abutments, and so on. Some experts have estimated that we could save more lives by investing in better roads than by paying the billions of dollars a year in additional costs for safer cars. You also should realize that sturdier cars that withstand accidents use up more resources and take more gas to drive—further costs of safety.

Another way of reducing highway accidents is to lower speed limits. There was a consensus among highway experts in early 1974 that the energy crisis-induced reduction in highway speed limits significantly reduced traffic fatalities. For some reason, advocates of safer cars did not, at least until then, strongly suggest lower speed limits as an alternative.

THE PRIVATE COST OF DRIVING

The cost of driving a car does not involve only making a monthly payment, although that is part of it. The private costs of driving include such things as wear and tear, repairs, gas and oil, insurance, and taxes, in addition to whatever payments are made and whatever the implicit cost is if you paid cash. (Remember the discussion in the previous issue when we talked about whether to buy or rent.) Table 11–1 shows the estimated cost of operating an automobile as given by the U. S. Department of Transportation. There are quite a few costs indeed—many more than you may have thought. It ultimately costs about 11¢ to 16¢ a mile to run a car. The repairs on cars can be quite expensive. And in addition, you have an information problem about whether or not you are being asked to pay for more than you need when your car breaks down.

TABLE II–1: COST OF OPERATING AN AUTOMOBILE

	SUBURBAN BASED OPERATION					
	CENTS PER MILE					
	Original Vehicle Cost Depreciated	Maintenance, Accessories, Parts & Tires	Gas & Oil (Excluding Taxes)	Garage, Parking, & Tolls	Insurance	State & Federal Taxes	Total Cost
Standard Size	4.2¢	3.4¢	3.2¢	2.0¢	1.6¢	1.5¢	15.9¢
Compact Size	2.9¢	2.7¢	2.6¢	2.0¢	1.5¢	1.2¢	12.9¢
Subcompact Size	2.3¢	2.5¢	2.0¢	2.0¢	1.5¢	.9¢	11.2¢

Source: U.S. Department of Transportation, Federal Highway Administration, April 1974.

THE REPAIR
INDUSTRY

The automobile repair industry is immense. There are at least 100,000 mechanic's garages in the United States, as well as 200,000 gas stations that also give repair service. In total, we spend probably $10 billion a year on automobile repairs. The labor costs for auto repairs have increased rapidly in the last few years. Obviously, it is important that you find a reputable repair shop for your car. If you know of none, ask your friends and acquaintances where they have gotten good repair work. Because repeat customers are generally going to be treated better, it is also advisable to take your car back to the same garage often if you are satisfied.

Some consumer economists believe that preventive maintenance avoids large repair bills. This is true, but you must take account of the maintenance costs themselves. In the long run, it may be cheaper not to keep your car in perfect condition, but rather to let some things (other than brakes, tires, and safety-related parts) wear out and replace them only when they do, or trade in your car every few years. Some state governments buy fleets of cars that they do no servicing on at all for a year and then trade in. This seems to be cheaper than trying to maintain the cars, and as the price of repair services rises, will become still cheaper by comparison. You will thus have two choices: (1) buy a car that you expect to keep only for a short period of time, or (2) buy a car that has a reputation of very low service requirements. The annual issue of *Consumer Reports,* for example, relays its readers' experiences with the repair needs of different makes and years of cars. This is an important aid when you try to assess the annual cost of operating an automobile. A Mercedes, for example, may be extremely expensive at the outset, but according to owners' reports, repairs are fewer and further between. Also, as you would expect, the actual physical depreciation of that car is much less than that of cars costing half the price. Hence, when checking out an automobile, look not at its list price, but rather at the implicit price you will have to pay per year. When viewed in this manner, a Mercedes is certainly not twice as expensive as a Ford.

THE AUTOMOBILE
INSURANCE INDUSTRY

When you buy a car, one of the first things you must think about is insuring yourself against theft, fire, liability, medical expenses, and damage. Very few people drive without automobile insurance. But whether most people have adequate insurance is another matter, and we will discuss what is adequate in the following consumer issue.

The insurance industry is a regulated one: every state has its insurance commissioner who passes judgment on the rates charged by various insurance companies. Although there is a tendency for any regulated industry to have quite a few regulations that stifle competition, the automobile insurance industry still remains competitive in many situations. It is not unusual for different prices to be charged for the same amount of insurance. But prices can be misleading, because different insurance companies offer different qualities of service: one company may be less willing to pay off claims than another; one may have an insurance adjuster at your house immediately if you have a small crack-up, while another may never send one out, leaving you to do the adjusting yourself. While insurance costs are not consistently related to quality of service, they do consistently differentiate among different classes of drivers.

Why? Simply because the probability that an accident will occur is different for these different classes. Competition among the various insurance companies has forced each one of them to find out which classes of drivers are safer than others and offer those classes lower rates. For example, because statistics tell us that single males from 16 to 25 have the highest accident record of all drivers, they pay a much higher price for auto insurance. And because statistics tell us that women drivers have fewer accidents overall than male drivers, women in a family often pay lower insurance rates for those cars that they use exclusively.

NO FAULT INSURANCE, PROS AND CONS

In May of 1974, President Nixon wired the National Governors Conference that **no-fault auto insurance** was "an idea whose time has come." The President added, though, that the place for no-fault action is at the state level, not at the federal level. Labor and consumer groups, however, were dissatisfied with the pace of state action and the lobbying tactics of no-fault opponents. Therefore, pressure was brought upon the Senate and the House to institute a federal plan. Supporters of such plans indicate that over a period of time it will save motorists a billion dollars a year in auto insurance premiums.

Under no-fault insurance, motorists are paid by their own insurance companies for medical and other costs arising out of an accident, regardless of who was at fault. This should be contrasted with the liability-based auto insurance systems that until recently were standard in most states; in a liability policy, a determination must be made as to who caused an accident and the insurer of the party deemed "at fault" pays the bills of the other.

Proponents of no-fault argue that their system provides speedier, more equitable compensation for losses and, as a result, premium costs are cut because legal fees and costly "pain and suffering" settlements are avoided.

By mid-1974, 22 states had adopted some form of no-fault insurance. However, only 14 of these had "true" no-fault statutes that provided for mandatory benefits by an injured party's *own* insurer and placed restrictions on lawsuits.

The first Senate version of a federal no-fault insurance bill included minimum standards that were much higher than the statutes on the books in 1974, in all but one state. The Senate bill called for payment by an insured party's *own* insurer of all medical costs arising out of an accident, up to $15,000 in lost wages, at least $1000 in burial expenses, and up to $5000 in death benefits for a victim's family. "Pain and suffering" suits

for further damages would be allowed only for accidents resulting in death, permanent injury, or disability of more than three months.

The objection most commonly made against no-fault insurance is the claim that no-fault would wrongly deprive most injured parties of the right to sue. One of the main lobbies fighting no-fault insurance was the Trial Lawyers section of the American Bar Association, for if no-fault became a reality everywhere in the United States the demand for their services would be reduced.

SHOULD YOU BUY AND HOLD

Frequently the question comes up as to whether it is better to buy a new car every year or so, or to buy and hold a car for, say, 10 years until it essentially has no resale value. A few years ago, the U.S. Department of Transportation conducted a study designed to come up with some exact answers to this question.

The Department of Transportation looked at the actual costs of depreciation, insurance, repair bills, maintenance, and so on for a 1970 full-sized, "big-three" (Ford, GM, Chrysler) four-door sedan equipped with V8 engine, automatic transmission, etc. They compared buying a car and keeping it for 10 years against buying a new car every year, or every two or three years. After a certain number of years, the car that is held for 10 years became a second car in a two-car family and was driven fewer miles. The study showed that to buy a new car every other year would cost you $4000 more over a 10-year period than keeping one for 10 years. The conclusion was that at least in this case it was cheaper to buy. and hold. Unfortunately, this conclusion is only a starting point for you in making your own decision about whether to buy a new car or not.

If you hold a car for 10 years and even keep it in very good condition, you have not purchased the same kind of transportation services as you would if you buy a new car every other year. If cars become safer every year, you do not have the benefit of new safety features. This is probably less important now since most basic safety features have been required for some time. But what if you had bought a car before dual brakes and safety laminated glass were required? You would be driving a much different piece of machinery than if you traded in your car every two years and got the benefits of the new safety features.

You lose the psychic benefits of styling changes, and of that new-car feeling or smell when you get into one. These are all very nebulous and hard to quantify; they might mean much to you or very little.

However, now with the pollution equipment required on new cars, the decision whether or not to buy one is even more complicated. Some automotive engineers maintain that 1971 or 1972 was the last good year to buy a car, because after that the pollution equipment has made the engine so bad and so expensive to run that you are better off not buying a new car.

THE SOCIAL COSTS OF DRIVING

When you get into your car and fire it up, you incur the private costs of driving, the ones we mentioned above. What you do not incur, or at least did not until recently, are the social costs. You are all aware of them, but particularly if you live in Los Angeles, New York, or Washington, D.C. One of the biggest social costs of driving has been air pollution. That engine of yours does not just pull your car around. It also emits by-products that, when added together, do little good for your lungs or mine. In some places, they can do so much harm that many people refuse to live there. Pollution from automobile exhaust contributes 60 percent to total pollution in the major U.S. cities today. This is, of course, why the federal government as well as individual states have started regulating the pollution output of automobile engines. And this is also why standard automobile engines with pollution abatement equipment do not run like the ones you were familiar with five years ago. It just has not been easy to eliminate the harmful by-products of internal combustion.

Thus, now you, the individual driver, are being forced to take account of the social cost you impose on the rest of society in the form of pollutin: you are forced to purchase automobile engines that have pollution abatement equipment, for which you pay directly in a higher purchase price and indirectly in the form of reduced power and higher gas consumption.

Private automobile transportation involves other social costs that are equally obvious: one of them is congestion. Congestion on bridges, highways, and in inner cities is a problem of social concern, even though private individuals, at least until now, were not forced to pay the full price of driving their cars. That price includes making other people late for work or making them spend more time in their own cars. In other words, by the mere fact that you get on a crowded bridge, you slow down everybody else a wee bit. When you add up the value of everybody else's time, you see that you impose a pretty high cost. And the same is true of every other person on that bridge.

The obvious solution is to make people pay the full cost of their driving by charging them more. Many will decide to cross the bridge at other than rush hours, or to go to work in car pools. Someday we may get to such a full costing solution. In the meantime, we build highways, freeways, expressways, bridges, underpasses, overpasses, parking lots—ad nauseam —until, if we keep on this way, eventually the landscape will be one massive automobile metropolis. Many people are clamoring for a change in this trend; they want mass transit. Unfortunately, mass transit on a large scale seems to be far off in the future.

MASS TRANSIT

The proposed solutions to the automobile problem are varied and many. In the San Francisco Bay Area, BART (Bay Area Rapid Transit) is busily developing an integrated rapid transit network. In Flint, Michigan, passengers have been enticed by a fleet of luxury buses, complete with air conditioning, stereophonic music, and in some cases even a "bus bunny" to handle complaints. *Fortune* Magazine found that, in 1972, 19 cities were building new subways, and 23 others, including London, Tokyo, and New York, were adding to existing systems. Planners throughout the world estimate that when all of their systems are finished, 12.5 billion passengers a year will be riding subways. Through its Urban Mass Transportation Assistance Act of 1970, the U.S. Congress provided $3 billion in federal funds for constructing subways. Congress stated that it intended to appropriate an additional $7 billion later.

Subways are not cheap to build. They typically cost about $6 million a mile to install, and many are even more expensive because soil conditions are so bad that pilings have to be driven, water has to be drained, and so on. In Washington, D.C., the subway system will have 98 miles of service and will cost at least $3 billion, making it one of the most expensive single public works projects ever undertaken in the United States.

However expensive subways seem to be, many engineers are convinced that they are the long-run solution to the urban congestion problem. In London, for example, it was concluded by a group of engineers that it would take an 11-lane highway to transport the 25,000 commuters who could be served hourly by a new subway line.

Some economists are not so optimistic about the future of mass transportation. In fact, some studies have shown that mass transportation will never effectively replace the auto and stop congestion if some current

conditions continue to exist in the future. Chief among those conditions is the fantastic amount of subsidization that private automobile drivers receive.

SUBSIDIZING
THE AUTOMOBILE

Highway travel that is most immediately competitive with mass transit—rush hour commuting in automobiles by private citizens—is subsidized to such an extent that mass transit may never be able to pay even its own operating costs, much less repay its construction costs. Urban motorists pay very little, perhaps only one-third, of the true cost of driving their cars to the city. For example, they do not pay for urban street maintenance and repairs, street cleaning, snow removal, traffic signals, or traffic police.

Most of these costs are incurred by all taxpayers because they are generally paid for out of city revenues. In addition, urban motorists who park in the streets use valuable land for which they pay no rent or property taxes, as must other people who occupy scarce land. Only a small parking meter fee is charged. Motorists use all of the capital invested in city streets but pay no tax comparable to the property or corporation income taxes imposed on users of these other forms of capital. When cities decide to improve streets and highways, the money is often borrowed and the interest costs are subsidized by the federal government.

It seems that until the private automobile is not so heavily subsidized, consumers are not going to respond to the mass transit attempts of public authorities. We are so wedded to that private way of getting around that we have to be forcibly induced not to use it. The best inducement is, of course, to make it more expensive, while making the alternative, mass transportation, more enticing. There have been attempts at making it more enticing, indeed. In downtown Seattle, there was free bus service, as in Everett, Washington, and in Los Angeles (Sundays only). In 1973, Pennsylvania initiated free fares for senior citizens, supplying the revenue differential from state lottery income. The Chicago Transit Authority temporarily cancelled fares for local riders in Evanston and Willamette. A system to phase out all fares in New York State by 1980 was proposed by Bronx Borough President Morris Abrams and has been sitting in Albany since 1971. His proposal included a 10 percent surcharge on the state income taxes for individuals and corporations to be returned to the various transportation districts based on transit use.

All of these attempts at enticing people onto mass transit may be in the "right" direction, but they seem to miss the point that we cannot be enticed onto mass transit facilities until we have been enticed out of our cars. Why continue to subsidize the private auto? Ending that subsidy is how we must start to reverse the paving of America.

Meanwhile, many of us still must buy and use cars in the absence of adequate mass transit, or of sufficiently forceful inducement to use mass transit. If you must buy a car, whether to meet your needs or satisfy your desires, the following consumer issue should give you some guidance as to how to go about it.

SUMMARY

1. Fully 85 percent of all American families own cars.

2. Multiple car ownership has increased to about 30 percent.

3. Highway deaths number around 50,000 a year, and property damage caused by the automobile exceeds $20 billion.

4. The National Highway Safety Administration sets standards for production of new cars. The cost of increased safety, however, is not insignificant.

5. An alternative to making a car safer is to make the highway safer by eliminating drunk drivers.

6. The automobile repair industry is indeed huge in the United States, accounting for perhaps $10 to $15 billion of consumer expenditures a year. Preventive maintenance is important in eliminating large repair bills; however, some preventive maintenance may be more costly than it is worth, particularly if you do not plan to keep your car very long.

7.   The automobile insurance industry is regulated, but there is enough competition to benefit you for shopping around.

8.   No-fault insurance, which may be federal law by the time you read this book, eliminates the liability-based system that has been in effect for so long.   Essentially, if you have no-fault insurance, your insurance company pays you in case of an accident no matter who was at fault.

9.   Buying and holding a car for many years may seem to be the least expensive way of obtaining transportation.   However, you lose out on the benefits of any improved product safety and quality found in newer model cars.

10.   The social costs of driving include the pollution, noise, and congestion caused by automobiles.

11.   As long as the automobile continues to be subsidized so heavily, it is doubtful that mass transit will ever become a reality throughout the United States as a substitute for the private automobile.

**QUESTIONS FOR
THOUGHT AND
DISCUSSION**

1.   Why do you think Americans spend so much for automobiles?

2.   Automobiles in America are much larger than in Europe.   Why?

3.   Even though they are told that speed kills, American drivers continue to drive as fast or faster than the speed limit on highways.   Why?

4.   Can you distinguish between safety features in a car that benefit only the occupants of a car and those that benefit so-called third parties?

5.   Why does safety cost?   Why has the automobile industry not provided a perfectly safe car?

6.   Do you think it would be difficult to eliminate drunk drivers?

7.   What cost do you, or would you, take into account when purchasing a car?

8.   Do you think there is a monopoly in the automobile insurance industry?

9.   Do you think no-fault insurance is "fair"?

10.   What has Congress been doing to reduce the social costs of driving?

11.   What are some ways mass transit could be furthered in the United States?

THINGS TO DO

1.   Write to the Federal Highway Safety Administration for a listing of safety requirements on cars.   Which ones do you think are appropriate or inappropriate?

2.   A few years ago a safety requirement was suggested that would oblige automobile manufacturers to relocate gasoline tanks and protect them from crashes in order to avoid fire. The Ford Motor Company asserted that the requirement would raise the price of each car by $11.20, and estimated that there were only 600 to 700 auto fire deaths annually. Ford concluded that the new safety standard would not be worth the price. Assume that 12 million cars are produced a year. What is the total cost of this new safety feature? If the Ford Motor Company is right about the number of auto fire deaths annually, what is the implicit value placed on human life? Is it too high or too low?

3.   Find out what the growth rate of bicycle and motorcycle sales has been in the past decade. Has this growth rate exceeded the growth rate of automobile sales? Can you think of reasons why?

4.   Write to your state's insurance commissioner for information on how the commissioner protects you from insurance companies.

**SELECTED
READINGS**

"How to Pay Less for an Auto Loan," *Changing Times,* April 1972.

Nader, Ralph, *Unsafe at any Speed: The Designed-in Dangers of the American Automobile* (New York: Grossman Publishers), 1972.

National Observer Staff, "Group Auto Insurance and Cutting Into Insurance Costs," *The Consumer's Handbook II* (Princeton, N.J.: Dow Jones Books), 1970.

O'Connell, Jeffrey, *The Injury Industry and the Remedy of No-Fault Auto Insurance* (Consumers Union, Commerce Clearing House), 1971.

"Will 'No-Fault' Bring Better, Cheaper Auto Insurance?" *Changing Times,* March 1972.

CONSUMER ISSUE VII
Buying Transportation

Liability insurance: Insurance that covers suits against the insured for such damages as injury or death to other drivers or passengers, property damage, and the like. It is insurance for those damages for which the driver can be held liable.

Umbrella Policy: A type of supplemental insurance policy that can greatly extend normal automobile liability limits to $1 million or more for a relatively small premium.

Zero Deductible: In the collision part of an automobile insurance policy, provision that the insured pays nothing for any repair to damage on the car due to an accident. Zero deductible is, of course, more expensive than, say, a $50 or $100 deductible policy.

SHOULD YOU BUY A NEW OR A USED CAR?

When most of us go out to purchase transportation, we face a problem: we are tempted to buy something new. There are certainly good reasons for buying a new car instead of a used one. A new car has never been touched by someone else and therefore you have to worry only about how you will treat it during its first few years, not about how it was treated beforehand. A new car may be safer, it may run smoother, it may be more stylish, and so on, although today these various aspects are not as subject to annual changes as they were in the past. On the other hand, new cars do not always run as well as used cars; to some buyers, they do not always look as nice; and they may not always be as comfortable. Nonetheless, you may choose a new car simply because you like to have things that are new. Be aware, however, of the price you are paying for that new car: a full-sized domestic car may automatically depreciate about $1000 when you take it off the dealer's showroom floor.

Nevertheless, in some cases, when you buy a new car you get the benefit of an extremely desirable warranty. American Motors, for example, had the following warranty for its 1974 automobiles: 12 months or 12,000 miles on the complete car, from windshield wiper blades to complete engine overhaul if needed. Volkswagen has a warranty which gives you 12,000 miles (or one year) of servicing on any parts that might need replacement, plus a total of 2 years or 24,000 miles on the internal parts of the engine and transmission; and Volkswagen will tow you to the nearest dealer or give you a rental car if yours has to be kept overnight for any warranty repair.

IF YOU DECIDE TO BUY A NEW CAR

If you decide to buy a new car, the questions are: where to buy it; which one to buy; and what accessories to purchase.

The Dealer

1. Location: Where to buy it depends on a number of factors, the most important being how far the dealer is from your job or home. After all, you must take the car in for servicing, and a new car, no matter how good it is, is going to have at least a few problems in the beginning. If you value time and convenience highly, if you can conveniently leave your car off at the dealer and walk to work or walk back home, you will be ahead of the game.

2. Dealer service facilities and personnel: To find out about the dealer's service facilities and personnel, ask specific questions about them, such as: what does the dealer do to make service easier for customers? What is the size and reputation of the service department? How long is service work guaranteed—0 days, 30 days, or 90 days? How much electronic diagnostic equipment does the shop have? Are there provisions for replacement transportation while your car is in service? When is the service department open? All of these questions are important and should not be glossed over because, as we all know, cars, whether they be new or used, require constant servicing.

3. Dealer reputation: Talk to customers who have bought from the dealer and have used his service department to find out how satisfied they are. Or, better yet, take your present car in for servicing and see how satisfied you are with their service department.

4. The deal offered: Obviously the deal offered is of utmost importance in all of the considerations above. You may be willing to pay a slightly higher price at a specific dealer whom you like very much and who has a

---

EXHIBIT:
Sample New-Car
Warranty

AMC BUYER PROTECTION PLAN ™

When you buy a new 1974 AMC car from an American Motors dealer, American Motors Corporation guarantees to you that, except for tires, it will pay for the repair or replacement of any part it supplies that is defective in material or workmanship. This guarantee is good for 12 months from the date the car is first used or 12,000 miles, whichever comes first. All we require is that the car be properly maintained and cared for under normal use and service in the fifty United States or Canada, and that guaranteed repairs or replacement be made by an American Motors dealer.

TABLE VII–1:
GAS MILEAGE
RATINGS BY CAR,
1974

Obviously, if you drive
much, which car you
buy can make a big
difference in the total
cost of your transporta-
tion services. The
gas mileage range for
the cars tested by
the Environmental
Protection Agency
varies widely from a
low of only 7 or 8 miles
to the gallon for big
American station
wagons and luxury cars
to a high of almost 30
miles a gallon for the
tiny Honda Civic.
(Note: M4 = 4-speed
manual transmission;
A3 = 3-speed auto-
matic transmission;
etc.)
Source: Office of Public
Affairs, Environmental
Protection Agency,
401 M Street, S.W.,
Washington, D.C.
20460.

	ENGINE SIZE [1] & NO. OF CARBURATOR BARRELS	WEIGHT CLASS (lbs.)	FUEL ECONOMY (mpg)
Alfa Romeo 2000 GTV (M4)	120–FI [2]	2,500	19.1
American Motors			
Gremlin (M4)	258–1	3,000	13.2
Javelin (A3)	304–2	3,500	12.1
Matador (A3)	304–2	4,000	12.4
Austin Morris BMC	78–1	2,000	22.4
MG Midget (M4)	98–2	2,500	22.5
Chrysler			
Dodge Colt Coupe (M4)	98–2	2,500	22.5
Dodge Sport Wagon (M3)	225–1	4,000	11.5
Chrysler (A3)	440–4	5,000	9.1
Chrysler Wagon (A3)	440–4	5,500	8.9
Ford			
Pinto (M4)	122–2	2,750	22.8
Capri (M4)	122–2	2,750	19.8
Mustang (A3)	140–2	3,000	16.9
Pinto Wagon (A3)	140–2	3,000	16.6
Comet (A3)	200–1	3,000	15.5
Maverick (A3)	200–1	3,000	15.0
Torino (A3)	302–2	4,000	11.8
Cougar (A3)	351–2	4,500	9.5
Fuji Heavy Industries			
Subaru Coupe (M4)	83–2	2,250	21.7
General Motors			
Chevrolet Vega Hatchback (M3)	140–1	2,750	24.6
Chevrolet Nova Hatchback (A3)	250–1	4,000	15.7
Buick Century 350 (A3)	350–4	4,500	10.4
Oldsmobile Cutlass Salon (A3)	350–4	4,500	10.1
Pontiac LeMans Sport (A3)	350–4	4,500	9.2
Cadillac Eldorado (A3)	500–4	5,500	10.4
Honda Civic (M4)	76–2	2,000	29.1
Jaguar E Type Series II (A3)	326–4	3,500	9.7
Mercedes Benz MB–450 SL (A3)	276–FI	4,000	10.6
Nissan			
Datsun 710 (M4)	108–2	2,500	20.0
Datsun 610 (M4)	119–2	2,750	20.6
Opel Manta Luxus (A3)	116–2	2,500	17.8
Peugot 504 Sedan (M4)	120–2	3,000	16.8
Porsche Roadster 914–4 (M5)	120–FI	2,500	17.5
Renault 15 Coupe (M4)	100–2	2,500	17.9

TABLE VII–1:
GAS MILEAGE
RATINGS BY CAR,
1974 (continued).

	ENGINE SIZE [1] & NO. OF CARBURATOR BARRELS	WEIGHT CLASS (lbs.)	FUEL ECONOMY (mpg)
Saab 99 (M4)	121–1	3,000	17.0
Standard Triumph Spitfire (M4)	91–1	2,000	23.1
Toyo Kogyo			
Mazda RX3 Wagon (M4)	70–4	2,750	10.8
Mazda RX2 Coupe (M4)	70–4	2,750	10.6
Toyota			
Corolla–1 Coupe (M4)	71–2	2,000	27.1
Mark II Wagon (A3)	156–2	3,000	19.4
Volkswagen			
Karmann Ghia 14 (M4)	97–1	2,250	21.7
Deluxe Sedan 11 (M4)	97–1	2,250	20.9
Volvo 145 (M4)	212–FI	3,500	18.4

[1] Measured in cubic inches.

[2] Fuel injection.

good reputation for service, but *only* a slightly higher price. Shopping around is, of course, a necessary part for most people when they buy a car.

When shopping around for the best price, do not be afraid to bargain. You can bargain on your trade-in, or on the list price, or on what accessories are offered. Remember, however, that you can find out the exact dealer (wholesale) price, which is about 25 percent below the list, or sticker, price. You will not get the price down much below a few hundred dollars above that price. A dealer who does not make a profit goes out of business. Hence, it is usually not worth your while to go to 25 dealers to bargain on a particular car. In fact, one study showed that after three dealers, the probability of getting a better deal was very small.[1]

Deciding on what new car to buy depends at least in part on how much money you want

[1] Allen F. Jung, "Price Variations Among Automobile Dealers in Metropolitan Chicago," *The Journal of Business,* January 1960.

to spend. You should figure out the exact yearly out-of-pocket costs you will incur for different price ranges and then decide which one you are willing to pay for. Remember, many times when you go up the ladder of car prices you are not buying any more safety or speed, but only styling, prestige, and so on. Be aware of the price you are paying for these qualities.

You should also be aware of the various operating costs of the new cars you look at. Compacts are cheaper to run than full-sized cars, as shown in Table VII–1, but they hold fewer people comfortably and less baggage, and they give you less protection in a big crash.

What options you should buy also depends upon your taste relative to your income. Some options are wise to take, even if you don't want them. It would be ridiculous to try to get a stick shift on a Cadillac because when you want to sell it, fewer people would want to buy it—which is why it is virtually impossible to get one with a stick shift. You should also consider things like power steering and

EXHIBIT: What are the Advantages, Disadvantages, and Seating Accommodations of the sizes? Generally:

SIZE	ADVANTAGES	DISADVANTAGES	SEATS
SUBCOMPACT	Lowest-cost available in U.S. Extremely easy to handle, park, garage. Excellent fuel mileage. Low operating, maintenance costs. Uncomplicated engines, usually 4-cylinder. Good second, or son-and-daughter car.	Slightly stiffer ride, usually because of short wheelbase and light weight. Limited space for passengers, cargo. Luxury interiors and some optional equipment not available on all models.	Two front, somewhat crowded. Two rear, crowded.
COMPACT	Low initial cost. Low operating, maintenance cost. Good fuel mileage. Easy to handle, park, garage. Fair cross-country car. Excellent for commuting. Good size for family of two adults, two small children.	Less-smooth ride than next sizes up. Less comfortable than larger cars for frequent long trips. Passenger and cargo space somewhat limited. Instruments, option choices somewhat limited.	Two to three, front. Two, rear.
INTERMEDIATE	Good room and comfort at low cost. Not as bulky as full-size cars. Easy to handle in traffic, to park, to garage. Relatively low-cost operation and maintenance. Well balanced for long-trip road car; gives good ride. Adequate passenger and cargo space. Good choice of engines, options, etc. Fairly good on fuel mileage.	Not as spacious for big families or those with lots of luggage. Not as well suited for heavy loads or heavy-duty trailer towing. May need V–8 engine for hill-country operation.	For normal trips: Three, front. Three, rear. For long trips: Two, front. Two, rear (or three children).

(continued on next page)

EXHIBIT: (continued from previous page).

SIZE	ADVANTAGES	DISADVANTAGES	SEATS
FULL SIZE	Most stability and riding comfort. Widest choice of options and equipment. Best long-trip car. Hauls heavy loads. Tows trailers easiest. Excellent for bigger families. Provides most space for passengers, cargo.	Costs more to buy, operate, maintain. Lower fuel mileage. A bigger size to handle, park, garage. More complicated and heavier.	Three, front (bench seats). Three, rear in comfort.

power brakes on the larger cars, because without these features they are again very hard to sell (and very hard to drive and park while you own them).

Tires are an important feature of any car and something that you probably will not want to compromise on. Radial tires seem to offer the most protection and to be the safest handling, and are sometimes the longest lasting. Today, many new cars come with radials; if the car of your choice comes without them, you should consider immediately trading in the standard tires for radials.

Another accessory that you may definitely want to consider is a rear window defogger. Most rear windows now have them as a standard equipment, but some do not. If you live in a cold climate, the extra $30 or $60 is well worth it on those cold mornings when you would not otherwise be able to see out the rear-view mirror. Of course, the assumption is that you are willing to pay for safety; only you can decide whether you are.

TRADING IN YOUR WHEELS

When you trade in your old car, you can be fairly certain you will get no more than the standard trade-in price listed by the National Automobile Dealers Association in its Official Used Car Guide, or "blue book." It might be a good idea for you to look up this information yourself.

Here is an area where private sellers are just as guilty of irresponsibility as dealers. How often have you heard of friends trying to trade in an old clunker with many things wrong with it? Usually, they assure the dealer that the old clunker is running perfectly and nothing is wrong with it.

IF YOU BUY A USED CAR

If you decide to buy a used car, there are a number of other things you must think about. Because you do not know how any given car was treated before you buy it, you must be especially careful about its condition. One way of making certain that no major things will go wrong is by having an independent mechanic check the car over before you commit yourself to buying it. You may be charged for this, just as you will be charged by a building inspector who checks out a house you want to buy. You are buying information from the mechanic. This information may save you hundreds of dollars in the future; the mechanic may point out that a transmission is about to go, that the gaskets leak, and so on.

Another way of insuring yourself against major repair expenses is by working with used car dealers who have 90-day written warranties on their products. Sometimes you have to pay for such a warranty and sometimes its price is merely included in the price of the used car. You are buying a type of insurance that costs you a little in the beginning but reduces the probability that you will pay out a wad in the future. Very rarely, a used car may still be covered by the manufacturer's one-year, 12,000-mile, or 2-year, 24,000-mile warranty. Because such a used car is worth more to you, the potential purchaser, than those without warranties, you will be willing to pay more.

One thing you can check out by yourself on a used car is whether it has been in a major accident. You look for mismatched colors in the paint; you look for ripples, bumps, and grainy surfaces on the bodywork. These will indicate extensive repainting and therefore extensive repairs. Such discoveries may not dissuade you from wanting to buy the car, but they should persuade you to have some shop testing done by an independent mechanic.

There are numerous methods of examining a prospective used car purchase. These can be found in the section on buying a used car in any annual *Consumer Reports Buying Guide.* It gives you eight to ten on-the-lot tests, and eight to ten driving tests that you can do yourself. It also tells you what each repair job will cost if you notice something wrong. However, since nothing can duplicate a shop test by a good mechanic, this step is highly recommended unless you have an extremely good warranty with the deal. You might also be able to get a helpful brochure from your local consumer affairs office.

WHEN THOSE REPAIRS GO WRONG

Every car owner is faced with the problem of having his or her car repaired. Finding a good repair shop or an honest mechanic may be a difficult job in your area. The Director of the Office of Consumer Affairs, Virginia Knauer, recently told a meeting of automobile dealers that "Every month complaints about automobiles head the list of problems that consumers write to me about." In order to counter the problems that customers have with dealers and with repairmen, a new organization, AUTOCAP, was recently formed.

How Does it Work?

Say you live in the state of Connecticut and you are dissatisfied with the car that you just bought from a dealer. You call a toll free number in your state (1–800–942–2276 in

TABLE VII–2 THE COST PER MILE FOR VARIOUS SIZES OF CARS
The Federal Highway Administration has developed cents-per-mile costs for operating subcompact, compact, and standard-size cars for 10,000 miles a year. They are useful as a guideline in figuring your own costs, but bear in mind that they may not take account of current prices of gasoline and costs which vary in different localities. The relative costs, however, will remain the same. The standard car costs you approximately 25 percent more per mile than a compact will. However, a compact may cost you only 10 percent more per mile than a subcompact.
Source: Federal Highway Administration. 1974

	CENTS PER MILE
Standard size	15.9
Compact	12.9
Subcompact	11.2

Connecticut), and register your complaint. You are immediately mailed a form on which to detail your problem. When you return the form to AUTOCAP headquarters in West Hartford, the dealer involved is notified by mail and urged to work out the problem with you, the customer. If this fails, the matter goes before AUTOCAP for arbitration. The panel arbitrating consists of four dealers and three public members.

It's a painless job to arrive at a "just" settlement when a dealer and a customer can agree. Obviously, the panel is not a court of last resort; it has no enforcement powers and relies on dealer cooperation to handle complaints satisfactorily. But, according to the Connecticut dealer and panel head, Richard D. Wagoner, dealer cooperation has been excellent: only two dealers had balked in the first year of operation.

When Things Get Sticky

When the going gets sticky on a matter of warranty or car performance, AUTOCAP goes directly to factory representatives. So far the results have been satisfying; manufacturers have cooperated in all respects.

And if you, the customer, feel that you did not get fair treatment at AUTOCAP's hands, you can still go to the state motor vehicle agency or take private legal action. The following automobile dealer organizations are operating AUTOCAP under sponsorship of the National Automobile Dealers Association as this book goes to press:

Kentucky Automobile Dealers Association, P.O. Box 498, Frankfort 40601.

Metropolitan Denver Automobile Dealers Association, 70 West 6th Ave., Denver 80122.

Automotive Trade Association of National Capital Area, 8401 Connecticut Ave., Chevy Chase, Md. 20015.

Central Florida Dealer Association, 1350 Orange Ave., Winter Park, Fla. 32789.

Idaho Automobile Dealers Association, 2230 Main St., Boise 83706.

Greater Louisville Automobile Dealers Association, 332 W. Broadway, Louisville 40202.

Cleveland Automobile Dealers Association, 310 Lakeside Ave., West, Cleveland 44113.

Oklahoma Automobile Dealers Association, 1601 City National Bank Tower, Oklahoma City 73102.

Oregon Automobile Dealers Association, P.O. Box 14460, Portland 97214.

Utah Automobile Dealers Association, Newhouse Hotel, Salt Lake City 84101.

Louisiana Automobile Dealers Association, 201 Lafayette St., Baton Rouge 70821.

Indianapolis Automobile Trade Association, 822 North Illinois, Indianapolis 46204.

Connecticut Automotive Trade Association, 18 N. Main St., West Hartford 06103.

FINANCING THAT PURCHASE

A new or used car is usually such a major purchase that at least part of it has to be financed by credit. Do not automatically accept the credit that the dealer offers you when you decide to buy a car. Shop around for credit just as you shop around for anything else. You may get a much better deal from your credit union or your local bank. Fortunately for you, the Truth-in-Lending Act of 1968 requires every lender to disclose the total finance charge you will pay and the actual annual interest rate to be paid. Thus, the credit offered you by the dealer can be compared to the credit offered you by competing sources such as banks and finance companies. Remember that in many cases if you default on your car payment, that car can be repossessed. This is a real possibility, because in some states finance companies can take your car away from you without a judicial hearing. Do not buy a car more expensive than you know you can afford. If the car is repossessed, you are bound to lose out.

GETTING AN ADEQUATE AMOUNT OF INSURANCE

The second most important step when buying an automobile is making sure you have adequate automobile insurance. Many kinds of insurance coverage can be offered to you. The most important is liability insurance.

Liability: This insurance covers bodily injury **liability** and property damage. Liability limits are usually described by a series of three numbers such as 25/50/5, which means that the policy will pay a maximum of $25,000 for bodily injury to one person, a maximum of $50,000 for bodily injury to more than one person, and a maximum of $5000 for property damage in one occurrence. Most insurance companies offer liability up to $300,000 and sometimes $500,000. The cost of additional liability limits is relatively small. It is wise to consider taking out a much larger limit than you would ordinarily expect to need, because today personal injury suits against automobile drivers who are proven negligent are sometimes astronomical. Sometimes dependents of automobile accident victims have been successful in suing for $1 million. Table VII–3 shows minimum insurance coverage required by state laws.

Some people are not even happy with the maximum liability limits offered by regular

EXHIBIT: **What your car loan will cost**

		12 MONTHS		24 MONTHS		36 MONTHS	
Annual Rate	Loan Amount	Loan Cost	Monthly Payment	Loan Cost	Monthly Payment	Loan Cost	Monthly Payment
8%	$1,000	$ 43.86	$ 86.99	$ 85.46	$ 45.23	$128.11	$31.34
	2,000	87.72	173.98	170.91	90.46	256.22	62.68
	3,000	131.58	260.97	256.37	135.69	384.33	94.02
9	1,000	49.42	87.46	96.43	45.69	144.79	31.80
	2,000	98.84	174.92	192.87	91.38	289.58	63.60
	3,000	148.25	262.38	289.30	137.07	434.37	95.40
10	1,000	54.99	87.92	107.48	46.15	161.62	32.27
	2,000	109.98	175.84	214.96	92.30	323.24	64.54
	3,000	164.97	263.76	322.43	138.45	484.86	96.81
11	1,000	60.58	88.39	118.59	46.61	178.59	32.74
	2,000	121.16	176.78	237.18	93.22	357.19	65.48
	3,000	181.74	265.17	355.76	139.83	535.78	98.22
12	1,000	66.19	88.85	129.76	47.08	195.72	33.22
	2,000	132.37	177.70	259.53	94.16	391.43	66.44
	3,000	198.56	266.55	389.29	141.24	587.15	99.66

automobile insurance coverage. These people can purchase a separate amount of coverage under a policy usually known as an **umbrella.** Umbrella limits sometimes go as high as $5 million.

Medical payments: Medical payments on an auto insurance policy will cover hospital and medical bills, and sometimes funeral expenses. Usually you can buy $2000 to $5000 for around $10 or $15 a year. This insurance protects all the passengers in the car.

Collision: Insurance of this type covers damage to your own car in any type of collision. It is usually not advisable to purchase full coverage (otherwise known as **zero deductible)** on collision. The price per year is quite high because the probability is so high that in any one year small repair jobs will be required, and will be costly. Most people take out $50 or $100 deductible coverage, which costs about one-fourth the price of zero deductible.

Comprehensive: Comprehensive auto insurance covers for loss, damage, or anything destroyed by fire, hurricane, hail, or just about all other causes, including vandalism. It is separate from collision insurance. Full comprehensive insurance is quite expensive. Again, $50 or $100 deductible is usually preferable.

TABLE VII–3: MINIMUM INSURANCE COVERAGE REQUIRED TO MEET FINANCIAL RESPONSIBILITY LAWS BY STATE

	AMOUNTS IN THOUSANDS						
STATE	Injury to Any One Person	Injuries in One Accident, to All Persons	Damage to Property	STATE	Injury to Any One Person	Injuries in One Accident, to All Persons	Damage to Property
Alabama	$10	$20	$ 5	Mississippi	$ 5	$10	$ 5
Alaska	15	30	5	Missouri	10	20	2
Arizona	10	20	5	Montana	10	20	5
Arkansas	10	20	5	Nebraska	10	20	5
California	15	30	5	Nevada	15	30	5
Colorado	15	30	5	New Hampshire	20	40	5
Connecticut	20	40	5	New Jersey	10	20	5
Delaware	10	20	5	New Mexico	10	20	5
District of Columbia	10	20	5	* New York	10	20	5
Florida	10	20	5	* North Carolina	10	20	5
Georgia	10	20	5	North Dakota	10	20	5
Hawaii	10	20	5	Ohio	12.5	25	7.5
Idaho	10	20	5	Oklahoma	5	10	5
Illinois	10	20	5	Oregon	10	20	5
Indiana	10	20	5	Pennsylvania	10	20	5
Iowa	10	20	5	Rhode Island	10	20	5
Kansas	15	30	5	South Carolina	10	20	5
Kentucky	10	20	5	South Dakota	15	30	10
Louisiana	5	10	1	Tennessee	10	20	5
Maine	20	40	10	Texas	10	20	5
Maryland	15	30	5	Utah	10	20	5
* Massachusetts	5	10	5	Vermont	10	20	5
Michigan	10	20	5	Virginia	20	30	5
Minnesota	10	20	5	Washington	15	30	5
				West Virginia	10	20	5
				Wisconsin	15	30	5
				Wyoming	10	20	5

* States with compulsory liability insurance laws.
Amounts shown as listed in "Best's Recommended Insurance Attorneys," 1972–1973 Edition. There may have been changes in some states since these data were published. For latest information, check your own state department of motor vehicles, or your auto insurance agent.

Uninsured motorists: This type of coverage insures the driver and passengers against injury by any driver who has no insurance at all, or by a hit-and-run driver. Many states require that it be in all insurance policies sold to drivers. The risk is small, so the premium is relatively small.

How to Shop for Insurance

Shopping for automobile insurance is usually easier than shopping for a car. You may want to look first to your local credit union, or some special insurance source available to you if you are a member of certain organizations. Sometimes companies get special rates for their employees. If you are a government employee, you can sometimes get special types of automobile insurance from a government employees' insurance company. However, when comparing insurance companies, remember that you should also look at the service they give. You can shop for insurance by figuring out the exact policy you want, including liability, uninsured motorist, medical, collision, comprehensive, and perhaps towing, with the specific limits you want, and then getting a written statement from several insurance companies' agents.

The insurance agent you work with is also important. If one in your area has the reputation of being fair and knowledgeable, you may want to take suggestions from that person. Again, you are being sold information as part of the package. (You may also be buying "clout" if you are dealing with a company agent rather than a broker for many different companies.)

There are special types of package policies you may want to look into, family rates, and the like. Also, you may be able to get safe driver policies, reductions if you have taken driver training, and so on. All of these possibilities should be discussed with prospective insurance agents.

SUMMARY

1. When looking for a new car dealer, consider (a) location, (b) dealer service facilities and personnel, (c) dealer reputation, and (d) the deal offered.

2. Generally, new cars have problems that you will want the dealer to take care of. Hence, the fact that the dealer is nearby and willing to handle such warranty problems is an important consideration when choosing a dealer.

3. Deciding on the size of a car should involve not only purchase cost, but running costs, as well as ride smoothness, acceleration, availability of options, and handling.

4. The purchase of a used car requires as much shopping as for a new car, or more, for the mechanical condition of the car is now in question. If you wish to have a warranty, purchase a used car from a dealer offering a one-month or 300 mile warranty. However, you will have to pay a higher price for that benefit.

5. Shop for automobile financing just as you shop for any other product. Shop on the basis of down payment required, setup charges, actual finance charge, and actual annual interest, as well as the number of months required to pay. Remember, the sooner you pay off the loan, the smaller the interest paid. On the other hand, the less money you will have for other purchases.

6. There is a minimum insurance required to drive an automobile in all states in the Union. However, it is generally quite cheap to purchase additional coverage. For example, it may cost you only $3 more a year to increase your liability from, say, $50,000 to $150,000.

7. Shop for automobile insurance systematically, asking each potential company its price for a standard policy, such as $25,000 for bodily injury to one person, a maximum of $50,000 for bodily injury to more than one person, and a maximum of $5000 for property, plus $10,000 medical payments, plus $100 deductible collision, full comprehensive and uninsured motorist. After you have received the different bids on such a policy, find out the pay-off procedures in case of an accident. Is there a claims department? How well is it set up? How fast will it operate? How soon can you get a loaner car in case of an accident, and so on?

QUESTIONS FOR THOUGHT AND DISCUSSION

1. For a few years, one car company had a 50,000 mile or five-year warranty on the drive train of its new automobiles. This warranty is no longer available. Why do you think it was discontinued?

2. Why do you think some automobile companies have longer warranty periods than others?

3. Many automobiles are obviously less safe than others. Why do you think people knowingly drive such unsafe cars?

4. Do you think that the most important factor in deciding which car to buy is the amount of gasoline it consumes?

5. In 1973 and '74, large American cars stopped selling well. Do you know why?

6. Why is the interest rate you pay for an automobile loan higher than what you would pay for a home mortgage?

7. Would you prefer to take out an automobile loan for 24 months or 48 months?

8. What is the most important safety feature a car can have?

9. Would it ever be considered rational to not carry automobile insurance?

THINGS TO DO

1. Even if you are not in the market for a new car, try shopping for one over the phone. Pick a particular make, body style, and set of accessories. Call five different new-car dealers in your area. See if you can get an actual quote on the phone. See if there are any big differences among the quotes you get. You will be surprised at how little they vary.

2. Make a list of the various new car warranties available for the largest-selling cars in the U. S., such as Ford, Chevrolet, Oldsmobile, Volkswagen, Volvo, Mercedes, and so on. See if the more expensive cars have a better warranty.

3. Write to the Federal Highway Administration in Washington, D.C., asking for their estimate of the current cost per mile for operating a subcompact, compact, and standard size car. Compare it with the figures in Table VII–2. Now, in percentages, figure out the relative costs. Is it now more or less expensive, in operating cost per mile, to have a standard-size car compared to a compact?

4. Find out from the National Highway Traffic Safety Administration what safety equipment this year's cars had to have. With this knowledge, would you feel safer in a newer car? How much would you be willing to pay for this additional safety?

5. Go to the library and get the latest December Annual Buying Guide of *Consumer Reports*. Look at the section on buying a used car. Could you perform the eight to ten on-the-lot tests given in that section? Have you ever tried the eight to ten driving tests given in that section when you were out looking for a used car?

6. Find out whether your area has a local office of AUTOCAP, which is under National Automobile Dealer Association sponsorship. See what AUTOCAP in your area has done.

SELECTED READINGS

Cost of Operating an Automobile (Washington, D.C.: U.S. Government Printing Office), 1972.

How to Buy a Used Car, Consumers Union, 1972.

"Used Car Dealers: How They Operate," *Changing Times*, September 1972.

"Will It Pay to Fix Up Your Old Car?" *Changing Times*, June 1972.

CHAPTER PREVIEW

☐ What has Medicare to do with the high cost of medical services?
☐ Why have there been so few medical doctors in the United States?
☐ What are the restrictions on entry into the medical care industry?
☐ How does the American Medical Association fit into all of this?
☐ What has the Food and Drug Administration done to protect the consumer from injurious drugs?
☐ What has the restriction on advertising drug prices done to the cost of drugs to consumers?
☐ What is group health all about?
☐ What are HMOs?
☐ How does diet affect your health?

GLOSSARY OF NEW TERMS

Consumer Price Index: An index of the prices of goods that consumers buy in the United States. Its change represents the average change in the price of things you buy.

Outpatient Services: The services of doctors and/or hospitals that do not involve the individual remaining as a registered patient in the hospital.

Inpatient Services: Services rendered to an individual by doctors and/or a hospital while the patient remains in the hospital at least for one night.

Naturopath: A practitioner of a system for treating disease that emphasizes assistance to nature and includes the use of natural medicinal substances and physical means (such as manipulation and electrical treatment).

Ethical Drug Industry: The industry that produces the drugs that are sold by prescription only. To be contrasted with patent drugs, which are sold over-the-counter without prescriptions.

Price Discrimination: Charging different people different prices for the same item.

The woeful lack of adequate health care for large segments of the American population has been long decried by Congresspersons, Presidents, laypersons, and even doctors. There have been many suggested solutions to our health care crisis, some of which have already been enacted in the form of Medicare and Medicaid. But even before those programs went into full effect, Senators and Congresspersons started demanding more comprehensive medical care insurance.

In addition to the problems of inadequate supplies of medical care, concerned legislators and citizens could not help noticing the spiraling costs of obtaining what medical care is available. Figure 12–1 shows the **Consumer Price Index** and the price indexes of various health care services, the latter having risen considerably faster than the overall CPI. Thus, not only is health care more expensive than it was, but its *relative* price is rising; it is more expensive in relation to other services than it once was.

THE HEALTH CARE DILEMMA

MEDICAL CARE EXPENDITURES

The expenditures for medical care in the United States have increased dramatically in the last four or five decades. We spent only $4 billion on medical care in 1929. We increased our spending to $40 billion by 1965. It is well over $80 billion today, and will reach $200 billion by 1980. In 1929, expenditures on medical care represented 4 percent of total national spending, but today's expenditures represent 7 percent or more. We can say, therefore, that as real incomes rise, Americans demand not just more medical care, but more than is in proportion to the rise in incomes.

WHY DOES MEDICAL CARE COST SO MUCH

Nobody expects medical care to be free. After all, it uses resources, and resources themselves are never free. But many people have wondered why medical care costs have been going up so much faster than all other costs. We can give several reasons why this is happening. The first has to do with the increases in demand brought about by government programs.

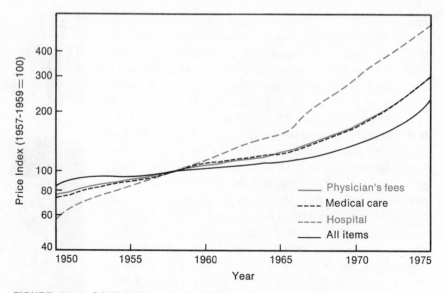

FIGURE 12-1 CONSUMER PRICE INDEX VS. MEDICAL PRICE INDEX
Here we show what has happened to the indexes of various prices in our economy. Hospital prices have risen the most rapidly, and both M.D.'s fees, as well as the overall index of medical care prices, have risen faster than the Consumer Price Index. Source: U.S. Department of Labor, Bureau of Labor Statistics.

WHEN MEDICARE
STARTED

Prior to Medicare—"free" medical care for the aged—Congressional estimates of what that program would cost were many times less than the actual cost turned out to be. This can be easily explained, for the demand for medical services is responsive to the price charged. When Medicare was instituted, the actual price of health care services to many people was drastically lowered. In some cases, the price was reduced to zero. As the price fell, the quantity demanded rose—and rose so much that the available supply of medical care services was taxed beyond capacity. The only thing that could give was the price, and it gave. Hospital room charges have skyrocketed since the imposition of Medicare. But Medicare is not alone in causing medical prices to go out of this world.

INSURANCE SCHEMES

Approximately 80 million Americans are covered by some form of private medical insurance. Most of this medical insurance pays a certain part of hospital expenses. Herein lies the problem: insurance rarely covers **outpatient service**. Rather, it covers only **inpatient service**. Individuals covered by insurance therefore have an incentive to go to the hospital to be taken care of by their private doctors. And their private doctors have an incentive to send them to the hospital in order to collect the insurance payments, knowing full well that fewer patients would be willing to have the services performed in their doctors' offices because they would not then be covered by insurance. Additionally, insurance plans generally have very little control over the number of tests and examinations that are performed on patients. Hospitals have an incentive, therefore, to use the most exotic techniques possible and doctors to order them, knowing full well that patients will have a large percentage of the costs reimbursed by insurance companies. The problem is that patients covered under insurance do not pay the *direct* costs of the medical care they receive in a hospital. Hence, they demand much more than they otherwise would. This increase in quantity demanded causes hospital expenses to go up, all other things held constant.

THE SHORT SUPPLY OF MEDICAL CARE

Medical care consists of a number of items, including but not limited to the services of physicians, nurses and hospital staff, hospital facilities, maintenance of the facilities, medications and drugs. What determines the supply of the most important item (at least up until now) in the total medical care package—physicians' services?

THE PRODUCTION OF MEDICAL DOCTORS

In 1972, 50,000 people took the Standard Medical School Admissions Test; only 12,000 were accepted in medical schools. Applicants to the Harvard Medical School run almost 3500, but the class size remains at fewer than 150. Some students apply to as many as 10 different medical schools, and when turned down reapply two or three times. Moreover, probably two or three times as many students do not bother to apply because they know the odds are so much against them. Why is there such a large discrepancy between those who want to go to medical school and those who are accepted? If you compare the number of students who wish to attend law school with the number of students who actually go, the discrepancy is much smaller than that for medical school. The reason for this greater discrepancy is not hard to find: the number of medical schools in the United States is severely restricted, as is the number of entrants into those schools.

RESTRICTIONS

The question is: restricted by whom? In principle, restriction on the number of medical schools is due to state licensing requirements which universally prohibit proprietary medical schools (schools run for profit). Also, it is difficult for a university that does not have a medical school to suddenly start one. A university can start a graduate department of romance languages without asking permission of any agencies or boards, just as it can start a law school without asking anybody. However, unless the medical school is accredited by the state, the graduates are not even allowed to take the licensing exam required for practicing medicine.

THE PAST

In the first decade in this century, there were 192 medical schools in the United States. By 1944, that number had declined to 69. The number of physicians per 100,000 people dropped from 157 in 1900 to 132 in 1957. It appears that the American Medical Association and the so-called Flexner Report (discussed below) were responsible for the reduced growth rate in the supply of physicians.

The AMA Wins Out. The American Medical Association was started in 1847. As it still does today, it represented then practitioners in the field of medicine. From the period of 1870 to 1910, there was a struggle between the AMA and medical educators over who should control the number of doctors allowed to practice. This became a battle over who should control medical schools themselves. The American Medical Association won the battle; it essentially has complete control over medical education in the United States. To become licensed in any particular state, a medical school graduate must have obtained a degree from a "certified" medical school. The certification is nominally done by the states themselves; however, in all cases the states follow exactly the certification lists of the American Medical Association. If the AMA were to decertify a particular medical school, you can be sure the state involved would also decertify that same school. Graduates coming out of that decertified school would find themselves barred from legal medical practice.

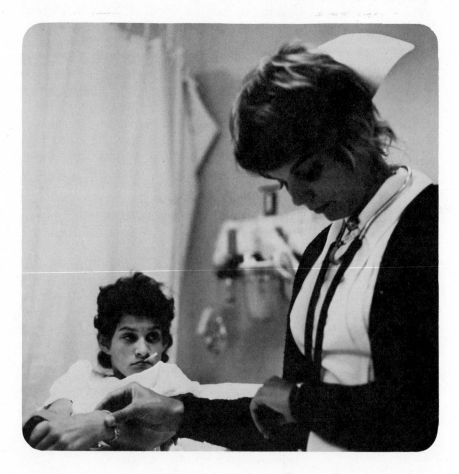

The Flexner Report. In all probability, the regulation and certification of medical schools was based on the outcome of the famous Flexner Report. In 1910, the prestigious Carnegie Foundation commissioned one Abraham Flexner to inspect the existing medical education facilities in the United States. Flexner's recommendations resulted in the demise of half of the existing medical schools of the day. He asserted that they were unqualified to teach medical education. It is interesting to note that Flexner had absolutely no qualifications himself for deciding which medical schools were to be rated class A. Flexner was not a physician; he was not a scientist; and he had never been a medical educator. He had an undergraduate degree in arts and was himself the owner and operator of a for-profit prep school in Louisville, Kentucky. Moreover, his evaluation of existing medical schools consisted of a grand inspection tour—nothing more, nothing less. Sometimes Flexner evaluated an entire school in one afternoon. He decided whether a medical school was qualified by estimating how well it compared with the medical school at Johns Hopkins University.

It is also interesting to note that Flexner was examining the *inputs* and not the *output* of these particular schools. Instead of finding out how well or how qualified the doctors were who *graduated* from the different schools, he looked at how doctors were taught. This would be equivalent to your instructor giving you a grade on the basis of how many hours you spent studying rather than on how well you did on the final exam (even though you might find that preferable).

WHY DID THE AMA SEEK CONTROL?

It is not hard to find the motive behind the AMA's desire to control medical schools. We merely need quote from an earlier head of the AMA's Council on Medical Education, Dr. Beven, who said in 1928:

> *In this rapid elevation of the standard of medical education . . . the reduction of the number of medical schools from 160 to 80, there occurred a marked reduction in the number of medical students and medical graduates. We had anticipated this and felt that this was a desirable thing. We had . . . a great oversupply of poor mediocre practitioners.*

Dr. Beven's statement can be rephrased to the effect that, if the supply falls, the price will therefore rise. On the other hand, if the supply increases, the price will fall.

AMA'S MOTIVES NOT SATISFIED

If we look at the American Medical Association's avowed motives, we realize that even those were not satisfied. The AMA maintained that the qualifications of many doctors were deficient—that is, the public was being disserved by doctors who were doing damage to unsuspecting patients. Medical school licensing was intended to weed out the most unqualified students and to eliminate the possibility that an unsuspecting sick person could be treated by an inadequately trained, yet licensed doctor. It is strange, therefore, that in 1910 the AMA did not seek to analyze the qualifications of the current crop of physicians. Closing one-half of the medical schools eliminated a *future* supply of supposedly unqualified doctors. But the then-current supply of supposedly unqualified doctors was allowed to continue practicing until retirement or death—as were those generations of unsuspecting citizens allowed to seek the aid of anyone who happened to have an M.D. degree, qualified or not. Somehow, this type of behavior does not seem consistent with the AMA's desire to raise the quality of medical services in the United States.

Moreover, it is difficult to understand why doctors are not reexamined periodically if they wish to continue practicing. Even a brilliant medical student from an excellent medical school could become lax in his or her medical practice and after a period of years become unqualified. Since there is no recertification procedure, the public can still be subjected to the malpractices of unqualified doctors.

SELF–TREATMENT

In addition, it is not obvious that the quality of medical care improved as much as the AMA professed. After all, there are two ways of obtaining medical services: one is self-diagnosis and self-treatment; the other is reliance on the medical care industry. If the price of a physician's diagnosis and treatment goes up, then one might expect that the quantity demanded would fall. Reliance on self-diagnosis and self-treatment would increase. People would decide to go to doctors only after their symptoms became alarming. It may be that the increase in quality and, therefore, price of doctors' services resulted in a decrease in the *total* quantity of medical care utilized because physicians were consulted less often. Moreover, we must presume that some people might forego the services of a licensed physician in favor of some alternative method which may be of "inferior" quality, such as **naturopaths** or faith healers. When the service of licensed physicians becomes more costly, there is an increase in the demand for substitute healing services from chiropractors, midwives, naturopaths, and so on.

And, of course, a real danger is present when consumers engage in extensive self-treatment. There are considerable numbers of over-the-counter medicines available to us all, many of which are quite powerful. And the tendency has been to become quite glib about self-prescription, even to the point of overuse of those medicines. It is one thing for a doctor to tell you to take three aspirin every four hours, and something else altogether for you to make that decision; you are often unaware of the possible side-effects and consequences of determining your own dosage. This problem becomes particularly acute with what children learn from their parents about taking medicines. If they see their parents taking a pill for almost everything, a certain appeal develops, and the result is usually dangerous and often fatal. You might have noticed that all recent advertisements for over-the-counter medications have been accompanied by the warning, "Use only as directed." This is an attempt to counter the serious health hazard presented by self-prescription. When in doubt, it is usually best to see a doctor.

THE FUTURE SUPPLY The current shortage of physicians has been figured at something like 50,000. However, recent rates of medical school graduation and the addition of foreign-trained physicians who are immigrating to the United States will eliminate this shortage. In addition, Congress has enacted a number of programs to increase the supply of medical personnel. For example, in 1971 the Comprehensive Manpower Training Act and the Nurse Training Act were passed; three billion dollars were provided for this purpose. Actually, some researchers believe that "there is a distinct possibility of excess capacity in medical schools and a surplus of physicians by the late 1970s." [1]

**DRUGS,
DRUGS,
DRUGS**
The ethical drug industry has always presented a problem to regulators and consumers alike. The information problems are sometimes insurmountable. Even the drug companies often do not know the effectiveness, or the side effects, of a drug. Doctors rarely take the time to get exact information on all the drugs they use, and in the past drug companies have

[1] Charles T. Stewart, Jr., and Corazon M. Siddayao, *Increasing the Supply of Medical Personnel: Needs and Alternatives*, (Washington, D. C.: American Enterprise Institute for Public Policy Research, 1972), p. 66.

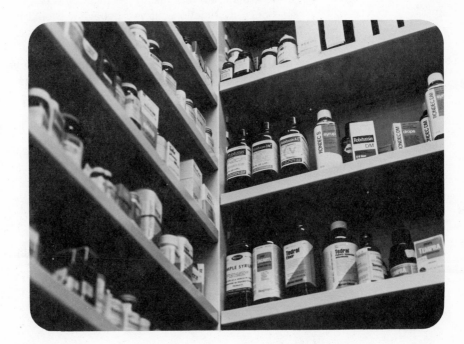

not always carefully screened the drugs they sold. The largest regulator of drugs in the United States is the federal Food and Drug Administration, established by the federal Food, Drug and Cosmetic Act of 1938, which replaced the federal Pure Food and Drug Act of 1906 signed by President Theodore Roosevelt.

Drug regulation is a difficult task. Consumers spend more than $7 billion for drugs a year, of which about $3 billion are sold only by prescription. Drugs save many lives and reduce the suffering for many illnesses. More than 90 percent of the prescriptions written today are for drugs that 30 years ago did not even exist.

WHAT THE FDA DOES

Since the Kefauver-Harris Amendment to the 1938 Act passed in 1962, the FDA has had quite detailed, extremely lengthy procedures that a company must go through before approval can be given for a new drug. The steps may take years for a drug company to complete before it can get approval for a new drug.

THE BENEFITS AND COSTS OF FDA REQUIREMENTS

Did you realize that if aspirin had to go through the current FDA requirements for drug certification, it would fail to pass muster? Do you know why? Because it is not known why it works, and it is known to have side effects if too many are taken. Certainly aspirin would at least require a prescription if it were under current rulings. Now ask yourself this: Do you think it should be dispensed only by prescription? Do you think it should be taken off the market because nobody knows how it works? Yet we are certain that taking too much of it can give you duodenal ulcers and kidney dysfunction. If you believe it should be taken off the market, then you will agree with the spirit of the 1962 Kefauver-Harris Amendment. If you have doubts, then read on.

A study was done by Dr. Sam Peltzman a few years ago. Among the costs of the 1962 FDA amendment, he found that the entry rate of new drugs into the market had slowed considerably. His conclusions were the following:

The 1952 Drug Amendment sought to reduce consumer waste on ineffective drugs. This goal appears to have been attained, but the costs in the process seem clearly to have outweighed the benefits. It was shown [in the study] that the amendments have produced a substantial decline in drug innovation since 1962.

The net effect of the amendments on consumers, then, is comparable to their being taxed something between 5 and 10% on their . . . drug purchases.[2]

[2] Sam Peltzman, "An Evaluation of Consumer Protection Legislation: The 1962 Drug Amendments," *Journal of Political Economy*, Vol. 81, No. 5 (September/October 1973), pp. 1089–1090.

As with all legislation, consumers have to weigh the costs against the benefits in deciding where they stand. The benefits of preventing certain drugs from entering the market are that no one suffers the side effects. The costs are those mentioned above. Dr. Peltzman believes the costs outweigh the benefits, but you may interpret his data differently. One thing is certain: we all have the same interpretation of the data about drug prices, and drug prices seem to be not insignificant.

RESTRICTIONS IN
PHARMACEUTICAL
SALES

Did you know that only 5 percent of prescriptions are compounded by the pharmacist? The other 95 percent the druggist fills by dropping pills into bottles and/or merely typing the patient's and doctor's names, and dosage instructions on the local druggist's label, which is then pasted on a bottle supplied by the manufacturer. Why, then, does it cost so much to get drugs? One reason is restriction of price competition among druggists: it is not considered "ethical" to advertise prescription drug prices. Thirty-seven states expressly prohibit drug price advertising. In most states, you cannot even get druggists to discuss on the phone what they charge for filling a prescription or what their prescriptions cost. They mention professional ethics.

Pharmacy practices came to light back in 1972 when the federal Price Commission then in existence was going to require that retailers display base prices of their best-selling drugs. The American Pharmaceutical Association got up in arms, claiming this would be a police state method of holding down prices. Unfortunately for us, the consumers, the Price Commission backed down; it did not require the posting of prices. Instead, pharmacies were told they could provide consumers with the standard list of wholesale drug prices and the store's professional fee or markup for filling a prescription.

Since most druggists do not post prescription prices, it is more difficult for us to shop around for bargains, as we can for other goods. It should not be surprising, then, that a 1967 AMA study in Chicago showed price differentials for exactly the same drug of 1200 percent! The U.S. Justice Department drew the obvious, logical conclusion:

Differentials such as these can only exist when they are unknown to potential customers; for a given choice, most consumers would refuse to pay 10 or 12 times the going price for a drug available elsewhere. The cost to the public of the lack of price competition is enormous.

BOSTON AN ANOMALY

As of 1973, Boston was one of the few jurisdictions in the country that required posting of prescription drug prices as an aid to consumers. (California is another, requiring the posting of prices on the 100 most frequently prescribed drugs.) The American Pharmaceutical Association (APA) opposes this Boston requirement, because price listing, the APA claims, encourages people to buy more drugs than they need and minimizes the valuable services of the pharmacist. A curious conclusion indeed, right?

It is interesting to note that the one large drug store chain in Massachusetts, Osco, was harassed with threats when it decided to comply with the new Boston ruling a few years ago. Osco found consumers overwhelmingly in favor of the program.

Osco, however, was also harassed by the Illinois Board of Pharmacy, which began proceedings to suspend licenses of Osco pharmacists on charges of "gross immorality." In many other states in which Osco showed its prescription prices in its pharmacy windows, the same harassment ensued. In North Dakota, rival pharmacists started telephoning Osco's director of professional services and called him a "prostitute" and a "traitor."

What will happen in this field is not clear. What is clear is that you, the consumer, are being taken for a ride by the American Pharmaceutical Association, which is attempting to keep the income of its members high by making you pay high prices for drugs. One way to avoid this is by getting your doctor to prescribe the generic form of the drug instead of a brand name.

ALTERNATIVE HEALTH-CARE DELIVERY SYSTEMS

The traditional health-care system has been the standard "fee for service" between doctor and private patient; but in recent decades alternatives to this system have become numerous. While we lack the space to go into all of them, we will discuss group health, and HMOs (Health Maintenance Organizations).

GROUP HEALTH

Group health service is basically a hospital made up of all different aspects of health care services in which doctors work for a salary, not for a fee. You become a member of a group health care plan by paying a specific fee determined by the number of members in your family. All group health services are then provided without charge, except for certain drugs. In some plans, you can pick your own doctors from among those on staff, in others you cannot. Group health plans stress preventive medicine in their practice. The AMA has fought tooth and nail against prepaid medical plans such as Kaiser, Group Health of Washington, Health Insurance Plan (HIP) of New York, and Ross Loos. With these medical plans, everybody is charged the same price for the same service. All plans are prepaid, and the charges are not a function of subscribers' incomes. There is no way to **price discriminate** as there is with the typical "fee for service" method of payment that most physicians use.

The AMA has used various tactics to discourage doctors from participating in group medical plans. Many doctors have been expelled from their county medical associations and therefore can practice specialties only with the group medical plan hospital. But the AMA has sometimes badly failed to squelch budding medical establishments that promoted competition with private physicians and did not price discriminate. For its efforts, the AMA has been prosecuted under the Sherman Antitrust

Act in Washington, D.C., and under other state antitrust acts. Nonetheless, about one-third of the states have declared group health plans illegal.

HMOs

Toward the end of 1974, many Americans were asked by their employers whether they wanted to drop group health insurance in favor of prepaid medical care. Those employees who chose that particular option became members of what the government calls an HMO, or Health Maintenance Organization.

HMOs run the range from group practice setups like clinics with such extras as specialists, affiliated hospitals, and dentists, all the way to individual practice foundations in which doctors continue to practice in their own offices but take HMO patients in exchange for a share of the premium.

Employees were given this opportunity to switch from group health to prepaid medical care by a provision in the Health Maintenance Organization Act signed by President Nixon late in December 1973. Under the law, any company of 25 or more workers that has some sort of group health insurance plan must negotiate a group HMO contract and offer it to employees. The legislation requires HMOs to accept individual members as well as groups of employees. (Note that this HMO concept is separate from national health insurance, which is discussed below.)

The list of basic services that must be covered by the monthly premium includes: hospital and physical care, including maternity; x-rays and laboratory tests; psychiatric treatment; emergency care; preventive health services, including regular check-ups; birth control services; alcoholism and drug abuse treatment; and, for children only, dental check-ups and eyeglass examinations.

Obviously, this coverage is more extensive than the typical health insurance program outlined early in this chapter. Thus, HMO premiums are anywhere from at least $5 a month more than a very good health insurance program, all the way up to $30 more than some group health plans.

Proponents of HMO legislation, however, point out that the higher premium cost is more than made up in savings in out-of-pocket medical expenses. Why? Simply because HMOs save considerable money on hospitalization, largely by treating people in the doctor's office instead of sending them to the hospital.

NATIONAL HEALTH INSURANCE

National health insurance is not a different way to provide medical services, but it pays for them in a different way. Note that insurance for everyone will do nothing for the supply problem in medical care. Its chief benefit will be to make sure that whatever medical services an individual obtains will be paid for by a national insurance plan. However, that plan has to be paid for somehow, and you know how it will be paid—by taxes. A national health insurance plan essentially benefits those people who are sick more often than those people who are not, unless it is organized around preventive health care.

At the writing of this book, national health insurance had not yet become a reality for all Americans. Numerous bills had been proposed in Congress, and no doubt one of them will be in effect during the first edition of this text. While Nixon was President, he proposed a Comprehensive Health Insurance Plan (CHIP). The leading alternative to Nixon's plan was identified with Senator Edward M. Kennedy. The contrast of the two plans was quite obvious. Nixon wanted to build on the existing system with private insurance companies maintaining their current role. Employees were to be offered private health insurance by their employers who would pay 75% of the premium. On the other hand, the Kennedy "National Health Security Act" would have been, in its first form, a completely public program financed by employer and employee payments to a trust fund and modeled on the Social Security system. The Kennedy plan was to offer much broader coverage than the Nixon plan.

Whatever our ways of paying for or receiving preventive health care or diagnostic medical care, one form of health care that many Americans have become increasingly conscious of—perhaps many of us even obsessed with—is the foods and nutrients we put in our bodies.

DIET AND HEALTH

Americans are becoming more and more nutrition and weight conscious. We have witnessed a veritable health revolution in the United States in the last decade. Sales of vitamins have increased by 482 percent in the last seven years. The number of health food establishments has increased by 700 percent in the same period.

HEALTH AND ORGANIC FOODS

Most of us are aware that so-called health foods are more expensive than their counterparts in regular supermarkets. Anything grown "organically" seems to cost more. Anything with that special health-food look to it and label seems to be a wee bit more expensive than its regular counterpart on the grocery shelf. Of course, you must decide whether you want to pay the extra price. Many people are concerned about the chemical natures of their diets and are therefore willing to go to great pains to have organic foods—even sometimes growing their own without the use of chemical fertilizers and pesticides. As long as you are aware of the possibility of being defrauded in your health food purchases, then you're okay if you decide to buy health foods.

There is obviously a real question as to the effectiveness of health foods and health fads. Most people in medical science indicate that you cannot expect miracles just by eating so-called natural foods and taking large quantities of vitamins. In fact, taking too many vitamins can do you harm. According to the FDA, this is particularly true for vitamins A and D. Most doctors now believe that if you eat a well-balanced diet, you are likely to get all of the vitamins you need to stay healthy.   Any supplements are generally superfluous.   If they make you feel better psychologically, however, you may still wish to take them.

DIETING

The dieting industry has also taken off by leaps and bounds.   It would have seemed amazing 15 years ago that diet books could ever be number-one best-sellers on the nonfiction list.   For example, Dr. Atkins Miracle Diet (which nutritionists and physicians say is one of the worst around) sold 1,400,000 copies in hardcover alone.   The number of diet books published every year must be in the hundreds, and the number sold in the millions.   Not only are people reading about diets, they are also increasingly visiting "diet" doctors, all of whom have a different way to help you be slim and trim.

There are numerous theories of weight gain, obesity, and weight loss. And all diets do work.   But unfortunately, none of them seems to work for very long.   All studies of the long-range effects of dieting show that within a year, about 90 percent of those who lose weight on a diet gain it all back.   That will not stop people from looking for "miracle diets." However, according to one authority on the subject, all successful diets hinge on one fundamental that is often denied:

Simply stated: calories do count.   In fact, calories are about all that count. If you take in more calories in 24 hours than you burn up in 24 hours, you'll gain weight.   If you take in fewer calories than you burn up you'll lose weight.   There is no way to get around this sad fact: it is a fundamental law of nutrition.[3]

The fact that Dr. Nolen says that eating less is the only way to lose weight does not mean you should not go to a diet doctor.   It may be psychologically important for you to obtain the counseling of a doctor or diet specialist to get you started on the right track.   You may need this additional impetus to get you going.   Again, nobody said you should not buy psychological support.

SUMMARY

1.   The relative price of health-care services has been rising.   In particular, hospital costs have gone up dramatically in the last few years.

2.   Medicare, which drastically lowered the price of health-care services to many aged people, as well as insurance schemes that do not show the consumer the direct costs of medical care, have caused the demand for medical-care services to rise dramatically.

[3] Dr. William A. Nolen, M.D., "Dr. Nolen's Magic Bringdown," *Esquire* (August 1973), p. 100.

3.   One of the reasons that medical-care services have always been so costly is because the number of medical doctors in the United States is restricted.

4.   The relatively high cost of medical care has caused many consumers to perform self-diagnosis and self-treatment.

5.   The federal Food and Drug Administration regulates the ethical drug industry in the United States.   A 1962 amendment to the Food, Drug, and Cosmetic Act has significantly lengthened the time that it takes for a drug company to get a new drug certified as safe.

6.   Until recently, in almost all states in the Union, prescription drug prices were not posted, and in fact could not be posted according to the rules of pharmaceutical associations.   This had the effect of reducing competition among pharmacies and increasing prices to consumers for prescription drugs.

7.   Alternative health-care delivery systems are now in use in the United States, such as group health and health-maintenance organizations.

8.   Health foods may not offer you the panacea you expected.

QUESTIONS FOR THOUGHT AND DISCUSSION

1.   Do you think it is fair that health-care services can rise in price?

2.   Should health-care services be a right and not a privilege?

3.   What is the difference between health-care services and other services performed in our economy?

4.   Why would insurance schemes increase the demand for hospital services?

5.   What is the argument for restricting the number of medical school graduates?

6.   The AMA has been called this nation's strongest union.   Why?

7.   Do you think more patent drugs should be sold by prescription only? Or do you think more prescription drugs should be sold without a prescription?

8.   What is the argument in favor of restricting advertising of prescription drug prices?

9.   What is the argument against that restriction?

10.   Do you think the future will see more group health-care facilities, or fewer?

11.   Why would the AMA try to stop group health care from proliferating?

THINGS TO DO

1. Discuss the argument in this chapter with someone in the medical care profession. What was left out of this argument? Is there a problem of vested interest here when you speak with someone who makes his or her livelihood by selling medical-care services?

2. Obtain a copy of a code of ethics for medical doctors, or for dentists. Is there any mention of the patient in such a code of ethics?

3. Ask a medical doctor you know why practicing MDs are not re-examined periodically.

4. Call up several pharmacies in your area to find out the price of, say, 50 capsules of 250 mgs. of tetracycline. If they will not give you the price on the phone, ask them why not. See if there is much difference among the prices quoted. If there is, ask why.

5. Visit a local health food store. See if you can determine whether the prices of fruit juice, nuts, milk, and so on are higher or lower in the health food store. If they are higher, can you figure out why?

SELECTED READINGS

"America's Health: Fallacies, Beliefs, Practices," *FDA Consumer*, October 1972.

Deutsch, Ronald M., *The Family Guide to Better Food and Better Health,* Creative Home Library, 1971.

"Diet and Coronary Heart Disease," *Nutrition Reviews,* October 1972.

First Facts About Drugs, 1712–0122 (Washington, D.C.: Consumer Product Information), 1970.

"Girth Control, Fat and Fads," *Everybody's Money*, Winter 1971–72.

Gwinup, Grant, *Energetics* (New York: Bantam Books), 1972.

"Health Insurance: A Drive to Make Policies Fit Promises," *Changing Times,* April 1973.

Hospital Expenses and Revenues: Pre-Medicare Inflation, Social Security Bulletin, October 1972.

Medicines: Participation and Over-the-Counter, FDA Fact Sheet 7700–024 (Washington, D.C.: Consumer Product Information), 1970.

1973 Heart Facts (The American Heart Association, 44 East 23rd Street, New York, New York 10010).

The Rising Cost of Hospital Care, 1955–1971 (Washington, D.C.: Bureau of Labor Statistics, U.S. Department of Labor) 1973.

Your Medicare Handbook (Washington, D.C.: U.S. Department of Health, Education, and Welfare, Government Printing Office) 1973.

CONSUMER ISSUE VIII
How to Keep Your Medical Costs Down

Waiting Period: The period during which an insurance policy is not in effect or for which you will be paid nothing on the policy. For example, if there is a waiting period of 30 days under a particular policy, you may have to be disabled for 30 days before a payment is made to you for loss of earnings.

Paramedic: A paraprofessional medical practitioner; a person with limited medical training who performs prescribed medical services, generally of a minor nature, under supervision.

Preexisting Ailment: A health defect or disease that afflicted you before you took out insurance. Generally, preexisting ailments are not covered by insurance policies.

HOW TO KEEP YOUR MEDICAL COSTS DOWN

There is no way that you can eliminate completely the costs of medical care for you and your dependents. However, you can insure yourself against at least extraordinary costs and, if you see fit, against all normal medical care expenditures throughout the year. In this consumer issue, we will give the pros and cons of different types of medical insurance coverage, including an explanation of how Medicare and Medicaid affect you.

KEEPING HEALTHY

One of the best insurance policies you can take out against excessive medical costs is a consistent, comprehensive program of keeping fit. All of us know what we *should* do, but many of us have a tendency to let ourselves become run down, hypertensive, overweight, and so on. This is not the place to go into detail about particular ideas on preventive care of the human body. Suffice it to say that the following are generally agreed to be important in keeping you out of the doctor's office for other than periodic health examinations:

1. Good diet: This means getting all the minimum amounts of vitamins and nutrients in a regular manner and in the right quantity. The right quantity is usually such that you do not become overweight, or for some persons, too much underweight. Good diet does not require a high income; as we pointed out in Chapter 8, even people with low incomes can obtain a nutritious diet if they are willing to sacrifice variety.

2. Adequate exercise: Medical men are fairly well convinced that if you exercise, you feel better, you sleep better, and you are less prone to serious cardiovascular illnesses. Again, this does not require money: For example, jogging is free in most parts of the country.

3. Moderation of foreign substances: There is much less agreement on this point than on the others, but many experts believe that if you want to play it safe, you should not abuse your mind and body with such drugs as nicotine, alcohol, hallucinogens, uppers, downers, and the like. They also counsel not becoming a patent medicine freak; hypochondria can lead to an overuse of medicines that may eventually cause serious bodily damage.

But how do you take care of the expenses when they come?

VOLUNTARY PREPAID MEDICAL CARE INSURANCE

Approximately 80 million Americans are covered under some form of voluntary, prepaid medical care insurance. These insurance plans may be either group or individual, and they cover a variety of possible expenses. We will first discuss the different coverages, and then discuss in some detail the most popular medical insurance plans in the country today: group health, Blue Cross, and Blue Shield.

TYPES OF MEDICAL INSURANCE

Below you will find five categories of medical service for which health insurance can be purchased. No doubt you can find other categories for special problems.

Hospital Expenses. Experts believe that over 90 percent of persons in the United States are now protected under some voluntary programs that will cover at least part of medical care costs arising from illness or accident. Hospital expense protection provides benefits toward full or partial payment of room, board, and services any time you are in a hospital. Usually it includes use of operating room, lab, x-rays, and medicines, and covers incidental care. Table VIII–1 shows a typical payment pattern for hospital expenses under the policy. Almost all insurance companies that issue any sort of total health insurance package will issue hospital expense insurance.

Disability Insurance. Almost 80 million persons are covered by this form of insurance which guarantees you benefits if you can no

TABLE VIII–1: TYPICAL HOSPITAL PAYMENTS UNDER A TYPICAL INSURANCE PLAN	HOSPITAL SERVICES	TOTAL HOSPITAL CHARGES	AMOUNT PAID BY INSURANCE COMPANY
	Room and Board 31 days at $65 per day	$2,015	$1,550
	X-rays, Laboratory Work, Medicines, etc.	800	400
	Use of Operating Room, Recovery Room, Cast, Dressings, etc.	150	150
	Physicians' Fees	425	180
	TOTALS	$3,390	$2,280

TABLE VIII–2:
SURGICAL INSURANCE BENEFITS

Appendectomy	$330
Gall bladder removal	500
Hernia repair	290
Tonsillectomy	140
Thyroid removal	473
Benign tumor	140
Prostate gland removal	330
Fracture, closed reduction of femur	330
Fracture, closed reduction of rib	55
Brain tumor	1,260
Intervertebral disc removal	756
Kidney removal	588
Eardrum incision	25
Boil, incision	17

longer work because of accident or illness. Such insurance compensates you for your wages lost. Sometimes this is called salary continuation insurance. Under many policies, you can expect to get 50 to 65 percent of your normal earnings if you are making average wages. Because the probability that illness will prevent you from working increases with your age, it is a good idea to get a noncancelable policy that offers you protection through your entire working life. Such a policy will be more expensive, of course. Many policies have a waiting period—that is, a period following your disability during which you receive no payments. The longer the **waiting period,** the less you have to pay for this type of insurance, obviously. Be careful when you buy health and disability insurance: find out how long the waiting period is. A one-year waiting period may render the policy useless to you except for permanent injuries. That may not be what you want; you may want the policy to go into effect 30 days after an accident or the onset of an illness.

Surgical Insurance. Almost all Americans who have some sort of hospital insurance also have surgical insurance, which pays for any of the services of a surgeon. Generally, there is a fee schedule that fixes the maximum amount;

Table VIII–2 gives an example. Any excess over the stipulated maximum must be paid either by another type of insurance policy or out of your own pocket. Since the higher the maximum limits for surgery, the higher is the cost of the insurance, you must decide what risk you want to take.

Regular Medical Protection. This type of protection pays for visits to the doctor's office as well as all x-ray, diagnostic, and laboratory expenses related to such visits. There is generally a maximum number of calls allowable for each sickness, and also a one-call deductible. In many cases, when you have your family covered under your medical insurance policy, only you, the subscriber, are covered under regular medical insurance provisions. Your spouse and your children are covered only in case of accidents.

Major Medical. What happens when a very serious or prolonged illness comes along, or a terrible automobile accident requiring $50,-000 worth of medical expenses? If you do not have major medical insurance, what happens is usually financial disaster, which may take years to pull out of. Essentially, then, major medical insurance takes over where all basic health plans discussed above stop. Over 85 million Americans are now covered under these policies. The limits range from $5000 to $50,000, and in some cases to a quarter of a million dollars. This maximum may apply to one illness or to the total of many illnesses during a policy year.

Major medical is cheaper if you have a basic policy, but often you can buy it alone, commonly in this way: after a specific deductible, say $100 to $1000, the insurance company will reimburse you for 80 percent of all your medical expenses for a single illness up to the maximum amount that you have contracted for. This is a feature called a coinsurance clause, requiring you, the policy holder, to pay 20 percent of the total bill. Most major medical coverage is sold under group plans as part of a comprehensive medical insurance scheme.

Dental Insurance

While few insurance policies cover dental work, such coverage is becoming an increasingly important part of all health insurance policies. Because it is generally provided only on a group basis, if you are not part of a group, such as a large company, government agency, labor union, and so on, you probably will be unable to buy dental insurance.

Most dental insurance is a standard prepayment plan that covers usually 80 percent of the cost of treatment after some sort of deductible, such as $50 or $100. There is a fairly low

TABLE VIII–3:
TYPICAL DENTAL INSURANCE BENEFITS

Cleaning	$12.00
X-ray	21.00
Extraction	11.00
Silicate filling	13.00
Removable Space Maintainer	56.00
Anesthesia	21.00
Crowns, Porcelain	105.00
Maxillary dentures	217.00

maximum that can be paid in any one year, usually $600 to $1000. Table VIII–3 shows the fixed allowances for different dental treatments.

Mental Health Insurance

While most health insurance does not cover this increasingly grave problem, the cost for mental health, some plans are starting to be considered. Several unions already have coverage for psychiatric services as a fringe benefit.

WHERE SHOULD YOU GO FOR HEALTH INSURANCE?

A variety of organizations will sell you health insurance. The largest are Blue Cross and Blue Shield; the next largest are the commercial insurance companies. In addition, there are labor union plans, community organization plans, and consumer cooperatives, as well as group health plans, one of which may be available in your locality.

BLUE CROSS AND BLUE SHIELD

Formed in 1929 by a group of Dallas school teachers, Blue Cross had a membership of over 500,000 by 1938. Today it has about 80,000,000 members with almost 80 Blue Cross plans throughout the nation.

Blue Shield, on the other hand, was established in 1946 by the coordinators of the Associated Medical Care Plans. Blue Shield, originally sponsored by the AMA, is sometimes known as the Doctors Plan, for the fact that Blue Shield subscribers can choose the doctor of their choice. While Blue Cross is concerned primarily with hospital insurance, Blue Shield is concerned with surgical and general medical.

Of all those who have any kind of insurance for hospital care, over 40 percent participate in one of the 63 autonomous Blue Cross plans.

Many Blue Cross group policies offer a 120-day Blue Cross plan which gives you full hospital protection for 120 days in a semiprivate room. Obviously, you save money if you can participate in a group Blue Cross plan. If you are not already aware of the possibility of joining a group plan, ask your employer, your fraternal organization, or any other organization that you may be a part of. Somewhere, some way, you ought to be able to get group coverage.

Many people take out Blue Shield as well as Blue Cross because Blue Shield covers the cost of physicians' services. Blue Shield plans contract with participating physicians to accept payment according to a preplanned fee schedule. If you select a physician who does not participate in the plan, Blue Shield gives you a cash refund up to a set amount on a given fee schedule; you make your own financial arrangements with that doctor. You can plan on paying a monthly rate of between $30.00 and $50.00 for family coverage, particularly if you are involved in a combination Blue Cross, Blue Shield arrangement.

In addition to Blue Cross/Blue Shield, there are almost 1000 nonaffiliated health insurance plans to choose from. All are independent of Blue Cross/Blue Shield, and insurance companies. However, these thousand plans cover only 5 percent of all persons receiving health care insurance. Among the most significant independent organizations are the various group health plans that you and your family can participate in for a fixed fee irrespective of your income.

GROUP HEALTH

In a group health plan, as a member you receive health care from a group health hospital where doctors are paid a salary (that is, their income is not based on the number of operations they do or the number of patients they see). Today there are about 30 to 35 community group practice plans. However, almost 95 percent of the total subscribers to group health plans belong to the largest nine. One of the largest is Kaiser Permanente Medical Care Program. It has over 2½ million members and operates in California, Oregon, Hawaii, Colorado, and Ohio. The cost varies. In 1974, for example, it cost $51.55 a month for a family of four in Washington State. This covers surgical and hospital care, but each visit to a doctor costs more and if a baby is born in the hospital, an extra charge of $150 is made. (Some group contracts may allow complete maternity coverage and free visits to the doctor.) Drugs are sold at below retail cost.

The Pros and Cons of Group Health

According to a 1967 report of the National Advisory Commission on Health Manpower, the quality of many group health plans was equal to the medical care available in most communities, and members' medical care costs were at least 20 to 30 percent less than those obtained elsewhere. Cost is controlled mainly by eliminating unnecessary health care, particularly hospitalization. One reason for this is that partner doctors generally get a year-end bonus, depending on the difference between total revenues and total costs. Doctors, therefore, have an incentive to prevent illnesses before they become serious enough to require hospitalization. It is not unusual, then, to find highly computerized testing services that check out for 50 to 100 possible medical ills and make a medical history that can be kept.

Detractors of group health care maintain that since the doctors are essentially profit sharers, they will stint on needed hospitalization. Moreover, many patients complain about the impossibility of seeing the same doctor every time. There also may be long waits for certain medical procedures.

Group Health Cooperative of
Puget Sound—Seattle

Group Health in Washington State is slightly different from many of the other group health plans. For example, it is a cooperative health care plan; all members have voting status and therefore set policy at the annual meetings.

The program serves more than 150,000 people, both members and those obtaining similar medical coverage through various group insurance plans, usually through their place of employment. The only difference between membership status and group membership status is being able to vote on policy.

Group Health Cooperative also covers all medications, including patent medicines if they are prescribed by a physician. The plan generally allows for an annual physical examination and unlimited office visits, including to specialists. There is an additional charge ($250) for delivery at the hospital, but the membership voted in 1973 to eliminate any extra charge for contraceptive services (at a cost of about 28¢ to all members). Unusual medical needs, such as dialysis, are often covered, but most apparatus (such as respirators, artificial limbs, or eyeglasses—though the latter are available at less than retail cost) that are not used in the hospital involve an extra charge. Much of the routine health care is provided by nurse practitioners and **paramedics,** but each patient is encouraged to select and regularly visit a family doctor.

WHEN YOU GET OLDER

When you get older, you may not have to bother about a private medical care insurance plan. You may be satisfied with Medicare or Medicaid benefits, although you might want supplemental health insurance as well to cover some of the aspects of medical care that those public plans do not provide for.

Medicare was created, in 1965, as an addition to the Social Security Act. It provides for hospital insurance and medical insurance, the latter being a supplementary plan for which you are charged.

Medicare Part A

The hospital insurance plan pays most of the cost of service in a hospital or extended care facility for covered people 65 years or older. You get the cost of nursing services, semiprivate room, meals, inpatient drugs and supplies, laboratory tests, x-ray and other radiology services, use of appliances and equipment, and medical social services. There is, however, a hospital deductible amount that is "intended to make the Medicare beneficiary responsible for expenses equivalent to the average costs of one hospital day." As of 1974, this deductible was $84 per hospital benefit period (defined as a period of illness not interrupted for more than 60 days). In other words, if a particular period of illness lasts for 18 days, and then the person is well for 45 days, and then ill again (that is, requiring hospitalization or confinement to a nursing home or other extended-care facility), the first and second illnesses would have occurred in the same benefit period. If the person were well for 75 days, then the new hospitalization would constitute another benefit period and again be subject to the $84 hospital deductible amount.

Under this program, any illness must commence with a hospital stay of at least three days if extended-care facilities are to be covered. After the hospital stay, any referral to an extended-care facility must commence within 14 days (except where a problem arises regarding space availability, etc.). If nursing care does not begin within 14 days, it is not covered under Medicare. And Medicare recipients are subject to later deductible amounts depending on the length of illness:

1. First 60 days: all specified benefits are covered except the $84 deductible.
2. Days 61 to 90: the same items are covered, but the deductible becomes $21 per day.
3. After 90 days: recipients are entitled to what Social Security calls their "lifetime reserve" of 60 days additional coverage, with a $42 per day deductible.

This "lifetime reserve" is just that—it can only be used once during the recipient's lifetime. If one illness requires 105 days of confinement in a hospital or extended-care facility, a subsequent illness would only have a remaining 45 days under that lifetime reserve; it does not "renew" itself, as do the other periods of coverage, with subsequent benefit periods.

Hospital insurance pays for all covered services in an extended-care facility for the first 20 days of such services in each benefit period, and all but $10.50 per day for up to 80 more days in the same benefit period provided that all of the following apply: you are in medical need of such care; a doctor has ordered such care; you have met the requirements indicated above (at least three days' hospital stay, and admittance to an extended care facility within 14 days of hospital discharge); and you are admitted for further treatment of the same condition for which you were treated in the hospital.

Subsequent to either a hospital stay or a covered nursing facility stay, you may be eligible for home health benefits, including occupational therapy, part-time services of home health aides, medical social services, and medical supplies and appliances, for as many as 100 home health visits.

All the benefits of Part A require treatment in participating health care facilities (most facilities do participate). And the law further specifies that the various dollar amounts charged to recipients, such as the $84 deductible and daily amounts, are subject to annual review, so that by the time you read this, the figures may have changed substantially. In no case does Part A cover doctor's services. But Part B does.

Medicare Part B

This supplementary medical insurance plan will help you pay for the cost of doctors' services, as well as other medical costs, if you are over 65 and a participant. There is a charge, however, which was $6.70 per month in 1974. You have to sign up as soon as you become eligible. Otherwise, when you sign up later (as you can *once* any year between January 1 and March 31), you pay a penalty fee of 10 percent for each year you were eligible but not enrolled.

Essentially, the federal government pays half of the cost of this medical insurance, and you as beneficiary pay the other half. The amount you pay is reviewed annually to insure that it is in keeping with current medical costs. Recently, however, changes in the law provided that your monthly payments cannot increase beyond the percentage increase in general Social Security benefits, so in the future the government may end up paying more than half of the coverage.

The medical insurance program helps pay for the following:

1. Doctors' fees in a hospital, office, or home for surgery and other services.

2. Home visits.

3. X-ray, surgical dressing, diagnostic services.

4. Drugs administered by a doctor or nurse as part of treatment.

5. Doctors' services for lab, x-rays, and other services (covered 100 percent if you are a bed patient in a hospital; covered as other benefits if you are not).

6. Limited services of chiropractors, ambulances, some physical therapist coverage (with a payment limitation), services of certain practitioners, such as Christian Scientists and naturopaths.

Under no circumstances should you be led to believe that the supplementary medical insurance under Medicare pays for the full costs of any of the above-listed services (with the single exception of doctors' lab, x-ray services). First, there is a $60 deductible every year. After that, you pay 20 percent and the insurance plan pays 80 percent, just as with major medical insurance. And the medical insurance does not cover routine checkups, eye examinations, hearing examinations, glasses or hearing aids, immunizations, routine

dental care, self-administered prescription drugs, nor the first three pints of blood received in any given year.

WHAT ABOUT MAIL-ORDER HEALTH INSURANCE?

You have probably seen many ads recently with pictures of famous people recommending different types of mail-order medical insurance. While some of them are not a very good deal, others are just as good a deal as any other type of medical insurance. Right now there are about 180 companies in the mail-order insurance business, covering only about 2½ percent of the total health insurance industry, but that percentage is growing. National Liberty Corporation, for example—the leader in mail-order health insurance—increased its sales about 20 to 30 percent a year for the past eight years. If you decide to buy, you must be careful about what you are getting. You should be aware that the IRS recently ruled that premiums for mail-order supplemental disability insurance policies are not tax deductible, whereas premiums for major medical and basic hospitalization policies such as Blue Cross are. (No reason has been given for this discrimination against mail-order companies.)

Reading the Ads

If you read an ad that touts coverage up to $1000 a month for hospital expenses, divide 30 into $1000 and you get the rate of $33.33 a day. Hence, you have to spend the entire month in the hospital to get that $1000. If you stayed in the hospital for only 10 days, you would get only $333.33. That is why you would never want to be caught with only mail-order supplemental insurance. It is meant to be just that—a supplement.

The premiums are low, but so, too, is the coverage. As an example, if you are 55 years old, you would be charged $120 for that $1000 a month supplemental coverage. But if you

HOSPITAL CASHIER

Albano

National Enquirer

also wanted it for your spouse who was about the same age, it would cost you about $240-$250.

Even if you buy the supplemental coverage, you may have difficulty in getting paid off because various companies have more or less strict definitions of **preexisting ailments,** by which they can reject your policy claims. Table VIII–4 shows the 10 leading mail-order health insurance companies and what percentage of premium dollars are returned in benefits. This table obviously tells you that the best deal around is group health insurance if you have no objections to its disadvantages, as outlined above.

If you pick one of the companies for mail-order insurance that gives you a pretty good payback on average—say, 60 percent or so—then you can expect to be paying for an insurance deal that is as good as any other. Mail-order insurance usually provides about one-fourth the benefits of regular insurance. But then again, it also costs about one-fourth what regular medical insurance costs. It is obviously not a superior "deal," but what many companies offer is not a gyp, either. To make sure of what you are getting into, get the Argus chart of health insurance from the National Underwriters Company, 420 East Fourth Street, Cincinnati, Ohio 45202. Or send away to the Research Institute for Quality Health Plans, Inc., 1611 Foster Street, Lake Charles, Louisiana 71601, and purchase a reformulation of the Argus chart. These two sources can serve as useful guides in choosing a health insurance company.

PROVIDING FOR THE ULTIMATE EXPENSE

We all know the cliche that nothing is certain except death and taxes. We will discuss taxes in a later chapter; first, let us briefly examine alternatives to the typical expensive American funeral.

The funeral business is indeed big business. The National Funeral Directors Association

TABLE VIII–4:

HOW TEN LEADING MAIL-ORDER HEALTH INSURANCE COMPANIES PAY OFF
(Percentage of premium dollar returned in benefits) Listed for comparison (in italics) are two companies that sell through salesmen only (Hartford and Mutual of Omaha). Also included for comparison are industry-wide averages on group health insurance (not including Blue Cross) and individual policies of all types—mail-order and non-mail order. Mail-order insurance is always an individual policy, not group. Policy type is guaranteed renewable unless otherwise noted.

90.3	*Group health insurance, average for all commercial companies*
67.2	Commercial Travelers Mutual Insurance (Utica, N.Y.)
65.8	Physicians Mutual Insurance (Omaha, Neb.), all individual policies
60.0	CNA Insurance group (Valley Forge Life, Continental Assurance, Continental Casualty), cancellable statewide.
59.4	*Hartford Life and Accident (Hartford, Conn.)*
54.8	*Mutual of Omaha (Omaha, Neb.)*
53.1	*Individual policies of all types, industry average.*
50.4	National Liberty Group (National Home Life Assurance of Missouri, National Liberty Life of Pennsylvania, National Home Assurance of New York)
49.7	Beneficial Standard (Los Angeles)
48.1	Colonial Penn Life (Philadelphia)
45.3	Bankers Life and Casualty (Chicago)
37.1	American Family Life (Columbus, Ga.)
36.0	J. C. Penney (Buena Park, Calif.)
33.5	Union Fidelity Life (Philadelphia)

Sources: 1972 Argus Chart of Health Insurance, published by the National Underwriter Co. Figures for the two groups, CNA Insurance and National Liberty, were supplied by the groups. They were not available from Argus. The figures represent 1971 business. The return listed is on the companies' major mail-order products or, in the case of Hartford and Mutual of Omaha, policies most similar to mail-order ones.

represents some 14,000 of the 27,000 funeral directors in the nation. The funeral industry as a whole is probably in for some economic difficulties in the future. The death rate is going down, and obviously the funeral market is limited by the death rate. Nonetheless, the over 25,000 funeral homes must share the less than 2 million deaths annually, and therefore the average number of funerals for each funeral home is not very large—around 80 a year. Over 60 percent of funeral homes average only one funeral a week. On the other end of the scale, there are some very famous ones —such as Forest Lawn Memorial Park in Los Angeles, which averages more than 5000 funerals a year.

The funeral industry of late has been facing increasing costs, not only for the kinds of equipment they need, such as coffins and hearses, but also for their labor needs. It is not surprising that the estimated price of a typical burial has been rising, nor that the funeral industry has become more competitive of late.

Prefinanced Plans

The Federal Trade Commission has accused a number of funeral directors of using high-pressure promotion to get people to sign up for prefinanced burial and funeral plans. Of course, there is nothing wrong with planning ahead, but you must be careful that the commission paid to a salesman who signs you up for a burial ahead of time is not excessive.

In 1975, the estimated total cost for a typical funeral service is approximately $1400. If you wish to provide for much less expensive funeral outlays for yourself or your family, a good investment would be purchasing *A Manual of Simple Burial* by Ernest Morgan.[1] This manual gives you a variety of choices which are open to you. You will find out about memorial societies, organ banks, etc.

[1] Burnsville, North Carolina: the Celo Press, Fifth Edition 1971, 63 pp., $1.50.

For example, the Continental Association of Funeral and Memorial Societies, of which there are over 100 members in operation, will arrange for a dignified but economical burial service for a member of your family. The Societies may arrange with a local firm for a cremation without embalming, which can cost less than $200.

SUMMARY

1. One of the best ways to reduce health care costs is to remain healthy by good diet, adequate exercise, and moderating the use of foreign substances.

2. Medical insurance consists of payment for hospital expenses, disability, surgery, and regular medical protection such as routine office calls.

3. In addition, major medical insurance will cover up to 80 percent of large medical expenses, sometimes up to $250,000.

4. Medical insurance can be purchased through your job, through various group plans, and individually from such companies as Blue Cross and Blue Shield, or commercial insurance agencies. If you are in doubt about the possibilities, call several insurance brokers to find out what policies are available.

5. The largest policy in effect today is Blue Cross/Blue Shield.

6. As an alternative, a group health plan may be appropriate. Generally it is cheaper than buying insurance either individually or through your place of employment. Group health services often pay for just about all medical expenses incurred except dental expenses. To find out about group health care in your area, you might check with any large employer that offers a variety of health options to its employees. Or write any of the large group health plans, such as Group Health Cooperative of Puget Sound or H.I.P. in New York City; most major group health plans have a policy of easy transfer among each other, so they are likely to maintain a listing of other similar programs.

7. Medicare is a hospital insurance plan that pays most of the cost of service in a hospital or extended-care facility for covered individuals 65 years of age and older. If this is something you are concerned about, it is best to call your Social Security Office to get the exact coverage that would be available for you. There are Social Security Offices in just about every major city in the United States. Or you can write the Social Security Administration, Washington, D.C., for this information.

8. If you are older, you may wish to partake in supplementary medical care insurance provided by Medicare Part B.

9. Mail-order health insurance is certainly not as good a deal as the advertisements indicate. However, it may be a useful supplement and should be looked into carefully for those who do not carry large amounts of medical insurance to begin with. Generally, though, mail-order insurance should be used as a supplement, not as a substitute for another insurance policy.

10. *A Manual for Simple Burial,* by Ernest Morgan (about $1.50) will give you information on simple, low-cost burials that can be provided for ahead of time.

QUESTIONS FOR THOUGHT AND DISCUSSION

1. Has exercise only recently been proven to be important for your health?

2. Teenagers are notorious for their poor diets. However, the teen years are generally the years when most individuals have the least amount of illness. Why?

3. Do you think that the medical insurance industry should be more strictly regulated in the premiums it charges individual members?

4. Why is it cheaper to be a member of a group insurance plan than subscribe individually?

5. When would it be worthwhile to purchase a major medical policy with a large limit, say $250,000?

6. Do you think group health is a workable concept?

7. Do you prefer to have a doctor whom you see all the time, or would you like to see a variety of doctors? Would this influence your answer to question 6?

8. Medicare costs much more than individual recipients put in. Who pays for the difference?

9. When would you want to have a mail-order insurance policy?

THINGS TO DO

1. Obtain the payment schedules for at least two medical insurance plans. Make comparisons between the two. If they are vastly different in coverage and payment, does this difference correspond to a distinct difference in the premiums that must be paid? If not, what do you think is the reason for the difference?

2. Find out about dental insurance in your area. Can you figure out why it has taken so long for dental insurance to catch on?

3. Order some of the free booklets from your local office of Blue Cross/Blue Shield. Read through them to see if the information there can give you an indication of why medical costs have been rising so rapidly.

4. Compare the coverage and payment schedule for a private insurance plan, such as Blue Cross/Blue Shield, with what would be covered under Medicare Part A and Medicare Part B.   Which is a better deal?

SELECTED READINGS

"An X-Ray Analysis of Doctors' Bills," *Money*, August 1973.

"Controversy on Pending National Health Insurance Proposal," *Congressional Digest*, February 1972.

Cooper, Barbara S., "The Who, What and Where of Medical Care Spending," *Family Economics Review*, March 1971.

Effect of Co-Insurance on Use of Physicians Services, Social Security Bulletin, June 1972.

"Group Therapy for Runaway Medical Bills," *Money*, May 1973.

"Health Insurance: Get the Facts Behind Those Ads," *Changing Times*, April 1972.

Simmons, Henry E., "Brand vs. Generic Drugs: It's Only a Matter of Name," *FDA Consumer*, March 1973.

CHAPTER PREVIEW

☐ What are the principles behind life insurance?
☐ What are the different types of life insurance?
☐ How does whole life compare with term insurance?
☐ What are the different types of living and death benefits and how can they be received?
☐ What are annuities, and why would you want them?
☐ What is Social Security all about and what are its defects?

GLOSSARY OF NEW TERMS

Term Insurance: Life insurance that is for a specified term (period of time) and has only a death benefit: it is a form of pure insurance with no savings aspect.

Whole Life Insurance: Insurance that has both death and living benefits. That is, there is a savings aspect to the policy by which part of your premium is put into a type of savings account.

Annuity: An amount payable yearly or at other regular intervals. Also, the right to receive or the obligation to pay such an amount.

Living Benefits: Benefits paid on a whole life insurance policy while the person is living. Living benefits include fixed and variable annuities.

Underwriter: The company that stands behind the face value of any insurance policy. The underwriter signs its name to an insurance policy, thereby becoming answerable for a designated loss or damage on consideration of receiving a premium payment.

Home Protection Plan: Another name for decreasing term insurance where the policyholder pays a uniform premium throughout the life of the insurance policy but the face value of the policy declines, much in the way the mortgage due on a house declines. That is why it is called a home protection plan.

Income Transfer: A transfer of income from some individuals in the economy to other individuals. This is generally done by way of the government. It is a transfer in the sense that no services are rendered by the recipients. Unemployment insurance, for example, is an income transfer to unemployed individuals.

We have discussed automobile insurance, home insurance, liability insurance, and medical insurance at some length. These are basically forms of protection, or income security. Two additional forms of protection not yet discussed are life insurance and social security, which we now turn to.

SECURITY

A sense of security is important for most families. In fact, psychologists contend that the average American wants a sense of security more than just about anything else in his or her life. Some of the major hazards to *financial* security are listed below with the ways that Americans provide for these hazards:

1. Illness: health and medical insurance; a savings account for emergency; Medicare and Medicaid
2. Accident: accident insurance; a savings account; state workmen's compensation; Social Security
3. Unemployment: a savings fund for such an emergency; unemployment compensation
4. Old age: private retirement pension plans; savings account; annuities; Social Security old age insurance
5. Premature death: survivors' insurance under the Social Security Act; life insurance

PREMATURE DEATHS

The mortality rate in the United States has been on the decline for many years now, as it has in the rest of the world. People are suffering from fewer fatal diseases than they used to, and are living longer, as can be seen in Figure 13–1. Nonetheless, every year there are at least 300,000 deaths. For example, in 1971, 282,034 males and females from the ages of 25 to 55 died. In many cases, a premature death can lead to financial hardship for dependents. This is true not only if a man dies, but also if a woman dies. Consider that when a woman who is responsible for a household and children, dies, those responsibilities must be made up after the premature death. This can bring financial hardship to a family unit. The same is true when the major wage earner dies, but in a more obvious manner. Both cases call for financial protection against the bur-

FIGURE 13–1

LIFE EXPECTANCY
At the start of the
twentieth century the
average American at
birth could expect to
live a little more than 47
years. By the middle of
the century this number
had jumped to almost
70. Source: *Historical
Statistics of the United
States*, U.S. Bureau of
the Census, p. 25, and
Department of
Commerce.

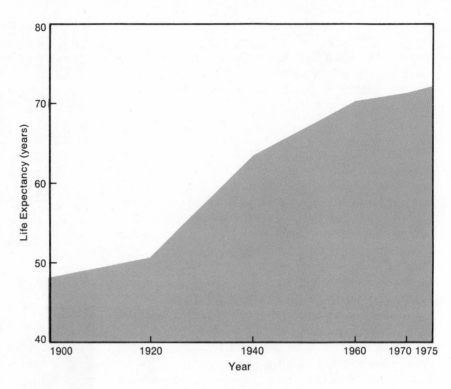

den imposed by such a premature death. Just about everybody will agree
with that, and therefore it is not unusual to find an extremely large life insurance industry in the United States.

**SELLING
LIFE INSURANCE**

The life insurance industry in the United States has grown by leaps and
bounds. In 1900, there were a mere 84 life insurance companies selling
some 14 million policies that had a total value of only $7.5 billion. By the
beginning of the 1960s, there were some 1441 companies selling 282 million policies, with a face value of $10,200 of life insurance per family.
By the beginning of the 1970s, there were 1800 companies and the average
American family had $20,900 in life insurance.

Employment in the insurance industry has also been growing by leaps
and bounds. In the last 30 years, it has increased from 600,000 to 1.53
million. We can expect that the industry will continue to grow as the
American economy grows.

**PRINCIPLES BEHIND
LIFE INSURANCE**

Life insurance is just like any other type of insurance: if the risk is spread
among a large enough number of people, the premiums that have to be
paid will be small compared to the coverage offered. In any particular
age group, only a very small number will die in any one year. If a large

percentage of this age group pays premiums to a life insurance company in exchange for a benefit payment in case of premature death, there will be a sufficient amount of money to pay off the survivors of those few who die.

Given a long enough time for collection of data about the group and about the particular disaster—in this case, premature death—insurance companies can predict with great accuracy the total number of premature deaths in any one year. They therefore can estimate exactly the total payout they will incur if they insure the group, and hence they can predict the rates for each member of the group in order to meet this payout, plus a profit for the company.

THE DIFFERENT TYPES OF LIFE INSURANCE

Although the insurance principles outlined above are simple to grasp, the variety of insurance programs that you can purchase are indeed many and complex. In this chapter we outline some of the basic types of life insurance policies. In the consumer issue following this chapter are some ideas to help you determine your own life insurance needs, and some recommendations about what is the appropriate type of insurance for you.

Life insurance falls basically into two types—term or whole life—but there is also a variety of others that we will discuss.

THE TWO BASIC TYPES OF INSURANCE

In one sentence, term insurance offers pure protection, whereas whole life combines protection with a savings plan. (Whole life is also called straight life or ordinary life; these are merely different names for the same life insurance.)

WHOLE, STRAIGHT, OR ORDINARY LIFE INSURANCE

Whole life insurance accounts for perhaps half of the total value of all life insurance in force in the United States. The average payoff value of such policies is around $10,000. Life insurance salespersons will almost always try to sell you a whole life policy because it is more profitable for them and their companies.

PREMIUMS

Whole life premiums generally remain the same throughout the life of a policy. As a result, the policyholder pays more than is necessary to cover the insurance company's risk in the early years, and less than would be necessary to cover the company's risk in later years. Table 13–1 gives an example of a $10,000 ordinary life insurance policy with an annual level premium of $222.70 for a male aged 35. In the first year, of the $222.70, $205.50 goes the the insurance company to cover insurance costs, and $17.20 goes to the savings fund for the purchaser of the policy. By the sixth year, the deposit to savings is greater than the level annual premium, and stays greater throughout the life of this particular policy. You can see in the summary of this policy that by the twentieth year—that is, when our policyholder is 55 years old—there is a total amount of cash value, or savings, in that policy of $5608.97, after having paid in $4454. The savings aspect of this policy, then, is $1154.97. That is, at the end of 20 years, the policy represents a type of savings account.

Owners of whole life policies often take comfort in the fact that their premiums are level and therefore represent one of the few costs that do not go up with inflation. True, the cost is relatively high to begin with, but it gets no higher. The exact level of premiums that you would pay for a $10,000 ordinary life insurance policy as represented in Table 13–1 depends on your age when you buy the policy; the younger you are the less it will be because the company expects to collect many years of premiums from you. The older you are, the greater it is.

As we will see when we compare whole life with term insurance (to be discussed below) whole life is relatively expensive because it is a form of financial investment as well as an insurance protection. The investment feature is known as its "cash value." In Table 13–1, the cash value at the end of 20 years was in excess of $5000, and at age 65, was actually in excess of the face value of the policy. You can, of course, cancel a whole life policy at any time you choose to and be paid the amount of cash value it has built in. Individuals sometimes "cash in" a whole life policy at the time of their retirement when the cash value can be taken out either as a lump sum, or in installments called **annuities**, which are discussed at the end of this chapter. These are the so-called living benefits of a whole life policy.

LIVING BENEFITS

Living benefits are the opposite of death benefits. The death benefit of a life insurance policy is obviously the insurance that you have purchased. The living benefit, on the other hand, includes the possibility of converting an ordinary policy to some sort of lump sum payment or retirement income. In any one year, up to 60 percent of all insurance company payments are in the form of these so-called "living" benefits.

Note that the level premium for a whole life policy is paid throughout the life of the policyholder—unless you reach the ripe old age of, say, 95 or 100.

BORROWING ON
YOUR CASH VALUE

One of the features of a whole life insurance policy is that you can borrow on its cash value any time you want. The interest rate on such loans is relatively favorable. However, if you should die while the loan is outstanding, the sum paid to your beneficiary is reduced by the amount of the loan. In any event, the borrowing power given you in the cash value of a whole life insurance policy can be considered a type of cushion against financial emergencies. However, if you ever have to drop a whole life insurance policy because you are unable to pay the level premiums, or because you are in need of its cash value, you most certainly will take a big loss. And, of course, you will give up the insurance protection.

TABLE 13–1:
COMPOSITION OF SAVINGS AND
OPERATING CHARGES IN 20-YEAR
ORDINARY LIFE PREMIUMS

$10,000 ORDINARY LIFE

Dividends [1] to Purchase Paid-Up Additions

Annual Premium: $222.70   Male Age: 35

YEAR	DEPOSIT TO SAVINGS	DEPOSIT TO INSURANCE	TOTAL SAVINGS
1	$ 17.20	$205.50	$ 17.20
2	179.71	42.99	196.91
3	190.43	32.27	387.34
4	201.97	20.73	589.31
5	213.47	9.23	802.78
6	225.43	2.73–	1028.21
7	237.14	14.44–	1265.35
8	250.35	27.65–	1515.70
9	262.61	39.91–	1778.31
10	275.17	52.47–	2053.48
11	270.17	47.47–	2323.65
12	282.60	59.90–	2606.25
13	294.64	71.94–	2900.89
14	306.82	84.12–	3207.71
15	320.64	97.94–	3528.35
16	333.21	110.51–	3861.56
17	346.11	123.41–	4207.67
18	360.95	138.25–	4568.62
19	376.12	153.42–	4944.74
20	391.60	168.90–	5336.34

SUMMARY

	20TH YEAR	AT AGE 65
Total Savings	$5608.97 [2]	$10,566.83 [1]
Total Deposits	$4454.00	$ 6681.00
Net Gain	$1154.97–	$ 3885.83–

[1] Dividends are neither estimates nor guarantees, but are based on the current dividend scale.
[2] Includes Terminal Dividend.

WHEN YOU REACH
RETIREMENT AGE

When you reach retirement years, you can discontinue premium payments on a whole life policy and choose one of the following:

1. Get protection for the rest of your life, but at a lower value;
2. Get full protection, but for a definite number of years in the future;
3. Get a cash settlement which gives back whatever savings and dividends that have not been used to pay off the insurance company for excessive costs it has incurred for your particular age group;

4. Convert the whole life policy into an annuity where a specified amount of income is given each year for a certain number of years.

DEATH BENEFITS

In most life insurance policies, you specify a beneficiary who receives the death benefits of that policy. If you bought a $10,000 ordinary life policy and have not borrowed any money on it, and you die, your beneficiary will receive $10,000. However, there are certain options that can be used for settling a life insurance policy. Before you purchase any insurance policy, the particular settlement terms that are available should be discussed with the underwriter of that insurance. There are generally four option settlement plans that can be decided upon:

Plan 1: Lump sum payment.
Plan 2: The face value of the insurance policy is retained by the insurance company, but a small interest payment is made to the beneficiary for a certain number of years or for life. At the end of a period, the principal is then paid to the children or according to the terms in the contract.
Plan 3: The face value is paid to the beneficiary in the form of installments, either annually, semiannually, quarterly, or monthly.
Plan 4: Regular life income is paid to the beneficiary. The insurance company guarantees a specified number of payments, or payments that will total to the face value of the policy. If, however, the beneficiary dies before the guaranteed payments have been made, the remainder goes to the estate of the beneficiary or as directed in the contract. This is sometimes called an annuity plan.

In sum, whole, straight, or ordinary life insurance gives you pure insurance plus forced savings and, hence, the possibility of retirement income as can be seen in Figure 13–2. Remember, though, that instead you can buy pure insurance, that is, term insurance, at a lower cost than whole life. You can invest the difference in your own saving and retirement plans and perhaps be better off (or at least no worse off) if you can get a higher rate of return on your savings than the insurance company offers. The latest research suggests that whole life can be a sensible long-term investment for those who could otherwise expect their own investments to earn only about 4 percent *after taxes*. But if, on your own investments, you can make 5 percent or more after taxes, whole life may not be the type of policy for you.

LIMITED-PAYMENT
WHOLE LIFE

Limited payment is whole life insurance with a slight twist: it is payable only at the death of the insured, and the premiums are payable only for a stated number of years, or until the insured reaches a certain age, such as 60 or 65. That is, the insurance is called limited because payments are limited to 10, 20, 25, or 30 years: if you took out a limited whole life policy with a 20-year payment life, you would have to pay premiums for 20 years,

Example based on $50,000 of ordinary life, age 35 (male)

(dividend accumulation plan 1)

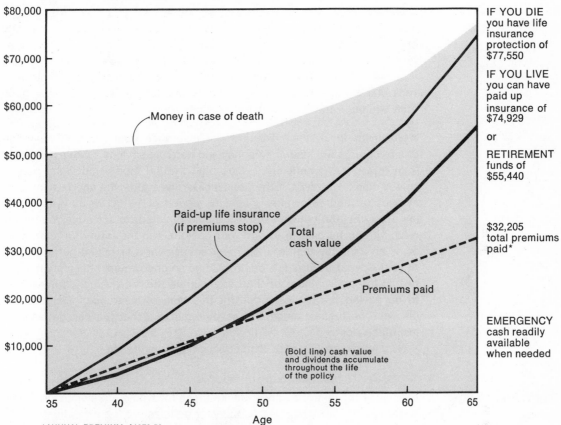

*ANNUAL PREMIUM: $1073.50

†Dividends and interest are computed on the 1973 dividend scale and are neither estimates nor guarantees for the future.

A terminal dividend is payable upon surrender, lapse or death after at least fifteen policy years, but only if declared by the Company at such time. Premiums and cash values in this illustration can not be prorated for other amounts.

FIGURE 13–2 HOW WHOLE LIFE INSURANCE WORKS TO PROVIDE BOTH SAVINGS AND PROTECTION
Here you see a typical whole life insurance policy for a 35 year old male with a face value of $50,000. It's "cash value" is represented by the bold line. The annual level premium is $1,073.50. Source: New England Mutual Life Insurance Company.

after which the entire policy would be paid up, while regular whole life premiums are paid until you, the insured, dies. Obviously, the premium rate must be considerably higher for this type of policy than for an ordinary life policy, because it is fully paid up at a much earlier date. The distinguishing feature between limited life and whole life is that while the premiums are level in both cases, they end after a specific time period with a limited policy, but continue until the death of the insured in a standard whole life policy.

Generally, for any fixed amount of money that you want to spend on insurance, limited-payment life policies give you less protection when you are young than either whole life or term insurance does. Limited-payment life insurance might be appropriate if you expect to have a very short career at a high income level, such as a professional athlete or a rock star does. For the rest of us mere mortals, it is not usually a good idea, although there are some exceptions.

Endowment Insurance. This type of insurance policy is a combination of a temporary life insurance policy and periodic savings. While the policy is in force, the beneficiary will be paid the full face value if the policyholder dies. However, if the policyholder lives after the endowment policy ends (at age 65 or after a specific period of 10, 20, or 30 years), you, the policy holder, get the face value paid to you or to someone you designate. It can be paid to you or your designate in the form of a lump sum, or as an annuity—that is, a payment either over a specified period or until your or your designate's death. Since an endowment policy guarantees to pay the policyholder or the beneficiaries the face value, you are sure to be paying the highest price for this type of insurance. But you will also get the highest amount of savings out of it that you can get with an insurance policy.

Now let us discuss pure protection, or term insurance.

TERM INSURANCE

Premiums for term insurance, unlike those for whole life, commonly go up every year or every five years (one-year policies are the exceptions) if you wish to keep the same face value on your insurance policy. The increased premium reflects the rising probability of death as age increases. Thus, it will cost you relatively little to buy term when you are 25 years old, but by the time you are 60, your premiums will have risen dramatically. However, by that time you probably will not want as much term insurance because your children will be well on the way to financial independence and you will have built up other forms of financial resources for any dependents you still have. That means that you can reduce the premium burden by reducing the amount of insurance carried to protect your family. Families often then choose term insurance that has a level premium, but a decreasing face value. (This is sometimes called a **home protection plan,** or decreasing term.)

Standard term insurance is often labeled one-year term, or five-year term, because those are common intervals, or terms, between premium increases. Other periods are also available. A term policy is called renewable if the coverage can be continued at the end of each period merely by payment of the increased premium without the need of a medical examination. The renewability feature must of necessity add to the cost of the policy, but if you wish to preserve your insurability despite any changes in your health, you certainly would want to pay the extra costs for this feature. Term policies are commonly renewable until the policyholder reaches some age of retirement, such as 65 or 70. All coverage then stops.

In one sense, the premiums for any term policy are constant for the life of the policy, but since most term policies are written with a one-year or five-year "life" the constancy of premium is not too meaningful. The premium is truly constant throughout a long period of time only with *decreasing* term insurance, in which the face value falls every year.

CONVERTIBILITY

Often, riders can be attached to term policies which give you the privilege of converting them into other than pure insurance without the necessity of a medical examination. You pay for this additional feature, however. If you have a convertible term policy, you can convert it into whole life without any problems. The main reason you might want to convert is to continue your coverage after you pass 65 or 70. After converting the policy, you would pay whole life premiums based on your age at the time of conversion. Most insurance experts believe that the two features mentioned above, convertibility and renewability, should be purchased. They give you much flexibility at a not inappropriate additional cost. Table 13–2 shows (a) $50,000 yearly renewable term insurance for a male aged 35. If this man keeps $50,000 of term insurance until age 65, he will pay in a total of $17,893. He will have no cash value in the policy, as he would in a whole life policy.

OTHER TYPES OF
LIFE INSURANCE
POLICIES

In addition to ordinary life insurance, which you buy as an individual, you may be eligible for certain other types of life insurance policies that are generally offered to you at more attractive rates.

Group Insurance. Group insurance is usually term insurance written under a master policy that is issued to either a sponsoring association or an employer. Some types of group insurance are currently offered to employees of universities and large businesses, to members of ski associations and professional associations, and the like. Per $1000 of protection, the cost of group insurance is generally lower than individually obtained insurance for many reasons, but the two main ones seem to be the lower selling costs and the lower bookkeeping costs. The selling costs are lower because the employer or sponsoring group does all the selling; there is no commission to be paid to a selling agent. And the bookkeeping costs are lower because, again, the employer or the association may do all the bookkeeping. Generally, no medical examination is required for members of the group unless they want to take out an abnormally large amount of group insurance. Today there are perhaps 400,000 master group life insurance policies outstanding in the United States.

TABLE 13–2:

A TYPICAL $50,000 YEARLY
RENEWABLE TERM POLICY

YEAR	ANNUAL PREMIUM
1	$165.50 [1]
2	172.50
3	181.00
4	192.00
5	204.50
6	219.00
7	235.00
8	252.00
9	270.50
10	290.50
11	312.50
12	339.00
13	368.00
14	400.00
15	435.00
16	473.50
17	515.50
18	560.50
19	609.50
20	642.50
20th Year Total	$6838.50
Total At Age 65	$17,893.00

[1] Dividends are neither estimates nor guarantees, but are based on the current dividend scale.

Industrial Insurance. This type of insurance involves weekly premiums, usually costing 10, 20, or 50¢, which are collected at the home by an insurance agent. The insurance agent visits the home and writes a receipt for these very small sums. Industrial policies are written for very small face values, usually $500, or no more than $1000. Believe it or not, there are 85 million industrial policies in force today. The average death payment is, of course, small and so the percentage of the total amount of life insurance in force is small.

Savings Bank Insurance. As of the mid-1970s, only three states offered savings bank insurance: New York, Connecticut, and Massachusetts. You must either live or work in those states in order to purchase the insurance. The rates are quite low because, again, there are no selling costs. You go directly to the savings bank to buy the insurance. Generally, savings bank life insurance gives you a better deal than other forms of life insurance offer, but, of course, you do not get the benefits of any information that salespersons from other commercial companies might be able to give you.

Credit Life Insurance. If you take out a loan, in many cases now you are forced to buy insurance, in the amount of the loan, on your life. The reason is simple: without such insurance, if you die with part of the loan outstanding, the creditor may have trouble collecting it. But if the creditor is named the beneficiary in the life insurance policy you are required to take out as part of the loan, then the creditor is assured payment of any remaining amounts due. Today there are almost 100 milion credit life insurance policies outstanding. The average amount per policy is small, being perhaps $1300. Since most credit life insurance is written on a group basis, it is relatively inexpensive. However, be careful, because a creditor may in fact be abusing the right to force you to take out insurance. Check to see that the rate you are actually paying is commensurate with other group policy rates. If it is not, then the difference you pay should be added to the total finance charge in order for you to figure out the true percentage rate of interest that you are paying on the loan.

ANNUITIES

Unlike life insurance, an annuity is issued on a bet that you will not live. An annuity pays the policyholder for living; it generally provides for periodic payment of a fixed sum, either yearly, monthly, or weekly. Certain kinds of annuities provide for partial retirement income and therefore eliminate the need to pay, for example, large life insurance premiums as in a level payment plan discussed above. Annuities can provide safe retirement income in a relatively easy manner (you cannot readily spend your savings), and can also provide tax advantages by deferring income tax payments until a later date, when most individuals are in a lower marginal tax bracket. There are several types of annuities, among them the relatively new variable annuities.

VARIABLE ANNUITIES

Under this type of annuity, you can either pay small sums into a plan over a period of years, or pay a large sum shortly before retirement to provide retirement income. This is the only type of annuity that may be "inflation-proofed," as the sum you receive on a fixed regular basis is not in itself fixed; it varies with the stock market return, for the money you pay in is invested in the stock market. Your payments depend on the market value of the common stocks in your account.

Variable annuities often yield a greater return than fixed annuities. Of course, this is in part due to the greater risk involved, because if the stock market declines during the period when you are collecting against your variable annuity, so, too, does the amount you receive in payments.

FIXED ANNUITIES

The commonest type of annuity is a fixed annuity. Fixed annuities are of two general kinds, named according to the time at which the income is to start:

1. **Deferred life annuity:** This type of fixed annuity is most often purchased a number of years before retirement age. It can be purchased either by making annual premium payments over a number of years, or by paying a lump sum some years before the annuity income would begin. Either way, payment is made some years before the date on which you desire income to begin.

2. **Immediate annuity:** This type of fixed annuity is usually purchased just before retirement, often in place of or in exchange for a level-payment whole life policy. Its premium must be paid in a single lump sum.

Whether you choose a deferred or an immediate annuity, there are several options, at different prices, as to the kinds of payments you will receive:

1. **Straight life:** You are guaranteed a fixed income for life, but all payments cease at your death (in this case, the company providing the annuity is clearly betting on your death);

2. **Temporary:** You are guaranteed a specified income for a certain length of time only.

TABLE 13–3: COMPARISON OF COSTS OF TWO KINDS OF ANNUITY

IMMEDIATE SINGLE PREMIUM ANNUITY (Income to Begin at Once)

Age		Monthly Income per $1000			Cost of $10 of Monthly Income		
Male	Female	Straight Life	10 Years Certain	Installment Refund	Straight Life	10 Years Certain	Installment Refund
50	55	$4.93	$4.88	$4.73	$2030	$2050	$2110
55	60	5.51	5.41	5.20	1838	1847	1920
60	65	6.30	6.08	5.81	1605	1644	1721
65	70	7.36	6.87	6.56	1375	1455	1524
70	75	8.80	7.73	7.50	1145	1293	1331

DEFERRED ANNUAL PREMIUM ANNUITY (For Men Age 65 When It Starts *)

	Monthly Income per $100 a Year Purchase			Cost per year of $10 of Monthly Income		
Age at Issue	Straight Life	10 Years Certain	Installment Refund	Straight Life	10 Years Certain	Installment Refund
30	$33.17	$31.33	$30.38	$ 30.15	$ 31.92	$ 32.92
35	26.49	25.01	24.50	37.75	39.98	40.82
40	20.57	19.42	19.03	48.61	51.49	52.55
45	15.34	14.49	14.20	65.19	69.01	70.42
50	10.71	10.12	9.92	93.37	98.81	100.81
55	6.62	6.26	6.13	151.06	159.74	163.13

* A woman would receive 15 to 20 percent less in annuity income per $100 of annual premium than a man of comparable age at issue.

TABLE 13–4: COMPARISON OF ANNUITY AGAINST SAVINGS OR INVESTMENT

		COST OF AN ANNUITY	RETURNS ON INVESTING OR SAVING THE SAME AMOUNT TO YIELD $100 A MONTH TO LIVE ON		
Purchaser:	Life expectancy:	$100 a month guaranteed for life costs:	You can live on dividends or interest only if your money earns:	With lower earnings, you can tap both interest and principal and your money will last:	And if still living, your life expectancy will then be:
A woman age 62	19½ years (49% live at least 20 years)	$17,300	7%	At 3%, 19 years At 4%, 22 years	At 81, 9 Years At 84, 7½ years
A man age 65	14½ years (27% live at least 20 years)	$13,750	8¾ %	At 3%, 14 years At 4%, 16 years	At 79, 7½ years At 81, 7 years

3. **Installments certain:** You are guaranteed income for the remainder of your life; in addition, you are guaranteed payments for a certain period—say, 10 or 20 years—even if you do not live that long. If you live longer than the guaranteed period, you still receive income, since this payment plan guarantees that period in addition to income for the length of your life.

4. **Installment refund:** In this case, you are again guaranteed payments for life. In addition, rather than a guarantee for a specific period, your heirs are guaranteed installment payments until such time as the balance on what you paid is returned.

5. **Cash refund:** This plan is similar to the installment refund, except that at your death the balance is paid to your heirs in a lump sum.

6. **Joint and survivorship:** Two or more persons (usually husband and wife) are guaranteed an income for life as long as either is living. This type of payment plan most clearly eliminates the need for life insurance.

It should be noted that annuities are a relatively expensive investment; that is, they yield a relatively low rate of return. Table 13–3 shows some average costs of annuities. And Table 13–4 indicates how annuities compare with other types of investment. As with whole life insurance, an important factor to consider when thinking about annuities is how well you could invest in alternative income-producing assets, and this includes considering the forced savings nature of annuities. In most cases, younger persons should invest in some form of life insurance before considering annuities. And it is perhaps best to diversify your investments anyway; there is no ideal investment designed to meet every individual's needs.

FIGURE 13–3
U.S. POPULATION
OVER 65

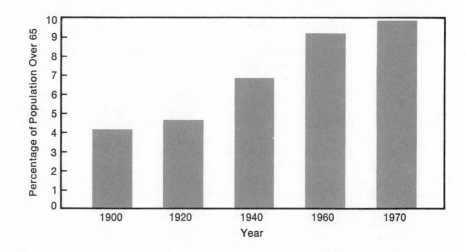

INVOLUNTARY BENEFIT PROGRAMS — THE CASE OF SOCIAL SECURITY

During the depths of the Depression, the nation realized that numerous people had not provided for themselves in case of emergencies. It was also realized that a large percentage of the elderly population, which could not rely on its children for support, became destitute. In an effort to prevent a recurrence of so much pain and suffering by elderly people, the Congress passed the Social Security Act of 1935. By January 1940, when the first monthly benefit started, only 22,000 people received payments. Today, however, well over 90 percent of people 65 or older are receiving Social Security benefits, or *could* receive them if they were not still working. Today, over 13 percent of the population is receiving all or part of its income from the Social Security Administration. If U.S. population growth continues to slow down, the average age of the population will continue to rise. Hence, the total number of people eligible and on Social Security will increase as a percentage of the total population. Figure 13–3 shows the past and projected percentage of the population 65 and over.

Now, why did we entitle this section "Involuntary Benefit Programs" ? The reason it is involuntary is because you and I, with few exceptions, have no choice. If we work, we must participate in the Social Security program. Self-employed people had been able to avoid it, but today they must pay self-employment Social Security taxes if they do not work for someone else. If you work for someone else, your employer must file Social Security taxes for you if you earn over $50 in any quarter. Of the people earning money in the United States, those who contribute to Social Security make up fully 95 percent. There is no way to escape it. Why Social Security has been made obligatory is sometimes difficult to decipher, but basically, according to supporters of the program, it is to insure that all older Americans have at least a basic living income and hence will not need welfare payments.

THE PROVISIONS OF
THE SOCIAL
SECURITY ACT

The Social Security Act provides benefits for old-age retirement, survivors, disability, and health insurance. It is therefore sometimes called the OASDHI. It is essentially an **income transfer** program, financed out of compulsory payroll taxes levied on both employers and employees, whereby those who are employed transfer income to those who are unemployed. One pays for Social Security while working and receives the old-age benefits later on in life after retirement. The benefit payments are usually made to those reaching retirement age. Also, when the insured worker dies, benefits accrue to his or her survivors. There are special benefits that provide for disabled workers.

Additionally, Social Security now provides for Medicare, which we outlined in the last chapter. The unemployment insurance provision of the Social Security Act of 1935 is not really a federally operated program of unemployment insurance. Rather, it is left to the states to establish and operate such programs. Although all 50 states have these programs, they vary widely in the extent and the amount of payments made. Programs are basically financed by taxes on employers. These taxes average less than 2 percent of total payroll. A worker who finds himself or herself unemployed may become eligible for benefit payments. The size of these payments and the number of weeks they can be received vary from state to state. In 1972, for example, over 1,840,000 workers were obtaining unemployment payments that averaged about $56 a week. Currently, about 70 million people are covered by unemployment compensation.

**BASIC BENEFITS
OF SOCIAL
SECURITY**

In the following Consumer Issue you will learn where to get information with which to tentatively figure the benefits that you are allowed under Social Security. (The predictions must be tentative because what future benefits will be is changed by Congress often.) But right now, to discuss the basic benefits you can count on, Social Security in essence is a form of life insurance. It is valued at something over $80,000 of the decreasing term type we talked about above. Every time you have a child, the maximum life insurance benefit of Social Security is automatically restored, and its term is automatically increased to a potential 21 years. Here is what you can expect from Social Security:

1. Medicare payments in the future.
2. If you should die, payments to your beneficiary.
3. If you should die, payments to your children until they have gone through college.
4. Payments to you or your dependents if you are totally disabled and unable to work.
5. A retirement annuity—that is, a payment of a certain amount of money every month after you retire until you die. This payment, however, is legislated by Congress and can be changed by Congress.
6. If you die, a modest lump sum payment, presumably to take care of burial expenses.

Whenever you figure out your insurance needs, you must first consult the basic coverage that you have on your Social Security. You will learn how to do that in the following Consumer Issue. Table 13–5 gives a detailed idea of benefits.

PROBLEMS WITH SOCIAL SECURITY

A number of respected researchers have looked into Social Security and come to some pretty depressing conclusions. In the first place, you have to remember that Social Security is not really an insurance policy in the sense that you are guaranteed a certain amount of money. You get that amount of money only if you die, just as with a regular insurance policy; but if you live, you get retirement payments that are a function not of how much money you have put in, but rather of what Congress legislates. Future Congresses may not be as kind as past Congresses. You may find yourself with a very small retirement income if you rely only on Social Security.

HOW SOCIAL SECURITY IS PAID

Social Security is paid by a tax on the employee's income that is matched by the employer. However, you must realize that generally you, the em-ployee, pay for much of the whole thing because your wages could be all that much higher if the employer did not have to contribute. The tax on Social Security for 1975 was set at 5.85 percent on the worker's income, and therefore an equal amount paid by the employer. This tax, however, is applied only to the first $14,100 a year.[1] After that, it no longer is applicable. Hence, the Social Security contribution, otherwise known as a payroll tax, is highly regressive. The tax rates, moreover, have been increasing rapidly, more than doubling since 1967. Nonetheless, few seem to have seen the regressive nature of this particular income tax, and the fact that for the majority of taxpayers it is greater than the income taxes they pay.

IF YOU WORK, YOU DO NOT GET PAID

The Social Security Act, as it currently stands, penalizes you tremendously if you decide to remain working past the retirement age (65), for you can earn only $2400, after which you get reductions in your Social Security check. If your earned income exceeds that figure, Social Security benefits are reduced $1 for every $2 earned. "Earned" has a very strict meaning here. It means income that is made as a wage-earner, not as dividends, interest, or pensions. If you decide to invest a lot of money, you can be making millions of dollars and still get full Social Security. But if you decide to be a hard worker and continue getting wages, you may lose all of your Social Security payments if you earn, for example, $5000

[1] By law this tax base automatically rises whenever the rate of inflation reaches specified levels.

TABLE 13–5: HOW TO FIGURE YOUR BASIC SOCIAL SECURITY COVERAGE PER MONTH

AVERAGE YEARLY EARNINGS AFTER 1950	$923 OR LESS	$1,800	$3,000	$4,200	$5,400	$6,600	$7,800	$9,000
Retired worker 65 or older; disabled worker under 65	$ 84.50	$134.30	$174.80	$213.30	$250.60	$288.40	$331.00	$354.50
Wife 65 or older	42.30	67.20	87.40	106.70	125.30	144.20	165.50	177.30
Retired worker at 62	67.60	107.50	139.90	170.70	200.50	230.80	264.80	283.60
Wife at 62, no child	31.80	50.40	65.60	80.10	94.00	108.20	124.20	133.00
Widow at 60	73.30	96.10	125.10	152.60	179.30	206.30	236.70	253.50
Widow or widower at 62	84.50	110.80	144.30	176.00	206.80	238.00	273.10	292.50
Disabled widow at 50	51.30	67.30	87.50	106.80	125.50	144.30	165.60	177.30
Wife under 65 and one child	42.30	67.20	92.50	157.40	217.30	233.90	248.30	265.90
Widowed mother and one child	126.80	201.50	262.20	320.00	376.60	432.60	496.60	531.80
Widowed mother and two children	126.80	201.50	267.30	370.70	467.90	522.30	579.30	620.40
One child of retired or disabled worker	42.30	67.20	87.40	106.70	125.30	144.20	165.50	177.30
One surviving child	84.50	100.80	131.10	160.00	188.00	216.30	248.30	265.90
Maximum family payment	126.80	201.50	267.30	370.70	467.90	522.30	579.30	620.40

a year. It is conceivable that you could work till the age of 70 and never get one penny of benefits from Social Security, even though you were forced to pay in your entire working life. Your decision to work after age 65 certainly will be influenced by this highly regressive taxation system. I say "taxation system" because you are obviously taxed if for every dollar you earn, you get to lose 50¢ in Social Security benefits. That sounds like a tax rate of 50 percent, does it not? (That is in addition to taxes that you pay already, such as Social Security and income.) This seems a bit steep since under the federal personal income tax system, the 50 percent marginal tax rate does not apply to individuals unless they make incomes of well over $30,000. But for people over 65, this 50 percent rate starts at $2400.

This is one aspect of the Social Security program that many observers feel is quite unfair. It penalizes work for older people. Professor Carolyn Shaw Bell, of Wellesley College, also points out that the Social Security system is not insurance, but rather a transfer. People who are working pay Social Security taxes. People who get Social Security benefits receive the income that is taxed away. Essentially, it is a subsidy from younger workers to older, retired people. There is also a transfer from those who continue to work after 65 to their peers who do not work. At the beginning of this decade, for example, there were 3 million people over 65 in the labor force, a full 22 percent of older men and 10 percent of older women. These 3 million people, according to Professor Shaw Bell, are "unjustly hemmed in between bleak job market prospects, on the one hand, and the necessity, on the other, of paying out of their meager earnings to support not only themselves but others of their own age." That is to say, of course, that these three million people who are working are continuing to pay Social Security taxes.[2]

**OTHER FACTS
ABOUT
SOCIAL SECURITY**

As Carolyn Shaw Bell points out, Social Security is not truly an insurance program: contributions do not go into a trust fund that is used to pay you an annuity when you retire.

Those who view the payroll tax as a contribution to a trust fund would have trouble understanding how Social Security actually works. The trust fund in 1974 was approximately $50 billion, enough to cover perhaps one year of benefits. A private insurance program or pension fund must, by law, have a trust fund that at any moment could finance all of the benefits promised to its members. But the benefits owed members of Social Security are valued at more than $2.1 trillion! Those who have suggested that individuals be allowed to voluntarily withdraw from the system have been lambasted by such supporters of Social Security as Nelson Rockefeller and the late President Johnson. Rockefeller predicted that such withdrawal would lead to the collapse of the Social Security system.

If this is so, then we must conclude the system is not actuarially sound, as trust funds are legally required to be. Rockefeller's prediction is unquestionably correct. Note, however, that at the system's inception in 1935 it was hoped that by around 1960 it would be actuarially sound. This hope was not realized because the trust fund built up huge surpluses immediately. Thus, although in 1940 the Social Security tax was to go up, it did not. The increase was delayed for a long time. In fact, it was not until 1950 that it did rise to 3 percent (1.5 percent on each party). Additionally, coverage has been greatly expanded.

What is actually taking place is that those who are working today are paying taxes to finance retirement payments to those who are no longer working. Each year there has been a slight surplus, which has been put into the relatively small trust. But what does the trust really do with those "surplus" social security contributions? It purchases U. S. Government bonds, thus helping to finance such things as military expenditures. If you and I were really contributing to a quasi-private trust fund, such use of our contributions would be deemed inappropriate, to say the least.

If you contribute to a private insurance or pension plan, what you ultimately receive is based on how much you put in. There is, to be sure,

[2] Carolyn Shaw Bell, *Challenge* (July/August 1973), p. 22.

a relationship between how much you put into social security and how much you get out, but it is a tenuous relationship at best. In 1971 the maximum wage-related benefit was about three times the minimum, whereas the maximum so-called average monthly wage on which benefits were based was eighty times the minimum sufficient to qualify. But the range would be even greater if account were taken of the total number of years the worker has paid into Social Security. The fact is that the benefits received are much more closely related to your marital status or the number of children in your family than to how much money you have paid in.

There are other anomalies in the benefit payment system that could not be justified if Social Security were truly an insurance system. For example, the later you enter the system, the better off you are, because as long as you worked the minimum number of quarters, you will receive the same benefits as someone else who has worked many, many more. Who profits by this? Generally, the wealthier in our society benefit because they start work later. But this is not the only benefit to the high-income class. People with higher incomes generally have longer life expectancies and will therefore tend to receive payments for a longer period. Blacks are discriminated against doubly because they go to

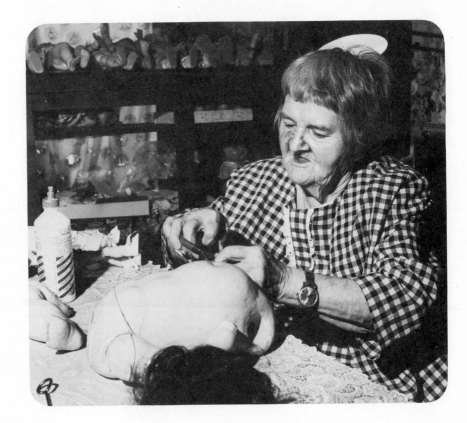

work sooner and die much earlier. And because of the regressive nature of the tax, the higher your income, the higher is the ratio of benefits received to taxes paid. It is not surprising that Social Security has been labeled the poor man's welfare payment to the middle class.

Clearly, then, Social Security pays very different benefits to individuals who have paid in "contributions" of exactly the same amount; and, on the other hand, Social Security will pay exactly the same benefits to individuals who have paid in vastly different "contributions."

The government has on occasion contradicted itself when referring to the insurance principle of Social Security—more precisely, it has been selective in its invocation of that principle. For example, in a court test of the constitutionality of the rule prohibiting benefit payments to persons deported for subversive activities, the Social Security Administration rejected entirely the insurance concept: "The OASI [Old Age, Survivors Insurance] is in no sense a federally-administered 'insurance program' under which each worker pays 'premiums' over the years and acquires at retirement an indefeasible right to receive for life a fixed monthly benefit, irrespective of the conditions which Congress has chosen to impose from time to time." There we have it. The insurance principle is officially endorsed in support of all Social Security *taxes* and rejected when benefits are denied.

To call Social Security an insurance scheme requires a special skill in deforming the meaning of words in the English language.

SUMMARY

1. The major hazards to financial security are illness, accident, unemployment, old age, and premature death of the person giving financial support.

2. Life insurance can take on many forms, the most popular being term and whole life.

3. Whole, straight, or ordinary life insurance involves pure protection in addition to a savings plan whereby part of your premiums are put into investments that return interest to the policyholder. At any time, a whole life policyholder has a cash value in his or her policy.

4. Whole life insurance has living benefits: you can, for example, borrow on your cash value; you can get protection for the rest of your life at retirement; you can get a cash settlement; and you can convert your whole life policy to a stream of income—called an annuity—over a certain period of time.

5. Death benefits can be paid to your beneficiaries in a lump sum equal to the face value, or as interest on the face value of the insurance policy plus principal at the end of a specific period, or in installments until the face value has been paid.

6. Term insurance is generally for a five-year period, after which time a higher premium must be paid to obtain the same face value in insurance because the probability of death has increased as the individual becomes older.

7. Term insurance is cheaper than whole life insurance. However, there is no cash value in the insurance policy—it is pure insurance.

8. An annuity can be obtained from an insurance company to provide income for retirement or for some other purpose. There are fixed annuities and variable annuities, the latter making a payout depending on the rate of return in the stock market whereas the former has a fixed payout because only fixed income investments, such as bonds, are purchased by the company issuing the annuity.

9. Social Security is a form of social insurance in the United States. It provides for living and death benefits.

10. However, Social Security is not an insurance policy in the normal sense of the word. Basically, contributions to Social Security are merely transfers from those who work to those who do not work.

11. Information about the basic benefits that you are allowed under Social Security can be obtained from the Social Security Administration, Washington, D.C., or your local office.

12. Social Security taxes are paid both by the employer and by the employee. However, in the economy as a whole, employees receive salaries that are lower by the amount that employers must pay to Social Security. After all, that payment is a cost of hiring employees.

13. Under current law, individuals from 65 to 72 who work often lose benefits from Social Security because their incomes are too high. In addition, they continue to pay Social Security taxes.

QUESTIONS FOR THOUGHT AND DISCUSSION

1. Who do you think should have life insurance?

2. Why would an insurance salesperson try to sell you a whole life policy?

3. Why is life insurance cheaper for college students than for older adults?

4. When would it be worthwhile to borrow on the cash value of a whole life insurance policy?

5. Do you know anybody who would be a good candidate for limited-payment whole life insurance? Would you ever be a good candidate?

6. Why would someone choose decreasing term insurance with a constant premium rather than level term insurance with an increasing premium?

7. When do you think it would be appropriate to have a convertibility feature in your term insurance policy? That is, when do you think it would be advantageous to pay the extra price to have the option of changing your term insurance into whole life insurance?

8. Why do you think group insurance is cheaper than individually written insurance?

9. If you had the choice, would you choose a variable or a fixed annuity?

10. Do you think Social Security is a good deal?

THINGS TO DO

1. Try to determine whether life insurance companies make a higher profit than other companies in the United States.

2. Phone several life insurance agents in your area and ask what the premium cost is of a $10,000 straight or whole life insurance policy. Is there great variation? Then see if you can find the actual costs to the companies involved in *A Shopper's Guide to Life Insurance* issued by the Pennsylvania Insurance Department in 1972. Comparing cost to the companies with premium rates, what can you infer?

3. Check newspaper ads for mail-order life insurance policies. In light of the analysis presented in this chapter, how do you interpret the claims made?

SELECTED READINGS

Annuities from the Buyer's Point of View, Economic Education Bulletin 10.7, American Institute for Economic Research, August 1970.

Belth, Joseph M., *Life Insurance Price Measurement* (Bloomington: Indiana University, Graduate School of Business, Bureau of Business Research), 1969.

Denenberg, Herbert S., "Insurance in the Age of the Consumer," *Best's Review,* April 1970.

Goodwin, Dave, *Stop Wasting Your Insurance Dollars* (New York: Simon & Schuster), 1969.

Lidster, Ralph E., *The Economics of Life Insurance* (10419 Bogardus Avenue, Whittier, California 90603).

Life Insurance from the Buyer's Point of View, Economic Education Bulletin X.6, American Institute for Economic Research, July 1970.

Pechman, Joseph A., Henry J. Aaron, and Michael K. Taussig, *Social Security: Perspectives for Reform* (Washington, D. C.: The Brookings Institution), 1968.

Report on Life Insurance, rev. ed. (Mount Vernon, N. Y.: Consumers Union), 1972. (New edition forthcoming.)

Steinhell, Charles M., "Variable Life Insurance," *Best's Review*, October 1970.

CONSUMER ISSUE IX
How to Meet
Your Insurance Needs

Before you go on in this Consumer Issue to figure out how much insurance you should buy, what type it should be, and where you should get it, first sit back and think about who should be insured in your family. You have to take into your account the Social Security benefits you have coming, and that sometimes is not easy. You then have to look at the actual economic (or financial) dependency that anybody has on a particular member of a spending unit. If you are a single college student, for example, it is usually not recommended that you have any insurance at all (unless you want to use it as a forced savings mechanism, or as insurance against becoming medically uninsurable later on in life). By the same token, it is usually absurd for a family to insure its children unless the children contribute a substantial amount to the family income. If the unfortunate day occurs when one of them dies, the family's earning power generally will not fall. This is not necessarily true for a wife, however; she frequently contributes explicitly to the family earnings stream by employment outside the home, or implicitly through the implicit value of her services rendered to the family. In this case, the family unit may want to take out an insurance policy on her life. The basic wage-earner should, of course, be the one with the most insurance because if he or she dies prematurely, the *spending* unit will suffer the greatest loss.

SOME INSURANCE BUYING RULES

1. Identify the major risks that you and your family reasonably face; insure them according to the *potential* loss that they can produce.

2. Insure big losses, not small ones.

3. Never buy an insurance policy of any type until you have compared at least two, and perhaps more, companies, not only on the costs but on the terms of coverage.

4. Limit your losses and control your risk through preventive measures.

ARE YOU UNDERINSURED?

There is a good chance that you are underinsured if anybody depends on you for even part of their livelihood. If, however, you live alone or are young and unmarried, or even are married but your spouse also contributes explicitly to the family kitty, then you may not need much (if any) life insurance. If, however, you are married, have children, or a spouse who depends on you for at least part of his or her income, then you probably should have some form of life insurance. You should first realize that Social Security is at the basis of all your protection needs. You will have to find out from your local Social Security office exactly what kind of benefits your dependents—or yourself, for that matter—have coming in case of your death.

In this Consumer Issue an assumption will be made that you yourself should make when trying to figure out your insurance needs: assume that you drop dead tomorrow. How much would be left for your dependents, in what form, and over what period? This is not an easy thing to figure out, so plan on spending some time. You may want to work it out with an insurance agent, but you can probably do it on your own.

GETTING YOUR SOCIAL SECURITY FIGURED OUT

The first thing you should do is write the Social Security Administration, giving them your Social Security number and the name on your Social Security card and asking for a current report of your account. After you have received this, take it to your local Social Security Office and request the following facts:

1. Survivors' benefit for a mother and one child under 18.

2. Survivor's benefit for a child 18 through 21 as a full-time unmarried student.

3. Survivor's benefit for a mother and two or more children under 18.

4. Maximum family payment allowed.

5. Widow's pension benefits starting at 62; widow's pension benefits starting at 60.

6. Total disability benefits for the wage earner, wife, and two or more children.

7. Total disability benefits for wage earner, wife, and one child.

The Social Security Administration will also gladly send you a booklet that will help you figure this all out yourself.

Now that you have this information, you can figure out the financial condition of your family. Go back to page 138 and see how a net worth statement was done when you applied for a loan. Figure out your net worth, for that gives you a starting point. The average net worth of American families in the United States is estimated at $25,000.

You now have two major details of your financial situation in case you have dependents and die tomorrow: Social Security payments to your dependents and a net worth that is left to them. Now you must figure out a monthly income goal for spouse and children under 18, a lump-sum education-fund goal for each child, a monthly retirement income goal for a widow (or widower) starting at age 62, and a monthly income goal, if any, for a widow (or widower) between child-rearing and retirement. This latter is optional depending on whether or not you want the widow (or widower) to have to work.

FIGURING OUT HOW MUCH INSURANCE YOU SHOULD BUY

Neither you nor anyone else can estimate *exactly* how much life insurance you should buy. That depends not only on all of the factors mentioned above, but also on how "safe" you want to be. After all, buying insurance means that part of your income can no longer be used for other purchases. You have to decide how much you want to give up in order to be "fully" insured. Nonetheless, you can get a general idea of how much life insurance you need by roughly estimating the income you would require to maintain the level of consumption you are used to. This means figuring out basic monthly expenditures for the entire family (minus expenditures that would have been made solely for the deceased), including such things as mortgage payments. In Table IX–1, we give a list that you might want to fill in to estimate your family's monthly expenses. Next you must estimate the monthly income (independent of any insurance benefits, of course) that would be available after the death of one of the income-earners in the family. These include all of the items listed in Table IX–2.

Putting it all together

What you next have to do is put together your estimated monthly income and your estimated monthly expenses to find out the deficit that must be made up by life insurance proceeds. In Table IX–3 are computed, as an example, the annual needs that must be made up by life insurance for a typical family with expenditures of $1040 per month. Table IX–3 is almost self-explanatory; all we have done is make predictions for a number of years into the future. These predictions included expenditures, benefits, and so on. What we have left out are the earnings that living members of the family can contribute to making up annual needs. That's why we have put in question marks. We have also put in a question mark about how much the proceeds from life insurance must be to make up the difference between annual needs and earnings of the living family members.

TABLE IX–1:
FAMILY MONTHLY EXPENSES

Housing	$_____
Utilities & Household Operation	$_____
Clothing	$_____
Food	$_____
Medical Care	$_____
Automobile Expenses	$_____
Recreation	$_____
Incidentals	$_____
Total Needed Per Month	$_____

TABLE IX–2:
MONTHLY AVAILABLE INCOME

Social Security	$_____
Income from Any Investments	$_____
Earnings of Living Members of the Family	$_____
Job-Connected Survivor Benefits	$_____
Trusts and Other Income	$_____
Total Income Per Month	$_____

Tomorrow is not the same as today

We all realize that tomorrow will not be the same as today. This is particularly true when we think about what our basic monthly expenditures will be. After all, in our current period of rising prices, it becomes difficult to predict from today's prices what the future cost of living will be. If this isn't complication enough, you must realize that an insurance policy, if paid off in one lump sum payment, can be invested to yield a stream of income. That means that if you require proceeds of, say, $10,000 a year for ten years, you need not buy an insurance policy with a face value of $100,000. Instead you can buy one with a lower face value, and if premature death occurs, a less than $100,000 lump sum payment could be invested so that $10,000 a year would be forthcoming and at the end of ten years nothing would be left of the lump sum payment. But the problem of trying to evaluate future dollars by today's dollars is a rather complicated problem, particularly when we don't know how well investments will do in the future. Table IX–4 presents one example of the monthly income(s) provided per $1000 of life insurance proceeds paid out by an insurance company as an optional alternative to the lump sum payment. You can get a rough idea of how much life insurance you need by taking an average of the monthly needs from Table IX–3 and using

Table IX–4 to decide how much insurance to buy. If, for example, you required $596 a month for the next 18 years, you would want to buy a $100,000 life insurance policy. Of course, that's probably too high a face value, given that you can receive higher than 3 per cent even from insurance companies. Note, though, that as the cost of living rises every year, you will need more than you planned. Even though the interest rate you can earn on the insurance proceeds will go up, the increase may just cover the increase in the cost of living, so using Table IX–4 may not actually be that conservative an approach to deciding how much insurance you need.

NOW THAT YOU HAVE FIGURED OUT HOW MUCH, WHAT SHOULD YOU BUY?

Say that you calculate that you need $50,000 worth of life insurance. What should you do? A number of life insurance plans were represented in the previous chapter, the most important being term, whole life, limited-payment whole life and endowment. All but term insurance include some element of saving. Thus, you are not only buying pure insurance, you are also investing and getting a rate of return. Your decision whether to buy pure insurance or to buy savings will determine the payments you must make to the insurance company. The cheapest way to buy insur-

TABLE IX–3:

Annual needs that must be made up by life insurance for a typical family with expenditures of $1040 per month

	Years in Future				
	1–3	4–10	11–13	14–30	Retirement
Basic monthly expenditures including house payments	$1040	$1240	$1100	$ 900	$ 700
Deduction of deceased's expenses	150	150	150	150	100
Expenditures without the deceased	$ 890	$1090	$ 950	$ 750	$ 600
Income not work-related Social Security	$ 400	$ 360	$ 300		$ 300
Job-connected survivor benefits Inheritance	200	200	200 280	200	200
Total benefits not work-related	$ 600	$ 560	$ 780	$ 200	$ 500
Monthly needs (expenditures minus benefits not work-related)	$ 290	$ 530	$ 170	$ 550	$ 100
Annual needs (monthly needs x 12)	$3480	$6360	$2040	$6600	$1200
Earnings of living family members per year	?	?	?	?	?
Life insurance needs	?	?	?	?	?

ance is, of course, to buy term: you buy only protection. If you already have a satisfactory savings program, you may not wish to save additional sums with an insurance company. Many insurance experts agree that the cheapest insurance you can buy is term, and if you want additional saving features, you will get a higher rate of return by going elsewhere than insurance companies.

Consumers Union points out, as do several other research organizations, that if purchasing whole life insurance is compared with buying term and investing the difference—that is, the difference between the whole life premium and the lower term premium—the combination of term and other investments will yield a larger sum of money at the end of any period. A critic of this conclusion, Mr. Herbert S. Denenberg, contends that this comparison is true only if you manage to get somewhere around a 6 percent rate of return on your savings (over a long period of time) if you invest them yourself. He contends that if you expect to get only 4 percent, you are better off buying whole life.[1] We will see in the following chapter on savings and investment that it is quite difficult *not* to get 6 percent on savings in a variety of ways. Therefore, we will stick to the conclusion that your best bet is buying term insurance and making your savings plan without involving an insurance company.

However, insurance salespersons have numerous arguments as to why you should not buy term insurance but, rather, whole life. They will say that whole life is a bargain, or even "free," because you eventually get back much or all of your money. Note, however, that if you die, your beneficiary will get only the face value on the policy and not the additional cash value. Salespersons use the cash value aspect of whole life to tout its de-

[1] Herbert S. Denenberg, "Consumers Union: No Help for Insurance Shoppers," *Business and Society Review*, No. 6 (Summer 1973), pp. 107–108.

TABLE IX–4:

MONTHLY PROCEEDS PER $1000
OF LIFE INSURANCE

The monthly income provided per $1000 of face value on a life insurance policy, based on an interest rate of 3 percent. This interest rate is obviously very low by today's standards, since a savings and loan account will yield much more than that. This table thus gives a very conservative idea of how much income would come from $1000 of insurance. If you had $100,000 of insurance, you would simply move the decimal point two places to the right: for example, $100,000 worth of life insurance would provide $596 a month in income at an interest rate of 3 percent, if this particular option were chosen from an insurance company.

NO. OF YEARS	
2	$42.86
3	28.99
4	22.06
5	17.91
6	15.14
7	13.16
8	11.68
9	10.53
10	9.61
11	8.86
12	8.24
13	7.71
14	7.26
15	6.87
16	6.53
17	6.23
18	5.96

sirability over term insurance. Since term has no cash value, salesmen will tell you that it is "just throwing money down the drain." This "down the drain" argument ignores the fact that the term premiums are lower than whole life premiums in the early years. For a man 25 years old, whole life premiums in the early years may cost three to four times more than term premiums.

What if You Need Someone to Force You to Save?

If you like the idea of having forced savings, then buying whole life insurance may be the way to do it. The insurance premiums are something you feel you have to pay and you know that part of the premium goes to a savings plan. The lower rate of return on savings left with an insurance company is compensated for by the fact that you have any savings at all, savings that you would not have had otherwise because you have no will power. This is something only you can decide.

If Your Income Is High

As another argument for favoring whole life over term, some insurance agents point out that for individuals in extremely high income brackets, it may be better to buy whole life insurance, borrow on that insurance to pay the premiums, and be able to deduct the interest payments on the borrowing from ordinary income so that taxes do not have to be paid.

SOME ADDITIONAL CONSIDERATIONS

A fact that we have not yet mentioned about permanent or whole life insurance policy contract is that it is essentially a piece of property and has certain characteristics that are perhaps unique. Under current law, provided that the permanent insurance plan is set up properly, it can accumulate income, tax free; dividends as well as interest on cash value are not taxable as current income. Essentially, then, you get a higher return than is actually shown in your life insurance saving plan because you are not paying a tax on the savings you are accumulating. Remember that if you have a regular savings account, you have to pay federal and sometimes state income tax on the interest earnings of that account.

Another fact that may or may not be important for most individuals is that death benefits on ordinary or straight life insurance

policies usually go to age 100, so that except in very rare cases there is always going to be a death benefit.

TAKE ADVANTAGE OF GROUP PLANS

Whenever you can take advantage of group term insurance plans, you probably should do so to take care of at least part of your life insurance needs. For reasons mentioned in the previous chapter, group insurance is generally cheaper than individually issued insurance.

SHOPPING AROUND FOR INSURANCE

One thing is certain: it generally is unwise to buy insurance from the first insurance salesperson who knocks on your door. Since large sums of money may be involved, it is usually advisable to look over several plans. Be warned, however: life insurance policies are incredibly complex. If you can find a knowledgeable insurance salesperson who represents a large number of companies and who can explain the benefits of each program and give you in simple language the average annual costs per $1000 of, say, five-year renewable term insurance, you are well on your way to being able to pick a company to insure you. To help you out, the average annual costs for a number of companies are listed in Table IX–5. These are not the only ones you can go to, and in fact, some of you are not eligible to participate in, for example, Teachers Insurance and Annuity Association of America, unless you are a teacher or staff member in a school or university, or an educational scientific institution.

SHOULD YOU GET A PARTICIPATING OR NONPARTICIPATING POLICY?

Any life insurance policy that you buy is either participating or nonparticipating. The former pays dividends to the policyholder and the latter does not.

A dividend is merely an annual payment

TABLE IX–5: FIVE–YEAR RENEWABLE TERM POLICIES

	POLICY SIZE	20–YEAR GROSS PREMIUM	20–YEAR DIVIDENDS [1]	20–YEAR NET PAYMENT	AVERAGE ANNUAL NET PAYMENT	AVERAGE ANNUAL COST PER $1000
New York State mutual savings banks	$30,000	$ 5,041.50	$1,950.30	$3,091.20	$154.56	$5.51
Massachusetts mutual savings banks	43,000	6,815.50	2,337.48	4,478.02	223.90	5.21
Institute of Electrical and Electronics Engineers (Washington, D. C.) group plan	50,000	8,412.50	2,903.77	5,508.73	275.44	5.51 [2]
National Life Insurance Co. (Montpelier, Vt.)	50,000	9,750.00	2,882.50	6,867.50	343.38	6.87
Teachers Insurance and Annuity Assn. of America (New York City), individual policy	50,000	9,815.00	2,653.50	7,161.50	358.08	7.16 [2]
Connecticut Mutual Life Insurance Company (Hartford, Conn.)	50,000	9,572.50	1,736.50	7,836.00	391.80	7.84
National Life Insurance Company (Columbus, Ohio)	50,000	12,347.50	4,159.00	8,188.50	409.43	8.19
Berkshire Life Insurance Company (Pittsfield, Mass.)	50,000	11,655.00	3,269.50	8,385.50	419.28	8.39
Prudential Insurance Company of America (Newark, N. J.)	50,000	11,515.00	2,916.50	8,598.50	429.93	8.60 [2]
Metropolitan Life Insurance Company (New York City)	50,000	11,280.00	2,665.00	8,615.00	430.75	8.62 [2]

[1] Based on 1966 dividend scales.
[2] Includes waiver of premium for total disability.

to the policy holder made at the company's discretion. Although the premiums for policies that pay dividends are higher than those that do not, the true or actual cost of a dividend-paying policy might be lower in the long run if the dividends are sufficiently high to compensate for the higher premium payments. When you buy a participating policy, the salesperson can only tell you the current scale of dividends. This does not, however, indicate what future scales may be, so you cannot get an accurate picture of the true payments you will be making on your policy. Note, however, that since World War II, the dividends paid in participating plans have generally been better than those projected.

If you do not want to take any chances, you will not opt for a participating plan, but, rather, a nonparticipating one. The initial premiums for a nonparticipating plan will be lower and you may consider that a virtue.

Should You Pay Monthly, Quarterly, or Yearly?

Your decision on how you should pay for insurance should be based on convenience. If it is inconvenient for you to pay annually, then perhaps you should pay on a quarterly basis, or even a monthly basis. But remember, like everything else, if you pay on other than a yearly basis, you usually pay a service charge, so it is best to compare the difference between, say, 12 monthly payments and one annual payment to see if you want to pay the implicit interest rate on the loan you are getting.

Alternatively, you can have some insurance companies arrange with your bank to send your insurance payment in directly every month. For example, Allstate has a plan whereby, for example, a 21-year-old male with $10,000 worth of life insurance would pay a monthly premium of $11.60 if he elected to handle the payment, but would only pay $10.98 per month for the same coverage if he elected to use what Allstate calls its "check plan." Under that plan, the smaller amount is deducted automatically by the bank each month from the individual's checking account. It saves Allstate some money in billing costs, and they pass part of the savings on to the customer. Often under such plans, the monthly payments cost no more per year than an annual or quarterly payment plan.

SUMMARY

1. In deciding whom to insure, make your decision basically on who is dependent on whom and what financial stress would be undergone when an individual prematurely dies.

2. Basic insurance buying rules are: **(a)** identify and insure major risks according to potential loss, (b) insure big rather than small losses, (c) always compare at least two companies on costs in terms of coverage.

3. If you want a forced saving plan, then you may wish to purchase whole life insurance. However, if you can save on your own, you generally will do better by purchasing lower-cost term insurance and putting the difference in high (long-run) income-yielding assets such as long-term savings certificates, the stock market, and so on.

4. Shopping for insurance requires the same skills as shopping for any other consumer product: information is the key. You may wish to consult *Consumer Reports'* special issues in 1974, which rate life insurance companies by their respective costs.

QUESTIONS FOR THOUGHT AND DISCUSSION

1. Can you think of any reason why children should have life insurance?

2. Can you think of any reason why a college student should purchase life insurance?

3. Are you underinsured?

4. Are you overinsured?

5. If you are relatively young, is it possible for you to figure out what Social Security will pay you on retirement?

6. Who should buy term insurance as opposed to whole life?

THINGS TO DO

1. Try to determine whether you are overinsured or underinsured. If you are underinsured, go to the next project.

2. Call at least two, preferably three or four, insurance agents. Take the time to sit down with each of them to discuss your insurance needs. Find out what their recommendations are for an adequate amount of insurance. Ask why they are not suggesting you purchase term or decreasing term insurance.

3. Take a look at the special reports in the 1974 issues of *Consumer Reports.* If you already have insurance, see where your insurance company rates relative to other ones. Would it be worthwhile for you to change policies?

SELECTED READINGS

Denenberg, Herbert S., *A Shopper's Guide to Life Insurance* (Harrisburg, Pa.: Pennsylvania Insurance Department), April 1972.

Denenberg, Herbert S., "The Decline and Fall of Cash Value Life Insurance," *Best's Review*, October 1970.

Denenberg, Herbert S., *The Insurance Trap: Unfair at Any Rate* (Racine, Wis.: Western Publishing Company), 1972.

Fogiel, Max, *How to Pay Lots Less for Life Insurance* (New York: Research and Education Association), 1971.

"Forces Reshaping Social Security," *Business Week*, July 15, 1972.

"How Much Life Insurance Do You Need?" *Changing Times*, January 1972.

"Six Fine Points to Check in Your Life Insurance Policy," *Changing Times*, July 1973.

CHAPTER PREVIEW

☐ How much do Americans save every year?

☐ Why do people save, and what determines how much they save?

☐ What is the nature of compound interest?

☐ What are the various types of savings institutions?

☐ What are some of the general facts about investing and the yields on investments?

☐ What is the stock market all about?

☐ Is it ever possible to "get rich quick" in the stock market?

GLOSSARY OF NEW TERMS

Saving: The act of not consuming or spending your money to obtain current satisfaction.

Stock Market: An organized market where shares in businesses are traded. These shares are generally called stocks. The largest stock market in the United States is the New York Stock Exchange. The second largest is the American Stock Exchange.

Securities: Another name for shares or stocks in a business.

Compound Interest: Interest that earns interest. For example, if you put a dollar in a savings account that earns 5 percent each year and you leave the interest in, it is compounded. At the end of the first year you would get 5 cents interest; at the end of the second year you would get interest of 5 percent times $1.05, or a compound interest of 5.25 cents.

Equities: A legal claim to the profits of a company. This is another name for stocks, generally called common stocks.

Bonds: A type of debt that a business or a government issues to investors. A bond represents a promise to pay a certain amount of money (called **interest**) each year. At the end of a specified amount of time, the principal on the bond is repaid to the bondholder.

Capital Gain: The difference between the buying and the selling price of something you own when the selling price is higher than the buying price.

Capital Loss: The difference between the buying and the selling price of something you own when the selling price is lower than the buying price so that in fact you take a loss.

Time Deposits: Another term for a savings account in a commercial bank. It is so called because in theory you must wait a certain amount of time after you have given notice of your desire to withdraw part or all of your savings. However, this requirement is generally not exercised by the bank.

Mutual Fund: A fund that purchases the stocks of other companies. If you buy a share in a mutual fund, you are in essence buying shares in all of the companies that the mutual fund invests in. The only business of a mutual fund is buying other companies' stocks.

Common Stocks: Another name for an equity. A common stock is a legal claim to the profits of a company. For each share owned, the common stock owner generally has the right to one vote on such questions as merging with another company and electing a new board of directors.

Preferred Stocks: Actually a type of debt obligation like a bond that a company sells to investors. Preferred stocks pay a specified dividend every year (or at some other interval). If the company goes bankrupt, preferred stockholders have the right to collect on their investment before common stockholders obtain any of the liquidated assets of the bankrupt company.

Inside Information: Information about a company's financial situation that is obtained before the public obtains it. True inside information is usually only known by corporate officials or other "insiders."

Almost two-thirds of all American families have savings accounts, and over 30 million Americans have stocks or bonds. In total, the amount of **saving** in the United States in any one year may exceed $55 billion for the rest of the 1970s. We see in Figure 14–1 the total amount of saving over time in the United States.

THE TENDENCY TO SAVE

The tendency to save in the United States has existed ever since the country started. Figure 14–2 shows the relationship between consumption and personal disposable income over the last three-fourths of a century. That relationship has been almost constant. It implies that what Americans do *not* consume, i. e., save, is about 12 percent of their income year in and year out. What they do with their savings will be discussed below. Why people save is a question many of you may be asking. The common answer is that we save for a rainy day.

WHY SAVE AT ALL?

If you think that saving is for a rainy day, you are right. The reason you may want to save is either to leave a large estate to your heirs, or to provide for yourself and your family during periods when your income is abnormally low. When are those periods? Obviously, at times when you are disabled or after you retire. We can look at saving, then, as a way to spread out your consumption over your lifetime so that it remains smooth even when your income fluctuates or sometimes falls to zero, especially after you reach old age. Even if you are very, very poor and just barely making a living, you know that some time in the future you will no longer be able to work. You will either reach mandatory retirement or you will become so unproductive that nobody will be willing to hire you. Your income stream will be cut off. Unless there are children, a benevolent government, or private charities that will take care of you, you will face starvation unless you have accumulated savings.

Therefore, you must decide today how much of your current meager income (assuming you are very poor) you want to set aside for those retirement years when

WHAT TO DO WITH YOUR PIGGY BANK

A man may, if he know not how to save, keep his nose to the Grindstone, and die not worth a Groat at last

Benjamin Franklin
Poor Richard's Almanac, January 1794

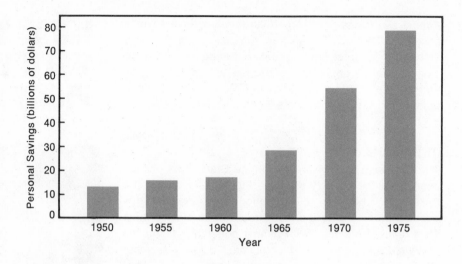

FIGURE 14–1   PERSONAL SAVING IN THE UNITED STATES FOR THE LAST 25
YEARS
Personal savings have been going up at fairly steady rates for the last quarter of
a century. Note, however, that part of this increase in savings is due to inflation,
because we have not corrected for it in this chart. Source: Department of Commerce.

you can no longer work. Unless you will literally starve if you reduce your
current level of consumption even by a very small amount, you probably
will attempt to save a little bit, however small, out of your meager income.
Most people would rather reduce current consumption by a small amount
to at least be able to exist after they can no longer work. Were they not
to reduce their current consumption at all, they might face certain starvation as soon as their income stream stopped.

Thus, saving is a method by which individuals can achieve an optimal
consumption stream throughout their expected lifetime—"optimal" not
meaning adequate or necessary, but rather the most desirable from the
individual's point of view. If you face the constraint of a very low income
for all of your life, in most cases you would still want to provide some
savings to live with when you can no longer work.

SAVING AMONG
THE POOR

There is a common notion that in many countries people are so poor
they cannot save at all because they are barely subsisting. This belief
is not true. Many anthropological studies of villages in India, for example,
have revealed that saving is in fact going on; but it takes forms that
we do not recognize in our money economy. In some places, for example, saving involves storing dried onions. In Table 14–1, which shows
the saving rates for different countries of the world, even the poorest
countries can be seen to have a saving rate that is positive.

**WHAT DETERMINES
HOW MUCH
YOU SAVE**

If you want to save something for that rainy day, it is interesting to specu-late on what determines the amount you save. We can offer a few ideas here. Obviously, the more money you can make on your savings, the more you will want to save (if nothing else changes). In other words, if a savings and loan association offered to give you 50 percent interest a year on anything you put in it, you probably would want to save more than you do now when a savings and loan association gives you an in-terest rate of less than 10 percent, and actually not much more than 5 or 6 percent.

Look at it this way: the only reason you save is so that you will have money later on to buy things. If you were to put $100 in a savings ac-count today and get $150 back next year, the price of buying something next year would be pretty low (assuming that the rate of inflation is relatively low). If, on the other hand, you put $100 in the savings account today and you got only $101 back next year because the interest rate

FIGURE 14–2 THE RELATIONSHIP BETWEEN CONSUMPTION EXPENDITURES PER CAPITA TO PERSONAL DISPOSABLE INCOME PER CAPITA, 1897 TO PRESENT

Here we are looking at personal disposable income in dollars per capita and personal consumption in dollars per capita. The line shows the direct relationship as being consumption = 0.877 × income. The line goes through the origin, which indicates that as real income goes up the percentage of it spent in consumption does not increase. Source: Raymond Goldsmith.

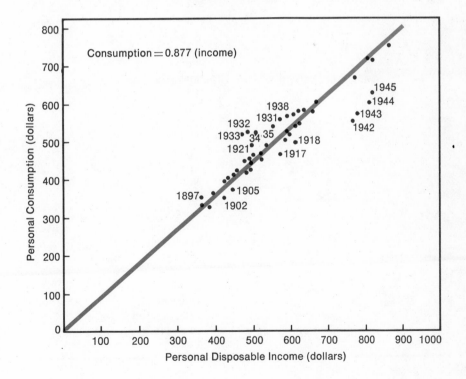

is 1 percent, then the implicit price of goods one year from now is not so cheap.

Of course, to decide whether to save, or how much to save, you look at more than the interest rate on your savings; you also look at how you value consumption today as opposed to consumption tomorrow. Obviously, when you put off spending $100, you do not get the pleasure from whatever you might have spent it on: you have to wait. If you are impatient, even a high interest rate on savings may not induce you to save much at all. Those of you who are not so impatient about consuming may save more.

Another major determinant of how much of your current income you think you should save is how variable your income is. For example, people who have stable incomes from secure government employment generally save a smaller percentage of their income than do people

TABLE 14–1:

SAVING RATES FOR DIFFERENT COUNTRIES IN THE WORLD

Amazingly, the saving rates for different countries in the world vary within a small range. A relatively poor country like Korea saves at about the same rate as a relatively rich country like the United Kingdom. Source: United Nations Statistical Year Books.

COUNTRY	TOTAL AMOUNT OF SAVINGS AS A PERCENT OF GROSS DOMESTIC PRODUCT
South Africa	13.4
Canada	12.0
Honduras	10.1
Jamaica	9.8
Panama	9.2
Venezuela	15.7
Korea	12.5
Malaysia	8.4
Philippines	10.2
Belgium	16.7
Denmark	10.3
Finland	20.1
France	17.9
Germany, Fed. Republic	17.5
Ireland	12.3
Italy	15.1
Luxembourg	13.4
Netherlands	18.8
Norway	16.4
Portugal	11.8
Spain	15.2
Sweden	14.9
Switzerland	18.9
United Kingdom	11.5
Australia	18.3
Fiji	16.0

who are in business for themselves. Obviously, the more variable your income, the more likely you are to have years when your income is lower than usual. Hence, during the years when it is higher than usual you will generally save more.

Moreover, how much you will save depends on how much future retirement income you decide that you should have. To fully understand how much you will have in the future, you must understand compound interest. Obviously, if you earned no interest at all, your total savings at the end of a specific saving period—say, 30 years—would be exactly what you put in. But that is not what usually happens: you should earn interest on whatever you save.

THE NATURE OF COMPOUND INTEREST

If you decide to save by not consuming all of your income, you can take what you save and, loosely speaking, invest it. You can put it in the **stock market** or you can buy **bonds**—that is, lend money to businesses. You could also put it in your own business. In any event, you might expect to make a profit or interest every year in the future for a certain period of time. To figure out how much you will have at the end of any specified time period, you have to compound your savings. To do so, you have to use a specified interest rate. Say you put $100 in a savings and loan association that yields 5 percent per year. At the end of one year, you have $105. At the end of two years, you have $105 plus 5 percent of $105, or $5.25. Thus, at the end of two years, you have $110.25. This same compounding occurs the third year, the fourth year, and so on.

THE POWER OF COMPOUNDING

The power of **compound interest** is truly amazing. Table 14–2 shows one dollar compounded every year for 50 years at different interest rates. At an interest rate of 8 percent, one dollar will return $46.90 at the end of 50 years. Thus, if you inherited a modest $20,000 when you were 20 years old and put it in an investment that paid 8 percent compounded annually, at 70 years of age you would have $938,000. Now it is not so hard to understand how some people become millionaires. It usually does not take much in brains or business acumen to get an 8 percent rate of return in the long run. Somebody who had invested in the stock market 50 years ago would have received much more than 8 percent. There are a number of people around who inherit moderate amounts of money when they are quite young. If this money is put in the stock market and left there to compound itself, it grows to quite unbelievable amounts after 30 or 40 years. Hence, we should be careful about assuming the astuteness of elderly millionaires; they could have been very conservative, done nothing with the money they inherited except put it in the stock market and leave it there. No business sense would be needed at all and the person could easily become a millionaire by the age of 65.

The power of compound interest should also tip you off as to the true worth of many investment schemes. Take high-priced paintings. Often art dealers will tell you that paintings are good investments. They will cite, for example, a Picasso that a couple purchased for only $5000 and then sold for $15,000. You have to find out, however, when it was purchased. Usually, if you look at the length of time for which the painting was held, the actual gain in value might be very modest, say only 3 percent a year. After all, if the painting cost $1000 in 1950, at a 3 percent compound interest, it would be worth over $2000 in 1975. The couple who sold it in 1975 could boast that they doubled their investment, while they probably could have done better if in 1950 they had put their $1000 into a savings account that yielded 4 or 5 percent; they would have done even better if they had put that money into the stock market, because then their rate of return would have been 8 to 12 percent. Usually, because people get some consumption pleasure out of having paintings in their homes, they are willing to receive a lower rate of return than they expect from money in some other type of investment.

TYPES OF SAVINGS INSTITUTIONS

The commonest savings institution, and the one familiar to people for the longest time, is the commercial bank. Commercial banks offer you what are called **time deposits**—so called because in principle you must allow time between the day you announce your intention to withdraw your savings and the day you withdraw them. Time deposits in commercial banks generally offer the lowest interest yields around.

The main purpose of some banks is to only accept deposits and lend these out for a long term to reliable borrowers at higher rates of interest than the banks pay depositers. These institutions are called *savings banks.* They are intended to provide a safe place in which the small investor can invest his or her savings. As with commercial bank time deposits, a savings bank deposit often requires that a notice be given before the money is allowed to be withdrawn. There are various types of savings banks, the main two being stock and mutual.

The *stock savings bank* is organized and conducted for profit by the owners of its capital stock. The greater number of stock savings banks are located in the midwestern United States. These banks are under the regulation of the state in which they are chartered.

The *mutual savings bank,* on the other hand, is owned by its depositors. In effect, the depositors simply pool their savings, which are invested by a board of trustees and a hired manager. Depositors are not paid a fixed rate of interest on their deposits; whatever earnings are made from the investment belong to the depositors, and are divided among them in proportion to their deposits.

The object of *savings and loan associations* is obviously to encourage thrift, but at the same time to assist present and future homeowners. The names by which these associations are known vary in different parts

TABLE 14-2:

**ONE DOLLAR COMPOUNDED AT DIF-
FERENT INTEREST RATES**

Here we show the value of the dollar at
the end of a specified period after it
has been compounded at a specified
interest rate. For example, if you took
$1 today and invested it at 5 percent,
it would yield $1.05 at the end of the
year. At the end of 10 years, it would
be equal to $1.63, and at the end of
50 years, it will be equal to $11.50.

In this table, interest is compounded
once a year at the end of every year.
There are other ways of compounding
interest, such as semi-annually (once
every six months), quarterly (once every
three months), daily, and continuously.
The actual compound factor in this
table would have to be altered for
each compounding scheme. Clearly,
the more frequently a given interest
percentage is compounded, the larger
the return after a given period of time.

YEAR	3%	4%	5%	6%	8%	10%	20%	YEAR
1	1.03	1.04	1.05	1.06	1.08	1.10	1.20	1
2	1.06	1.08	1.10	1.12	1.17	1.21	1.44	2
3	1.09	1.12	1.16	1.19	1.26	1.33	1.73	3
4	1.13	1.17	1.22	1.26	1.36	1.46	2.07	4
5	1.16	1.22	1.28	1.34	1.47	1.61	2.49	5
6	1.19	1.27	1.34	1.41	1.59	1.77	2.99	6
7	1.23	1.32	1.41	1.50	1.71	1.94	3.58	7
8	1.27	1.37	1.48	1.59	1.85	2.14	4.30	8
9	1.30	1.42	1.55	1.68	2.00	2.35	5.16	9
10	1.34	1.48	1.63	1.79	2.16	2.59	6.19	10
11	1.38	1.54	1.71	1.89	2.33	2.85	7.43	11
12	1.43	1.60	1.80	2.01	2.52	3.13	8.92	12
13	1.47	1.67	1.89	2.13	2.72	3.45	10.7	13
14	1.51	1.73	1.98	2.26	2.94	3.79	12.8	14
15	1.56	1.80	2.08	2.39	3.17	4.17	15.4	15
16	1.60	1.87	2.18	2.54	3.43	4.59	18.5	16
17	1.65	1.95	2.29	2.69	3.70	5.05	22.2	17
18	1.70	2.03	2.41	2.85	4.00	5.55	26.6	18
19	1.75	2.11	2.53	3.02	4.32	6.11	31.9	19
20	1.81	2.19	2.65	3.20	4.66	6.72	38.3	20
25	2.09	2.67	3.39	4.29	6.85	10.8	95.4	25
30	2.43	3.24	4.32	5.74	10.0	17.4	237	30
40	3.26	4.80	7.04	10.3	21.7	45.3	1470	40
50	4.38	7.11	11.5	18.4	46.9	117	9100	50

of the country; they can be called savings and loan associations, cooperative banks, or building and loan associations.

Generally, when you put money into a savings and loan association,
you get a passbook which indicates that you are a shareholder in that
organization. As a member, you are entitled to receive interest on your
deposits. Savings and loan associations are not generally authorized
to handle checking accounts. Currently, the savings in these associations
are insured up to a maximum of $40,000 per account.

Credit unions are one of the fastest growing savings institutions in the
nation. Credit unions are owned by their membership. They have three
purposes:

1. to help their members save.
2. to enable their members to borrow money for "good" purposes at
lower than market interest rates.
3. to educate members in money management.

As a member in a credit union, you usually buy shares that are marked
on your share booklet. In effect, credit unions are really cooperative

small-loan banks that lend amounts to their members at reasonable rates of interest. Federal and state laws vary as to the maximum amount that may be loaned by the credit union.

Not just anybody can join a credit union. Generally, you must be a member of some organization because the credit union is usually for a particular group.

Even when you have decided how much to save, your problems have not yet ended. You must decide what to do with your accumulated savings. That is, how should you invest them?

THE SIMPLE FACTS ABOUT INVESTING

There are many things that you can do with your accumulated savings: you can keep all or part of them in cash, which earns no interest at all and in fact loses value at the rate of inflation. You can put them into a savings and loan account which gives a relatively low rate of interest but is extremely secure. You can invest your money in a **mutual fund,** which is a corporation that buys the shares of stocks of various other corporations. You can invest your money in U. S. Savings Bonds, which yield a relatively low rate of interest and in fact are only a slightly better deal than just keeping your savings in a savings and loan association or a commercial bank. You can purchase land. You can purchase what are called consumer durable goods, such as cars, houses, and stereos, which yield a stream of services over their lifetime. You can do an infinite number of things with your savings. The question is what should you do? Well, to start with, that depends on your goals; what your goals are will tell you how much risk you want to take.

There is an unfortunate fact that we have alluded to time and again: you cannot get anything free. If you go into an investment deal in which you expect to make a killing, you may be sure that the risk you are undertaking is relatively high.

RISK AND RATE OF RETURN

There is no way out of the dilemma that the higher the prospective rate of return you expect to get on any investment, the higher the risk you take. That is why if you are offered a "deal" that you are told will make you 50 percent a year, you may be certain that the risk of losing everything is pretty high. On the other hand, if you take your savings and invest them in a savings and loan association you may make only 6 percent a year, but you do not risk losing your entire savings.

A better way to understand why you cannot get a high rate of return without a high risk is to understand why no particular investment "deal" is necessarily any better than any other, at least unless you have some pretty specialized information. Let us explain this by taking a specific example—making money on the stock market. But first, we need a few facts.

SOME FACTS ON THE STOCK MARKET

The stock market is the general term used for all transactions that involve the buying and selling of **securities** issued by companies. What is a security? A security is a piece of paper giving the owner the right to a certain portion of the assets of the company issuing the security. Security·is another name for stock. Most stocks are **common stocks,** called **equities.** Say a company wishes to expand its operation. It can obtain the money capital for expansion by putting up part of the ownership of the company for sale. It does this by offering stocks, usually common stocks, for sale. If a company worth $1 million wants $200,000, it may sell stocks. Suppose one person, you, owns the company and you arbitrarily state that there are 100,000 shares of stock that you own completely; you would then have to put out on the market about 20,000 shares of your stock, which you would sell at $10 a share. You would get the $200,000 for expansion and the people who paid the money would receive 20,000 shares of your stock. They would have claim to one-fifth of whatever the company earned as profits.

There are many different submarkets within the stock market. At the top of the ladder are the big ones: the New York Stock Exchange and the American Stock Exchange. Measured by dollar value, about 80 percent of all stock transactions are carried out at the New York and the American. There are also regional stock exchanges throughout the country as well as the national over-the-counter market and regional over-the-counter markets. These markets are somewhat less organized than the New York, American, and regional exchanges. The stocks are usually not traded as often in the over-the-counter market as those on the big exchanges. Stocks in companies that are small and less well known than bigger companies are usually traded in the over-the-counter market.

PREFERRED STOCKS AND BONDS

Preferred stock is a fancy name for what is simply the debt of a company. It is called "preferred" because, in the event of distributable earnings, or in the event of liquidation or bankruptcy, the holders of that stock have a preferred claim against the company prior to that of the common stockholders. That is, whatever assets can be retrieved are distributed first among preferred stockholders. A preferred stock is actually a type of **bond** that can be defined very simply. A bond is basically an I.O.U. or promissory note of a corporation, usually issued in multiples of $1000. A bond is evidence of a debt in which the issuing company usually promises to pay the bondholders a specified amount of interest for a specified length of time and then to repay the loan on the expiration date. In every case, a bond represents debt: its holder is a creditor of the corporation and not a part owner, as is the shareholder or stockholder. So you can see that preferred stock is merely a bond, except that failure to pay the interest or dividend on preferred stock does not legally allow the preferred stockholder to sue the company. The preferred stockholder simply has preference to the earnings, if any, for payment of interest before any dividends can be paid to the common stockholders. Sometimes the preferred stock is "cumulative": if any arrears of unpaid dividends (or interest) accumulate, the common stockholders cannot take any dividends until the preferred stockholders have been paid.

Preferred stock may also be convertible, which means that the preferred stockholder has the option to exchange—that is, convert—it into common stock at a preset exchange rate. There are also such things as convertible bonds, which can be exchanged for common stock at some preset exchange rate, also.

CAPITAL GAINS AND LOSSES

Stocks can go up and down in price. If you buy a stock at, say, $10 and sell it at $15, you make a **capital gain** equal to $5 for every share you bought and then sold at the higher price. That is called an appreciation in the price of your stock, which you realized as a capital gain when you sold it. If the value of your stock falls and you sell it at a loss, you have suffered a **capital loss** because of the depreciation in the market value of your stock. Some stocks pay dividends, but not all do. (Dividends are paid by checks mailed to the stockholders.) Normally, when you buy a stock that has never paid a dividend, you expect to make money on your investment by increase in the value of the stock. That is, if the company is making profits but not giving out dividends, it must be reinvesting those profits. A reinvestment in itself could pay off in the future by higher profits. The value of the stock would then be bid up in the market. Your profit would be in the form of a capital gain rather than by dividend payments.

EXHIBIT:
**Comparison of stocks
and bonds**

STOCKS	BONDS
1. Represent ownership (except preferred stocks).	**1.** Represent owed debt.
2. Have no fixed dividend rate (including preferred stocks).	**2.** Require interest be paid whether or not any profit is earned.
3. Allow holders to elect board of directors, who in turn control the corporation.	**3.** Usually entail no voice in or control over management.
4. Have no maturity date; the corporation does not usually repay the stockholder.	**4.** Have a maturity date when the holder is to be repaid the face value.
5. Are issued by all business corporations (and are purchased by stockholders).	**5.** Need not be issued by corporations.
6. Allow holders to have a claim against the property and income of the corporation after all creditors' claims have been met.	**6.** Give to bondholders a prior claim against the property and income of the corporation, which must be met before the claims of stockholders.

WHAT AFFECTS
THE PRICE
OF A STOCK?

Some observers believe that individual psychological or subjective feelings are all that affect the price of a stock. If people think a stock will be worth more in the future, they will bid the price up. If they think it will be worth less in the future, the price will fall. However, that is not a very satisfactory theory. What are psychological feelings based upon? Usually, such feelings are based upon the expected stream of profits that the company will make in the future. Past profits may be important in formulating a prediction of future profits. However, past profits are bygones, and bygones are forever bygones. A company could lose money for 10 years and then make profits for the next 15.

If a company gets a new management team that has a reputation for turning losing companies into winning ones, people in the stock market might expect profits to turn around and go up. If a company has a record

number of sales orders for future months, one might expect profits to go up. Whenever profits are expected to rise, we typically find a rise in the value of the stock. That is, people bid up the price of the stock. Any information about future profits should be valuable in assessing how a stock's price will react.

**MAKING MONEY IN
THE STOCK MARKET**

You have probably heard of the infamous J. P. Morgan: he was supposed to have made his fortune by manipulating the stock market. You have also probably heard of persons becoming millionaires overnight by making astute investments in securities. You may even have a parent who talks much about the stock market, follows the *Wall Street Journal,* reads the financial page of the local newspaper, talks about the prices of various stocks going up or down. Making money in the stock market seems as easy as calling up your stockbroker for the latest "hot" tips.

**GETTING ADVICE
ON THE MARKET**

If you want to make an experiment, try the following: look in your Yellow Pages under "Stock and Bond Brokers" and pick any phone number at random; call it; ask to speak with a registered representative or an account executive (in the old days, called "customers' men"). Talk to this broker as if you had, say, $10,000 to invest. Ask him or her for advice. You will probably be asked what your goals are. Do you want income from your investment? Do you want growth in your investment? Do you want to take a chance? Do you want to be safe? After you tell the broker the strategy you wish to pursue, you will be told what are the best stocks to buy. If you ask the broker what he or she thinks the market in general will be doing over the next few months, you are bound to hear an opinion, and an authoritative one at that. After all, if you want to know what to do with your garden, ask the person who runs the local nursery. If you want to know about your car, you ask your local mechanic. That is, you generally seek out specialists in whatever is your interest. Why not seek out a specialist, then, when you are interested in making money?

It may seem strange that you will not benefit much from seeking the advice of a stockbroker concerning the stocks you should buy. A broker is a specialist, one from whom you can get much useful information. A broker can tell you all about stock market, can give you quotes on all the different stocks—that is, what their prices are and how many of them were sold in the last few days and what the history of the prices was. You can be told about the various types of securities you can buy —stocks listed on the big exchanges like the New York and the American, over-the-counter stocks that are sold only in very restricted sections of the country, preferred stocks, bonds, convertible debentures, puts, calls, warrants, and so on and so on. A stockbroker is the person you should ask concerning all these different avenues of investment.

But the broker is *not* the one you should ask about which particular stock to buy. *The broker is no more likely to be right than are you.* You might even select the stocks to purchase by throwing a dart at a list of stocks in the New York Stock Exchange. If you are shocked by this revelation, consider that the stock market is the most highly competitive market in the world, and information costs there are perhaps the lowest of any market in existence.

PUBLIC
INFORMATION

Information flows rapidly in the stock market. If you read in the *Wall Street Journal* that International Chemical and Nuclear (ICN) has just discovered a cure for cancer, do you think you should rush out and buy ICN stock? You might, but you will be no better off than if you had bought any other stock. By the time you read about ICN's discovery (which will mean increased profits in the future for the company), thousands and thousands of other people will have already read it. A rule that you should apply, and one that will be explained several times in this chapter, is that *public information does not yield an above-normal profit or rate of return.* Once information about a company's profitability is generally known, that information has a zero value for predicting the future price of the stock. The only information that is useful is what we call **inside information**.

CAPITALIZATION

True inside information is just that: it is information that is not generally known. Information that becomes public is capitalized upon almost immediately; people consider what it means for future profits and bid up the price of the stock to a level that reflects the expected future increase in profits. Information is used almost immediately in the stock market because it flows so rapidly. There have been studies on the value of information contained in the *Wall Street Journal* or the *New York Times,* and it turns out that this information is useless for assessing which stocks to buy. Even information about national or world events cannot tell you whether the market in general will go up or down.

Studies have also been done on the profitability of information acquired by insiders in companies—that is, by corporate officers. Officers in a company are required to file statements of their transactions in their own company's stocks with the Securities and Exchange Commission, the regulator of the stock market industry. Statistical studies have shown that when insiders (corporate officers) sell their stocks in their company, the price of the stock usually falls within 30 days; when insiders buy their own company's stocks, the price of the stock usually rises within 30 days. Obviously, there is a value to having inside information. (Note that it is illegal for officers to tell outsiders any inside information that can then be used to make money on the company's stock.)

HOT TIPS

What about the hot tips your broker might have? It is highly dubious that it will be true inside information. After all, if it were really inside information, why would it be given to you? Why would the broker not take advantage of it himself or herself, get rich quick, and quit being a stockbroker? The broker's information might have come from the brokerage's research department. Almost all stock brokerage companies have large research staffs that investigate different industries, different companies, and the future of the general economy. These research departments issue research statements on different companies and industries in the economy. There are recommendations as to which stocks are underpriced and, therefore, should be bought. *The value of this research information to you as an investor is zero.* You will do no better by following the advice of research branches of your stock brokerage company than you will by randomly selecting stocks—particularly stocks listed on the New York and American stock exchanges. Nevertheless, the amount of research on those companies that is completed by firms, individuals, organizations, governments, and so on is indeed staggering. Since information flows so freely, by the time you receive the results of research on a particular company, you can be sure that thousands and thousands of other people have already found out. And since so many brokerage firms employ research analysts, you can be sure that there are numerous analysts investigating every single company that has shares for sale in the open stock market.

THE RANDOM WALK

Recall, from your high school physics course, your study of Brownian motion of molecules. They jumped around randomly; there was simply no way to predict where a molecule would jump next. This is exactly what happens when something follows a random walk; it goes in directions that are totally unrelated to past directions. If something follows a random walk, no amount of information of the past is useful for predicting what will happen in the future. The stock market would be expected to exhibit a random walk merely because it is so highly competitive and because information flows so freely. Examining past prices on the market as a whole or on individual stocks would not be expected to yield any useful information as to prices in the future. Years and years of academic research on the stock market have left little doubt that the stock market is, indeed, a random walk. (If you find out otherwise, you may be able to get rich very quickly.)

A stock is not like a dog—which is to say, it will not eventually come home to its former price. Indeed, because a stock does not know where its home is, and does not have a mind or a purpose, what has happened to that stock in the past does not matter. You can find no usable information by examining past stock prices. Or, according to Nobel Prize winning economist Paul Samuelson:

Even the best investors seem to find it hard to do better than the comprehensive common-stock averages, or better on the average than random selection among stocks of comparable variability. *

WHAT ABOUT
INVESTMENT PLANS? Investment plans and sophisticated investment counselors are numerous. In their advertising, they guarantee you a higher rate of return on your stock dollars than anyplace else. A typical piece of advertising might show, for example, the average rate of return for investing in all of the stocks on the New York Stock Exchange. An investment counselor would show you that his stock portfolio makes 15 percent a year, rather than the average 8 percent by buying all stocks together. However, these investment counselors usually neglect to point out that the 15 percent rate of return does not take account of the investment counseling fees nor the trading costs—that is, brokers' commissions—for buying and selling stocks. Investment services usually do much trading: they go in and out of the market—buying today, selling tomorrow. Each time someone buys a stock or sells a stock, that person pays a commission to the broker. Thus, the more trading your investment counselor does for your account, the more trading costs you incur. In fact, in almost all cases that have been thoroughly examined, investments made through counselors do no better than the general market averages because any special profits they make are eaten up by brokerage fees and their own counseling fees. Thus, you would be better off just paying brokerage fees and not using the services of an investment counselor.

This fact was confirmed in a study of mutual funds. Mutual funds take the money of many investors and buy and sell large blocks of stocks; the investors get dividends or appreciation in their shares of the mutual

* Paul Samuelson, *The Bell Journal of Economics and Management Science*, Vol. 4, No. 2 (Autumn 1973), pp. 369–374.

fund. The mutual fund, then, is a company that invests in other companies but does not sell any physical product of its own. You can buy shares in mutual funds just as you can buy shares in General Motors. The study of mutual funds mentioned above concluded that mutuals that did the least amount of trading made the highest profits, an expected result if one understands the competitive nature of the stock market.

THE TWO TYPES OF MUTUAL FUNDS

A mutual fund or investment trust is principally either of two types: the closed end and the open end. Shares in closed end investment trusts, some of which are listed on the New York Stock Exchange, are readily transferrable in the open market and are bought and sold like other shares. These companies are called closed end because their capitalization remains the same unless action is taken to change, which is seldom. Open end funds sell their own new shares to investors, and stand ready to buy back their old shares, and are not listed on the stock exchange. Open end funds are so called because their capitalization is not fixed; they issue more shares as people want them.

The only commission you pay to buy closed end mutual funds is the standard commission you would pay on the purchase of any stock. On the other hand, there are two types of open end mutual funds, a no-load and a load. The no-load mutual fund charges no setup or loading charge for you to get into the fund, while the load mutual fund charges you about 8 percent to get into the fund. The salesperson or stockbroker who sells you an open end mutual fund with a loading charge usually keeps most of that charge as commission.

IS THERE NO WAY TO GET RICH QUICK?

The general conclusion to be reached from our analysis of the stock market is that all of the investing schemes everybody talks about are really quite useless for getting rich quickly. That does not mean, of course, that some people will not get rich by using them. Luck has much to do with making money in the stock market—just as it does with winning at poker or craps. If you do make money with your particular scheme, it does not mean you are extra smart, a better investor, or a prophet. You may just be lucky. You may, however, make more than a normal rate of return on your invested capital if you spend a tremendous amount of time searching out areas of unknown profit potential. But then you are spending resources—your own time. Your fantastic profits can be considered as payment for the time you spent—the value of your opportunity cost—analyzing the stock market and different companies.

The question still remains: How can you make money? You know that you can make a normal rate of return by merely throwing a dart at the listing of stocks in the New York Stock Exchange. Pick eight stocks, for example, and just keep buying them with your investment dollars. Never sell until you need money for retirement. Over the long run, you will probably make around an 8 to 15 percent rate of return. On the other hand, you might want to pick particular stocks if you have inside information or information that is better than the tips anybody else has. In such a case, you stand to gain more than by randomly picking stocks. Also, if you think you can somehow evaluate public information better than anybody else can, you may want to do more than select random stocks. But before you decide whether you can evaluate better than others, you had better think seriously about how many others there are in the world. The stock industry is huge. Why do you think that you can do better than everybody else at evaluating public information?

OTHER SUREFIRE SCHEMES

By now, you ought to be quite suspicious about any special investment deals that come up. Because there is so much competition in the investment markets, and because you, as a single consumer, are not likely to be smarter than any of the experts around, you should consider every single investment as a trade-off between risk and rate of return. The higher the potential rate of return, the higher the risk. There is no reason why you should expect you can do better than average unless you have some special information. Real estate is a good example.

REAL ESTATE

Will Rogers once said, "It's easy to make money, just figure out where people are going and then buy the land before they get there." Now, how does that fit in with our discussion? Obviously, if Will Rogers knew this astute proposition, all of the experts know it, too. What do you think happens when it is known where people will be going? That information will be used by others, who will thereby bid up the price of land in the

places where people are going. Only if you think you have such information ahead of everyone else can you expect to make a higher than normal rate of return in any type of land investment.

Do not be taken in by such statements as "land is always a safe investment." The value of land can fall like the value of anything else. The fact that the overall price of land has been going up for a long time does not mean that you will make more than what you could make, say, investing money in a savings and loan association. Although on average you might make more in land, on average you also take a greater risk because many times land deals fall through completely.

You can think of a thousand and one other investment opportunities to which the same logic applies. Just remember that you do not get something for nothing: any time you do something with your savings, you are going to be subjected to the rigors of a competitive marketplace. Only special information is valuable. Otherwise, you will get no more, on average, than a normal rate of return.

**PENSIONS AND
RETIREMENT PLANS**

If you are involuntarily or voluntarily covered by a retirement or a pension plan, you are saving: that retirement or pension plan is in fact a savings plan. Moreover, if you have anything other than term insurance, you are also saving, because the cash value of whole or ordinary insurance can be turned into retirement annuity.

How to be a wise investor is outlined in the following Consumer Issue. But remember that your spending much time researching investment possibilities does not necessarily mean that you are wise. Only if you think you have acquired special information can you, on average, expect to get a higher than normal rate of return. You also must consider all the time spent in researching that information. If your time is worth something, it may not be worth your while to spend it in that manner. You may want to pay somebody else to do it, or you may want to play it safe, as you will see in the following Consumer Issue.

SUMMARY

1. Individuals save in order to provide for income during periods when their earnings capacity falls, such as during sickness or after retirement. Hence, even in poor countries individuals save a positive amount of income every year. In addition to the rate of return or interest you obtain from your savings, the variability of your income will also determine how much you save. The higher the interest paid and the higher the variability of your income, the more you will save.

2. In our competitive society, very few things come free of charge. Hence, any investment deal you go into with your savings cannot guarantee you a higher than normal rate of return unless a large amount of risk—that is, a high chance of losing everything—is involved.

3. When trying to figure out how much savings you will have accumulated after a certain amount of saving, you should consult a compound interest table such as we have presented in Table 14–2. If, for example, your savings were invested at an average yield of 8 percent, at the end of 20 years every dollar invested will have grown to $4.66.

4. There are numerous types of savings institutions, such as savings banks (stock and mutual), savings and loan associations, and credit unions.

5. In the stock market, shares of American businesses are bought and sold just about every weekday throughout the year. When you buy and sell stocks, you may either sell them for more than you paid and experience a capital gain, or sell them for less than you paid and experience a capital loss.

6. When you buy a share in a company, there is no guarantee that you will receive dividends or that you will make any particular rate of interest on your investment. However, if you loan money to the company—that is, buy one of their bonds—you are guaranteed, as long as the company does not go bankrupt, a specified dollar interest payment every year and a specified principal payment when the bond matures or when the bond's life runs out. It is important to purchase bonds only if the interest rate paid at least compensates you for inflation that you anticipate.

7. It is generally a waste of time to consult stock market analysts in deciding which stocks to buy for your investment portfolio. This is because the stock market is one of the most highly competitive markets in the world and any useful information is immediately used by those who perceive it. Thus, the price of a stock represents all of the information (properly discounted) that exists about the company, the industry, or the economy as a whole.

8. Stockbrokers can be useful to explain how the stock market works, what are different types of securities you can buy, and so on.

9. Do not be taken in by so-called investment plans that purport to guarantee you a higher than normal rate of return in the stock market. Generally, these investment plans consume any above-normal rates of return in the fees they charge you or the commissions you must pay to buy and sell stocks often.

10. Mutual funds may be an easy answer to your investing problems, for they purchase a wide variety of stocks. It is generally advisable to buy into a no-load mutual fund, which has no sales charges. Also, it may be possible to buy into mutual funds which purchase a nearly random selection of stocks and therefore do not have any management expenses. At some time in the future, these mutual funds will be offered to you at a lower management fee than those currently in existence.

11. All schemes to make you richer should be investigated thoroughly, for, on average, they very rarely guarantee you a higher than normal rate of return unless you accept a higher amount of risk. For example, even though the amount of land is fixed and the population is growing, real estate is not always a good investment. That is an example of public information that has zero value as a guide to where to invest your accumulated savings. The same would be true for any arguments telling you that the best investments are antiques, oil and gas wells, old paintings, cans of food, and so on.

QUESTIONS FOR THOUGHT AND DISCUSSION

1. "Poor people barely have enough to survive on and therefore cannot save anything for a rainy day." Do you agree or disagree?

2. What determines how much you save?

3. Would it make a difference whether the interest on your savings were compounded daily, weekly, monthly, semiannually, or every year? If so, what difference?

4. Why do you have to worry about the rate of inflation when you invest your savings?

5. What is the maximum yield you can obtain from putting your money in a savings and loan association today? Is that yield greater than the rate of inflation? Are you taxed on the interest you receive?

6. "Risk and rate of return are positively related." Do you agree with that statement? Why or why not?

7. The New York Stock Exchange has been called one of the most competitive markets in the world. However, it has also been called a monopoly. Which aspect of the NYSE do you think is monopolistic? (Hint: Can anybody become a member of the NYSE?)

8. Which do you think are a better investment—stocks or bonds?

9. Do you think stockbrokers have more information about which stocks to buy than you have?

10. What is the value of public information?

11. Do you think the small investor should be given special treatment by the stock exchanges and brokerage houses?

12. "The stock market is the backbone of American capitalism." Comment.

13. Do you believe the so-called random walk theory of stock prices?

14. Why do you think there were no mutual funds in existence 50 years ago?

15. The value of land has always gone up. If that is true, why do investors not put all their money in land?

THINGS TO DO

1. Try to figure out what percentage of your income you save. Remember that the purchase of a so-called consumer durable, such as a television set, a stereo, a house, or a car, is a form of saving because you receive income from that consumer durable for a long period of time. The income you receive is the satisfaction you obtain from the durable.

2. Assume that by the time you retire at age 65, you want to have $100,000 saved up. Also assume that you can earn 10 percent per year on your savings. Determine from Table 14–2 how much you have to put in the bank today to have $100,000 at age 65 at a 10 percent rate of return.

3. Call up an antique dealer and ask that person about the investment opportunities in antiques. Find out what the rate of return is on investing in antiques. Is this rate of return higher or lower than what you could expect if you put your money in a savings and loan association?

4. Find out the different rates of return offered by the various savings institutions. Why do you think there is a difference?

5. Call up a local credit union—say one for labor union employees or school teachers. Get a copy of the credit union's requirements. Try to find out why there is a restriction on who can use the credit union. Compare the rates on a car loan or a personal loan from that credit union with what you would have to pay at a commercial bank. Why do you think the difference exists, if it does? (It usually does.)

6. If you live in one of the large cities that has a stock exchange, go visit it. You will be able to see a competitive market in action. Also, you can usually pick up information on stock markets and how they work. Call up a brokerage firm in your area to ask if there is a national or regional exchange near your place of residence.

7. Look at the financial page of any newspaper. Find out what all of the various financial quotations actually mean, either from your instructor or from a stockbroker.

**SELECTED
READINGS**

Baruch, Hurd, *Wall Street: Security Risk* (London: Acropolis Books), 1972.

Friend, Irwin, Marshall Blume, and Jean Crockett, *Mutual Funds and Other Institutional Investors: A New Perspective* (New York: McGraw-Hill), 1970.

"Settling an Estate Could Be Faster and Cheaper," *Changing Times*, November 1972.

"The Need for Truth-in-Savings," *Everybody's Money*, Summer 1972.

"Why So Many Lawsuits against Mutual Funds?" *Changing Times*, November 1972.

Wiesenberger, Arthur, *Investment Companies* (New York: Arthur Wiesenberger & Company), published annually.

CONSUMER ISSUE X
How to Be a Rational Investor

Real Rate of Return: The rate of return received on any investment after the effect of inflation has been taken into account. For example, if you receive a 10 percent rate of return on an investment and the rate of inflation is 5 percent, your real rate of return is only 5 percent.

Dow Jones Industrial Average: A stock market performance indicator that consists of the price movements in the top 30 industrial companies in the United States.

Tax Exempts: Investments that yield income that is tax exempt. Generally, tax exempts are municipal bonds with an interest rate that is not taxed by the federal government.

Liquidity: The "moneyness" that an investment has. The most liquid asset you can own is, of course, cash; it trades dollar for dollar. The next most liquid asset you could own might be a savings account. A house would be an illiquid asset.

As you saw in the last chapter, the various schemes you supposedly could follow to get rich quickly in the stock market are useless, since the stock market is so highly competitive. That happens to be true for just about every other conceivable investment opportunity that you could partake in with your savings. Nonetheless, you must do something with your savings if you want to insure yourself against inflation. In Consumer Issue XI you will receive more specific tips on how to deal with inflation, but we can start pointing them out right here.

INFLATION AND THE INTEREST RATE

You should make sure that the **real rate of return** on your investments is at least positive. For example, you should not be content with buying a Series E Savings Bond from the U.S. government at, say, 5½ or 6 percent interest if the rate of inflation is 5½ or 6 percent. If you do such a thing, your real rate of return will be *negative,* because you have to pay taxes on those earnings. In a period of uncertainty about the future rate of inflation, you should probably invest in mutual funds that buy only short-term debt. You will read about those in more detail in Consumer Issue XI, which follows Chapter 15. Suffice it to say now that these mutuals yield you in the area of 8 to 11 percent. You get essentially the same interest rate that the big money market people get. Right now, if you have very small amounts of savings to invest, there is little else that you can do to protect yourself against inflation. If, however, your goals are long range, the stock market has been shown to be (at least until recently) a relatively safe investment.

EVIDENCE ON THE STOCK MARKET

Numerous studies on the stock market have shown that on the average you can expect to make 8 to 15 percent per year if you reinvest all dividends and refrain from trading for a long period of time. As long as you assume that what has happened in the past will keep on happening, then a stock market investment can be reassuring. For Columbia University economist Phillip Cagen, who, under the auspices of the National Bureau of Economic Research, conducted one of the most recent studies of the stock market, found that in the United States, and in most other countries of the world, the rate of return on common stocks over long periods has been positive, even allowing for inflation. Only during periods of very rapid inflation have stock prices lagged considerably behind consumer prices. Of all the world's stock markets, according to Professor Cagen, the U.S. market

has done especially well in outpacing inflation.[1]

What does this mean for the buyer of stocks? If you decide to buy common stocks, the easiest thing you can do is randomly pick and then hold them until you want to retire. Do not look at the newspaper every day to see what the price of the stock is doing. Do not call a broker for advice on what to do. Just pick at random; do not worry about your choices; and in the long run you will get 8 to 15 percent, which is hard to beat.

However, if you ever have a desperate need of those savings for something like a medical emergency, you may be in trouble. Figure X–1 shows what the stock market did from 1968 to 1974. Its performance was not very impressive. In fact, Figure X–2 shows the **Dow Jones Industrial Average,** which is a composite indication of the value of the top 30 industrial shares in the New York Stock Exchange. But in this figure the averages have been corrected for inflation and the amount of profits the companies pour back

[1] Phillip Cagen, "Common Stock Values and Inflation—The Historical Record of Many Countries," Supplement, No. 13, 1974 (National Bureau of Economic Research, New York, N. Y. 10016).

FIGURE X–1 COMMON STOCKS STAND STILL

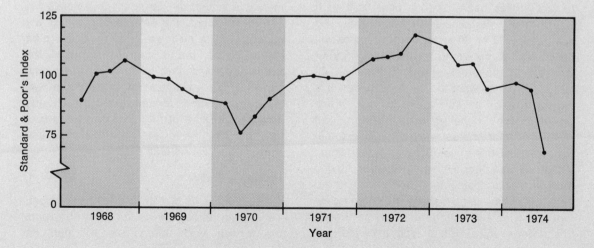

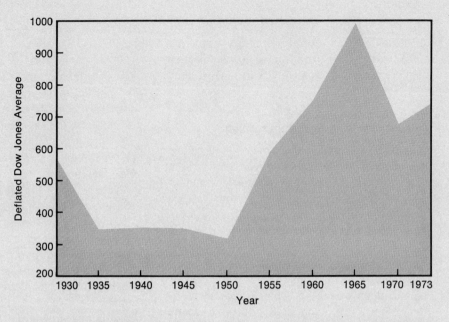

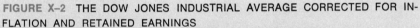

FIGURE X–2 THE DOW JONES INDUSTRIAL AVERAGE CORRECTED FOR IN-
FLATION AND RETAINED EARNINGS
In this figure the Dow Jones depicted in Figure X–1 has been corrected for inflation since 1930, using 1967 as the base. The averages also show correction
for the 3 percent retained earnings that is the average for the economy. The
figures given are the closing highs for each year. The corrected Dow Jones hit
its peak back in 1965 and 1966, and has done little since then. Source: *The Dow
Jones Averages, 1885–1970.* Annual High Closing quotation. Dow Jones & Company, 1972; and Bureau of Labor Statistics.

into the company. This, then, is the Dow
Jones average in *real* terms. It has not been
very impressive over the last five or six years.
In fact, it has been lower in the 70s than it
was in 1959. Nonetheless, those of you who
are looking 20 or 30 years into the future will
find it hard to go wrong by just plunking your
money into the stock market randomly. Of
course, you may want to use the services of a
mutual fund or an investment service, which
we discussed in the previous chapter. But
remember that mutual funds or investment
counselors are not going to help you much
if high service charges are involved in buying
their shares or using their services, particularly if they have a philosophy of "churning"—
that is, buying and selling frequently on special
tips. However, a mutual fund that you can

now buy is offered by Wells Fargo Bank; in
this fund, stocks are purchased "scientifically,"
in proportion to their weight in another stock
market average, the Standard and Poors 500.
For the moment, the service charge for that
mutual fund is no lower than those for other
mutual funds, but it can be predicted that
eventually it will have to come down as more
mutuals take advantage of the random walk
theory presented in the previous chapter.
Anyway, the kind of fund you should favor is
one that has the lowest service charge possible or is of the no-load type.

Picking a Broker

If you decide to buy stocks, you usually can
do so only through a broker. But if you use
the random walk theory, you will need the

EXHIBIT:
Cut-rate
brokerage
fees

Commissions

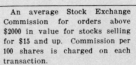

Ours	Theirs
$22 maximum per 100 shares	**$50 average per 100 shares**
Applies to the Top 500 Exchange Listed Stocks and all over-the-counter stocks. Commission per 100 shares is pro-rata portion of a prepaid fee covering commissions for round-lot transactions.	An average Stock Exchange Commission for orders above $2000 in value for stocks selling for $15 and up. Commission per 100 shares is charged on each transaction.

Let's say you want to buy 200 shares of U.S. Steel.

You can either go to a conventional Exchange Member broker to buy it or you can come to us.

If you go to them, it will cost you about $130 in commissions. If you come to us it will cost you $44, maximum.

You pay the same price for the stock and get the same account services, either way.

That kind of difference, more than ⅜ths of a point per 100 shares, can make trading in the market worthwhile again.

And over the long run, it can materially increase your overall returns.

Here's how we do it.

First, we save you from paying for stock analysts you don't use. We simply give no advice.

Second, we use the tried and true account practices and services of an Exchange Member firm to safeguard and maintain your accounts.

And, third, we add a new dimension to save you time as well as money, the Third Market.

When you place your order for any one of the Top 500 Listed stocks in the Third Market it is executed at the Exchange price and confirmed to you in minutes, and in one phone call. Plus all the shares in your market order are executed at the single market price you have agreed to before execution.

When we use the Third Market, you don't wait to find out if you bought something or wait to find out what you paid for it.

That's the gist of what you save at Source and how we do it.

For all the details read our brochure, "Saving Money on Commissions."

Send for it by mailing the coupon below. Or call us and we'll put one in the mail today.

Call toll free: (800) 221–2251 (212) 425–3420 (N.Y. State residents)

Please send me your free brochure:
"Saving Money On Commissions"

SEND TO:
Source Securities Corporation
70 Pine Street, New York, N.Y. 10005

NAME _____

ADDRESS _____

CITY _____ STATE _____ ZIP CODE _____

Members Securities Investor
Protection Corporation

Members National Association
of Securities Dealers

SOURCE SECURITIES CORPORATION
70 PINE STREET, NEW YORK, NEW YORK 10005 (212) 425–3420

**EXHIBIT:
Sample rates
for small stock
orders**

In 1974, the Securities and Exchange Commission ended fixed commission rates on trades of $2000 or less. New rates were immediately put into effect by some of the very large stockbrokerage firms, such as Merrill Lynch; Paine, Webber; and Bache and Company. The new rates announced in 1974 were 16 to 25 percent lower than earlier levels, as given in the table below. However, to qualify for these new rates, you, the investor, must send in your money in advance. Obviously, if you plan to make any small investments, it would pay you to shop around among brokerage houses.

New and old rates for stock transactions up to $2,000

Shares Traded	Stock Price	Total Investment	Old Commissions	Merrill Lynch's Sharebuilder Plan	Paine, Webber's Econo-Trade	Bache & Co.
50	$5	$250	$10.34	$7.50	$9.48	$17.00
50	20	1,000	25.30	20.90	22.48	30.00
100	5	500	18.04	14.25	16.32	22.00
100	20	2,000	41.80	34.65	37.15	40.00
200	5	1,000	36.08	32.65	36.17	40.00
200	10	2,000	55.00	44.65	48.88	50.00

services of a broker only for executing your order. In New York and elsewhere, there are some cut-rate commission places like the one in the accompanying exhibit, but they usually are not available to small investors. Eventually, the stockbrokerage industry should become more competitive and less regulated, but right now, regulations imposed on member firms of the New York and American stock exchanges prohibit complete competition on the basis of price for other than very large orders. However, the stock market regulatory agency —the Securities and Exchange Commission— seems to be in the mood to change this.

In any event, you should pick a broker who meets your needs. If, as many people do, you like the psychological benefit of having a broker call you often with hot tips, then you want to get an outgoing one who will be calling you all the time. But if you value your time and get few kicks out of the stock market *per se,* then just call any broker in the book, let it be known that you never want to be called, and that all you want is for your orders to be executed. Since there is a penalty in the form of higher service charge for smaller orders, wait until you have enough saved to order your shares of stocks in blocks of 100 or more.

If you want to know more about the ins and outs of the stock market, there are hundreds of books to consult. Most will give you different schemes, but if you believe what you read in the previous chapter, you will ignore them. Probably, the most widely read and most informative book on the stock market is *How to Buy Stocks*, by Louis Engel, available (sometimes free) from Merrill Lynch, Pierce, Fenner and Smith Inc. and also (for about $1.50 in paperback) from Bantam Books.

What about Bonds?

As you learned in the previous chapter, bonds are an alternative to stocks, and many people have them as a form of savings. However, for the reasons mentioned above you must be careful. Unanticipated inflation can make bonds a bad deal. This is particularly true, of course, for low-interest U.S. Savings Bonds, but it may also be true for any other type of bond—federal, state, and municipal government, plus corporate—that is long term and has an interest rate that fails to fully reflect the decreasing purchasing power of the dollars you loaned the people who gave you the bond. Remember, if you expect the inflation rate to be 5 percent a year and you buy a long-term bond that yields only 6 percent, you will make only 1 percent rate of return in real terms. That is not very much, is it? (But, of course, it is better than not buying any asset at all.)

In effect, bonds are fixed income-bearing types of investments. You buy a bond and it yields you a specific annual interest rate or return in dollars. In other words, if you buy a bond that yields you $50 a year and it cost you $1000, you receive a 5 percent rate of return; if it cost you only $500, you get a 10 percent rate of return. Generally, as with all investments, the higher the rate of return, the higher is the risk. What is the risk? The risk is that the issuer of the bond will not be able to pay interest—or will not be able to pay at all.

If you decide to buy any bonds at all, make sure you go through a broker who knows what he or she is doing in the bond market. Tell the broker how much risk you are willing to take and when you want the bonds to mature.

You can buy bonds that mature in 1990, 2000, 2010, or in six months if you want. Bonds are issued by the U.S. government, by state and local governments, and by corporations. For some people, there is an advantage to buying local municipal bonds.

Tax Exempt Bonds

Municipal bonds generally are **tax exempt**— that is, the interest you earn on those bonds is not taxed by the federal government, and in some cases it is not taxed by state governments, either. Nevertheless, these bonds are not always a special deal. Unless you are in a higher income-tax bracket—in fact, unless you are in about the 32-percent or above income tax bracket—tax exempt bonds offer you no advantages over nonexempt bonds. Since the bond market is highly competitive, and everybody knows of the savings in not having to pay taxes on interest from these municipal bonds, their price is therefore bid up so that only people in the higher tax brackets get any special benefit. In fact, if you were in the 14 percent tax bracket and you bought a tax exempt bond, you would be worse off than if you bought nonexempt bonds, because the effective yield would be so low.

To decide whether a tax exempt bond is worth buying, you first determine how the yield compares with the rate you can earn on another investment that is not tax exempt. Table X–1 shows the yield in your particular tax bracket. Say that you are in the $16,000 to $20,000 bracket and the tax exempt yield was 6.0 percent. That would be equivalent to a 8.33 percent rate of return from some other investment that did not have this special tax advantage. On the other hand, if you were in the $32,000 to $36,000 bracket, the 6.0 percent would be equivalent to 10.34 percent of taxable interest. (State taxes are not figured in the table because the rates and rules governing taxability of municipal bonds vary widely.)

Tax exempt bonds are usually available in both $1000 and $5000 denominations. Unfortunately, most of the newer bonds are being issued in $5000 denominations, so small investors cannot directly purchase them. However, you can buy shares in tax exempt bond mutual funds instead of buying the bonds themselves.

Financial Backing Differs

Note that tax exempt bonds are classified not only according to the organizations that issue them—states, territories, cities, towns, villages, counties, local public housing authorities, port authorities, water districts, school districts— but also according to the sources of funds that the issuing organizations can utilize to pay interest and principle. As an example, general obligation tax exempt bonds are backed by the full credit, and ordinarily by the full taxing power, of the state or municipality. On the other hand, *revenue* tax exempt bonds are backed only by revenues from a specific activity, such as a water supply system or a toll road. In addition, bonds are rated according to their riskiness, all the way from very risky to not risky at all.

REAL ESTATE DEALS

Of course, by now you will be suspicious of any "special" high-yield real estate deals. But you should not necessarily rule out real estate as a possible investment for your savings, as long as you avoid being taken in by any real estate scheme—particularly those introduced by door-to-door salespersons or mail ads. If you have any interest in land in the middle of Arizona or Texas or Florida, investigate before you invest. Generally, you are locked into those deals for many, many years before you can get any money out at all—that is, they are extremely illiquid. Moreover, the selling charges may be incredibly high and many of them border on being frauds. If you do decide to go into real estate, remember that rate of return is positively related to risk: the higher the potential rate of return that someone offers you on a real estate deal, the higher the risk you are going to take. Just as long as you are aware of that, you will never be duped.

VARIETY IS THE SPICE OF INVESTMENT

It is generally advisable to seek variety in your savings plans, for several reasons. First, not all of your savings should be in illiquid

TABLE X–1:
THE AFTER–TAX RETURN ON TAX EXEMPT MUNICIPAL BONDS

Market Yield	AFTER–TAX YIELD * Taxable Income				
	$16,000–20,000	24,000–28,000	32,000–36,000	44,000–52,000	64,000–76,000
4.50%	6.25%	7.03%	7.76%	9.00%	10.00%
5.00	6.94	7.81	8.62	10.00	11.11
5.50	7.64	8.59	9.48	11.00	12.22
6.00	8.33	9.37	10.34	12.00	13.33
6.50	9.03	10.16	11.21	13.00	14.44
7.00	9.72	10.94	12.07	14.00	15.56
7.50	10.42	11.72	12.93	15.00	16.67
8.00	11.11	12.50	13.79	16.00	17.78

* Based on Joint Return.

TABLE X-2: VARIOUS SAVINGS OUTLETS. Here we show the various saving outlets, ranging from cash to unimproved real estate. Column 1 lists how well your principal is protected. In column 2 we list how good these particular investments have been as an inflationary hedge. In column 3 are average rates of return in the mid-1970s. Column 4 indicates how well you can expect that return to continue year in and year out. Column 5 indicates what kind of transactions costs are involved in getting in and out of the particular types of investments. Column 6 indicates whether or not you have a liquid asset. And column 7 gives you your chances for long-term growth.

SAVINGS INVESTMENT	(1) PRINCIPAL	(2) INFLATION	(3) RATE OF RETURN, %	(4) CERTAINTY OF CONTINUED RETURN	(5) SMALLNESS OR LACK OF SELLING CHARGE OR OTHER FEES	(6) LIQUIDITY UNDER ALL CONDITIONS	(7) CHANCE FOR LONG-TERM GROWTH
Cash	Exc.	Poor	0	—	—	Exc.	None
Life Insurance	Exc.	Poor	3–5(a)	Exc.	Fair	Exc.	Poor
United States savings bonds	Exc.	Poor	6	Exc.	Exc.	Exc.	Poor
Savings account in commercial bank*	Exc.	Poor	4½	Exc.	Exc.	Exc.	Poor
Bank savings certificates	Exc.	Poor	(b)	Exc.	Exc.	Exc.	Poor
Mutual savings bank*	Exc.	Poor	5	Exc.	Exc.	Exc.	Poor
Federal savings and loan association*	Exc.	Poor	5¼	Exc.	Exc.	Good	Poor
Credit Union	Exc.	Poor	5½(c)	Good	Fair	Good	Poor
Corporate bonds	Good	Poor	4–7, 7½, 9	Exc.	Fair	Good	Good
Corporate stock	Fair	Exc.	3½–8	Good	Fair	Good	Good
High-grade preferred stocks	Good	Poor	7½–9	Good	Fair	Good	Poor
High-grade convertible preferreds	Good	Good	4–4½, 5–9	Good	Fair	Good	Good
Convertible bonds	Good	Good	3–4½, 5–9	Good	Fair	Good	Good
Investment companies (mutual funds)	Fair	Exc.	3½–5½	Fair	Poor	Good	Good
Common trust funds	Fair	Fair	4–6	Fair	Fair	Good	Fair
Real estate mortgages (as investments)	Fair	Poor	6½–7¼, 7–9	Fair	Poor	Poor	Poor
Unimproved real estate	Fair	Good	—	Poor	Poor	Poor	Good

* Insured up to $40,000 FDIC or FHLIC.

SOURCE: Adapted from "What to Do With Your Savings," *Changing Times.*

(a) depends on your tax bracket
(b) under $1000:
  5% @ 30–89 days
  5½% @ 90–364 days
  6% @ 1–2½ yrs.
  6½% @ 2½–4 yrs.
  7¼% @ 4 yrs. or longer
(c) industry average

assets. If you have a disaster that requires money quickly, you would like to have some cash or savings account reserve that you can take out immediately without losing anything. Remember, however, that for keeping cash you pay a cost—the cost of the rate of inflation that shrinks the purchasing power of those dollars.

The second reason is that you can reduce your overall risk by having a large variety of different investment assets. There are no fixed rules to follow, although many investment counselors have their own. They might say to have a certain fraction of your assets in cash, a certain fraction in a savings account, and so on. But there is no scientific rule or reason behind any advice like this. You must decide yourself how much **liquidity** you want, how much risk you want to take, how many long-term investments you want, how many short-term investments you want.

Remember, as you increase the variety of risks that you have in your investment portfolio, you lower the overall risk involved in that whole portfolio, but you also lower the overall rate of return you will receive. You may want to gamble as part of your investment program. You may want to buy, for example, penny stocks that sometimes jump tremendously in value. You may want to buy stocks on local over-the-counter markets that have a high variability and sometimes really hit. But you certainly should not put all your eggs in this basket because if you lose you will have nothing. On the other end of the spectrum, you could be absolutely safe by keeping everything in the savings account; but since you would be unable to make a higher rate of return, you probably do not want to do that, either. Remember, successful investment does not mean making a killing. It means preventing yourself from suffering losses that deprive you of retirement savings and, at the same time, being reasonably certain that you will get a normal rate of return on

those savings. Any other goals that you choose will cost you.

SUMMARY

1. Whenever you try to ascertain the rate of return from any investment, subtracting the rate of inflation from the interest rate you receive on your investment will give you some notion of the real rate of return.

2. Even though the American stock market did not perform very well during the first part of the 1970s, historically it has been an excellent hedge against inflation. Anybody putting savings into the stock market and leaving them there and reinvesting all dividends obtained would have received an 8 to 15 percent rate of return from the 1920s through the 1960s.

3. It is advisable to diversify your investments: have some in cash, some in a savings account, some in the stock market, some in bonds, and some in mutual funds that buy only short-term government securities or certificates of deposit and bankers acceptances. (These funds are discussed in the following Consumer Issue.)

4. It pays to shop around for the best deal in the commission you must pay to purchase stocks, since different brokerage firms have different rates.

5. Unless you are making enough income to be in a relatively high income tax bracket, it is not worthwhile for you to purchase tax exempt municipal bonds. Leave them to the wealthier Americans.

6. Be wary of real estate deals, particularly those touted by door-to-door salespersons or mail advertising announcements. You never get something for nothing. No investment deal can truly offer you a higher than normal or competitive rate of return unless you are willing to take a higher amount of risk.

QUESTIONS FOR THOUGHT
AND DISCUSSION

1. Why do you think so many people have bought U.S. Savings Bonds?

2. Why do you think the stock market did so poorly in the early part of the 1970s (and perhaps may still be doing poorly)?

3. The rate of return on the stock market is basically the rate of return to American business. So long as American business continues to make a rate of return of around 10 percent, so, too, should investors in the stock market. Do you agree or disagree?

4. Why do you think you can obtain so much free research from various brokerage houses?

5. What do you think determines the price of a stock?

6. What is the difference between a corporate bond and a government bond?

7. Why do you think the interest earned on municipal bonds is not taxed by the federal government?

8. Why is there so much diversity of opinion about what are appropriate investments?

THINGS TO DO

1. Write a list of any investments you have. Figure out which one of them has any hedge against inflation. Figure out what your average yearly rate of return is on those investments.

2. Find the Consumer Price Index increase for last year: that is, find out what the rate of inflation was. Then compute the real rates of return on Series E Savings Bonds, savings accounts, and any other investment you have information on. Can you explain how some real rates of return are actually negative? Why would any investor leave money in such an investment?

3. Call a stockbroker and have information sent to you on mutual funds in the United States. Find out the characteristics of growth funds versus income funds versus high-risk funds versus low-risk funds. How would you decide which mutual fund to buy? Find out the difference between load and no-load mutual funds. Why would anybody want to pay the sales commission to buy a load fund as opposed to a no-load fund?

4. Look at the next to the last page of the *Wall Street Journal*, which shows the Dow Jones Industrial Average. Can you see any pattern in what has happened to the average price of stocks?

5. Find out the latest rates for purchasing less than $2000 worth of stock. Try to determine why some investment brokerage houses charge less than others.

6. Read a book on the stock market, such as *How to Buy Stocks* by Louis Engel. Now read a book on how to get rich quickly in the stock market. What is the difference in the information obtained from these two books? How valuable is the information from the second book?

7. Find out from a stockbroker or a local financial service what the interest rate is for tax-exempt municipal bonds. Does that interest rate exceed the rate of inflation?

SELECTED READINGS

American Research Council, *Your Investments*, eighteenth edition (New York: McGraw-Hill), 1970.

Amling, Frederick, *Investments: An Introduction to Analysis and Management*, second edition (Englewood Cliffs, N. J.: Prentice-Hall), 1970.

Doane, C. Russell, and Charles W. Hurll, Jr., *Investment Trusts and Funds from the Investor's Point of View*, Economic Education Bulletin XI.2, American Institute for Economic Research, March 1971.

Reilly, F. K., G. L. Johnson, and R. E. Smith, "Inflation, Inflation Hedges, and Common Stocks," *Financial Analysts Journal*, January/February 1970.

CHAPTER PREVIEW

☐ What has been the history of prices in the United States?
☐ How does inflation in the United States compare to that in the rest of the world?
☐ Does inflation hurt everybody equally?
☐ Why is it important to look at *relative* prices?
☐ What has happened to income as prices have gone up?
☐ What is the effect of inflation on interest rates?
☐ How does inflation affect your income taxes?

GLOSSARY OF NEW TERMS

Hyperinflation: An inflation that has gotten out of hand. In the United States, we have experienced a hyperinflation in the South during the Civil War. Germany experienced a hyperinflation after World War I when it required literally wheelbarrows full of German marks to buy a loaf of bread.

Nominal Dollars: Dollars that you pay out as measured by their face value which does not take account of their purchasing power.

Relative Prices: The price of something relative to the price of other things. For example, if the price of apples goes up by 50 percent and the price of oranges goes up by 100 percent, then even though apples have a higher absolute price, they have a lower relative price with respect to oranges.

Cost of Living or **Escalator Clause:** A clause in a labor contract giving automatic wage increases tied in some way to cost of living rises in the economy. Cost of living is usually measured by the Consumer Price Index.

The constant increase in the cost of living in the United States is a phenomenon none of us has been able to avoid noticing. Rising prices now seem as inevitable as death and taxes. We are continually reminded by newspaper and magazine articles that today's dollar is worth only 30 percent of 1939's dollar. Although prices have not always gone up at such rapid annual rates, they have been rising at a compounded rate of almost 1 percent per year from 1867 to the 1970s. The pace of inflation (defined as a *sustained* rise in prices), however, has not been even.

HISTORY OF PRICES

The erratic behavior of prices is shown in Figure 15–1. After shooting up at a rate of 25 percent per year during and after the Civil War, the price index *fell* at the rate of 5.4 percent from 1867 to 1879. That is equivalent to a halving of the price level in less than 15 years. During those years of falling prices, farmers and businessmen cried out, strangely enough, for higher prices —inflation and "greenbackism," as it was later called. Farmers thought that inflation would cause the prices of their products to rise faster than the prices of the products they bought. However, politicians apparently did not listen very well, for prices kept on falling, averaging a decline of 1 percent per year from 1879 to 1897. Prices then rose 6 percent per year continually until a few years after World War I. For several years after the war, prices fell drastically and then remained fairly stable until the Great Depression, which started in 1929. Wholesale prices dropped at an average rate of 8 percent a year from the stock market crash until Roosevelt declared a "banking holiday" in March 1933. Roosevelt's attempts to raise prices were successful, and there was general inflation until 1937. Then prices leveled off until the beginning of World War II.

The rate of price rises during World War II was lower than those during both the Civil War and World War I. The wholesale price index rose 118 percent from August 1939 through August 1948—about 9 percent per year. From 1948 until the mid-60s, prices remained quite stable except for a jump during the Korean War at the beginning of the 1950s. Since the Vietnam involvement around 1965, inflation has accelerated.

THE HIGH COST OF LIVING

HISTORY OF PRICES
IN THE UNITED
STATES, 1770–1975
Here we see the
wholesale price index
for the past two
centuries. As can be
seen, prices have not
always been rising, even
though the experience
of the past few years
might lead us to that
conclusion. Almost
every war in our history
has been associated
with a rise in the
wholesale price index.
Source: U.S. Depart-
ment of Commerce.

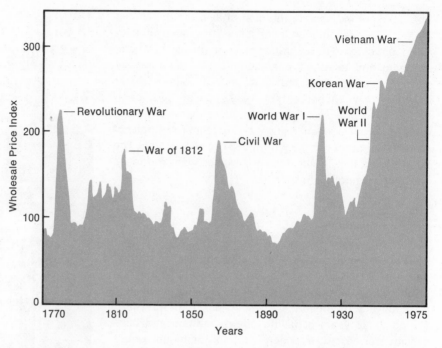

INFLATION IN OTHER COUNTRIES

The United States is not alone in its history of rising prices. Inflation seems to be a worldwide problem, as can be plainly seen in Table 15–1. In fact, our rate of inflation is mild compared to those in many other countries. Some countries have had periods of **hyperinflation** that make our wartime episodes look like ripples in the monetary ocean. In 1939, Hungary had a price index set at 100; by January 1946, it was almost 5,500,-000. A half year later, it was 20,000,000,000,000, or 2×10^{13}! This means that a commodity with a 1939 price tag of 100 forints would have cost 5,500,000 forints in January 1946, and by August of the same year it would have cost 20,000,000,000,000 forints. Imagine having to carry a wheelbarrow full of money to the store just to buy a loaf of dark bread!

WHO IS HURT BY INFLATION?

Misery may love company, but numerous international bedfellows will not alter the effects of inflation. The question is: Do we necessarily suffer because of inflation, and, if so, is the suffering "equitably" distributed? Although we have observed that falling prices (deflation) generally bring misery, inflation certainly does not always mean prosperity. Even if it did, not everyone would benefit. When prices rise unexpectedly, those persons who have given credit to others are repaid in "cheaper" dollars— that is, dollars that cannot buy as much as before. When the price level goes up unexpectedly before account can be taken of its rise, any obligation fixed in terms of **nominal dollars** will cause creditors to lose and debtors to gain. The moral, of course, might be to borrow all you can, if you expect an inflation that nobody else expects.

If everyone anticipates rising prices, the cost of borrowing (interest rate) will go up. People who lend money will demand higher interest rates as compensation. They know if prices rise, the money they are repaid will buy less than when they lent it. If a person lends $5000 (enough money to buy a Buick Riviera) when prices are rising, by the time he is repaid, $5000 may buy only a Dodge Dart. Debtors anticipating this decreased purchasing power will pay the higher interest rate. If you know that prices will rise 5 percent by the end of next year, you will not lend money unless you are compensated for the loss in purchasing power. You will charge 5 percent more than if you had expected no inflation, instead of 3 or 4 percent interest, you will demand 8 or 9 percent.

POCKET MONEY

All of us, in some sense, are bondholders because we carry cash with us. A dollar bill is basically a noninterest-bearing bond from the government. Its expiration date is infinity, and it pays zero cents a year in interest. Anyone holding cash during an inflation loses part of his or her real (as opposed to nominal) wealth when prices rise. The real value of your cash is what it can be traded for—what it can buy. When the price level goes up, the same amount of cash no longer buys as much. If you kept an average checking balance (which is considered to be like cash) of $100 in 1974, its purchasing power would have fallen by about 8 to 10 percent by the end of the year.

Inflation therefore causes people to lose purchasing power in proportion to the amount of cash they generally keep on hand. The only way to avoid this loss of purchasing power is to keep no cash balances. But, as we have discussed previously, life without cash can be very inconvenient.

OTHERS WHO SUFFER
FROM INFLATION

In addition to the specific groups of people who can be hurt by inflation— creditors, bondholders, and those with cash balances—people with fixed incomes have suffered at least in the past. (Others, believe it or not, have actually benefited.) During the first part of the inflationary '60s, there was price stability; during the second part, prices started to increase at 1.3 percent a year and then at as much as 6 percent a year.

TABLE 15–1:
WORLD RATES OF INFLATION, 1973
Source: First National City Bank

United States	5.0%
Sweden	5.8
France	6.3
Austria	7.1
Spain	7.8
United Kingdom	7.8
Mexico	9.9
Brazil	13.1
Argentina	41.7

The aged, who generally rely on fixed incomes, saw their real level of living fall during the period between 1964 and 1968. Social Security payments rose more than the price level, but the payoff from other retirement plans—bonds and fixed dollar-value financial assets such as savings and loan shares—did not. These payments actually fell.

Fixed Income People. Historically, all persons who have income that is fixed in nominal terms (that is, set at a dollar amount not altered to maintain a certain real level of living) will lose during unexpected inflation. Bonds and retirement payments usually pay a set amount of dollars a year. But if people were certain that prices would rise in the future, they would demand retirement plans that offered a constant real standard of living during their retirement years. Some are doing just that now.

Union Workers. Union workers also lost out during the latter part of the 60s. Union workers are usually covered by long-term contracts; hence, when prices started to rise, many unions still had to wait to get wage in-

creases. For the three-year period between 1966 and 1969, union wage rates, after taxes, hardly rose at all in purchasing power. Since then, unions have attempted to make up for lost growth in real wages and have also tried to build into their contracts their expectations of a continuing inflation.

Ultimately, no general statement can be made that people are better or worse off during inflation. Individually, we must look at our wages and also at the value of all our assets such as a house, stocks, and so on. We must compare any changes in nominal quantities with changes in the purchasing power of the dollar in order to arrive at an idea of the real increase in our income and assets. If your house is worth 50 percent more, but prices have risen 55 percent, your house has actually decreased in real value.

CONTRACTS
NEGOTIATED
IN REAL TERMS

It appears that real wages did not rise in the latter part of the '60s, so many workers did not actually improve their lot. We can easily see why this happened: no one expected prices to rise as rapidly as they did. If everyone feels that prices will keep rising at their current rate, workers will demand contracts that include purchasing power adjustments every year; bondholders will demand a yield (interest rate) which includes an inflationary adjustment; and retirement plan purchasers will demand variable, inflationary adjusted, future incomes. The only people who cannot completely avoid all negative effects of long-term, anticipated inflation are those who hold cash—which means all of us. We have to pay the tax imposed by inflation on the use of our currency and checking account balances as long as we continue using them.

**RISING PRICES
AND YOU**

All of the general information about inflation may be interesting in and of itself, but of course what you want to know is how inflation affects you. First of all, you know that prices are rising, for that is the definition of inflation. How much prices have been rising in your area is, of course, more specifically applicable to decisions you make. Let us look at some of the average increases in prices of various consumer items over the period 1960 to 1972. Table 15–2 shows the price rise of refrigerators, TVs, cars, and washing machines, as well as the price rise over the same period for the average of all prices, as represented by the Consumer Price Index. The Consumer Price Index is compiled by the Department of Labor, Bureau of Labor Statistics, which collects a market basket of goods and services every so often and finds out what the price is, and then computes an index based on how these prices compare to those of some base period (1967 in Table 15–2).

Do you notice something strange? The prices of the goods have risen less than the Consumer Price Index. That tells you that the relative prices (given in parentheses below the observed price indexes in Table 15–2) of certain goods are lower today than they were 15 years ago. This is an

TABLE 15-2: PRICE CHANGES FOR CERTAIN CONSUMER GOODS

The first column lists the Consumer Price Index for all items that consumers bought from 1960 to 1972. A price index for televisions, washing machines, electric refrigerators, and new and used cars is given for each year. Underneath each price index is what we call the relative price index, or the price of these consumer durables relative to the price of all other goods. Our base year is 1967 for both the relative price index and for the observed price index. So you see in the row after 1967 all the indices are 100. Obviously, the observed price index for many consumer durable goods has been rising at rates less rapid than the overall Consumer Price Index. In fact, the price index for television sets remained relatively constant after 1967, while the Consumer Price Index rose 25 percent. Thus, at the end of the period, the relative price of TVs had fallen around 25 percent.

Sources: U.S. Department of Labor, Bureau of Labor Statistics, *Handbook of Labor Statistics, 1972; Monthly Labor Review*, Feb. 1973.

1967 = 100, relative index given in parentheses underneath

YEAR	CPI ALL ITEMS	TELEVISION SETS	ELECTRIC AUTOMATIC WASHING MACHINES	ELECTRIC REFRIGERATORS	AUTOS NEW	USED
1960	88.7	127.1 (143.3)	110.7 (124.8)	116.8 (131.7)	90.6 (102.1)	104.5 (117.8)
1961	89.6	123.8 (138.2)	107.4 (119.9)	115.2 (128.6)	91.3 (101.9)	104.5 (116.6)
1962	90.6	117.7 (129.9)	104.5 (115.3)	112.5 (124.2)	98.0 (102.6)	104.1 (114.9)
1963	91.7	114.7 (129.9)	103.0 (115.3)	109.6 (124.2)	93.4 (102.6)	103.5 (114.9)
1964	92.9	112.1 (120.7)	101.6 (109.4)	107.4 (115.6)	94.7 (101.9)	103.2 (111.1)
1965	94.5	107.3 (113.5)	100.2 (106.3)	104.2 (110.3)	96.3 (101.0)	100.9 (106.8)
1966	97.2	102.1 (105.0)	99.7 (102.5)	100.2 (103.1)	97.5 (100.3)	99.1 (103.2)
1967	100.0	100.0 (100.0)	100.0 (100.0)	100.0 (100.0)	100.0 (100.0)	100.0 (100.0)
1968	104.2	99.8 (95.8)	102.5 (98.4)	101.3 (97.2)	102.8 (98.7)	— —
1969	109.8	99.6 (90.7)	104.6 (95.3)	103.1 (93.9)	104.4 (95.1)	103.1 (93.9)
1970	116.3	99.8 (85.8)	107.3 (92.3)	105.8 (91.0)	107.6 (92.5)	104.3 (89.6)
1971	121.3	100.1 (82.5)	104.1 (85.8)	108.1 (89.1)	112.0 (92.3)	110.2 (90.8)
1972	125.3	99.5 (79.4)	110.5 (88.2)	108.7 (86.7)	111.0 (88.5)	110.5 (88.2)

important distinction that you as a wise consumer should always make. It does not matter to you what the *absolute* (or observed) price level is; what matters to you in your purchases is the *relative* prices of those things you buy. If all other prices went up by 500 percent, but the price of washing machines went up only by 100 percent, then even though the *absolute* price of washing machines would be higher, they would have become a very good deal because their *relative* price would have fallen dramatically.

AND INCOME, TOO

So far, our argument has been academic. If everything went up in price except your wages or income, you would really be in trouble. But Figure 15–2 shows the average income in the United States. It has been going up at 9.1 percent a year for the last 5 years. In other words, incomes generally go up not only as much as prices do, but even a little more every year. Thus, even though prices have risen, most of us are actually better off at the end of the year, because our wages or total incomes have risen even more. Now, you may be convinced that rising prices are killing you, but you must take stock of what your real standard of living is: if your income went up by 7 percent and prices went up only by 5, your real standard of living went up by 2 percent, in spite of the inflation. Do not be taken in by arguments that we are all worse off because of inflation. Only those of us who do not have income increases that match or exceed the rate of inflation are truly worse off, and, historically, the incomes of few people have failed to keep up with inflation. Those who generally suffer are the ones mentioned above—people on fixed incomes and the like.

ANTICIPATING INFLATION

To avoid being hurt by inflation, you must anticipate it. And we generally anticipate inflation by looking at the behavior of past prices. Generally, if we think that inflation will continue, we will act accordingly. We will demand—if we have the power—higher salaries to take account of the inflation; we will realize that things are going to cost us more in the future; and we will not be satisfied, for example, with keeping constant levels of insurance or retirement benefits available for us, because we know that the real value of those items will be lowered by rising prices. Remember, the real value of anything is its implicit purchasing power. As prices rise, the real value of, say, a $50,000 insurance policy falls, because $50,000 buys less and less every year.

INTEREST RATES AGAIN

We talked about interest rates before, and we also mentioned the relationship between market interest rates—that is, the ones you have to pay —and the rate of inflation. But so important a point is worth repeating. Every time you borrow money, you must pay a price for the use of that money. Whenever an inflation is anticipated, creditors wish to be compensated for the cheapening of the dollars that they will be repaid. That is, creditors tack on an inflationary premium to take account of the depreciation in the dollars they will get back, for those dollars will buy less. For example, if you borrow $1000 and one year later repay your creditor $1000 plus interest, and there has been no inflation at all, then the purchasing power of the principal—that is, $1000—is exactly what it was a year before. However, if there has been a 10 percent inflation, your creditor will be able to purchase only $900 worth of goods and services because of that inflation: the purchasing power of that $1000 will have fallen 10 percent. No one will want to loan out the money unless in addition to the normal interest rate there is also an inflationary premium.

Moreover, debtors are willing to pay that inflationary premium because they know that they are going to pay back their debt in depreciated dollars. If you subtract the anticipated rate of inflation from the interest rate charged you for a loan, you get the real rate of interest; that is the

FIGURE 15-2
PER CAPITA
PERSONAL
DISPOSABLE INCOME
Per capita personal
disposable income is
expressed in current
dollars. That is, it is not
corrected for changes in
the price level. Notice
that it has been going
up steadily from 1919
until the present, except
for the Great Depression
when it started going
downhill. Source:
*Business Conditions
Digest,* U.S. Department
of Commerce, August
1974, *Survey of Current
Business.*

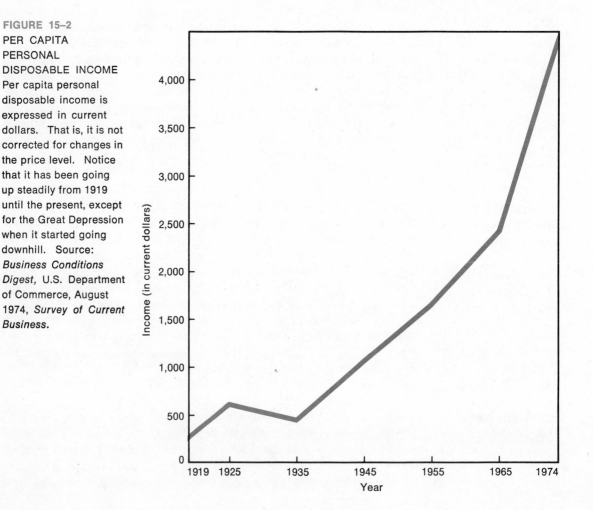

real cost to you in terms of what you are giving up in purchasing power to have command over goods and services today instead of waiting. If the rate of inflation in the United States went to 100 percent a year, you would not be surprised, then, to see interest rates of 105 percent, if people thought that rate of inflation would remain in effect forever.

HOW TO TELL WHERE YOU STAND

How can you tell where you stand with respect to inflation? The easiest way is to try to figure out how many hours it takes you to earn enough income to buy your essentials. Compare the number of hours, for example, it might take you to work in order to pay for a good restaurant meal with how many hours of work it took to pay for that same meal, say, five years ago. Do the same thing for other items you buy. In all probability, most of you will find that it takes fewer hours now to purchase essentials than it did 5 or 10 years ago. What does that mean? That means that your real standard of living may have gone up, in spite of the inflation. Inflation *per se* is only bad to the extent that you and I do not anticipate it and/or cannot take account of it. Once it is fully anticipated, then everything adjusts with it: wages, interest rates, investment plans, and so on. Witness what has happened in Israel, a country with a fairly steady 7 percent a year rate of inflation for the last 10 years. Cost of living clauses are added on to just about all contracts. We are starting to see this in the United States also, where, in 1974, an estimated 2½ million workers were covered under contracts which had cost of living clauses.

WHAT IS A COST OF LIVING CLAUSE?

A cost of living, or escalator, clause in a wage contract is inserted to guarantee workers that they will not be hurt by unexpected inflation. A clause may read that workers' wages will go up 3 percent a year plus whatever percentage the Consumer Price Index went up. That way workers know that their real standard of living will go up by 3 percent a year no matter what happens to overall prices. As inflation becomes a more permanent part of American economic society, you will probably see more and more cost of living clauses inserted in contracts of all sorts.

IF YOU KNOW PRICES ARE GOING UP, SHOULD YOU BUY NOW?

Many people think that in a period of inflation, all purchases for houses, stereos, cars, and the like should be made right away since prices will be higher in the future. This belief may or may not be true: if inflation is fully anticipated, then your basic decision about when to purchase a house or a car depends not in the least on inflation itself. Your timing of purchases should be based on your expected income, how much you want something, whether you are willing to wait, and so on. For example, say that you do not want to buy a car until next year, but you know the price is going to go up 4 percent because that has been the rate of inflation for a long time. If you buy the car this year, you will most likely borrow the money just as you would next year. Thus, for this year you will have to pay an interest rate on whatever you borrow. That interest rate will take account of the expected inflation of 4 percent, so you will be no better off by buying now than by waiting until next year and paying a higher price.

The key to understanding this entire analysis is that if you think inflation is more or less anticipated by everybody, you are not any better off buying now rather than waiting and paying a higher price in the future. And, as we have seen, as prices go up through inflation, income usually goes up also, and often even more so. In other words, the increased price of those potential purchases may be no greater relative to your income.

INFLATION AND INCOME TAXES

As we will see in the next chapter, we Americans have a progressive income tax system: as your income goes up, you have to pay a higher rate of taxation on the last several thousand dollars you earn. This has grave implications in a period of inflation. Suppose that all prices and wages went up every year by 20 percent. Your real income would not increase; that is, your level of living would be the same. Nonetheless, you *would* pay higher federal income taxes, because as your *nominal* dollar income rose due to inflation, you would jump into higher and higher income tax brackets. Hence, inflation can hurt you in that respect even if you anticipate it in all other respects. The only way out of this box is to persuade the government to take account of this fact by continuously lower federal income tax rates for given sizes of income. You could also persuade the government to express your personal exemption and the size of each tax bracket as a number of dollars times the price index: say that prices rose by 20 percent, and the personal exemption today is $750; when prices rose 20 percent, it should become $750 plus $150, or $900. The first tax bracket, taxed at 14 percent, should rise to 0 to $600 instead of the current 0 to $500.

WHAT HAS HAPPENED?

Actually, income tax rates have come down as inflation has increased. Figure 15–3 shows the average amount of taxes paid as a percentage of income from 1941 to 1970. Latest data, however, show that the government is starting to collect a higher percentage of our income in taxes during the 1970's.

ARE YOU BETTER OFF OWNING A HOUSE DURING INFLATION?

Many people think that during inflation it is better to own a house because its value will go up. That sounds so obvious, so inevitably true. Well, it is not true. For example, you bought a $30,000 house. There is an inflation in home values of 10 percent a year. At the end of one year, you could sell that house for $33,000. Now, are you better off by owning it? Well, the cost to you of staying in the house is the same whether you own it or not. If someone else owned it and you were renting, you would be

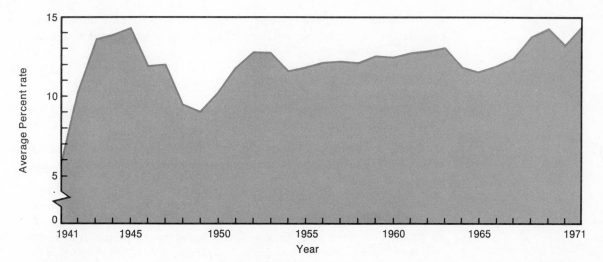

15

10

5

0

Average Percent rate

1941   1945   1950   1955   1960   1965   1971

Year

FIGURE 15–3
AVERAGE EFFECTIVE
TAX RATES

charged a higher rental fee. But since you own it, you in fact obtain an implicit rental value from having the house. You incur a higher opportunity cost for staying in it. The implicit rental value of that house will go up by 10 percent. You will implicitly be paying more to live in it. So on the one hand you gain, but on the other hand you lose in an equal amount. After all, you could sell the house for $33,000 and invest the money to get an explicit rate of return. The higher the value of the house, the higher that opportunity cost you are incurring by not selling it. It does not matter to you, actually, if you were given a house free. You are paying for the services rendered by that house whether you like it or not, because you always have the opportunity of selling it and investing the money. You are not made better off by the fact that inflation has caused the value of your house to go up, for it has caused the value of all housing services to go up. Hence, if you sold your house, you would have to pay a higher price for anything you moved into. (However, if the value of your house went up faster than the rate of inflation, you are obviously a wealthier person.)

But if the *relative* cost of housing has gone up, you may decide to purchase less of it; you may decide to sell your house, which has appreciated in value, and move into smaller, less expensive quarters, and do something with the money difference. That is a decision many of us rarely have to make because the *relative* price of housing generally does not change, although it has somewhat in the last few years. It may also change for you if you happen to live in an area that suddenly becomes a boom town. If this is the case, you may decide that it is too expensive to live in that boom town, *whether or not you own the house and no matter what you paid for it.* The funny thing about an opportunity cost is that it is there even if it is not written in your checkbook ledger. A rational consumer takes account of opportunities even if they are only implicit.

SUMMARY

1.   Prices have not always risen in the United States; in fact, during some periods they have fallen. A falling of prices over any period of time is called a deflation.

2.   Not everyone is hurt equally by inflation. However, everyone who holds cash is hurt by a rise in prices because that cash has a lower purchasing power. Inflation, in a sense, taxes the cash that you hold in the form of currency and checking accounts.

3.   Whenever there is an unanticipated inflation, individuals on fixed incomes suffer because the purchasing power of those fixed incomes falls as inflation remains.

4.   It is important to distinguish a general rise in all prices and a specific or relative rise in the price of a commodity you are buying. Even though all goods have gone up in price recently, some have gone up at a slower rate than the average of all prices as expressed in the Consumer Price Index. Such things as televisions, cars, stereos, refrigerators, and washing machines now have a lower relative price than they had 15 years ago.

5.   If incomes did not rise along with inflation, we would all be worse off. However, in the United States incomes have consistently risen at a slightly faster rate than inflation, thus leading to a rising standard of living for Americans. The key to not getting hurt by inflation is to anticipate it.

6.   Whenever inflation is anticipated, nominal interest rates will rise to take account of that inflation. In other words, an inflationary premium will be tacked on to interest rates to take account of the reduced purchasing power of the dollars paid back. In order to figure out the real rate of interest, you must subtract what you expect will be the rate of inflation over the period of the loan.

7.   More and more workers are being covered by cost-of-living or escalator clauses, which automatically increase nominal salaries whenever there is an increase in the Consumer Price Index. In addition, the workers' contracts usually are negotiated to include a real increase in wages of several percent a year or more.

8.   With our progressive system of taxation, inflation can put individuals in higher income tax brackets even though their *real* income has not gone up. Thus, in real terms, the after-tax income falls and the individual is worse off. Until around 1970, tax rates fell enough to take account of the inflation that occurred, but in the 1970s this has not been the case and the government's "take" from personal income has been increasing as inflation puts individuals in higher tax brackets.

9.   In general, you are not any better off owning a home during a period of inflation as opposed to a period when there is no inflation. Only if the relative price of housing goes up is it better to own.

1. Why would anybody want inflation?

2. How can inflation be so terrible, since our paying a higher price for something yields somebody else that higher price as an increased income?

3. Do you have any idea of what a repressed inflation could be?

4. How many Americans do you think are covered by some form of cost-of-living clauses? (Hint: Social Security payments are now tied to the Consumer Price Index.)

5. Why would anybody sign a long-term contract if it had no cost-of-living clause?

6. Is it important to know the rise in absolute prices—that is, what has happened to the Consumer Price Index—or to find out what has happened to the relative prices of the things you buy?

1. Go to the reference section of your library and look at *The Federal Reserve Bulletin, The Survey of Current Business, Business Conditions Digest,* or *The Monthly Labor Review.* Find out what inflation has been during the past year or so. These government documents contain several indicators that give different types of price indexes. Find out the meanings of those different types of indexes. Does it matter which one you use?

2. Find out what has happened to the relative price of television sets, washing machines, refrigerators, and automobiles since 1972. (Hint: Find the Consumer Price Index for all items and divide it into the price index for the four items just listed.)

Bach, G. L., *The New Inflation: Causes, Effects and Cures* (Providence, R. I.: Brown University Press), 1973.

"Bad News, and Good, About Inflation," *U.S. News & World Report,* March 11, 1974, pp. 56–58.

"Fuel for Another Burst of Inflation," *Fortune,* February 1974, p. 89ff.

"Here's What's Been Happening to Your Living Costs," *Changing Times,* April 1971.

Holt, Charles C., et al., *The Unemployment–Inflation Dilemma: A Manpower Solution* (Washington, D. C.: Urban Institute), 1971.

"Inflation, the Big Squeeze," *Newsweek,* March 4, 1974, pp. 58–62.

Koretz, G., "Global Inflation: A Disease in Search of a Cure," *Business Week,* March 16, 1974, p. 71ff.

Lerner, Abba P., *Flation: Not Inflation of Prices, Not Deflation of Jobs; What You Always Wanted to Know about Inflation, Depression and the Dollar* (Baltimore, Md.: Penguin Books), 1973.

CONSUMER ISSUE XI

Protecting Yourself Against Inflation

Negotiable Orders of Withdrawal (NOW): A type of check drawn on a special NOW savings account offered in a couple of states in the United States; it is a request to withdraw funds from a savings account and transfer them to a third party, just as you do with a check on your checking account.

Treasury Bills: Short-term obligations of the federal government. Treasury Bills are for specified terms of three, six, and twelve months. If the term on government debt is from one to seven years, the certificates are called Treasury Notes; for periods greater than seven years, Treasury bonds are issued, such as U.S. Savings Bonds.

Bankers Acceptance: A bill of exchange draft payable at maturity that is drawn by a creditor against his or her debtor. Bankers acceptances are short-term credit instruments most commonly used by persons or firms engaged in international trade. They are comparable to short-term government securities (for example, Treasury Bills) and may be sold on the open market at a discount.

It is not easy for you to protect yourself against inflation, but there are some ways in which you can at least improve the protection you might have already.

MINIMIZING THE COSTS OF CASH

Remember that if you have an average checking account balance of $100 a year and there is a 10 percent inflation, the purchasing power of that checking account balance is going to fall by 10 percent. You will implicitly be paying an inflationary tax on holding cash. One way that you can reduce the size of this inflationary tax is to reduce the level of cash that you use. In other words, you can economize on the amount of cash you hold and put the difference in an interest-bearing asset. There are now several ways in which you can do this that were not available in the past. We discussed them in Chapter 6. They are usually known as NOW, **negotiable orders of withdrawal,** or such things as transfunds or other similar arrangements whereby all or part of your excess cash that you are not using earns interest while you are not using it. Obviously, the higher the rate of inflation, the more incentive you have to try these systems out, for you are losing money every day on that checking account balance that earns no interest, or on those dollars you keep in your wallet or purse.

INVESTMENTS

Avoid investments that have not adapted to our inflationary times. One of the worst investments of all is the purchase of U.S. Savings Bonds, or Freedom Shares. Until recently, they yielded a negative rate of interest —right, negative!—because your rate of return on them, after taxes, was lower than the rate of inflation; you had less purchasing power than when you bought the bonds themselves.

Until you can be certain that interest rates, for example, on long-term bonds fully reflect the rate of inflation that you anticipate will occur over the next decade, do not buy those long-term commitments, because if the rate of inflation stays at present levels, you are going to lose out. What do you think the rate of return is on a bond that pays you 7 percent a year for the next 10 years if the rate of inflation is 6 percent? Well, first, you will be taxed on that 7 percent, and second, your real rate of return will be almost negligible. Some people like to bet that the future will be better than today, and that if they buy 7 percent bonds and the rate of inflation falls to zero, they will be sitting pretty. It is not recommended that you bet that inflation will slow down to anything like zero percent a year.

The Stock Market

As we pointed out on page 361, for most countries and for most periods, the stock market has been one of the best hedges against inflation in the long run. The *real* rate of return to investing in the stock market has consistently been positive over any long period. However, from the 1960s through the middle of the 1970s, the stock market did not do well at all. By the time you read this text, it may be back on its long-run growth course. In any event, if you are investing for the long haul, you can probably do no better than to put many of your investment dollars into common stocks. The other alternative—particularly for the short run when the stock market doesn't seem to be reflecting current rapid rates of inflation—is to put at least some of your investment dollars in a special type of mutual fund, which we describe below.

FUNDS FOR INVESTING IN SHORT-TERM SECURITIES

Starting a few years ago, interest rates on short-term bonds such as 90-day U.S. **Treasury Bills** began rising. The rates quoted on other short-term financial instruments like commercial bank certificates of deposit were even higher. The stock market was at that time (and may still be) languishing, with rates of return that were either barely positive or, in fact, negative. It was not surprising, then, that mutual funds got into the action to provide small investors with the opportunity to partake in the relatively high interest rates on certain short-term securities such as those mentioned above. The reason that small investors have always been unable to partake in these short-term financial securities is because the minimum amount required is usually too large. For example, certificates of deposit are usually in denominations of $100,000 or more. **Bankers acceptances** are sold only in denominations of $5000 or more. And, more recently, Treasury Bills are sold in denominations of only $10,000 or more, although for a number of years they were sold in $1000 units. In any event, mutual funds that invest their assets—that is, the mutual fund shareholders' dollars—into short-term securities have been flourishing. We will describe a few of them below, but basically they are all the same. They will buy such things as certificates of deposit, bankers acceptances, commercial paper, U.S. Treasury Bills, notes, and bonds, and so on. They buy no common stocks or anything that is very long term; at least they did not when the funds first started in business.

Hedge Against Inflation. These funds, at least in 1974 and '75, seemed to be one of the best hedges against inflation that was available for a small investor. Why? Simply because the interest rates on the short-term bonds that these funds bought seemed to reflect better than other investments the relatively high rates of inflation that were experienced at that time, and which are probably being experienced now. The rates of return on these funds varied from 8 to 9½ percent in 1974. And some of them enabled investors to invest as little as $50 a time after an initial larger investment was given to the fund. This is certainly preferable to the alternative of putting your money into a savings and loan association where the interest rates are regulated by the Federal Reserve System at unreasonably low levels that do not compensate at all for the inflation rates of the 1970s.

Some Representative Funds

Listed below are some representative funds that specialize in short-term securities. This list is not exhaustive, and should not be taken in any way as a recommendation for those listed.

1. Fund for Investing in Government Securities, Inc., American Express Investment Management Company Advisor and Distributor.

   Minimum initial purchase is $1000.

Sales Charges. Sales charges are indicated in Table XI–1.

Table XI–2 shows the sale charge in dollars:

The scale of reduced sales charges shown here is applicable to a single purchase made at one time and to the aggregate of purchases of $10,000 or more made within a 13-month period. The scale is applicable on a cumulative basis: the dollar amount of a current purchase may be added to the value of the shares the investor owns. The sales charge on the shares being purchased will then be at the rate applicable to the aggregate. For example, if the investor held shares valued at $9000 and purchased an additional $6000 of Fund shares, the sales charge for the $6000 purchase would be at the rate of 1.25 percent. There is also a management fee of approxi-

mately one percent of the annual average net assets, in addition to the sales charge which is once and for all.

Automatic Dividend Reinvestment. Shareholders of the Fund automatically receive dividends and capital gains distributions in additional shares of Fund unless the management company is notified by the shareholder that he or she wishes to receive dividends and/or capital gains distributions in cash.

TABLE XI–1

	Sales Charge as a Percentage of the	
Amount of Purchase	Offering Price	Amount Invested in the Fund
Less than $10,000	1.75%	1.78%
$10,000 but less than $25,000	1.25%	1.27%
$25,000 but less than $50,000	0.75%	0.76%
$50,000 but less than $100,000	0.50%	0.50%
$100,000 but less than $250,000	0.30%	0.30%
$250,000 but less than $500,000	0.20%	0.20%
$500,000 or more	0.10%	0.10%

(Dealers selling Fund shares will receive from AEIMCO, the Fund's underwriter, approximately 95% of the sales charged.)

TABLE XI–2

To Invest:	Sales Charge
$ 1,000	$ 17.50
$ 10,000	$125.00
$ 25,000	$187.50
$ 50,000	$250.00
$100,000	$300.00
$250,000	$500.00
$500,000	$500.00

2. Dreyfus Liquid Assets, Inc.
600 Madison Avenue
New York, New York   10022

Minimum initial investment is $1000 if forwarded by a securities dealer (stockbroker), or $5000 if done individually. Subsequent investments must be in the amount of at least $1000.

Sales Charge. There is no actual sales charge for either investing or withdrawing money in this fund. However, a management fee of approximately one percent per year on the total amount of market value of the assets in the fund is assessed to the shareholders. Note that this one percent fee is charged year in and year out.

3. Fund for Federal Securities
A Wellington Management Company Mutual Fund
P.O. Box 823
Valley Forge, Pennsylvania   19482

A minimum initial investment of $1000 is required, but additional investments of $50 or more may be made at any time.

Sales Charge. The sales charge is the same as for the Fund for Investing in Government Securities, Inc.

Management Fee. The management fee is approximately one-half of one percent of the asset value of the fund, paid to the management company year in and year out.

4. Oppenheimer Monetary Bridge, Inc.
1 New York Plaza
New York, New York   10004

The minimum initial investment is $1000 with minimum subsequent investment of $25.

Sales Charge. Sales charges vary as shown in Table XI–3.

Management Fee. Approximately one-half of one percent is charged on the value of the fund at the end of each year, year in and year out.

If you are interested in any of these funds, you can contact them directly, or talk to your stockbroker. In many cases, your stockbroker

TABLE XI–3

Amount of Purchase	Sales Charge as Percentage of Offering Price	Sales Charge as Approximate Percentage of Amount Invested	Dealer Discount as Percentage of Offering Price
Less than $25,000	4.25%	4.4%	4.0 %
$25,000 or more but less than $50,000	3.0 %	3.1%	2.85%
$50,000 or more but less than $100,000	2.0 %	2.1%	1.90%
$100,000 or more but less than $250,000	1.5 %	1.5%	1.45%
$250,000 or more but less than $500,000	1.0 %	1.0%	0.95%
$500,000 and over	0.5 %	0.5%	0.49%

receives 90 percent of the sales charge and, therefore, would be interested in informing you about the various attributes of each of the funds. A stockbroker, however, apparently does not get any commission on selling the Dreyfus Liquid Assets, Inc., mutual fund shares. Also, while that fund appears to have essentially a lower sales charge, it is not completely certain, for its management fee has a maximum of one percent a year that you pay year in and year out, whereas the other funds have management fees that may be only one-half of a percent a year and sometimes lower. So for those other funds, you may pay an initial higher sales charge, but the management fee each year is presumably smaller. Your decision as to which fund to invest in would then have to depend on how long you thought you were going to keep your investment dollars in these specialized types of mutual funds.

ADJUST YOUR LIFE INSURANCE

Once you have figured out your life insurance needs, realize that they do not take account of inflation. Hence, adjust your life insurance policies every once in a while to take account of the decreased purchasing power implicit in the face value of those policies. Many insurance companies are now issuing "agreements for cost of living benefit," by which every year you are charged a fee to have your existent life insurance policies increased in value to take account of inflation. Usually, the Consumer Price Index is used as a basis. For example, say that you have $10,000 worth of term life insurance a year which costs you $5 per $1000. Your total payment at the end of the year would be $50. Now, say that in one year the Consumer Price Index went up by 10 percent. You would get a bill from the insurance company for $5. If you agreed to pay it, this would give you a life insurance policy worth $11,000 in face value. You would still have the same real amount of protection and it would still cost you the same real

amount, although the nominal or dollar payment would go up by 10 percent to take account of the inflation. Whenever possible, you might wish to purchase cost of living benefit agreements for whatever insurance you have. Or every few years, make sure you take out more insurance to take account of inflation.

TAKING OUT LOANS

Whenever you take out a loan of any type, you obviously benefit if the future inflation rate is higher than that anticipated by the creditor. But do not bet on your being able to outsmart creditors; usually, the interest rate that you will pay reflects future rates of inflation. If, however, you are fairly confident that the rate of inflation today is higher than it will be in the future, you may attempt to get variable-interest-rate loan contracts, particularly if you happen to be taking out a home mortgage. At the very minimum, you would want your mortgage to have a no-penalty for prepayment clause put in so that you could pay it off and refinance it at a lower rate if interest rates in the future in fact fall. What is nice about variable interest rates is that no one loses (and no one gains) from any changes in money-market interest rates that reflect changes in the rate of inflation.

RETIREMENT PLANS

You had better make certain that the retirement plan that you take out is not of the fixed-sum type, unless that sum is so large that you will be able to live on it even if inflation continues until you retire. Variable annuities for retirement and life insurance policies are generally available. However, these are usually linked to the stock market, and the stock market, as we have seen in the last chapter, is an imperfect protection against inflation, although in the long run it does not do too badly. What you would really prefer is to

EXHIBIT:

The Effect of Inflation on Take-Home Pay

Because of graduated income tax rates, even families lucky enough to get raises matching the big increase in living costs wound up losing purchasing power. Here we show how a 9.4% inflation outruns a 9.4% pay raise.

	GROSS INCOME	FEDERAL INCOME TAX	EFFECTIVE RATE	AFTER–TAX INCOME IN 1972 DOLLARS
1972	$14,000	$1,600	11.4%	$12,400
1973	15,316	1,890	12.3	12,164
1972	20,000	3,010	15.1	16,990
1973	21,880	3,506	16.0	16,646
1972	30,000	6,020	20.1	23,980
1973	32,820	7,035	21.4	23,361

have the face value of your retirement annuity plan automatically adjust for inflation, and you would have to pay a higher premium each year to compensate for that adjustment. When you discuss your pension plan, your retirement plan, or whatever, with your employer or your insurance agent, be sure that all of these things are openly treated so that you can choose the deal that best enables you to avoid being surprised by a high rate of inflation in the future.

YOUR WAGES

One way to make sure that you do not get caught unprepared by an unexpected rise in prices is to have an escalator clause, which adjusts your wages automatically to changes in the cost of living. You may want to bargain for this individually with your employer or get your union representative (if you have one) to have an escalator clause put in the next contract.

TAXES

There is very little you can do to avoid the effects of inflation on raising your effective tax burden. The only thing you can do is always vote for candidates who ask for lower taxes. That way, you can perhaps have the current trend continue into the future, where the effective tax burden has remained the same over the last 25 years, as evidenced in Figure 15–3. This has been accomplished by lowering tax rates over this same period.

MINIMIZING CASH HOLDINGS

Since inflation can also be defined as the rate of reduction in the value or purchasing power of cash, the faster the rate of inflation, the more costly it is for you to hold cash in the form of dollar bills and checking account balances. Hence, one way you can fight against a rising rate of inflation is by reducing your average cash holdings. You can do this by, for example, keeping excess cash in interest-earning savings accounts (which still may not be a good deal, but certainly gives you a higher interest rate than zero). You can spend more time planning your expenditures so as to match the receipts of your income. In this way, you will not be required to carry as large an amount in your checking account or in your wallet. Of course, the larger your average checking account or currency balance, and the greater the rate of inflation, the more important this consideration is.

IN CONCLUSION

The key to protecting yourself against inflation is to realize the decline in the purchasing power of money paid you in the future. If you think through all of the exchanges you make or are going to make and include an inflationary factor, you will be ahead of the game. There is no way that you can completely protect yourself against inflation in a world where inflation has different rates that people cannot completely anticipate. If everything were written in real terms—that is, with purchasing power clauses or escalator clauses— then you would not have to worry. But not everything is, at least not yet. So you do have to worry. Do not lose sleep over it; just make sure you take advantage of every new inflation protector that you can buy, such as cost-of-living benefit additions to your life insurance, cost-of-living escalator clauses on your wage contracts, checking accounts in which you can earn interest on unused balances, variable interest rate bonds, and so on. You can learn to live with inflation. You may never like it. You may never be able to make it your friend. But you can make sure that it does not destroy your well-being, now or in the future.

SUMMARY

1. During an inflation it is important to minimize the cost of holding cash by reducing the cash you hold that does not bear interest and the balance you have in your checking account.

2. During an inflationary period it is important to avoid investments that do not yield an interest which at least equals the rate of inflation. For that reason, U. S. Savings Bonds are to be avoided unless you want to buy them out of patriotism.

3. It would be advisable to adjust your life insurance to take account of inflation (as well as all other insurance you have, such as on your home and on your personal effects).

4. One relatively new way to obtain a rate of return on your investment during inflationary times that will at least compensate you for inflation is to purchase shares in mutual funds which buy only short-term investments such as U. S. Treasury Bills. A list is presented in this Issue, but you can get further information from a stockbroker.

5. Any retirement plans that you participate in, such as pensions and so on, should be set up to take account of inflation. Therefore, at least part of your retirement income should be in the form of variable annuities that will reflect increases in the stock market. In the past, the stock market has reflected inflation, although it did not during the earlier part of the 1970s.

6. Whenever possible, a cost-of-living clause inserted into a labor contract will minimize any negative effect that inflation could have on your standard of living.

QUESTIONS FOR THOUGHT
AND DISCUSSION

1. Inflation has been called a tax on cash. Why?

2. If you have purchased a level term insurance policy, do you need to adjust it for inflation? (Remember what happens to your need for being insured as you get older.)

3. Why would the stock market be expected to reflect over the long run any rate of inflation that we have?

THINGS TO DO

1. Get information on recent rates of return to mutual funds that specialize in short-term securities such as U. S. Government Treasury Bills, bankers acceptances, and certificates of deposit. Compare those rates of return with rates of return on long-term corporate bonds, which can be found in the *Wall Street Journal* or on the financial page of any newspaper.

2. Find out what the current rate of interest is on U. S. Savings Bonds. Write your senator or representative for an explanation of why the interest rate on U. S. Savings Bonds is less than the rate of inflation.

3. Call an insurance broker to ask about cost-of-living clauses for term insurance poli-cies. See if you can get a copy of one of the agreements for a cost-of-living clause. Find out what the clause is tied to. Is it the Consumer Price Index, the Wholesale Price Index, or the implicit GNP deflater?

SELECTED READINGS

"How to Head Off Today's Soaring Costs," *Better Homes and Gardens,* January 1970.

"Inflation's Bite, Any Relief in Sight?" *U.S. News & World Report,* January 28, 1974, pp. 15–17.

"Inflation's Relentless Squeeze; How Five Families Try to Cope with It," *U.S. News & World Report,* April 15, 1974, pp. 30–32.

"Seeking Antidotes to a Global Plague," *Time,* April 8, 1974, pp. 72–76.

Wolinsky, L. J., "What Can We Do About Inflation?" *The New Republic,* March 2, 1974, pp. 21–25.

CHAPTER PREVIEW

☐ What are the different theories that justify taxation?
☐ What type of tax system do we have in the United States?
☐ How important is the federal personal income tax as a source of government revenues?
☐ What is the history of our progressive tax system?
☐ What are tax "loopholes" all about?
☐ How do special interest groups affect what the government does with our tax dollars?

GLOSSARY OF NEW TERMS

Proportional Taxation: A system of taxation in which the rate of taxation is uniform no matter what the size of income. For example, proportional taxation of 20 percent would take 20 percent of an income of $100, and also 20 percent of an income of $1 million.

Progressive Taxation: A taxing system in which the higher one's income, the higher the tax bracket one is put in to. In a progressive system, you pay a higher rate on the last dollar you earn than on the first dollar you earn.

Regressive Taxation: A system in which, unlike progressive taxation, as you earn more and more income, your tax rate falls.

Average Tax Rate: Simply the total amount of taxes you pay divided by your income.

Free Rider Problem: The problem that, with certain types of goods and services, individuals attempt to get a "free ride" by not paying for what they use. For example, many persons, if asked how much they were willing to pay for national defense, would say "nothing," hoping that others would pay for national defense. Those who don't want to pay want a free ride.

Special Interest Groups: Groups in society that have a special interest in common. Special interest groups generally attempt to influence government legislation to benefit their own particular groups.

The government provides you with numerous goods and services. It generally provides you with a court system, policemen, firemen, public schools, public libraries, and a million other varied and sundry programs to help specific groups in the nation. Governments do not run on thin air, however; they have to be financed. And in the end the only way a government can be financed is by having you, the consumer, give up part of your income to it. You have to do it now to the tune of about 40 percent of every dollar you make. Figure 16-1 shows the percentage of income that has been collected each year by federal, state, and local governments. Right now it is up to 40 percent. Much of that, of course, is returned to you in the form of transfers such as Social Security, unemployment compensation, and the like, but at least 24 percent is direct expenditures by governments. That is fully $350 billion in 1975. Government is big business. We will give you a few ideas on how you can expect governments to behave based on some simple economic principles that you apply to your own day-to-day decision-making. Before we do that, however, let us look at various methods of taxation and some of the principles behind them.

PAYING FOR GOVERNMENT

THE WHYS AND WHERES OF TAXATION

Governments—federal, state, and local—have various methods of taxation at their disposal. The best known, of course, is the federal personal income tax, which generates fully 42 percent of all taxes collected by Uncle Sam. At the state and local levels, personal income taxes are not as popular; property taxes make up the bulk of the taxes collected. In addition to these taxes, there are corporate income taxes, sales taxes, excise taxes, inheritance taxes, and gift taxes. We will not attempt to investigate all of these taxes in detail.

FIRST, A LITTLE THEORY

Naturally, everybody would prefer a tax that someone else pays. Since we all think that way, no tax could be invented that everyone would favor. Economists and philosophers have come up with alternative justifications for different ways of taxing. The three most-often discussed principles of taxation are: (a) benefits, (b) ability to pay, and (c) sacrifice.

THE BENEFIT
PRINCIPLE

One doctrine of taxation that has been widely accepted is the *benefit principle.* According to this principle, people should be taxed in proportion to the benefits they receive from government services. The more they benefit, the more they should pay; if they benefit little, they should pay little. This principle of taxation has problems in application, however. First of all, how do we determine the value people place on the goods and services the government provides? Can we ask them? If people think that others will pay their way, they will claim, upon being asked, that they receive no value from government services. For example, they will tell the interviewer they are unwilling to pay for national defense because they do not want any of it—it is of no value to them. Here is the free rider problem. We all want to be free riders if we think we can get away with it. If you think everybody else will pay for what you want, then most likely you will gladly let them do so. The problem is schematized in Figure 16–1. How much national defense will you benefit from if you agree to pay and everyone else also pays? $90,000,000,100. How

FIGURE 16–1
WHERE $1 IN
FEDERAL
GOVERNMENT
REVENUE COMES
FROM AND WHERE
IT GOES, FISCAL
YEAR 1975
Source: Office of
Management and
Budget.

Getting and Spending the New Budget Dollar

Fiscal Year 1975

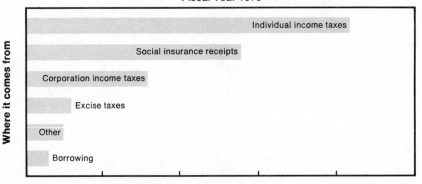

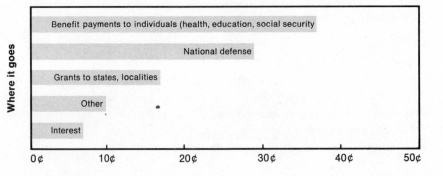

	If you pay	If you do not pay
If everyone else pays	$90,000,000,100	$90,000,000,000
If no one else pays	$100	$0.00

FIGURE 16–2 SCOREBOARD FOR NATIONAL DEFENSE
The free rider is the one who will gladly let everyone else pay for him.
If you don't pay your share of national defense but everyone else
does pay, there will still be $90,000,000,000 available for the country's
defense. Whether you pay or not seems to make very little difference.

much will there be if you do not pay but everyone else does pay? $90,-
000,000,000. If you think everyone else will pay, would you not be tempted to get a free ride?

One way out of this dilemma is to assure that the higher a person's income, the more services he receives, and, therefore, the more value he
gets from goods and services provided by the government. If we assume
that people receive increases in government services that are *proportional* to their incomes, then we can use this benefit doctrine to justify
proportional taxation.

Proportional Taxation. This approach to taxation is merely a system by
which taxpayers pay a fixed percentage of every dollar of income. When
their income goes up, the taxes they pay go up. If the proportional tax
rate is 20 percent, you pay 20 cents in taxes out of every dollar you earn.
If you earn $1000, you pay $200 in taxes; if you earn $1 million you pay
$200,000 in taxes.

Progressive Taxation. At this point, we should contrast proportional
taxes with **progressive taxation.** If a tax is progressive, the more you
earn, the more you pay in taxes, as with the proportional system, but in
addition, the *percentage* taken out of each additional dollar earned goes
up. In the terminology of marginal and average, we can describe progressiveness as a system by which the marginal tax rate goes up. (So
does the **average tax rate,** but not as much.) In the example illustrated
in Table 16–1, the first $100 of income is taxed at 10 percent, the next
$100 at 20 percent, and the third $100 at 30 percent. The average rate
is always equal to or less than the marginal rate with a progressive tax
system. With a proportional system, the marginal tax rate is always the
same, and it equals the average tax rate.

Can the benefit principle of taxation be used to justify progressiveness?
Yes, it can. The only additional assumptions needed are: (a) the *value*
people obtain from increased goods and services provided by the government goes up faster than their income, and/or (b) the *amount* of government goods and services received goes up faster than income. The

TABLE 16–1:
A PROGRESSIVE
TAX SYSTEM
The percentage of tax taken out of each additional dollar earned goes up; that is, the marginal tax rate increases progressively.

INCOME	MARGINAL RATE	TAX	AVERAGE RATE
100	10%	$10	$\dfrac{\$10}{\$100} = 10\%$
200	20%	$10 + $20 = $30	$\dfrac{\$30}{\$200} = 15\%$
300	30%	$10 + $20 + $30 = $60	$\dfrac{\$60}{\$300} = 20\%$

benefit principle alone, without one of these two assumptions, cannot be used to justify progressive taxation.

Regressive Taxation. As you can imagine, **regressive taxation** is the opposite of progressive taxation. Any tax system that is regressive takes away a smaller and smaller additional percentage as income rises. The marginal rate falls and is usually below the average rate. As an example, imagine that all revenues of the government were obtained from a 99 percent tax on food. Since we know that the percentage of income spent on food falls as the total income rises, we also know that the percentage of total income that would be paid in taxes under such a system would likewise fall as income rises. It would be a regressive system.

THE ABILITY
TO PAY DOCTRINE

The second principle of taxation considers people's ability to pay. It states that those who are able to pay more taxes *should* pay more taxes. Obviously, people who make more money should generally be able to pay higher taxes. But do we make them pay taxes which go hand in hand with income (a proportional system)? Do we make them pay taxes at a higher rate, the higher is their income (a progressive system)? Or do we make them pay taxes that go up, but at a rate that is not in proportion to their income (a regressive system)? To answer the questions, we must decide whether their ability to pay rises faster than, in proportion to, or slower than their income. Whatever assumption we make determines whether we use a progressive, proportional, or regressive tax system. The ability to pay doctrine would lead us to recommend progressiveness only if we assume that ability to pay rises more rapidly than income.

THE SACRIFICE
DOCTRINE

The third principle of taxation holds that the sacrifice people make to pay their taxes should be equitable. It is generally assumed that the sacrifices people make when paying taxes to the government become smaller as their incomes become larger. When a $100 tax is paid, a millionaire is surely sacrificing less than a person who only earns $1000 a year. The pleasure that the millionaire gives up for that last $100 is less than the pleasure that the other person gives up for that last $100. Again, we are faced with the problem of determining how fast satisfaction from income rises as income itself rises, and this involves a value judgment. If the satisfaction from income rises at a rate that is less than, equal to, or more than in proportion to income, we will end up justifying a system of progressive, proportional, or regressive taxes, respectively.

THE PERSONAL FEDERAL INCOME TAX

You are probably all aware that the personal income tax system in the United States is of the progressive kind. In Table 16–2 we see part of the 1975 tax schedule. Notice that, as income rises, the marginal tax rate goes up. The rate applicable to the previous lumps of income stays the same, however. Many students think that if you are in the 50 percent tax bracket you pay 50 percent of all your income to the federal government. That is not the case. You may pay 50 percent of your income to the government on your last (marginal) $15,000 earned. However, income made before that last bracket is taxed at progressively lower and lower rates. Even in the 50 percent bracket, you will pay only 32.6 percent of your taxable income to the government. As we see in Table 16–3, personal income taxes account for over 40 percent of all federal revenues. They should not be taken lightly.

TABLE 16–2:
FEDERAL PERSONAL
INCOME TAX FOR A
CHILDLESS COUPLE, 1975
Here we show the different income brackets and the marginal tax rates along with the average tax rates. As you can see, the marginal tax rates go up to a maximum of 70 percent. However, if income qualifies as being "earned," the maximum is 50 percent. All wages are considered earned income, but interest on bonds or dividends from stocks is not.

NET INCOME BEFORE EXEMPTIONS (BUT AFTER DEDUCTIONS)	PERSONAL INCOME TAX	AVERAGE TAX RATE, PERCENT	MARGINAL TAX RATE
Below $ 1,500	$ 0	0	0
2,000	70	3.5	14
3,000	215	7.2	15
4,000	370	9.2	16
5,000	535	10.7	17
10,000	1,490	14.9	22
20,000	3,960	19.8	28
50,000	16,310	32.6	50
100,000	44,280	44.3	60
200,000	109,945	55.0	69
400,000	249,930	62.5	70
1,000,000	669,930	67.0	70
10,000,000	6,969,930	69.7	70

TABLE 16–3:

FEDERAL REVENUES ACCOUNTED FOR
BY PERSONAL INCOME TAXES

During the depression, individual income taxes accounted for less than 20 percent of federal revenues. Now, however, individual income taxes account for almost 45 percent of federal revenues. The importance of the personal income tax has increased. *Source:* U.S. Department of Treasury.

FISCAL YEAR	PERCENT OF FEDERAL REVENUES ACCOUNTED FOR BY PERSONAL INCOME TAXES
1927	25.7%
1932	19.0
1936	16.7
1940	15.5
1944	39.5
1950	40.7
1955	45.1
1960	45.6
1965	43.8
1969	44.9
1971	43.0
1974	42.3

HOW OUR PROGRESSIVE SYSTEM CAME INTO BEING

The Constitution gives Congress the authority "to lay and collect taxes, duties, imports and excises. . . ." No reference was made to an income tax at the time the Constitution was drafted. But in 1894 the Wilson-Gorman Tariff Act provided for individual income taxes of 2 percent on incomes above $4000. The country knew about income taxes from the period during the Civil War, when $4.4 million of such taxes were collected. Nonetheless, the concept of income taxation set forth by the Wilson-Gorman Tariff Act was violently challenged and had to be settled by a Supreme Court decision in 1895. Finally, in 1913, the Sixteenth Amendment was passed. The Amendment reads as follows:

AUTHORIZING INCOME TAXES. The Congress shall have power to lay and collect taxes on incomes, from whatever source derived, without apportionment among the several states, and without regard to any census or enumeration.

Section 2 of the Underwood-Simmons Tariff Act of 1913 provided for a one percent rate on taxable income with an exemption of $3000 plus $1000 more to a married head of household. Notice the concept of exempting the first several thousand dollars of income from taxes. Today we have personal exemptions equal to $750 for every member of the family. A single person is allowed a $750 exemption, whereas the head of a family with a wife and three children is allowed a $3750 exemption.

The Underwood-Simmons Tariff Act also provided for a surtax that was levied progressively on income over $20,000 with a maximum total tax rate of 7 percent on income over $500,000. These taxes may seem paltry in comparison with today's rates, but they were considered quite large in those times. The concept of progressiveness was first introduced and met with considerable debate in 1913; the debate raged for several years thereafter. Today, there is no doubt that progressiveness is here to stay, at least in principle. However, the apparently progressive nature of our personal income tax system has declined somewhat in recent years. Up to 1961, the maximum tax rate was a whopping 91 percent. Today it is only 70 percent, and if you receive all your money by the sweat of your brow, you face a 50 percent maximum rate.

LOOPHOLES

Our progressive tax schedule does not bear a very close relationship with what actually happens in the United States. Everybody knows that there are a tremendous number of *loopholes* in our tax laws. Attempts at closing these loopholes have been resisted by those most strongly affected. When the 1969 Tax Reform Act was finally put into law, it had been altered with so many amendments that even attorneys and accountants could not figure out how to use it. Wise persons renamed the 1969 legislation the "Lawyers' and Accountants' Relief Act"; it was certain that these professionals would see a great increase in the business of helping mere mortals figure out how to complete their tax forms.

Tax shelters or loopholes are devices that allow individuals in high-income brackets to take advantage on their personal income tax return of various business incentives such as accelerated depreciation, the deduction of intangible oil-drilling expenses, capital gains preferential rates (discussed below), and so on. A group of, say, dentists can form a partnership to drill an oil well. From that moment on, they will be able to pay for part or even all of their investment by deducting a combination of these special incentives just mentioned against their dental income. By merely giving up dollars that otherwise would go in taxes, or at least so it seems, they have a chance to bring in a well and strike it rich.

Using similar reasoning, many, many people have invested in tax shelters or loopholes. In 1965, partnerships in the major tax shelter industries of livestock, real estate, petroleum, and natural gas reported $900 million in net losses and $1.4 billion in net profits. By 1971, losses were $4.2 billion and profits were only $2.4 billion. The reason for this growth is quite obvious: the once sparsely populated upper-income brackets, where people start to look seriously for tax shelter (say 40 percent or 50 percent and up), have become increasingly crowded as inflationary forces and rising real incomes have begun to move much larger numbers of people into such high levels of taxable income. No longer the domain of a limited number of financial sophisticates, the market for tax shelters has become a mass market.

CAPITAL GAINS

One of the biggest loopholes in personal income taxation has concerned capital gains rates. A capital gain is defined as the difference between the buying and selling price of a capital asset, such as a stock, a bond, or a house. If you buy a share of Silver Syndicate Mining stock for $13 and, being a financial wizard, are able to sell if for $67, your capital gains are $54. In the past, capital gains have been taxed at one-half a person's marginal tax rate, up to a maximum of only 25 percent. Recently, however, there have been changes in the tax laws so that capital gains are not treated so favorably. Over the years, special interest groups have succeeded in getting more and more of their income classified as capital gains. Today the following types of income, for example, are eligible for preferential capital gains tax treatment: patent royalties, oil exploration, and cattle raising.

If we look at taxes as a percentage of income, without including capital gains as part of income, we come up with a set of tax payments similar to those given in Figure 16–3. When we include capital gains, the figures change quite drastically. All the progressiveness of our tax system disappears. Look, for example, at Table 16–4, which was taken from total

FIGURE 16–3 TAXES AS A PERCENTAGE OF INCOME
Here we show total taxes paid as a percentage of income taken from a survey done in 1965. The average tax rate for the under $2000 per annum income level is somewhat deceiving because those people receive transfer payments. In fact, if you take account of those transfer payments, such as public assistance, their average tax rate is minus 83%. When you take account of the public assistance and other transfers given to the income earners in the $2000–$3999 category, their effective tax rate drops from 26.6% to 15.7%. Average tax payments aren't progressive until $15,000 and over. Source: Economic Report of the President.

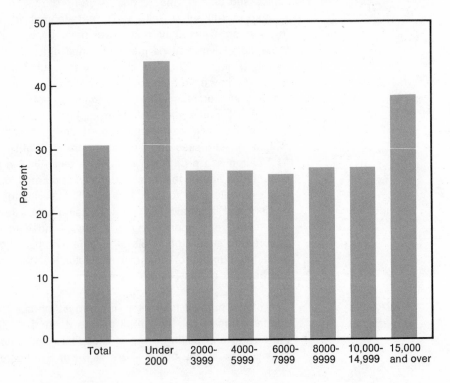

1968 INCOME	TAXES AS A PERCENT OF TOTAL INCOME	TAXES AS A PERCENT OF TOTAL INCOME AND CAPITAL GAINS
Less than $4,000	27.5%	26.6%
4,000–5,999	26.0	25.4
6,000–7,999	25.8	24.5
8,000–14,999	24.2	21.9
15,000 and over	38.1	26.0

income data and from the Tax Foundation Incorporation studies on 1968 incomes. Included are state and local taxes as a percentage of income.

INCOME
REDISTRIBUTION

The progressive income tax is deemed desirable by many people because they feel it will help redistribute income from the rich to the poor. Back in 1952, social historian Frederick Lewis Allen stated: "We had brought about a virtually automatic redistribution of income from the well-to-do to the less well-to-do."[1] This does not seem to be the case, however. The poor still seem to be poor. Joseph Pechman, former president of the American Finance Association, stated in his inaugural address in 1971 that the lowest one-fifth of American families gets only 3.2 percent of the total national income, while the top fifth (earning $12,000 or over) gets a whopping 46 percent. In other words, the top fifth gets 15 times as much as the bottom fifth. The top 1 percent—that is, people with incomes of over $32,000—get 6.8 percent of the total pie. If we compare these income distribution figures with those, say, after World War II, we will find there has not been too much change. This can be seen in Figure 16–4.

**HOW YOU SHOULD
EXPECT
GOVERNMENT TO
SPEND YOUR
TAX DOLLARS**

When any of us analyze the behavior of persons in business, we generally assume that they will do whatever is in their own best interests. Of course, there are exceptions, but it is best not to count on them. If we look at individual economic behavior, we generally will not go too far astray if we assume that people act in their own best interests and not necessarily in those of society. This is not to say that people are inherently bad; it is just human nature. If we take these same ideas about human behavior and apply them to how politicians and government officials will act, we realize that it will *not* be in their best interests to look out *only* for general welfare. You and I as consumers are a diffuse group made up of millions and millions of people with millions and millions of

[1] Frederick L. Allen, *The Big Change: America Transforms Itself* (New York: Harper & Row, 1952).

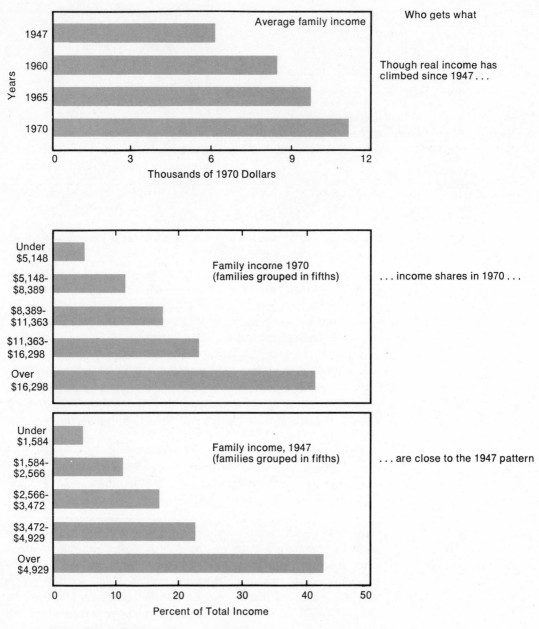

Who gets what

Though real income has climbed since 1947 . . .

. . . income shares in 1970 . . .

. . . are close to the 1947 pattern

Data: Census Bureau

FIGURE 16–4 INCOME SHARES IN THE UNITED STATES THROUGH TIME
We see that the income shares in 1970 are quite close to the 1947 pattern. After
23 years of rising income, the distribution of income has hardly changed at all in
the United States. Source: *Business Week*, April 1, 1972, p. 56.

different tastes, wants, and needs. How could politicians satisfy all of us? Impossible, right? They can, however, satisfy special interest groups. That is what our political system is all about—special interest groups have very defined, clear-cut interests in specific pieces of government legislation. They can see the direct benefit and measure it in dollars and cents. They therefore know how much it is worth for them to spend in order to get that legislation passed. If we were to analyze the legislation now on the books, we would find that most of it was indeed sponsored by special interest groups, and in fact benefits special interest groups only.

When it was discovered, for example, that various milk associations contributed perhaps up to $2 million to the reelection campaign of President Nixon, it was also discovered that just before this contribution was given, milk support prices were raised, benefiting the dairy industry to the tune of about $600 million. This kind of behavior should not surprise you, however. That is exactly what you would expect, because special interest groups are going to look out for their own interests, and if it means influencing government actions, that is what they will do. As long as you are aware of this, then you as a citizen can guard against it by carefully considering all propositions and referenda up before you to vote on. If you first ask the question, "What special interest group is this legislation for?" then see if it in fact benefits you, you will be on your way to a good analysis. If, however, you start reading the slogans attached to the proposed or passed legislation, you are going to get lost in contradictory and often meaningless arguments. The same is true if you want to decide whether or not to vote for a particular incumbent candidate. You can look at his or her legislative record and find out what special interest groups he or she has catered to. This does not mean, however, that you as an individual will not benefit by special interest legislation. We showed, for example, that usury laws will benefit all those people with very good credit ratings who will continue to get credit at the lower interest rate. If you happen to be a plumber, you are obviously going to benefit from very strict building codes that require sophisticated plumbing for all new houses.

It should also not surprise you that regulatory agencies in general end up working on behalf of the regulated firms instead of on behalf of you the consumer. You the consumer generally know nothing about the industry in question because the technical details are too complicated and it would not be worth your while to learn anything about them. However, the firms themselves know the most about their own industry and have the most incentive to influence the regulators. Hence, few are shocked to find out that the Interstate Commerce Commission has worked to preserve noncompetition in the transportation industry; it should not surprise you that the Civil Aeronautics Board fights tooth and nail against competition in the industry; it should not surprise you that just about all regulatory agencies act to dampen instead of encourage competition. You the consumer generally lose out by this government/business marriage. However, in some cases you may win out. It is up to you to decide by seeing the benefits and the costs of different types of regulatory activities.

CAN WE IMPROVE OUR TAX SYSTEM?

Any of you who have tried to fill out a federal income tax form know that our tax system is incredibly complicated. When one President's life-long valet asked him to help out with his taxes, the President could not. It was too complicated to figure out. It is estimated that the cost of filling out forms, measured in people's time, is somewhere between $3 and 5 billion a year! Additionally, there is all the money spent on accountants and lawyers. Why has this all happened? Just as you would expect, because of special interest groups getting special benefits for themselves and thus adding complications to our tax laws.

One of the reasons why special interest groups find it worthwhile to attempt to get special legislation that reduces their tax burden is the high progressive income tax rates. The higher the rate you pay, the greater incentive you have to find a loophole or, as a member of a group with other people in the same situation, to influence tax legislation to benefit your group. If all taxes were only 2 percent, nobody would try very hard to find loopholes. But if you are in the 70 percent tax bracket, you had better believe it is worthwhile to find one. Every dollar of income you can have declared nontaxable nets you 70¢ in cash, for that is the tax you do not have to pay. With all the incredible numbers of loopholes and complexities, our so-called progressive tax system really is not progressive at all, or at least not very much, as evidenced by Table 16–4. Given this fact, there are some obvious tax reforms that could benefit the majority of Americans. When we talk here about tax reform, we certainly do not mean the kind that goes through Congress every few years. A tax reform act was passed back in 1969, as we previously mentioned. Only lawyers and accountants benefited. Just about everybody else lost. The only meaningful way to talk about tax reform is to forget about all special interest groups and do something drastic but simple, such as the following proposal that I have put forth for a number of years now:

1. Eliminate all deductions except an absolute minimum number of bona fide business expenses.
2. Increase the exemption, say to the poverty line of income, meaning that the first $3000 or $4000 of income is not taxed at all.
3. Establish a uniform 15 to 20 percent straight tax rate on all income, no matter where it is from and no matter who earns it.

This is certainly drastic in comparison with what we now have. Notice, however, that the tax rate of 15 to 20 percent is lower than the actual taxes paid as a percentage of total income right now in the United States.

WALL STREET JOURNAL

"**Your tax money is returned to you in many
ways. . . my salary as well as the prosecuting
attorney and the maintenance of the Federal
prison system.**"

How could this be, you might ask. Easy: if you eliminate the high, complicated progressive tax system, you eliminate people's wasted efforts
trying to avoid taxes. There would be a proportionately higher degree
of work effort and higher national income on which to base our taxes.
That is how we could actually lower the overall tax rate and still get as
much revenue as we now get.

Believe it or not, many rich people would be against lowering tax rates
because they know that with all of the loopholes now, they pay very few
taxes anyway. Some pay much less than 15 or 20 percent of their total
income.

Few observers of the tax system acknowledge the virtue in simplicity
of a tax system. It could avoid so many complications, perhaps make
life so much easier for all of us, reduce the incentive for any of us to
cheat, and increase the amount of work that many of us want to do because our tax rates would be lower. Since we do not have a progressive
tax system anyway, it is ridiculous to argue against a uniform nonprogres-
sive tax system on the basis of the "need" for "soaking the rich." We
do not soak them anyway, so why should all of us suffer for some imagi-
nary reasoning?

Unfortunately, you and I still have to suffer. Pure tax reform is a long way off. Until then, it behooves you to know the ins and outs of tax reporting and tax payments. After all, there is nothing wrong with your taking advantage of every single legal way to reduce the taxes you owe your government. You have a right to spend what is legally yours. After all, you earned it.

SUMMARY

1. The three most often discussed principles of taxation are the benefits principle, the ability-to-pay principle, and the sacrifice principle.

2. In both the benefits and ability-to-pay principles, an additional assumption is necessary to use them to justify a system of progressive taxation in which progressively more is taken away from those who earn higher incomes. This additional assumption is that benefits and ability to pay increase *more* than in proportion to income.

3. It is important to realize that in a progressive tax system, you pay a higher tax rate only on the last dollars earned. For example, that you are someone in the 50 percent tax bracket in our progressive tax system does *not* mean that you pay 50 percent of your income in taxes. Rather, you pay 50 percent on the last tax bracket of income only.

4. The personal federal income tax is the most important source of government revenues in this country. It accounts for over 40 percent of all federal revenues.

5. Tax loopholes or shelters are usually available only for higher income earners. In other words, the benefit of a tax loophole is directly proportional to your marginal tax bracket. And unless you are making a high income, your marginal tax bracket isn't very high.

6. Capital gains tax rates are usually lower than tax rates on income. That is why it is beneficial to have any of your income received as a capital gain.

7. In spite of our progressive tax system, income differences have not narrowed in the United States since World War II.

8. In analyzing any prospective government legislation, you must realize that it has probably been influenced by special interest groups. Therefore, informed voters must analyze the legislation to see who will benefit and who will pay. Very little legislation proposed and supported by special interest groups is made with the general welfare in mind. In fact, most of this legislation by necessity must hurt the consumer. Many restrictions on economic activities are of this nature, as well as the subsidies that are legislated for particular industrial and agricultural groups in our society.

9. It would be possible to improve our tax system by true reform in which all loopholes were eliminated, a large exemption were instituted, and a flat proportional tax of 15 to 20 percent were used in place of our very complicated system today.

QUESTIONS FOR
THOUGHT AND
DISCUSSION

1. Why do you think the concept of progressive taxation is so popular in the United States?

2. Which aspect of government expenditures do you think is most important for your own well-being?

3. Which principle of taxation do you think best justifies progressive taxation?

4. Would you prefer to have most taxes collected from individuals or from corporations?

5. Who really pays the corporate income tax?

6. How do tax loopholes hurt or help you as a consumer?

7. Do you think that tax loopholes should exist?

8. Why has our progressive tax system failed to eliminate income differences in the United States since World War II?

9. Is there any way to prevent special interest groups from affecting government legislation?

THINGS TO DO

1. Get a copy of next year's individual income tax schedule from your local office of the Internal Revenue Service. Compare it with the one in this book. Is there any difference?

2. Call up a local stockbroker and ask if he or she has any recommendations about tax shelters. Have that stockbroker send you copies of information on any tax shelters for sale. Do you think they would be beneficial for you if you were making $5000 a year? $50,000 a year? $500,000 a year?

3. Write a letter to your senator or representative asking for copies of legislation that he or she has supported during the last year. Try to figure out why such legislation was supported by that legislator. If you are in doubt, write another letter asking why. Try to discover where special interests might be affecting his or her decision. Write your other senator or another representative in your area asking how a bill is proposed and eventually passes in Congress. Try to figure out at what point the bill's initiation or chance for passage can be affected by special interest groups.

**SELECTED
READINGS**

Dietsch, R. W., "How Private is Your Tax Return?" *Nation's Business*, December 1973, pp. 66–67.

"Do Our Taxes Need a Shake-Up?" *Saturday Review*, October 21, 1972.

Friedberg, S., "Tax Shelters: Doing Well by Doing Good," *Esquire*, November 1973, p. 32ff.

"How Rich People Escape Taxes," *U.S. News & World Report*, June 3, 1974, pp. 49–51.

"Many Companies Work to Avoid Local Taxes," *The Wall Street Journal*, July 17, 1972.

"New Crackdown on Tax Shelters," *U.S. News & World Report*, December 24, 1973, pp. 47–49.

Pechman, Joseph A., and Benjamin A. Okner, *Who Bears the Tax Burden?* (Washington, D. C.: Brookings Institution), 1974.

People and Taxes, monthly newsletter (Washington, D. C.: Ralph Nader's Research Group).

Thurow, Lester C., *The Impact of Taxes on the American Economy* (New York: Frederick Praeger), 1971.

CONSUMER ISSUE XII

Easing Your Tax Burden

In this short Consumer Issue it will be impossible to give you a complete course in how to ease your tax burden. If you are really interested in getting all the details, you might want to buy one of the various tax books such as Laser's *Tax Guide,* or H&R Block's *Income Tax Workbook,* or The Research Institute of America's *Individual Tax Return Guide,* all of which are published yearly. You can also get *Your Federal Income Tax* free from the Internal Revenue Service in your area. You can get numerous booklets from the Internal Revenue Service for every imaginable loophole that you might be eligible for. If that is not enough for you, you can buy the services of sophisticated tax lawyers or certified public accountants.

Of course, if you do not want to have anything to do with filling out your tax forms, you can pay one of the many services to do it. Be careful, however, for often the people who fill out your returns are not any better trained in the subject than you are. Just to be safe, you ought to go through the most basic parts of your tax returns with the person you are paying for the service to find out if he or she knows what is happening. Of course, once you find a good tax person, stick with that person, for he or she can be a valuable friend when April 15th rolls around.

THE MINIMUM

If you have no expenses that qualify as legitimate deductions, you will merely take the so-called standard 15 percent deduction.

But if your legitimate deductions are greater than 15 percent, you must keep good records to support those deductions. This is one minimum thing you must do to take advantage of all of the benefits in the tax laws. If the Internal Revenue Service conducts a tax audit and you cannot adequately substantiate the deductions you have taken on your tax returns, they will be disallowed and you may have to pay a penalty or, at a bare minimum, interest on the taxes that are now overdue. And just because you keep records does not mean you can throw them out as soon as you have used them. You have to keep them for at least three years after the date your return was filed, or at least three years from the date your tax was paid, whichever occurred later. In fact, it is a good idea to keep them even longer, just in case you want to make sure what you did, although they cannot legally be subpoenaed by the Internal Revenue Service after three years.

What Kind of Records

A good rule to remember is: when in doubt, keep a record. You should have records for all medical expenses, for all business expenses, for all taxes paid, everything that could possibly be used to reduce your effective tax burden. The best way to keep records, of course, is to write checks. If you do any amount of business for which the expenses are tax deductible, you also should keep a complete diary of those expenses. If you move because of a change of job, you are

EXHIBIT:
Possible income deductions that can lower your tax liability

Accounting and auditing expenses paid for preparation of tax returns

Alterations and repairs on business or income-producing property

Attending conventions

Attorneys' fees in connection with your trade or employment

Automobile expenses incurred during business trips, trips for charitable organizations, and trips for medical care

Burglary losses

Business expenses of employees in excess of amounts received as reimbursements

Campaign contributions

Charitable contributions

Child care expenses

Condominium owners' interest and realty taxes

Depreciation of property used in business

Dues for professional societies and organized labor unions

Educational expenses if required to keep your employment or professional standards

Fees paid to secure employment

General sales taxes (state and local)

State and city income tax

Interest you paid or finance charges for any loans or retail installment contracts

All medical expenses in excess of 3 percent of adjusted gross income

Moving expenses

Home office expenses if you use part of your home as a place to do work that you are paid for

Property taxes

Safe deposit box expenses

Pro-rata share of automobile expenses if used for your business

Automobile license

allowed to deduct moving expenses. Make sure you have records for all of those. When you sell your house or other major things, keep a record of that transaction.

The best way to keep records, of course, is to do it regularly. Every month when you go through your check stubs to balance your statement, separate the checks into individual envelopes, marked business expenses, telephone, medical expenses, and so on. If in fact you can prove that you use part of your home as a place of business, then you must keep records on all the expenses on your house: rental or mortgage payments, heating bills, light bills, telephone bills, electricity bills. Again, the best way to do this is to pay everything by check. The next best way is to keep a receipt for everything you pay for in cash. Here is where charge cards also come in useful. You get a receipt every time a charge is made on your card. If it is a receipt for a tax deductible item, it will be useful in your record-keeping endeavors.

What if You Are Uncertain?

Whenever you are uncertain about the acceptability of the deduction, it is not always unwise to take a chance. Many of the deductions are subject to interpretation by the IRS—that is, they are not cut and dried, and if you are audited you stand as good a chance of winning your case as of not winning it. At the most, since this action does not involve fraud or anything illegal, you only pay an interest rate penalty on the taxes due. At least until 1975, that interest rate was somewhat less than the rate of inflation, so you really do not lose out by owing the government money for back taxes. However, it might prove inconvenient to pay any interest fine in one lump sum. You have to keep that in mind, too.

If, in fact, you do not think that you have many deductions at all, it is generally not worth your while to do anything except the simplest amount of work on your tax form.

That is, you take a standard 15 percent deduction, fill in the rest of the lines, and pay your taxes. That way you do not have to keep any records except those of the income you made. That certainly simplifies life, but it may not ease your tax burden. It only eases your tax work.

KEEPING DOWN YOUR TAXES

Below are listed possible deductions that you can use to help reduce your federal income taxes. You of course may find others in many of the excellent guides to filling out your tax forms. But remember, it certainly is not worthwhile for you to spend weeks filling out your tax forms that might save you another $25. You must figure out at what point you should *stop* trying to figure out ways to reduce your tax burden. This, of course, is a function of your marginal tax bracket. If you are in the 14 percent bracket, every extra dollar that you can find as a legal deduction saves you only 14¢. The incentive is not very much: if it takes you an extra hour to find $10 more of deductions, the benefit to you of those $10 of deductions is only $1.40. Is your time worth more than $1.40 an hour?

AMERICANS ARE HONEST

Americans in general are very honest. The IRS estimates that fully 95 percent pay their lawful due to the government. Being honest, though, does not prevent you from taking advantage of what is legally your right. That is, you can be very honest and report all income, but at the same time make sure that you take all deductions that are due. You owe that to yourself and to your family.

SUMMARY

1. As a basic reference for doing your own taxes, it would be useful to obtain one of the better known tax guides, such as *Laser's Tax*

Guide, or *H&R Block's Income Tax Workbook.* At the first of every year, a number of these tax guides become available in most bookstores throughout the country.

2. If you have complicated tax problems, it is best to get a certified public accountant and/or the advice of a tax lawyer. However, weigh the cost with the potential benefits—good tax advice does not come cheap.

3. If in fact you do not anticipate being able to deduct a large number of items from your income before you pay taxes, it may be cost-saving for you to use the standard 15 percent deduction and a short form for filling out your taxes.

4. If you decide to keep records and fill out a long form, you must have a record for everything you decide is a legitimate deduction.

5. The easiest way to keep records is to write checks for everything. Note, however, that in many cases you must substantiate those checks with receipts.

6. If you decide to take business expenses, you must keep a diary of expenses for which you do not obtain receipts, such as meals with business colleagues.

7. Whenever you are uncertain about the legitimacy of a deduction, it is best to decide in your own favor, for generally it is a matter of interpretation by the IRS agent who might audit your returns. And his or her interpretation could be the same as your own.

8. You can call your local office of the Internal Revenue Service and have many, many free booklets sent to you explaining all facets of our taxing system. Additionally, for small fees you can have some of the more complete tax guides written by the Internal Revenue Service sent to you directly. If there is no local IRS office nearby, write the nearest major city for these booklets.

QUESTIONS FOR THOUGHT AND DISCUSSION

1. When would it not pay to be careful about keeping records for tax purposes?

2. When is it definitely a waste of time to have a CPA fill out your tax returns?

3. What is the cost to you of deducting an expense from your income before paying taxes if upon a tax audit it is determined that that is not a legitimate deduction?

4. "It is cheaper to give things to charity than to sell them." How could this be true?

THINGS TO DO

1. Send away for all the free booklets from the Internal Revenue Service. See if you can find information that will be useful for your own tax planning.

2. Try to find out from the IRS what percentage of taxpayers are audited every year.

3. Buy one of the best-selling tax guides. Read through it to see if you can get a general feeling for how our tax system works. Do you think we have a complicated system or not?

4. Write down a list of reforms you think would make ours a better tax system.

SELECTED READINGS

How to Prepare Your Personal Income Tax Return (Englewood Cliffs, N. J.: Prentice Hall), published annually.

Lasser, J. K. *Your Income Tax* (New York: Simon and Schuster), published annually.

"New Tax Rules You Need to Know About," *Changing Times,* December 1972.

"Outfoxing the Internal Revenue Service: That Tax Reform Act Left Shelters Intact Many People Find," *Wall Street Journal,* April 14, 1972.

"You Can Save Now on Next Year's Taxes," *Changing Times*, July 1973.

Your Federal Income Tax (Washington, D. C.: Superintendent of Documents), published annually.

"Ways to Save on Your Income Tax," *U.S. News & World Report*, February 26, 1973.

CHAPTER PREVIEW

☐ Is the consumer movement a new one?
☐ What are antitrust policies all about and how do they affect the consumer?
☐ Have recent U.S. presidents been interested in consumer protection?
☐ How do state and local consumer protection agencies compare with federal ones?
☐ Can the private sector do anything to protect the consumer? If it can, has it?
☐ What is the essence of consumer activist groups?

GLOSSARY OF NEW TERMS

Antitrust Policies: Government policies to prevent business monopolies. Antitrust policies are aimed at establishing and maintaining competition in business to assure the consumer fair prices and goods of adequate quality.

Common Law: The unwritten system of law governing the rights and duties of persons, in the courts of England, from decisions based on custom and fixed principles of justice. Common Law is the foundation of both the English and U.S. legal systems (excluding Louisiana).

Case Law: The law set by decisions in court cases, as distinct from statutes and other kinds of law.

Statutory Law: The law declared by statute—that is, put on the books by a legislature.

Like the policeman who tries to break up a family fight and suddenly finds himself the target of both the husband and the wife, the concept of consumer protection is constantly in the middle of an argument. On one side of the argument are those who believe that the only consumer protection needed is what arises out of competition in the marketplace, and that consumer protection insults consumers by implying that they are helpless. On the other side are those who believe that consumerism or consumer activism is what is needed. Although most people have become aware of consumer protection only in the last 10 years, it has a long history.

THE CONSUMER GETS A VOICE[1]

A HISTORY OF CONSUMER PROTECTION

The earliest forms of consumer protection were really attempts to make market protections effective. Since in a competitive market there are many buyers and many sellers, no one of them can individually influence the price of a particular good. Buyers and sellers are assumed to know what they are doing, and also to know what product they are bargaining for. But even if you know what you are bargaining for, it may be difficult to determine exactly how much you are bargaining for and how much you are getting. And so, from earliest recorded times, we find ourselves involved in the setting of standards of weights and measures.

POLICING STANDARDS

As you might expect, once the standards of weights and measures are established, the next problem is to make sure they are being met. So the second development in consumer protection was policing the standards of weights and measures. Once fraud in the marketplace has been made illegal, not only must the market be policed, but the police work must be evaluated. Thus, the courts and administrative bodies came into the consumer protection system. The principle which is being supported here is the principle of competition. If enough consumers have enough information, they can protect themselves in the marketplace.

[1] I am deeply indebted to Professor Phillis Basile for her help on this chapter and the following issue. She is responsible for much of what follows.

BUSINESS WANTED
THEM, TOO

But of course, even this system was not purely a consumer protective system. It was not the consumers who worked hardest for standards of weights and measures, police work, and courts, but rather producers who found themselves engaged in competition that they deemed detrimental to their own interests. Remember, *everyone* is a consumer. We tend to think of consumers as being found in supermarkets, department stores, car showrooms, and so on; that is, we think of the consumer role as being played only at the retail level. But businesses are consumers, too, when they buy goods and services to be used in further production. Businesses, then, have two reasons for being interested in the enforcement of standards:

1. To protect themselves when they go into the market to buy, and
2. To protect themselves against fraudulent competitors who may be more successful in selling to the individual consumer than the traditional business.

ANTIMONOPOLY
POLICIES

At the same time that standards were being set and enforced, another concept was becoming prominent—the concept of antimonopoly, or **antitrust policies** on the part of the government. The rights of buyers and other competitors had long been protected in **common law** because the courts refused to enforce monopolistic contracts. But before the Sherman Antitrust Act was passed in 1890, there had been no stated public policy that monopoly and price-fixing were in and of themselves unacceptable in the American economy. Again, this legislation was designed to protect the interests of all competing producers in the market, but it had consumer implications, because for competition there must be many buyers and sellers in the market so that no one alone can influence price.

Thus, 75 years ago, at the turn of the century, consumer protection, as we mean it today, did not really exist. The set of rules to provide the seller protection as a competitor in the marketplace had only an incidental effect on consumers, because the information and antimonopoly requirements might make it easier for consumers to operate in the market. In the years between 1900 and World War I, however, there was a distinct change, not only in the consumer area, but throughout the social and economic concerns of the period. This was the period of the "muckrakers"; the period of the first wage and hour laws; the period of the first women's and minors' protective legislation; and the period in which the first federal law designed specifically to protect consumers was passed. This was the Food and Drug Act of 1906, dealing with the production, transportation, and sale of foods, drugs, and medicines.

FOOD AND DRUG ACT

Although 30 years earlier Congress had rewritten the postal laws to make fraud through the mails illegal, the emphasis still was on the transaction at the retail level of the marketplace. The Food and Drug Act of 1906 began to look behind the practices in the retail market and into how food actually was being produced, as well as sold. Upton Sinclair's book *The Jungle* awoke the general public to the fact that consumer protection meant more than information at the point of sale. Groups now began seeking some form of "consumer protection" in those products that were processed before they arrived at the marketplace.

But the Food and Drug Act of 1906 was not the beginning of a strong, continuous surge in consumer interest or in consumer protection. Not until 1914 was the Federal Trade Commission Act passed to provide administrative machinery to enforce antitrust laws, and to spell out unfair methods of competition, including deceptive advertising. And it was fully 32 years later that the 1938 Food, Drug and Cosmetic Act was passed to enlarge the protective features of the 1906 legislation.

The passage of the 1938 legislation was the last significant federal activity on the consumer protection issue until 1958, 20 years later. But unlike the earlier period, the federal interest in consumer issues in 1958 was a beginning, not an end. And in the years following the mounting interest in consumer issues, a flood of legislative activity resulted, not only at the federal, but at the state and local levels as well. In the 10 years between 1965 and 1975, more than twice as many laws were passed in the consumer area as had been passed in the previous 90 years.

What happened to make the interest in consumer protection, which had flared and died in earlier periods, become a strong continuing flame of concern?

Some people have pointed to Ralph Nader, whose 1965 book *Unsafe at Any Speed* brought to public attention the issue of automobile safety. But Upton Sinclair's *The Jungle,* which preceded the passage of the Food and Drug Act of 1906, and Stewart Chase's *Your Money's Worth,* which preceded the activity in the 1930s, had not led to continuing streams of consumer protection activity. Something else was operating in the system, and that something else, according to some, was the complexity of modern economic life. By the early 60s, the explosion in technology, in production, in transportation, and in information systems had been fully felt by the American consumer. The developments in plastics, frozen foods, and dried foods had made preprocessing and prepackaging an everyday fact of American life. The American automobile had become a complex, accessory-loaded machine that could no longer be easily understood by the buyer. Consumers found themselves at the center of an increasing mass of information—so much information, in fact, that now they not only had to look for the information, but to discriminate among all of the kinds of information available. In addition to all this was the impersonality of the modern American marketplace. The small community has been replaced by the large city; most of our goods are moved by mass marketing techniques, and are prepackaged and today even machine-delivered; markets have extended to a national and even an international scope. All of this has left us individual consumers in a complex world feeling helpless as we attempt to determine what to buy, how to use it, and to whom to complain if the product failed us.

The legal system that had developed over the years as a matter of both case law and statutory law was not geared to handle the problems of millions of individuals with small sums of money at stake, each sum important to the individual but no one large enough to pay for the costs of litigation. The mounting sense of helpless frustration led consumers to look for a new form of consumer protection: protection *after* the fact. The new emphasis in consumer protection became consumer redress: the right of each of us consumers to legitimately air our grievance and to seek satisfaction for damages incurred through a system that would not penalize us because the individual sum involved is small. This is not the same as the earlier consumer protection against fraud. We consumers can now ask for redress, not because we have been deliberately defrauded, but because the complexity of the marketplace makes it impossible, in our eyes, for us to protect ourselves adequately before the fact of purchase.

Moreover, in making buying decisions, consumers spend much time seeking and evaluating information. In a relatively simple system, consumers may know enough about the products they are buying and enough about the people from whom they purchase them to feel that they need spend little time to make a good decision. But in the complex technology of today, seeking information may become a very time-consuming job. To know enough to make completely satisfactory consumer decisions in every field takes a lifetime. This, by the way, is not a new thought: Wesley Mitchell, a prominent economist of the turn of the century, in a 1912 article, "The Backward Art of Spending Money," pointed up the difference between a business firm, which hires experts to carry out its many functions, and the family unit, which makes all of the same and even more complex decisions through a single buyer or two. Mitchell concluded that if the family had developed as well as the production unit, we would by now have homemakers who specialized in each of the different aspects of family buying. In effect, consumers in the 1960s began to ask government to perform some of these specialist functions by establishing standards of packaging and disclosure that would enable us to readily compare claims from many sellers. There was also a strong movement to provide government standards of safety so that consumers could eliminate such concerns from their information-gathering task.

THE PRESIDENTS SPEAK UP

In 1962, President John F. Kennedy sent the first consumer protection and interest program to Congress. In that message, he stated four consumer rights:

1. The right to safety—a protection against goods that are dangerous to life or health.
2. The right to be informed—not only to discover fraud, but also to make rational choices.
3. The right to choose—a restatement of the need for many firms in a competitive market and for protection by government where such competition no longer exists.
4. The right to be heard—the right of consumers to have their interests heard when governmental policy decisions are being made.

To these four rights as stated by President Kennedy, most consumer representatives would add the fifth mentioned earlier:

5. The right to redress for reasonable damages incurred when dealing in the marketplace.

Presidents Johnson and Nixon reaffirmed the consumer rights stated by President Kennedy and the strong tide of consumer legislation at the federal level continued.

Legislation, of course, is not the end of the story. Legislation must be administered and the administration must be efficient if the concept of consumer protection is to be effective. In 1964, President Lyndon B. Johnson made a gesture in this direction when he appointed the first Special Presidential Assistant for Consumer Affairs. Although this person, a member of the staff of the Office of the President, had no direct authority, the fact that such a position existed made certain that consumer interests would have some representation at the federal policy level. The office was continued by President Nixon until 1973, when it was transferred to the Department of Health, Education, and Welfare. The transfer of the office from the direct contact of the President appeared to some consumer activitists to be a sign of weakening federal support. However, in 1974 the prospects for passage of a law that would set up an independent federal agency appeared more favorable than in the past.

In the 100 years from 1872, when the mail fraud postal law was passed, to 1972, when President Nixon sent the third consumer message to Congress, the federal government had slowly but certainly increased its role on the consumer side of the marketplace. But this does not begin to be the whole story of consumer protection. State and even local governments have become increasingly involved in the issues confronting consumers, and the private sector of the economy has been involved with consumer issues in a vast array of groups and activities.

STATE AND LOCAL GOVERNMENT AND PRIVATE CONSUMER PROTECTION

We have spent a good deal of time detailing the history and developments in federal consumer protection in the United States. While federal action is important, because once adopted it expresses the policy of national importance in the field, nevertheless the policy often is the result of prolonged activity at the state and local government level, or in the private sector of the economy. This has been especially true of consumer protection policy. In fact, in some areas even today, states, localities, and private groups have gone far beyond the limits now set by federal policy.

State and local governments have always been involved in setting standards, weights and measures, and marketing standards, as well as standards that define the term "fraud." Even today, enforcement of consumer fraud statutes is left largely to state and local governments. Many of the areas of fraud are most commonly dealt with under criminal fraud statutes arising out of the criminal fraud case decisions of earlier years. And these are primarily state and local law. Furthermore, in the areas of credit, insurance, health and sanitation, and all issues dealing with contract rights, it has been primarily state governments that have dealt with consumer problems. In fact, state response has sometimes been much earlier than federal response. For example, as early as 1959, both New York and California had legislation on the books to protect the rights of consumers in credit transactions. And not until Massachusetts passed the first truth-in-lending law was federal action on this important issue likely to succeed. The federal Truth-in-Lending Law was passed in 1968. Massachusetts, in effect, became a pilot case for the national legislation.

*"It's my observation that more and more consumers are looking
after their own interests these days."*

The same pattern is currently being followed in "no-fault" automobile insurance: state legislation has provided a testing ground for the feasibility of federal action. If the problem is a significant one, federal action tends to come eventually, because of the United States has an interstate economy.

THE PRIVATE SECTOR   How does the private sector of the economy fit in with the public activities for consumer protection? As you might expect, activity in the private sector of the economy has been varied, and in many cases short-lived and uncertain in its effect. But in some specific areas, private activities have been most important. The first of these is *product testing.* Only very recently has government at any level begun to test products and reveal the results of those tests in a way that makes it possible for consumers to use the information in making their own purchases. But private product testing groups have been around for a long, long time. We are all familiar with some of them. We have already mentioned Consumers Union and Consumers' Research, which exist primarily for the purpose of providing consumers with information on products they may buy.

But there are other product testing groups, too, whose interest may not be directed toward consumers but whose activities produce information that consumers can use. The American Standards Association is an example of this kind of private agency. The ASA, organized in 1918, exists primarily to develop standards and testing methods which may be used by manufacturers. By setting a common level of performance, these standards and testing methods can protect manufacturers themselves against unfair competition. But, of course, they also provide protection to consumers who are buying products the safety of which may be important. Using the standards developed by the ASA, other private laboratories or testing groups certify the efficiency and/or safety of such items as electrical appliances, gas appliances, textiles, and many other products as well. In addition to the product testing that takes place at the manufacturing level, a wide range of product testing is done by retailers who wish to perform a consumer service and provide themselves with a competitive advantage at one and the same time.

For a period of time, the testing by many private firms resulted in "seals of approval" given to products that supposedly were acceptable by these tests. Unfortunately, in recent years legal action has been taken which indicates that some of the better-known seals of approval, such as Parent's Magazine and the Good Housekeeping Seal of Approval, can be of doubtful value to consumers. In fact, some of this legal action is what produced much of the pressure for government to do more public standard setting.

PRODUCT STANDARDS

Any discussion of product testing implies, of course, that there are product standards, and the setting of such standards has become one of the most important and most controversial areas of consumer protection. We have noted the federal development, and that the state and local governments have been quite busy in this area. Because products and services have become both complex and expensive, consumers are more and more demanding of standards that are both reliable and relatively easy to judge. Some of the most important forms of standard setting

at the state level have been in the area of services, an area that is not covered at the federal level. Although not seen as a consumer protection issue in its earlier years, state licensing of the performance of services has become increasingly oriented towards this issue.

In addition to setting standards, states have been particularly active in enforcing them, particularly the standards of legitimate versus fraudulent selling practices. In most states of the country, the Attorney General's office has become a major arm of the consumer protection movement by seeking patterns of consumer complaint that permit action against sellers who are violating either the old or the newer fraud statutes. As a result of these activities by the state attorney generals, the states have led the federal government in passing legislation that more clearly defines fraudulent practices and that gives consumers some new legal rights. Probably one of the most important areas of recent activity has been contracts. An example of the kind of protection consumers now enjoy in some states is the "cooling off period" we mentioned in Chapter 3. Finally, the states and localities have moved into an area in which the federal government still has not acted.

That is the area of seeking redress for consumers for damages they have suffered from either a fraudulent activity or, even more significantly, from an unsatisfactory purchase.

RECOVERY OF DAMAGES

Recovery of damages for the individual consumer is a major issue in the consumer protection movement today. States have generally provided this kind of service only in special types of sales that have presented special problems. For example, in California again, the state has provided for registration, for disclosure standards, and for administrative procedures on consumer grievances about service and repair for radios and TVs, automobiles, and major appliances. In cities and counties all over the country, the concern with consumer damages has been expressed more broadly: in such areas as New York City, Dade County, Florida, Orange County, California, the City of Los Angeles, agencies of the local government are acting as the mediators in disputes between consumers and sellers. The activities of these agencies are different from any public agency activity in the past. These agencies will refer consumers or handle the referral of the case for the consumer to the correct public agency which administers any law that has been violated as a condition of the consumer's complaint; they will sometimes appear on behalf of the consumer as a friend of the court in a small claims or larger action; but most importantly, they investigate the consumer's complaint and then attempt to achieve a mutually agreeable settlement between the consumer and the seller.

The makeup and the authority of these local agencies vary dramatically. In some areas, the authority is lodged in an "old line" agency, such as the Bureau of Weights and Measures, which already has operations in the consumer field. In other cases, the agency is made part of a department of social services. But in its most effective form, the local consumer agency is independent and owes responsibility to no one but consumers and the public at large.

PRIVATE AGENCIES   Local government agencies are new participants in the public area of consumer protection, an area that has traditionally belonged to the private sector. Probably the best known of such private agencies is the Better Business Bureau. The National Better Business Bureau has been in existence since 1916 and has local affiliates in all major cities and counties. The Better Business Bureau has a multiple purpose:

1. To provide information on products and selling practices to consumers.
2. To provide businessmen with a source of localized standard setting as to acceptable business practices.
3. To provide a technique for mediating grievances between consumers and sellers.

Since the Better Business Bureau has no enforcement powers, all actions must be voluntary. And since the Better Business Bureau is dependent on the business community for its membership, it cannot afford to antagonize those in business more than it antagonizes consumers. The weaknesses in the voluntary system were felt most strongly when the consumerist movement began to press for protection, not only against the fly-by-night, illegal, fraudulent firm, but against marketing practices that were generally accepted by the business community. Once consumers began to seek redress for damages suffered from exaggerated advertising, ineffective warranties and guarantees, safety hazards, and poor choices made by consumers because of the structure of the market in which goods were sold, the private business organization was unable to effectively police its members. But the Better Business Bureau continues to survive and to thrive as the organization has sought to improve communication with the consumer.

Although the Better Business Bureau is the oldest of the private agencies that seek to mediate grievances, it is by no means the only one. As consumerism has grown, the media have been both criticized for their performance and mobilized for consumer protection. The media have been criticized for the type of advertising they have carried and for their lack of interest in providing time for countercommercials, or public service consumer information. But newspapers, radio stations, and TV stations have all been in the forefront of attempts to help consumers who have legitimate complaints; these media have provided column space or air time for "consumer action." These programs have been highly successful in obtaining results for those consumers who are able to make use of them. Affiliates of both the ABC and NBC networks have run regular consumer report and consumer action series, as have many of the independent television stations. These programs typically use publicity as the powerful weapon to resolve the consumer's grievance.

Thus, looking back, we can see that the concept of consumer protection has developed from a mere set of standards necessary to protect both buyers and sellers in a fair exchange; next, standards were set for health and safety, to protect consumers primarily; later, both the consumers and businesspersons were protected against fraud; finally, the concern became the techniques of marketing and the problems of consumers in finding their way through the maze of technological detail in a highly industrialized society. No longer are consumers to be protected only up to the point of purchase; protection past the point of purchase is now a goal. This new area of consumer protection of groups that seek, both publicly and privately, to provide mechanisms for settling consumer grievances without the need for going to court has now opened up.

ACTIVE CONSUMER GROUPS

But is there anything newer than new in consumer protection? Yes: as we noted at the beginning of the chapter, many people feel strongly that the term "consumer protection" is insufficient, if not downright insulting; they seek consumer policy participation. While Ralph Nader, through both his own activity and the activities of the organizations founded through his energies, has become the symbol of consumer activism in the 1960s and '70s, consumer organization at the state and local level actually began well before Ralph Nader appeared on the scene. It is well to remember that the consumer cooperative movement began many years ago. And although it has never successfully defeated the corporation as a business form, it has succeeded in helping some consumers solve some of their problems.

During the 1930s, consumer groups sprang up over the country as many people found it necessary to stretch precious few dollars to cover the cost of living. The burst of consumerism, of course, occurred in the 1960s, and by the early 1970s, organizations existed at state and local levels throughout the country. And in 1967, the Consumer Federation of America was formed to coordinate the efforts of such groups at the national level. Local consumer activist groups have been in the forefront in pressing for legislation on credit, packaging, no-fault insurance, and adequate labeling of food and drugs. They have been active as well as in seeking protection of consumers in such fields of major abuse as automobile and appliance repair services.

While acting at their own levels to try to seek redress for consumers who felt that they have been damaged in private transactions, the state and local groups have also worked to provide education and representation to consumers in hearings before government legislative and admin-

istrative bodies. The ultimate goal of these groups is to have consumer participation in the policy decisions made by government. (To this end, these groups have actively supported the proposal for a federal Department of Consumer Affairs.) In addition, they seek for consumers the strength to indirectly participate in the policy decisions of business firms by their power in the marketplace, if they act as a single group. Thus, at least some consumers seek to participate in the functioning of the marketplace in the same way that large corporations and major trade unions do.

The development of this kind of consumer activism is significant because it illustrates that consumers can also have points of view. In any public policy issue, there may be a business interest; there may be a labor interest; there may be a consumer interest. The price of food, for example, is a major issue that has involved all of these interests in recent years. The question is: What is the public interest? From this point of view, where is consumer protection heading? What issues must be resolved as we expand, or try to expand, the concept of consumer protection?

COST vs. BENEFITS

An immediate issue, of course, is the cost of consumer protection versus its benefits. The issue of cost versus benefits cannot be viewed only from the individual's point of view. We must consider the social benefits—that is, benefits to all of us as a group—versus the private benefits or the private damages that may result from consumer protection policy. For example, say you, the consumer, are knowledgeable about tires and are able to judge their quality. If you are willing to run the risk of making an ineffective purchase to determine whether or not your standards are correct, perhaps you resent the cost to you as a taxpayer of providing a government agency to set, enforce, and review standards. But is there not a value to society at large in providing such standards so that all drivers will buy new tires with a reasonable degree of safety? Is there not a benefit to society as a whole in saving the dollars that might be lost through unwise tire purchases by consumers unable to determine when a tire is a good tire?

On a much broader scale, the issue of social benefits versus private losses involves the issues of environmental pollution, resource conservation, and consumer protection. Should consumer protection be meant to protect the individual buyer in the individual purchase, or instead to protect the ability of all consumers in the country to maintain or to achieve a satisfactory life style?

Some consumer activists believe that the consumer issue is the primary issue facing society today because, in its largest sense, it involves all the major issues concerning us today. Whichever way you view consumerism—as a matter of providing for an effective buyer in a marketplace, or as a matter of providing for an effective consumer society—one thing is clear: the scene is complex. The following Consumer Issue is an effort to simplify some of the complexities of organizations and functions in the consumer protection field.

SUMMARY

1. Among the first consumerist activities ever engaged in was the formation of standards of weights and measures. Following this was the policing of these standards.

2. Businesses were interested in enforcing such standards to protect themselves when they were buying materials or products and also to protect themselves against fraudulent competitors.

3. Among the first purely consumer-oriented activities were antitrust or antimonopoly policies, aimed at preventing or breaking up existing monopolies that fixed prices at higher than competitive levels to the detriment to the consumer.

4. Although the first food and drug act was passed in 1906, not until the 1938 Food, Drug, and Cosmetic Act was legislated did consumer protection become a strong aspect of federal government activity. The most recent development in the consumerist movement is consumer redress after a wrong has been committed.

5. In the 1960s and 1970s, starting with President John F. Kennedy and extending through every succeeding president, the rights of consumers

and the need for increased consumer protection have been popular executive topics.

6. Consumer protection continues to exist at the federal, state, and local levels of government, as well as being maintained by private agencies.

7. The best-known private agencies are Consumers Union and Consumers Research, Inc., both meant chiefly to provide information to consumers. In addition branches of the Better Business Bureau attempt to help consumers as well as businessmen. There are also private testing agencies such as American Standards Association, Parent's Magazine, The Underwriter's Laboratory, and so on.

8. States and localities have recently set up numerous devices to help consumers recover damages for fraudulent business activities. At the very minimum, local government mediators act in disputes between consumers and sellers and will often refer both parties to an appropriate agency if specific laws have in fact been violated.

9. Recently, activist consumer groups have engaged in consumer advocacy at all levels of government. The ultimate goal of consumer participation in the policy decisions of business firms, at least indirectly by their power in the marketplace, has been sought through the formation of certain segments of the marketplace into a single advocacy group.

QUESTIONS FOR THOUGHT AND DISCUSSION

1. Why is the consumerist movement thought to be relatively new even though it started many years ago?

2. Exactly what are antimonopoly policies? Why do monopolies hurt the consumer?

3. What is the difference between consumer protection before the fact and consumer protection after the fact?

4. If you had to set up a model consumer protection act, what would you include in it?

5. What do you think that the current administration's stand on consumer protection is?

6. Do you think the consumerist movement is still as strong as it was a couple of years ago?

7. Should the government engage in product testing and present the results of those tests to consumers?

8. What private sources of consumer information do you use in making your decisions about what to buy?

THINGS TO DO

1. Engage in a research project in which you outline the history of consumer activism back through its origins in England. What groups have been around longest? What principles of consumerism have been with us longest?

2. If you happen to know a lawyer, talk to him or her about recent developments in laws affecting the consumer. Ask what has happened to the number of laws affecting the consumer and to the "sanctity" of contracts entered into by both consumer and seller.

3. Call your local Better Business Bureau and ask for its booklet that describes the bureau, its activities, and all of the areas in which it is active.

4. Obtain a list of the books put out by Ralph Nader and his associates. Read one or two of them and then read Upton Sinclair's *The Jungle.* Do you see any similarities? Have things gotten better or worse in the United States?

**SELECTED
READINGS**

"Consumers are Rewriting the Rule Book," *Fortune,* March 16, 1974, p. 41ff.

"Consumers May Get a Break," *Nation*, May 4, 1974, pp. 550–551.

Greider, W., "How Far Can a Lone Ranger Ride?", *Ramparts*, March 1974, pp. 21–23.

Jones, L. F., "Consumerism and One Small Businessman," *National Review*, May 10, 1973, p. 535ff.

Nader, Ralph, "Ralph Nader Reports," *Ladies Home Journal*, February 1972 through January 1973.

Peterson, E., "Consumerism as a Retailer's Asset: Program at Giant Foods," *Harvard Business Review*, May 1974, pp. 91–101.

CONSUMER ISSUE XIII

How to Get Help from the Government

Knowing what kind of services are available is the first step in taking advantage of consumer service agencies. Generally, government agencies and private voluntary and business groups provide the following four consumer services:

1. information to consumers before purchase is made. This service, designed to help you, the consumer, help yourself, includes standard setting, inspection, investigation of marketing techniques, product testing, publication of results, and, finally, formal teaching.

2. aid to consumers after purchase is made, generally through the enforcement of public policy to prevent unsatisfactory or fraudulent practices from being repeated. This service includes accepting complaints, investigating the complaints, possibly instituting legal proceedings followed by a judgment, and imposing either injunction against the action or penalty for breaking the law. This kind of action does not help individual consumers make up their own losses.

3. redress to individual consumers for their individual losses as a result of purchases. Now we are involved with a complaint, an investigation, possibly publicity or mediation, sometimes settlement, or legal action followed by a judgment and enforcement of the judgment.

4. representation of consumers in issues with a consumer interest before a legislative body, government administrative agencies, and private business leadership. Here again we are generally concerned with the complaint, with investigation and research regarding the complaint and the problem that it reflects, and developing and publicizing plans for remedy; often these result in changes in legislation.

WHERE TO GO?

Knowing when, where, and how to go for consumer services may turn out to be just as big a job as learning how to buy in the first place. There are over 30 federal agencies involved in consumer issues, and an equal number of state, local, and private agencies with which you might have to deal. We will be primarily concerned with the problems that you face when something goes wrong, rather than how you get information before you buy a product. But even this limitation does not significantly reduce the number of agencies or organizations with which you will have to contend, for many of the agencies that provide information before you buy are the same ones that provide the protection after you buy. And, of course, when you are concerned with complaints about products, you are most likely going to be dealing with a business firm, and there are some 12 million business firms in the United States. Thus, if you are going to deal successfully in the market and with consumer service agencies, you will have to develop a strategy.

A STRATEGY

You should always first figure out a strategy for trying to get your grievances straightened out without going to an outside party. After all, it takes additional time and effort to get somebody else involved in your disputes with a seller. Thus, whenever you buy anything, keep a receipt if you are worried that there may be problems later on. But before you make the purchase, be certain to have everything put in writing about any take-back provisions, warranties, guarantees, etc.

Say you buy something and it falls apart a week later. A call back to the store, and preferably a talk with the person that you bought it from, will tell you immediately whether or not you will have problems. Many times, reputable stores will either give you an identical article that is in good working condition, repair the one you have, or refund your money. If the salesperson does not agree, then you next look higher up: find the manager or the owner. If you still do not get satisfaction and you are dealing with a nationally advertised product or with a large chain store, you may want to find the address of the president or the chairman of the board and write him or her directly to complain. Personal letters to the presidents of large companies get quick responses surprisingly often. But sometimes they do not. If your effort fails, where to next?

To answer this question, you may also have to decide how much you want to put into it. Do you just want your money back, or your own satisfaction, or do you want to make sure that this never happens again?

GETTING YOUR MONEY BACK

If getting your money back or solving your own problem is your primary goal, then you will probably do best to work with those at the local level who are also concerned with that. So you should see whether there is a local consumer affairs agency or a consumer affairs office in your local government. The

telephone book is probably your nearest source of information. In most major cities today, there is a Yellow Pages listing, under "consumers," of the major public agencies that provide consumer services. A call to the administrative officer of the county or city in which you live should quickly turn up the information on the availability of public consumer services. If you find no local consumer agency, look under the state listings; if no listing looks promising under the state, call the state attorney general's office. If there is a consumer agency in the state, the attorney general's office will be sure to know. That office and such agencies always work closely because a large amount of consumer fraud that is uncovered by the consumer agency is prosecuted through the attorney general's office.

Private Organizations

While your state and your community may have no public consumer affairs agency or office, there may be a private organization —whether an organization of consumers, a local newspaper, radio, or television station— that provides a consumer service. It usually is not hard to find out about the newspaper, radio, and TV services because they are advertised over the media that perform them, although it may be more difficult to learn about a private consumer organization. But if it is having any success at all, you probably will have read about it in the newspapers and you will find it listed in the telephone book. If you have to hunt too hard for it, it probably is not yet an effective group. If so, it may not be too helpful to you in getting your own money back, but you should probably consider joining it if you want to make sure that your problem does not happen again. Finally, getting your own money back may depend on private legal action. We discuss the use of the small claims court later. If you find that you have to go to a higher court, you will

EXHIBIT:
THE RIGHT WAY
TO COMPLAIN

If you have a problem that you haven't been able to get satisfactory action on locally, write or call the manufacturer, giving all details. If that doesn't solve the difficulty, write or call collect, MACAP, 20 N. Wacker Dr., Chicago, Ill. 60606. Telephone: 312 236–3175.

Include the following information:
☐ Your name, address and telephone number.
☐ Type of appliance, brand, model, serial number.
☐ Date of purchase.
☐ Dealer's name and address and service agent's name and address if different from dealer.
☐ Clear, concise description of problem and service performed to date.

MACAP cautions that it's important to keep receipts of repairs even when a service call is in warranty. The receipts may be required to prove an appliance needed excessive repairs and should be replaced.

have to face the fact that legal fees must be paid. However, even if you are unable to pay them, you need not give up, because in many cities the traditional legal aid society has been augmented by special legal services for low-income families, and these services often have a strong emphasis on consumer problems. In some states, too, group legal practices have been approved, and you might obtain help through your union or some other organization that has contracted with such a group legal service. On some college campuses, the student body government has set up or arranged for legal services to be available to students; these may permit students to pursue some of the consumer problems that beset them.

Specific Industry Agencies

If your problem lies in some industries, there may be a specific industry program to help resolve disagreements between buyers and sellers, as in the dry cleaning industry and in the appliance industry, for example. In your area, the local chapter of the American Medical Association and the American Dental Association may also provide such a mediation service. Generally, these professional associations provide for some form of self-discipline, either through a county committee of physicians or dentists, or through the appointment of independent arbitrators. Remember, however, that like the Better Business Bureau, the professional or industrial policing organization often finds that it can police only some of its members, or can police them only to a point acceptable to the members of the organization. For if the organization ceases to exist, the policing effect of the organization will die also.

What to Do When Your Major Appliances go on the Blink

For more than half a decade, the appliance industry has used an independent advisory panel to resolve consumer complaints about appliances. The panel is called the Major Appliance Consumer Action Panel, or MACAP.

MACAP is sponsored by the Association of Home Appliance Manufacturers, the Gas Appliance Manufacturers Association, and the National Retail Merchants Association. The appliances that are under its jurisdiction are:

1. dishwashers
2. dehumidifiers
3. dryers
4. electronic ranges
5. disposers
6. freezers
7. gas incinerators
8. humidifiers
9. ranges
10. refrigerators
11. room air conditioners
12. trash compactors
13. washers
14. water heaters

If you have one of these appliances and you have been unable to get satisfaction on some problem from the dealer or the manufacturer, MACAP will seek to remedy the fault. When your complaint is received and acknowledged, a staff member of MACAP will contact the company involved, outlining the problem and requesting an answer. The company, it is hoped, will resolve the difficulty and let MACAP know the action that has been taken within two to three weeks. If you are not satisfied with the solution, you are asked to let MACAP know.

MACAP's track record has been pretty good. By the beginning of 1974, the panel had received 10,446 complaints, and 93 percent of the consumers were satisfied by the action taken. If you need help, just follow the rules given in the accompanying exhibit.

WHAT HAPPENED TO ME SHOULDN'T HAPPEN TO ANYBODY

If you feel strongly enough not only about getting your own satisfaction but also about making sure that nobody else suffers your experience, then you will find yourself involved with a whole series of additional service organizations. Sometimes, unfortunately, this is the only satisfaction that you, the consumer, can get—or at least your only satisfaction without spending endless sums of money for private lawyers. Most of the federal and state agencies are designed not to provide help to the individual consumer, but rather to make sure that the laws on the books are properly enforced. In making this kind of a complaint, it is again important that you have a record of your purchase and your payment. And if you are complaining about the performance of a product, you should have the product itself or the container in which you purchased it. If your problem arose from a service that was provided, you must have your records of the service, the name of the person or firm that provided it, and some evidence for your claim that the service was unsatisfactory. Although states and localities have used an infinite variety of ways to deal with these problems of enforcing the rules of the marketplace and protecting the general welfare, they have relied most heavily on four types of agencies:

1. **The department of agriculture:** important in consumer protection because it deals with food. Many departments of agriculture also are concerned with the problem of weights and measures, with pesticides, and with the setting of prices at which some commodities, such as milk, are sold.

2. **The public health department:** concerned with the safety of food and the sanitariness of its handling, processing, and display for sale, and whether or not any of its contents might sicken or kill humans.

3. **The state agency or agencies that license occupations and professions:** may be called by different names. And some licensing boards, such as those for medicine and the law, may be entirely separate from each other.

4. **The state attorney general's office or the local district attorney's office:** concerned with

practices that are illegal through fraud or deceptive advertising.

If your problem with a product or a service involves food, health, licensed services, or possible fraud, you can start with these four kinds of agencies, which you will find at every local and state level.

Remember, though, that all of these agencies have many duties not specifically oriented to serving a complaining consumer. Obviously, the DA's office considers violent crimes more serious than problems of small fraud carried out against consumers. In health and agriculture, the agencies have to be concerned with issues that may affect the health of the industry or the public health in an emergency situation; they also provided services to others of the public besides consumers. Licensing agencies have to maintain standards that have been set to protect not only consumers but also other practitioners in the same industry. In recent years, however, most of these agencies have assigned at least one unit to consumer complaints. These are typically called consumer relations, consumer services, or consumer affairs offices, and you usually will find someone who is willing to listen to you and who is responsible for taking some action on consumer complaints. Even in the energy crisis in 1974, the office of the energy "czar" set up a consumer services section. And that brings us to the federal government.

THE FEDERAL GOVERNMENT

If your problem is with a product that is sold nationally, or if your problem is large enough that it affects people all over the country, you will want to go to a federal agency.

Office of Consumer Affairs

The Office of Consumer Affairs, which once advised the president directly, is now within the Department of Health, Education, and Wel-

fare. It analyzes and coordinates all federal activities on behalf of consumers. To this purpose, it, among other things, conducts investigations and surveys, and it holds conferences. The Office also supplies policy guidance to the General Services Administration in its role of making consumer product information publicly available. The Office of Consumer Affairs is also involved in a consumer education program. Any time you have an inquiry, comment, or suggestion, send it to the Director, Office of Consumer Affairs, Department of Health, Education, and Welfare, Washington, D.C. Although the agency has no power to redress grievances, if enough letters are sent about the same problem, the Director will try to do something about it by suggesting government policy changes or new legislation. Usually, though, if you think you have a grievance worth being taken care of, you should direct yourself to one of the many federal agencies. As a help in this task, it might be worth your while to send away for a booklet called "Consumer Information," catalog number PL86, from the Superintendent of Documents, U.S. Government Printing Office, Washington, D.C. 20402. It costs 10¢. We list below some of the agencies you may have occasion to complain to.

When you write, direct your letters to the chairman, the agency's name, Washington, D.C., and the zip code, which we give after each of the agencies.

THE OLD GUARD

The Office of Consumer Affairs in the Department of Health, Education, and Welfare performs a relatively new function at the federal level. But the Old Guard, the agencies that have been around the longest, fall into the same general categories as do those we mentioned for states and local governments: agriculture, health, antifraud, and licensing. Although we call them the Old Guard, many of these agencies have dramatically changed in the last few years. Once agencies that typically represented the interests of the industries they regulated, they have begun to see themselves as champions of the consumers who buy the products or use the services the agencies oversee. Some have been much more responsive to consumers than others, not always because they chose to be, but because they have been forced to be by consumer activists. For example, a survey of the Federal Trade Commission by Ralph Nader and his associates was the reason why the FTC changed its attitude. When the Nader survey was reinforced by a survey made by the American Bar Association, the change in the Federal Trade Commission was assured. Changes in the Food and Drug Administration reflected not only changes in the attitude of the agency, but changes in the laws under which it operated as well. Several events and changes—passage of the Truth in Packaging law in 1966 and the Truth in Lending law in 1968, revision of the meat packing regulations in 1967, the promise of requirements for nutritional labeling, introduction of care labeling on garments in 1973, and creation of the new Product Safety Commission in 1969—provided a whole new framework within which the old line agencies would operate, and the new agencies would perform new functions. Let us take a look at some of these agencies from the point of view of the consumer who has a complaint to make. How do you make it? Where do you make it? And what can you expect to happen?

The Food and Drug Administration (Department of Health, Education, and Welfare 20201)

The Food and Drug Administration has regional offices in many cities. In each of these offices there is a person who is specifically charged with consumer services. Many of the FDA's 5000 employees are technical experts working in specific fields under FDA jurisdiction. Any complaint about a food or a drug (or a cosmetic) that you purchased should be made either to your regional office or directly to Washington, D.C. The agency will

ask for as much information as you can give them, and they are particularly interested in seeing the container or the food or drug about which you are complaining. If they believe your complaint is justified, they will have a member of their staff visit the firm in question to observe and to check out its production and packaging procedures. They will check the labeling on the container and the contents of the product to determine whether or not it meets all of the legal requirements. If you do not have the product—because you used it up or it was destroyed—you may still make your complaint. The FDA will seek additional supplies of the product on which to base its decision. The FDA is always very interested in receiving reports of consumers even though the complaints may not turn out to have legal standing. Through such consumer reports, the FDA often discovers new problems developing in foods and drugs and new instances or new outbreaks of old problems. In those areas in which the FDA sets and/or enforces standards, consumers can play a very important role because it is for them that these standards are ultimately set. Unless the agency is hearing from consumers, it may make avoidable mistakes.

Federal Trade Commission (Washington, D. C. 20580)

The FDA largely enforces standards of product and performance. But the Federal Trade Commission standards are essentially those of practice—competition in the marketplace; false, misleading, and deceptive advertising by sellers to buyers; and packaging and labeling of firms engaged in nonfood sales. In recent years, the FTC has become quite demanding in its rulings on advertising practices: it has begun to require something more than merely stopping the practice, and has sometimes required the seller of a deceptively advertised product to make a positive public statement on the product's limitations. To assure competition in the marketplace, the

FTC has in recent years looked hard at merchandising methods long considered fair and competitive. For example, the Commission has studied whether or not the control of advertising and the resultant brand loyalty of consumers can be grounds for an antitrust suit in the cereals industry. The Commission has also been much interested in the general effect of advertising on consumer buying habits. This is a whole new approach, for in earlier years, the Commission looked only at specific advertising issues, and only after consumers, or another seller or advertiser, had complained.

The FTC has regional offices in major U.S. cities, and also has consumer service representatives. It has established a special office to serve consumers, and provides a wide range of informative pamphlets for consumers. If you have a complaint to the FTC, you may make it either to the regional office, or to the Washington, D.C. headquarters office. If it believes you have a valid complaint, the FTC will send an investigator out to check with both you and the firm. Typically, the FTC works in two ways: first, it investigates whether or not a particular seller or advertiser has violated a particular law that the agency enforces, and if so will take action to stop the practice by the single firm. Second, the agency looks for new patterns of practice or new areas that may mislead consumers. If it finds any such patterns or areas, the FTC may act against an entire industry, rather than a single firm, to stop the practice altogether. Sometimes such investigation leads to a new interpretation of an old law; other times it leads to information on which new legislation will be based. As with the FDA, individual consumers can play an important role in the work of the FTC because, again, they are the persons for whom this work is ultimately carried out.

U. S. Department of Agriculture (Washington, D. C. 20250)

Although the U.S. Department of Agriculture primarily provides services to farmers, it also protects consumers in very important ways, notably by inspecting and grading meat, poultry, and fish. In recent years, the agency has also become a primary source of information for consumers on the best ways to spend their food dollars. The USDA does this through its Agricultural Extension Service, operated in conjunction with universities throughout the United States. Any complaint you have on the grades of meat that you are buying or the quality of the poultry that is shipped interstate, is best reported to your local health department or your local department of agriculture. The Department of Agriculture has long operated on a federal, state, and local cooperative basis. On the other hand, if you are a militant consumer who wishes to change the entire framework within which meat grading is carried on, then you will want to join an organization and attack the entire USDA head on. In 1971, and again in 1973 and 1974, when meat prices soared to new highs, consumers around the country organized in many groups to pressure the market to bring meat prices down. Because of the many levels of industry involved in bringing meat from the farmer to the consumer, these consumer efforts generally failed. Through it all, the Department of Agriculture played the role of the farmers' advocate rather than the consumers' advocate—an excellent example of the conflict of interest that can arise when a government agency is expected to represent more than one interest group.

CONSUMER PROTECTION BY THE CPSC

One of the newest federal agencies designed to protect the consumer, the Consumer Product Safety Commission, set up in 1972, has been given sweeping powers to regulate the production and sale of consumer products that are potentially hazardous. The agency eventually will have a staff of over 1000 persons, which will make it one of the major federal regulatory agencies for consumer protection.

Creating the Agency

The Consumer Product Safety Act of 1972 came out of a trend that began back in 1953 with the enactment of the Flammable Fabrics Act (see page 192), designed to protect consumers from hazards created by the use of consumer products. In the intervening period, Congress has seen fit to enact legislation that regulates specific classes rather than broad categories of consumer products. On the other hand, the CPSC is designed to regulate all potentially hazardous consumer products. Its creation came out of the 1970 recommendations of the National Commission on Product Safety.

Products Subject to the Act

The 1972 Act states that ". . . any article, or component part thereof produced or distributed for sale to a consumer for use in or around a permanent or temporary household or residence, a school, in recreation or otherwise, or for the personal use, consumption or enjoyment of a consumer" shall be subject to regulation by the CPSC. As further evidence of how comprehensive the Act is, the authority to administer other Acts is transferred to the CPSC. These Acts include the Federal Hazardous Substance Act, the Child Protection and Toy Safety Act, the Poison Prevention Packaging Act, the Flammable Fabrics Act, and the Refrigerator Safety Act.

Purposes of the Act

As stated in the Act, the CPSC was created:

1. To protect the public against unreasonable risk of injury associated with consumer products;

2. To assist consumers in evaluating the comparative safety of consumer products;

3. To develop uniform safety standards for consumer products and to minimize conflicting state and local regulations; and

4. To promote research and investigation into causes and prevention of product related deaths, illnesses, and injuries.

Form and Functions of the CPSC

To achieve all of these purposes, an independent regulatory commission was set up, consisting of five commissioners appointed by the President and subject to Senate confirmation for seven year terms. Not more than three of the commissioners can be of the same political party. The President decides which one of the commissioners will be chairman. Most of the early commissioners have been persons with scientific training or with previous experience in consumer protection activity.

The Commission was set up to conduct research on product safety and maintain a clearinghouse to "collect, investigate, analyze, and disseminate injury data, and information, relating to the causes and prevention of death, injury, and illness associated with consumer products. . . ." To this end, the CPSC immediately started gathering data on the 200 most hazardous consumer products in the nation. The data have been obtained by requiring hospital emergency wards to indicate the particular cause of any injury, illness, or death related to a consumer product. After the initial CPSC survey, the most hazardous consumer product was the bicycle.

It was hoped by the CPSC that the data obtained, and the resulting hazard index for consumer products, would move manufacturers to voluntarily improve the most hazardous products and also forewarn consumers about which products they must be most careful about.

POWERS OF THE CPSC

Not only can the CPSC set safety standards for consumer products, it also can ban the manufacture and sale of any product deemed hazardous to consumers. It has, for example, banned some adhesive sprays and other such consumer items.

The Commission also has authority to seize products from the market which are deemed "imminently" hazardous. The process of seizure resembles that provided for under the Food, Drug, and Cosmetic Act discussed on pages 285/6.

The CPSC also has made use of its power to require manufacturers to report information about any products already sold or intended for sale which have proven hazardous.

Impact of the CPSC

Congress sought to create an agency with broad powers to regulate the sale and manufacture of all consumer products. The CPSC is likely to have increasingly profound effects upon the consumer products industry. At the very least, we can expect that the CPSC, if it continues its present effectiveness, will give consumers more certainty about the safety of the products they buy. That is, the CPSC may in fact increase the amount of information available concerning consumer products.

HOW TO GET IN TOUCH WITH THE CPSC

If you think that there is an unsafe product on the market, or if you have any questions whatsoever about product hazards and safety, you may want to get in touch directly with the CPSC hot line. That number is toll free from anywhere in the United States, (800) 638-2666, or, in Maryland, (800) 492-2937. You can also write directly to the Consumer Product Safety Commission in Washington, D.C. 20207 and explain your concern over a particular product or products.

EXHIBIT: **Today's Top hazards.** **Data: Consumer Prod-** **uct Safety Commis-** **sion**	Estimated injuries 1973 *
Bicycles and bicycle equipment	372,000
Stairs, ramps, landings, (indoors, outdoors)	356,000
Nails, carpet tacks, screws, thumbtacks	275,000
Football-related equipment and apparel	230,000
Baseball-related equipment and apparel	191,000
Basketball-related equipment and apparel	188,000
Architectural glass	178,000
Doors (other than glass)	153,000
Tables (nonglass)	137,000
Swings, slides, seesaws, playground climbing apparatus	112,000
Beds (including springs, frames)	100,000
Non-upholstered chairs	68,000
Chests, buffets, bookshelves, etc.	68,000
Power lawn mowers	58,000
Bathtub and shower structures (except doors, panels)	41,000
Cleaning agents, caustic compounds	35,000
Swimming pools and associated equipment (in-ground only)	32,000
Cooking ranges, ovens and equipment	25,000
Fuels, liquid, kindling, illuminating	25,000
Space heaters, heating stoves	22,000

* Based on injuries treated in 119 hospital emergency rooms

DO YOU WANT TO DO IT YOURSELF?

Finally, a consumer complaint—a problem with a faulty product or an unsatisfactory service, or a feeling that there is no way that you can make a good bargain for yourself in the marketplace—may lead you to feel that changes must be made. Such changes may have to be accomplished by yourself. But it can be done.

FCC Reacts

An example of what we individually can do by ourselves is set by John Banzhaf, a professor of law at George Washington University, in Washington, D.C. In 1967, Banzhaf took advantage of the FCC's "equal time" doctrine, which the television industry must follow. Since the doctrine requires that equal time be given to opposing sides of controversial issues, Banzhaf requested the FCC to require television stations and cigarette advertisers to provide time for antismoking commercials in response to cigarette commercials. For many years there had been controversy over cigarette advertising on television; the evidence was mounting that lung cancer was associated with heavy cigarette smoking, and that advertising cigarettes on TV encouraged more people to smoke.

The Federal Communications Commission ruled that for every three cigarette commercials shown, one antismoking commercial should be shown, free. When the FCC ruling was challenged, the Commission was upheld in court, and the antismoking ads are thought to be what significantly reduced cigarette sales. Finally, as a result of the changing attitudes brought about in some part by the antismoking ads on television, Congress required in January 1971, that advertising of cigarettes on television be dropped nationwide.

National Activist Organizations

Although Banzhaf's efforts had dramatic effects, he did not really act entirely alone. Before 1967, many organizations had been involved in the controversy over the association betwen cancer, smoking, and cigarette advertising. One of these was Consumers Union, which we discussed in an earlier chapter. You can join Consumers Union simply by participating in the annual voting for its directors, or by informing CU that you want to join. Becoming a member of CU does not necessarily involve you directly in active consumer advocacy, but it does enable you to help choose the future directions of this large organization. In recent years, Consumers Union has broadened its concerns; in addition product testing, it now also studies problems affecting consumers generally. In 1973, Consumers Union opened an office in Washington, D.C., with the special responsibilities of watching over the activities of federal administrative

agencies and the Congress, and of keeping in touch with the participants.

Another national organization is the Consumer Federation of America, which represents almost 250 national, state, and local consumer groups, unions, churches, and farm organizations. The goal of the CFA is to build a unified effort towards a threefold aim: to foster consumer education, to gain consumer legislation, and to encourage consumers to actively affect consumer-related decisions. While you do not become individual members of the CFA, you can consult it for information on state and local consumer organizations and activities throughout the country. It is a good source of information for you if you are interested in becoming active in your own area.

Other Consumer Interest Groups

Other consumer groups are active around the country. In 1974, when the Consumer Price Index was rising at an annual rate of 9 percent, and shortages of oil, gasoline, and other energy sources became acute, consumer groups sprang up all over the country to fight individual issues of stress in the marketplace. State and local consumer groups usually attempt to cover the problems within a state and often emphasize state legislation as a tool and a goal. About half the states in the country have had such groups at one time or another; New York, California, Pennsylvania, Washington, Oregon, Arizona, and Massachusetts have been leaders in this form of consumer organization. But because of the problems of distance and population size, it can be hard to keep consumers actively interested in a state organization. As a result, there are often local consumer organizations which may or may not be affiliated with the state group. Some such groups arise, as we said, over a single issue, and remain in existence only for as long as the issue is alive. Sometimes, the most effective consumer organizations are not interested only in consumer issues. For example, the American Home Economics Association and its state and local branches have many interests, but include consumer issues among them, as does the American Association of University Women. Many labor unions and some church organizations have a consumer organization within their frameworks. So, if you are interested in participating in policymaking on consumer issues, you may have to look around to find a consumer group or a consumer interest group to join. Or you may have to try to form your own consumer group.

Local consumer groups have undertaken all kinds of activities that range from publishing food price information to picketing retailers whose practices and policies they disagree with. Throughout the country, local consumer organizations have appeared before city, county, state, and federal legislative bodies that are considering legislation, and before administrative bodies considering changes in regulation. In 1974, 19 California consumer organizations formed a coalition to appear before the California State Department of Agriculture milk stabilization hearings to protest an increase in milk prices. While the price of milk was increased, the consumer organizations felt that the raise would have been more had they not been heard from.

Consumer groups are needed most in consumer representation before administrative bodies. It is very hard for individual consumers to do this with any success. For, rather than looking towards administrative action, most consumers have thought of consumption as buying in the store, and were aware only after the fact that some changes occur through administrative action. But the energy crisis of 1974 focused everyone's attention on how utility rates and gasoline prices are set, and created a new interest in consumer representation in administrative bodies. But because it is hard to focus the attention of millions of consumers on a single issue, the interest aroused at that time is not likely to result in

a strong consumer organization. Typically, when Americans have become aroused on consumer issues, they have turned to the government for satisfaction. Thus, the consumer organizations that are effective at the national level have sought to establish a federal Department of Consumer Affairs.

Traditionally, too, federal government regulatory agencies have tended to favor the interests of the industries that they attempt to regulate rather than consumer interests. It is hoped that the only group with which the federal Department of Consumer Affairs would readily identify would be consumers themselves. It would therefore provide the kind of consumer representation at the administrative level that seems to be out of reach of the consumer groups themselves.

SUMMARY

1. When you have purchased a faulty product or been given inadequate services for money spent, you should develop a strategy for your redress of grievance. That strategy will involve the following: (1) before you purchase any good or service, make sure that all guarantees, warranties, and take-back provisions are in writing; (2) if you are dissatisfied after purchase, speak with the person who sold the good or service to you; (3) if no satisfaction is obtained there, speak with the manager or owner; (4) if still no satisfaction is obtained, contact the president or chairman of the board if your purchase was a nationally advertised product or one from a large chain store; (5) when you cannot obtain satisfaction directly from the company, you may wish to seek out a local consumer-affairs agency or an office of consumer affairs from your local or state government. In the yellow pages, look under consumer to find out if there is one in your area, or call the state attorney general's Office to get information on the possibility of contacting a particular agency in your local or state government.

2. Private organizations may help you. These are difficult to find, however, in certain areas. If there is a college campus in your area, a call to the home economics department may be useful.

3. Certain specific industries have consumer-oriented agencies such as The American Medical Association, The American Dental Association, The American Bar Association, The Association of Home Appliance Manufacturers, The Gas Appliance Manufacturers Association, and The National Retail Merchants Association. Directly contacting one of these associations might be your best step when you seek redress for an applicable grievance.

4. Each state has the following departments that you can contact directly for specific areas of help: agriculture, public health, occupational licensing, and attorney general's office. In addition, your local district attorney general's office may be helpful in cases of fraud or deceptive advertising.

5. The federal government may be of assistance to you or can refer you to the appropriate agency at the state or local level. You may wish to contact one of the following: the Office of Consumer Affairs in the Department of Health, Education, and Welfare; the Federal Trade Commission; the Food and Drug Administration; the U. S. Department of Agriculture; the Consumer Product Safety Commission; or the Federal Communications Commission.

QUESTIONS FOR THOUGHT AND DISCUSSION

1. Who do you think benefits most from consumer-protection agencies?

2. Should there be an agency to inform lower-income consumers that other agencies exist to help them?

3. If you were head of the Consumer Product Safety Commission, how would you determine which products should be banned from the market?

4. When do you decide it is time to seek help for a consumer grievance?

5. How do you decide when to seek help against fraudulent activity on the part of businesses?

6. What is the difference between consumerism and consumer advocacy?

THINGS TO DO

1. Draw up a list of consumer-affairs agencies in your area. First look in the yellow pages under the heading *Consumer* to see what is listed there. Then contact the district attorney general's office. Next contact the state attorney general's office.

2. Write to various industry organizations such as The National Retail Merchant's Association. Find out what kind of grievance procedure is set up for consumers who feel they have been wronged.

SELECTED READINGS

"Consumer Agency's Targets," *Business Week*, March 30, 1974, p. 29.

"Help for Consumers: Government Agencies," *Today's Health*, April 1974, pp. 64–65.

Karpatkin, R., "Advocate's Advance," *Time*, June 28, 1974, p. 66.

Louviere, V., "Getting Relief from Consumer Headaches," *Nation's Business*, June 1974, p. 40ff.

"New Centurions: Government Consumer Offices," *Time*, September 18, 1972 p. 86ff.

"New Hotline for Product Safety: Consumer Product Hazard Index," *American Home*, April 6, 1974, p. 38ff.

"New Kind of Consumer Watchdog: Neighborhood Based Aides in Boston Program," *Business Week*, July 22, 1972, pp. 42–43.

CONSUMER ISSUE XIV

How to Use a Small Claims Court

Do you think that your former landlord gypped you by keeping your security deposit when you moved out? Did a dry cleaner ruin or lose your clothes? Did you make a claim to your insurance company that it refused to pay? Did a company issue you a warranty on one of its products and then charge you for a repair job while it was still covered?

If you felt helpless when any of these things happened to you, you need not have. To right such wrongs, you could have used the small claims court in your area. However, before you use a small claims court, you may first want to exhaust some of the available alternatives, which include such things as the consumer hot lines available in many states and cities; consumer advocates, who will take up your gripes with the appropriate people and print the results in newspaper columns; and, in some cities, radio and TV newspersons who narrate complaints over the air. They often are very effective. We discussed some other ways you can complain and get redress of your consumer grievances in the last Consumer Issue. If you still feel you need judicial help, then you might want to use a small claims court. Before you do that, you should know what a small claims court is all about.

WHY WERE THEY FOUNDED?

In 1913, a noted professor of the Harvard Law School, Roscoe Pound, gave a justification for small claims courts. He said, "It is a *denial of justice* in small causes to drive litigants to employ lawyers, and it is a shame to drive them to legal aid societies to get as charity what the state should give as a right." In most states today you have the right to use the services of small claims courts to litigate, usually, claims under $400.

CRITICISM OF THE COURTS

Small claims courts are not appreciated by everyone. Former Federal Trade Commissioner Mary Gardner Jones once said:

> Our courts are for all practical purposes foreclosed to the individual citizen with the typical grievance involving nondelivery or unsatisfactory service of goods, landlord defaults or indifferent performance under a lease, or even personal injury or property claims which involve relatively minor amounts.

She apparently does not believe that small claims courts usually serve these purposes. Neither does Judge J. Shelly Wright of the U. S. Court of Appeals in Washington, D.C. He contended that "the promise of the small claims courts has not been fulfilled, for in actual operation there is little correspondence between the professed aims of these courts and the ends they serve." Judge Wright believes that most small claims courts have been used as collection agencies by businesspersons.

Businesspersons are indeed the plaintiffs in many cases; they bring suit against consumers who have defaulted in payments for goods already delivered. In 1966, for example, eleven ghetto retailers in Washington, D.C., reported

TABLE XIV–1: SMALL CLAIMS COURTS CHARACTERISTICS IN SELECTED STATES

	Name and location of court	Maximum amount of suit	Are lawyers ordinarily allowed?	Is court procedure formal?	Who can appeal? Plaintiff	Defendant	What does it cost to sue?
CALIFORNIA	Small Claims Branch of Municipal Court, Sacramento	$500	No	Yes	No	Yes	$2.00 +
DISTRICT OF COLUMBIA	Small Claims Branch of Superior Court, Washington, D.C.	$750	Yes	Yes	Yes	Yes	$1.00 +
FLORIDA	Small Claims Court, Miami	$2,500	Yes	Yes	Yes	Yes	$3.50 +
GEORGIA	Small Claims Branch of Civil Court, Atlanta	$100	Yes	Yes	Yes	Yes	$6.50 +
ILLINOIS	Circuit Court, Springfield	$1,000	Yes	Yes	Yes	Yes	$8.00 +
IOWA	Small Claims Div. of Municipal Court, Des Moines	$1,000	Yes	Yes	No	No	$3.00 +
MAINE	Small Claims Div. of District Court, Augusta	$200	Yes	Yes	Yes	Yes	$5.00
MASSACHUSETTS	Small Claims Div. of Municipal Court, Boston	$400	Yes	Yes	No	Yes	$3.55
MICHIGAN	Small Claims Div. of District Court, Lansing	$300	No	Yes	No	No	$5.00 +

TABLE (Continued)

	Name and location of court	Maximum amount of suit	Are lawyers ordinarily allowed?	Is court procedure formal?	Who can appeal?		What does it cost to sue?
					Plaintiff	Defendant	
MINNESOTA	Small Claims Div. of Municipal Court, St. Paul	$500	Yes	Yes	Yes	Yes	$2.00
NEW JERSEY	Small Claims Div. of District Court, Trenton	$200 to $500	Yes	Yes	Yes	Yes	$2.70 +
NEW YORK	Small Claims Div. of Civil Court, New York City	$500	Yes	Yes	Yes	Yes	$3.20
NORTH CAROLINA	Small Claims Div. of District Court, Raleigh	$500	Yes	Yes	Yes	Yes	$7.00 +
PENNSYLVANIA	Small Claims Div. of Municipal Court, Philadelphia	$500	Only if corporation	Yes	Yes	Yes	$11.00
TEXAS	Justice Court, Houston	$150 to $200	Yes	Yes	Yes	Yes	$5.00
VIRGINIA	Civil Div. of District Court, Richmond	$5,000	Yes	Yes	Yes (If over $50)	Yes (If over $50)	$5.00 +
WASHINGTON	Small Claims Div. of Justice Court, Seattle	$300	No	Yes	No	Yes (If over $100)	$1.00
WISCONSIN	Small Claims Div. of County Court, Madison	$500	Yes	Yes	Yes	Yes	$5.00

2690 court judgments, one for every $2200 of sales that year. Things are changing, however, mainly because consumers are becoming aware of their rights in small claims court proceedings, and they are using small claims courts today in order to right their grievances. A 1970 study by Consumers Union showed that the small claims courts in the four cities investigated did indeed help consumers. For example, of the 153 suits filed by consumers against landlords, repair shops, stores, car dealers, and other businesses, 100 were definitely settled in favor of the plaintiff.

BUT YOU HAVE TO WATCH OUT

Complications can arise in any small claims court proceedings. In many states, the defendant can automatically and routinely have a case transferred to a civil court. In most civil courts, without an attorney your efforts are worthless. So, if a case in which you are plaintiff is transferred to the civil court, you must incur the expense of an attorney or drop out of the suit.

Further, a small claims judgment in your favor does not mean you will get full satisfaction for your loss. The judge may tell the defendant to pay you $100 on a $150 claim (which, of course, is still $100 more than you started with). But no matter what the defendant is told to pay you, the small claims court does not act as a collection agency. You do not always collect when you win. For example, in the 1970 study by Consumers Union, of the 62 cases which the consumer plaintiff won, 13 proved uncollectable. You must realize that a defendant who does not show up in court is not likely to pay. You may be able to obtain a so-called "writ of execution" from the small claims court if you can show that the defendant is not paying you off. But this writ of execution against the defendant's property, bank account, or wages is oftentimes not effective.

HOW THEY WORK

The first thing you do is find the small claims court in your area. Ask the court clerk whether the court can handle your kind of case. For example, some large cities have special courts to handle problems between renters and landlords. Then make sure that the court has jurisdiction over the person or business you wish to sue. Usually the defendant must live, work, or do business in the court's territory. If you are trying to sue an out-of-town firm, you may run into real problems. You probably should go to the state government, usually the secretary of state, and find out where the summons should be sent. Remember that since the small claims court is not a collection agency, if you are filing suit against a firm that is no longer in business, you will have a very difficult time collecting.

Make absolutely certain that you have the correct business name and address of the company being sued. Frequently, courts require strict accuracy, and if you do not abide by that requirement, the suit is thrown out.

Once you file suit, a summons goes out to the defending party, either by registered mail or in the hands of a sheriff, bailiff, marshal, constable, or sometimes a private citizen. Once a company receives the summons, it may decide to resolve the issue out of court; about one-fourth of all cases for which summons are issued are settled this way. Many times, however, the defendant company may not even show up for the trial, in which case you stand a good chance of winning by default. (But, as we said, no-shows are usually also hard to collect from.)

PREPARING FOR TRIAL

How should you prepare for trial? Obviously, if you know a lawyer, you can get some quick advice. In any event, you should have all necessary and pertinent receipts, canceled checks, written estimates, contracts, and any other form of documentary evidence that you can show the judge. The best way to do things is to have the entire affair set down in chronological order with supporting evidence so you can show the judge exactly what happened. Make sure that your dates are accurate. Inaccurate dates would prejudice your case against you.

If you are disputing something like a repair job, you may have to get a third party as an "expert." Generally, this third party will be someone in the same trade. It is often difficult to get persons to testify against their fellow workers in the same trade. He or she may, however, be willing to give a written statement. Sometimes this is viewed as acceptable evidence. If possible, when you are suing over disputed workmanship, bring the physical evidence of your claim into court. If your local dry cleaner shrunk that wool sweater of yours to a size 3, do not fail to show it to the judge.

WHAT HAPPENS IN COURT

The judge will generally let you present your case in simple language without the help of a lawyer. In fact, in many states, neither you nor the defendant can bring a lawyer to help you. You may get the judge's decision immediately or by notice within a few weeks. In some states, you can appeal the case, but in many situations the small claims court plaintiff does not have the right to appeal a case that is decided against him or her. Remember, whatever action you decide to take after the judgment should be weighed against the costs of that action. Your time is not free, and the worry that may be involved in pursuing a lost case further might not be worth the potential reward of eventually winning.

If your opponent tries to settle the case out of court, make sure everything's written down in a manner that can be upheld if he reneges on the offer. Anything should be signed by both of you and filed with the court so that the

agreement can in fact be enforced by the law. What is better is to have him appear with you before the judge to tell of the settlement terms. Generally, if you win or if you settle out of court, you should be able to get him to pay for the court costs, which range from $3 to $20, depending on the state.

WHERE, WHAT, AND HOW MUCH?

In the next few pages we give you a brief rundown of the name of the court in selected states, where the court is located, the maximum amount of the suits, and some other information such as the costs to you of filing a small claims suit. Remember, you want to be a rational consumer decision maker. Weigh the potential benefits of going to court against the potential costs. Opt for small claims court when you think on net you'll be better off. If, however, the potential gain to you is less than the value you place on your time and the worry and fear that will be involved when you in fact get before a strange judge in a strange setting, it may be just best to forget the whole thing. On the other hand, if you are convinced that your case is just, that you have indeed been gypped, and the sum of money involved is not insignificant, by all means take advantage of the information presented in this consumer issue and start the proceedings.

SUMMARY

1. If you feel that a local retailer has cheated you out of more than a few dollars (but less than $500 to $1000, depending on your state of residence), you might find it worthwhile to go to a small claims court.

2. A judgment in your favor from a small claims court does not guarantee payment of the claim. Many successful suits lead to uncollectable payments.

3. If you decide to file suit in a small claims court, ask the clerk of your local small claims court whether your kind of case can be handled there—that is, whether the court has jurisdiction over the person or business you wish to sue.

4. Once a summons is issued to whomever you are suing, you may find that the person or company will decide to resolve the issue out of court.

5. If you go to court, make sure you have the events and actions of the entire affair set down in chronological order with supporting evidence so that you can show the judge exactly what happened. Supporting evidence includes receipts, canceled checks, written estimates, contracts, and correspondence.

6. When you enter a dispute over workmanship, bring physical evidence of your claim into court, if possible.

QUESTIONS FOR THOUGHT AND DISCUSSION

1. In your opinion, who makes most use of small claims courts?

2. Why would you decide in some cases not to go to a small claims court?

3. Do you think that small claims courts should take on bigger cases? That is, do you think that the maximum amount of money at issue in a suit should be raised in many states? Why or why not?

4. Do you think that legal services should be provided to lower-income individuals free of charge or at prices below cost?

THINGS TO DO

1. Find out what is the current maximum amount of money that it is permissible to enter a suit over in the small claims court in your state. Are lawyers allowed in Small Claims Courts in your state today? Can both plaintiff and defendant appeal? What does it now cost to sue?

2. Go to a local small claims court and observe some of the action. Do you think that all of the cases should necessarily have been brought into court? What would determine whether some of them should not have been brought into court?

3. Talk to a lawyer about the advisability of using the small claims court in your area.

SELECTED READINGS

"Caveat Venditor; Suing in Small Claims Court; Advice of D. Matthews," *Time,* September 10, 1973, pp. 70ff.

Cratchit, B., "Tell us about Small Claims Courts," *Ramparts,* September 1972, pp. 47ff.

Hirsch, D., "The Case of the Shrunken Coat," *Saturday Review of the Society,* May 1973, pp. 71ff.

MacDonald, S., "Sue Me, Said Mr. Kass to Mrs. Blustein; New York's Small Claims Court," *New York Times Magazine,* April 7, 1974, pp. 32ff.

"Small Claims Courts," *Consumer Reports,* December 1973, pp. 383–385.

"So Give Her the Money," *Newsweek,* January 14, 1974, pp. 50–51.

CONSUMER ISSUE XV

Do Consumers Have Responsibilities, Too?

Throughout this text we have discussed the responsibilities of businesses and business-persons toward consumers. We have not yet discussed the possibility that consumers have responsibilities also.

If you do not think that this is a real issue, read the following article by Barbara Katz.

REVERSE RIP–OFFS: CONSUMERS WHO CHEAT BUSINESS PEOPLE

The well-dressed, well-coifed woman paid for her $250 dress with a signature and a smile. She walked out of the high-priced suburban store, stepped into her Lincoln Continental, and drove straight to her dressmaker's. A few days later, she returned, picked up the store-bought dress and the look-alike that her dressmaker had copied from the original, and headed back to the store, sales slip in hand. Explaining briskly that she'd changed her mind about the purchase, she watched as the full price was credited to her account—no questions asked—and then headed home with her $50 copy.

The woman, a frequent shopper at expensive stores, would probably have reacted indignantly had anyone suggested she was doing anything wrong. After all, isn't the customer always right?

Well, not quite always, say spokesmen for retail stores, hotels, utilities, airlines and others in the business of providing goods and services to the public. In an age of consumerism these spokesmen often hear their businesses portrayed as bilkers, while customers are portrayed as

Source: *Media & Consumer*, Vol. 2, No. 1 (January 1974), p. 2. © Dow Jones & Co., Inc., 1973. Reprinted with permission of *The National Observer*.

loyal, honest, and trustworthy. But sometimes, say business people, it's the customer who is thoughtless, sneaky or downright dishonest.

Rip-offs by consumers range from modest "oversights" to wild flim-flams and blatant thievery.

On the modest side, ever see anyone call the waitress back after noticing she's charged for only one instead of two martinis? A discount house in New York conducted an experiment a few years ago, deliberately overcharging 20 customers 40 cents and undercharging another 20 customers the same amount. The results painted a dark picture of the average customer's honesty: Of those overcharged, 18 called attention to the matter; only 2 of those undercharged did so.

Returned goods also can be a headache to store managers. Every clothing store has to deal with the customer who buys a dress or suit on Saturday, wears it to a dance on Sunday, and returns it to the store on Monday. And then there's the penny pincher who buys a stereo system at a discount store, hauls it over to a store where the full price is maintained, and tries to get a "refund."

More common, though, is the customer who simply takes a store's liberal return policy at face value. At Rich's Inc., a 107-year-old Atlanta department-store chain, a woman recently returned a pair of high-button shoes—an item the chain hadn't sold in decades. The woman said it was "the first chance she'd had" to get downtown since buying the shoes. The store made the refund without asking whether the customer had worn the shoes.

Retail stores suffer also from a practice known as tag-switching. In this rip-off the customer removes the price tag from a low-price item and attaches it to a high-priced item. A $30 shirt thus becomes a $10 bargain. Stores are now fighting back with new, harder-to-remove price tags.

Even supermarkets are tag-switching victims. "There's nothing as weird as watching a woman in a thousand-dollar mink coat switching the tag from the chuck steak to the sirloin," says one Washington, D.C., supermarket manager. There's also package-switching: Customers will painstakingly remove all the eggs from a carton reading "small" and replace them with a dozen "extra large"—all to save 7-cents.

Hospitals and hotels have their share of consumer rip-offs, mostly in the form of pilferage. The American Hospital Association reports that patients are almost as likely to take their sheets and pillowcases home with them as their pills.

John Romero of Las Vegas' Sahara Hotel says that guests steal not only the expected "souvenirs" like towels and ash trays, but just about everything they can get their hands on. "We've lost TVs that have been bolted to the floor," he says. "We've lost drapes and shower curtains. We've even had people walk out with the lobby chairs."

Airlines, too, have problems. One major airline estimates that only about one-third of its lost-baggage claims are legitimate. While some travelers submit claims for nonexistent luggage, others inflate the value of their lost property. "Why is it that we never lose old clothes from J. C. Penney?" asks one airline representative. "Why is it always new $350 suits from Saks Fifth Avenue?"

A favorite technique some consumers use when dealing with large enterprises like utilities and credit-card companies is the "8-cent rip-off." The customer simply "forgets" to attach a postage stamp when he mails in a bill payment.

Most large companies pay the postage rather than refuse mail that is likely to contain checks or money orders. But Pacific Telephone of San Francisco has announced that it will no longer accept postage-due mail. The decision came when the company estimated it was heading for a $140,000 postage-due bill this year.

And then, of course, there is the Great Insurance Rip-off. There are those who, after getting involved in a minor auto accident, work out a deal with the body shop to inflate the damage estimate, and then collect enough in insurance to have the whole car overhauled.

Or there's the fellow whose automobile engine finally gives up. He leaves the car where it broke down, comes home, and reports the car stolen. When the car is found a few days later, he insists it was running fine when he last saw it and tries to collect for engine overhaul from his car-theft insurance. "It's not easy to prove he's a liar," says an East Coast insurance appraiser, "but when you look at the car and see how old the parts are and how poorly it's been maintained, it strikes you as awfully convenient."

Even used-car salesmen are complaining about consumers. Ralph Williams, the Southern California new-and used-car salesman who advertises as the biggest Ford dealer in the country ("Hi there, Ralph Williams here"), moans that consumers have taken over—and they're not all playing fair.

Williams says he gets about 10 customers a month who "buy" a car with a small down-payment, apply for a loan on the balance, drive the car for three weeks, then pull out of the deal before the loan is approved. They go from one dealer to another, Williams says, never really buying anything, but always driving a new car.

"The consumer is king," Williams bellows. "He gets away with murder, and we roll over and play dead because we don't need the heat. All the buyer-beware has been taken out of the business. The consumer is king."

What Do You Think?

After reading some of the abuses that consumers heap on businesses, perhaps you might agree that there are at least a few responsibilities that each of us as consumers must agree to. Perhaps all of these responsibilities can be best summed up as honesty toward the people with whom we do business.

SELECTED READINGS

"Customer Gripes, Industry's Side of the Story," *U. S. News & World Report,* October 23, 1972, 94–95.

Morganstern, Stanley, *Legal Protection for the Consumer* (Dobbs Ferry, N. Y.: Oceana Publications), 1973.

A. Shenfield "A British View of Consumerism, *Consumers' Research Magazine,* September 1973 pp. 35–37.

Raymond A. Bauer, 'Consumer Behavior as Risk Taking', in *Consumer Behavior: Selected Readings* edited by James F. Engel, American Marketing Association Reprint Series, (Homewood, Illinois; Richard D. Irwin, Inc., 1968) pp. 138–146.

S. R. Campbell, 'The Concerned Consumer', *Better Homes and Gardens,* September 1972 p. 24ff.

CHAPTER PREVIEW

☐ Is destruction of our ecology a new problem?
☐ How important is air pollution in the total environmental problem?
☐ What are the major air polluters?
☐ What do private and social costs have to do with ecological problems?
☐ What is the future of the automobile?
☐ How has federal legislation affected the pollution picture?
☐ Will there ever be an end to air and water pollution?

GLOSSARY OF NEW TERMS

Waste By-products: Substances that are produced by an activity but are not the intended, useful products of the activity. For example, the waste by-product from manufacturing paper might be a sticky, smelly, gooey mess. All activities involve some type of waste by-product.

Particulates: Things you can feel or see in the air that are generally associated with pollution, such as soot.

Common Property Resource: A resource that nobody owns (but everybody owns) as compared with a private property resource which a person or persons owns specifically. An example of a common property resource is air.

Private Cost: The cost incurred by an individual in the use of some economic resource.

Social Cost: The cost incurred by society when one or more individuals use an economic resource. Social costs include private costs.

Ecology: The branch of biology that deals with the relations between living organisms and their environment.

Biological Oxygen Demand (BOD): A measure of how much dissolved oxygen must be in water before any organic polluting matter can be biologically destroyed.

Lake Erie is dying; certain rivers are fire hazards; and every year a number of beaches become fouled from oil spills. The air in Gary, Indiana (especially where the poor live), is said to be as thick as pea soup with pollutants, while the smog in Los Angeles on a *good* day may smell unpleasant to some unaccustomed visitors. The list of examples could go on and on. Clearly, air and water pollution have become part of our everyday lives.

How bad is the problem really? What caused it? How can it be improved? These questions, which we shall deal with in this chapter, are some of the most pressing of our times. For air and water pollution are already serious enough that many scientists believe irreversible damages may cause national disasters.

IS THE PROBLEM AS NEW AS IT SEEMS?

We all seem to think that the problem of pollution is something new to the 1960s and 1970s, but this is not so. London had smog well over a century ago because its inhabitants burned soft coal. Los Angeles has been smog-filled for many, many years, and Pittsburgh used to be dark during the day in some sections of the city. In fact, we know there has always been some pollution because nothing can be produced without **waste by-products**. In the past, the natural cleansing action of the earth's waters and air seemed fairly able to cope with the waste products that we created. And until only 10 or 20 years ago, pollution in most parts of the United States did not apparently exceed the vast absorptive capacities of water and air. But it seems this is no longer so. U. S. population increased by 24 million between 1960 and 1970, and it is projected to increase by the same amount during this decade. Also, following a trend that goes back to the beginning of our country, people have increasingly concentrated in urban areas. Right now, over half of the population is crowded into 1 percent of our land, and two-thirds crowd themselves into less than 10 percent of the land. In these urban environments, there are many manufacturing plants, power plants, and transportation facilities, which are so highly concentrated that the natural environment can no longer absorb their waste products.

ECOLOGY AND THE MARKETPLACE

Even though air and water pollution seem to be getting worse, we should remember that cities have always been places of pollution concentration. Before the automobile, horses (averaging 27½ pounds a day of waste by-products) made city streets unusable for all pedestrians except those wearing high-topped boots. The burning of coal with high sulfur content polluted the air in London for many, many years until that particular type of coal was banned. Believe it or not, the amount of air pollution in London today is lower than it was 100 years ago. Some economic historians contend that the quality of life in our crowded cities is not necessarily lower today than it was in years past. While we will not attempt to argue this controversial point, the fact remains that many believe our levels of pollution to be too high. Let us look specifically at air pollution.

AIR POLLUTION

Figure 18–1 shows that the largest physical quantity of pollution consists of over 130 tons of carbon monoxide, of which over 60 percent is generated by transportation: cars, buses, planes, and so on. Every year, we are showered with 60 million tons of **particulates.** (Particulates are things you can see: bits of ash, carbon, oil, grease, and metallic substances.) In some cities the level of particulates in the air is so high that their citizens have come to believe the saying, "We don't trust any air we can't see."

The major contributor of carbon monoxide is transportation. Motor vehicles, a prime source of air pollution, number over 135 million on the road today. Internal combustion, gasoline-powered cars, trucks, and buses emit unburned hydrocarbons, lead compounds, nitrogen oxides, carbon monoxide, and compounds of phosphorus, lead, and additional unburned organic compounds. Why have manufacturers not yet developed a cleaner burning engine so that auto exhaust fumes do not choke our precious air? Why do motorists ignore the pollution problem they are causing?

THE UNPAID SOCIAL COSTS

The answers to these questions are easy. Until very recently, auto manufacturers and motorists were not forced to pay the costs they imposed on the rest of society by stinking up our air. Each of us who got into our cars could ignore the pollution problem we were adding to. In any event, each of our single contributions is, for all practical purposes, negligible. If any one of us decided not to drive or use any engine, the total quantity of pollution would remain almost the same because each of us, *individually,* is such a small part of the total problem. Air is a **common property resource;** we all seem to want to use it in any manner that suits us best. While the **social cost** of driving includes air pollution from internal combustion engines, the **private cost** of driving, until recently, did not, because nobody had to take account of what his or her exhaust fumes did to society.

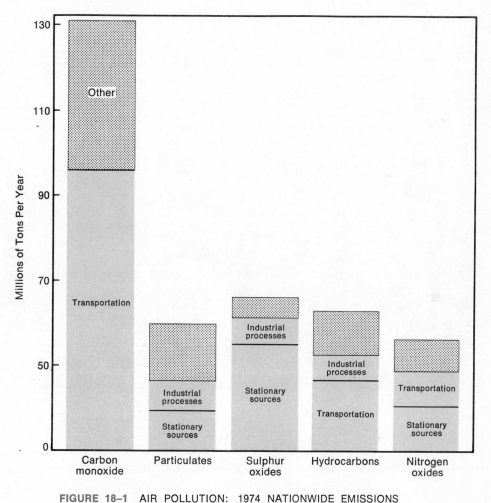

FIGURE 18–1 AIR POLLUTION: 1974 NATIONWIDE EMISSIONS
In 1974 over 130 million tons of carbon monoxide were spewed out into the air.
Over 60 percent of that was accounted for by transportation. Transportation also
accounted for a large part of hydrocarbon emissions and nitrous oxide emissions.
Source: U.S. Department of Health, Education, and Welfare.

NEW REGULATIONS

Now things have changed. Air is still a common property resource, but
the federal and state governments have stepped in to enforce emission
control regulations. The federal government, for example, has set specific maximum levels of pollutants that can be emitted from any car's
exhaust. But these standards apply only to new cars, and it is quite
obvious that they will not eliminate the problem completely because of
all the older cars on the road. Moreover, unless cars are systematically
checked periodically to make sure that their engines have been tuned
properly and that their exhaust control systems have not been disconnect-
ed, we will probably not drastically alter the level of air pollution caused

by vehicles. (Disconnecting pollution control devices, which it is illegal to do, is now a big business.) In any event, automobile manufacturers have been developing cleaner burning engines and have even been experimenting with external combustion cars, such as steam engines.

NO–LEAD GAS   The development of no-lead fuel created one potential way to eliminate some forms of air pollution from automobiles. The lead or ethyl in high-octane gasolines for high-compression engines contributes substantially to air pollution. While it had therefore been suggested that the lead content of gasoline be taxed, this method of pollution control was dropped in favor of requiring all new cars to be built with engines that could run acceptably on low-octane, no-lead fuel. (These engines have low compression ratios.) This requirement most affected the performance of imported cars which historically have smaller engines and higher compression ratios than most American cars. Here we find again that reduction of pollution is not costless. A good point to remember is that *eliminating pollution will always involve a cost.* To find out the entire cost, we must be careful to dig out all of the ways in which individuals pay for pollution abatement.

THE FUTURE OF
THE AUTO

What does the future hold for the automobile? Perhaps we will have electric cars in the future; but even here we will not eliminate all pollution. After all, an electric car's batteries have to be recharged with electricity, which has to be generated somewhere. The process of generation itself causes pollution. In fact, electric power plants account for almost one-half of the emissions of sulfur oxides and one-fourth of the emissions of particulates in our air. Let us see what we can expect to happen in that sector of the economy to ease our pollution problem.

ELECTRICITY
GENERATION

The amount of electricity generated annually has been doubling every 10 years. In 1970, over 16 billion kilowatt hours were generated. Ten years earlier, less than 8 billion kilowatt hours were generated. It is estimated that at current relative prices for electricity, by the year 2000 the demand will be six or six times what it is today.

Right now, most electricity is generated in steam power plants that burn fossil fuels. That is, some form of fuel such as oil, coal, or natural gas is burned to generate steam to run large turbines that then create the electricity for the nation. In the process of burning fossil fuel—except for natural gas, which burns with almost no pollution at all—sulfur oxides and particulate matters are injected into the air.

Clean Air Act. The government has stepped in to force electric power companies to account for the pollution they create by generating their product. The Clean Air Act, passed in 1970, is the strictest air quality measure ever legislated. This Act provides for setting up standards for stationary polluters such as electric utilities. The standards will be based on what emission controls are at the time technologically practical. Some states have gone further than the Clean Air Act by requiring that the sulfur content of the fuel burned must be 1 percent or less. The Executive branch first suggested a sulfur content tax but later changed its mind and proposed a tax on the sulfur emissions. This is obviously a much more economical way of controlling pollution, for we usually do not care what goes into generating power; instead, we care what pollution comes out of generating the power. A sulfur emissions tax allows producers to find the most efficient ways of eliminating pollution—whether by burning lower sulfur content fuel, or instead by installing pollution equipment on the smokestack or by some other similar means.

WATER POLLUTION

In 1970 the government issued a report indicating that millions of Americans may be drinking water with potentially hazardous contamination. A few years ago there was a mercury scare: certain types of fish contained such high levels of mercury that they were presumably unsafe for human consumption. The mercury they obtained was from effluent discharged by industrial plants.

The pollutants of water are numerous and complex and in many cases hard to identify and isolate. Among the pollutants are inorganic and chemical compounds. These include fecal bacteria, lead, arsenic, barium, cadmium, chromium, and selinium. Heat itself is another type of water pollutant, producing what is called thermal pollution. This type of pollution, which is known to disturb the ecology in surrounding waters, relates in particular to the electric utility industry, which wants to build a large number of nuclear power plants that may heat the surrounding water.

One collective measure of water pollutants that scientists often talk about is Biological Oxygen Demand (BOD). This is a measure of how much dissolved oxygen must be in water before any organic polluting matter can be biologically degraded. Thus, scientists refer to the pollution outputs of manufacturing plants as a certain number of BOD per day. The larger the BOD for a given quantity of water, the less likely will the water be able to cleanse the pollution away naturally.

THE HARM FROM
WATER POLLUTION

There are numerous medical reasons for wanting to eliminate or reduce the level of water pollution in the United States. Certain types of pollution, such as the sewage of human beings and livestock, may spread disease. Synthetic organic chemicals like pesticides may be directly harmful to both humans and other animals such as fish. Certain forms of inorganic chemicals and minerals destroy aquatic life. They also produce excessive hardness in water; they will corrode metals; and, in many cases, they are poisonous if taken in large enough quantities. In addition, any radioactivity contained in water may be harmful not only to present but to future generations as well. This is a particular problem with nuclear power plants. Such plants normally release no nuclear or radioactive waste at all. But it is feared that some critical malfunction could have disastrous, long-term consequences.

Municipal Wastes. Municipal sewage is still a major source of BOD and suspended solid pollutants. While rivers no longer carry visible lumps of human excrement, some rivers continue to be highly contaminated by relatively unprocessed sewage. In fact, there are still well over 1000 municipalities in the United States that do not treat their sewage at all before dumping it into a river or lake. And many others continually bypass their plants. In 1970, the Federal Water Quality Administration indicated that almost 40 percent of the nation's sewage treatment systems were inadequate.

There are two types of waste water treatment—primary and secondary. Primary treatment involves removal of solids, grease, and scum. Over 30 percent of municipalities provide only primary treatment. Secondary treatment involves the controlled degradation by micro-organisms of organic matter. But even secondary treatment does not remove such things as nitrogen and phosphorus that come from detergents.

The federal government estimated that $25 billion would have to have been spent between 1970 and 1975 in order to achieve what it called "adequate" levels of primary and secondary treatment of municipal wastes. However, we know this figure means nothing, because the standards that the government sets are as arbitrary as the standards that you or I could have set. The fact is that the purer we want our water, the more expensive the process will be. At some point it becomes prohibitively expensive to try to make the water any closer to absolutely pure.

Unfortunately, how much money a municipality decides to spend on sewage treatment is often totally unrelated to the economic damages caused by relatively untreated sewage. If a city on a river dumps untreated sewage into the river, that city does not bear the consequences. Rather, the downstream users of the river do. If there are only two cities involved, it may be possible for the downstream city to bargain with the upstream city to provide more sewage treatment. However, when there are large numbers of polluters on a river, it may be difficult to find out which cities are doing the polluting. The policing costs would be very high, even if some agreement were reached. Again, we are talking about a common property problem. Here, the resource is a moving body of water that, in most cases, nobody owns.

The federal government wants all rivers and lakes to be clean enough to swim in by a specified year—say 1980 or 1985. This amounts to a uniform purity requirement that all municipalities will have to comply with. Again, such a uniform requirement runs into problems of economic inefficiency. It may be better to devote resources to cleaning up only selected rivers instead of trying to make them all fit for swimming. Some rivers may have so many industrial plants on them that no one would want to swim in them anyway. So it would be economically inefficient to require that the polluters on those rivers stop all water pollution activities.

Heating the Water. When a large body of water is heated several degrees, it sometimes changes the balance of the aquatic ecology. Certain fish cannot survive in warm water. They will perish or move to other areas if possible. Other fish thrive in warmer water and will therefore become more populous when the water is warmed. How does water get warmed in large bodies? If you put a large nuclear power plant on the ocean, it sends billions of gallons of heated water into the surrounding waters. This heated water will raise the average temperature all around. Water impounded behind dams also becomes warmer than the nearby free flowing river.

WILL THERE EVER BE AN END TO AIR AND WATER POLLUTION?

Is it too late? Are we already headed for disaster? Or can we assume that somehow pollution abatement will turn the tide and allow us in the future, or at least our children or grandchildren, to live in a cleaner environment? Apparently, we have not yet gone "too far." We can improve our environment, but it does take resources, and we will have to spend part of our income in the process. A clean environment can be treated like any other good or service. Presumably, all of us or most, of us desire a cleaner environment. But a clean environment is less desired at a higher price than at a lower price. We would expect that if somehow an optimum solution were reached, we would still have some pollution in our air and water, but it would be the maximum quantity tolerated by the paying public. Again, this may be upsetting to some people who wish to see our environment perfectly cleaned up. But that would be prohibitively expensive, and not many people are willing to pay the costs. They would rather live in a not-so-perfect environment and have that extra income to spend on other things. We can not simultaneously have a perfectly clean environment and the current amount of goods and services we consume, because at any one time, we are faced with a fixed amount of resources. Environmental clean-up involves a trade-off with other goods. Scarcity follows us wherever we go.

SUMMARY

1. The problem with pollution is not a recent one. Over a century ago, London had smog and many centuries ago Romans complained of soot on their white togas.

2. Pollution seems to have become more evident as over half of our population has crowded into one percent of our land and two-thirds crowd into less than 10 percent. Such high concentration in crowded urban environments exceeds the ability of the natural environment to absorb everyone's waste products without some help.

3. Pollution of the air is generated mostly by transportation—cars, buses, and planes.

4. The internal-combustion engine automobile is responsible for a large amount of air pollution; however, current efforts to reduce the amount of pollution from engines may lead to less in the future.

5. Basically, pollution problems arise when individuals are not required to take account of the full costs of their activities. They take account only of the cost to themselves, their private costs. Such a situation occurs when no one has control over something like our air, which is a common property resource.

6. Government legislation such as the Clean Air Act will require an increasing amount of pollution-abatement equipment on all phases of economic activity.

7. Pollution abatement requires the use of resources, and hence requires Americans (and others throughout the world) to give up part of their current consumption activities in order to have a cleaner environment. Hence we are faced with a trade-off.

**QUESTIONS FOR
THOUGHT AND
DISCUSSION**

1. What is the difference between private costs and social costs?

2. If the automobile were banned from the United States, do you think we would still have a pollution problem?

3. Can electricity be generated without making pollution of some kind?

4. "It is not cost effective to require all rivers to be swimmable by 1985." Discuss this quotation.   What does cost effective mean?

5. If a city dumps its sewage into a stream that pollutes a city further downstream, does the polluting city pay any costs for such pollution?

THINGS TO DO

1. Read some of the latest ecology books. Compare them with some of the books written in the 1960s and early 1970s. Do you notice a difference in the tone of the arguments? Does that mean things are getting better or worse?

2. Write to the Environmental Protection Agency in Washington, D. C. Ask for their free literature on what is being done to clean up the environment.

3. Write the Council on Environmental Quality in Washington, D. C. Ask for literature on what it is doing to help clean up the environment.

**SELECTED
READINGS**

"Clean Air Act Keeps its Teeth," *Business Week,* June 8, 1974, 23–24.

"Crackdown Starts on Filing for Pollution Permits," *Farm Journal,* May 1974, pp. 6ff.

Edel, Matthew, *Economics and the Environment* (Englewood Cliffs, N. J.: Prentice-Hall), 1973.

Ehrlich, Paul R., and Anne H. Ehrlich, *Population, Resources, Environment,* second edition (San Francisco: W. H. Freeman), 1972.

Harris, R. H., and E. M. Brecher, "Is the Water Safe to Drink?" *Consumer Reports,* June-July 1974, 436–443; 538–542.

Hobbs, P. V., *et al.*, "Atmospheric Effects of Pollutants," *Science,* March 8, 1974, 909–915.

Holden, C., "Clean Air: Congress Settles for a Restrained Coal Conversion Plan," *Science,* June 21, 1974, 1269–1270.

Mead, M., "Pollution: The Need to Think Clearly About Clear Water," *Redbook,* May 1974, pp. 38ff.

"Utilities Fight Costly Water Rules: Effect of Water Pollution Control Action," *Business Week,* July 13, 1974, pp. 22–23.

Wolozin, Harold, *The Economics of Pollution* (Morristown, N. J.: General Learning Press), 1973.

CHAPTER PREVIEW

☐ Were the good old days as good as everyone says?
☐ Has life become a more certain prospect in our society?
☐ How has our society become more complex?
☐ Are consumers expending more resources on recreation?
☐ Are workers retiring earlier?

GLOSSARY OF NEW TERMS

Indentured Servants: Persons whose labor was contracted for a length of time to pay the cost of their coming to this country.

Tangible Property: Property that can be felt, seen, and touched, such as land or a building.

Intangible Property: Property that represents wealth but is not physical. Stocks and bonds are examples of intangible property.

Most of what you have read in this book is based on the present or the past. Now we must discuss the future. What can you anticipate happening to your life style as a consumer? Right off the bat, you and everybody else are fairly certain that your life is going to get more complicated, because the choices available to you seem to be getting more complicated all the time.

YOUR FUTURE AS A CONSUMER

A MORE COMPLEX LIFE

Certainly, today's consumer products, and hence today's living experience, seem incredibly more complex than those of our ancestors. At the beginning of these United States, although life was hard, it certainly did not appear to be as complicated as it may appear today. For almost everyone, it was either do or die, eek out a bare existence tilling the ground, or forget about staying around. Back then, over 90 percent of the population was engaged in agriculture. One of the most complicated things about living then was coping with the vagaries and vicissitudes of the weather. Of course, all of the day-to-day problems involved in human relationships existed then as they do now and as they will in the future. But as both consumers and producers, Americans had much less choice and, hence, faced less complicated decision-making. Times have changed. Today, less than 5 percent of the population is engaged in agriculture, and the standard of living is many times higher than it was at the beginning of this country. The number and variety of products available to us seems to approach infinity. And the number of different types of economic pursuits we can engage in also seems overwhelming.

THE NOT SO GOOD OLD DAYS

Now, many people contend that America should go back to the good old days, when we were happier and less alienated from our environment. Many believe that during its beginnings, this nation was presumably composed of happy farmers who owned their own land and who all shared equally in the economic pie, but that somehow things have changed. Today there is, according to many, an extreme maldistribution of income and wealth as compared to those good old days. To be sure, the extreme inequality in income today is undeniable. But does the past in fact resemble the description above? Only when we have answered this question can we determine whether we are now better or worse off.

Go back, for example, to the year 1800 or to any year before the Civil War. There was certainly much more inequality in income then, partly because many people in the South were slaves. Their income was in fact very, very small. If you go back as far as colonial days, you find that over half of the working members of the population were either slaves or indentured servants (persons whose labor was contracted for a length of time to pay the cost of their emigration to this country). When you look at the wealth statistics—that is, information on how much of the tangible and intangible property was owned by what percent of the population—you get a striking picture. In 1860, the top one percent of families held 24 percent of the total wealth in the U. S., the top 5 percent held 53 percent, and the top 10 percent held almost three-fourths. That picture seems to have very little room for many self-employed farmers all getting their little share of the action, does it?

INCOME UNCERTAINTY

Something else not so good in the good old days was the extreme variability in the income of farmers. After all, farmers were at the mercy of pestilence, drought, bumper crops (with their resultant low prices), competition in the world market from farmers of other countries, floods, hailstorms, frosts, and every other conceivable natural calamity that could cause an income that was great in one year to be small the next. Today, an extremely small portion of our population is now subject to such variability in income.

AND LIFE ITSELF

Not only has income become more certain for the vast majority of Americans, but today life itself has become a more certain prospect; that is, people are more likely to live longer than their ancestors. Back in the so-called good old days at the turn of the century, expected lifetime was about 47 years. By the beginning of the 1970s, it had risen to about 71 years. Certainly not all Americans benefit equally from improved health conditions, but even those who benefit least still lead healthier lives than most of our ancestors.

OUR COMPLEX SOCIETY

Although longevity and income have become more certain, the living process appears, as we stated above, to have become more complex. Technology changes every day, and according to some, at such rapid a pace that it has made day-to-day living more difficult. If you do not know from one minute to the next what technological advance is going to alter your optimal choices as a consumer, then you are obviously in a fix. One thing to remember, however, is that technology responds not to the absolute dictates of some higher power, but rather to the

profit incentives that rest on the desires of consumers taken as a whole. Technology will develop products that it hopes consumers will buy, but if no consumer wants to buy them, then there is no profit in continuing production (unless the government decides to subsidize such technology).

Individually, we may be confused by the mass of products that modern technology allows to be shoved before us. But on the whole we are getting more or less what we want, because in fact we are buying these new products. Nobody forces us to buy them; we are doing so voluntarily. In fact, if you were able to choose products only out of a 1908 Sears and Roebuck catalog or a current one, most of you would probably choose a current one because the choices would be so much greater and so much closer to your tastes and preferences. Many things listed in the 1908 catalog you cannot buy today—buggies, horseshoes, tapeworm remedies, and so on—but there are even more things that you could not buy in 1908 that you can buy today. Technology is obviously at one and the same time a curse and a blessing.

It is not, however, a monster that is totally uncontrolled. As a matter of fact, technology has often simplified rather than complicated our lives.

For example, the newest jet airplanes are extremely complex compared to airplanes of, say, 20 years ago. However, have you ever seen what a pilot must do to control a 747? Today, pilots do little more than make certain that the computer that runs the plane is working right. The machinery they are operating is extremely complex, and of course their responsibility for lives and expensive machinery is great, but their work tasks are not that complicated once they have mastered them. In other words, technology can provide us with very complex and sophisticated products that are not difficult to use. Is our life more complicated or less because we have these products? Only you, of course, can ultimately decide.

One thing you can be sure of: the more complicated consumer products become, the more incentive there will be for information agencies to tell you what are the best buys. It is predictable that we should see more organizations like Consumers Union giving out information about consumer products as (or if) they get more complicated.

WHAT CAN YOU DO AS A CONSUMER?

What can you do as a consumer in the face of an ever-increasingly complicated array of consumer products that you either can or must purchase? Obviously, you apply the same rules of decision-making to this problem as you do to any other. For example, you should invest in as much information as is worthwhile. How do you figure out how much is worthwhile? You try to estimate the gains from acquiring the additional information, and the costs of doing so. The costs usually involve your time. Sometimes they may involve money, like subscriptions to information services or paying some expert to give you an opinion—as we suggested you do when buying a house, to make sure it is structurally sound, or when buying a used car, to make sure you will not have unanticipated major repairs. One thing is certain: as the world becomes more complicated, more people will specialize; you will find experts to help you out in the consumer decision-making problems of a modern technological society.

Another feature of our modern society appears to be a trend towards taking it easy sooner in life.

RECREATION AND CALLING IT QUITS SOONER

Did you know that the average retirement age in the United States has fallen? In 1890, 68 percent of all the men in the country aged 65 were working; by 1972, only 23 percent of those aged 65 worked. The trend toward earlier retirement is increasingly evident every day, as is the trend toward the leisure society. For example, Figure 19–1 shows the rising percentage of personal consumption expenditures that go to recreation. People are buying more recreational vehicles, more vacations, more stereos—people are, in short, buying a lot more leisure-oriented consumer products.

The trend towards early retirement points to one certainty: those who decide to retire early must obviously have planned for that early retirement many years ago by providing for sufficient income to cover all those nonworking years. After all, if you decide to retire at 55, and you live to the ripe old age of 70, you need 15 years of retirement income. You would have had to build up a pretty big nest egg in the form of a pension plan or some other retirement scheme. If you have any desire whatsoever to retire early (before 65 for men, 62 for women), there is no escaping the fact that to do so you will have to save more today. Do not plan on Social Security as a help to you: first, it would not start at

55 years of age, and second, it does not provide you with a very comfortable living standard (or at least it has not in the past).

To fully enjoy a long retirement period, you have to be equipped to take advantage of 100 percent leisure time. You might be ill equipped if all of your working years were spent without developing outside interests. Hence, it could be important for your happiness in retirement to lead some sort of balanced life before retirement. That is, at least moderate amounts of leisure activities should have been worked into your working time periods. The man or woman who spends 65 hours a week working until age 55 and hopes to truly enjoy a long retirement period on a large pension plan may be sadly disappointed, for their only interest will have been in work, not play. (A person can, however, develop new interests *after* retirement.) It is not surprising that some people who work their heads off while they are young end up working their entire lives because they become addicted to the excitement of a full day of work, at least five and sometimes six or seven days a week. Of course, there is nothing necessarily wrong with this: each of us has the right to pursue our own values and preferences. But if work is not what you think you want to do the rest of your life, it is wise to start young in figuring out a balanced diet of work and play. If you always put off doing what you would like to do during leisure time you will probably never do it. Hobbies may sound corny to some, but they are an integral part of a life style that leads to a happy retirement that seems fulfilling, whether it be early or late.

In sum, then, successful early retirement requires two ingredients:

1.   an exceptionally large saving program while you are working.

2.   a personal development program for acquiring interests outside of work activities to be expanded when retirement comes around.

FIGURE 19–1   PERCENTAGE OF PERSONAL CONSUMPTION EXPENDITURES
DEVOTED TO RECREATION
Back in 1933, only 4.7 percent of personal consumption expenditures was devoted to recreation. This percentage has been rising ever since, today reaching 7 percent or more.   Source: *Survey of Current Business*.

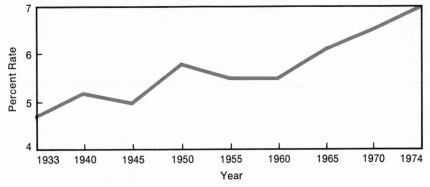

**ALTERNATIVES TO
EARLY RETIREMENT**

Obviously, there are many alternatives to early retirement. For one, you can work less and retire later in life. You do not have to work 50 weeks a year every year until you retire at age 65. You can work 40 weeks a year, or 35, or even six months. Now, it takes a very special job for that to be possible, but if that is really what you want in life, you can start your search right now to find the appropriate situation. You generally will not make as much money, but you will have more leisure time, which is a good in itself for most people. It has a value just as income does. Of course, here again you have to get just the right mix to suit yourself. For if you work too little, you have too little money to make your leisure time satisfying, such as by purchasing records, books, movie tickets, boats, restaurant meals, skis, trips, etc.

Some people, for example, think that a motor home or a trailer is an excellent way to take advantage of increased leisure. You can go to many national parks and many private campgrounds. But be careful: buying a trailer or a motor home involves a large *implicit* cost, a cost that you pay whether you like it or not. Say you buy a motor home and only use it two weeks a year; you are paying for it the rest of the year in the form of depreciation, wear and tear, etc., and also in the form of the opportunity cost of the money invested in that recreational vehicle. What if it cost you $10,000? Well, your opportunity cost is at least what you could get by investing the $10,000 in a savings account, and probably higher, so it is costing you a good $600 to $1000 just in that implicit opportunity cost. It is also costing you the additional money for maintenance, gas, and however much it depreciates. Now figure out what that two-week vacation in your "own" motor home is going to cost you. It might be tremendous, equivalent to what you could pay to go first class and stay in luxury hotels. You may not like luxury hotels and may prefer the privacy of a motor home or a trailer. But again, if you are a rational consumer, you will figure out all of the implicit costs and make your decision accordingly. Find out whether you really want to pay that much for privacy and the love of the open road.

WRAPPING IT UP

We could go on about the different aspects of your future life, as a consumer, a wage-earner, and as a retiree. Basically, though, the principles outlined in the previous chapters and issues can be used and applied to all situations in your life. As an intelligent, informed consumer, you can apply these principles to your decision making now and in the future. But you will also need to acquire more information about the society around you tomorrow, the next day, and the day after that. In other words, a complete understanding of consumer economics today will not be sufficient 10 years from now, for institutions and facts change in our society. But the process of acquiring the needed additional information should not scare you. In fact, given the tools you now have, it will be easier for you to selectively choose areas where you need to acquire more information in order to be a rational consumer.

SUMMARY

1. At the beginning of our country, there were much greater differences in income and wealth than there are today.

2. At the beginning of our country, there was much more uncertainty about the constancy of income because the vast percentage of the population engaged in farming. Farmers were at the mercy of pestilence and drought.

3. At the beginning of this nation life itself was quite uncertain; The average expected lifetime was less than 50 years.

4. As our society has become more complex and the consumer products we buy more complicated, so too has technology devised methods to make their use less complicated.

5. In a more complex society, consumers generally spend more time and resources to acquire information about what to purchase than about how to use the things they have purchased.

6. A larger fraction of consumer income is being spent on recreation today than it was 50 years ago.

7. The average age of retirement is falling steadily in the United States.

8. In order to retire earlier an individual must (a) save more when he or she is working and (b) develop a life style that is adaptable to a situation in which work is not the predominate factor.

QUESTIONS FOR THOUGHT AND DISCUSSION

1. Why are people retiring earlier now than they were 50 years ago?

2. Do you think it is necessary to plan for retirement?

3. Do you think life is becoming more complex each year?

4. What is the difference between complexity in operation and complexity in purchase? Making that distinction, has a consumer's life become more complex in either or both of these areas?

5. Do you anticipate a change in your consuming life style as you grow older? In which direction?

6. Is it necessarily true that more affluence leads to more consumption?

THINGS TO DO

1. Chart your future as a consumer. Are you worried about what your life will be like in the future, or do you think that "things will work out"?

SELECTED READINGS

"Cost Squeeze: Plight of Retired People," *U.S. News & World Report,* March 27, 1972, pp. 38–40.

Heilbroner, R. L., *An Inquiry into the Human Prospect* (New York: Norton & Co.), 1974.

Maddox, George L., ed., *The Future of Aging and the Aged* (Atlanta, Ga.: Southern Newspaper Publishers Association Foundation), 1971.

"No Big Rush to Retire Early," *Business Week,* December 2, 1972, p. 62.

"Outlook: Higher Prices, Slower Growth," *Time,* October 1973, 10.

"Retirement Living: How Two Couples Make Ends Meet," *Changing Times,* September 1974, pp. 24–28.

Schuchat, T., "Government Steps up Protection for Elderly Consumers on Fixed Incomes," *Harvest Years/Retirement Living,* June 1972, pp. 6–7.

"Some Guesses about the Next 25 Years," *Changing Times,* March 1974, pp. 4ff.

Swinnerton, A. R., "Let's Get Organized," *Retirement Living,* November 1973, 40–41.

Toffler, Alvin, *Future Shock* (New York: Random House), 1970.

"Want to Retire Early? Could You? Should You?" *Changing Times,* March 1974, 31–34.

APPENDIX A
Estate Planning: Wills, Trusts, and Taxes

Briefly, estate planning is an attempt to analyze an individual's present and future assets, liabilities, and desires relative to the event of his or her death. The commonest goal in estate planning is to minimize the inheritance taxes levied on a person's estate at death. An additional goal is to lower the nontax costs associated with dying, such as legal and accounting fees.

Estate planning can be done by the individual, but attorneys have traditionally handled the bulk of the more sophisticated estate plans. However, trust companies, banks, and even life insurance salespersons will offer estate planning advice.

ESTATE PLANNING IS NOT JUST FOR THE RICH

Of course, it is imperative that rich persons engage in estate planning to minimize the tremendous inheritance taxes due upon death. But the average individual fails to undertake some form of estate planning, and therefore the heirs endure the hardship of unnecessary costs and problems, all because he or she failed to seek professional advice.

THE BASICS

It is difficult to get into the mood to plan for your death because it is such an undesirable topic of thought or discussion. It is also diffi-cult to plan for what happens after your death since you will not be around to absorb the gratitude of your heirs or dependents. But anyone who is the head of a household or who lives in a state where married individuals have equal rights to all property of the family should in fact engage in some form of estate planning.

What Is Your Estate?

A person's estate can be defined as those material assets existing at his or her death. Homes, cars, cash, securities, and the like make up your estate. It is how these assets are taxed and given to your heirs that you must worry about. Therefore, it is important than you designate who is to inherit your estate and to do it in such a way that it minimizes the cost and the bother. In general, you designate who inherits your estate by making up a will, which we describe below. If you do not have a will when you die, all of your estate, your assets, will be subject to state laws governing inheritance. These laws, instead of your own desires, will decide who gets your property and what procedures (called probate) must be followed in the distribution of your estate. In most instances, the state laws would distribute and administer your estate in a manner that you would not have anticipated. Thus, by executing a will, the most basic element of an estate plan, you can designate who gets which assets and in which manner.

BASIC WILLS

Every state in the Union has a maze of rules and regulations pertaining to the proper content and execution of a will, so it is generally recommended that you contact an attorney, at least to advise you what formalities exist. Most people have an attorney draft their will. The following are the basic wills:

1. If you are not married, the commonest scheme divides your estate among your mother, father, brothers and sisters.

2. If you are married and without children, the disposition is generally to your spouse.

3. If you have children, you will want to provide for them in the event that you and your spouse die in a common disaster. This latter event is usually handled through a device called a trust.

4. If you are divorced with children, you might also consider leaving your estate to a trust with your children as beneficiaries. This would eliminate any worry that your ex-spouse might obtain resources you had wished to go to the children.

What Makes a Will Valid?

In most states, the following are necessary to make a will legally valid:

1. Signature—each page of the will must be signed by the maker or testator, and it must be signed in the presence of witnesses.

2. Witnesses—usually two or three witnesses are required for a will to be valid. The will should state that all witnesses signed in the presence of each other, and the addresses of all witnesses might profitably be included in the document.

3. Alterations—sometimes alterations or erasures cause a will to be deemed invalid. Therefore, any time these have to be made it is usually worthwhile to have the entire will redrafted.

4. Terms—the will should specifically state how the estate should be distributed.

Wills Should Be Reviewed

A will can be changed whenever you want. That you decided on one aspect in your will a few years ago does not mean you cannot change it today. In fact, you can change your will right up to the time of your death. You can supplement it or modify it with an amendment.

It is not unwise to reread and reconsider your will each year or so. You would want a different will if you had additions to your family or a change in marital status. You might want a different will if you suddenly became poorer or richer. You might want a different will if you changed your mind about wanting to support your children through college.

The will should be reviewed in the presence of the attorney who drew it up, or a new one if you have moved.

WHAT TO DO WITH YOUR WILL

As with all valuable documents, the safest place for a will would be in a safe deposit box. But since a safe deposit box may be sealed for a while after your death, it is preferable to place the original will with the trust company or with your attorney.

LETTER OF LAST INSTRUCTION

In addition to a will, you should have a separate letter of last instruction. The letter, which is opened at death, should contain the following information:

1. the location of your will

2. instructions about how you should be buried

3. the location of all of your relevant documents, such as your Social Security card, marriage certificate, and birth certificate

4. the location of all safe deposit boxes

5. a list of your life insurance policies and where they are deposited

6. pension statements

7. a list of all stocks and bonds, real and other property, and bank accounts and their locations

8. any instructions concerning a business you might be engaged in

9. a statement of reasons for not giving part of your estate to someone who would normally be expected to receive it.

TRUSTS

In its commonest form, a trust is an arrangement whereby you leave your property to an individual, a bank, or a trust company to manage for the benefit of your heirs. Most trusts are set up because there are minor children surviving a parent or parents. The funds are usually invested by the trustee (the designated holder of the trust) in order to support and educate the children. After a given period of time, which is designated in the Will or Trust Agreement, the remaining assets are distributed, usually to the beneficiaries of the trust.

Trusts can be created for anyone's benefit, including your spouse or a charity, and are not necessarily designed for the protection of children. For example, a surviving spouse may not have the interest or ability to manage the deceased spouse's estate after death and therefore a trust agreement may be the most desirable method of arranging for use of the assets.

It should be kept in mind that trust can also be established while you are still living, and these can provide at least as many benefits

as a trust created at death. Below we list a number of the more popular trusts available today.

Life Insurance Trust

A life insurance trust is administered by a bank or any other trustee, but not an insurance company. The trustee is named to manage the insurance proceeds after death for any heirs inexperienced in handling large sums of money.

Funded Trusts

The funded trust is a method by which funds or assets other than life insurance can be put under the same expert management that the life insurance trust is under. This way, estate administrative expenses can be reduced and taxation can be averted. That is, taxes do not have to be paid first by a surviving parent and then by the children who would inherit the same funds from her or him.

Testamentary Trust

A testamentary trust is one that is tailor-made for you. In your will, for example, you can create a testamentary trust that makes certain your property will be managed expertly and used as you desire. The trustee, which is usually a bank, is given broad investment powers.

Living Trust

A living trust is a legal instrument in which you make the income from your assets payable to yourself while you are alive, or have them reinvested for your future benefit. This type of trust is not subject to probate (legal procedures for deciding the disposition of your estate at death). But if the living trust can be revocable—that is, altered or canceled at any time—then it will be subject to estate taxes.

TABLE A–1:
FEDERAL ESTATE
TAX BURDEN ON
REPRESENTATIVE NET
ESTATES

AMOUNT OF NET ESTATE *	MAXIMUM GROSS TAX †	MAXIMUM CREDIT FOR STATE TAXES	NET TOTAL TAX	EFFECTIVE RATE ‡
$ 5,000	$ 150	$ 40	$ 110	2.2%
20,000	1,600	160	1,440	7.2
50,000	7,000	400	6,600	13.2
100,000	20,700	1,200	19,500	19.5
200,000	50,700	3,600	47,100	23.5
600,000	180,700	18,000	162,700	27.1
1,000,000	325,700	38,800	286,900	28.7
5,000,000	2,468,200	402,800	2,065,400	41.3
10,000,000	6,088,200	1,082,800	5,005,400	50.0
50,000,000	36,888,200	7,482,800	29,405,400	58.8

* Includes amount of net estate after all deductions and exemptions.
† Totals are for both the basic and additional tax.
‡ Based on net tax.

MINIMIZING ESTATE TAXES

The federal government and all states impose a tax on one's estate. (Minimizing these estate taxes is one of the basic reasons for having trusts, mentioned above.) The taxes are generally levied on the net value of the assets remaining after miscellaneous expenses and standard exemptions are deducted. For federal tax purposes, the first $60,000 of net estate is exempt from tax. The federal estate tax is progressive, running from the rate of 3 percent on taxable estates of less than $5000 to 77 percent on taxable estates of $10,000,000 or more. Estate tax rates are shown in Table A–1. Since federal estate taxes are relatively high for wealthier individuals, they sometimes turn to an alternative way to dispose of an estate—that is, by way of gift, because the gift tax is usually lower.

GIFT TAXES

The federal and state governments also impose a tax on gifts, as shown in Table A–2. The tax is levied on the fair market value of the object transferred. Under federal law, each donor receives a $30,000 lifetime tax exclusion plus a yearly exclusion of $3000 per donee. Thus, a married couple with two children could gift each child $30,000 in a lump sum plus $3000 per year per child.

Gift tax rates, although progressive, are, as mentioned above, substantially lower than estate tax rates. The federal gift tax runs from 2¼ percent on taxable gifts under $5000 to 57¾ percent on gifts of $10,000,000 or more.

Because the gift tax is generally lower than the estate tax, and because it could be costly to administer an unplanned estate, one object of estate planning would be to get rid of as much of an individual's assets as possible before death. This could be done, for example, by gifting a large part of it to individuals who would be designated as your heirs in your will anyway. (Note, however, that gifts received by donees within three years of an individual's death are considered to be gifts in contemplation of death and are taxed at the regular estate tax rates.)

What Might You Need?

If you are 30 years old and have a net estate of $60,000 or less, all you really need is a will. If you are 90 years old and have a net estate of $120,000, you might, for example, want to give $60,000 tax-free, which would leave $60,000 in your estate, thereby also avoiding estate taxes.

Anyone falling between the 30-year-old and the 90-year-old in age and wealth is a candidate for estate planning. It would be dangerous in this short an appendix to attempt to

TABLE A–2:
FEDERAL GIFT TAX

AMOUNT OF GIFT	A FEDERAL GIFT TAX (*unmarried donor*)	B FEDERAL GIFT TAX (*married donors to third parties*)	C FEDERAL GIFT TAX (*married donor to spouse*)
$ 30,000	$ 0	$ 0	$ 0
60,000	2,250	0	0
100,000	9,225	2,400	1,200
150,000	20,025	8,850	4,425
200,000	31,275	18,450	9,225
250,000	42,525	28,950	14,475
300,000	54,075	40,050	20,025
350,000	66,075	51,300	25,650
400,000	78,075	62,550	31,275
450,000	90,075	73,800	36,900
500,000	102,075	85,050	42,525
600,000	127,650	108,150	54,075
700,000	153,900	132,150	66,075
800,000	180,450	156,150	78,075
900,000	208,200	180,150	90,075
1,000,000	235,950	204,150	102,075
1,500,000	386,700	334,050	167,025
2,000,000	554,775	471,900	235,950
2,500,000	737,625	617,250	308,625
3,000,000	935,475	773,400	386,700
5,000,000	1,836,975	1,475,250	737,625
10,000,000	4,549,050	3,673,950	1,836,975

Amount of Gift: This column represents the amount of gift *after* deducting the annual exclusion or exclusions but *before* deducting the lifetime exemption or exemptions.

Column A Gift tax payable on gifts to third parties where donor is unmarried or prescribed consent of spouse has not been given.

Column B Combined gift tax payable on gifts by married donors to third parties where prescribed consents have been given.

Column C Gift tax payable on gifts by one spouse to the other.

TABLE A–3:
ESTATE TAX SAVINGS
DUE TO MARITAL
DEDUCTION

NET ESTATE BEFORE $60,000 EXEMPTION	TAX WITHOUT MARITAL DEDUCTIONS *	TAX WITH MARITAL DEDUCTIONS *	TAX SAVING
$ 100,000	$ 4,800	....	$ 4,800
150,000	17,500	$ 1,050	16,450
200,000	31,500	4,800	26,700
250,000	45,300	10,700	34,600
500,000	116,500	45,300	71,200
750,000	191,800	80,500	111,300
1,000,000	270,300	116,500	153,800
2,500,000	830,000	351,400	478,600
5,000,000	2,038,800	830,000	1,208,800
10,000,000	4,975,000	2,038,800	2,936,200

* After maximum credit for state inheritance taxes.

discuss the many estate plans that could be developed. We do point out, however, in Table A–3, the tax advantages with trusts from a marital community. That is, the chart shows the tax advantage of using a trust in a community property state where each spouse is treated as owning one-half of the property. Note that the point made by this illustration in Table A–1 applies to all taxing jurisdictions. When reading this illustration, keep in mind that additional sums might be saved through other devices, such as gifts and lifetime trusts.

APPENDIX B
All You Need to Know about Metric (for your everyday life)

METRIC IS BASED ON DECIMAL SYSTEM

The metric system is simple to learn. For use in your everyday life you will need to know only ten units. You will also need to get used to a few new temperatures. Of course, there are other units which most persons will not need to learn. There are even some metric units with which you are already familiar: those for time and electricity are the same as you use now.

Common Prefixes (to be used with basic units)

Milli: one-thousandth (0.001)
Centi: one-hundredth (0.01)
Kilo: one-thousand times (1000)

For example:
1000 millimeters=1 meter
100 centimeters=1 meter
1000 meters=1 kilometer

(comparative sizes are shown)

1 Meter

1 Yard

BASIC UNITS

Meter: a little longer than a yard (about 1.1 yards)
Liter: a little larger than a quart (about 1.06 quarts)
Gram: about the weight of a paper clip

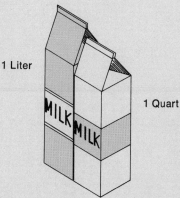

1 Liter

1 Quart

OTHER COMMONLY USED UNITS

Millimeter: 0.001 meter=diameter of paper clip wire

Centimeter: 0.01 meter=width of a paper clip (about 0.4 inch)

Kilometer: 1000 meters=somewhat further than ½ mile (about 0.6 mile)

Kilogram: 1000 grams=a little more than 2 pounds (about 2.2 pounds)

Milliliter: 0.001 liter=five of them make a teaspoon

Other Useful Hints

Hectare: about 2½ acres

Tonne: about one ton

For more information write to: Metric Information Office, National Bureau of Standards, Washington, D.C. 20234

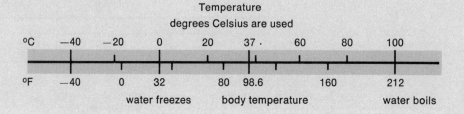

Temperature degrees Celsius are used

Here is where you can find all of the new terms used throughout this book.

INDEX TO GLOSSARY OF NEW TERMS

Acceleration Clause, *135*
Advertising:
    Comparative, *30*
    Competitive, *30*
    Corrective, *30*
    Informative, *30*
Age-earnings Profile, *68*
Annuity, *306*
Antitrust Policies, *414*
Assets, *135*
Average Tax Rate, *392*

Bait and Switch, *30*
Bankers Acceptance, *384*
Bankruptcy, *110*
Barter, *10*
Biological Oxygen Demand (BOD), *452*
Bonds, *338*

Capital Gain, *204, 338*
Capitalist, *next to page 1*
Capital Loss, *338*
Case Law, *414*
Cease and Desist Orders, *184*
Collateral, *110*
Common Law, *414*
Common Property Resource, *452*
Common Stocks, *338*
Comparative Advertising, *30*
Comparison Shopping, *30*
Competitive Advertising, *30*
Complementary Resources, *171*
Compound Interest, *338*
Conspicuous Consumption, *10*
Consumer Durables, *110*
Consumer Price Index, *278*
Consumers, *next to page 1*
Consumption Good, *63*
Consumption or Consuming, *next to page 1*
Corrective Advertising, *30*
Cost of Living or Escalator Clause, *370*
Credit, *10*
Crypto-servant, *52*

Dow Jones Industrial Average, *360*
Discount Points, *227*

Earnest Money, *227*
Ecology, *452*
Engel's Law, *148*
Equities, *338*
Escalator Clause—See Cost of
   Living
Ethical Drug Industry, *278*

Fixed Expenses, *99*
Flexible or Variable Expenses, *99*
Free Rider Problem, *392*

Generic Name, *184*
Good:
   Consumption, *63*
   Luxury, *78*

Home Protection Plan, *306*
Housing Voucher, *204*
Hyperinflation, *370*

Income Transfer, *306*
Indentured Servants, *462*
Inflation, *next to page 1*
Inflationary Premium, *110*
Informative Advertising, *30*
Inpatient Services, *278*
Inside Information, *338*
Intangible Property, *462*
Investment in Human Capital, *68*

Lease, *204*
Liabilities, *135*
Liability Insurance, *264*
Liquidity, *360*
Living Benefits, *306*
Luxury Good, *78*

Marginal Buyers, *148*
Marginal Tax Bracket, *204*
Monopoly, *10*
Motivational Research, *10*
Mutual Fund, *338*

Naturopath, *278*
Negotiable Orders of Withdrawal,
   384
Net Worth, *135*
No-Fault Auto Insurance, *250*
Nominal Dollars, *370*
Nonrecourse Loans, *148*
NOW—See Negotiable Orders of
   Withdrawal

On-the-job Training, *68*
Opportunity Costs, *63*
Outpatient Services, *278*

Pair Bonds, *52*
Paramedic, *294*
Parkinson's Law, *10*
Participation Rate, *68*
Particulates, *452*
Patriarch, *52*
Preexisting Ailment, *294*
Preferred Stocks, *338*
Price Discrimination, *278*
Private Costs, *250, 452*
Productive Asset, *63*
Progressive Taxation, *392*
Proportional Taxation, *392*
Pro Rata, *204*
Purchasing Power, *next to page 1*

Rational Consumer Decision-Mak-
   ing, *10*
Real Level of Living, *next to page
   1*
Real Rate of Return, *360*
Recommended Dietary Allow-
   ances (RDA), *148*
Regressive Taxation, *392*
Relative Prices, *370*
RDAs—See Recommended Die-
   tary Allowances
Right of Rescission, *110*

Saving, *338*

Scarcity, *78*
Securities, *338*
Service Flow, *110*
Service Sector, *next to page 1*
Site Value, *204*
Social Costs, *250, 452*
Special Interest Groups, *392*
Specialization, *52*
Statutory Law, *414*
Stock Market, *338*
Stocks:
   Common, *338*
   Preferred, *338*
Sunk Costs, *10*
Support Prices, *148*

Tangible Property, *462*
Target Prices, *148*
Taxation:
   Progressive, *392*
   Proportional, *392*
   Regressive, *392*
Tax Exempts, *360*
Term Insurance, *306*
Time Deposits, *338*
Title, *227*
Title Insurance, *227*
Trade-Off, *78*
Transfer Payments, *78*
Transactions Costs, *110*
Treasure Bills, *384*

Umbrella Policy, *264*
Underwriter, *306*
Unit Pricing, *171*

Variable or Flexible Expenses, *99*

Waiting Period, *294*
Waste By-products, *452*
Whole Life Insurance, *306*

Zero Deductible, *264*

AAA. *See* Agricultural Adjustment Administration

Abrams, Morris, 261

Abstract (title insurance), 237

Acceleration clauses, 142; *see also* Loans

Acts
consumer protection, 41, 119–126, 140–142, 151–155, 192–196, 252–253, 272, 286–287, 416–417, 420, 437
farmer protection, 160–163
health care, 289
housing, 210–212
medical personnel, 285
pollution, 258, 455, 457
Social Security, 320–326
taxation, 398–399

Advertising
and brand names, 33–35
comparative, 36–37
competitive, 36
corrective, 41–42, 439–440
of drug prices, restrictions on, 287
expenditure on, 2–3, 5, 31–32
false, 3, 37–38
informative, 6, 35–36, 195
and motivational research, 16–17
regulation of, 36, 39–45, 123, 195
types of, 30, 35–37

Age-earnings profile, 70–75

Aging. *See* Retirement

Agricultural Adjustment Act, 160–163

Agricultural Adjustment Administration, 160–163

Agriculture, Department of, 124, 437
and meat grading, 154–155, 437
and nutrition, 155–159, 175
and produce grading, 155, 156
see also Agricultural Adjustment Administration

Air pollution, 8, 214–215, 258, 453–457

Allen, Frederick Lewis, 401

Allstate Insurance Companies, 336

American Bankers Association, 129

American Bar Association, 43, 257

American Home Owners Association, 244

American Motors Corporation, 264–265

American Medical Association
and Blue Shield, 297–298
and group health plans, 288–289
and medical school licensing, 281–284

American Pharmaceutical Association, 287–288

American Standards Association, 421–422

American Stock Exchange, 347; *see also* Stock market

Annuities, 310, 312, 314, 317–319, 388; *see also* Life insurance

Antitrust policies, 163, 416

Apartments, 206
and burglaries, 213–214
condominium, 208–209
cooperative, 207–208
renting, 244–245

Appliances, and consumer redress, 432–433

Argus Chart of Health Insurance, 302

Arkansas, and usury laws, 121–122

Aspirin, 286

Assets, 136–140, 147
and estate planning, 471–477
see also Loans

Atkins Miracle Diet, Dr., 291

Atlanta, Ga., 130

Attorney General's office (state), and consumer protection, 422, 431

AUTOCAP, 270–272

Automobiles, 251
and accidents, 251–254
and air pollution, 454–456
buying: and inflation, 379–380;
new, 257–258, 264–269; used, 269–270
dealers of, 265, 267, 270–272
and insurance, 255–257, 272–275
and gas mileage, 266–267
loans for, 113–117, 119, 135, 143, 272, 273
and no-fault insurance, 256–257, 421
operating costs of, 254, 255, 257–258, 267, 270, 273
and pollution equipment, 258, 455–456
and price index, 376
and repairs, 254–255, 270–272
and safety features, 252–253
sizes compared, 268–269, 270
social costs of, 251–252, 253, 258–259, 260, 454–456
subsidization of, 260–261
taxes, 232
warranties, 264–265, 270

Baby Trap, The, 66

"Backward Art of Spending Money, The," 419

Bacteria, in food, 177–179

Bait and switch, 37–38

BankAmericard, 114, 144

Bankers acceptances, 385; *see also* Short-term securities

Banking and Currency, Senate Committee on, 122; *see also* Truth-in-Lending Act

Bankruptcy (personal), 112, 142, 146–147

Bankruptcy Act, National, 112, 147

Banks, 128
and cashless society, 130–131
and certificates of deposit, 385
and checking accounts, 126, 128–130, 336, 373, 384, 389–390

and contingency clauses, 142
and Fair Credit Reporting Act, 140–141
and finance charges, 117–119, 144, 388; restrictions on, 119–122; and Truth-in-Lending Act, 122–125, 272
and loans, 113, 137–144, 231, 240, 272, 388; *see also* finance charges (above)
and net worth, determining, 137–140
and NOW accounts, 129, 384
regulation of, 126, 128–129
and time deposit savings, 344, 367
and total services, 129–130
see also Mortgages; Savings and loan associations
Banzhaf, John, 439–440
BART, 259
Bell, Carolyn Shaw, 323–324
Better Business Bureau, 424
Beven, Dr., 283
Blue Chip Accounts, 129–130
Blue Cross, 297–298
Blue Shield, 297–298
Bonds, 343, 348, 349, 367
in inflationary periods, 365, 374, 385
short-term, 385–388
tax exempt, 365–366
see also Stock market
Borrowing. *See* Loans
Boston, Mass., 287–288
Brand names, 33–36, 46–47, 202
Brokers. *See* Stockbrokers
Budgets, 79–81, 185
average, family, 84–89
and clothes, 185, 186, 188–189
college student, 101–103
and court-supervised debt repayment, 147
examples of, 100, 101–102, 104–108
and family councils, 81–84
and goals and value clarification, 89–92, 93
and housing services, 205
and keeping records, 103
and lifetime plans, 93–96
and saving, 103
steps in making, 99
and sudden changes in income, 92–93

see also Clothes; Food; Loans
Building codes, 215–216
Building suppliers, 216
Burglaries, 213–214
Burial, A Manual of Simple, 303
Burial expenses, 303
Buyer protection plans (auto), 264–265
Buying habits, 15–16; *see also* Consumption

Cagen, Phillip, 361
California
and consumer protection, 420, 423
and milk prices, 441
and small claims court, 444
Cancellation, Notice of, 40
Canning industry, 154
Capital gains, 219, 348, 399–400, 401
Capital losses, 348
Cash, and inflationary periods, 373, 375, 384, 389–390
"Cash" cards, 114–115
Cashless society, 130–131
Cereals, as protein sources, 176
Certificate of Title, 237–238
Certificates of deposit, 385; *see also* Short-term securities
Changing Times, 47
Charge accounts, 125–126, 142, 144n, 201
Checking accounts, 126, 128–131, 336
and inflationary periods, 373, 375, 384, 389–390
Chicago Transit Authority, 261
Children, 63–65, 82–85, 155–156, 194
Civil Aeronautics Board, 5–6, 124, 403
Civil Rights Act, 60, 73
Clean Air Act, 457
Cleaning deposits, 244–245
Closed end mutual funds, 354; *see also* Mutual funds
Closing costs, 237–238; *see also* Mortgages
Clothes, 4, 185–186, 189–191
cleaning, 192, 196
durability, 191–192, 202
government regulation of, 192–196

labeling, 194–196
as percent of budget, 84, 86, 87, 185
shopping for, 199–202
and social class, 187–188
College
affect on income, 69–72, 74
budgeting while in, 101–103
Collision insurance, 273, 274
Commerce, Department of, 193, 194
Commerce, Secretary of, 152
Commercial banks. *See* Banks
Commissions (stock), 353, 354, 363, 364
Common stocks. *See* Stocks
Comparison shopping, 19, 32, 172–173, 199–200; *see also* Rational consumer decision-making
Comparative advertising, 36–37
Competition, business, 18, 416, 417
Competition, Bureau of, 41; *see also* Federal Trade Commission
Competitive advertising, 36
Complaints. *See* Consumer redress
Compound interest, 343–344, 345
Comprehensive auto insurance, 273–275
Comprehensive Health Insurance Plan, 290
Comprehensive Manpower Training Act, 285
Condominium apartments, 208–209
Confession of judgment, 244
Conformity, 15, 187–188, 189
Congress. *See* Federal government
Connecticut, 125, 316
Constitution (U.S.), and taxation, 398
Construction workers, 217, 218
Consumer abuses and rip-offs, 449–450
Consumer action (media), 424–425; *see also* Consumer redress
Consumer affairs agencies, 431; *see also* Consumer redress
Consumer Affairs, Office of, 270, 420, 434

Consumer Affairs, Special Presidential Assistant for, 420
Consumer Credit Protection Act, 122–126, 140–142
Consumer durables, 116, 346, 375–377; *see also* Automobiles, loans for; Loans; Mortgages
Consumer Federation of America, 425–426, 440
Consumer finance companies, 113–114, 116, 137–144,
  and contingency clauses, 142
  and Fair Credit Reporting Act, 140–142
  and finance charges, 117–119, 140, 142–144; restrictions on, 119–122; and Truth-in-Lending Act, 122–125
  and net worth, determining, 137–140
"Consumer Information" (federal), 47–48, 175, 195; *see also* Information
Consumer policy participation, 425–426
Consumer price index. *See* Price index
Consumer Product Safety Act, 437–438; *see also* Flammable Fabrics Act
Consumer Product Safety Commission, 194, 437–439; *see also* Flammable Fabrics Act
Consumer protection, 5, 415–427; *see also* Consumer redress; Regulatory agencies
Consumer Protection, Bureau of, 39, 41; *see also* Federal Trade Commission
Consumer redress (recovery of damages), 246, 418, 423–424, 430–431, 433, 443, 446
  and industry agencies, 432–433
  and private agencies, 424, 431–432, 440–441
  and public agencies, 246, 423–424, 430–431, 433–440
  and small claims court, 443–447
Consumer Reports, 46–47; *see also* Consumers Union
Consumer Reports Buying Guide, 270

Consumer rights, 6, 419; *see also* Consumer protection; Regulatory agencies
Consumer services, 430–431, 443
  and industry agencies, 432–433
  and private agencies, 424, 431–432, 440–441
  and public agencies, 430–431, 433–440
  and small claims courts, 443–447
  see also Information
Consumerist movement, 5–6, 417, 419, 424, 425–427, 440–441
Consumers. *See* Consumption
Consumers' Research, Inc., 47
Consumers' Research Magazine, 47
Consumers Union, 46, 440
  on drained weights of canned fruits, 153–154
  on frankfurters, 174
  on regulation of interest rates, 128
  on hamburger, 177, 179
  on life insurance, 333
  on small claims court, 446
Consumption, 1–3
  abuses of, 449–450
  and advertising, 2, 16–17, 32–33, 35–45
  of automobiles, 251, 252, 264–270
  and bankruptcy, 112, 142, 146–147
  and brand names, 33–35, 36
  and budgeting, 79–96, 103–108
  and buying habits, 15–16
  cashless, 130–131
  and children, 63–65, 83–84
  and choice, 4, 464–466
  of clothes, 185, 186–192, 196, 199–202
  conspicuous, 15
  and consumerist movement, 5–6, 120–121, 417, 419, 424–427, 440–441
  of convenience food, 165–166, 173–174
  and credit investigation protection, 140–142
  of diets, 291
  and discount stores, 166
  of food, 149–151, 155–158, 159, 164–166, 171–181

  and food labeling, dating, and packaging, 151–155, 156, 158–159
  and fraudulent practices, 37–40; *see also* Consumer protection; Consumer redress; Regulatory agencies
  and goals, 13–14
  of hamburger, 177–179
  of housing services, 217–219, 227–244
  and inflation, 373, 440–441; *see also* Inflation
  and information, 6, 18–19, 31–48; *see also* Information
  and installment buying, 112–127, 135, 142–144; protection, 39–40, 122–126, 142
  of life insurance, 308, 330–336
  and loans, reasons for, 115–117, 135
  and marriage, 55
  of medicines, 286
  and poor diets, 174–177
  rational decision-making, 10–19; *see also* Rational consumer decision-making
  and recreation, 466, 467
  and redress of grievances, 418, 423–424, 430–441, 443–449
  and regulatory agencies: *see* Regulatory agencies
  and safe debt load, determining, 136–140
  and saving, 103, 339–343
  and supermarket shopping, 179–181
  and small claims court, 443–447
  teenage, 83–84
Continental Association of Funeral and Memorial Societies, 303
Contingency clauses, 142; *see also* Loans
Contracts, labor, 374–375, 379, 389
Convenience foods, 165–166, 173–174, 179
Convertible bonds, 348, 367; *see also* Stocks
Convertible preferred stocks, 348, 367; *see also* Stocks
Convertible term insurance, 315
"Cooling off" laws, 39–40, 123
Co-op City, Bronx, 208

Cooperative apartments, 207–208, 209

Corporate bonds, 365, 367; *see also* Bonds; Stocks

Corporate stocks, 367; *see also* Stocks

Corrective advertising, 41–42, 439–440

Cost of living, 371; *see also* Inflation

Cost of living benefit, 388

Cost of living clauses, 379, 389

Costs
opportunity, 64–65, 72, 79–80, 82–96 *passim,* 227–228, 380–381, 468–469
per service flow, 115–117, 192, 201, 206, 207, 221
sunk, 23–34
see also individual items

Courts, 416
and consumer redress, 431–432, 443–447
small claims, 443–447
and supervised debt repayment, 147

Credit. *See* Loans

Credit bureaus, 140–142

Credit cards, 114, 120–121, 123, 130, 144

Credit investigations, 140–142

Credit life insurance, 317

Credit unions, 345–346
and contingency clauses, 142
and Fair Credit Reporting Act, 140–142
and finance charges, 117–119, 140; restrictions on, 119–122; and Truth-in-Lending Act, 122–125, 272
as investment, 367
and loans, 113–114, 137, 272
and net worth, determining, 137–140

Crime, 213–214, 233

Customs, 4, 14–15, 185–186

Dairy products
dating of, 158–159
and price supports, 162–163, 403, 441
as protein, 176

Dating
of clothes, 191
of food, 158–159

Death benefits, 310, 312, 334; *see also* Estate planning; Life insurance; Retirement

Death rate, 303, 307

Debt, 111
aggregate, 112–113
and bankruptcy, 112, 142, 146–147
business, 348
and buying: an auto, 113–117, 119, 135, 143, 272, 273; a house, 227–231, 238–242
and cashless society, 130–131
and checking accounts, 126–130
and contingency clauses, 142
and cost per service flow, 115–117
counseling, 144–145, 147
and credit, sources of, 113–115, 143–144, 310
and credit cards, 125–126, 142, 144n
and credit life insurance, 317
and Fair Credit Reporting Act, 140–142
and finance charges, 116–127, 142–144, 218–219, 388; *see also* buying a house (above)
and inflation, 118–119, 120, 372–373, 377–379, 388
installment, 112–113, 115–117; *see also* finance charges (above)
interest on: *see* finance charges (above)
and life insurance loans, 115, 310
and net worth, determining, 137–140, 146–147
reasons for borrowing, 115–117, 135; *see also* inflation (above)
repayment, as per cent of income, 113
and repossession, 142
and revolving credit: *see* credit cards (above)
and safe amount of, determining, 136–140
and tax deductions, 142–143, 218–219
and Truth-in-Lending Act, 122–126, 142, 272

Deferred life annuity, 318, 319

Deflation, 371, 372

Denenberg, Herbert S., 333

Dental insurance, 297

Department of Agriculture. *See* Agriculture, Department of

Department stores, and revolving credit, 125–126

Depression, Great, 371, 378
and Agriculture Adjustment Act, 160–161
and Social Security Act, 320

Diet, 155–159, 175–177, 290–291, 294–295

Diet for a Small Planet, 176–177

Dieting, 291

Disability insurance, 295–296

Disclosure statement, 127; *see also* Revolving credit

Discount points, 241; *see also* Finance charges

Discount stores, 166, 185, 199

Discrimination, sexist, 59–61, 72–73

Dividends (stock), 348, 353; *see also* Stocks

Divorce, 54, 57–58

Doctors
and dieting, 291
and group health plans, 288–289, 298–299
and medical insurance, 280–281, 297–298, 300–301
supply of, 281–284, 285

Door-to-door sales, 39–40

Dow Jones Industrial Average, 361–362; *see also* Stock market

Dreyfus Liquid Assets, Inc., 387, 388

Drugs. *See* Medicines

Earnest agreement, 237

Ecological problems, 8, 453, 459–460
of air pollution, 214–215, 453–457
of water pollution, 457–459

Economics and the Public Purpose, 56

Education
affect on income, 69–72, 74
medical, 281–284
and property taxes, 219–220

Electricity, and pollution, 457, 458

Endowment insurance, 314

Engel, Ernst, 150
Engel, Louis, 365
Engel's Law, 150
Engels, Friedrich, 55
Environment, quality of. *See*
    Ecological problems
Equal Rights Amendment, 59
"Equal time" doctrine, 439–440
Equities. *See* Stocks
Equity Club International, 115
Estate planning, 471–476
Estate taxes, 473, 474–476
Ethical drug industry, 285–288
Everett, Wash., 261
Executive Accounts, 129–130

Fabrics
    information about, 195
    labeling of, 194–196
    nonflammable, 192–194
    see also Clothes
Fair Credit Reporting Act, 140–
    142
Fair Package and Labeling Act,
    151–155
Family
    annuities for, 317–319; *see also*
        estate planning (below); life
        insurance (below)
    budgeting, 81–96, 103; aver-
        age, 84–89; decisions on,
        81–84, 89–96, 103; examples
        of, 104–108; goals and val-
        ues helped by, 89–92, 93
    and clothes, 188–189, 194
    costs of having, 63–65
    council, 82–84, 95, 189
    estate planning, 471–476
    Food Plans, 155, 159; *see also*
        Nutrition
    income, 56, 81, 87, 402, 408;
        sudden changes in, 92–93
    and life insurance, 308–317,
        329–336
    and lifetime plans, 93–96
    planning, 65
    premature deaths in, 57, 307–
        308; *see also* estate plan-
        ning (above); life insurance
        (above)
    problems of, 64
    and saving, 339–343
    and Social Security, 320–326;
        see also Retirement
    trusts for, 472, 473

Family Food Plans, 155, 159
Farmers
    and deflationary periods, 371
    and price supports, 160–163
    variable income of, 160, 161–
        162, 464
Fashion industry, 18, 189–190
"Fast-food" stands, 179
FDA. *See* Food and Drug Ad-
    ministration
Federal Communications Commis-
    sion, 43–45, 439–440
Federal Deposit Insurance Cor-
    poration, 124
Federal government, 393, 398
    and antitrust policies, 163, 416,
        417
    and automobile regulations,
        252–253, 258, 455
    budget (1975), 394
    and checking account interest,
        126, 128
    and consumer information, 47–
        48, 175, 195
    and consumer protection, 246,
        415–421, 430, 433–440, 441;
        see also Regulatory agencies
    and consumer rights, 419
    and credit regulation, 39–40,
        119–126, 140–142
    and defense, 395
    and ethical drug regulation,
        285–287
    and equal employment, 59
    and fabric labeling, 194–196
    and farmer protection, 160–163
    and flammable clothes, 192–194
    and food: dating, 158–159;
        labeling and inspection, 150–
        155, 156, 416–417; nutrition,
        155–158, 159, 174–177; pack-
        aging, 151–155
    and health care and insurance,
        280, 285, 289–290, 299–301
    and income redistribution, 2,
        401; *see also* Income taxes;
        social security (below)
    and mass transportation, 259
    and Medicare, 299–301
    and mortgages, 208, 240–241
    and moving industry, 221–222,
        245
    and nutrition, 155–158, 159,
        174–177

    and pollution standards, 258,
        455, 457–459
    and price supports, 161–163,
        403
    regulatory agencies of: *See*
        Regulatory agencies
    and Social Security, 320–326
    and special interest groups,
        162–163, 256–257, 403–404
    and stock commission regula-
        tion, 352, 364
    and taxation, 393–406; *see
        also* Taxes
    and transportation regulation,
        5–6, 221–222, 246, 403–404
    and urban renewal, 210–212
    see also Taxes
Federal Home Loan Bank Board,
    124
Federal Housing Administration,
    208, 240–241
Federal Price Commission, 287
Federal Reserve Board, 124–130
Federal Trade Commission, 38,
    417, 435–436
    and advertising regulation, 36,
        39, 41–43, 417, 435
    and consumer redress and
        services, 435–436
    and cooling off laws, 39–40
    criticisms of, 42–43
    and fabric labeling, 194–196
    and flammable clothes, 193,
        194
    and food packaging and label-
        ing, 152
    and funeral industry, 303
    and Truth-in-Lending Act en-
        forcement, 124–126
Feminine Mystique, The, 58
Fibers, labeling of, 41, 194–196;
    see also Clothes
Finance charges, 117–119, 140,
    142–144, 273
    and inflationary premiums, 118–
        119, 120, 372–373, 377–379
    and mortgages, 229–231, 237–
        242
    and points, 241
    restrictions on, 119–122
    and revolving credit, 125–126,
        142, 144n, 201
    and Truth-in-Lending Act, 122–
        127, 142, 272

Finance companies
  and contingency clauses, 142
  and Fair Credit Reporting Act,
    140–142
  and finance charges, 117–119,
    140, 144, 273; restrictions on,
    119–122; and Truth-in-Lend-
    ing Act, 122–125, 272
  and loans, 113–114, 116–117,
    137–144
  and net worth, determining,
    137–140
  and repossession, 272
Financial advisers, 135–137, 200–
    201
  and debt counseling, 144–145
  see also Loans
Financial Crisis Clinic, 144
Financial institutions. See Banks;
    Mortgages; Savings and Loan
    Associations
Financial protection. See Health
    care, insurance; Life insurance
"First Hundred Days," 160
Fixed annuities, 317–319
Fixed expenses, 99
  in budgets, 100–108
  to repay loans, 137
  see also Loans
Fixed income and inflation, 373–
    374; see also Retirement
Flame-retardant clothing, 194
Flammable Fabrics Act, 192–194
Flexible expenses, 99–108
Flexible mortgage plans, 241–242
Flexner, Abraham, 283
Flexner Report, 283
Flint, Mich., 259
Florida, small claims court in, 444
Food, 149
  bacteria in (hamburger), 177–
    179
  dating of, 158–159
  and dieting, 291
  in discount stores, 166
  frozen, 165–166, 173–174
  and government inspection,
    labeling, and regulation of,
    150–156
  health and organic, 290
  and nutrition, 155–159, 174–
    177, 294–295
  as percent of family budget, 84,
    86, 87; of U.S. income, 149
  price index of, 150

price supports of, 161–163
  protein content of, 158, 174,
    175–177
  retailing of, changes in, 163–164
  shopping for, 172–173, 180–181
  short-weighing of, 179–180
  specials, shopping for, 172–173,
    181
  unit pricing of, 171–172
Food and Drug Act, Pure, 286,
    416–417
Food and Drug Administration
  and consumer redress and
    services, 435
  and ethical drug regulation,
    286–287
  and food inspection and label-
    ing, 150–155
  and nutrition standards, 155–
    158, 159
Food, Drug, and Cosmetic Act,
    286, 417
"Food Is More than Just Some-
    thing to Eat," 175
Fraud, 3, 37–38
  advertising, 3, 37–38
  door-to-door sales, 39–40
  consumer, 449–450
  and federal regulations, 39–45,
    179, 416, 420
  and state and local regulations,
    420, 423–424
  in supermarkets, 179–180
Freedom Shares, 385; see also
    Savings Bonds, U.S.
Freidan, Betty, 58
Frozen food, 165–166, 173–174
Fruit
  canned, 153–154
  grading of, 155, 156
FTC. See Federal Trade Com-
    mission
Fund for Federal Securities, 387,
    388
Fund for Investing in Government
    Securities, Inc., 386, 388
Funded trusts, 473
Funeral business, 302–303
Fur Products Labeling Act, 41, 195

Galbraith, John Kenneth, 17, 56
Georgia, small claims court in,
    444
Gift taxes, 474, 475
GNP, 80

Goals, 13–14, 55
  clarified by budgeting, 89–92,
    93, 95–96
Gold Accounts, 129–130
Government. See Federal gov-
    ernment; Local government
    agencies; State regulations
Grading, of food, 154–155, 156
Grains, as protein sources, 176
Group Health Cooperative of
    Washington, 288, 298–299
Group health service, 288–289,
    297, 298–299, 302
Group life insurance, 315, 334

Hamburger, bacteria in, 177–179
Hazardous products. See Prod-
    uct safety
Health care
  cost of, 279–280
  and dental insurance, 297
  and ethical drug regulations,
    285–288
  and funeral industry, 302–303
  and group health services, 288–
    289, 298–299
  and Health Maintenance Organ-
    izations, 289
  insurance for, 279–280, 289–
    290, 295–302
  Medicare, 299–301
  as percent of income, 84, 86,
    87, 279
  prepaid, 289
  preventive, 294–295
  and self-treatment, 284–285
  and supply of doctors, 281–284
Health, Education, and Welfare,
    Department of, 193, 194
Health foods, 290
Health Insurance Plan. See
    Group health services
Health Maintenance Organization
    Act, 289
Hidden Persuaders, The, 16
Higher education. See Educa-
    tion
Home owners' insurance, 242–243
Home-protection devices, 214
Hospitals, and insurance plans,
    280–281, 288–289, 295–302
Housing Act, 210
Housing and Urban Development
    Act, 210–212

Housing industry, 205–206, 209, 211, 219
Housing services, 135, 205–206, 227–228
apartments, 206, 207–209, 213
and building codes, 215–216
and burglaries, 213–214
buying, 207–209, 214–218, 221–244
and closing costs, 237–238
construction of new housing, 206, 208–212, 216–217, 228
and inflationary periods, 380–381
and inspecting prospective homes, 234, 237
investing in, 216–218, 219, 227–228
insurance for, 242–243
low-income, 210–212
maintenance and improvements, 206, 207, 221, 243–244
middle-income, 208, 210
and mobile homes, 206, 207, 216–217, 468–469
mortgages, 135, 143, 208, 228–231, 238–242
and moving, 221–222, 245–246
as percent of family budget, 84, 87
and property taxes, 214, 219–220
and real estate brokers, 233–234
renting, 208–210, 228, 235, 244–245
single family, 205, 214
substandard, 210–212
Housing vouchers, 212
Hyperinflation, 372

ICC. *See* Interstate Commerce Commission
Illinois, small claims court in, 444
Illinois Board of Pharmacy, 288
Illness. *See* Health care
Immediate annuity, 318
Impulse buying, 15
Income, 1
at different ages, 75
from different occupations, 74
disposable, 4, 113, 151, 341, 378
education's affect on, 69–72, 74

family, 56, 81, 402, 408
and health insurance, 295–297
inequalities, 2, 17–18, 69, 74, 87, 396–397, 401, 402, 463–464
and inflationary periods, 373–381, 389, 390
and investments, 227, 312, 319, 331, 333, 343–344, 346–356
and mortgage payments, 228
per capita, 80
real, per capita, 4, 205
redistribution, 2, 86, 87, 400, 401; see also Social Security (below)
and saving, 17, 339–343
sexist differences in, 60, 61, 72, 74
share spent on: autos, 251; clothes, 185; food, 86, 149–151, 175; health care, 84, 86, 87, 279
and Social Security, 322–323
sudden changes in, 92–93
taxes: *See* Income taxes
see also Budgets; Loans
Income taxes, 381
and ability to pay doctrine, 396
deductions, 142–143, 208, 209, 218–219, 334, 399, 410, 411
history of, 398–399
and inflation, 380–381, 389
information on, 409
joint, 61, 397
loopholes in, 399–400, 401, 404
as percent of: family budget, 84, 86, 87; federal revenue, 393, 398; of total personal income, 400–401
progressive, 395–401
proportional, 395
proposed reforms of, 404–406
regressive, 396
record keeping for, 409–411
and sacrifice doctrine, 396–397
on savings, 334
and Social Security, 87, 320–324
state, for different cities, 232
and transfer payments, 2, 86, 87, 321, 323–324, 400, 401
Industrial life insurance, 316
Inflation, 8, 371
anticipation of, 373, 375, 377, 379–380, 388–390

and consumer action groups, 440–441
and fixed-incomes, 373–374
and interest rates, 118–119, 120, 372–373, 388
and life insurance, 388
and owning a home during, 380–381
protecting oneself against, 384–390
and purchasing power, 373, 375–377, 378–380, 389
and real rate of return on investments, 360–362, 365, 384–385
and retirement plans, 374, 375, 388–389
and union contracts, 374–375, 379
worldwide, 372, 373
Inflationary premiums, 118–119, 120, 372–373, 377–379
Information, 6–7, 31–33, 418
by advertising, 35–37, 41–42, 439–440
by brand names, 33–35
on crime rates in areas, 233
on fabrics, 195
from federal government, 47–48, 409
on food dating, 158–159
on food packaging and labeling, 151–155
on income taxes, 409
inside (stock market), 351–352
on land values, 355–356
on mail-order health insurance, 302
on nutrition, 155–158, 159, 174–177
privately produced, 45–47
by real estate brokers, 233–234
on repair persons, 244
searching for, 18–19
on Social Security, 330
on stock market, 350–353
on used cars, 269–270
Informative advertising, 35–36, 195
Inside information (stock market), 351–352
Inspection
and building codes, 215–216
of food, 150–151, 179, 180
of prospective home, 234, 237

Installment buying
and American median debt, 112–113
and bankruptcy, 112, 142, 146–147
and contingency clauses, 142
contracts, 39–40, 123
and debt counseling, 144–145, 147
and door-to-door sales, 39–40
and Fair Credit Reporting Act, 140–142
and finance charges, 116–127, 142–143, 144; restrictions on, 119–122
and net worth, determining, 137–140
reasons for, 115–117, 135, 137, 200–201
repayment as percent of income, 113
and repossession, 142
restrictions on advertising for, 123
and revolving credit, 125–126, 142, 144n, 200–201
and safe debt load, determining, 136–140, 146–147
and sources of credit, 113–115, 143–144
and tax deductions, 142–143
and Truth-in-Lending Act, 122–126, 142
see also Mortgages
Institutional buyers, 152–153
Insurance
agents, 275, 333, 334
annuities, 317–319
automobile, 255–257, 272–275; no fault, 256–257, 272–275; state requirements for, 274
Blue Cross and Blue Shield, 297–298
credit, 317
dental, 297
group health, 288–289, 298–299, 301, 302
for hospital expenses, 295–298
house, 242–243
and inflationary periods, 388
life, 308–317, 329–336, 388; loans on, 115, 310
mail-order health, 301–302
medical, 279–280, 288–290, 295–302

Medicare, 299–301
mental health, 297
national health, 289–290
no-fault auto, 256–257, 272–275
salary continuation, 296
surgical, 296, 297–298
tax deductions for, 201, 334
unemployment, 321
voluntary prepaid medical, 295–298
see also Social Security Act
Interest
on bonds, 348, 365, 385; short-term, 385–386
and checking accounts (zero), 128
compound, 343–344, 345
on loans: see Finance charges
on savings, 116, 129, 341, 343–344
on stocks, 348, 353
and tax deductions on payments, 142–143, 218–219, 334
see also Finance charges; Investment; Life insurance
Internal Revenue Service, 301, 409; see also Income taxes
Interstate Commerce Commission, 5–6, 124, 221–222, 246, 403
Investment, 367
in bonds, 343, 348, 349, 365–366; short-term, 385–388
compared with buying life insurance, 319, 331, 333
and compound interest, 343–344
counselors, 353, 362, 368
in housing, 217–218, 219, 227–231
in human capital, 69–72, 74
and inflation, 360–362, 365, 384–388
in mutual funds, 346, 353–354, 362, 367; short-term, 385–388
in paintings, 344
plans, 353–354
rate of return from, 360–361, 367, 384–386
in real estate, 355–356, 366, 367
and risk, 346–347, 355, 365, 366, 368
and Social Security, 322

in stocks, 343, 347–355, 360–365, 385–386
variety of, 346, 366–368
see also Saving
Iowa, small claims court in, 444
Israel, 379

Job discrimination (sexist), 59–61
Johnson, Lyndon B., 122, 324, 420
Jones, Mary Gardner, 443
Jungle, The, 417, 418
Justice Department, 163, 287

Kaiser Permanente Medical Care, 288, 298
Katz, Barbara, 449–450
Kefauver-Harris Amendment (Food, Drug, and Cosmetics Act), 286
Kennedy, Edward M., 290
Kennedy, John F., 6, 419
Knauer, Virginia, 270

Labeling
of fabrics, 194–196
of food, 150–155, 156, 158–159
Labor force, sexism in, 59–60, 72–73
Land
investing in, 355–356, 366, 367
site value of, 214–215, 217–218, 228
Landlords, 244–245
Last instruction, letter of, 472–473; see also Estate planning
Laws. See Legislation
Leases, 209–210, 244–245
Legislation
Agricultural Adjustment, 160–163
antitrust, 163, 416
on automobiles: insurance, 256–257, 274; pollution, 455; safety, 252–253
Clean Air, 457
on clothes, 41, 194–196
consumer protective, history of, 415–427
cooling off, 39–40, 423
on credit regulation, 122–126, 142, 272, 420
on ethical drugs, 286–287, 416–417
Fair Package and Labeling, 151–155

Flammable Fabrics, 192–194
on food inspection, packaging, labeling, 150–155, 416–417
on fraud, 423
to increase medical personnel, 285
Medicare, 299–301
on prepaid medical care, 289
on postal fraud, 416, 420
on price supports, 160–163
on product safety, 437
Social Security, 320–326
and special interest groups, 216, 256–257, 403–404
on taxation, 398–399
Truth-in-Labeling, 41
Truth-in-Lending, 122–126, 142, 272, 420
wage and hour, 416
women and minors' protective, 416
Wool, Fur and Textile Fiber Products, 41, 194–196
on urban renewal, 210–212
Legumes, as protein sources, 175, 176
Leisure, 467, 468–469
Liabilities, 136–140; *see also* Loans
Liability insurance, 272, 274
Licensing
and consumer protection, 423
of medical schools, 281–284
occupational, 5
Life expectancy, 308
Life insurance, 308–309, 329, 332–333, 367
annuities, 317–319
cash value of, 310, 313
credit, 317
death benefits, 312
dividends, 334–335
endowment insurance, 314
figuring how much to buy, 330–332
group, 315, 334
industrial, 316
and inflation, 388
and low-cost loans, 115, 310, 334
participating, 334–336
payment plans, 336
policies and companies compared, 335
salespersons, 333, 334

as savings, 309–310, 311, 313, 314, 332, 334
savings bank, 316
settlement terms, 312
tax benefits, 334
term, 309, 312, 314–315, 316, 332–333, 335, 388
trust, 473
whole, 309–315, 316, 333–335, 388
see also Social Security Act
Life styles, 20–26, 187–188
Lifetime plans, 93–96
Limited-payment whole life insurance, 312–314
Lincoln, Nebr., 130
Liquidity, 366–368
Living arrangements
divorce, 57–58, 60
family, 63–66
marriage, 53–57, 60
single, 60–61
Living trust, 473
Loading charges, 354; *see also* Mutual funds
Loan officers
and determining net worth, 137–140
and refusing loans, 140–142
Loans, 111–112
and acceleration clauses, 142
automobile, 113–117, 119, 135, 143, 272, 273
and bad credit ratings, 140–142
and bankruptcy, 112, 142, 146–147
business (preferred stock as), 348
and cashless credit, 130–131
and checking accounts, 126–130
and contingency clauses, 142
and debt counseling, 144–145, 147
and Fair Credit Reporting Act, 140–142
and finance charges, 116–127, 142–144; restrictions on, 119–122; *see also* Mortgages
housing, 231; *see also* Mortgages
and inflation, 118–119, 120, 372–373, 377–379, 388

life insurance, 115, 310, 317
and net worth, determining, 137–140, 146–147
NOW accounts as, 129
reasons for, 115–117, 135, 137
regulation of advertising for, 123
repayment as percent of income, 113
and repossession, 142
revolving credit as, 125–126, 142, 144n, 200–201
safe debt load, determining, 136–140, 146–147
single woman's problem getting, 60
student, 119
and tax deductions, 142–143, 218–219, 334
see also Mortgages; Truth-in-Lending Act
Local government agencies, and consumer protection, 423–424, 431
London, 453, 454
Los Angeles, Calif., 258, 261
Low-income housing, 210–212, 216, 241

MACAP, 432–433
Macon, Ga., 130
Mail-order buying
of clothes, 199–200
of health insurance, 301–302
Maine
and credit regulation, 125
small claims court, 444
Maintenance
of automobiles, 254–255, 270–272
of clothes, 192, 196
and consumer protection, 422–424
of co-op apartments, 207
of houses, 206, 221, 243–244
redress and small claims court, 448–449
Major medical insurance, 296–297
Man-made Fiber Producers Association, 195
Marginal buyers, 152–153
Marginal tax brackets, 219
Market research, 16
Marriage, 53–54
dissolution of, 54, 57–58
economic value of, 55–57

specialization in, 55, 60
tax costs of, 61
see also Family
Mass media, and consumer protection, 424–425; *see also* Television
Mass transit, 259–260, 261
Massachusetts
and credit regulation, 125, 420
and savings bank insurance, 316
and small claims court, 444
Mastercharge, 114, 144
Mead, Margaret, 66
Meat
bacteria in, 177–179
government grading of, 154–155
and nutrition, 155, 174, 177
rising prices of, 437
short-weighing of, 179–180
Medical care. *See* Health care
Medical schools, 281–284
Medicare, 280, 299–301
Medicines
ethical, regulation of, 285–287
over-the-counter, 284–285
and price listing, 287–288
Mental health insurance, 297
Metric system, 477–478
Michigan, small claims court in, 444
Middle-income housing, 208, 210; *see also* Single-family houses
Milk, and price supports, 162–163, 403, 441
Minerals, RDAs, 157
Minnesota, small claims court in, 445
Mitchell, Wesley, 419
Mobile homes, 206, 207, 216–217, 468–469
Money, 47
Money management. *See* Budgets
Moore, Frances, 176–177
Morgan, Ernest, 303
Mortgages, 135, 143, 228–231, 238–239
of co-op apartments, 208
and flexible payment plans, 241–242
kinds of, 239–242
and points, 241

and tax benefits, 208, 209, 218–219
and variable interest rates, 388
Motivational research, 16
Motor homes. *See* Mobile homes
Motor Vehicle Safety Act, 252–253
Mutual funds, 346, 353–354, 362, 367, 385
and short-term securities, 360, 385–388
Mutual savings bank, 344, 367; *see also* Banks; Saving
Moving, 221–222, 245–246
Moving companies, 221–222, 245–246
Municipal bonds, 365–366
Municipal sewage, 458–459

Nader, Ralph, 45, 252, 425
criticisms of FTC, 42–43
National Advisory Commission on Health Manpower, 298
National Automobile Dealers Association, 269
National Bankruptcy Act, 112, 147
National Canners Association, 154
National Credit Union Administration, 124
National Defense Education Act, 119
National Funeral Directors Association, 302–303
National Health Insurance, 289–290
National Health Security Act, 290
National Highway Safety Bureau, 252–253
National Liberty Corporation, 301, 302
National Organization for Nonparents, 66
National Organization for Women, 59
National Underwriters Company, 302
Negotiable Orders of Withdrawal, 129, 384
Net worth, 137–140, 330; *see also* Loans
New Jersey, small claims court in, 445
New York State
and consumer credit protection, 420

and savings bank insurance, 316
small claims court in, 445
New York Stock Exchange, 347; *see also* Stock market
Nixon, Richard M., 256, 290, 403, 420
No-fault auto insurance, 256–257, 421
"No fault" divorce, 58
No-load mutual funds, 354; *see also* Mutual funds
Nolen, William A., 291
North Carolina, small claims court in, 445
North Dakota, 288
NOW accounts, 129, 384
Nuclear power plants, 458, 459
Nurse Training Act, 285
Nutrition, 155–159, 165, 174, 175–177, 290, 294–295
Nuts and seeds, as protein sources, 177

Obsolescence, in clothes, 191–192
Occupational licensing, 5
Occupational planning, 69–72, 74–75
Ohio, and cooling off laws, 39
On-the-job training, 70
Oklahoma, and credit regulation, 125
Old age. *See* Retirement
Open dating systems (food), 158–159
Open end mortgage, 239
Open end mutual funds, 354; *see also* Mutual funds
Open-ended credit, 125–126, 142, 144n, 201
Oppenheimer Monetary Bridge, Inc., 387, 388
Opportunity costs
of education, 72
of housing, 227–228, 380–381
of raising children, 64–65
of recreational vehicles, 468–469
of spending, 79–80, 82–96 *passim*
Ordinary life insurance, 309–314; *see also* Life insurance
Organic food, 290

Origin of the Family, The, 55
OSCO, 288
Over-the-counter markets, 347–348; *see also* Stock market
Over-the-counter medicines, 284–285

Package mortgage, 239
Packaging (food), 151–154, 174
Packard, Vance, 16
"Pain and suffering" suits, 256–257
Paintings, as investments, 344; *see also* Investment
Palace Guard program, 244
Parkinson's Law, 10, 26
Participating life insurance, 333–335; *see also* Life insurance
Patent drugs, 284–285
Patriarch, 54
Payroll taxes, 321, 322, 324
Pechman, Joseph, 401
Peck, Ellen, 66
Pelfzman, Sam, 286–287
Pennsylvania, small claims court in, 445
Pension plans, 324, 356; *see also* Retirement
Pharmacists, and price listing restrictions, 287–288
Physicians. *See* Doctors
Planned Parenthood, 65–66
Planning, 14, 16
    and budgets, 79–96, 99–108
    and education, 72, 74
    of families, 64–66
    long term, 93–96
    menu, 180–181
    occupational, 71–72, 74–75
    of time, 26–27
Plumbers union, 216
Points, 241; *see also* Finance charges
Pollution, 8, 453, 459–460
    air, 8, 214–215, 258, 454–457
    and automobiles, 258
    and land values, 214–215
    water, 8, 457–459
Population
    birth rate, 64
    growth, 3, 453
Postal fraud, 416, 420
Poultry
    grading, 155

as protein source, 177
and short weights, 179–180
Pound, Roscoe, 443
Preferred stock, 348, 349, 350, 367; *see also* Stocks
Premiums, life insurance. *See* Life insurance
Prepayment privilege, 239, 240
Prescription drugs, 285–288
Price discrimination, 288
Price index, 371, 372, 375–376, 388
    food, 150
    medical care, 279, 280
Price listing (ethical drugs), 287–288
Price supports, 161–163, 403
Prices
    costs built into, 33
    relative, 375–377
    supported, 161–163, 403
    unit, 171–172
    see also Inflation; Price index
Prime grade, 154
Private schools, 219–220
Privacy, invasion of, and credit investigations, 140–142
Pro rata shares, 207–208, 209
Produce
    dating, 158–159
    grading of, 155, 156
    and nutrition, 155, 159
Product safety, regulation of, 192–194, 437–439; *see also* Automobile safety; Medicines, ethical, regulation of; Food, and government inspection
Product testing, 421–423
    American Standards Association, 421
    Consumers' Research, 47
    Consumers Union, 46–47, 128, 153, 174, 177, 179, 255, 270, 333
Productivity
    and age, 75
    and education, 69
    and on-the-job training, 70
Property taxes, 214, 219–220, 231, 232
Protein, 158, 174, 176–177
Public housing, 210–212
Public school systems, and property taxes, 219–220

Purchasing power, 2–3
    in inflationary periods, 373, 375–380, 389
Pure Food and Drug Act, 286, 416–417

Radio, regulation of, 43–45
Random walk, 352–353; *see also* Stock market
Rate of return, 343–344, 345, 346, 367
    and bond investment, 365–366, 385; short-term, 385–386
    and real estate investment, 366
    real rate, 360–361, 365
    and risk, 347, 355, 365, 366, 368
    and stock investment, 354–355, 360–361, 385
    see also Investment
Rational consumer decision-making, 11–14
    about automobiles: buying new, 264–269, 272; buying used, 269–279; insurance, 272–275; repairs, 270–272
    about bonds, 265–266
    about budgets, 79–96, 101–108
    about burial expenses, 303
    about children, 63–66
    about clothes, 186–192, 196, 199–202
    about consumer redress, 430–441, 443–447
    about estate planning, 471–476
    about food, 171–181
    about houses, buying, 227–244
    and inflation, 373, 375, 377, 379–381, 384–390
    and information, 18–19, 45–48
    about insurance: auto, 272–275; health care, 295–302; life, 329–336
    about investment, 350–353, 360–365, 366–368
    and legislation, 403
    about loans, 115–117, 135–144
    about moving, 245–246
    about renting, 244–245
    about retirement, 466–469
    and special interest groups, 403–404
    steps in, 12–14
    about the stock market, 350–353, 360–365

RDAs, 157–158

Real estate
brokers, 233–234
investing in, 355–356, 366–367; *see also* Housing services

Real estate taxes. *See* Property taxes

Recommended Dietary Allowances, 157–158

Recreation (retirement), 466–469

Redress, consumer. *See* Consumer redress

Regional over-the-counter markets (stock), 347–348; *see also* Stock market

Regional stock exchanges, 347; *see also* Stock market

Regular medical insurance, 296

Regulatory agencies, 5–6, 163, 441
and advertising, 36, 39, 41–45, 417, 439–440
and automobile safety, 252–253
and checking account interest, 126, 128–129
and consumer redress, 434–440
and cooling off laws, 39–40
and credit investigation bureaus, 140–142
and equal employment, 59
and ethical drugs, 286–287
and fabric labeling, 194–196
and finance charges, 119–126, 142, 272
and flammable clothing, 192–194
and food dating, inspecting, labeling, packaging, 150–155, 156, 158–159
and funeral industry, 303
and moving industry, 221–222
and product safety, 437–439
and special interest groups, 403–404
and the stock market, 352, 364

Renewable term insurance, 314–315, 316, 335

Rent vouchers, 212

Renting, 208, 209–212, 228, 235, 244–245

Repairs. *See* Maintenance

Repossession, 142, 272; *see also* Loans

Regulation Q, 128, 129

Rescission, right of, 39–40, 123

Research analysts (stock), 352

Retail stores, and buying clothes, 199, 200, 202

Retirement, 307, 330, 466
and annuities, 317–319, 388
and inflation, 374, 375, 388–389
and life insurance, 310–312, 356
and leisure, 467–469
and pension plans, 324, 356
and saving, 339–340, 343, 466
and Social Security, 320–326
and stock market investment, 361
and trust funds, 324
see also Estate planning; Investment; Life insurance; Medicare

Revolving credit, 125–126, 142, 144n, 201

Rockefeller, Nelson, 324

Roosevelt, Franklin D., 371

Ross Luce plan. *See* Group health service

Rural costs of living, 87–89

Safety regulations
and automobiles, 252–253
and ethical medicines, 285–287
and food, 150–151
products, 192–194, 437–439

Salaries. *See* Income

Salary continuation insurance, 296

Sales taxes, 232

Salespersons
door-to-door, 39
insurance, 275, 333, 334
real estate, 233–234
in stores, 199, 200

Samuelson, Paul, 353

San Francisco Bay Area Rapid Transit, 259

Sauter, R. F., and D. C. Walker, Jr., 121

Savers Clubs of America, 115

Saving, 17
compared with annuities, 319
in different institutions, 344–346, 367
interest on, 116, 341, 343–344, 347
life insurance as, 309–310, 311, 313, 314, 332, 334

rate of, 333, 339, 340–341, 342
reasons for, 103, 339–343
and risk, 346–347
taxes on, 334
see also Investment

Savings banks, 129, 344–345, 367, 384; *see also* Banks; Savings and Loan Associations

Savings bank life insurance, 316

Savings and loan associations, 17, 344–345
and housing loans, 231, 239, 240, 241–242; *see also* Mortgages
and interest on savings, 116, 341, 343, 345, 347
as investment, 367
and life insurance, 316
and Negotiable Orders of Withdrawal, 129, 384
and prepaying house insurance and taxes, 242
and tax on savings, 334

Savings Bonds, U. S., 346, 365, 367, 384–385

Schools
law, 281
medical, 281–284
and property taxes, 219–220
see also Education

Seafood, 176–177

"Seals of approval," 422

Seattle, Wash., 216, 261, 298–299

Second-hand stores, 186

Securities. *See* Stocks

Securities and Exchange Commission, 352, 364

Security, 307; *see also* Insurance; Saving; Social Security Act

Security industry, 213–214

Self-employment social security tax, 320

Self-treatment (medical), 284–285

Service sector, 3–4
and consumer protection, 422–424, 433

Sewage treatment, 458–459

Sexism, 58–61, 72–73, 74

Shays, Daniel, 111

Sherman Antitrust Act, 416

Shopping
for clothes, 199–202
for food, 172–173, 180–181

Short-term securities, 360, 385–388

Short-weighing practices, 179–180

Sinclair, Upton, 417, 418

Single-family houses, 205, 214
buying, 207–209, 214, 217–218, 221, 227–244

Site value, 214–215, 217–218, 228, 355–356

Sixteenth Amendment, 398

Slums, 210–212

Small claims court, 443–447
in various states, 444–445

Social class, and clothes, 187–188

Social Security Act, 320–326, 329–330, 374

Soybeans, 175, 176

Special interest groups, 403–404
and building codes, 216
and moving industry hearings, 222
and no-fault auto insurance, 256–257
and tax loopholes, 404

Specialization
in jobs, 71
in marriage, 55–56, 60

Standard & Poor's Index, 361, 362

Standard of living, 377, 378, 379

State regulations, 420
on automobiles: emissions, 455; insurance, 255, 256, 274, 421
on consumer protection, 420, 431
cooling off laws, 39–40
on credit contracts, 39–40, 125, 420
on divorce, 58
on estate taxes, 474
on fraud, 420
on gift taxes, 474
against group health plans, 289
on income taxes, 232
on inheritance, 471
on interest rates (usury), 120–122
on medical schools, 281–284
on service and product standards, 422–423
and small claims courts, 444–445

on sulfur fuel, 457
and unemployment insurance, 321
on women's rights, 82

State taxes, 232, 474

Stigler, George, 175

Stock market, 347–348, 354–355, 368
and brokers' commissions, 353, 354, 363, 364, 387–388
and factors affecting stock prices, 349–350
information on the, 350–353, 354–355, 364–365
and investment counselors, 353, 362
and mutual funds, 353–354, 362, 367, 385; short-term, 385–388
performance of the, 361–362
and rate of return, 354–355, 360–362, 367, 385
and stockbrokers, 350–351, 352, 362–364
and types of stock, 347–348, 349

Stock savings bank, 344; see also Saving

Stockbrokers, 350–351, 352
commissions of, 353, 363, 364
picking, 362–364
and short-term securities, 387–388
see also Investment, counselors; Stock market

Stockholm, Sweden, 163

Stocks, 1, 343, 347–348, 349, 354–355, 368
commissions on, 353, 354, 363, 364
common, 347, 348, 361
dividends, 348, 353
factors affecting prices of, 349–350
information on, 350–353, 354–355, 364–365
and investment counselors, 353, 362
mutual funds, 353–354, 362, 367, 385; short-term, 385–388
preferred, 348, 367
and rate of return, 354–355, 360–362, 367, 385

and stockbrokers, 350–351, 352, 362–364, 387–388
see also Bonds

Stocks, How to Buy, 365

Straight life insurance, 309–314

Student budgets, 101–103

Student loans, 119

Subsidies
for automobiles, 260–261
to farmers, 161–163
for low-income housing, 212, 241

Subways, 259

Sulfur emissions tax, 457

Sunk costs, 23–24

Supermarkets
and bacteria in hamburger, 177–179
shopping in, 180–181
and short-weighing, 179–180

Support prices, 161–163, 403

Surgical insurance, 296

Sweden, 253

Target prices, 161

Tax exempt bonds, 365–366

Tax Reform Act, 399

Tax shelters, 399–400; see also Income taxes

Taxes, 232, 393
automobile, 232
and capital gains, 219, 399–400, 401
estate, 473, 474–476
and exempt bonds, 365–366
gift, 474, 475
and implicit subsidies, 219
income: see Income taxes
payroll, 321, 322
property, 214, 219–220, 231, 232
sales, 232
self-employment social security, 320
social security, 320–324
state and local compared, 232
on sulfur emissions (proposed), 457
unemployment, 321

Technology, 464–466

Teenagers, 83–84, 85

Television
and antismoking commercials, 439–440

and closed-circuit food shop-
ping, 164
pay, 44
regulation of, 43–45
Term insurance, 309, 312, 314–
315, 316, 332–333, 335, 388
Testamentary trust, 473
Texarkana, 122
Texas, small claims court in, 445
Textile Fiber Products Identifica-
tion Act, 195
Textile Labeling Act, 41, 195–
196
Theory of the Leisure Class, 15
Time deposit savings account,
344
Time values, 18–19, 24–25
and convenience foods, 164,
172–173
and personal plans, 26–27
Tires (auto), 269
Title insurance, 237–238
Torrens certificate, 238
Trade-ins (auto), 269
Trade-offs, in budgeting, 80, 82–
83, 89–92, 95–96
Trans fund accounts, 129
Transactions costs, 130
Transfer income payments, 2, 86,
87, 321, 323–324, 400, 401
Transportation
and air pollution, 454–456
mass, 259–260, 261
moving industry, 221–222, 246
as percent of family budget,
84, 86, 87
regulation of, 5–6, 124, 221–222,
246
see also Automobiles
Transportation, Department of,
257–258
Treasury Bills, U. S., 385; *see
also* Short-term securities
Trust funds, 324, 367
Trusts, 472, 473; *see also* Estate
planning
Truth-in-Labeling Act, 41
Truth-in-Lending Act, 122–123,
142, 272, 420
enforcement of the, 124–125
and revolving credit, 125–126

Underwood-Simmons Tariff Act,
398
Unemployment insurance, 321
Uninsured motorist insurance, 275
Unions
and building costs, 216–217
construction workers, 217, 218
and inflation, 374–375, 379, 389
Unit pricing, 171–172
United Housing Foundation, 208
United International Club, Inc.,
115
Unsafe At Any Speed, 252
Urban costs of living, 87–89
Urban Mass Transportation As-
sistance Act, 259
Urban Problems, National Com-
mission on, 211
Urban renewal, 210–212
Usury laws, 119–122

Values
and budgeting, 79, 80, 82, 89–
92, 93
clarifying, 25–26, 90–92
and clothes, 186–189
economic, of marriage, 55–57
and life styles, 20–26
of saving, 342
of time, 18–19, 24–25, 164, 172–
173
Variable annuities, 317, 388
Veblen, Thorstein, 15
Vegetables, 155, 156, 159
Veterans Administration mortgages, 240
Virginia, small claims court in,
445
Vitamins, 157, 290–291
Volkswagen, 264–265

Wage Earner Plan, 147
Wages. *See* Income
Waiver of tort liability, 244
Warranties, auto, 264–265, 270
Washington, George, 111
Washington, D. C., 258, 259
small claims court in, 443, 444,
446
Washington, State of
group health service in, 298–
299
small claims court in, 445

and usury laws, 120–121
and wife's legal rights, 82
Waste treatment, 458–459
Water pollution, 8, 457–460
Weatley, John J., and Guy G.
Gordon, 121
Weights and measures inspec-
tors, 179–180
Wells Fargo Bank, 362
Whole life insurance, 309–312,
313, 315, 333, 334, 388
limited-payment, 312–314
tax benefits of, 334
Wholesale price index. *See*
Price index
Wholesome Poultry Products Act,
155
Wills, 471–473; *see also* Estate
planning
Wilson-Gorman Tariff Act, 398
Wisconsin, small claims court in,
445
Wives, economic value of, 56–57,
82, 307; *see also* Family;
Women
Women
and decision to have children,
64–66
and divorce, 57–58
economic value of (as wives),
56–57, 307
and family budget decisions,
81–96 *passim*
liberation movement of, 56, 58–
59
and marriage, 54–57, 64
median income of, 60, 74
single, 60–61
working, 56, 60, 72–73, 74
Women's liberation movement,
56, 58–59
Wool, Fur and Textile Fiber Products Acts, 41, 194–196
Wool Products Labeling Act, 194–
195
Wright, J. Shelly, 443
Wyoming, and credit regulation,
125

Your Money's Worth, 47

Zero Population Growth, 66